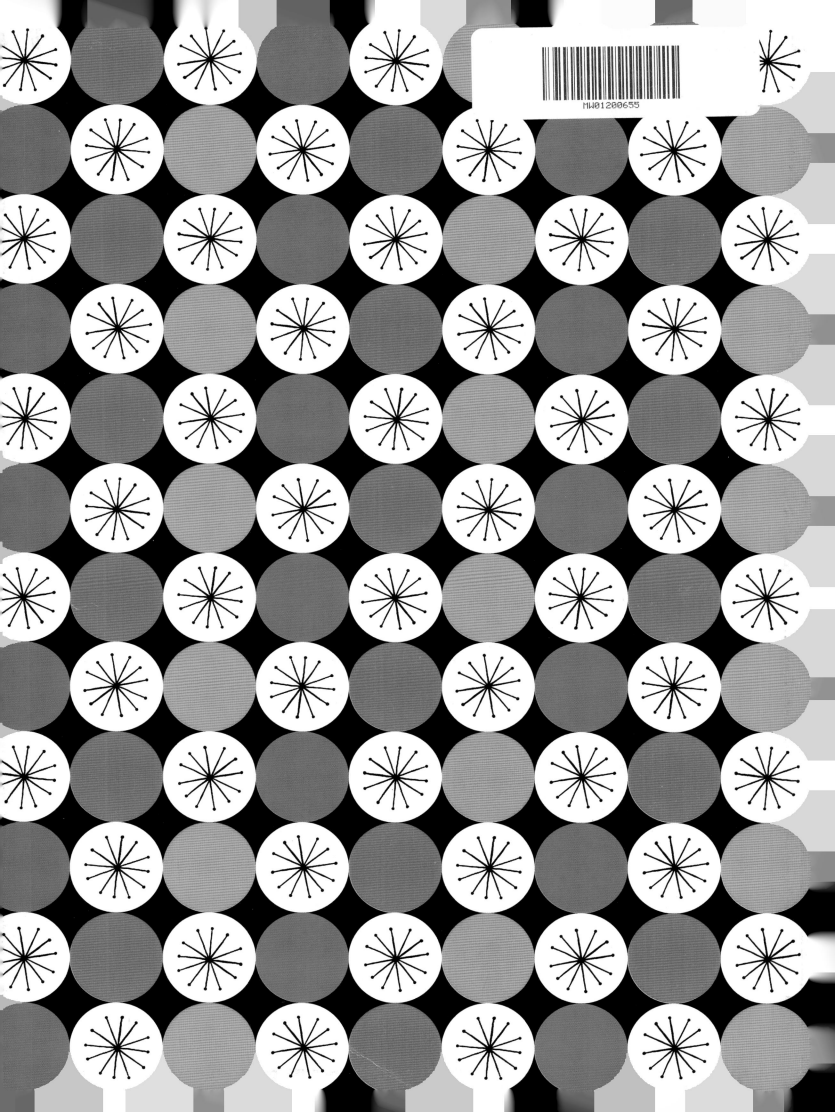

AMMO

AMMO

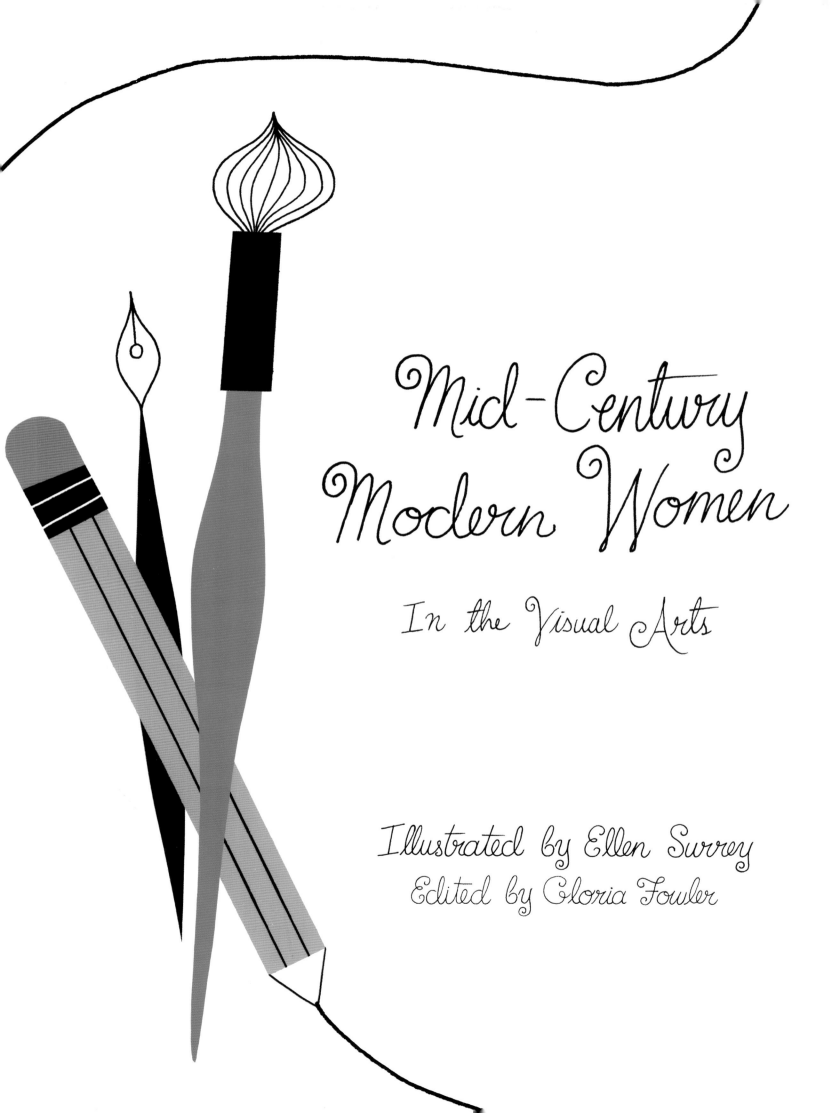

# Mid-Century Modern Women

## In the Visual Arts

Illustrated by Ellen Surrey

Edited by Gloria Fowler

# Introduction

When I first came across Ellen Surrey's delightful illustration of Peggy Moffitt, it was love at first sight. The connection was twofold. First, Ellen Surrey is an incredibly talented, young illustrator who is a recent graduate of the renowned Art Center College of Design, which coincidentally is also my alma mater and a place I called home in the twenty years I taught there. Secondly, Peggy Moffitt is not only one of the most iconic fashion models of the mid-twentieth century but also a dear family friend. Her late husband, the celebrated photographer William Claxton, was my husband Steve Crist's close friend and mentor. In fact, one of our favorite vintage photographs of Peggy by Bill hangs in our home.

During the 1960s, Peggy Moffitt caused a sensation as the model and muse for Rudi Gernreich's bold and graphic clothing designs, perhaps none more so than the monokini, the topless swimsuit she so elegantly modeled. Peggy's background in dance gave a fluidity to her movements that was captured on film by William Claxton. Together they created what is considered the first fashion video: *Basic Black*, which is now in the permanent collection at MoMA in New York. Coupled with her Kabuki-style makeup she created herself and her geometric Vidal Sassoon haircut, Peggy invented a look all her own. Indeed, Peggy was more than just a model; she was an aesthetic collaborator and communicator.

This made me think about all the other amazing, creative women from this era that I adored—women like Ray Eames, who I came to admire even more so after designing and editing the monograph *Eames: Beautiful Details*. I realized there were so many more remarkable women from this era who were sometimes overlooked, and I knew right away that Ellen and I should create a book together that celebrated women in the visual arts from the mid-twentieth century. It felt like serendipity, and the result of our collaboration is this exhibit-in-a-book: an eclectic list of twenty-five real-life heroines across multiple disciplines whose work and whose lives continue to inspire today. From Edith Head to Edith Heath, from Eva Hesse to Eva Zeisel, the twenty-five talented women featured here are influential for both their artistry and determination. Ellen Surrey's exquisite portraits of these women are accompanied by quotes from each of them, imparting both wit and wisdom from their own life experiences.

Mid-twentieth-century modernism, long celebrated for its much-lauded designs by mostly male designers, architects, and artists, was also a time of groundbreaking work in the visual arts by extraordinarily talented women. Predominantly focused on the 1940s to the 1960s, with the influence of the Bauhaus beforehand and foreshadowing the emergence of the feminist movement afterwards, this book celebrates an era that saw unprecedented accomplishments in the arts by women. In architecture, illustration, animation, textile design, graphic design, industrial design, furniture design, painting, sculpture, ceramics, costume design, and fashion, every one of these unique women pursued her own distinct vision in fields that were largely underrepresented by and inaccessible to women. This book shines the spotlight on a diverse sampling of talented women across all of these disciplines, who created wonderful works with wit and willfulness. Amongst the women featured here are some of the most recognizable names in the arts from this time period, such as fashion maven Coco Chanel, and painters Frida Kahlo and Georgia O'Keeffe, as well as lesser-known but equally impressive women such as Disneyland's It's a Small World designer Mary Blair, sculptor and Japanese-American internment survivor Ruth Asawa, and children's book illustrator Alice Provensen, who at ninety-seven is our longest-living lady featured here.

All of the women included in this book had to overcome significant obstacles in society and their personal lives in order to pursue their dreams and realize their artistic ambitions. One inspirational artist featured here that broke from convention was Sister Mary Corita Kent. Sister Corita was part of the progressive order of nuns at Immaculate Heart in Los Angeles during the 1960s. Sister Corita not only taught art but created hundreds of original, colorful, and graphically bold silkscreened works that often incorporated clever references to advertising as well as spirituality. She was dedicated to the ideals of helping the poor and underserved, and to uplifting the values and desires of a just society through her artistic messages of love and peace. In one of her pieces from 1969 she depicted Martin Luther King Jr. with her signature handwritten text that reads, "The King is dead. Love your brother." Eventually, the Immaculate Heart nuns were deemed too radical for the archdiocese in their quest for modest changes and self-governance, ultimately resulting in their decision to leave the Catholic Church altogether. Luckily, Corita Kent continued to paint her optimistic and beautiful hopes for humanity until the end of her life.

Artist Yayoi Kusama has lived an eccentric life of devotion, one might say obsession, to her work. Beginning in the 1950s through the 1960s, Yayoi Kusama began painting surfaces with her now-signature polka dots. These paintings, performance art pieces, and installations, including her amazing and immersive *Infinity Mirrored* rooms, were all manifestations of the hallucinations she has experienced for most of her life. In fact, since the 1970s, Yayoi Kusama has voluntarily lived in a mental hospital in Japan a short distance away from her studio. Despite this unusual setup, or more likely because of it, Yayoi Kusama has emerged as one of the most prolific and recognized artists of our time, with recent retrospective shows at both MoMA and the Whitney Museum of American Art in New York, as well as the Tate Modern in London. Now in her late eighties, Yayoi Kusama continues to create magic with her singular vision.

While some of the women featured here have had long, productive lives, others, like Eva Hesse, were tragically taken from us much too soon. In Eva's brief thirty-four years of life she suffered and survived through many seemingly insurmountable circumstances. Born to an observant Jewish family, as a young child Eva and her family escaped Nazi Germany and ultimately immigrated to New York. When Eva was ten years old, her mother committed suicide. Despite these traumatic events in her childhood, Eva Hesse went on to study art and received her undergraduate degree from Yale. She was a contemporary of minimalist artists Sol LeWitt and Donald Judd. But unlike the rigidity of much of these minimalist artists' works, Eva brought a handmade, organic, and almost sensual quality to her sculpture that emanated from her innovative use of materials. By experimenting using latex and fiber-glass, Eva Hesse created series of slightly irregular yet repetitive forms in her compelling installations. In a career spanning just ten years before she sadly succumbed to cancer, Eva Hesse's soulful and ephemeral work continues to inspire artists to this day.

As difficult as it was during this time period for women artists in general, it was even more so for African-American women in the visual arts—all the more reason that Alma Thomas was so remarkable. Alma Thomas was born in the South, but her family relocated to Washington, D.C. to flee racial violence. As a girl growing up she had dreamed of becoming an architect, which was seemingly impossible at the time, but instead graduated from Howard University with a degree in fine arts. Alma Thomas went on to have a thirty-five-year career teaching art in junior high school. Upon her retirement in 1960, at the age of sixty, she embarked on her fine art career while the civil rights movement was still in its infancy. Influenced by Abstract Expressionism she created her own beautiful Color Field paintings, developing a bold, multi-hued, mosaic-like technique. In 1972, Alma Thomas became the first African-American female artist to have a solo exhibition at the Whitney Museum of American Art. Recently, President Obama and First Lady Michelle Obama proudly unveiled an Alma Thomas painting at the White House, the first artwork by an African-American woman to be featured there.

All of these women forged new territory in a day and age without many, if any, female role models in their given fields. It is a testament to their talent, enthusiasm, and determination that we luckily have them and their inspired work to look back on today. As artist Helen Frankenthaler said, "Go against the rules or ignore the rules. That is what invention is about." Here's to all of these rule-breaking and inventive women, and may they inspire the next generation of talented women to find their own artistic voices. Enjoy!

*Gloria Fowler*

New York, New York
October 28, 2015

# Featuring

# 25

## mid-century modern women

*in the visual arts*

*Ray Eames*

*Edith Head*

*Peggy Moffitt*

*Yayoi Kusama*

*Frida Kahlo*

*Maija Isola*

*Sister Corita Kent*

*Coco Chanel*

*Bridget Riley*

*Ruth Asawa*

*Twiggy*

*Mary Quant*

*Louise Nevelson*

*Elaine Lustig Cohen*

*Helen Frankenthaler*

*Eva Zeisel*

*Georgia O'Keeffe*

*Florence Knoll*

*Edith Heath*

*Alma Thomas*

*Vera Neumann*

*Eva Hesse*

*Alice Provensen*

*Greta Magnusson-Grossman*

*Mary Blair*

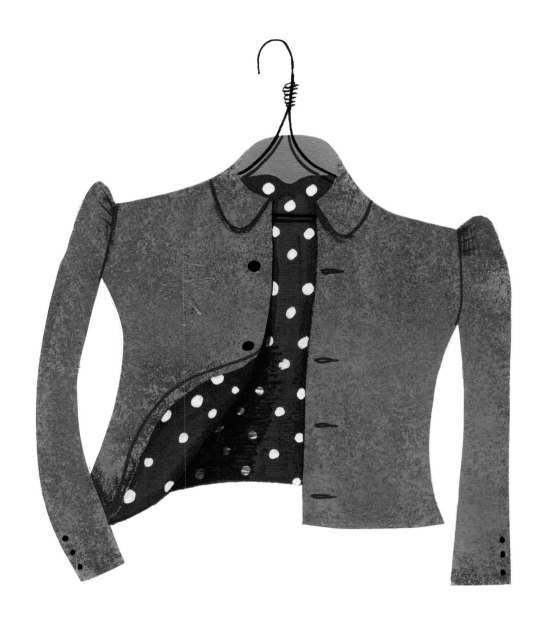

Ray Eames

"What works good is better than what looks good, because what works good lasts."

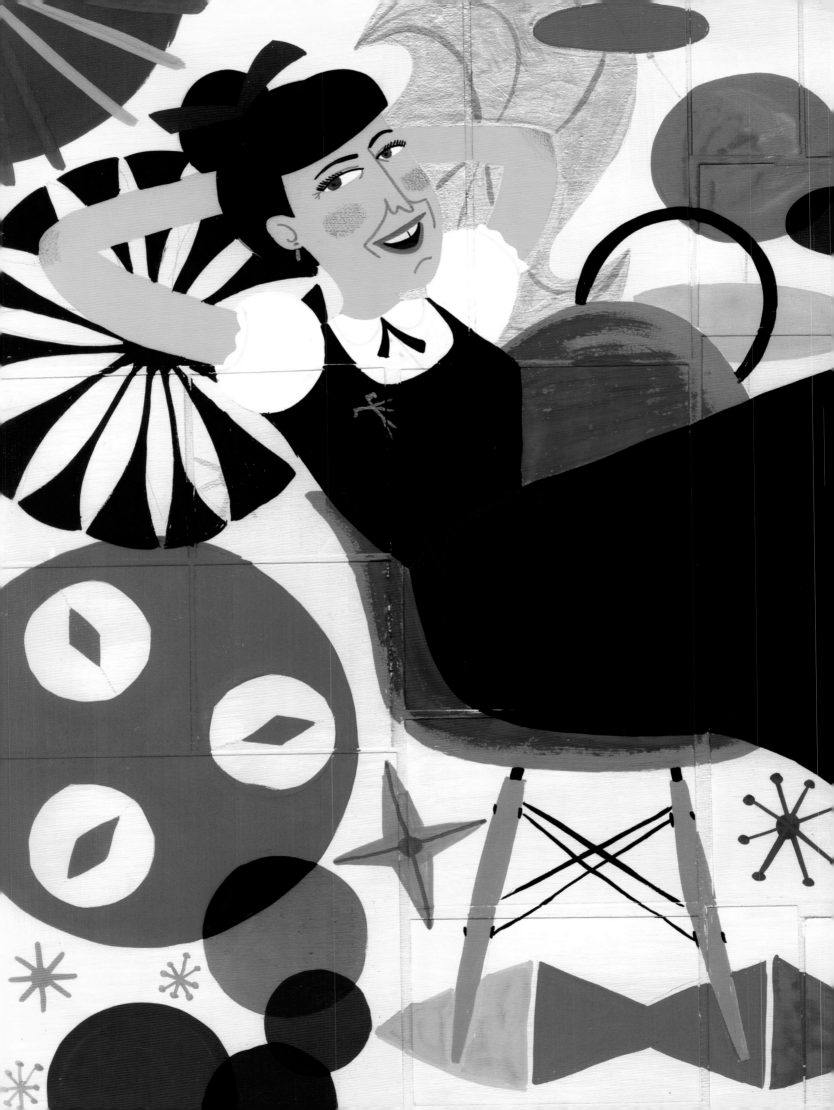

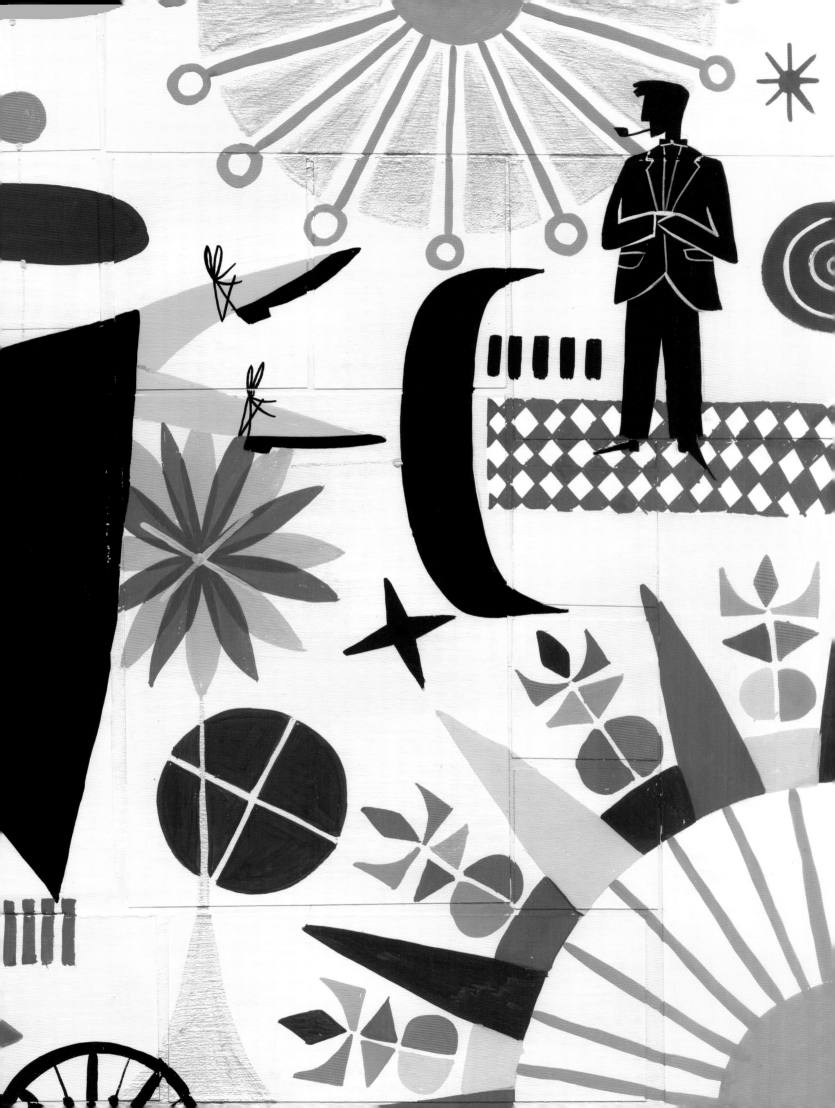

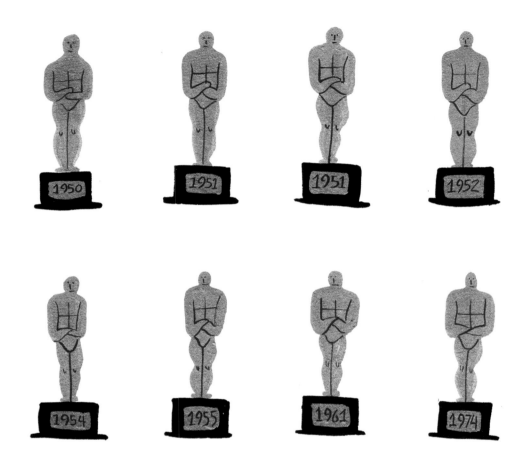

Edith Head

"You can lead a horse to water and you can even make it drink, but you can't make actresses wear what they don't want to wear."

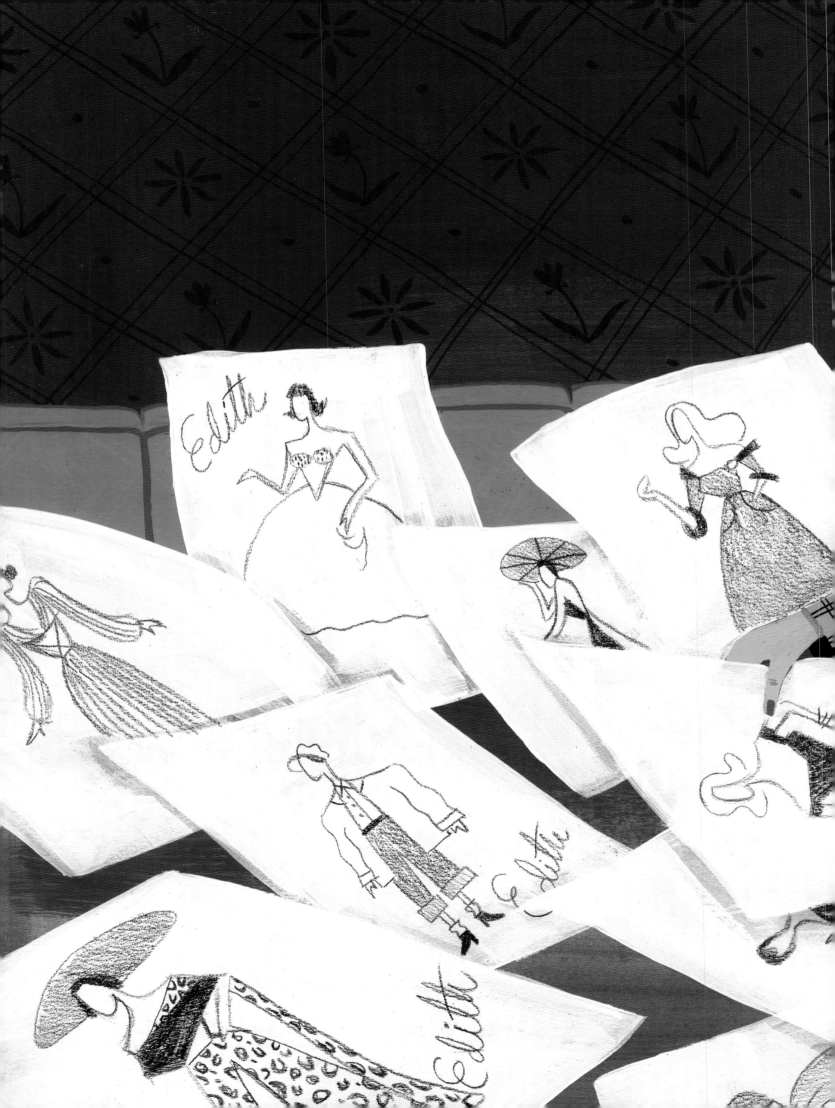

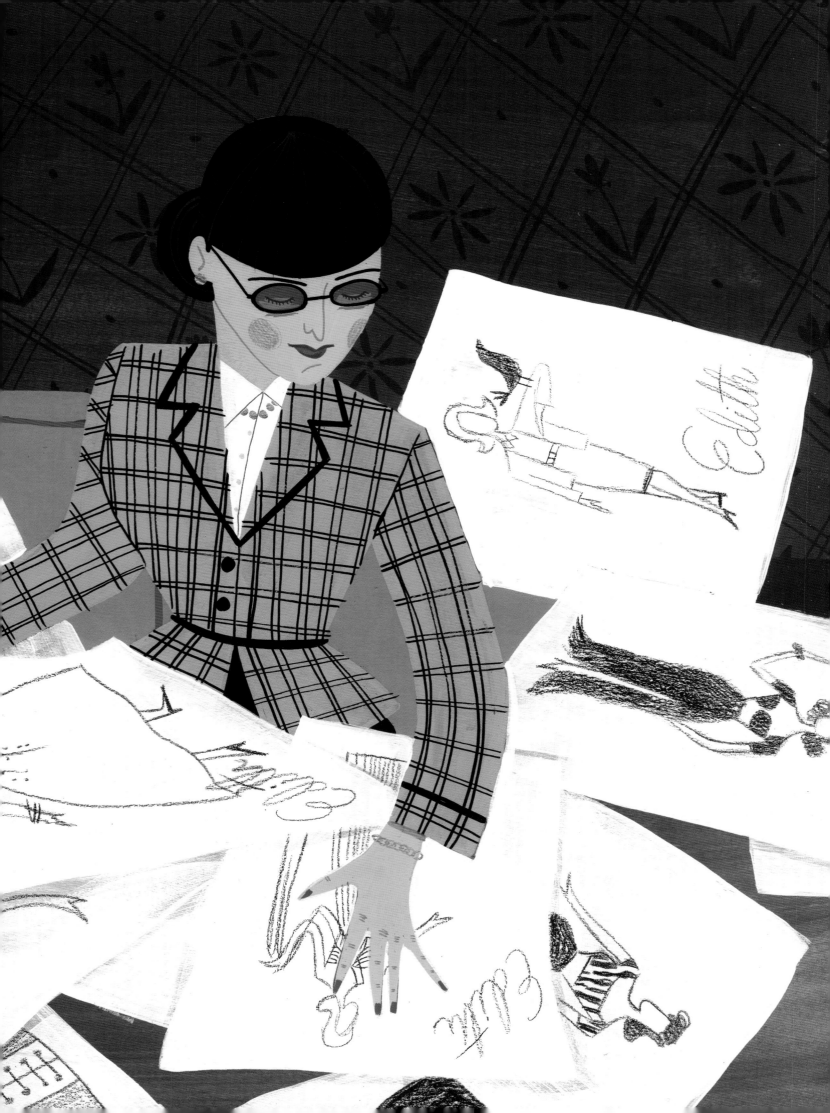

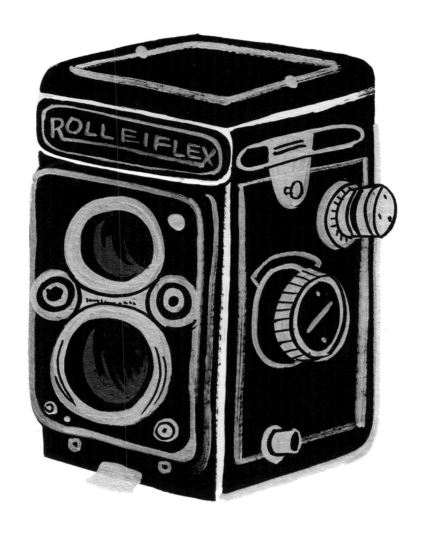

Peggy Moffitt

"I never held back. It was the height of freedom and liberation."

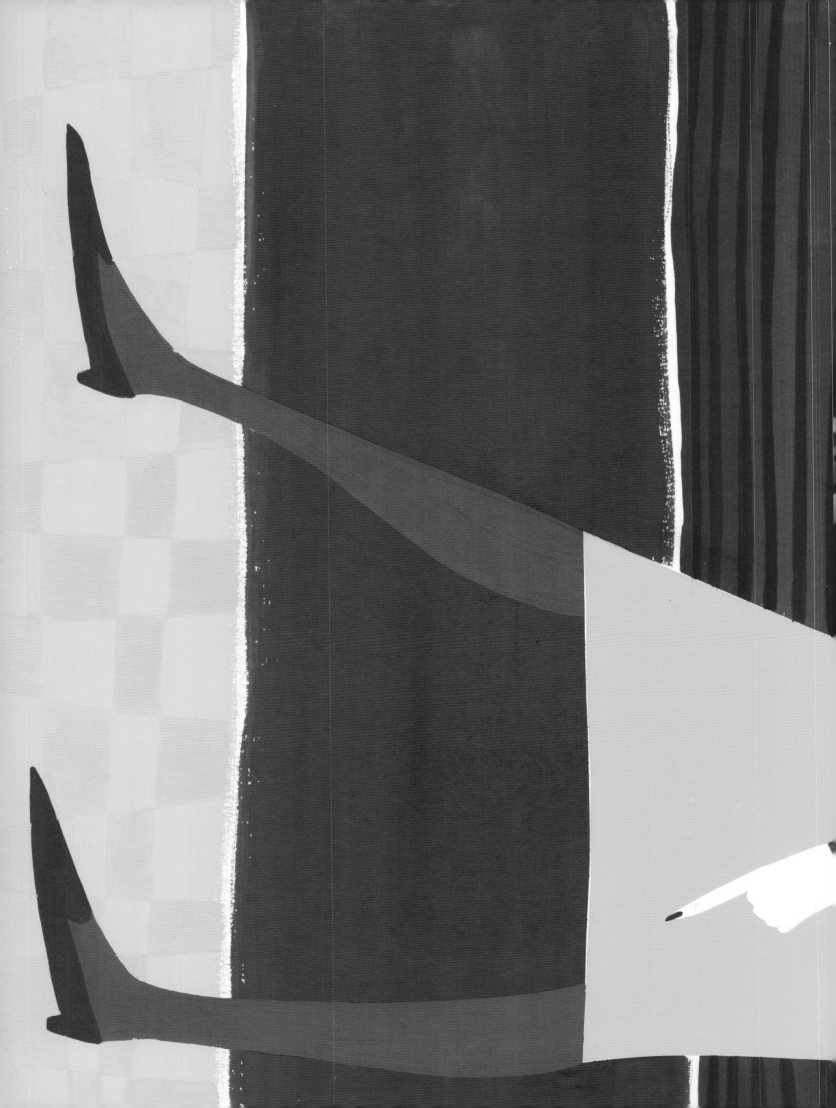

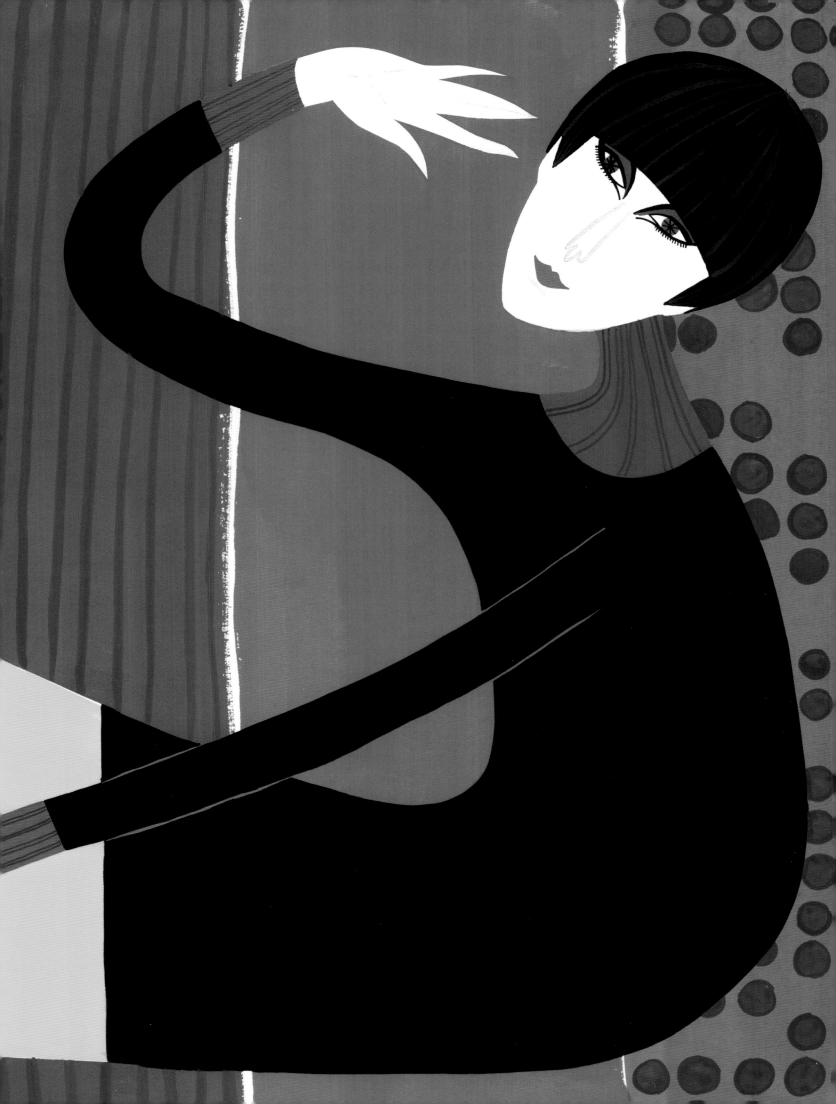

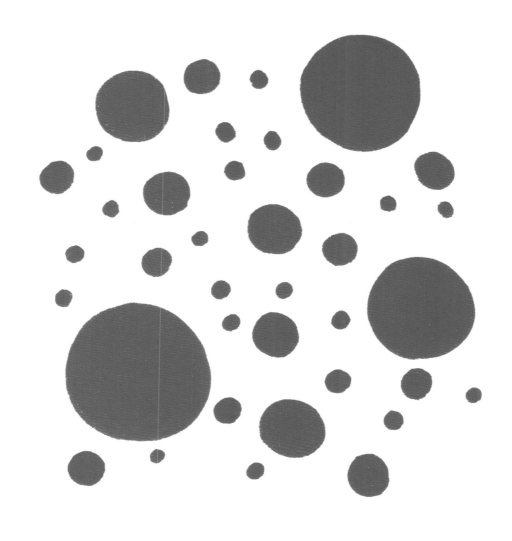

Yayoi Kusama

"Since my childhood, I have always made works with polka dots. Earth, moon, sun, and human beings all represent dots; a single particle among billions."

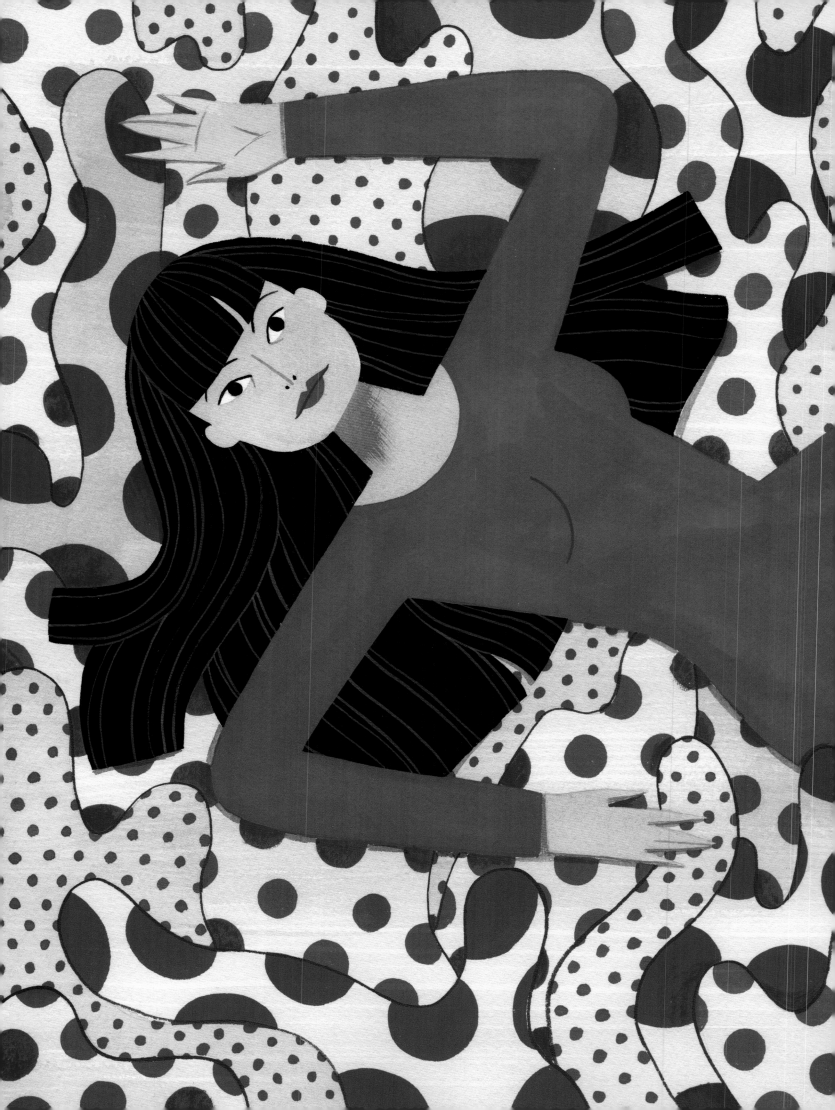

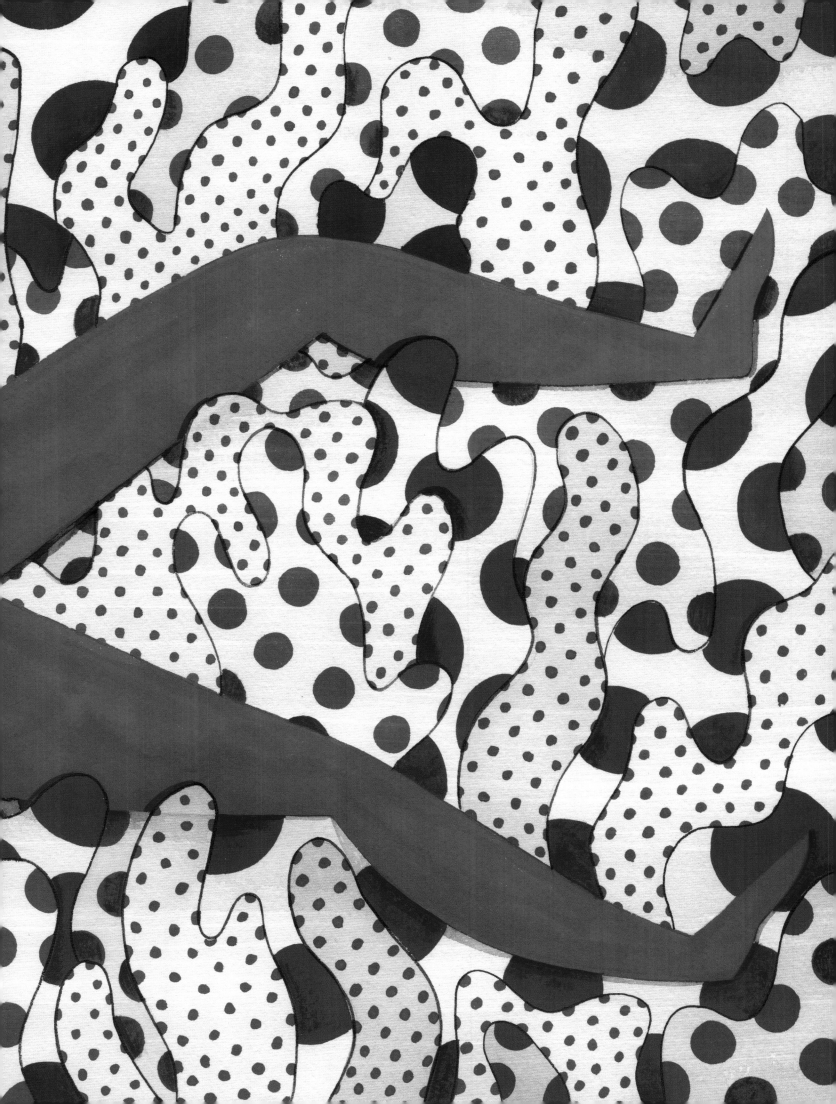

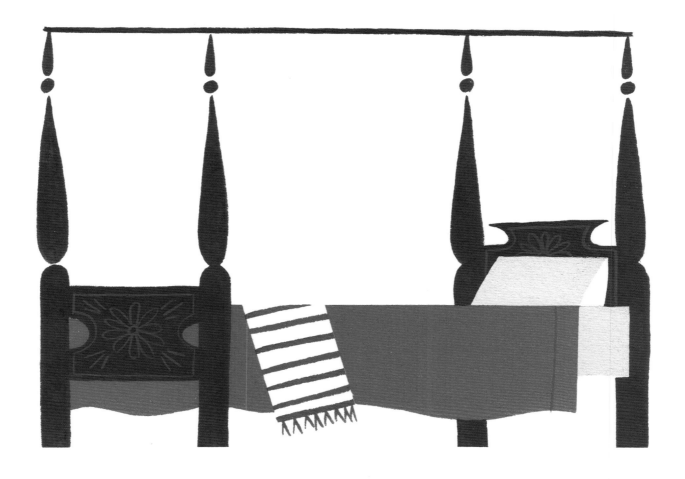

Frida Kahlo

"I never paint dreams or nightmares. I paint my own reality."

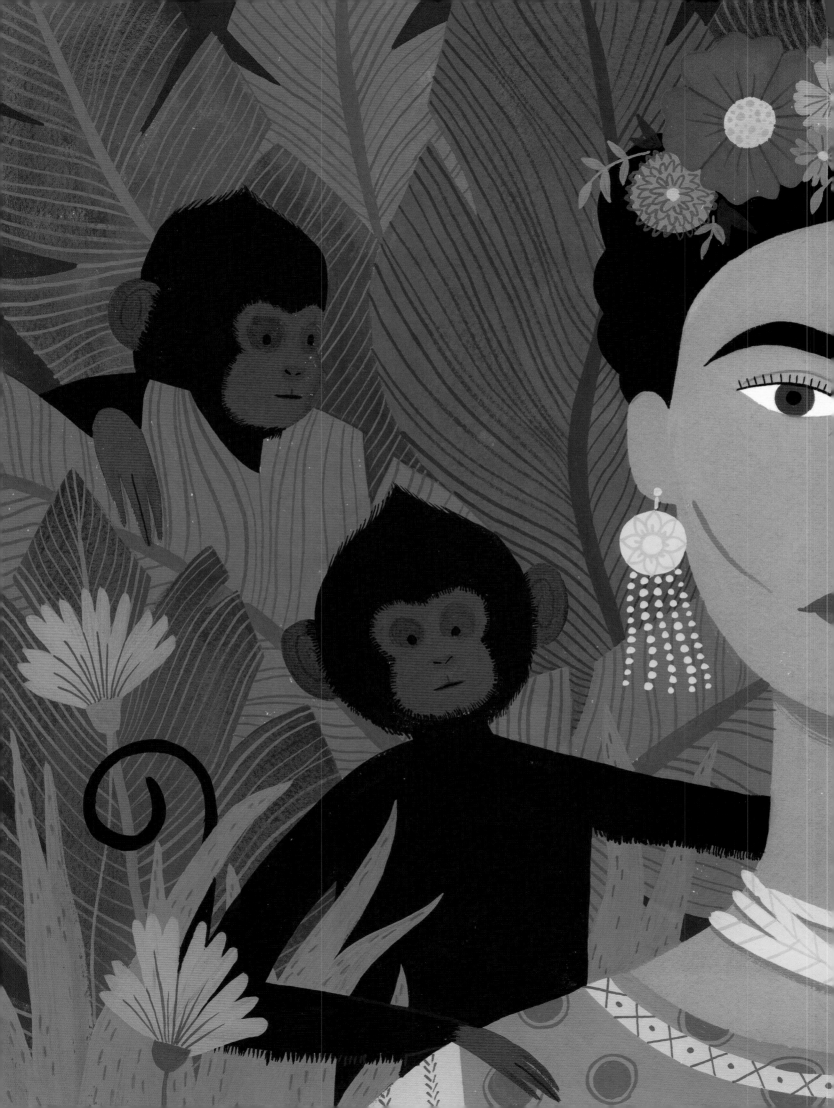

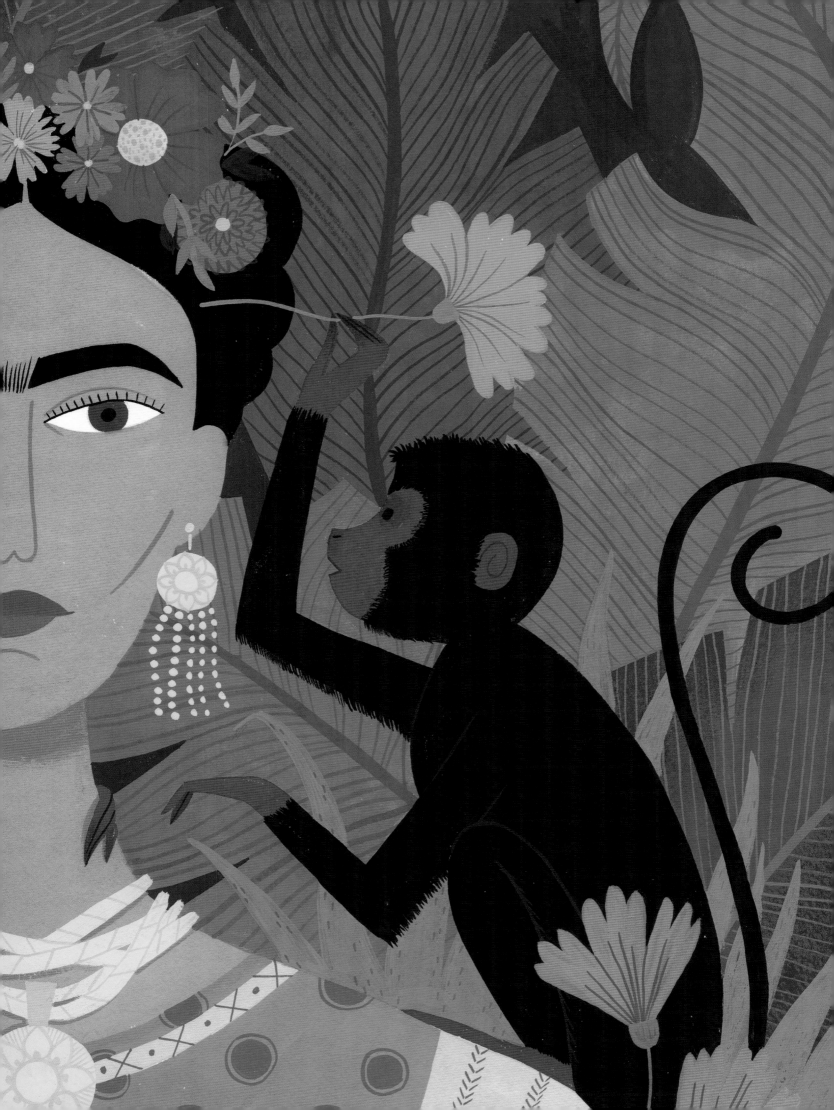

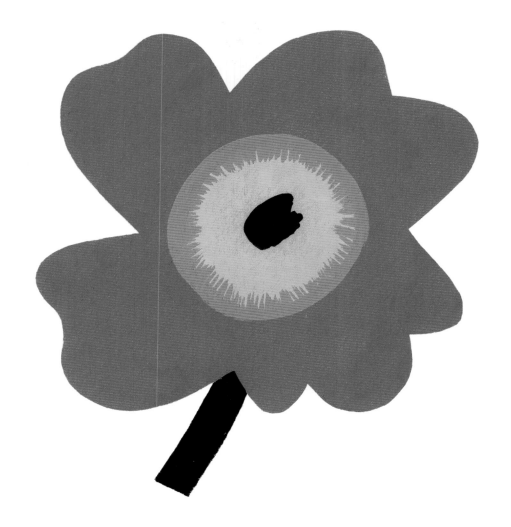

Maija Isola

"I tend to see everything in patterns ... when I go see a film, look at snow and ice, wash dishes, or maybe the most when I am in love."

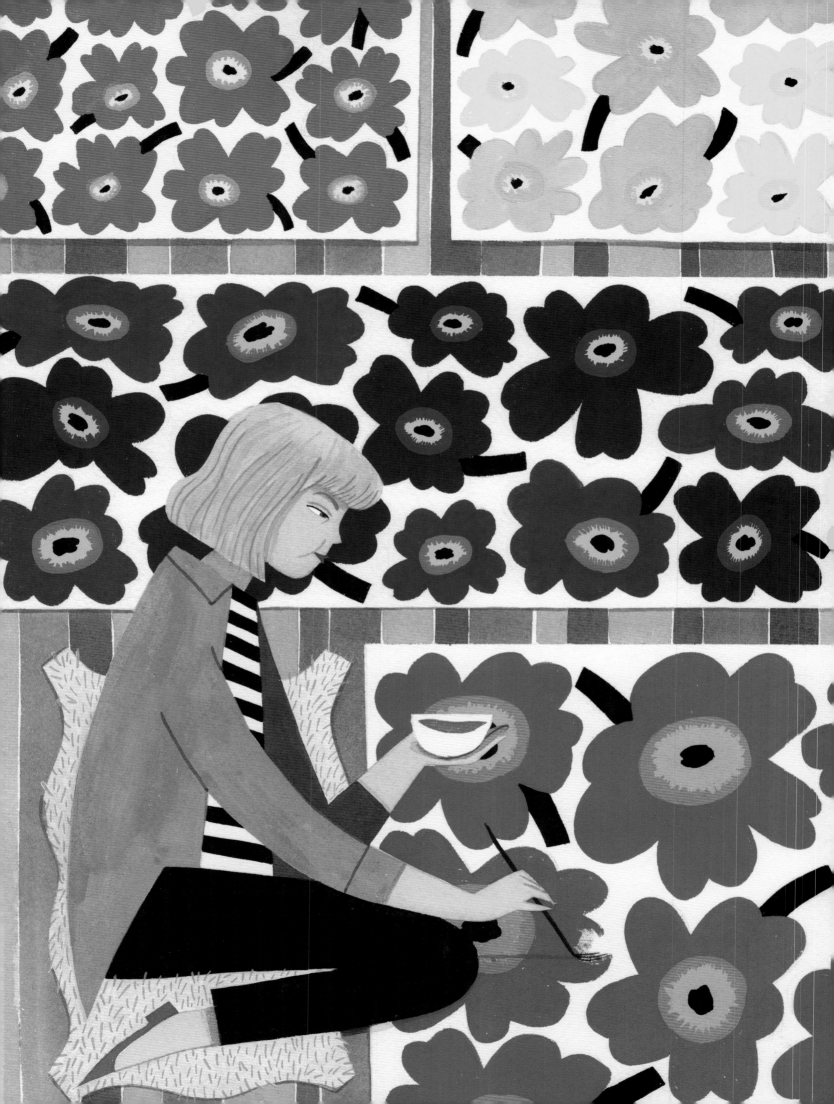

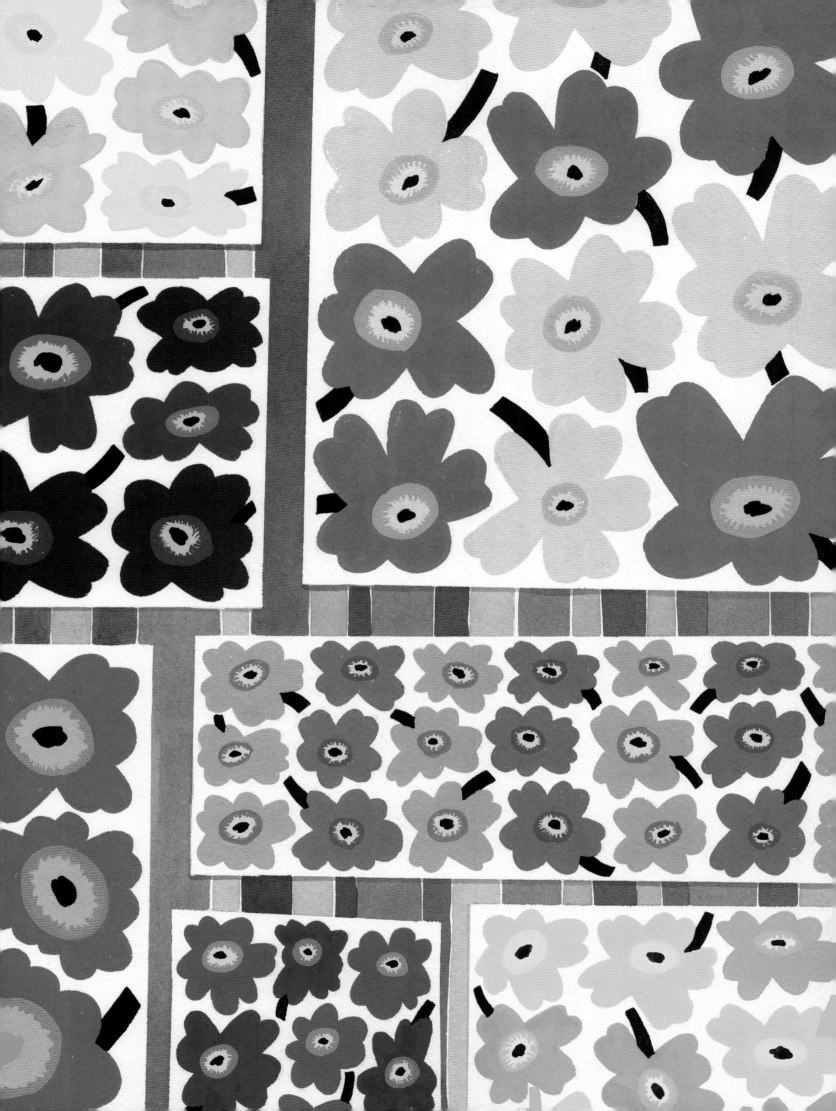

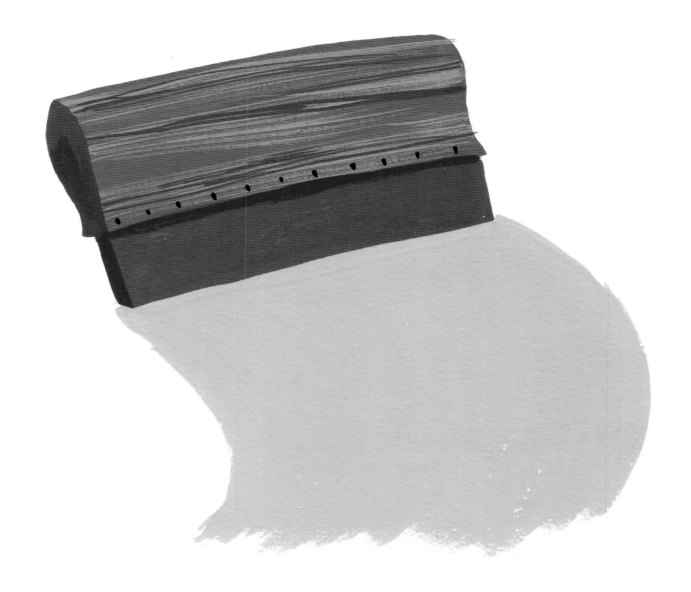

Sister Corita Kent

Rule 9:
Be happy
whenever you
can manage it.
Enjoy yourself.
It's lighter than
you think."

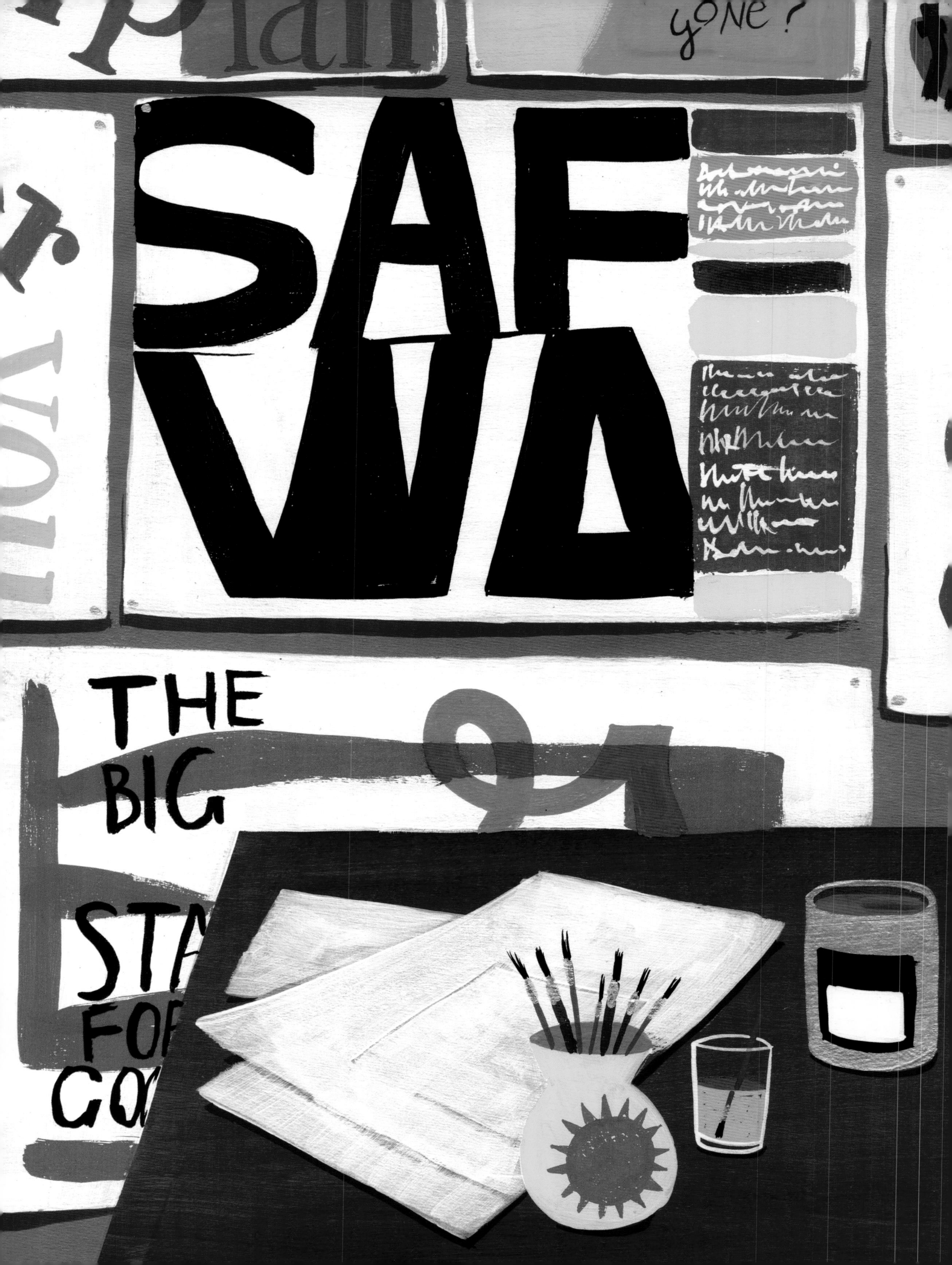

gone?
SAFWA
THE
BIG
STA
FOR
GO

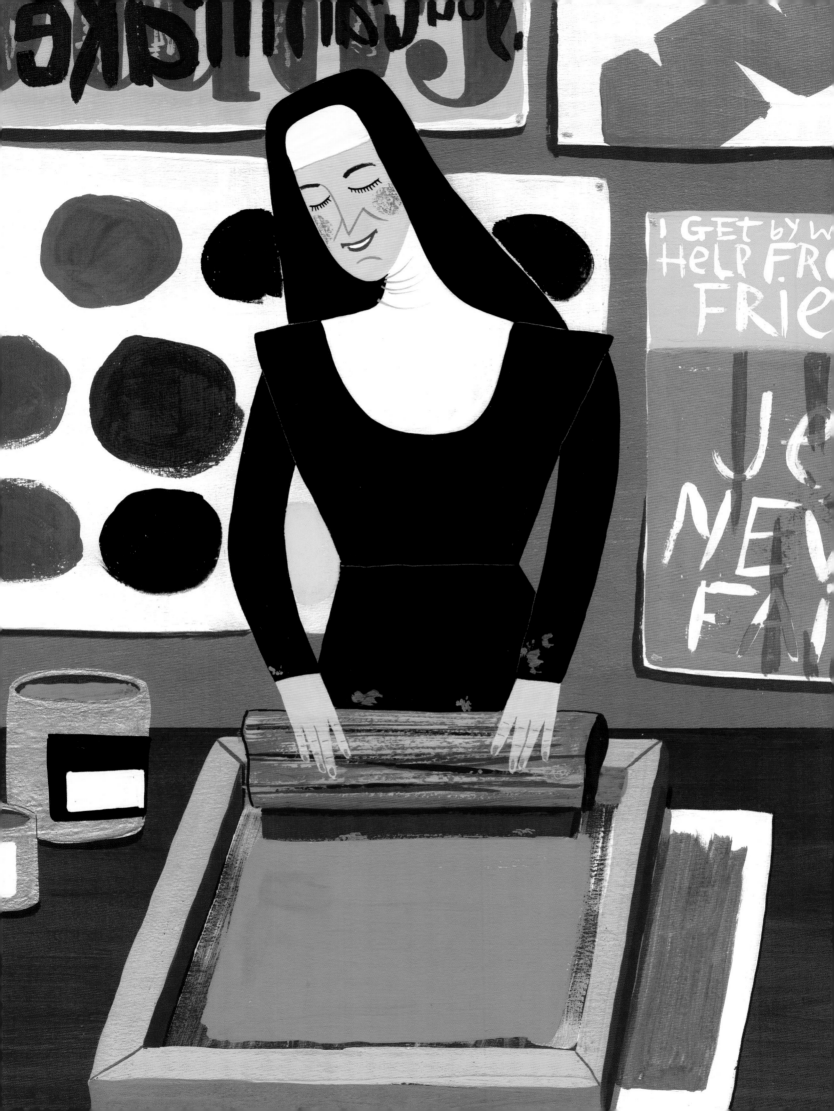

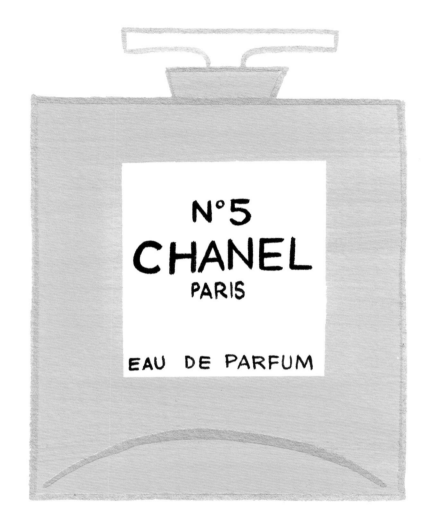

N°5
CHANEL
PARIS

EAU DE PARFUM

*Coco Chanel*

"A girl should be two things: classy and fabulous."

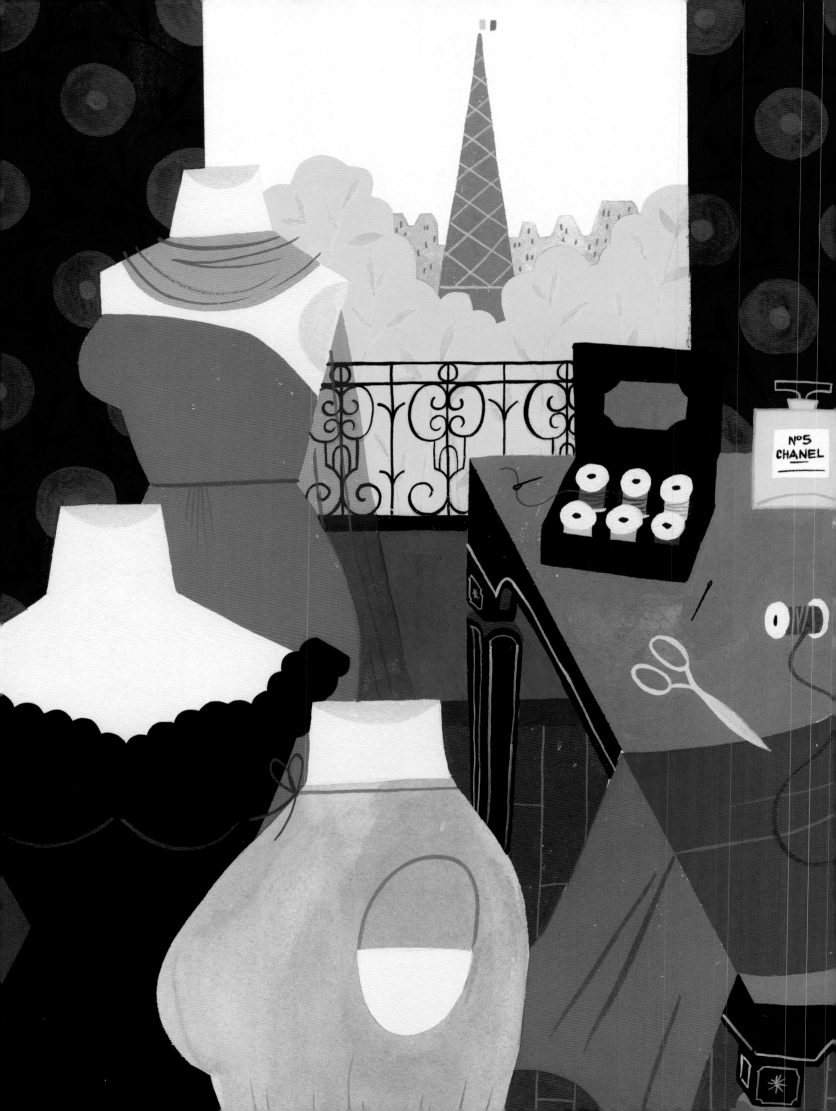

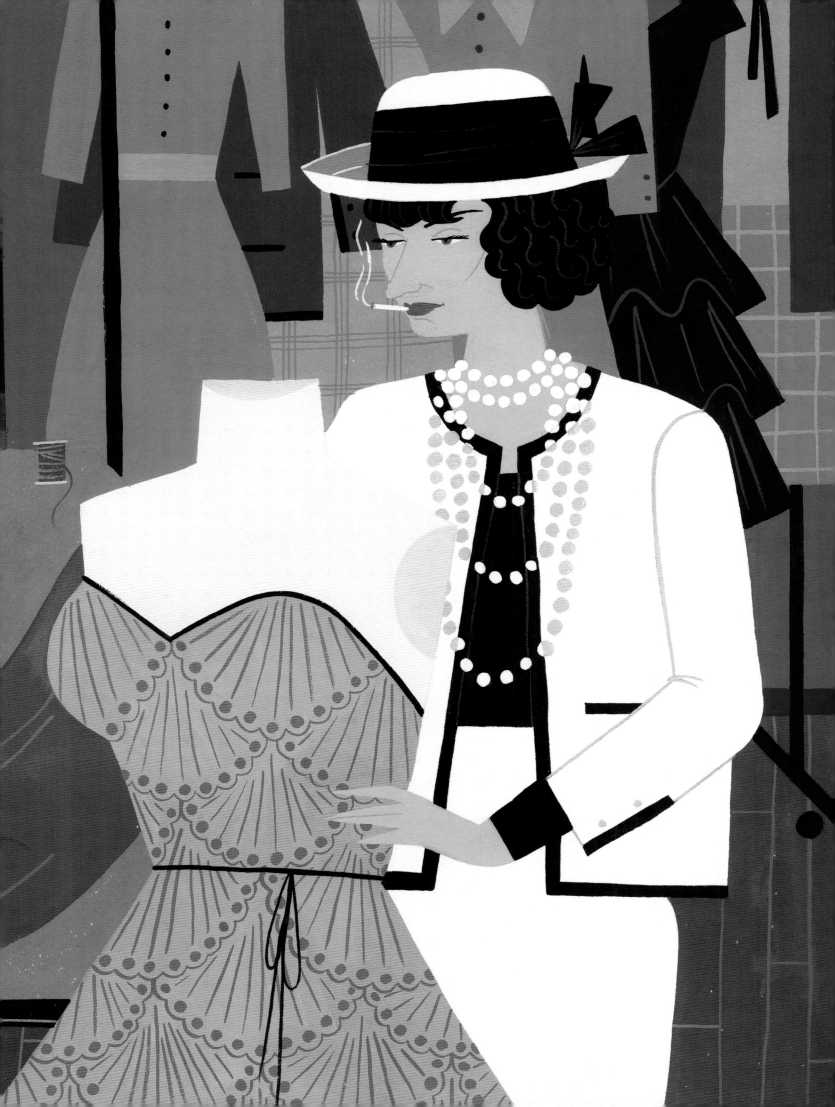

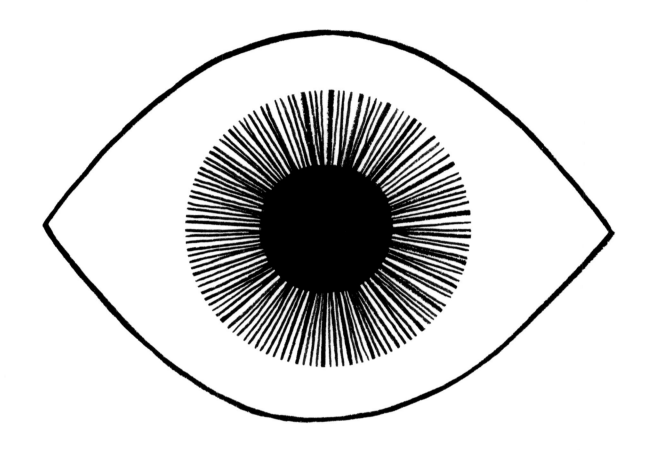

Bridget Riley

"Focusing isn't just an optical activity, it is also a mental one."

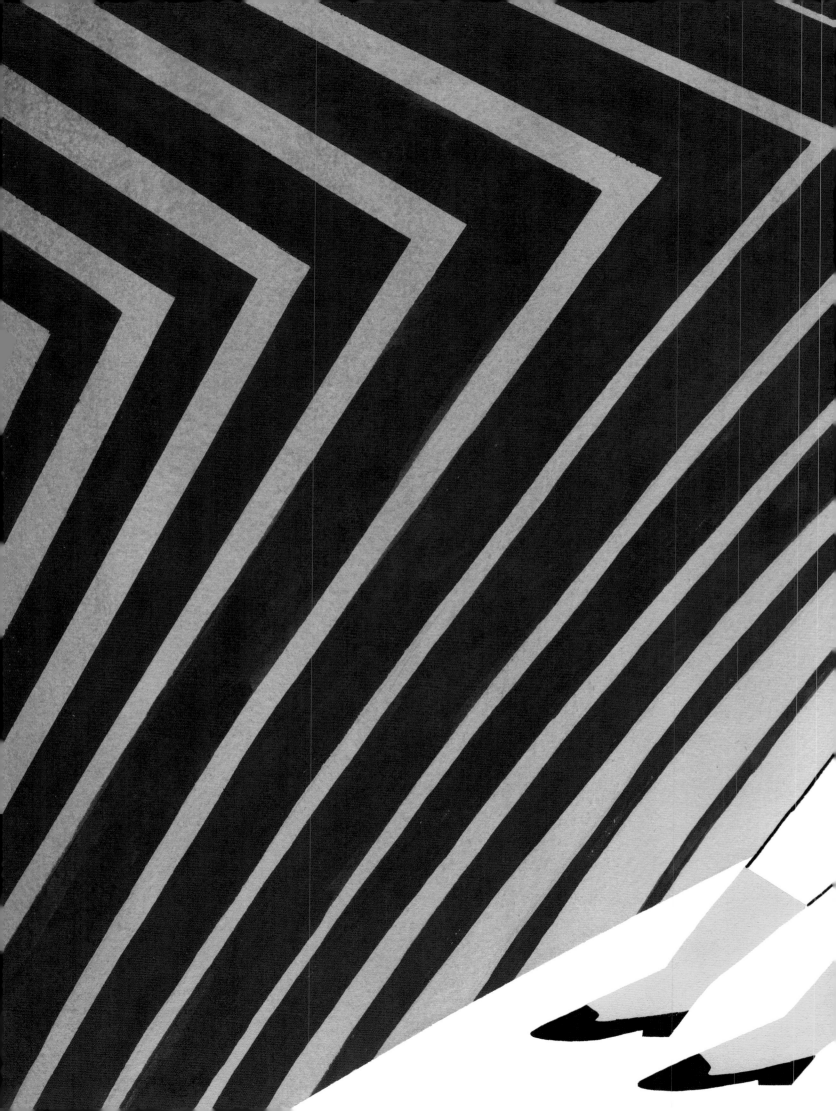

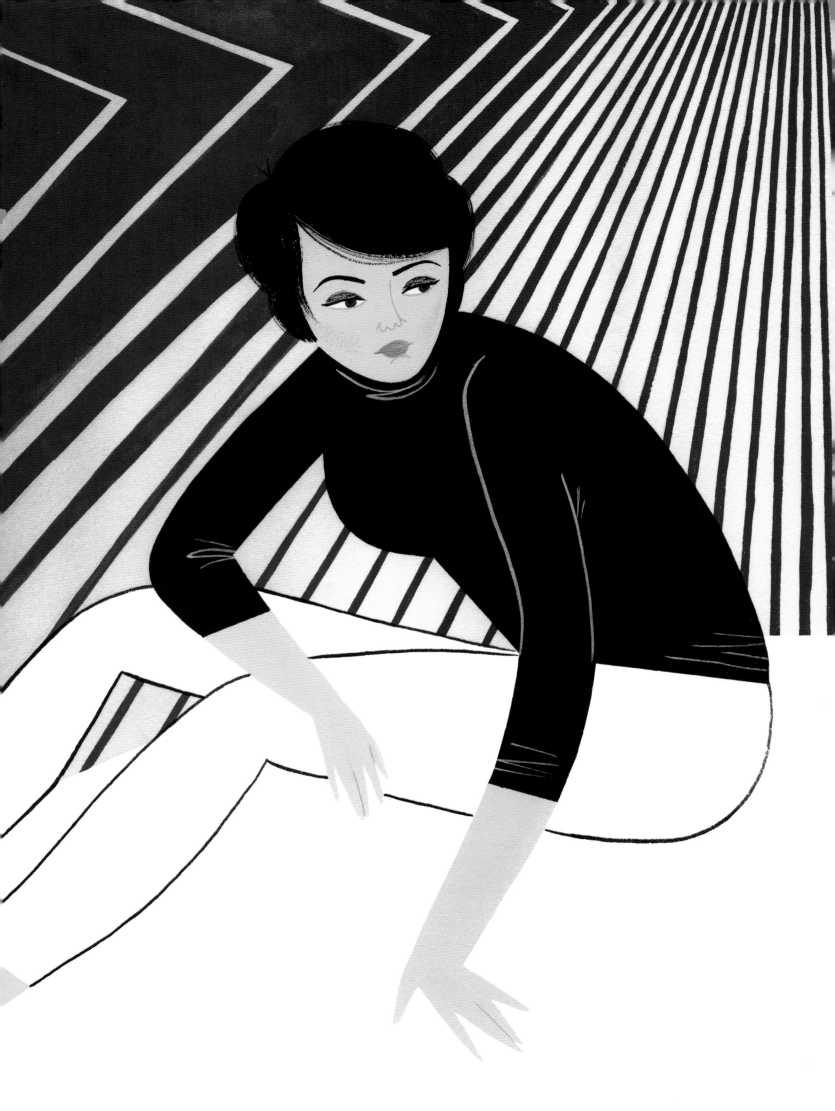

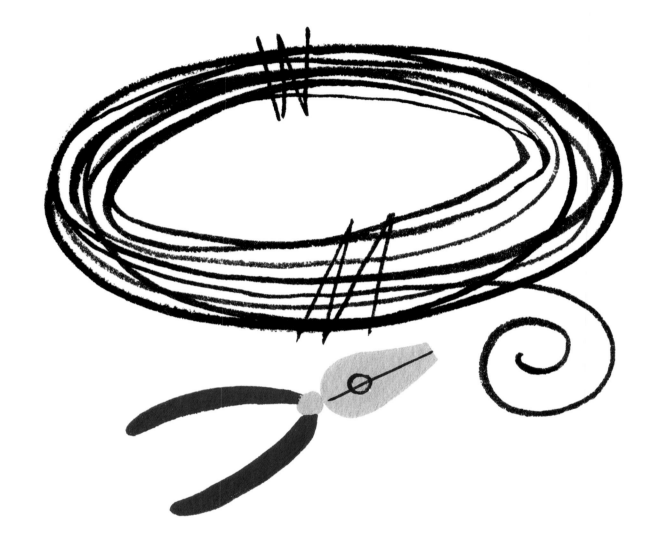

Ruth Asawa

"Sculpture is like farming. If you just keep at it, you can get quite a lot done."

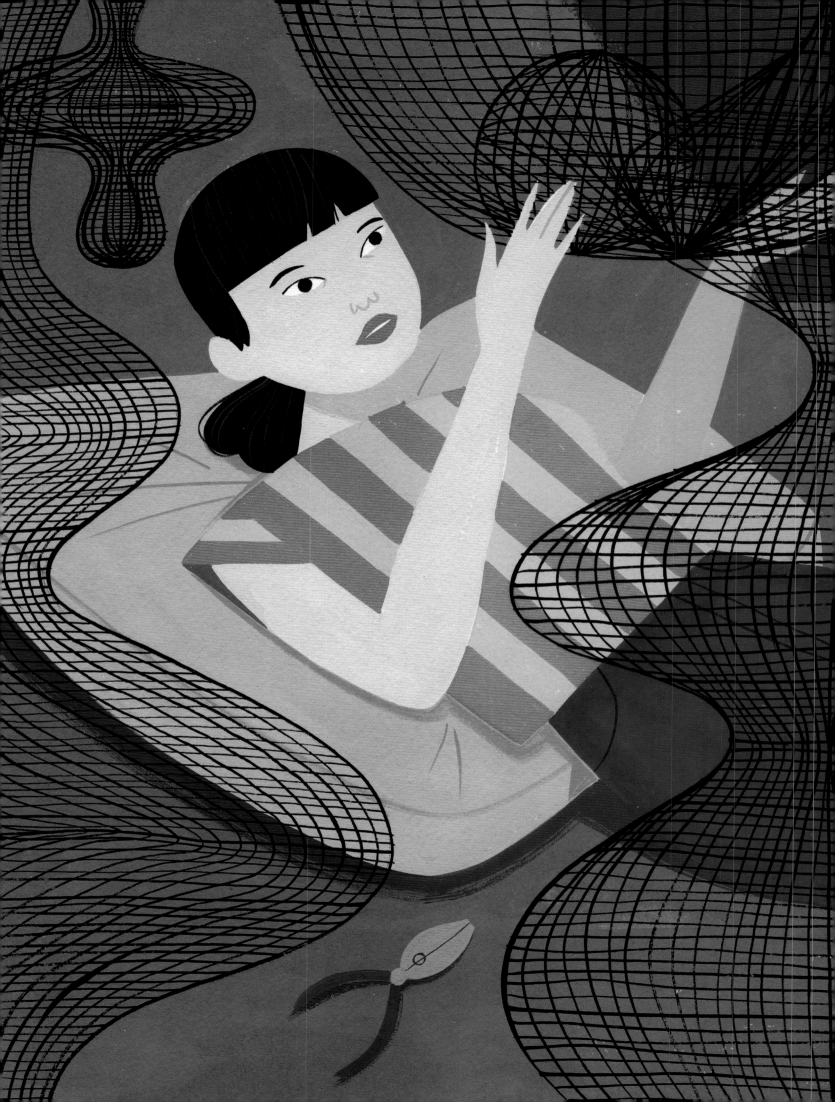

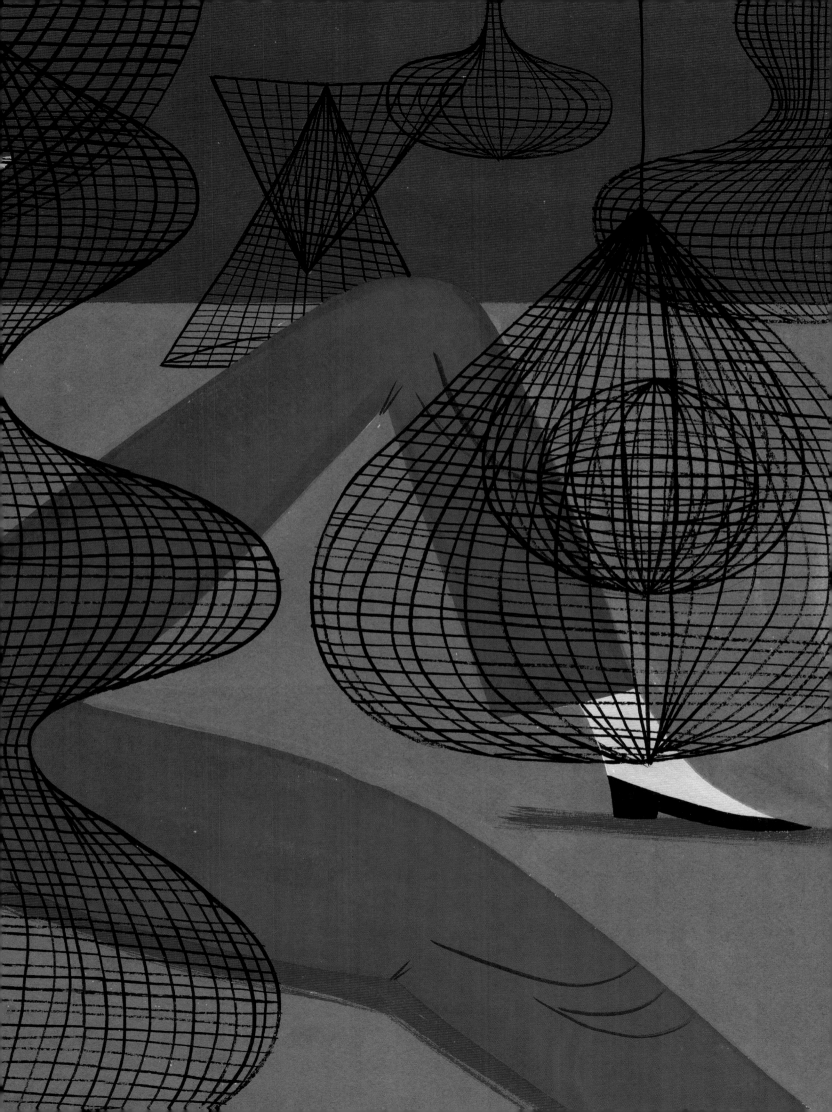

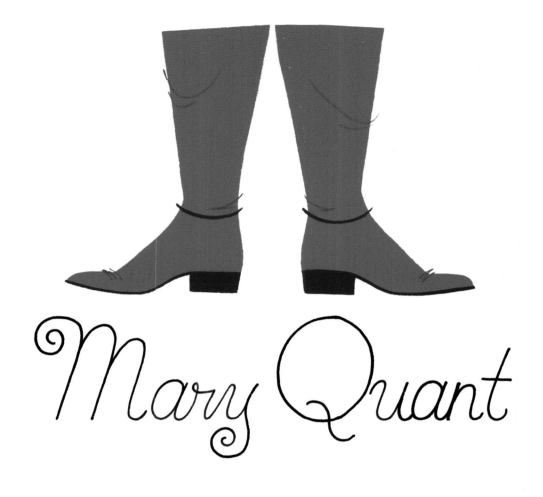

Mary Quant

and

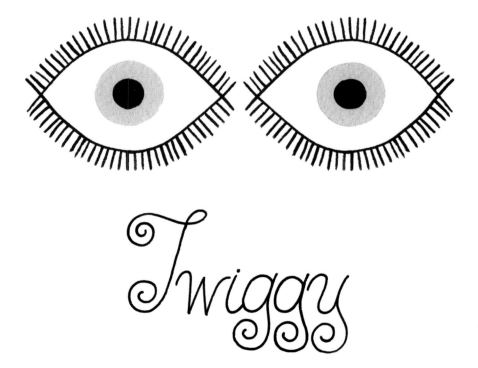

Twiggy

"The fashionable woman wears clothes. The clothes don't wear her."

"At sixteen, I was a funny, skinny little thing, all eyelashes and legs. And then, suddenly people told me it was gorgeous. I thought they had gone mad."

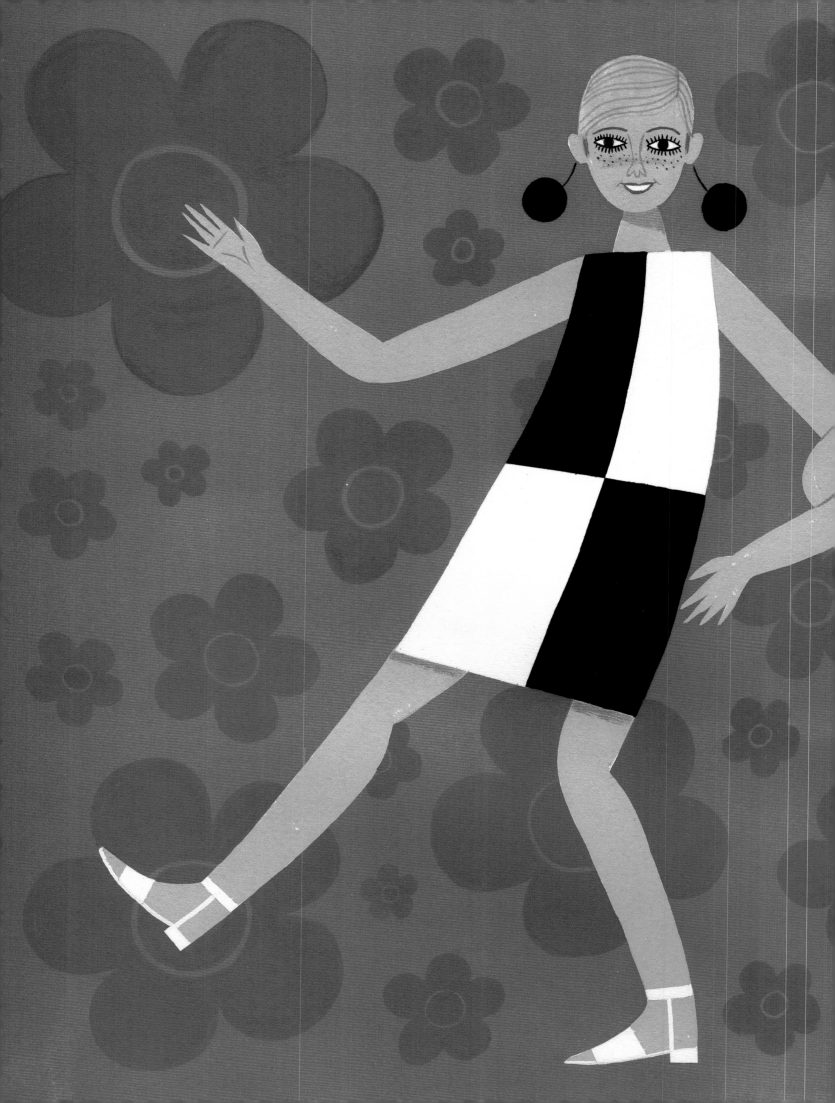

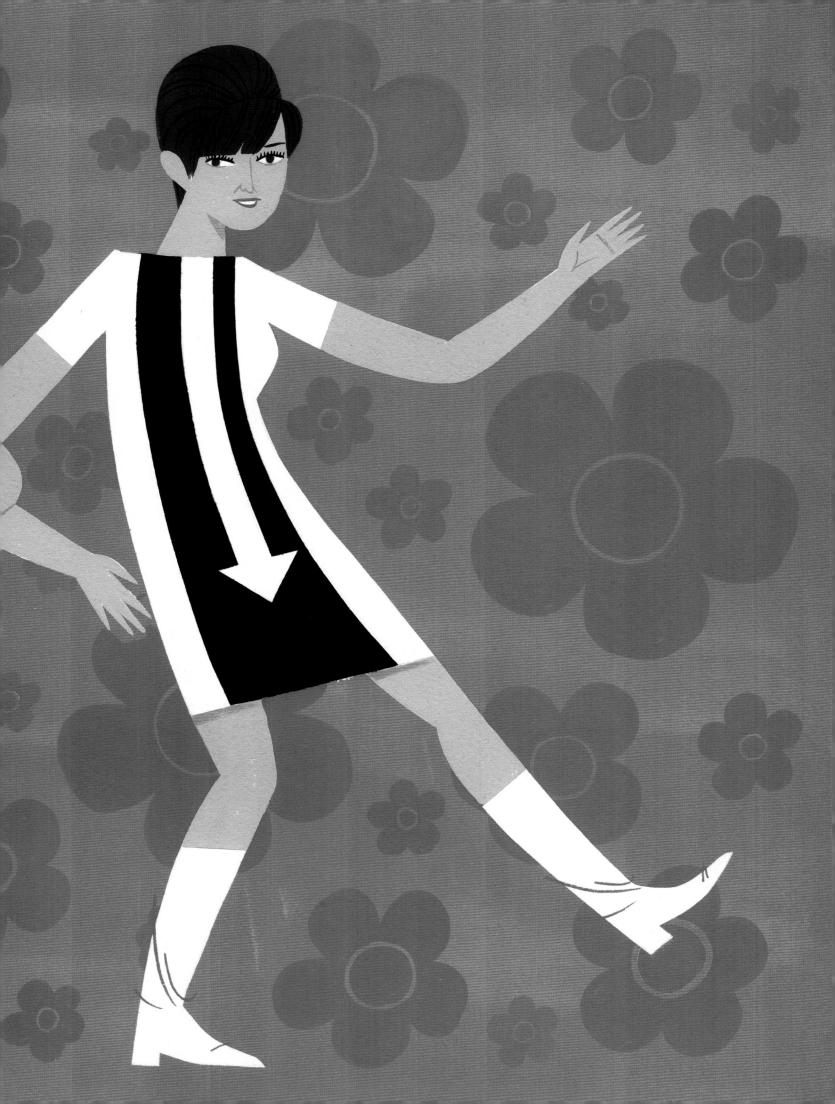

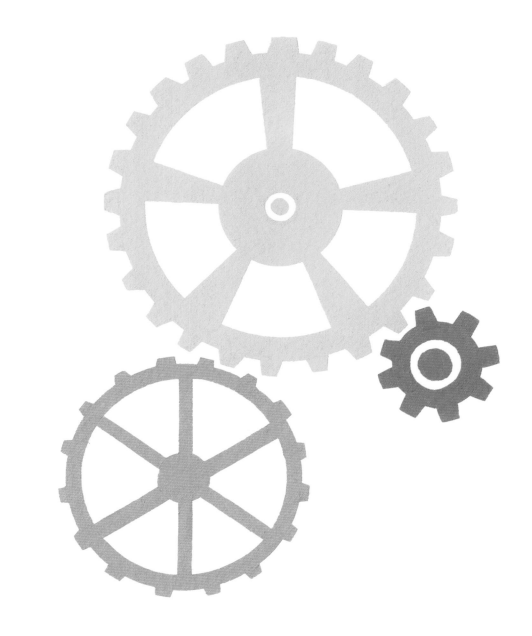

Louise Nevelson

"I never feel age.
... If you have
creative work, you
don't have age
or time."

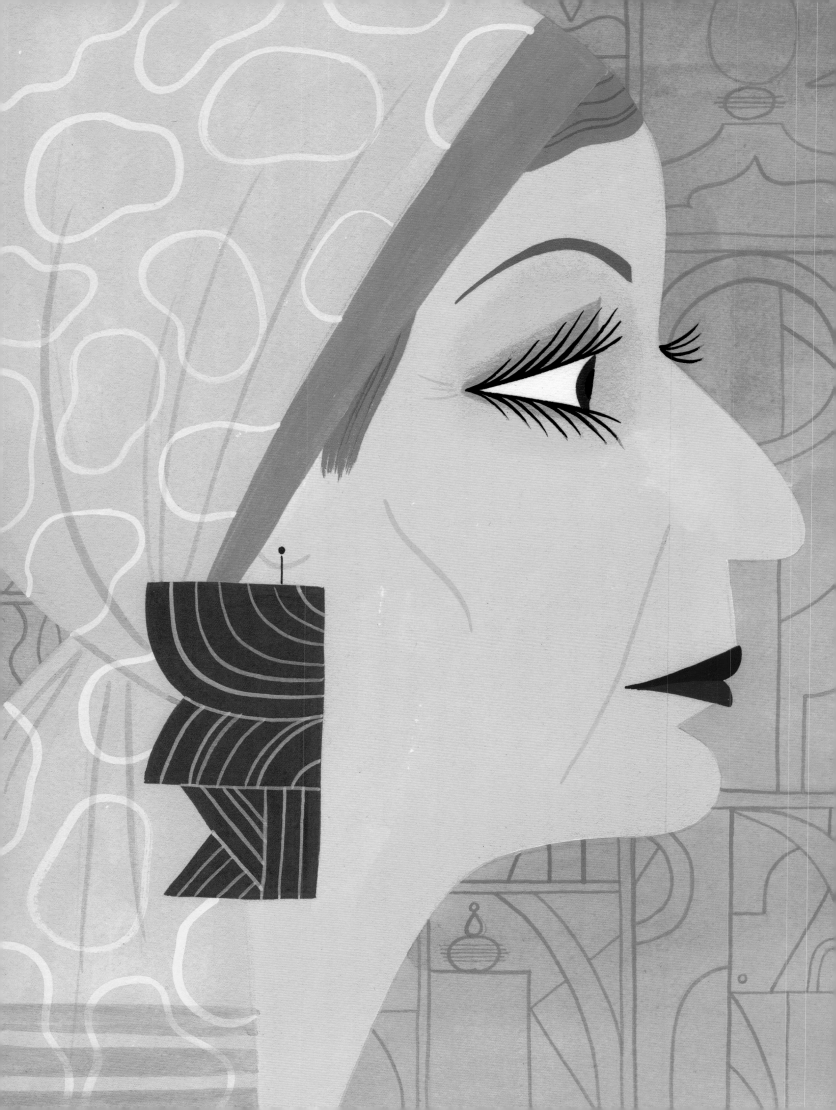

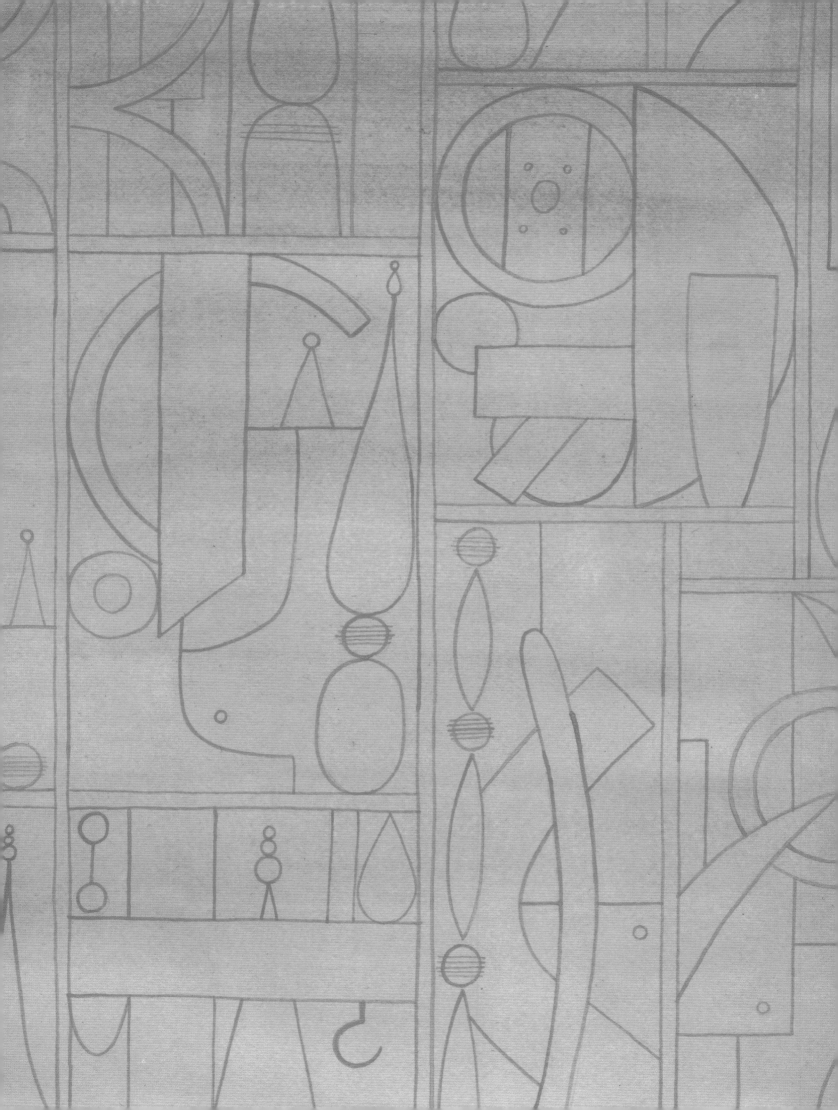

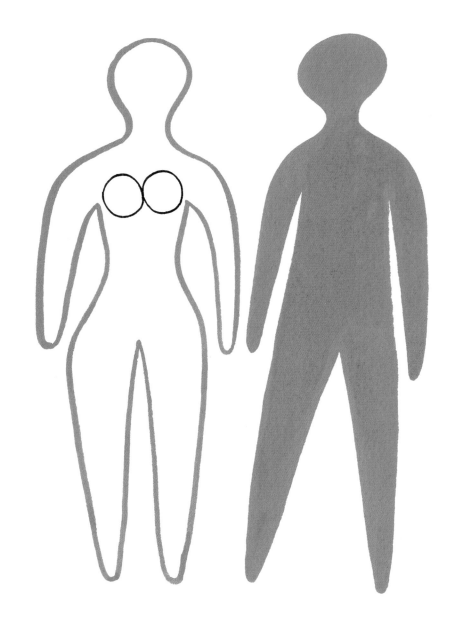

Elaine Lustig Cohen

"My gender may have been an issue for other designers, but not for my clients."

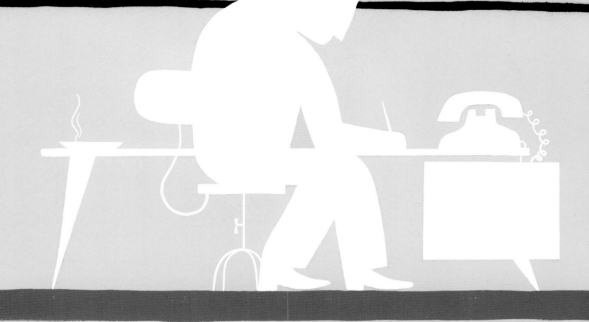

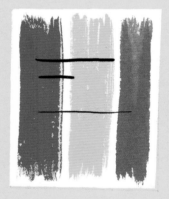

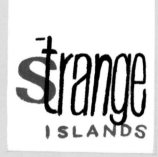

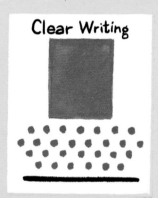

Clear Writing

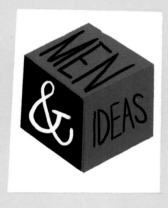

MEN & IDEAS

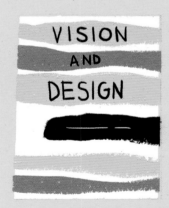

VISION AND DESIGN

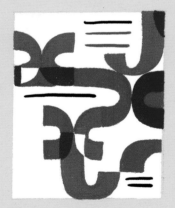

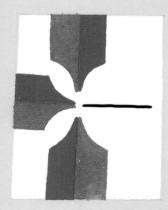

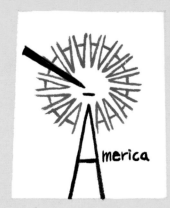

America

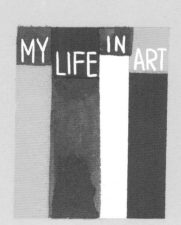

MY LIFE IN ART

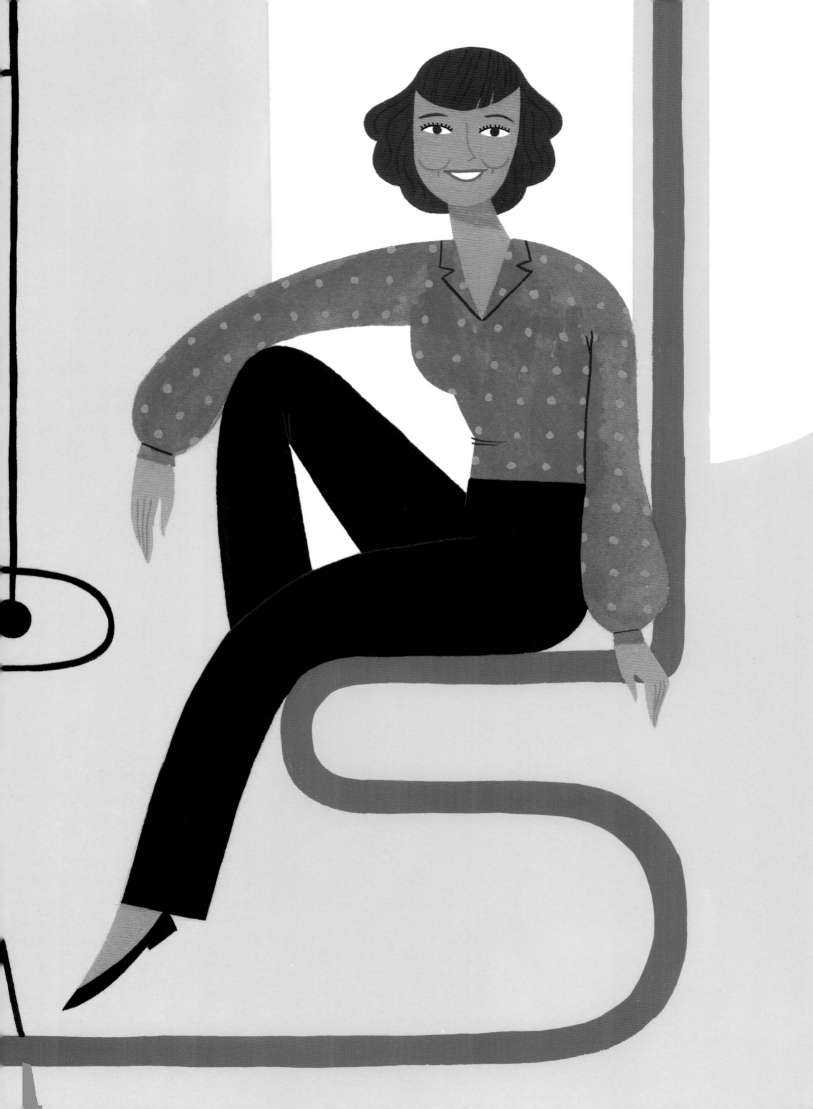

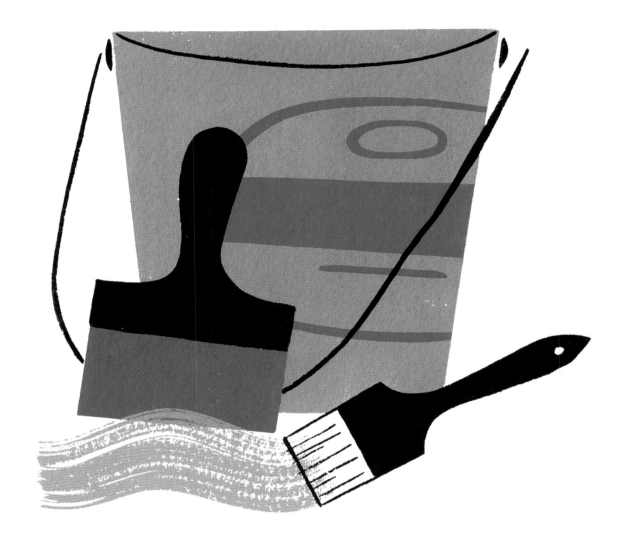

Helen Frankenthaler

"Go against the rules or ignore the rules. That is what invention is about."

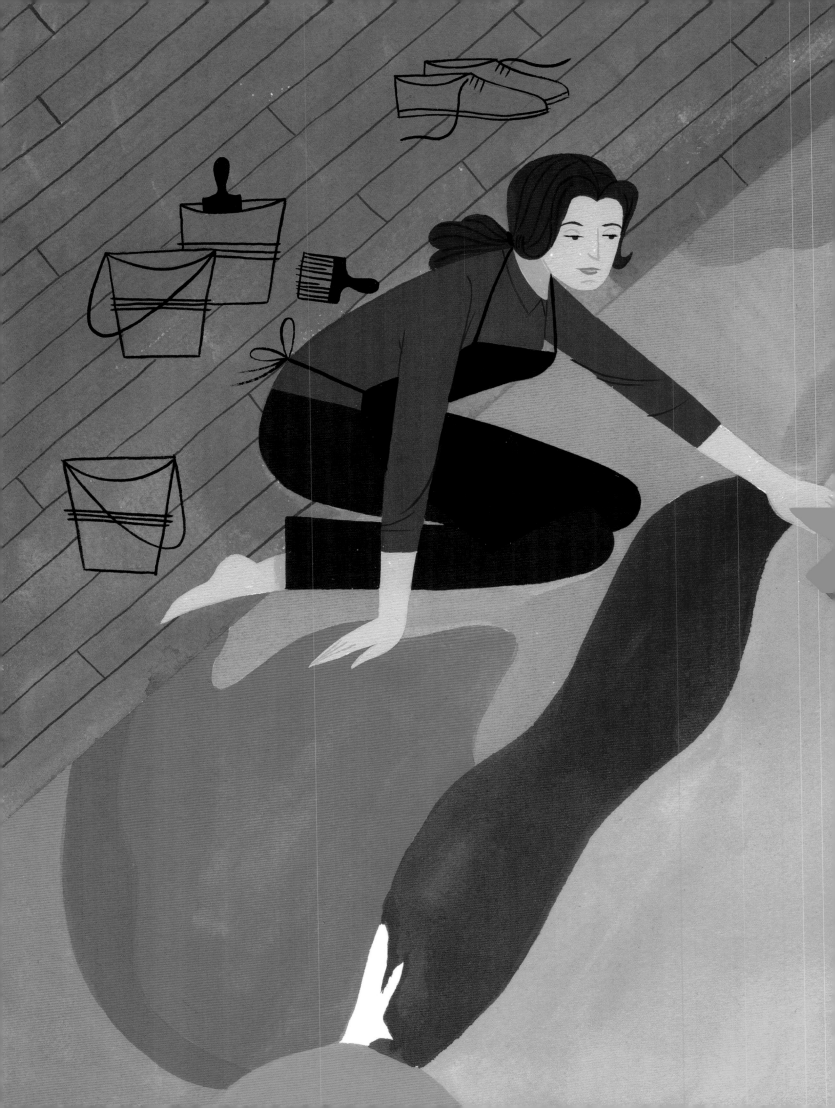

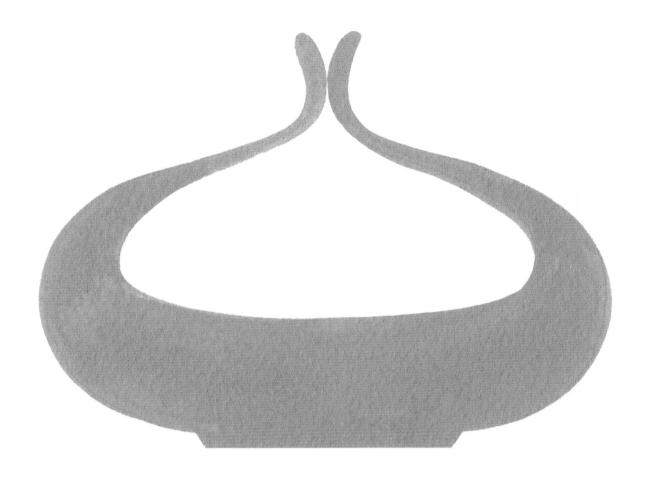

Eva Zeisel

"Beautiful things make people happy."

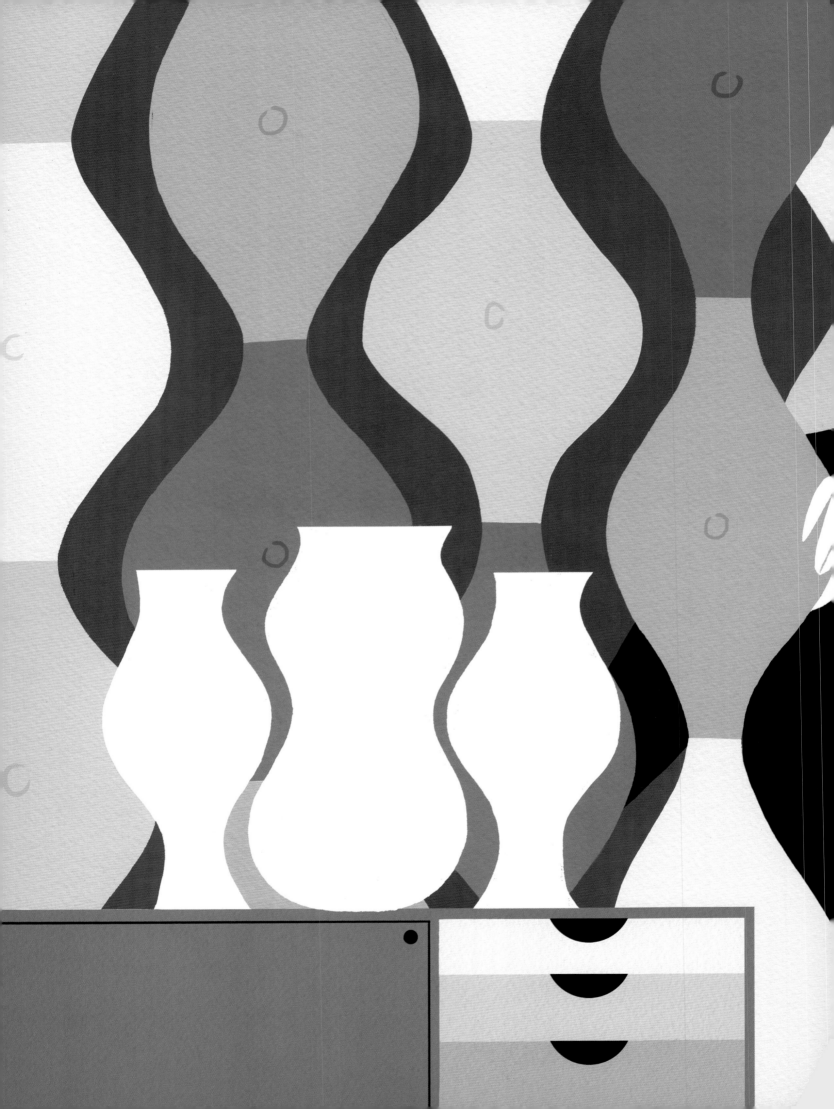

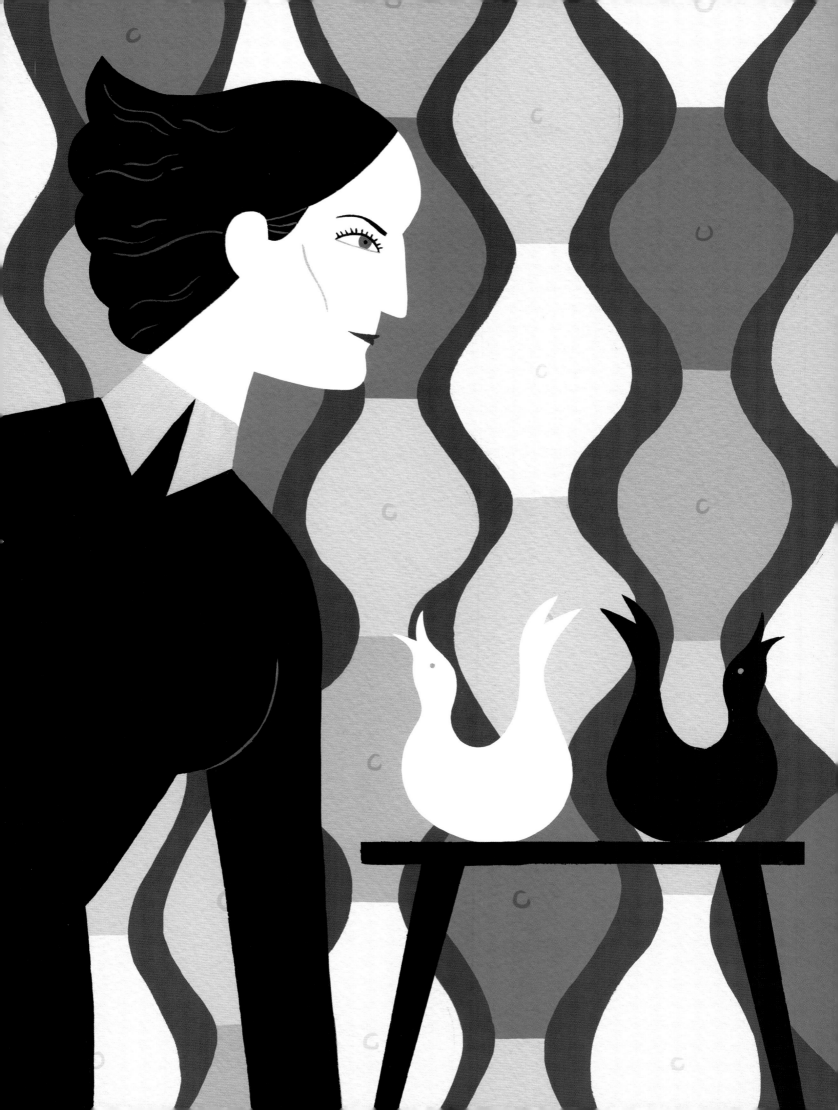

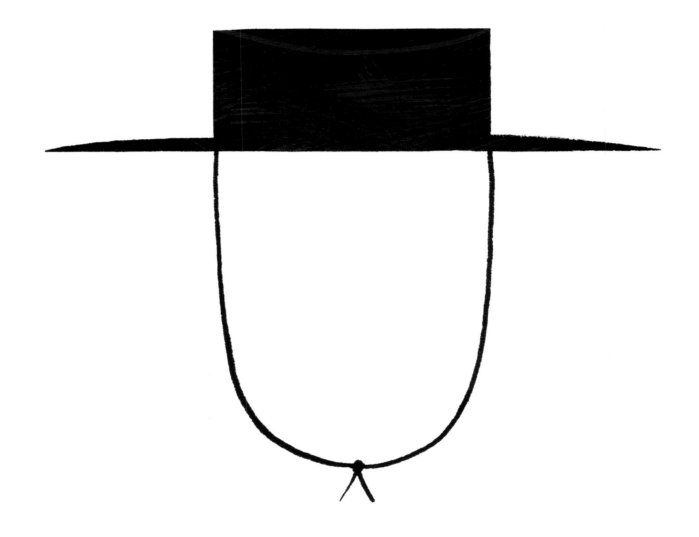

Georgia O'Keeffe

"I found I could say things with color and shapes that I couldn't say any other way— things I had no words for."

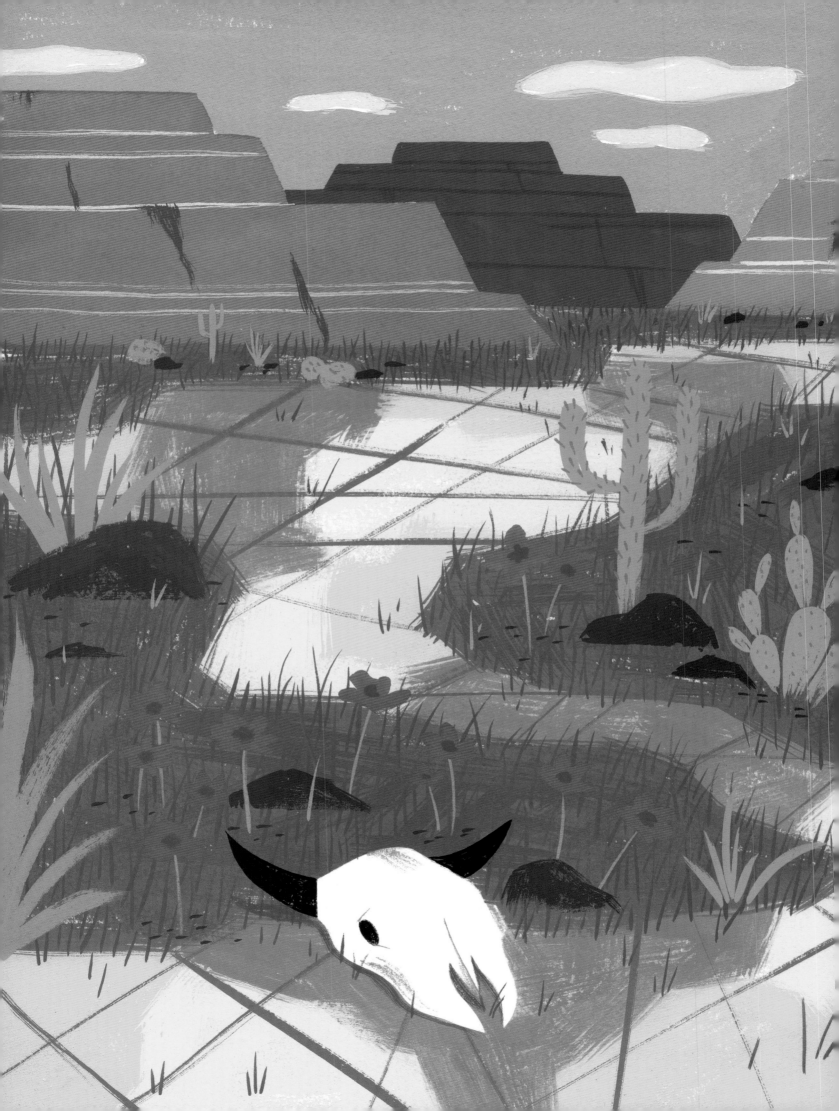

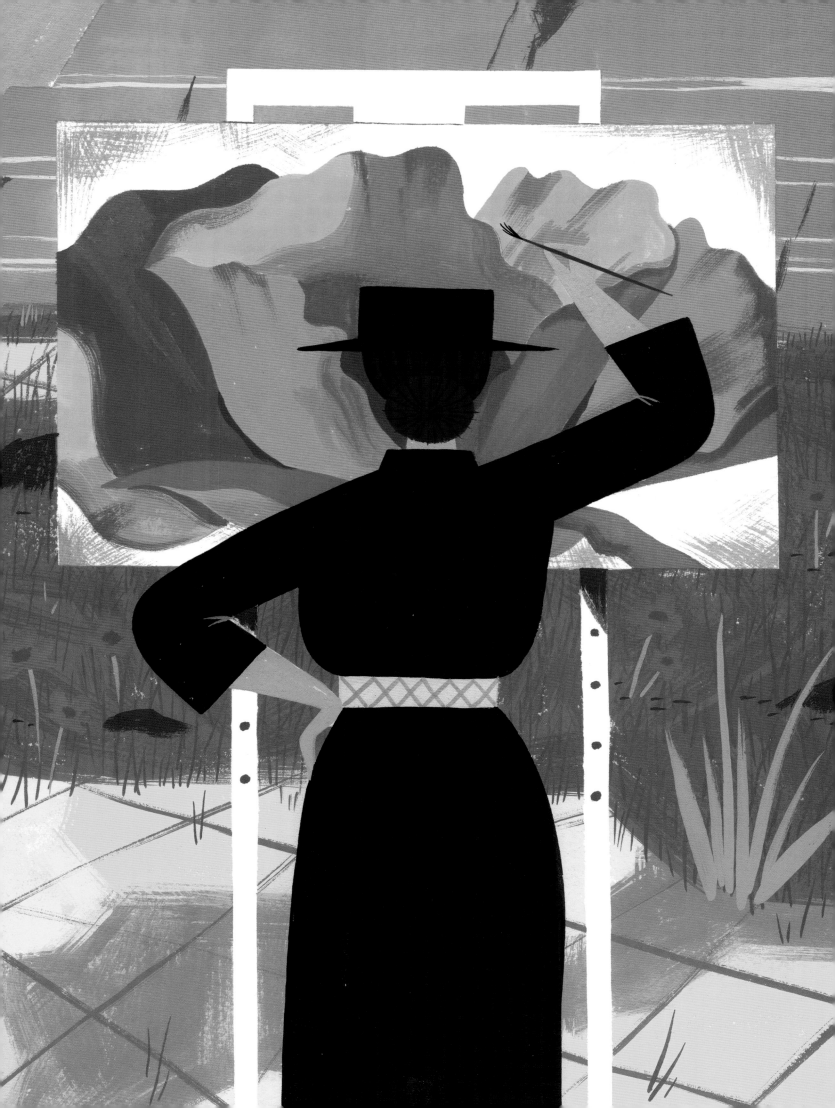

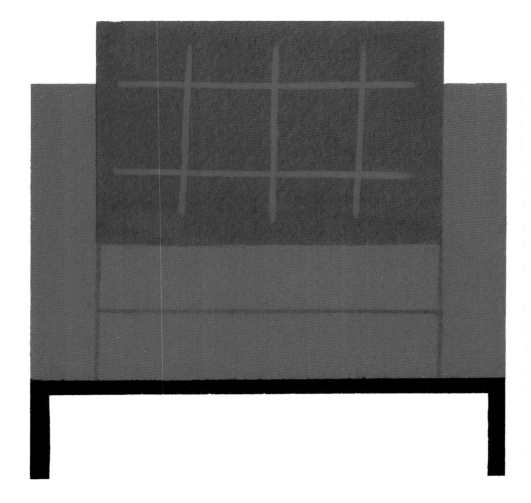

Florence Knoll

"Good design is good business."

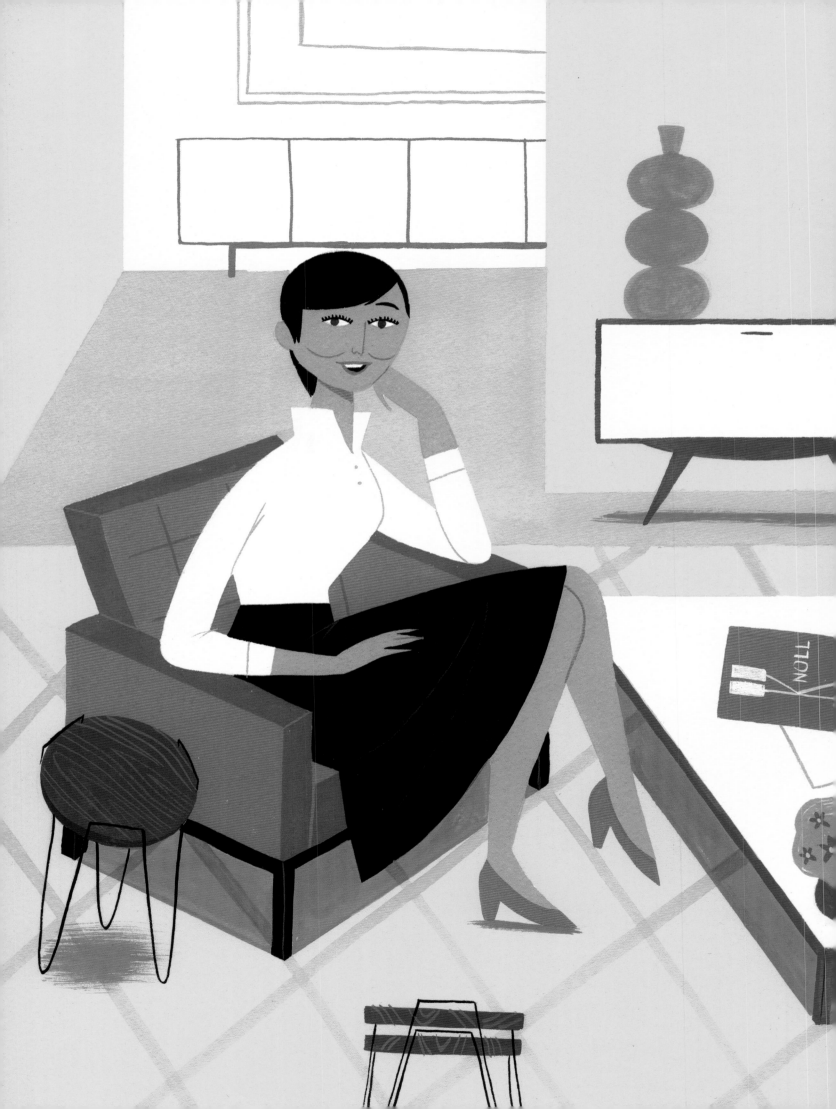

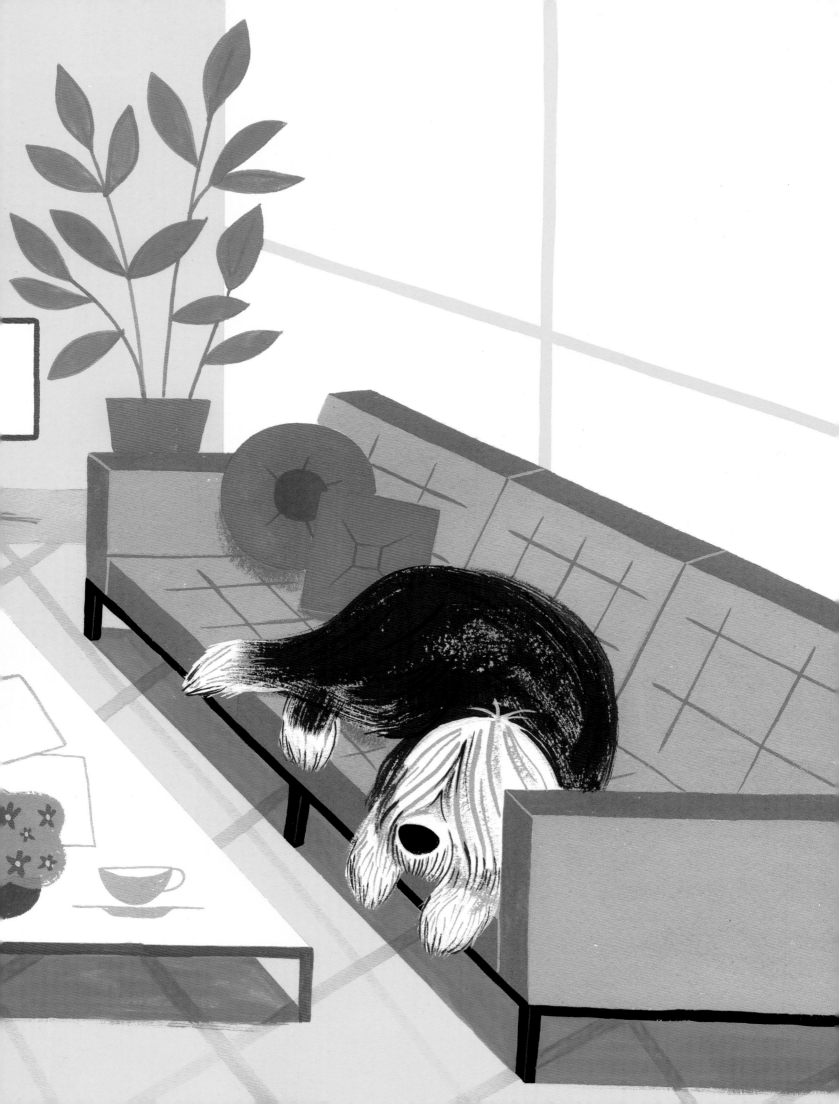

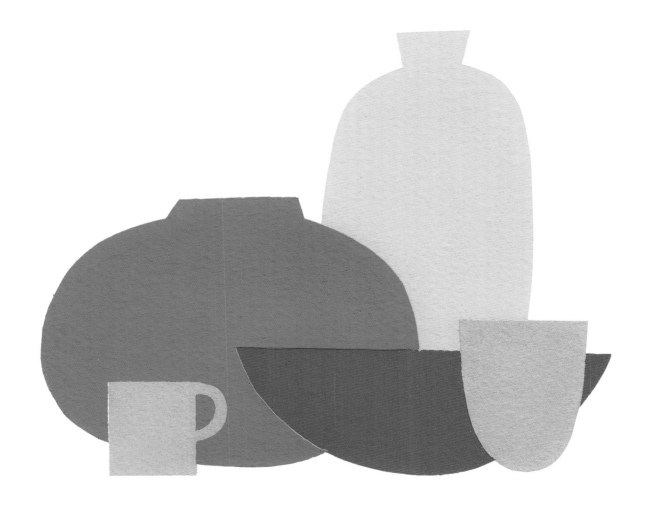

Edith Heath

"I was trying to do something that was more egalitarian rather than aristocratic."

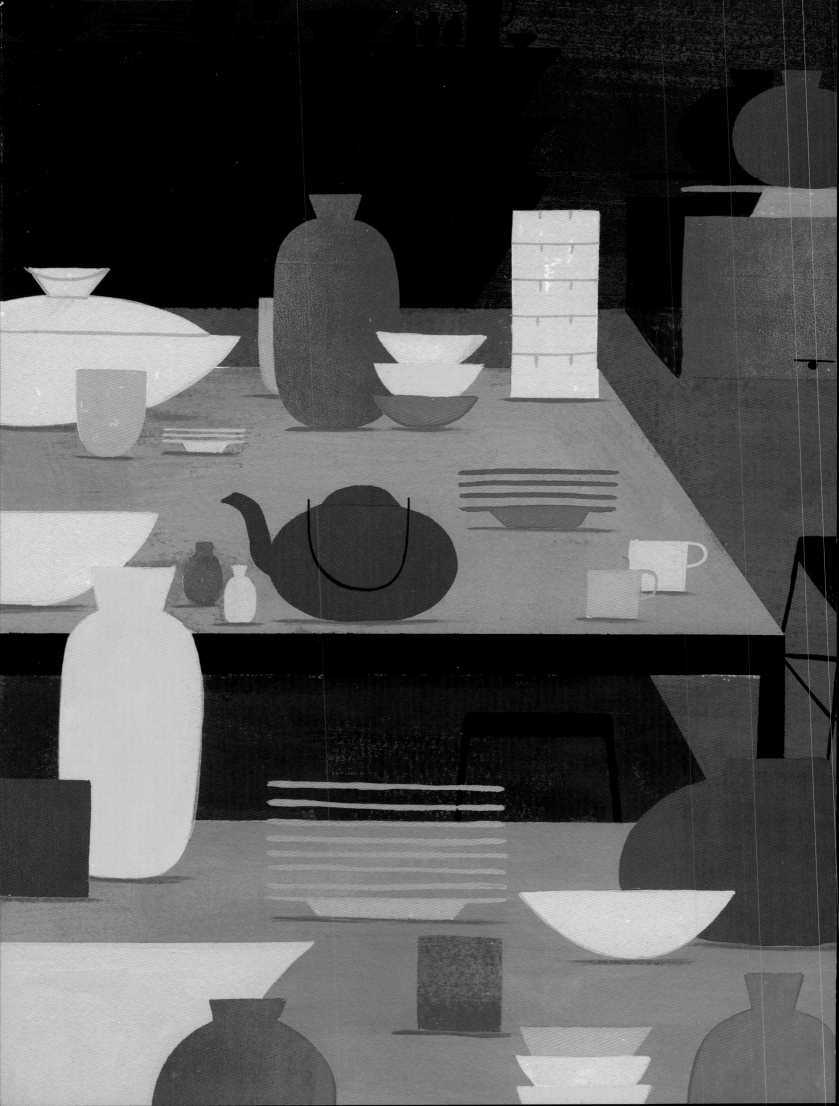

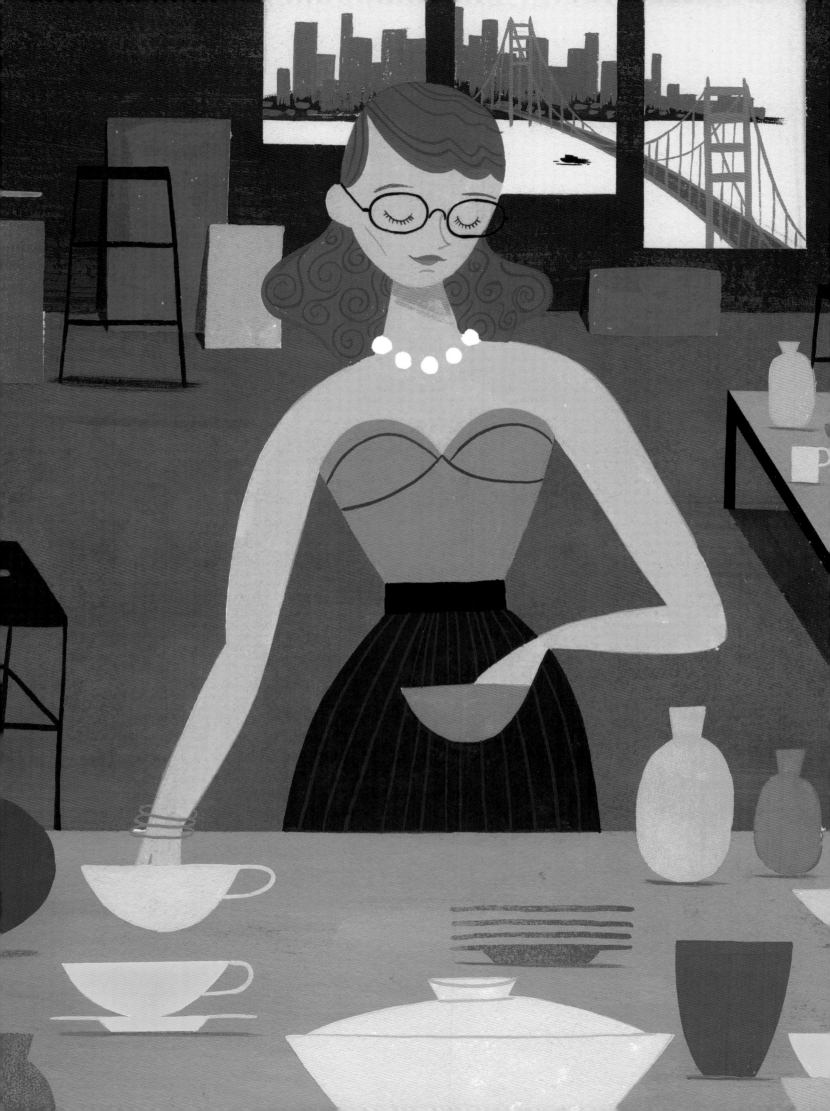

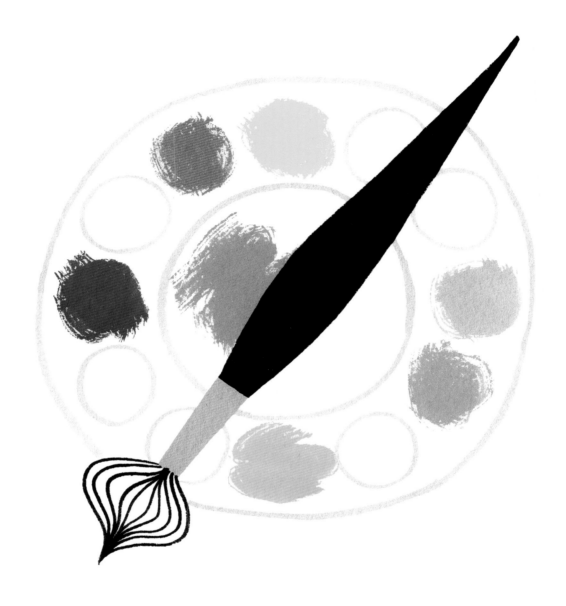

Alma Thomas

"What I would rather do is to paint something beautiful."

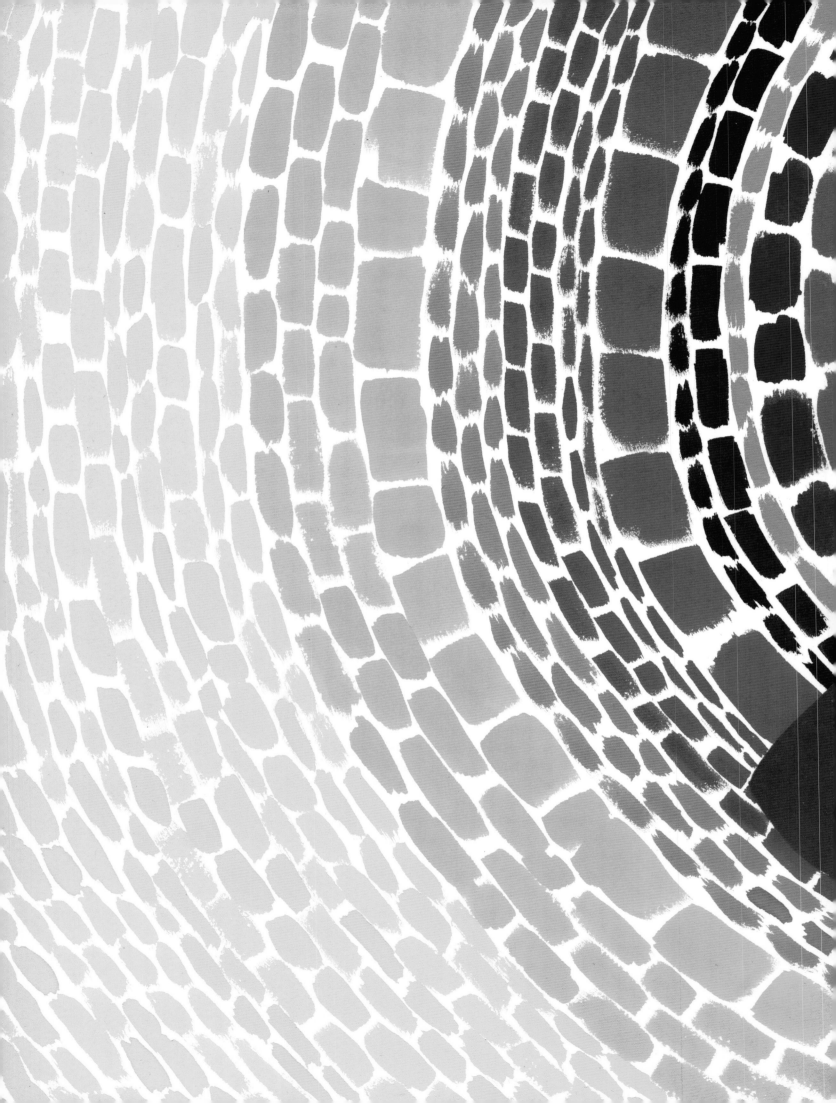

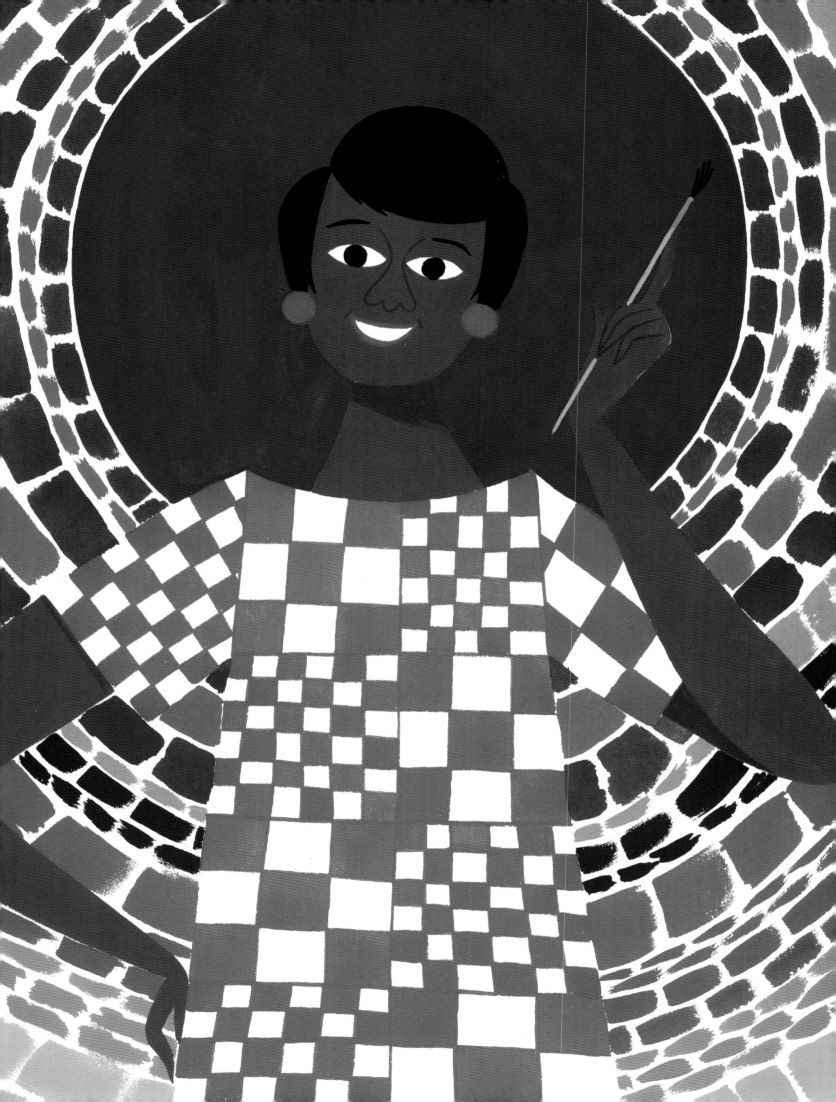

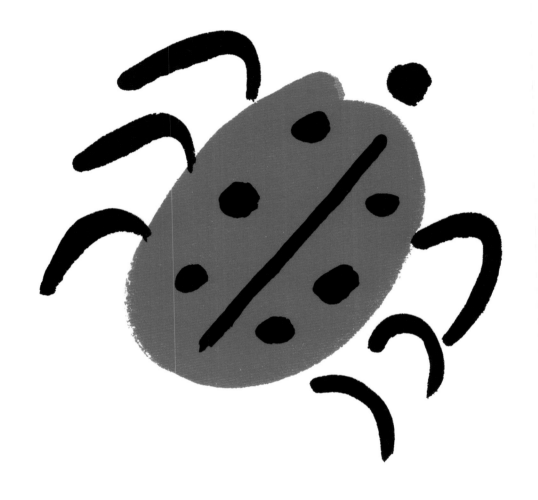

Vera Neumann

"As a child drawing wildflowers, ferns, and butterflies ... I dreamed that someday I would be an artist."

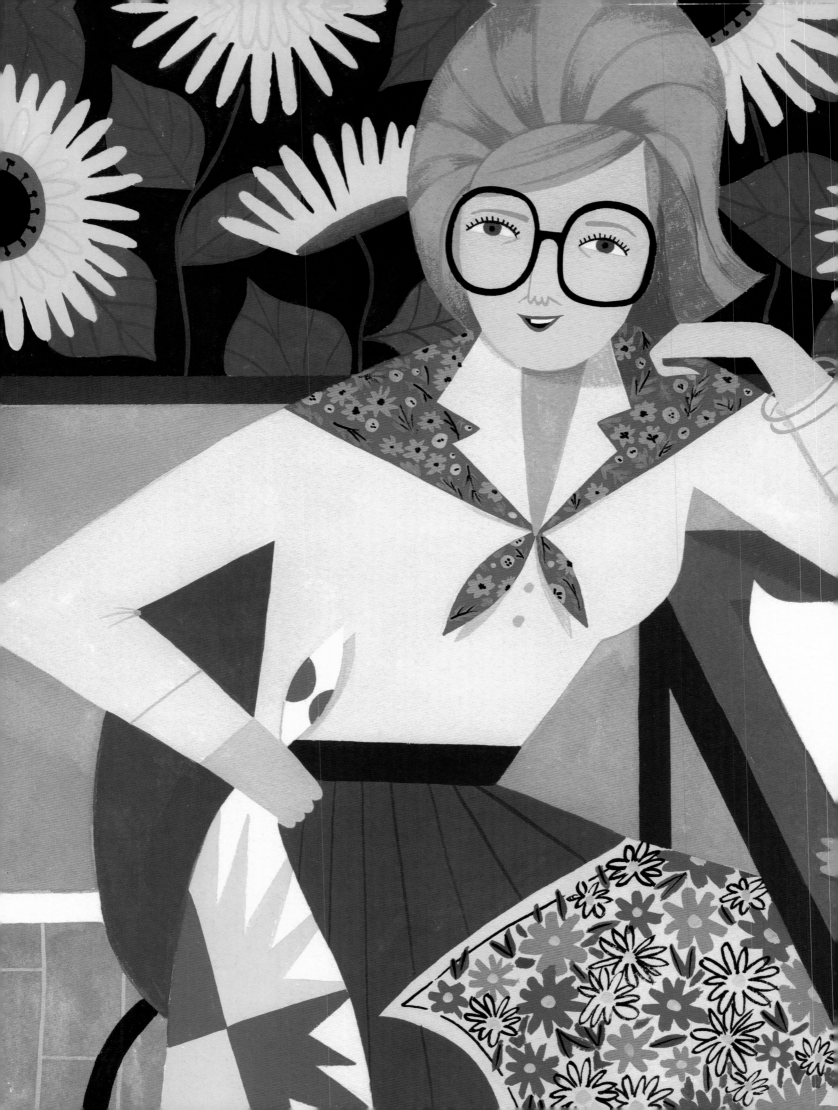

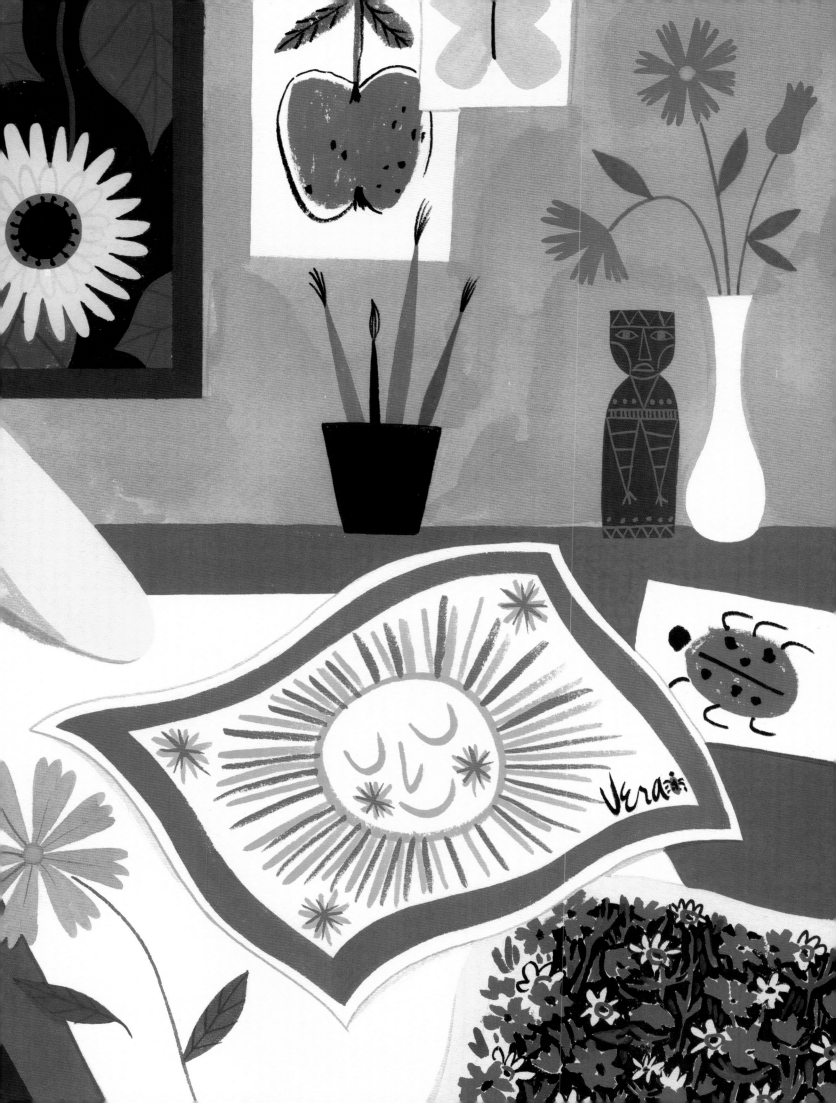

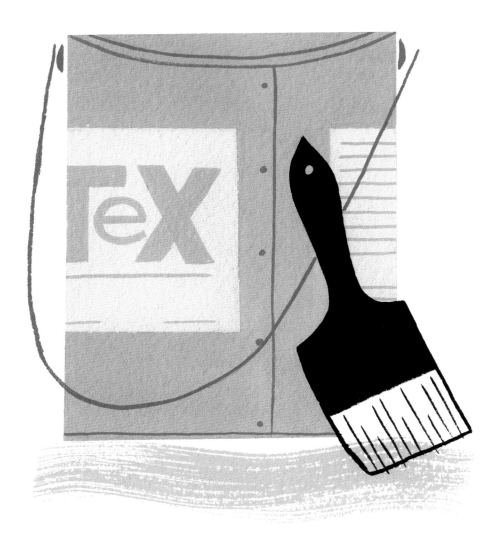

Eva Hesse

"In my inner soul art and life are inseparable."

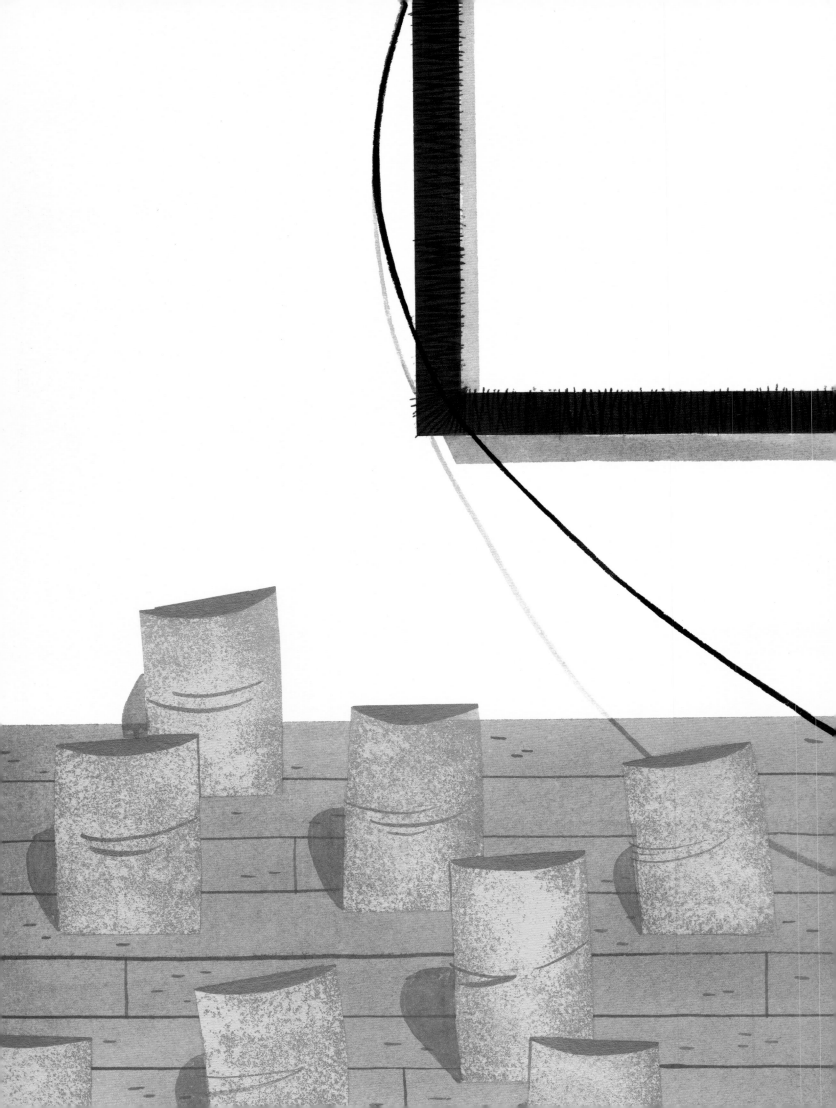

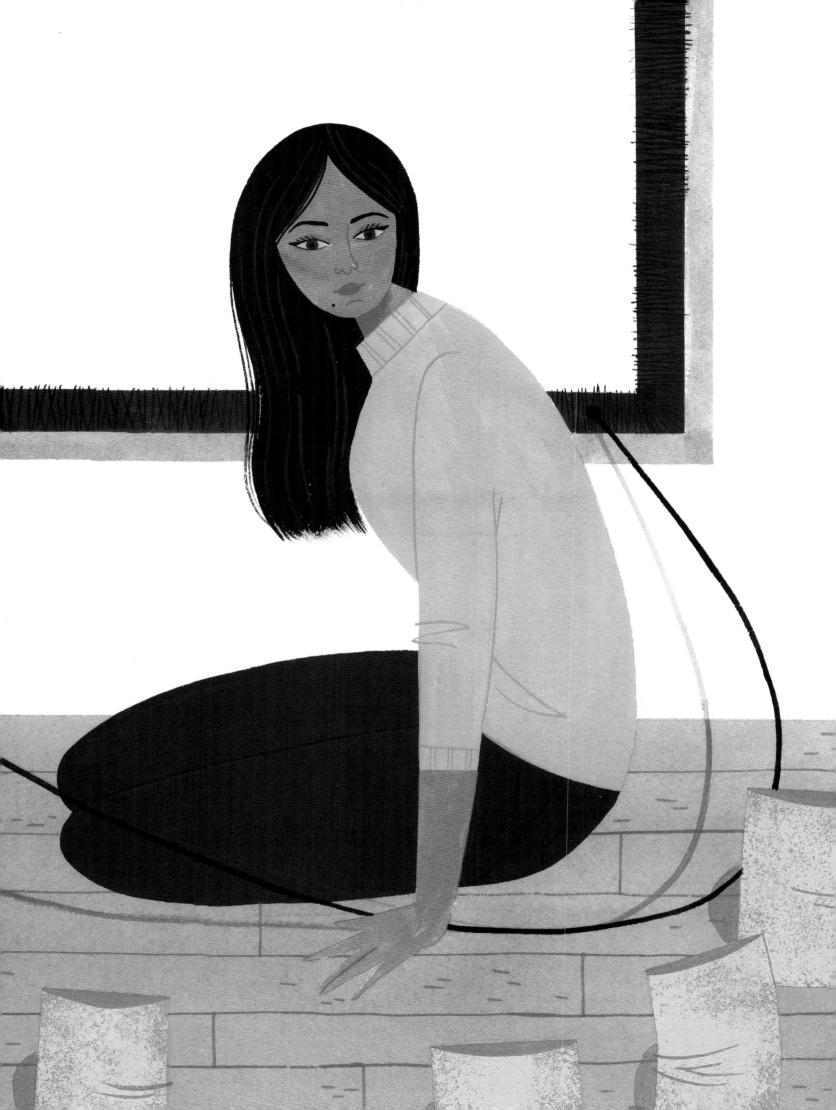

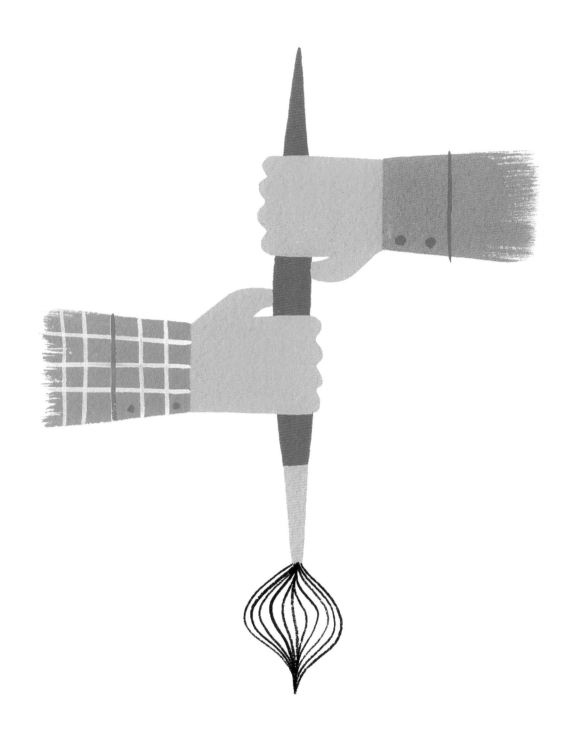

Alice Provensen

"We were a true collaboration. Martin and I really were one artist."

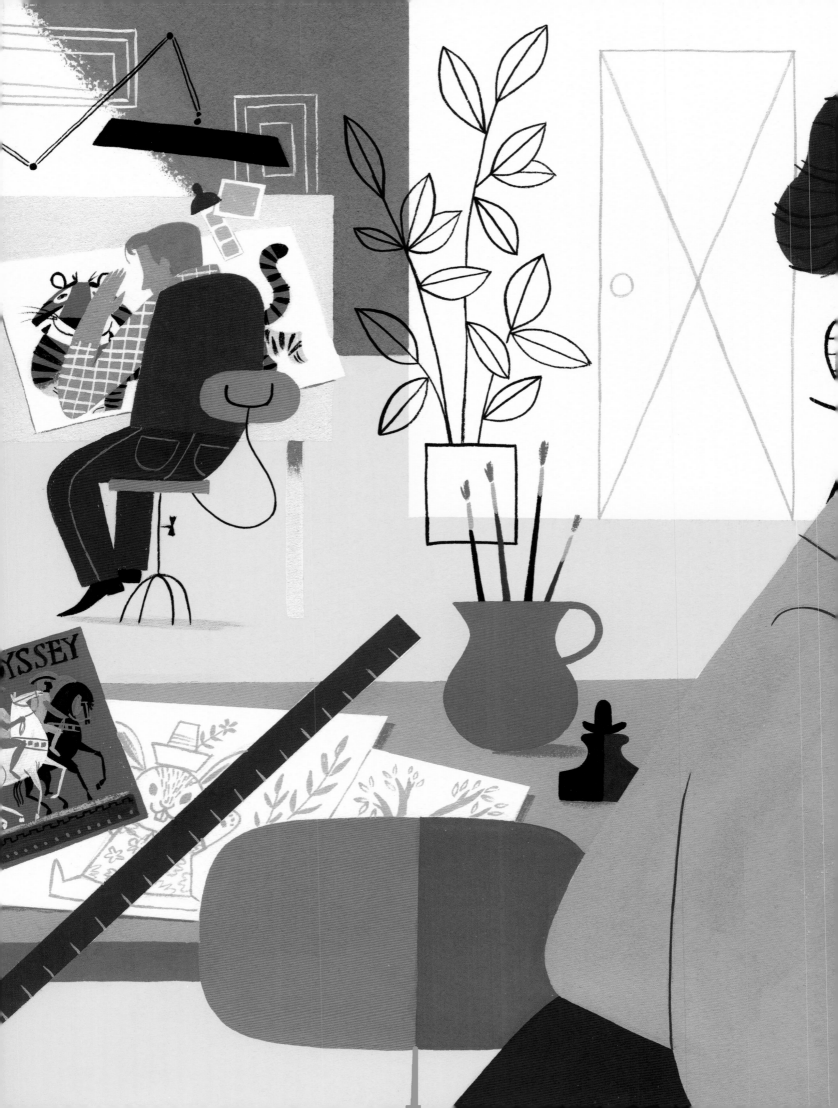

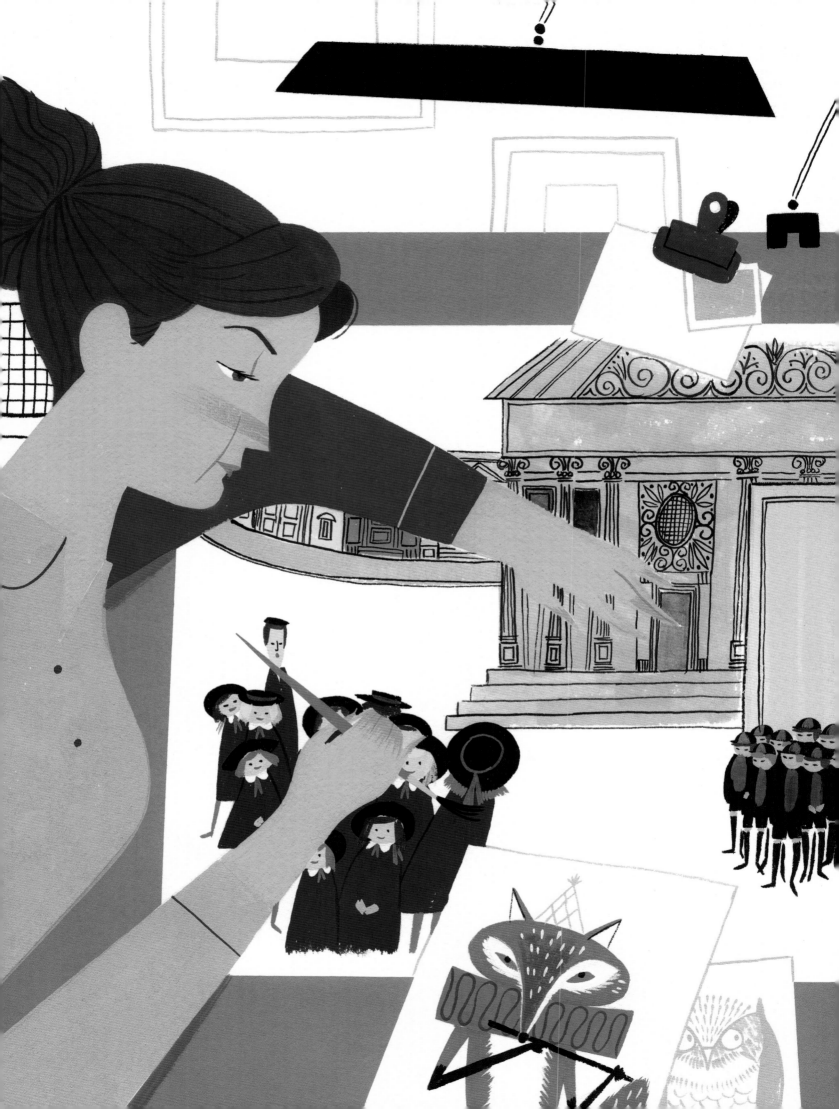

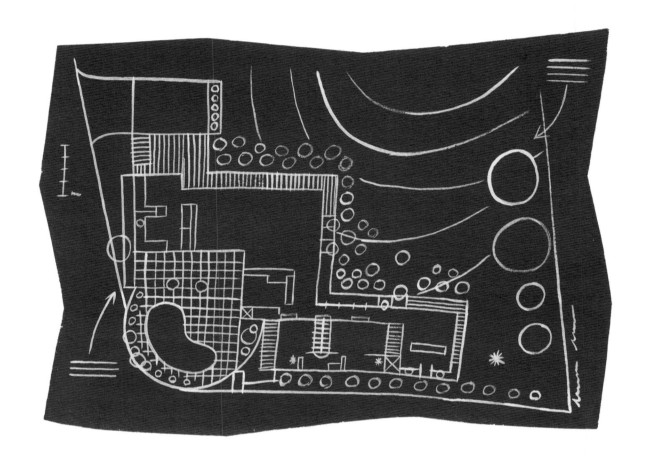

# Greta Magnusson-Grossman

"The easiest way to show what you can do is to do it on your own."

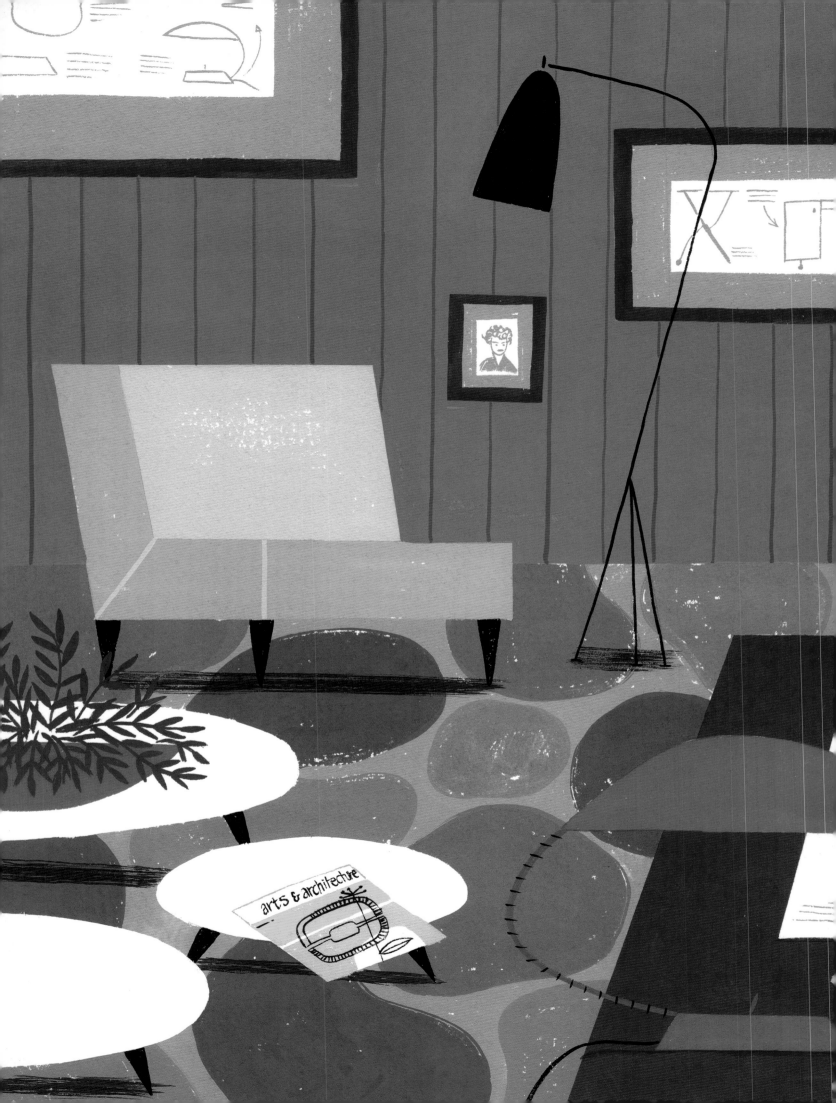

arts & architecture

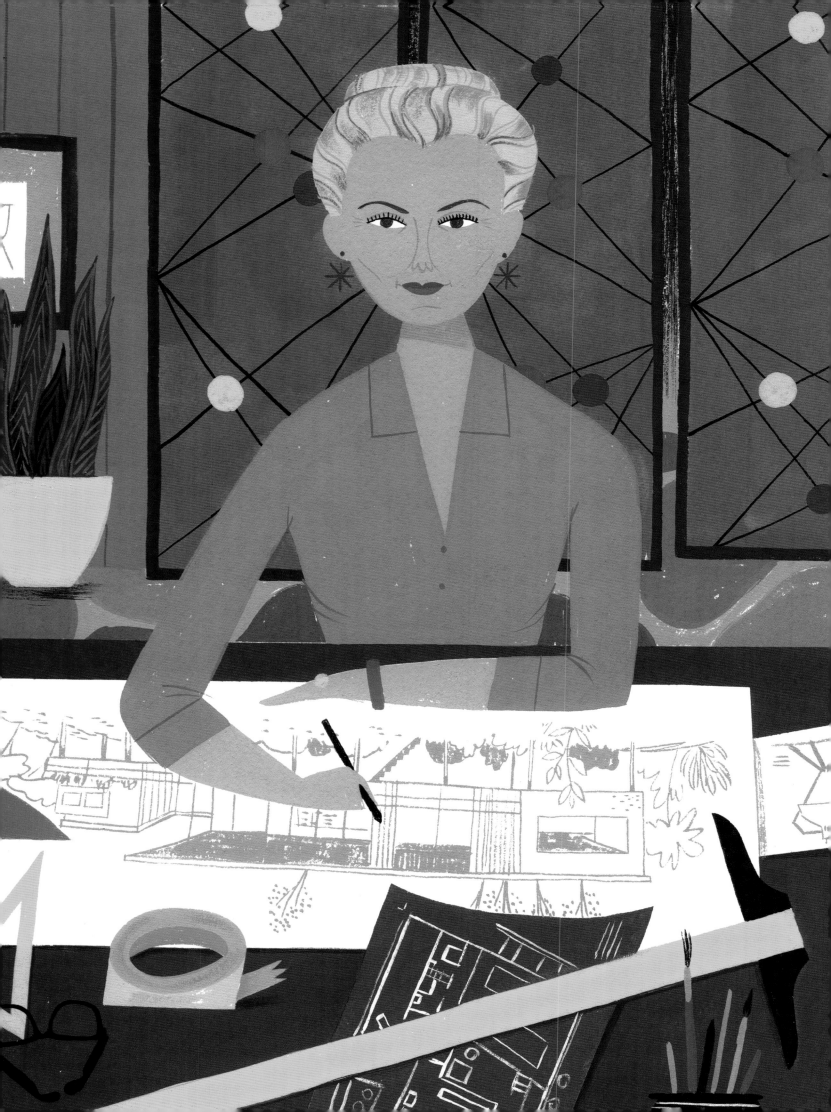

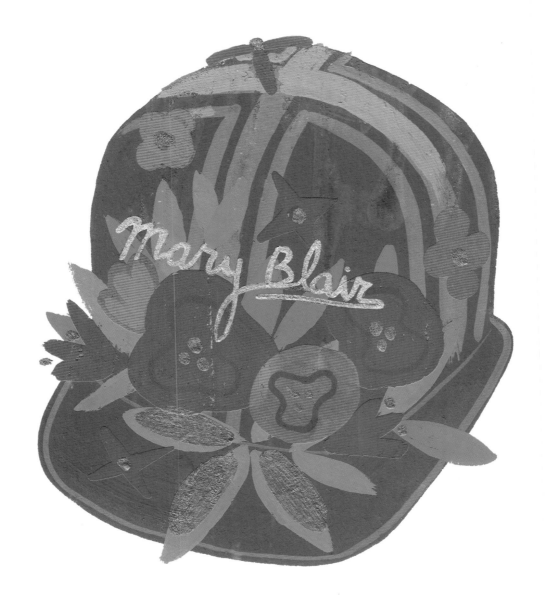

Mary Blair

"Walt [Disney] said that I knew about colors he had never heard of before."

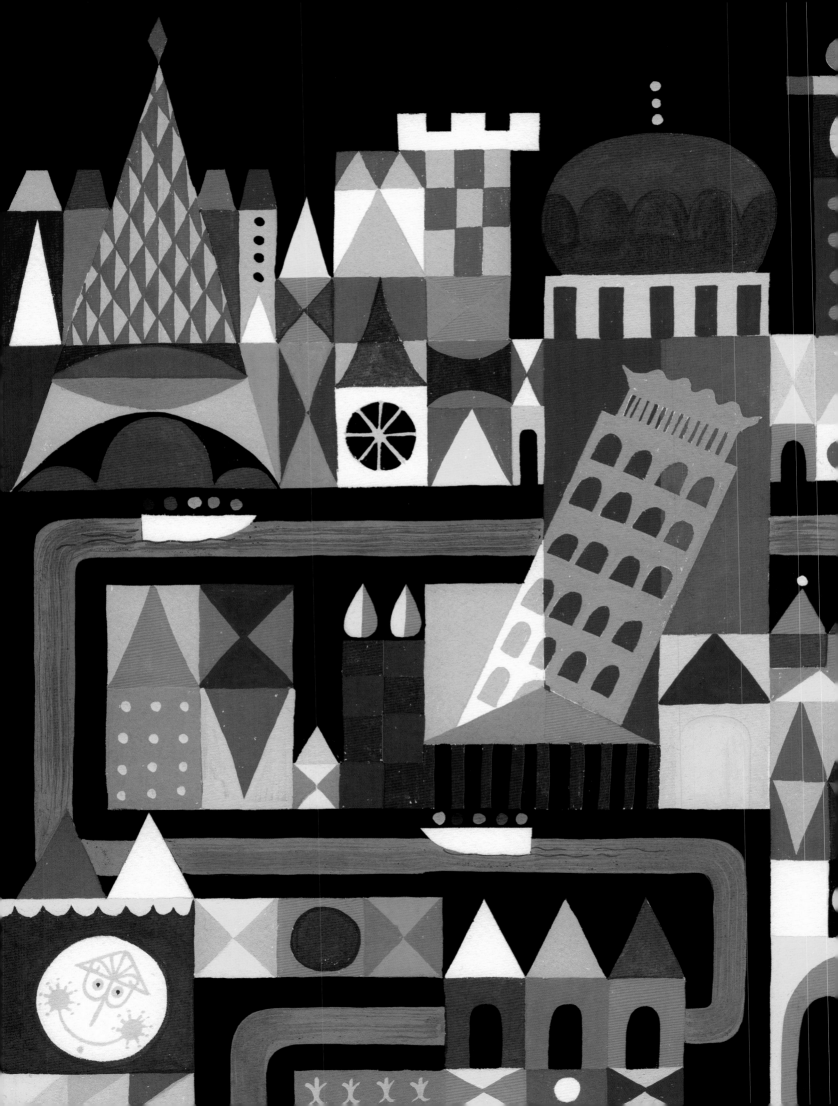

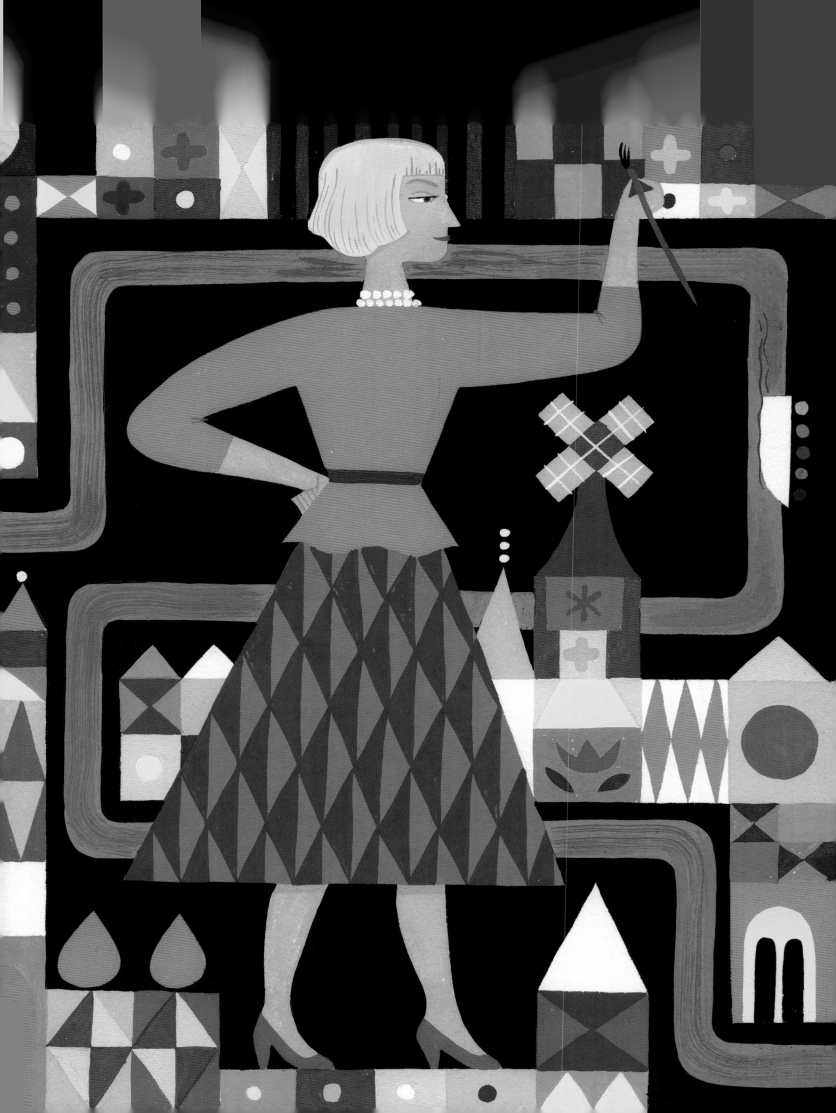

# Biographies

## 1 *Ray Eames*  (12.15.1912–08.21.1988)

Ray Eames was an artist, designer, and filmmaker most well known for the collaborative work she created with her husband, Charles Eames, and the Eames Office. Ray studied painting with the Abstract Expressionist artist Hans Hoffman in New York, and studied design at the Cranbrook Academy of Art in Michigan. At Cranbrook, Ray delved into many creative pursuits, foreshadowing the multi-disciplinary work of the Eames Office. As Ray later said, "I never gave up painting, I just changed my palette." It was also at Cranbrook that Ray met Charles, and within a year, in 1941, the two were married. The Eameses then moved west and set up the Eames Office in Venice, California, producing some of the most seminal furniture designs of the twentieth century, including Ray's sculptural, walnut stools for the Time-Life building that are still manufactured by Herman Miller to this day. During this time, Ray also designed many covers for the very influential *Arts & Architecture* magazine, created textile designs that are still produced by Maharam, and collaborated with Charles on numerous exhibits, films, toys, and more. In 1949, together they created the Case Study House #8, the landmark mid-twentieth-century residence that was to become their home for the rest of their lives. Ray meticulously displayed her folk art collection and treasures from their travels throughout their home. Far from the starkness that many associate with Modernism, the Eameses' home was, and still is, a space filled with warmth, personality, and delightful details curated by Ray Eames. Underscoring their lifelong partnership and connection to each other, Ray passed away ten years to the day that Charles died.

## 2 *Edith Head*  (10.28.1897–10.24.1981)

Edith Head is probably the most well-known costume designer in Hollywood, even to this day. She was nominated for thirty-five Academy Awards, including every year from 1948 through 1966, and won eight times—more Oscars than any other woman. Despite earning degrees in French and Romance Languages from UC Berkeley and Stanford universities in Northern California, Edith Head was completely self-taught in the field of costume design. At Paramount Pictures in Hollywood, she quickly became a favorite of movie stars and directors, and created memorable costumes for Grace Kelly in Alfred Hitchcock's *To Catch a Thief*, as well as Audrey Hepburn's quintessential look in *Breakfast at Tiffany's*, to name just a few. Unlike her male contemporaries, Edith was known for consulting with her female stars extensively. It was because of this practice that she became a favorite amongst some of the biggest leading ladies in Hollywood. There were even a few stars for whom she designed a personal wardrobe. One of those stars was Barbara Stanwyck, whose son Dion secretly offered Edith $6 to make a "nice dress" for his mommy's Christmas present. When Edith agreed, Stanwyck supplied the remaining several hundred dollars. When Edith was asked about her favorite star to dress, she said, "I've dressed thousands of actors, actresses, and animals, but whenever I am asked which star is my personal favorite, I answer, 'Grace Kelly.' She is a charming lady, a most gifted actress, and, to me, a valued friend." With her signature bangs, thick-rimmed, round glasses, and tailored two-piece suits, Edith Head's personal style was a serious and consistent uniform that was in stark contrast to her elaborate and feminine designs.

## 3 *Peggy Moffitt*  (b. 05.14.1940)

During the 1960s, the California born-and-raised model Peggy Moffitt caused a sensation as the muse for both fashion designer Rudi Gernreich's bold and graphic clothing designs, and her photographer husband William Claxton's classic and stunning photographs of Peggy in these designs. Perhaps none more so than Gernreich's monokini. The monokini was a bathing suit that revealed a woman's top half and was a symbol of the freedom and liberation that was emerging around that period of time. The striking black-and-white photograph of Peggy modeling the monokini was taken by her renowned photographer husband, whose images immortalized the likes of Jazz legend Chet Baker, film star Steve McQueen, and so many other notable artists of the era. It became a worldwide news event when *Women's Wear Daily* published the photograph in 1964, catapulting Peggy into the media spotlight. Peggy's background in dance gave a fluidity to her movements that was captured on film by William Claxton. Together they created what is considered the first fashion video: *Basic Black*, which is now in the permanent collection at MoMA in New York. Additionally, in 1966, Peggy appeared alongside Vanessa Redgrave and Veruschka in italian director Michelangelo Antonioni's cult classic *Blow Up*, a film that captured the zeitgeist of the the swinging sixties in London through the lens of a fashion photographer. Coupled with her Kabuki-style makeup she created herself and her five-point, geometric Vidal Sassoon haircut, Peggy invented a look all her own. Indeed, she wasn't just a model; she was also an aesthetic collaborator and communicator whose signature visual style helped define an era.

## Yayoi Kusama  (b. 03.22.1929)

Straying from tradition all of her life, Yayoi Kusama has flourished with an artistic career based largely on her obsession with polka dots. As a young girl in Japan, her parents did not support her creative pursuits, so Yayoi used sacks from the family's plant business as painting canvas. Even as she began her training at the Kyoto Art Academy, Yayoi rejected the school's traditional teachings and began to infuse her now-famous polka dots into her artwork. Over the course of her lifetime, Yayoi has endured effects of mental illness, including hallucinations, but rather than be burdened by these experiences, she has used them as inspiration, and her artwork as an escape. In fact, since the 1970s, Yayoi has voluntarily lived in a mental hospital in Japan a short distance away from her studio. Despite this unusual setup, or more likely because of it, Yayoi has emerged as one of the most prolific and recognized artists of our time. Beginning in the 1950s and 1960s, Yayoi began painting surfaces with her now-signature polka dots. She has created paintings, performance art pieces, and installations, including her amazing and immersive *Infinity Mirrored* rooms that have become celebrated, must-see events in world-class museums around the world. Yayoi has had recent retrospective shows at both the Museum of Modern Art and the Whitney Museum of American Art in New York, as well as the Tate Modern in London. And at eighty-six years young, she continues to create new pieces, and work with her beloved polka dots: "Polka dots can't stay alone. When we obliterate nature and our bodies with polka dots we become part of the unity of our environments."

## Frida Kahlo  (07.06.1907–07.13.1954)

One of the most important artists of the twentieth century, Frida Kahlo is known for her striking appearance, her turbulent marriage to painter Diego Rivera, and her vibrant paintings. Frida often incorporated the lush colors, vegetation, and wildlife of her native Mexico, and her self-portraits often depicted references to the body and physical pain and injury, a reference to a childhood of polio and a debilitating bus accident at the age of eighteen. Frida is quoted as saying, "I paint myself because I am so often alone, and because I am the subject I know best." Despite experiencing such physical pain, she forged a life and a career on her own terms and was openly bisexual in a time and a culture where this was taboo. Frida received her first solo exhibition in 1938 in New York City at the Julien Levy Gallery. From there she began to receive further recognition for her artwork, traveling to Paris and befriending Pablo Picasso. After returning to Mexico, Frida continued to paint, as well as teaching art and becoming a member of the Seminario de Cultura Mexicana—to promote Mexican art and culture. Throughout her life, Frida continued to face health issues, and when she received her first solo exhibition in Mexico in 1953, her doctor forbid her from attending. Too determined to miss such an important event, she was carried on a stretcher and lay on a bed in the center of the gallery. Still, it was not until after Frida's death, at age forty-seven, that her life and her paintings became truly famous and appreciated worldwide.

## Maija Isola  (03.15.1927–03.03.2001)

Known for her bright, floral and geometric patterns produced for Finnish design house Marimekko, Maija Isola created brilliant textile designs for more than three decades. She began her career at the esteemed company, formerly Printex, in 1949, and during her thirty-eight years with the firm, she designed more than 500 pieces. Maija found inspiration from her travels abroad and was very influenced by folk art, modern visual art, and nature. Often thought of as a recluse, Maija preferred working at home alone, sitting on a sheepskin on the floor, surrounded by her paint and brushes. Maija designed her most well-known pattern, Unikko (Poppy) in 1964, against the wishes of Marimekko founder Armi Ratia, who disliked and forbid floral patterns. Thankfully, since its inception, the pattern has been in continuous production, appearing everywhere from Nordic walking poles to Hong Kong tram cars, a hot air balloon, and everyday objects, including aprons, shower curtains, lunch bags, and tea towels. In the 1980s, Maija began working with her daughter Kristina, who was just three years old when her mother first started her career at Printex. Kristina wrote of her mother's time and legacy as a designer, "When I was a child, Maija would work and take care of me at the same time. She would tell me a story while drawing a textile pattern. … My mother taught me to be methodical and plan my work beforehand. She would say that it's better to sit and think before you do anything." Maija spent the later years of her life focusing on painting, rather than textile design, harkening back to her time in the 1940s studying art at the Helsinki Art School.

## Sister Corita Kent  (11.20.1918–09.18.1986)

Sister Corita Kent was not your average nun. Corita was an icon for the "rebellious modern nun" during the tumultuous 1960s as the head of the art department at the progressively minded Immaculate Heart College in Los Angeles. Encouraged by the social reforms of the day, Sister Corita encouraged her students to look at the world differently by gathering inspiration from the world around them. Sister Corita drew most of her inspiration from billboards, hand-painted signs, and pop culture. During her three-week vacations from school she was known to create anywhere from thirty to thirty-five different silk-screened prints in editions of 100 each. Her work consisted of bright neon colors and typography, which mirrored many different advertising slogans, as well as pop culture references of the time. But what made each print cohesive was the way in which she would alter the meaning of the advertising slogans to no longer reflect a commercial product, but instead to reflect an uplifting message of spirituality. Sister Corita enjoyed a mutual admiration from some of the biggest names in the arts of that period, including Alfred Hitchcock, John Cage, Saul Bass, Buckminster Fuller, and Charles and Ray Eames. She became such a friend of Charles and Ray that she and her students often frequented their studio. By the end of the 1960s, the Immaculate Heart nuns were deemed too radical for the archdiocese in their quest for modest changes and self-governance, ultimately resulting in their decision to leave the Catholic Church altogether. Luckily, Corita continued to paint her optimistic and beautiful hopes for humanity until the end of her life.

## Coco Chanel  (08.19.1883–01.10.1971)

Her name conjures up images of haute couture clothing, classic perfume, and pure elegance. She was Coco Chanel: a style inspiration, a fashion pioneer, and a formidable business presence. Known for reinventing herself and her past, certain details of Gabrielle Chanel's young life are a mystery, including when and why she became "Coco" instead of Gabrielle. Despite a childhood in poverty, the loss of her mother when she was just eleven years old, followed by life in an orphanage, Coco overcame her hardships to become the legend we know of today. It was at the orphanage where Coco began learning to sew, followed by more lessons at the Notre Dame school she attended when she turned eighteen. Coco opened her first shop in Paris in 1910, selling hats and then gradually making and selling her own clothing. In the 1920s she created Chanel No. 5 perfume and introduced the firsts in a famous collection of Chanel suits and little black dresses, transforming black from something mournful into a chic evening style: "I imposed black; it's still going strong today, for black wipes out everything else around." Additionally, she also designed costumes for stage productions, and struck up friendships and romances with notable figures like Igor Stravinsky. The 1930s brought economic hardship, and Coco was forced to close her business for some time. But in 1953, at the age of seventy, Coco relaunched her fashion career—and the House of Chanel continues to thrive today, more than forty years after her death. Her legacy lives on, perhaps just as she predicted: "May my legend prosper and thrive. I wish it a long and happy life."

## Bridget Riley  (b. 04.24.1931)

Bridget Riley is known for her graphic, bold, geometric Op Art paintings that she began creating in the 1960s, quickly rising to fame as a young artist still in her thirties. Bridget had studied at the Royal College of Art in London, but her time there was a struggle, as she desired to develop her own style. Eventually Bridget discovered the work of Abstract Expressionist painters, and she began to experiment with new directions. In the early 1960s, while teaching and studying at London's Hornsey College of Art, Bridget explored a new area: painting geometric shapes in black and white—her first Op Art paintings. This series of works would launch her career on a new path; she began to receive significant recognition for pieces like *Movement in Squares* (1961) and *Where* (1964). These paintings often tricked the eye, and their graphic visuals became iconically linked to the hallucinatory and pop-art aesthetics of the era. Bridget's solid standing in the Op Art movement made her a celebrity in Great Britain's art world. Of her process for creating art, she said, "In the early 1960s I realized that the most exciting way of setting about work was to establish limits, in terms of each particular piece, which would sometimes push me and the work as we evolved together into such tight corners that they yielded surprising riches. ... Through limiting oneself, even severely, one discovers things that one would never have dreamt of." Bridget eventually brought color into her work, and expanded in other areas as well, including murals and ballet set design. Now in her eighties, Bridget continues to create as her work has become even more revered.

## *Ruth Asawa* (01.24.1926–08.05.2013)

Born to Japanese parents, with six brothers and sisters, Ruth (Aiko) Asawa was raised on a vegetable farm in California during the Great Depression. Following the attack on Pearl Harbor in 1941, the family was forced from their homes into internment, first at horse stables at the racetrack in Santa Anita, California. A few Japanese artists from Disney Studios were also interned there and were the first to teach Ruth how to draw. Ruth's family was transferred to an internment camp in Arkansas, where she finished high school, earning her admission to attend the Milwaukee State Teachers College. There she took every art course offered but ultimately was unable to graduate when no school in Wisconsin would hire a Japanese-American woman to complete her student teaching requirement. Afterwards, Ruth attended Black Mountain College in North Carolina, where she met her husband, architect and designer Albert Lanier. Staying home to raise their children, Ruth began to sculpt, working on a wire piece she had started at Black Mountain. She was inspired to use wire after a visit to Mexico, where she observed baskets in the markets for eggs and produce: "My materials were simple, and whenever there was a free moment, I would sit down and do some work."Ruth became known for her weaved, wire sculptures, as well as her public fountain installations throughout San Francisco. She co-founded a public school for the arts in 1982, now known as the Ruth Asawa San Francisco School of the Arts; and in 1998, the University of Wisconsin-Milwaukee, previously the Milwaukee State Teachers College, awarded Ruth the bachelor's degree she had been prevented from earning so many years before.

## *Twiggy* (b. 09.19.1949)

Known for her slender frame, giant eyes, and blond bob, Twiggy and her distinct, androgynous look became a sensation in the 1960s and '70s in London's mod scene—earning her the groundbreaking title of the first international supermodel. Unlike the curvaceous, full-figured, and overtly sexualized models of the 1950s, Twiggy's look was nonconformist, boyish, and thoroughly modern. Twiggy modeled many of British fashion designer Mary Quant's clothes, and her look became synonymous with the designer's famed miniskirts. Born Lesley Hornby, the stunning Twiggy received her iconic nickname at the beginning of her career, as a thin teenager with long limbs growing up in England. And it wasn't long before her name was known in households worldwide. Twiggy's popularity was instant, as she appeared on the covers of successful fashion magazines, including *Elle* and *British Vogue*, working with established photographers like Richard Avedon. Her images defined the era, and she became an idol and inspiration for young women across the globe. Using her fame to her business advantage, Twiggy branched out to create a clothing line, began acting on the stage and screen, and inspired consumer products, including a Barbie doll, lunch box, and board game. For her performance in the stage production *My One and Only* she earned a Tony nomination, and as Polly Browne in the film *The Boy Friend*, she received two Golden Globe awards. In recent years, Twiggy has served as an animal activist and supporter of breast cancer research groups. And her striking appearance and cheeky personality have granted Twiggy an iconic and lasting presence in the annals of fashion.

## *Mary Quant* (b. 02.11.1934)

Bold, graphic, colorful, and patterned, Mary Quant's fashion designs were synonymous with the Mod aesthetics of the 1960s. She may not have invented the minidress, but Mary Quant brought fame and recognition to the fashionable style, even wearing a minidress herself to accept an OBE from the Queen of England in 1966. International supermodel Twiggy wore the style frequently, and the girls who came into Mary's Chelsea shop asked for their hems to be shorter and shorter. But this garment wasn't her only contribution to the fashion industry; with her signature Vidal Sassoon bob and plastic boots, she modeled and marketed her own innovations—from her shop, Bazaar, in London to her tour through America. Her youthful lines appealed to a large demographic, and J.C. Penney purchased 6,000 of her garments in the early 1960s. Her carefully arranged shop windows in Bazaar drew in interest and customers, and the rise in popularity allowed Mary to open a second branch of her store in 1963. Success continued, including a hot pants trend, and Mary later launched the Ginger Group to offer her designs to a wide range of consumers at more affordable prices, with her label appearing worldwide on beauty products and accessories as well. In her 1966 autobiography, *Quant by Quant*, she commented on her preference for mass appeal: "What ready-to-wear does today, the couturiers—even the Paris couturiers—confirm tomorrow. It has happened several times already. I think it will go on happening." In the 1960s and '70s Mary added makeup and household goods to her repertoire, even designing the interior of the Mini Designer car in 1988.

## *Louise Nevelson*  (09.23.1899–04.17.1988)

Louise Nevelson is known for her large-scale, collage-like sculptures that house multiple com-partments and objects in relief united by a single color. Louise was born in Czarist Russia to a Jewish family in 1899. Her family immigrated to the United States in 1905, and by 1920, Louise was married and living in New York. By 1929 she became a full-time student at the Art Students League. Two years later she traveled to Munich to study with Hans Hofmann, walking by Adolf Hitler's house every day on her way to the school. While in Europe, Louise was influenced by Picasso's Cubism, and was inspired to create her own three-dimensional sculptures, initially in wood, that often incorporated found objects, such as table legs, into her pieces. One of her most important piec-es, *Sky Cathedral* (1958), is a large-scale, wooden, interior sculpture painted black, which now lives in the permanent collection of MoMA in New York City. Louise's first solo exhibition occurred in 1941, but it wasn't until almost reaching sixty that her body of work earned the respect and recognition she'd struggled for over decades. In her seventies, Louise began working on even larger-scale outdoor sculptures and utilized Corten steel. Beyond her larger-than-life sculptures, Louise's personality was much the same—she was known as strong, flamboyant, bisexual, and striking, with a penchant for false eyelashes and vibrant scarves. Of her single-minded pursuit of art creation she said, "I never got caught [up] in making a living. That would have seemed to be a little bit out of order to a creative mind such as mine."

## *Elaine Lustig Cohen*  (b. 03.06.1927)

A recipient of the distinguished American Institute of Graphic Arts medal in 2011, Elaine Lustig Cohen has earned a reputation as a talented graphic designer and artist over the past eighty-eight years. Growing up in New Jersey, Elaine's mother instilled in her a sense that she could accomplish anything of interest, no matter her gender. Elaine took drawing lessons and eventually earned a bachelor's degree in fine arts. In 1948 she married designer Alvin Lustig, and the two were together for seven years, until Alvin's untimely death at age forty. During their marriage Elaine worked as an assistant to Alvin, who owned his own Manhattan design firm. Upon Alvin's death, it became Elaine's responsibility to fill her husband's shoes. Thus at age twenty-eight, with no formal graphic design training, Elaine took the reins and proved herself a talented designer in her own right. Architect Phillip Johnson commissioned her to design the signage for the Seagram Building. Eventually, she began to specialize in signage, book jacket design, catalogs, and other pursuits. Alvin had designed twenty-five book covers for Meridian Books, and Elaine went on to design more than a hundred. At this time she was one of very few women to own and run her own high-profile graphic design firm. Throughout her life Elaine has continued to change and evolve, and she continues to explore new avenues of design, including printmaking and digital work. In a 2013 interview, she spoke about her artistic methods: "The wonderful thing about being an artist is you never know exactly where you are going with a process. ... You're always opening another door and finding something unexpected."

## *Helen Frankenthaler*  (12.12.1928–12.27.2011)

Helen Frankenthaler was one of the foremost painters of the mid-twentieth century. Early in her career, Helen was influenced by many of the major artists of Abstract Expressionism she was fortunate enough to meet, including  Jackson Pollock, Franz Kline, and Robert Motherwell—whom she went on to marry. Helen had a privileged upbringing that garnered many opportunities that helped shape her artistic voice. While still in high school at Dalton she studied with Mexican painter Rufino Tamayo, and later at Bennington College she studied with Paul Feeley. Helen developed her own method of painting referred to as the "soak-stain" technique, where she would pour turpentine-thinned oil paint onto oversized canvases, creating large, luminescent areas of color. This breakthrough was hailed by critics and seen as an instrumental part of what was called the new Color Field movement. Helen often found inspiration for her works in landscapes of nature, as was the case for *Mountains and Sea* (1952), which she painted after returning home from a trip to Nova Scotia. As an abstract artist, her focus was not on literal interpretation of her subject matter: "What concerns me when I work is not whether the picture is a landscape, or whether it's pastoral, or whether somebody will see a sunset in it. What concerns me is: did I make a beautiful picture?" Both Helen and Robert came from well-to-do families and were known to live a lavish lifestyle; they were fond of entertaining at their home on the Upper East side of New York. In New York, Helen's work is part of the permanent collections at MoMA and the Guggenheim, as well as many more museums around the world.

## Eva Zeisel (11.13.1906–12.30.2011)

A prolific and accomplished modern designer, Eva Zeisel lived a remarkable and long life. She was falsely imprisoned in the 1930s for plotting against Joseph Stalin, and she narrowly escaped the German army in 1938, leaving Vienna for America: "I saw the Statue of Liberty and my fears came down. It was a very touching reception." When Eva was a child, her mother, Laura, opened a progressive kindergarten, where Eva learned about art, music, and movement. Her parents emphasized playfulness in her early life, and certainly encouraged her creativity. During her time at the Budapest Royal Academy of Fine Arts, her mother suggested that she switch from painting to a more practical career in ceramics—a path that would ultimately lead her to great success. As soon as she moved to the United States, Eva began receiving ceramics commissions, as well as becoming the first person to teach ceramics as industrial design for mass production at the Pratt Institute. Eva believed in producing quality products at an affordable price for many people to enjoy and appreciate. Living to 105 years old, Eva continued to design even after her centennial birthday. Upon her death, *The New York Times* wrote of Eva as "a ceramic artist whose elegant, eccentric designs for dinnerware in the 1940s and '50s helped to revolutionize the way Americans set their tables. … [She] brought the clean, casual shapes of modernist design into middle-class American homes with furnishings that encouraged a postwar desire for fresh, less formal styles of living." Indeed, after a career that spanned over eighty years, Eva's sculptural and distinctive dinnerware is still commercially available to this day.

## Georgia O'Keeffe (11.15.1887–03.06.1986)

American painter Georgia O'Keeffe found inspiration in nature, focusing on various regions of the United States. From a young age, she enjoyed spending time outdoors, touching and feeling everything on her family's Wisconsin farm. Her mother instilled in her a love of art, and Georgia pursued further art education as she grew up. She went on to teach art in Texas before famed photographer Alfred Stieglitz invited her to New York to paint. After working together for some time, the two were married in 1924, and moved into a high-rise hotel in the city, where Georgia could paint views of the sprawling metropolis. Alfred had a summer home in Lake George, New York, as well, and there Georgia drew from the rural setting for her work in the 1920s. Her paintings covered a varied range of subjects, including abstract views, brightly colored flowers, and the New Mexico desert, where she traveled frequently. She used bleached animal bones from that area as subject matter for her artworks, pairing them with foliage and other landscapes. Her paintings rarely featured people or animals, but rather focused on natural objects, including flowers, seashells, clouds, or simply shapes she imagined in her mind's eye. Following her husband's death in 1946, Georgia settled in New Mexico permanently—there she felt the blue skies and desert flowers, among other elements, best served her work. During her ninety-eights years, Georgia also lobbied for women's equal rights for several decades, even telling Eleanor Roosevelt that she "would like each child to feel … that no door for any activity that they may choose is closed on account of sex."

## Florence Knoll (b. 05.24.1917)

Born of German ancestry and raised in Michigan, Florence Knoll found an interest in architecture and design early in life, at the Kingswood School for Girls. At the Cranbrook Academy of Art next door, Florence met and eventually studied under architect Eliel Saarinen, later becoming close friends with Eliel's son, an architect and designer in his own right, Eero Saarinen. Florence continued her education and studied under a host of esteemed industry figures, including renowned architect and the head of the Bauhaus school Mies van de Rohe, whose "less is more" philosophy she noted as having "a profound effect on my design approach and the clarification of design." Upon her move to New York City in 1941, Florence met (and eventually married) furniture designer Hans Knoll, and the two grew the Knoll company into an internationally respected success. Florence herself pioneered the Knoll Planning Unit, which provided modern, efficient interior design for corporate offices, depending on the needs of each individual client. In addition, she provided what she called the "meat and potatoes" of Knoll Associates' furniture offerings, in contrast to the more specialized pieces that were created by revered outside designers and by others within the company. Her own designs may have seemed like basics to her, but they are now considered Modernist classics in their own right. Following the untimely death of Hans in 1955, Florence took over as president of the company. As an architect, interior designer, industrial designer, and business woman, Florence helmed one of the most esteemed and successful furniture businesses in America. More than half a century later, Florence Knoll and the business she created are still going strong.

### Edith Heath (05.24.1911–12.27.2005)

The founder of the esteemed Heath Ceramics, Edith Heath was born and raised on a family farm near Sioux City, Iowa. The daughter of a headstrong mother, Edith learned to diligently pursue her own interests, a trait that served her well later in life. She took her first ceramics class at the Art Institute of Chicago. In 1938 she married Brian Heath and traveled through New Mexico, where she encountered the work of a famous Native American potter, later saying, "We visited a pueblo and I fell in love with the ceramic work of Maria Martinez. Although I had little training in ceramics, I decided then, 'this is what I want to do.'" She began teaching art in San Francisco, and after converting her laundry room into a studio, Edith experimented with various materials and techniques, and began creating dishes and vases. Soon Edith was creating pieces for the well-known retailer Gump's. In 1948, Heath Ceramics was founded after Edith exhibited a solo pottery show at San Francisco's Legion of Honor. As her company grew and production was streamlined, Edith observed: "Good design doesn't depend on whether something is made by hand. In fact, there are some very junky things that can be made by hand. ... It was okay while I was learning and getting a feel for the clay. But after all, a machine doesn't decide what the shape is going to be. A human being has to decide that ... so I felt I was in as much control as ever." By 1949, Heath Ceramics was producing 100,000 pieces a year, and the Sausalito, California-based company continues to thrive today more than half a century later.

### Alma Thomas (09.22.1891–02.24.1978)

Alma Thomas was born in Columbus, Georgia, in 1891, but her family was forced to relocate to Washington, D.C. in 1906 to flee racial violence in the South. As a girl growing up she had dreamed of becoming an architect, which was seemingly impossible at the time, but instead graduated from Howard University with a degree in fine arts in the 1920s, becoming the first graduate of the university's art department. She also studied at Columbia and New York universities in the 1930s. Alma Thomas went on to have a thirty-five-year career teaching art at Shaw Junior High School in Washington, D.C., often bringing her students to art exhibits at the Smithsonian Institution. Upon her retirement in 1960, at the age of sixty-eight, she embarked on her fine art career while the civil rights movement was still in its infancy. Influenced by Abstract Expressionism she created her own beautiful Color Field paintings, developing a bold, multi-hued, mosaic-like technique. But it wasn't until 1972, when Alma was more than eighty years old, that she was fully recognized for her own artistic contributions, after being "discovered" by the Whitney Museum of American Art and awarded their first solo exhibition of an African-American woman's artworks. In the last years of her life, esteem for Alma only grew, with September 9th declared Alma W. Thomas day in our nation's capital in 1972, and an invitation from President Jimmy Carter to visit the White House in 1977. Recently, President Obama and First Lady Michelle Obama proudly unveiled an Alma Thomas painting at the White House, the first artwork by an African-American woman to be featured there.

### Vera Neumann (07.24.1907–6.15.1993)

Vera Neumann created wearable art with her stylish scarves, elegant designs, and recognizable ladybug logo. Creating a brand based on her own original artworks, this entrepreneur thrived for decades, with pieces appearing virtually everywhere throughout the 1960s. Vera found art at a young age in the meadows and woods near her Stamford, Connecticut, home. Her father encouraged her passion, and he took her weekly to the Metropolitan Museum of Art, as well as hiring a sign painter to give her art lessons. She attended The Cooper Union for the Advancement of Science and Art and the Traphagen School of Design, where she learned about the potential for developing her creativity into a viable career and business. During this time, Vera began to illustrate children's books, design textiles, and create murals for children's rooms. After marrying George Neumann, Vera and her new husband formed a creative partnership, and he suggested she create fabrics from her vibrant paintings. From there they launched a successful business of many years, producing placemats and napkins, aprons and pot holders, dish towels and bed sheets, not to mention brilliant fabrics and her exquisite scarf collections. In the 1960s, Vera expanded to clothing lines, with celebrities wearing her designs in magazines and Marilyn Monroe collecting Vera's scarves. In fact, by the 1970s, what started out as a kitchen table business had grown to a $100 million international business. Vera's art and entrepreneurship succeeded in delighting a wide audience. Later in life Vera summed up an inspirational career to *The Washington Post* with a spot-on sentiment: "The creative part of the business is like a fountain; it keeps going, going, going. I never repeat myself."

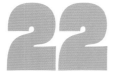

### Eva Hesse (01.11.1936-05.29.70)

In Eva Hesse's brief thirty-four years of life she suffered and survived through many seemingly insurmountable circumstances. Born in 1936 to an observant Jewish family, Eva and her family escaped Nazi Germany and ultimately immigrated to New York. When Eva was ten years old, her mother committed suicide. Despite these traumatic events in her childhood, Eva pursued her passion for art, studying at The Cooper Union for the Advancement of Science and Art, as well as with Josef Albers at Yale University. Eva began her career in the 1950s as a painter, and then moved into sculpture as well in the next decade. Eva is known for pieces like *Hang Up*: a mixed media Minimalist sculpture about which she said, "It has a kind of depth I don't always achieve and that is a kind of depth or soul or absurdity or life or meaning or feeling or intellect that I want to get. ... It is the most ridiculous structure I have ever made and that is why it is really good." She was a contemporary of minimalist artists Sol LeWitt and Donald Judd. But unlike the rigidity of much of these minimalists artists' works, Eva brought a handmade, organic, and almost sensual quality to her sculpture that emanated from her innovative use of materials. By using latex and fiberglass, Eva Hesse created series of slightly irregular yet repetitive forms in her compelling installations. In a career spanning just ten years before she succumbed to cancer, Eva Hesse's soulful and ephemeral work continues to inspire. In response to comments of the fragility of her work, Eva once said "Life doesn't last; art doesn't last."

### Alice Provensen (b. 08.14.1918)

Encouraged at a young age by her mother and sixth-grade teacher, Alice Provensen always had art supplies at the ready for her childhood creations. When her teacher entered Alice's picture into a contest, she won a scholarship to the Chicago Art Institute's program for public school children, and she's been drawing ever since—encouraging other youngsters to do the same: "Young children make marvelous pictures. There is nothing they can't draw. They paint and draw from their imaginations and the world around them. And they are not afraid to draw anything." As men left to fight in World War II, Alice was able to secure an animator position at Walter Lantz Studios, working on Woody Woodpecker cartoons. She met her future husband, Martin Provensen, and the two moved from Los Angeles to Washington, D.C. They began to work together to illustrate children's books, earning contracts for Golden Books like *The Fuzzy Duckling*; and their careers flourished. Together they created Kellogg's beloved Tony the Tiger. After a few years, the Provensens moved to a farm in the Hudson River Valley and began creating their own books. Eight of their titles earned placement on *The New York Times* list of the Ten Best Illustrated Books of the year, and they earned a Caldecott Medal in 1984. After Martin's death in 1987, Alice eventually returned to her studio to begin illustrating again. Even into her nineties, Alice has continued to develop new ideas for children's books. At ninety-one, she earned a lifetime achievement award from the Eric Carle Museum of Picture Book Art and commented, "Let's face it, it's not a jab in the eye with a stick!"

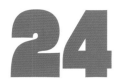

### Greta Magnusson-Grossman (07.21.1906-08.28.1999)

With varied talents and a proven reputation for quality, Swedish-born Greta Magnusson-Grossman enjoyed a prolific career of more than four decades as a designer and architect living and working first in Europe and then in Los Angeles. As a young adult just starting out, Greta completed a one year woodworking apprenticeship and earned a scholarship to attend the Stockholm arts institution Konstfack, where she learned furniture, ceramics, and textiles design. She received an award for furniture design in 1933, and the same year she opened Studio, a store and workshop, with a Konstfack classmate. With Studio, Greta earned interior and furniture design commissions, including designing a crib for Sweden's Princess Birgitta. Greta immigrated to Los Angeles with her bandleader husband, Billy Grossman, in 1940, and opened her own design shop in Beverly Hills. Her "Swedish modern furniture, rugs, lamps, and other home furnishings" attracted celebrity and industry clients, including Greta Garbo and Gracie Allen. For Barker Brothers' Modern Shop, in the late 1940s, she designed lamps with flexible arms, which were included in the "Good Design" exhibition at MoMA in New York City. During the next ten years, she designed fourteen homes in California and Sweden, many of which have been featured in *Arts & Architecture* magazine, including several still standing today. Of her experience working in Los Angeles, she is known as saying, "[California design] is not a superimposed style, but an answer to present conditions. ... It has developed out of our own preferences for living in a modern way." Greta's work has been featured in countless exhibitions, and in the 1950s, she taught industrial design at UCLA and the Art Center College of Design.

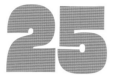

## *Mary Blair* (10.21.1911–07.26.1978)

Mary Blair was inspired to become an illustrator by Pruett Carter, an illustrator and professor of hers at the renowned Chouinard Art Institute in Los Angeles. It was while she was at school that she met her husband, Lee Blair, the brother of Disney animator Preston Blair. Originally Mary and Lee sought out a career in fine art, but after facing the struggles of that world the two began working for Ub Iwerks, creator of Mickey Mouse, painting animation cels. By 1940 both Mary and Lee were working at the Disney studios doing visual development work for feature films, such as *Dumbo, Lady and the Tramp,* and *Fantasia*. Then, as a part of Franklin D. Roosevelt's Good Neighbor policy, Walt Disney invited a handful of artists on a research tour of South America. Among those artists were Lee and Mary Blair. On that trip Mary became inspired by the color and pattern of the continent. She also quickly became one of Walt's favorite artists in attendance. Upon her return from South America, Mary went on to do visual development for many projects, most notably *Cinderella, Alice in Wonderland*, and *Peter Pan*. Mary then took time off from Disney to raise a family and did advertising work on the side, as well as illustrating many Little Golden Books, including *I Can Fly*. It wasn't until Walt came to Mary with an idea for a ride at his new theme park, Disneyland, in Los Angeles, California, that Mary went back to work for Disney. The ride ultimately became Disney's beloved attraction: It's A Small World, which delights and inspires millions of visitors every year.

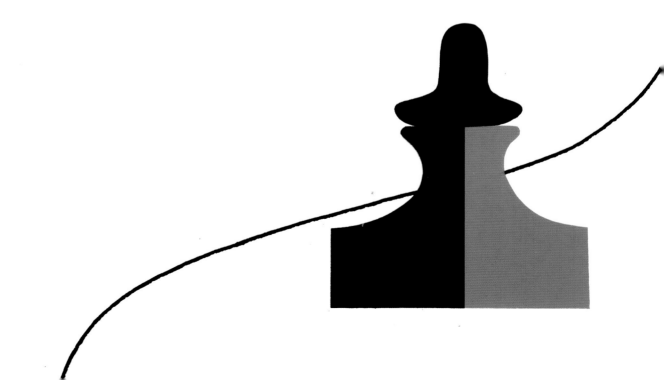

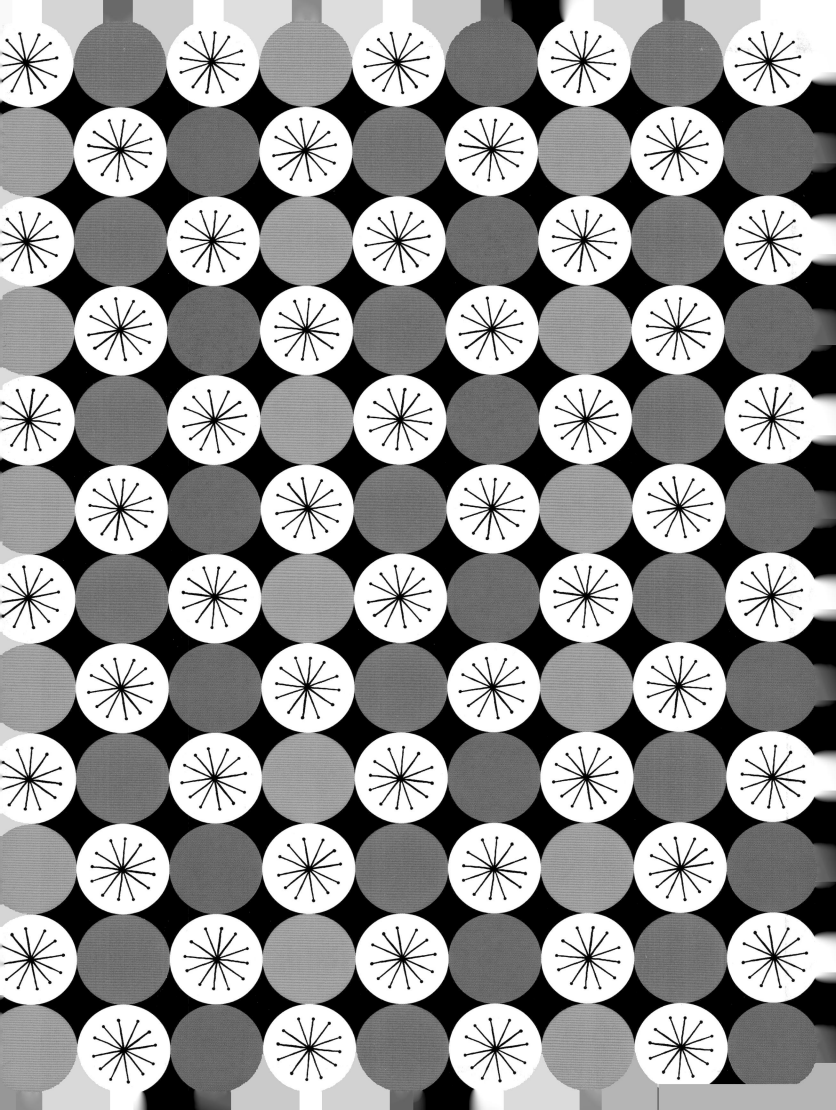

from Ellen Surrey:
for my mother and grandma Jean: two women who always encouraged me to stay true
to who I am and pursue my dreams.

from Gloria Fowler:
for my lovely Lola Rae Crist and all her future creative endeavors, and to the memory
of her grandmothers Leonor Gaviria Fowler and Donna Lois "Rae" Bentzen Crist.

Illustrated by Ellen Surrey
Edited, written, and art directed by Gloria Fowler

Biographies: Sara DeGonia, Gloria Fowler, Ellen Surrey
Copy Editing: Sara DeGonia
Production: Megan Shoemaker

For more books and products visit us at:
www.ammobooks.com

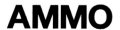

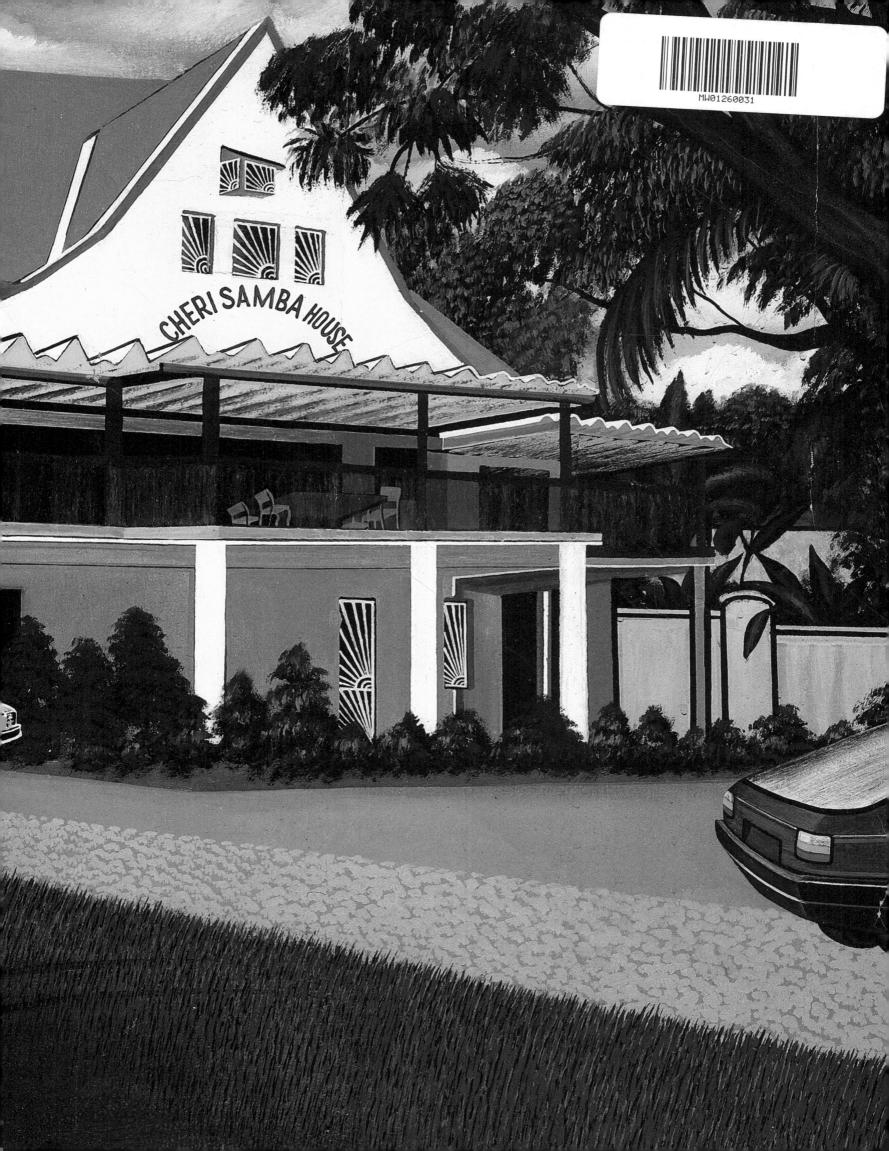

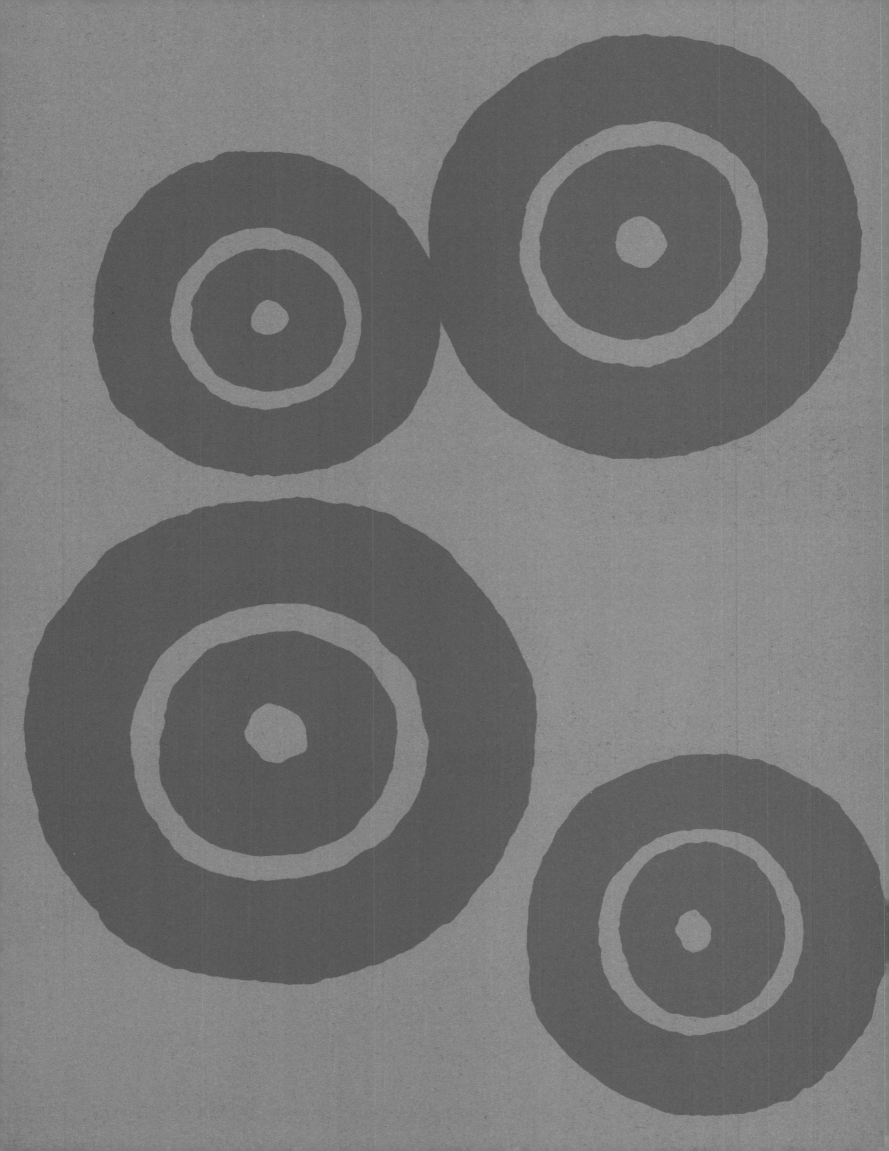

# INSIDE AFRICA
## SOUTH & WEST

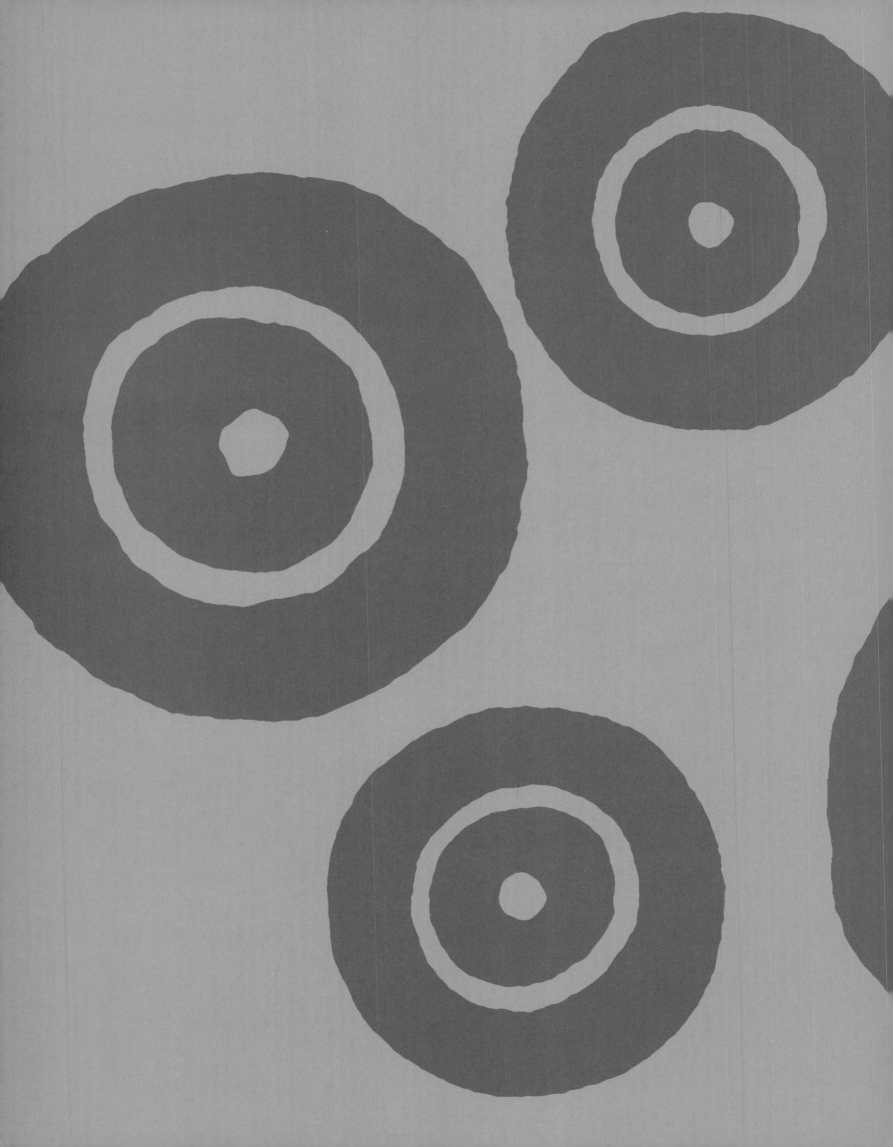

PHOTOS BY DEIDI VON SCHAEWEN
TEXT BY FRÉDÉRIC COUDERC & LAURENCE DOUGIER
EDITED BY ANGELIKA TASCHEN

# INSIDE AFRICA

## SOUTHERN

TASCHEN

KÖLN LONDON LOS ANGELES MADRID PARIS TOKYO

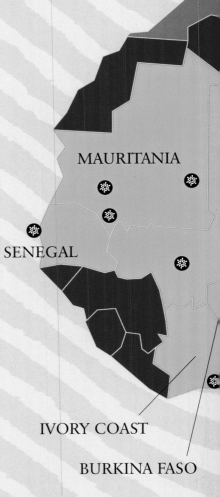

MAURITANIA

SENEGAL

IVORY COAST

BURKINA FASO

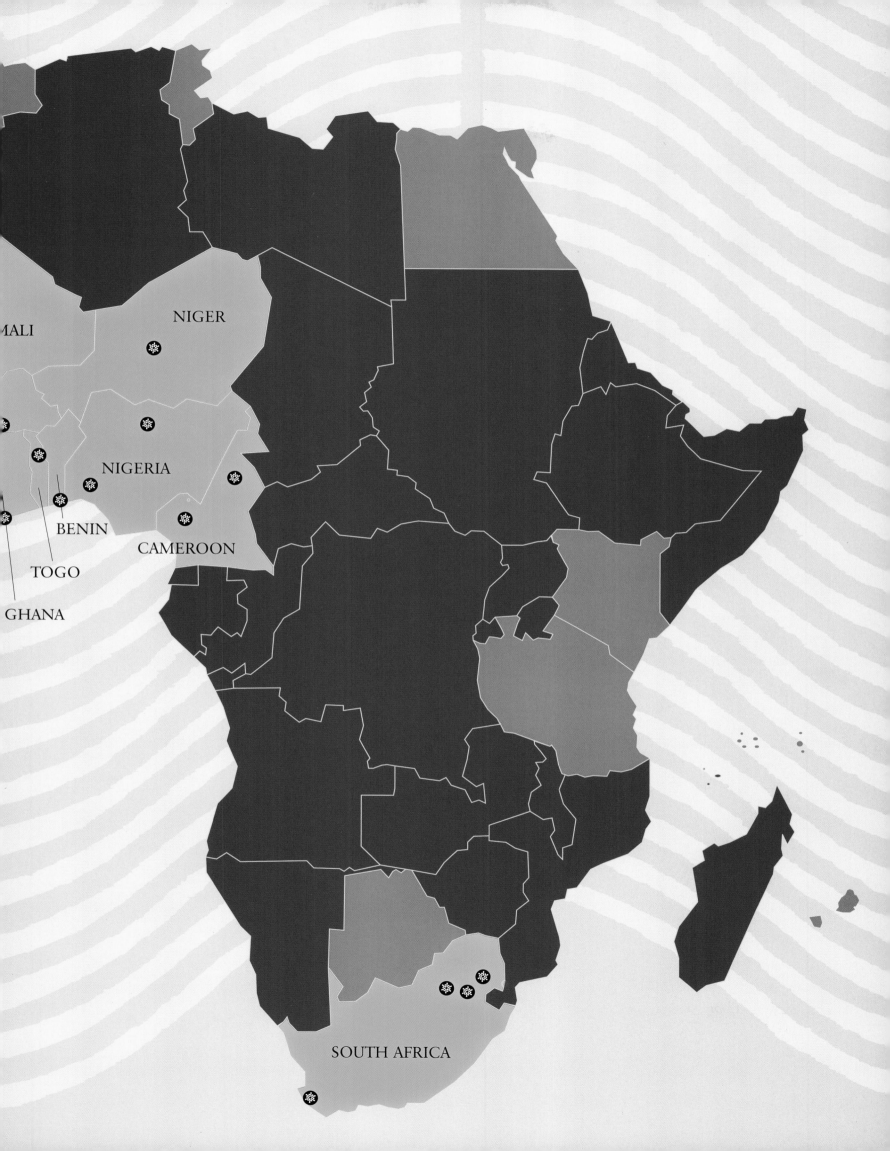

MALI

NIGER

NIGERIA

BENIN

TOGO

GHANA

CAMEROON

SOUTH AFRICA

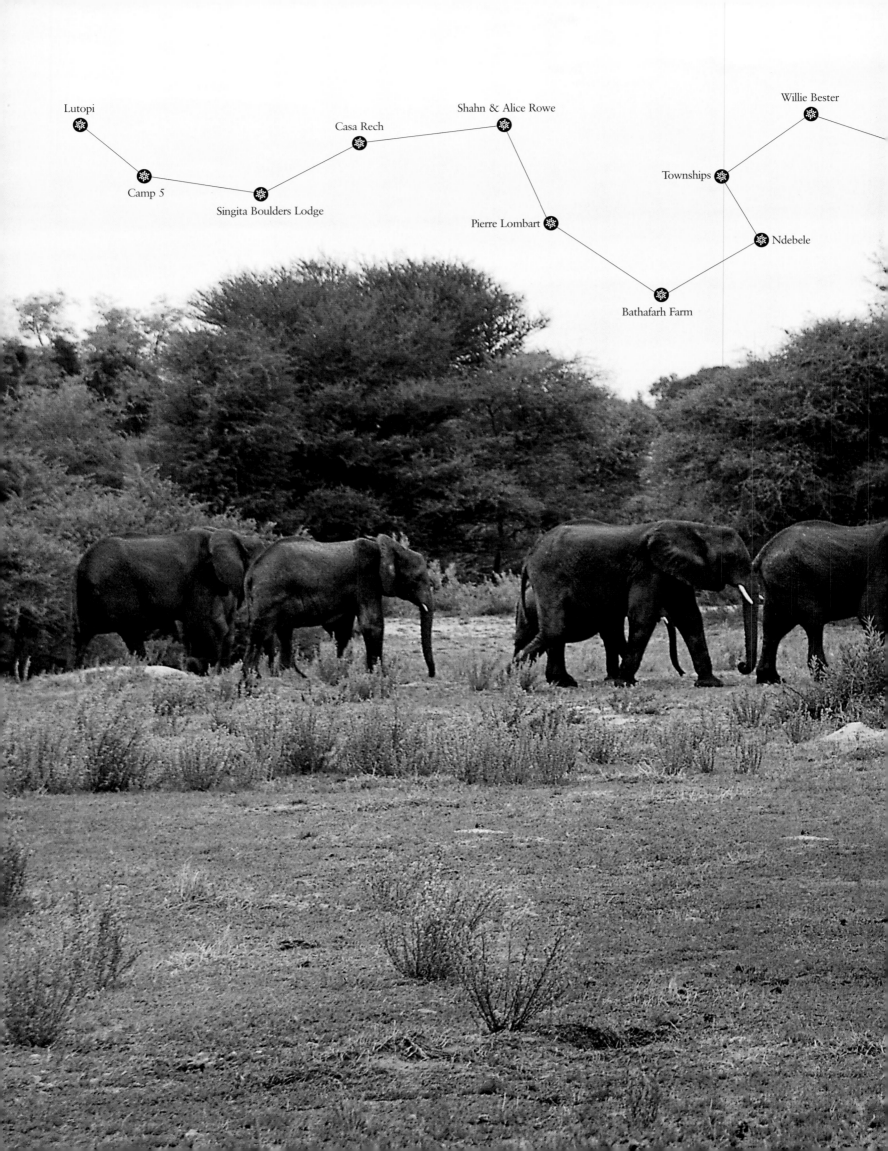

Lutopi

Camp 5

Singita Boulders Lodge

Casa Rech

Shahn & Alice Rowe

Pierre Lombart

Bathafarh Farm

Townships

Willie Bester

Ndebele

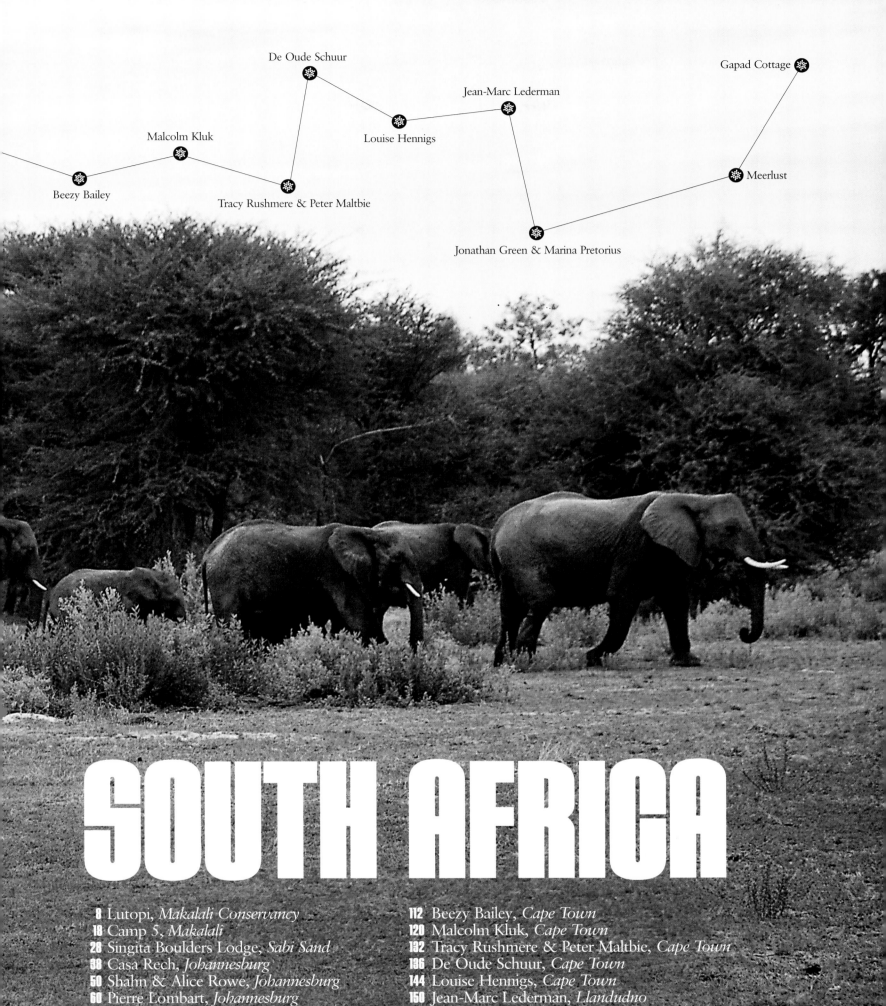

De Oude Schuur

Jean-Marc Lederman

Gapad Cottage

Malcolm Kluk

Louise Hennigs

Meerlust

Beezy Bailey

Tracy Rushmere & Peter Maltbie

Jonathan Green & Marina Pretorius

# SOUTH AFRICA

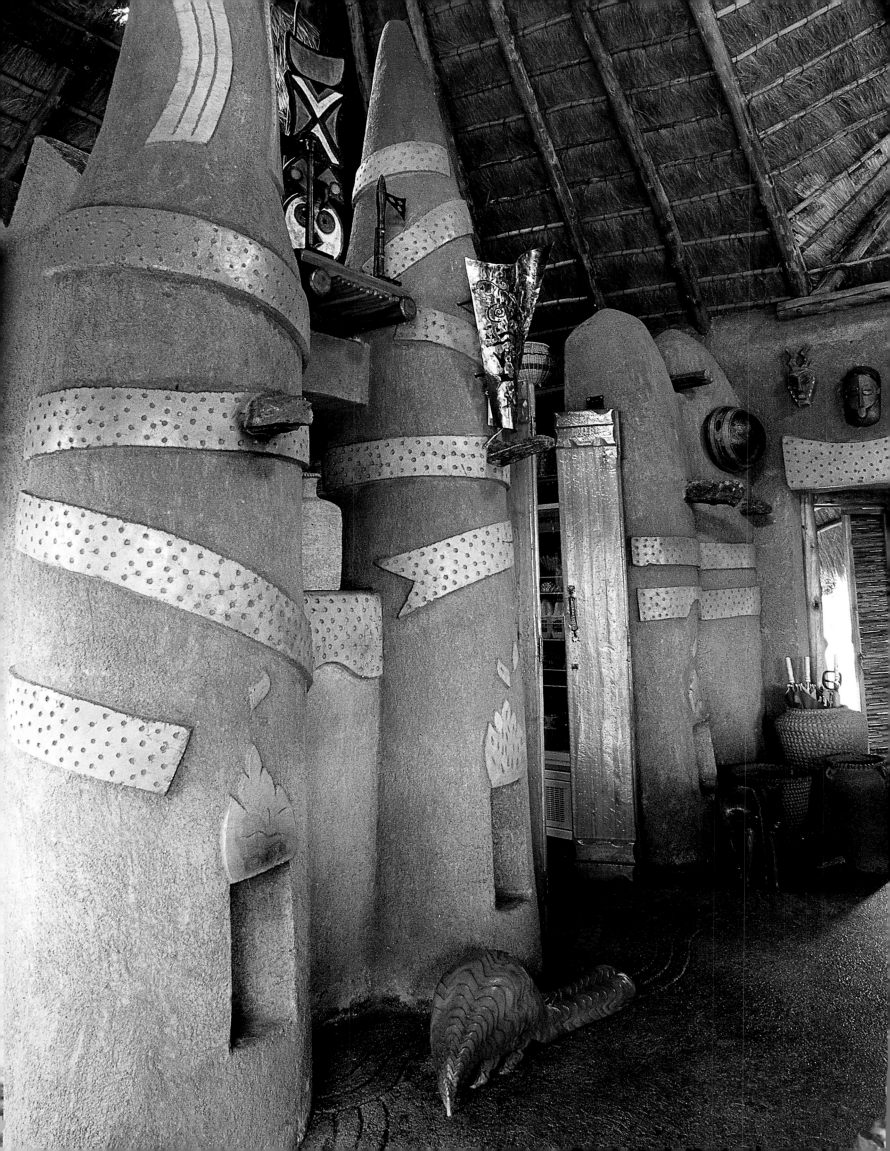

# Lutopi
## MAKALALI CONSERVANCY

A private lodge inspired by every conceivable African influence.

In the sky, the cries of hundreds of birds. The ochre earth here makes you think your feet might just be the first that ever trod here.

The spirit of Juvalapa is one of total respect for nature and animal life, but also of free forms and fantasy, pushed to their extremes by the architect Silvio Rech in a lodge that would not disgrace a movie set. Private pools overlooking the savannah, love-beds under the stars, wrought iron fireplaces, a suspension bridge, mixed clay and mosaic surfaces – all in all, a multi-referenced folly. Every conceivable African influence is present here. The walls evoke the surrounding soil. Local artisans created all the furniture and inlaid the floors with naïve designs. Everything breathes harmony and sobriety. A massive tree trunk projects through the living room floor, as if to remind us that the extreme care lavished on the decoration here means nothing without the symbiosis with Africa. Every bedroom has its own bathroom and its own terrace among the mighty jackalberry trees.

Der ockerfarbene Boden lässt einen glauben, man sei der erste Mensch, der die staubige Erde feststampft. Am Himmel singen Hunderte von fröhlichen Vögeln.

Hier weht ein besonderer Geist: Uneingeschränkter Respekt vor der Natur und den Tieren in Verbindung mit einer Freiheit der Form und einer zum Extremen neigenden Fantasie, die der Architekt Silvio Rech in diese filmreife Lodge einbrachte. Private Swimmingpools, die über der Savanne schweben, Liebeslager unter Sternen, schmiedeeiserne Kamine, Hängebrücken, Verbindungen von Lehm und Mosaik – Verrücktheiten mit Sinn für Humor. Einflüsse aus ganz Afrika kommen zum Tragen. Die Wände erinnern an die Erde ringsum. Wie die gesamte Einrichtung wurden auch die mit naiver Malerei verzierten Böden von Handwerkern der Umgebung gefertigt. Die Anlage strahlt Harmonie und Zurückhaltung aus. Ein dicker Baumstamm, der aus den Dielen im Salon wächst, lässt erkennen, dass das besonders sorgfältig gestaltete Interieur nur in Symbiose mit der afrikanischen Natur zu verstehen ist. Alle Räume verfügen über ein großes Badezimmer und eine in den riesigen Jackalberry-Bäumen versteckte Terrasse.

Par terre, c'est un sol ocre qui donne au visiteur l'impression d'être le premier homme à fouler la poussière.

Au ciel, c'est le chant joyeux de centaines d'oiseaux. Esprit des lieux: le respect absolu de la nature et de la faune, mais aussi la liberté des formes et la fantaisie poussée à l'extrême par l'architecte Silvio Rech, dans ce lodge qui se veut digne d'un décor de cinéma. Piscines privées suspendues au-dessus de la savane, lits d'amour sous les étoiles, cheminées de fer forgé, pont suspendu, argiles et mosaïque mélangés, l'endroit est une «folie» aux multiples clins d'œil. Toutes les influences africaines se retrouvent ici. Les murs évoquent la terre qui les entoure. Comme l'ensemble du mobilier, les sols incrustés de dessins naïfs ont été réalisés par des artisans de la région. Tout respire l'harmonie et la sobriété. Et si un robuste tronc d'arbre perce le plancher du salon, c'est pour nous rappeler à l'ordre: le soin extrême apporté à la décoration n'a de sens que dans la symbiose avec la terre d'Afrique! Chaque chambre dispose d'une grande salle de bains et d'une terrasse nichée au creux des grands arbres de Jackalberry.

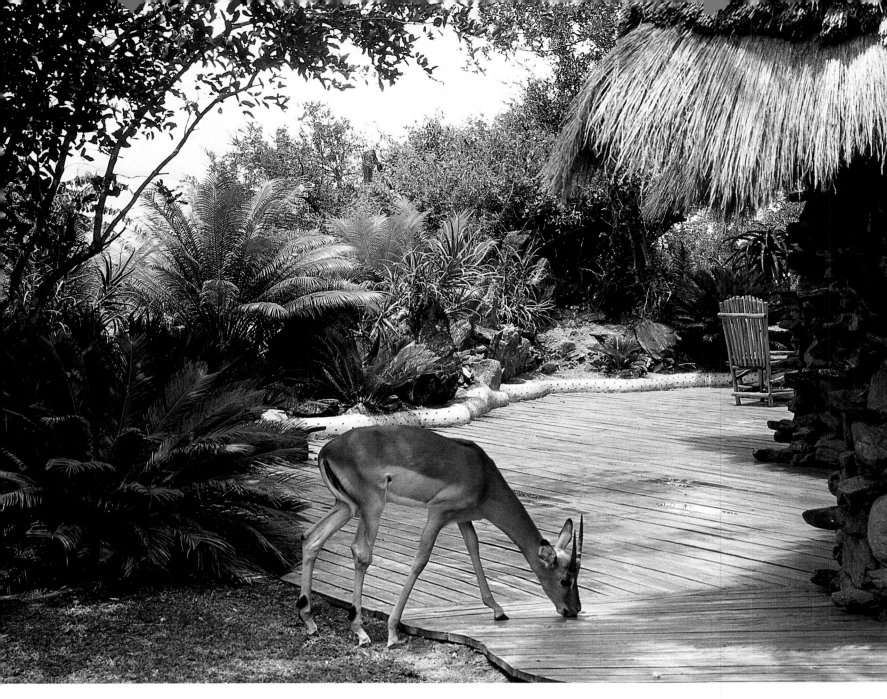

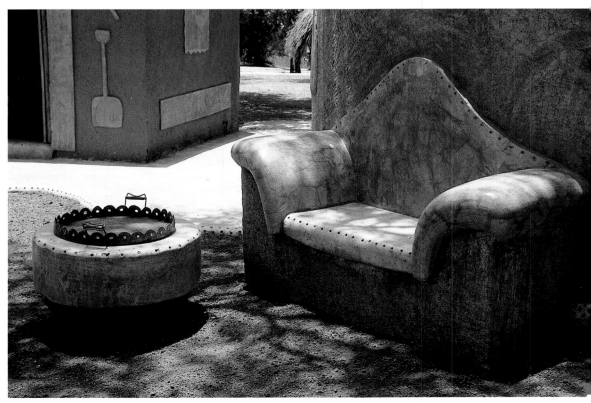

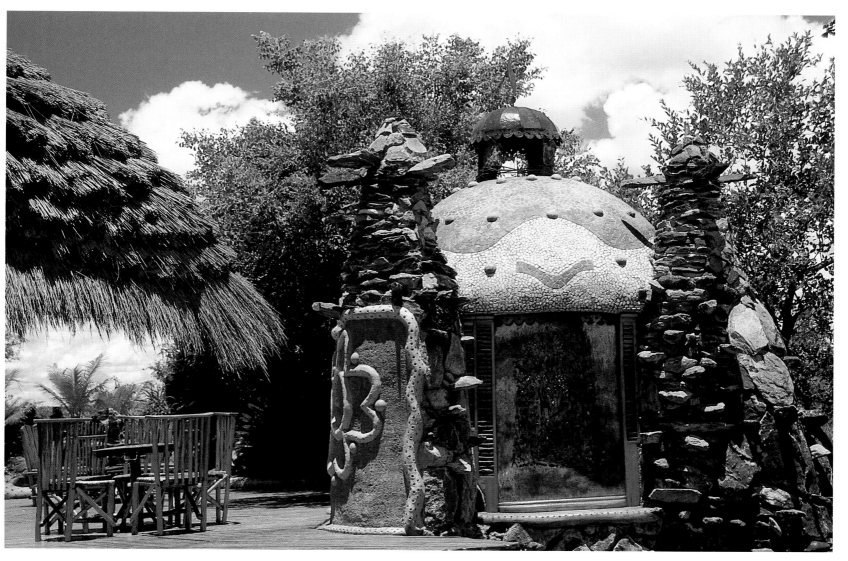

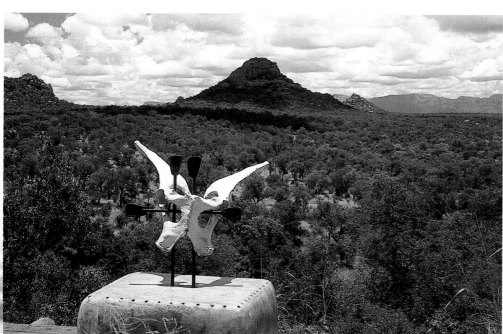

❋ **FACING PAGE** This private lodge is ideal for relaxing and observing wild animals – especially impalas, gazelles, gnus and giraffes. Often in the evenings you can hear lions roaring nearby. **LEFT** The savannah is everywhere, with the fabulous Drakensberg mountain landscape in the background. ❋ **LINKE SEITE** Diese Privatlodge eignet sich bestens zur Entspannung oder zur Beobachtung von Wildtieren wie Impalas, Gazellen, Gnus oder Giraffen. An manchen Abenden kann man sogar Löwen brüllen hören. **LINKS** Ringsum Savanne und im Hintergrund die großartige Landschaft der Drakensberge. ❋ **PAGE DE GAUCHE** Ce lodge privé est idéal pour la détente ou l'observation de la faune, impalas, gazelles, gnous et girafes. Certains soirs on entend même rugir les lions! **À GAUCHE** Partout la savane et, en toile de fond, les fabuleux paysages des montagnes du Drakensberg.

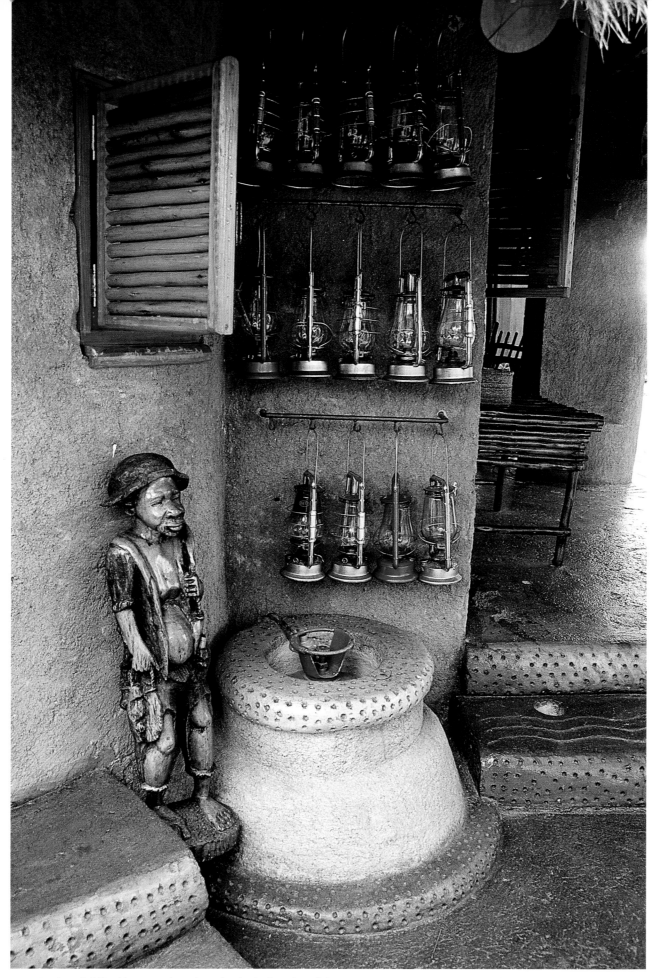

✳ **ABOVE** At nightfall, oil lamps are hung from the slender branches of the mopau trees. **FACING PAGE** No amount of mosaic and metal can make us forget that the lodge is built according to the criteria of traditional houses of the region. The living room is of less importance, because the *boma*, where everyone eats by the fire, is the convivial centre of the lodge.   ✳   **OBEN** In der Abenddämmerung werden Öllampen an die dünnen Äste der Mopanebäume gehängt. **RECHTE SEITE** Trotz des Einsatzes von Metall und Mosaik wird deutlich, dass die Privatlodge in Bezug zur Region und ihren Traditionen erbaut wurde. Hier spielt der Salon keine so große Rolle, im Gegensatz zur *boma*, dem eigentlichen Kommunikationszentrum, wo rund um die Feuerstelle gegessen wird.   ✳   **CI-DESSUS** À la nuit tombée, les lampes à pétrole sont suspendues aux frêles branches des arbres mopane. **PAGE DE DROITE** Mosaïque et métal ne peuvent faire oublier que ce lodge privé est bâti selon les critères de l'habitat régional traditionnel: le salon a moins d'importance puisque le *boma*, où l'on dîne au coin du feu, est le centre de la convivialité.

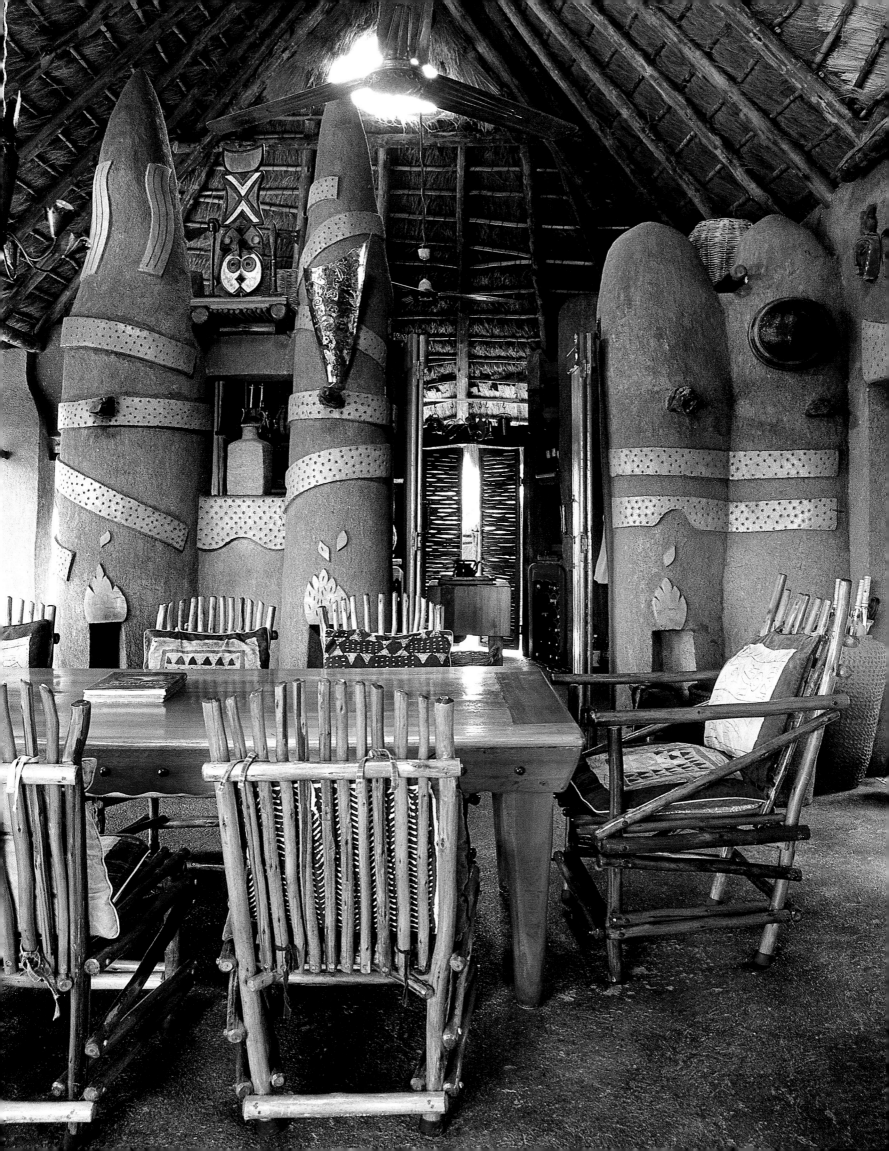

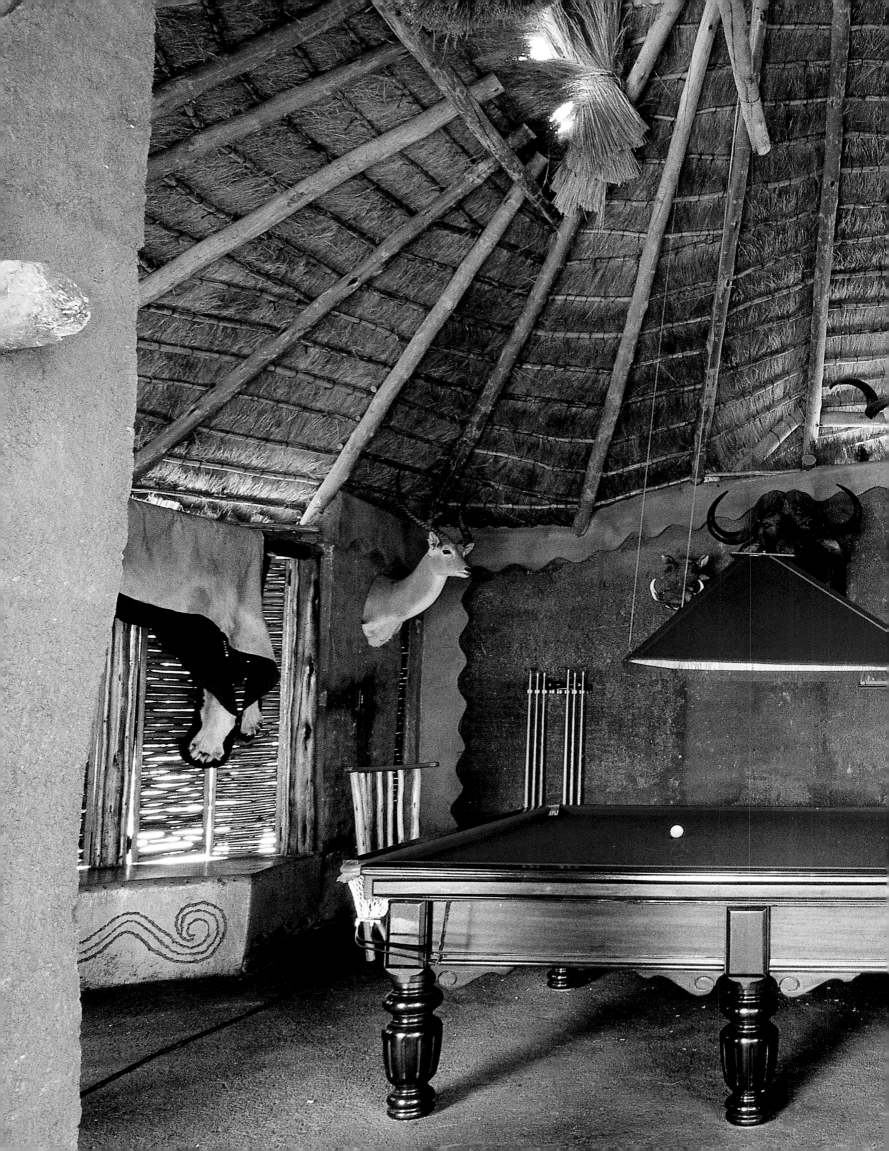

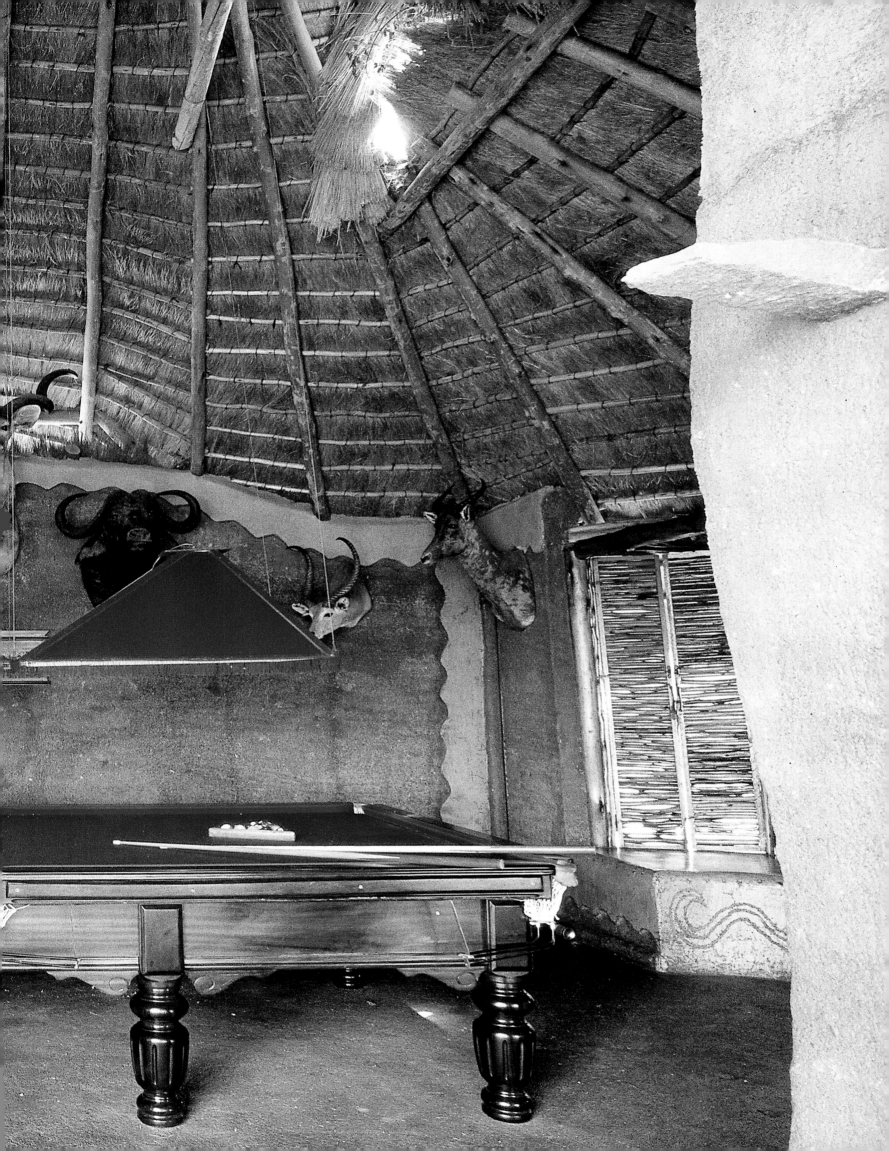

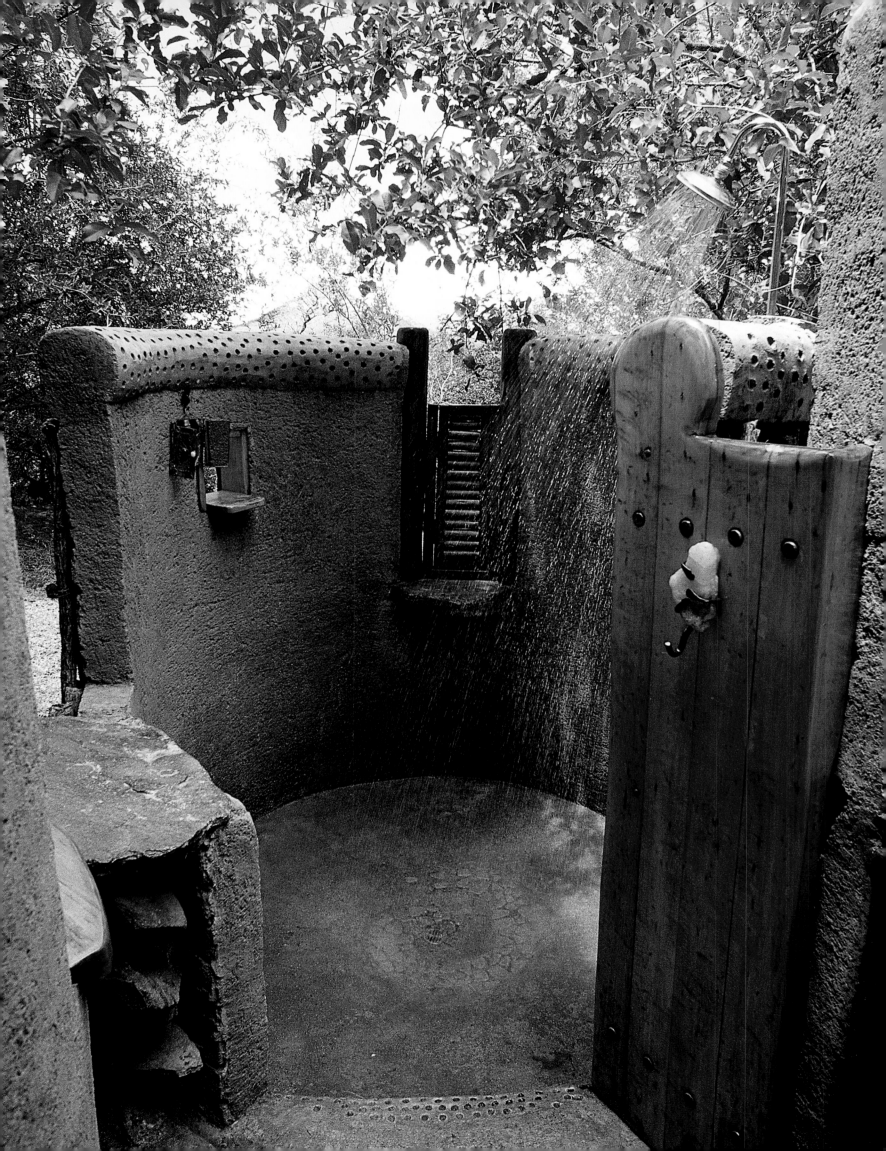

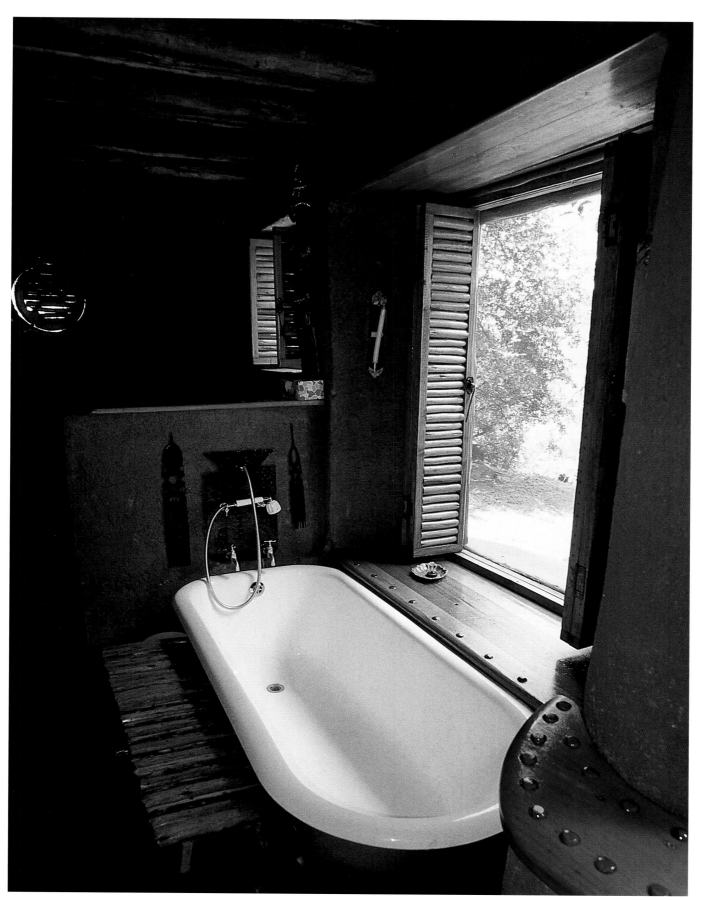

✻ **FACING PAGE** The outside shower, with walls of natural colour of the soil. **ABOVE** In the bathrooms, as elsewhere in the lodge, the warm shades of wood and earth contrast with the coolness of wrought metal. ✻ **LINKE SEITE** Die Freiluftdusche mit den erdfarbenen Wänden liegt mitten in der Natur. **OBEN** Wie überall in der Lodge stehen auch im Badezimmer die warmen Holz- und Erdfarben im Kontrast zur kalten Ausstrahlung des bearbeiteten Metalls. ✻ **PAGE DE GAUCHE** La douche extérieure aux murs couleur terre joue la communion avec la nature. **CI-DESSUS** Dans la salle de bains comme ailleurs dans le lodge, les couleurs chaudes du bois et de la terre contrastent avec la froideur du métal travaillé.

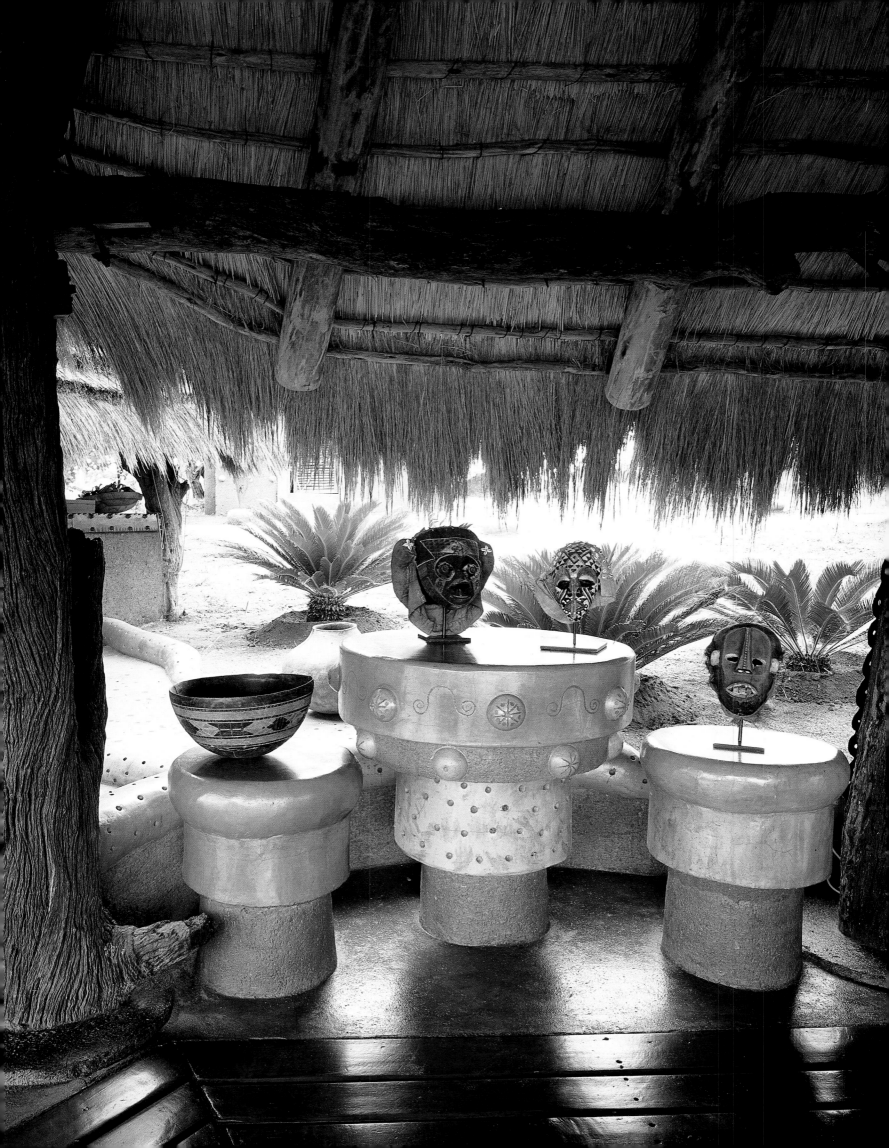

# CAMP 5
## MAKALALI

From a couple of hundred yards away,
you'd never guess that these brown anthills conceal a comfortable safari lodge.

Impeccable in his bush jacket, the guide awaits you at the door of the little plane which left Johannesburg, with you aboard, about an hour earlier. In the Land Rover, there's a sign just above the game rifle on the dashboard, which reads "Makalali".

That's the name of this private 75,000-acre reserve with its four separate safari camps, as well as this erstwhile private camp, each of which has six rooms. Makalali isn't some kind of African Disneyland, but a natural reserve with facilities that take those who go there to the very source of Africa's wildlife. And even that doesn't quite do it justice; much of the originality of the place rests on the work of the architect Silvio Rech, who set out to put together something "thoroughly sensual". He has succeeded. The fabrics, the cushions, the rattan chairs and the mattresses on the floor are an enticement to relax. By night, the soft lights, the candles and the oil lamps tinge everything a rich gold. Exhausted by a full day in the bush, you find yourself falling asleep on the spot, oblivious to the savannah and its perils. The whole thing seems to be lifted straight from *Out of Africa* – only here Meryl Streep isn't at the beck and call of a film director, she's right here with you. She's spent the day at Makalali observing animals as they move about according to the direction of the wind or the ambient scent of water. And here she is, like you, back again at nightfall.

Der Führer in tadellos sitzender Buschkleidung erwartet den Reisenden vor dem kleinen Flugzeug, das eine Stunde zuvor von Johannesburg abgeflogen war. An dem Landrover weist ein Schild direkt über dem schweren Gewehr am Armaturenbrett auf »Makalali« hin.

So heißt das private Naturschutzgebiet, das auf 30000 Hektar vier separate Camps, sowie dieses ehemals private Camp 5, mit je sechs Zimmern beherbergt. Makalali ist kein afrikanisches Disneyland sondern ein Naturschutzgebiet, wo Touristen den Ursprung allen Lebens in der Wildnis erleben können. Dabei verdankt sich die Originalität der Anlage einzig und allein dem Architekten Silvio Rech. Der Künstler wollte einen sinnlichen Ort schaffen und das ist ihm gelungen. Stoffe, Kissen, Korbsessel und Matratzen direkt auf dem Boden laden zur Entspannung ein. Nachts verleiht das gedämpfte Licht der Kerzen und Öllampen dem Camp einen goldenen Schimmer. Erschöpft von einem Tag auf Safari schläft man auf der Stelle ein, ohne sich weiter um die Gefahren der Savanne zu sorgen. Man wähnt sich in der Kulisse des Films *Jenseits von Afrika*, aber Meryl Streep gehorcht der Inspiration keines Autors oder Regisseurs. Sie ist hier. In Makalali hat sie den Tag damit verbracht, zu beobachten, wie sich die Tiere am Wind oder dem Geruch der Wasserlöcher orientieren. Und nun steht sie da in der Abenddämmerung. Es sei denn …

Impeccable dans sa tenue de brousse, le guide attend le voyageur au pied du petit avion qui a quitté Johannesburg une heure auparavant. Dans la Land-Rover, juste au-dessus d'un gros fusil fixé sur le tableau de bord, une pancarte indique «Makalali».

C'est le nom de cette réserve privée de 30000 hectares formée de quatre camps bien distincts et de cet ancien camp privé, abritant chacun six habitations. Le Makalali n'est pas un Disneyland africain mais une réserve naturelle dont les racines plongent le voyageur au plus profond de la vie sauvage. L'adjectif est d'ailleurs bien faible, car l'originalité des lieux repose entièrement sur le travail de l'architecte Silvio Rech. L'artiste voulait composer un lieu sensuel, et l'entreprise est réussie! Tissus, coussins, fauteuils en rotin et matelas posés sur le sol invitent à la détente. De nuit, la lumière tamisée, les bougies et les lampes à pétrole donnent à l'ensemble une teinte dorée. Épuisé par une journée de safari, on s'endort sur-le-champ, ignorant la savane et ses périls … On jurerait le décor tiré de *Out of Africa*. Mais Meryl Streep n'obéit pas à l'inspiration d'un auteur ou d'un metteur en scène. Elle est à vos côtés. Au Makalali, elle a passé le jour à observer les animaux poussés par le vent ou l'odeur des points d'eau. Et puis, la voici à la nuit tombée. À moins que …

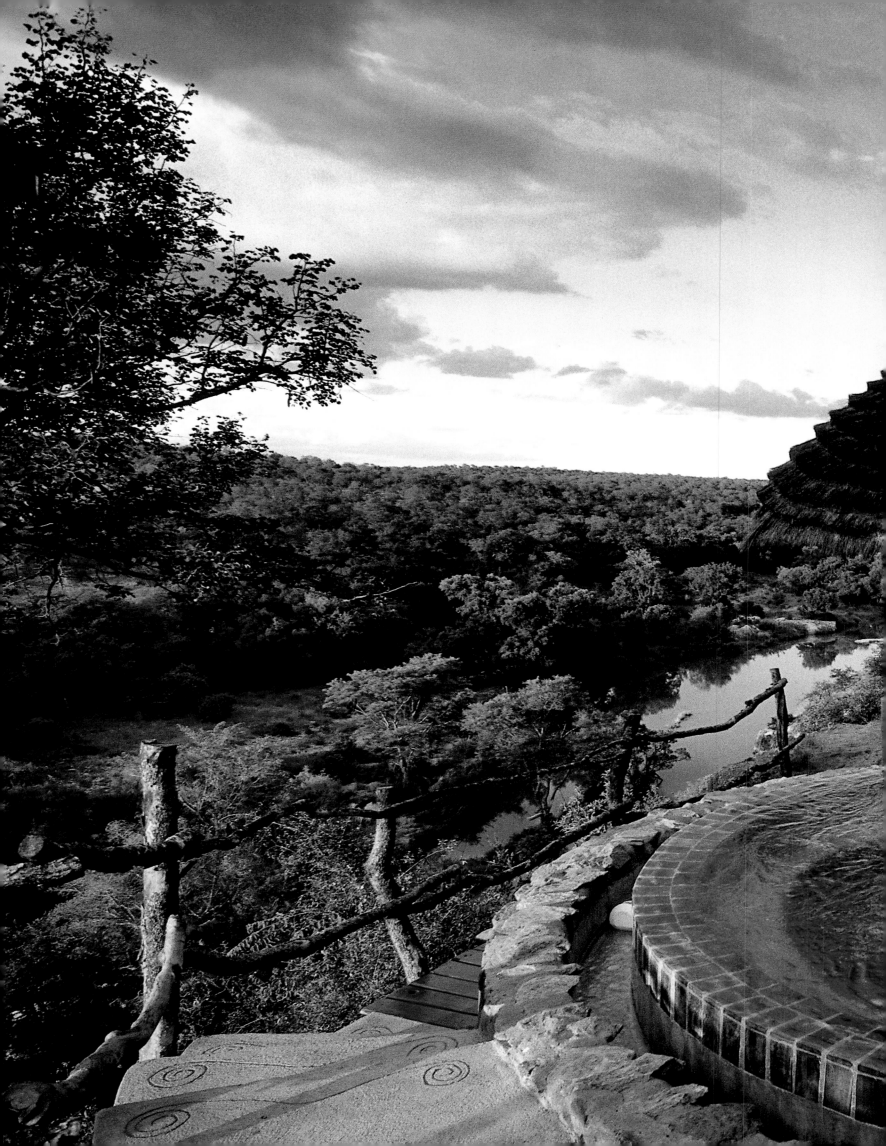

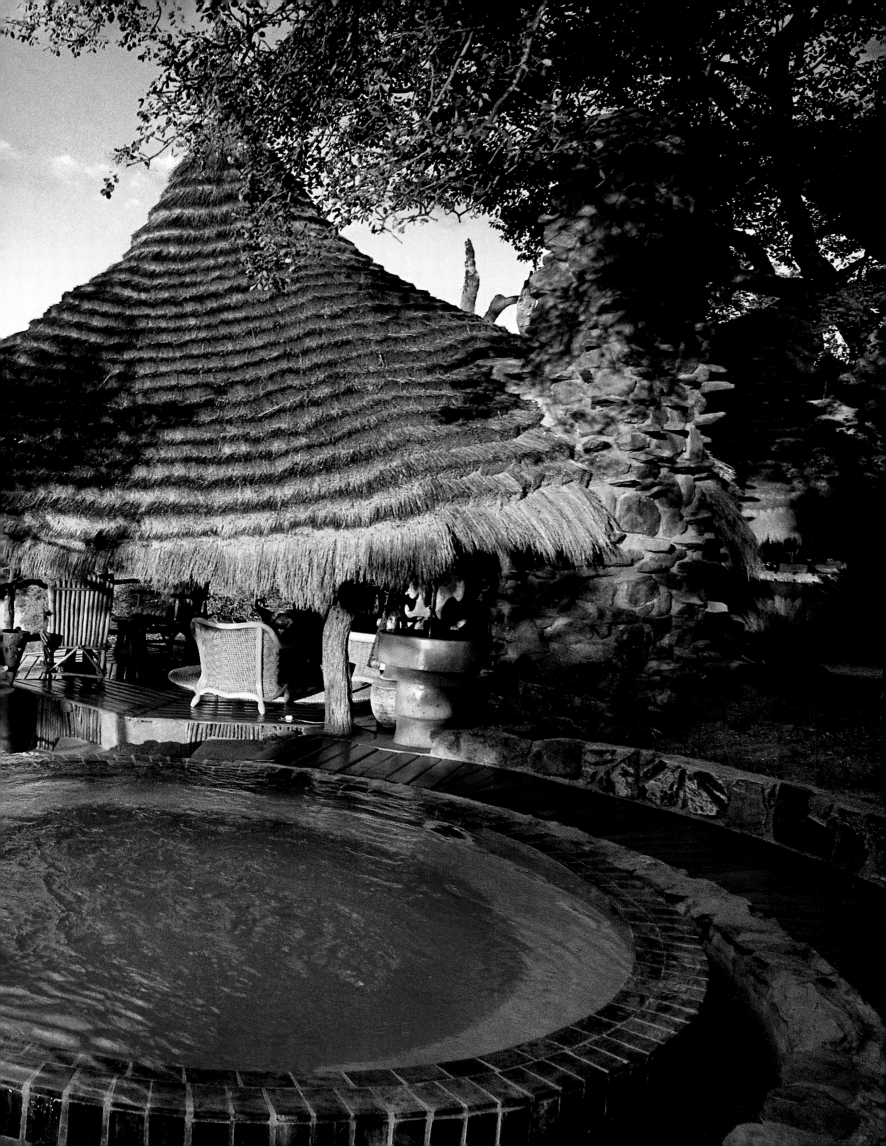

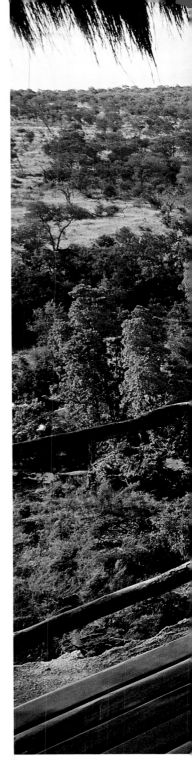

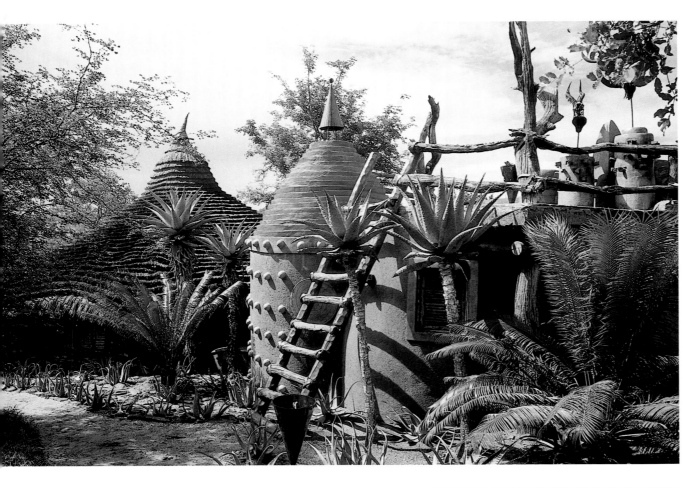

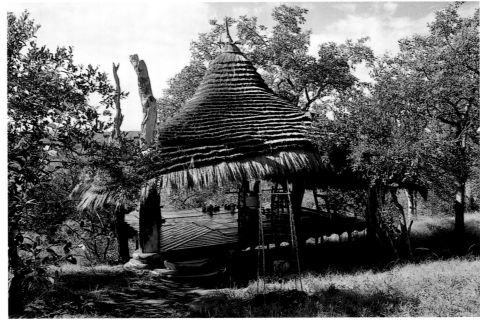

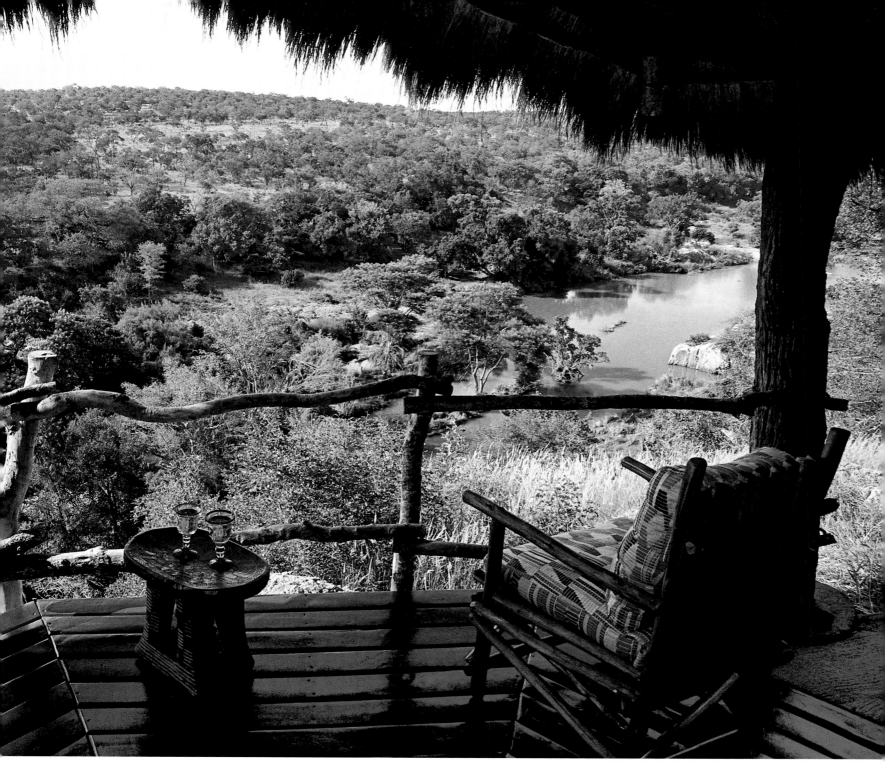

※ **PREVIOUS PAGES AND FACING PAGE** The camp's miniature swimming pool. With its mosaics and domes, Makalali is a cross between something created by Antoni Gaudí, and mythical Darkest Africa. **ABOVE** The terraces in the tops of the jackalberry trees are ideal for relaxing and watching the animals come down to drink in the river. ※ **VORHERGEHENDE DOPPELSEITE UND LINKE SEITE** Im Camp gibt es einen kleinen Swimmingpool. Makalali ist ein eigenes Universum, irgendwo zwischen Antoni Gaudí und Afrika. **OBEN** Auf den in den Jackalberry-Bäumen versteckten Terrassen kann man sich entspannen und zuschauen, wie die Tiere am Fluss trinken. ※ **DOUBLE PAGE PRECEDENTE ET PAGE DE GAUCHE** Ce camp dispose d'une piscine miniature. Avec ses mosaïques et ses dômes, le Makalali a su inventer un univers à mi-chemin entre Antoni Gaudí et l'Afrique. **CI-DESSUS** Les terrasses nichées au creux des arbres de Jackalberry sont idéales pour se détendre et observer les animaux qui s'abreuvent à la rivière.

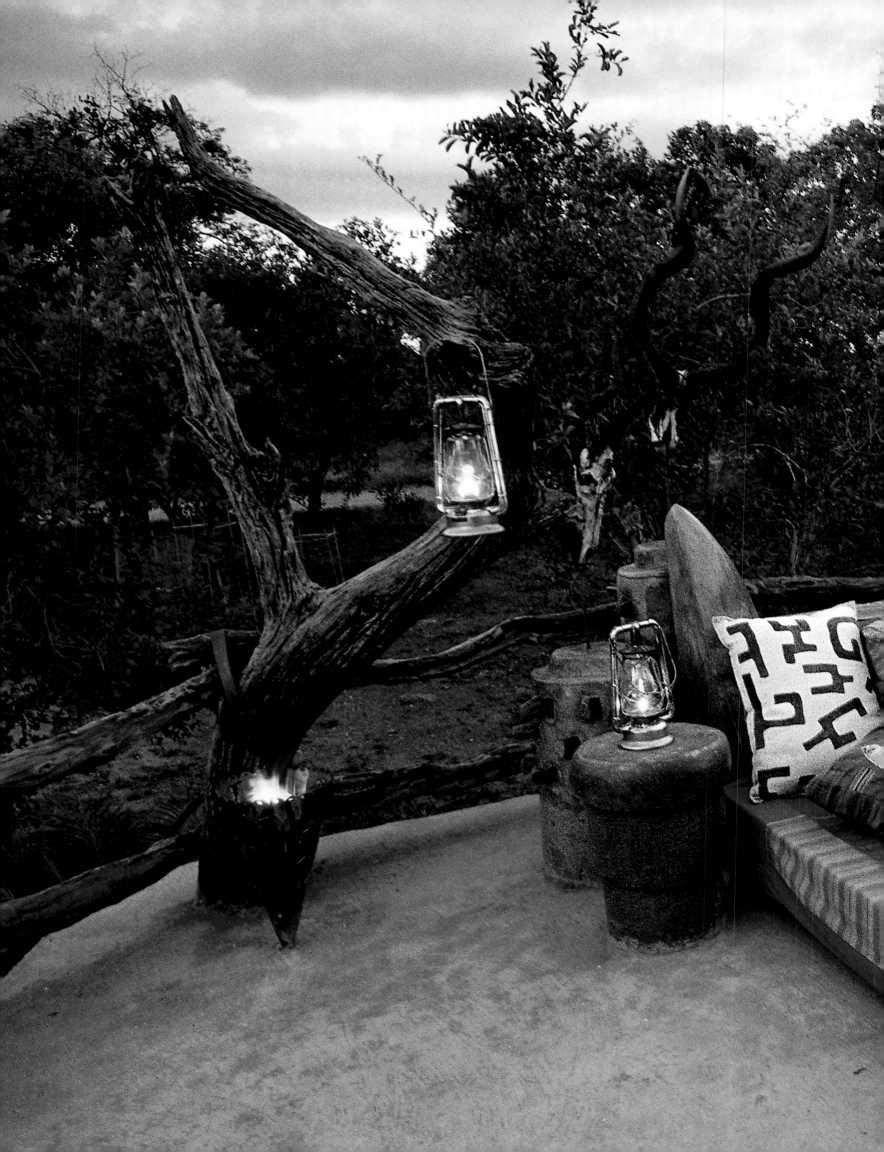

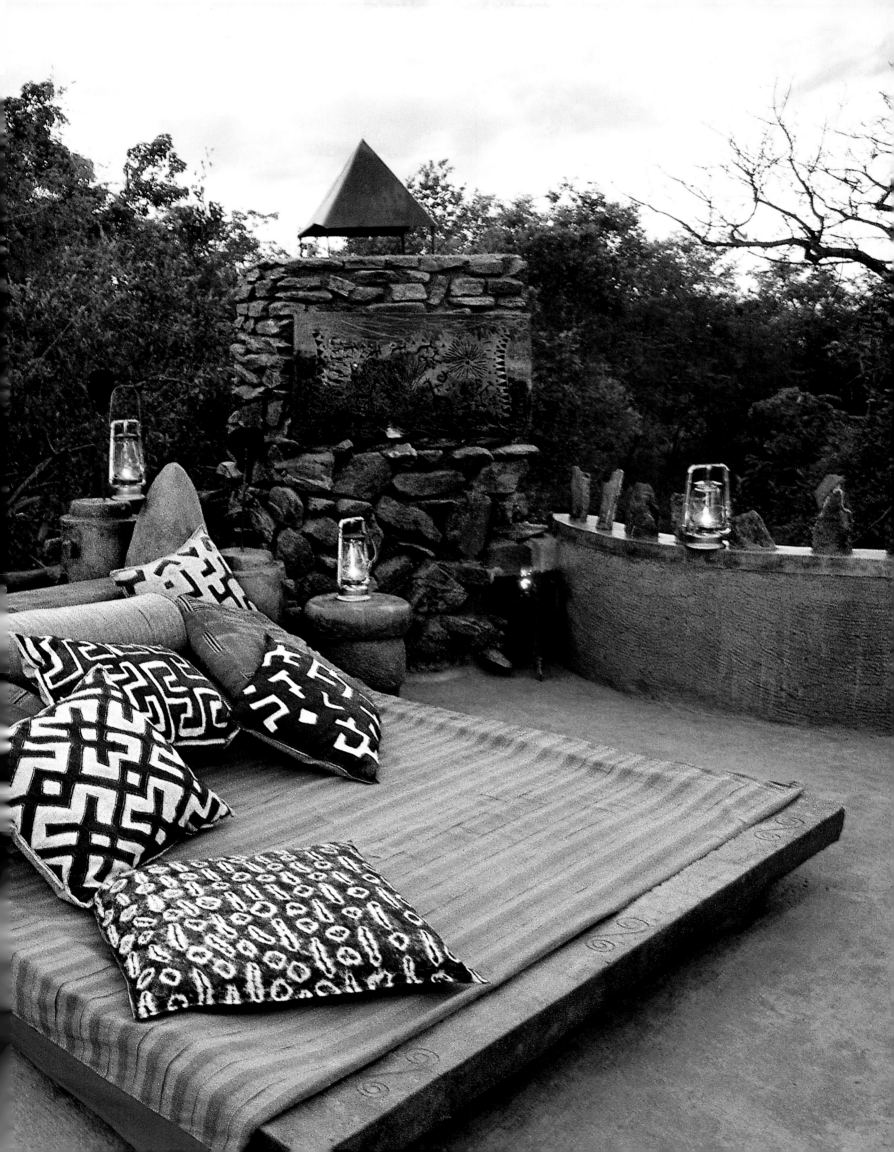

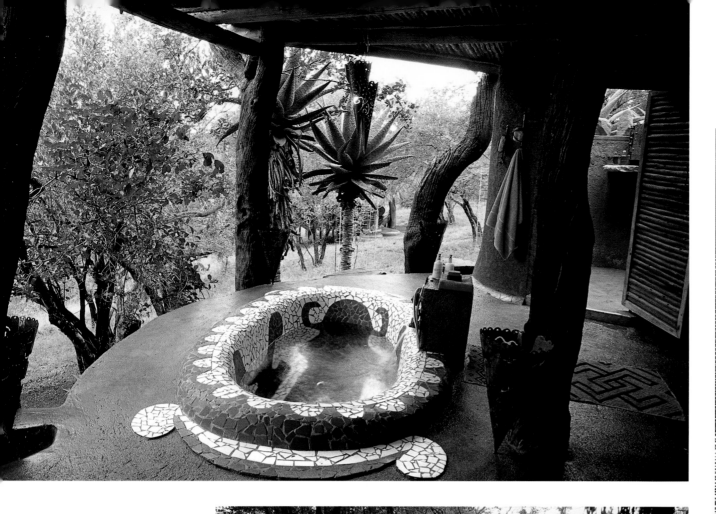

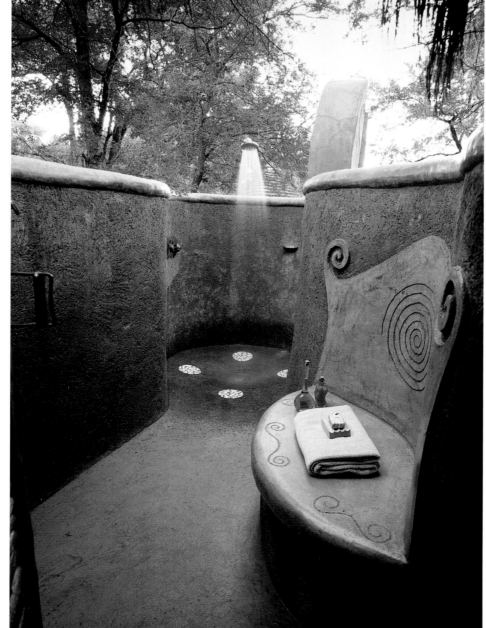

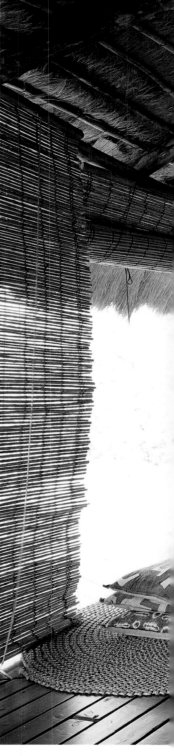

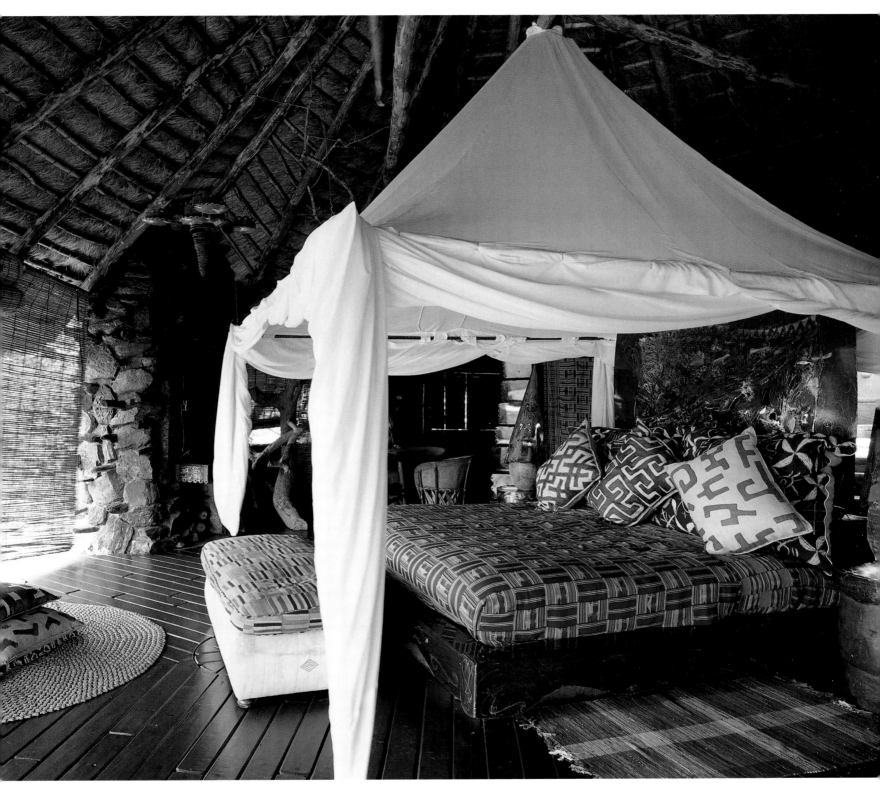

✳ **PREVIOUS PAGES** More adventurous guests can spend the night under the stars, by the light of spirit lamps, with lions in the darkness nearby. **FACING PAGE** Framing the mosaic tub, the trees also support the roof. **ABOVE** A bedroom, with the traditional cotton mosquito net and raffia cushions. On the teak floor, a sisal mat. ✳ **VORHERGEHENDE DOPPELSEITE** Besonders Mutige können die Nacht auch ganz in der Nähe der wilden Tiere im Freien verbringen, im Licht der Öllampen. **LINKE SEITE** Die Bäume, die das Dach stützen, umringen die Mosaik-Badewanne. **OBEN** Ein Zimmer mit dem üblichen Moskitonetz aus Baumwolle sowie Bastkissen. Auf dem Teakholzboden liegt ein Sisalteppich. ✳ **DOUBLE PAGE PRECEDENTE** Les plus courageux peuvent passer une nuit à la belle étoile, sous la lumière des lampes à pétrole et à proximité des grands fauves. **PAGE DE GAUCHE** Encadrant la baignoire en mosaïque, des arbres supportent le toit. **CI-DESSUS** Une chambre avec la traditionnelle moustiquaire en coton et des coussins en raphia. Sur le sol en teck, un tapis de sisal.

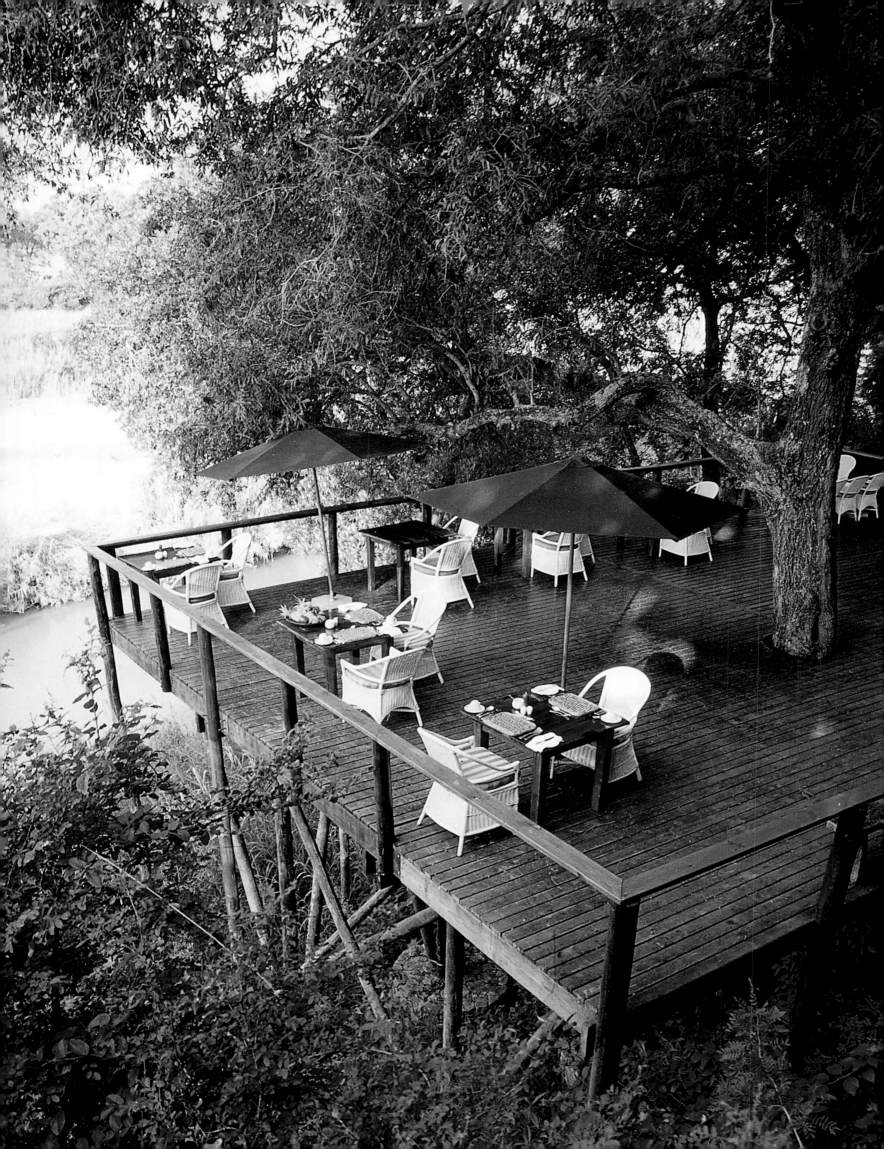

# Singita BOULDERS LODGe

# SaBi SanD

A room with a view:
a camp that has been immaculately integrated into the surrounding landscape.

Before it was turned into a lodge, Singita was a private house, and it is perhaps in the one or two objects and books remaining from earlier times that the enduring charm of the place resides.

Singita, which means "miracle", overlooks a 40,000 acre reserve. Its architect, Bruce Stafford, set out to achieve a view of the plain and its fauna from a point of vantage similar to a box at the opera, from the front and from the side. He designed the buildings overlooking the site accordingly, in the conviction that man's presence should have the minimum effect on the environment. From these vantage points the illusion is perfect: the undisturbed existence of the wild, and the sophistication of mankind, create a mysterious harmony. At the heart of this Eden is a main living room that once constituted the entire original residence here and served Stafford as the blueprint for the rest of the project. Guests eat among the trees, or beside the big fireplace. There are eight thatched chalets artfully sited in the vegetation around the main house. Materials, colours, furniture and bedrooms are all handled in an elegant, ethnic style, while statuettes, glass, masks, earthenware, polished stone and fabrics play their traditional role. For the safaris, there is a choice of "targets" – the big five of African fauna are all plentiful in the reserve.

Bevor es in eine Lodge verwandelt wurde, diente Singita als Privatwohnsitz. Es mag an den Hinterlassenschaften der ehemaligen Besitzer oder auch an der Hand voll Bücher liegen, die wie ein Gebetbuch weitergegeben werden – jedenfalls ist Singita eine Lodge voller Zauber und Charme.

Singita, übersetzt ein »Wunder«, geht auf einen 15000 Hektar großen Park hinaus. Das Konzept des Architekten Bruce Stafford besteht darin, seine Gäste in einer Art Opernloge zu platzieren, mit Blick auf die Savanne und ihre Tiere. Stafford legte Wert darauf, den Eingriff des Menschen in die Natur so gering wie möglich zu halten und entwarf Gebäude, von denen man die Landschaft überblicken kann. Die wilde Welt der Tiere und die Eleganz des menschlichen Daseins verbinden sich auf geheimnisvolle Weise. Der Salon im Zentrum dieses Paradieses, der eigentlich aus der alten ansehnlichen Residenz entstand, hat Modellcharakter. Hier speist man unter Bäumen oder an dem mächtigen Kamin. Acht strohgedeckte Chalets verteilen sich auf die Landschaft. In Bezug auf das Baumaterial, die Farben und Möbel sind alle Zimmer im ethnisch-eleganten Stil eingerichtet. Kleine Statuen, Glaswaren, Masken, Keramik, polierte Steine sowie Stoffe dienen der üblichen Dekoration. Auf Safari kann man zwischen verschiedenen Schießscheiben wählen. Die berühmten »Big Five«, Büffel, Elefant, Leopard, Löwe und Nashorn leben im Reservat.

Avant d'être transformée en lodge, Singita était une résidence privée, et c'est peut-être dans les quelques objets et la poignée de livres transmis comme un bréviaire, que réside ce supplément d'âme qui fait le vrai charme.

Singita, traduisez «le miracle», s'ouvre sur un parc de 15000 hectares. Voir la savane et sa faune, comme au balcon d'un opéra, de face, de profil: tel est le concept défendu par l'architecte Bruce Stafford. Tenant d'un impact minimal de l'homme sur son environnement, il a conçu des bâtiments qui surplombent le site. De ces promontoires, l'illusion est parfaite. Le monde brut de la faune et les sophistications du genre humain se marient mystérieusement. Au cœur de cet éden, un grand salon qui n'était autre, précisément, que l'ancienne résidence cossue, fait figure de modèle. On y mange entre les arbres ou au coin de l'immense cheminée. De part en part, huit chalets au toit de chaume sont dispersés dans la végétation. Matériaux, couleurs, mobilier, les chambres ont toutes été décorées dans un esprit ethnique et élégant. Statuettes, verreries, masques, céramiques, pierre polie et tissus jouent leur rôle traditionnel. Pour les safaris, on a le choix des «cibles». Les fameux «Big five» des amateurs gambadent dans la réserve.

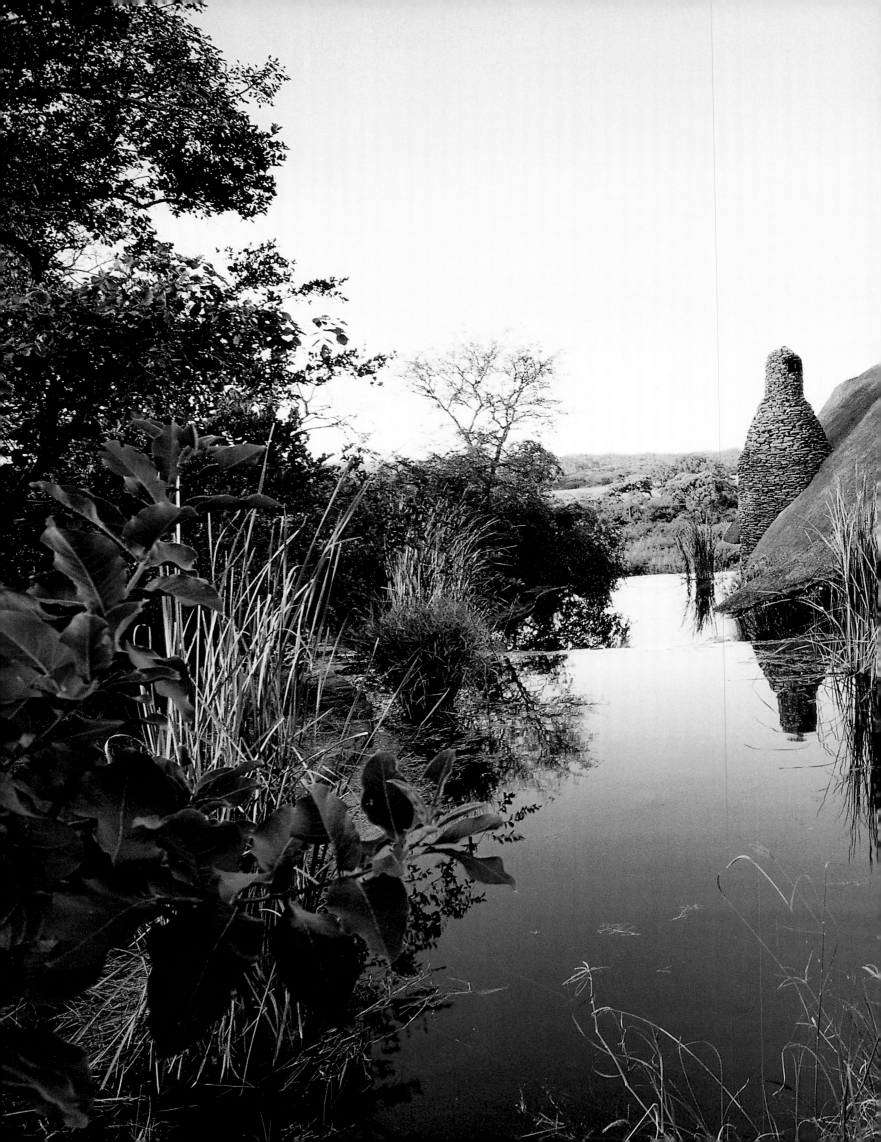

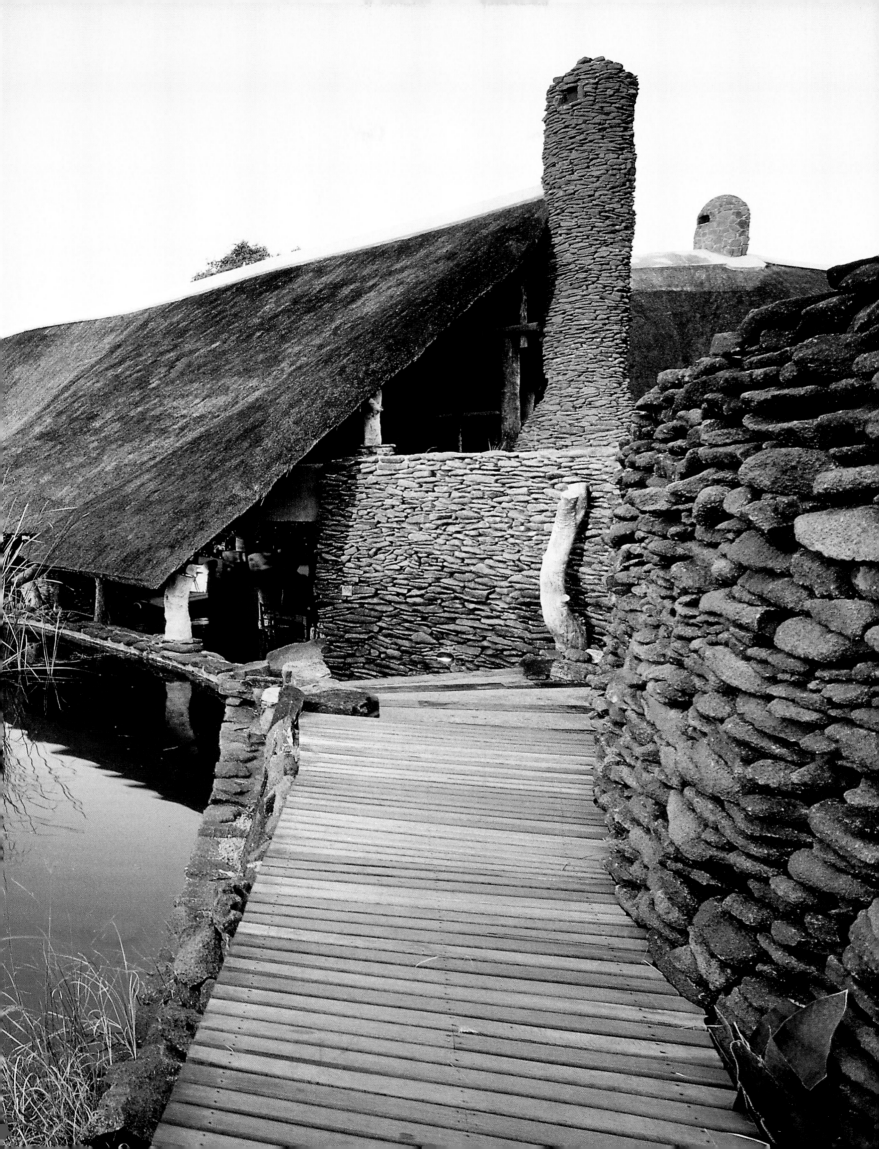

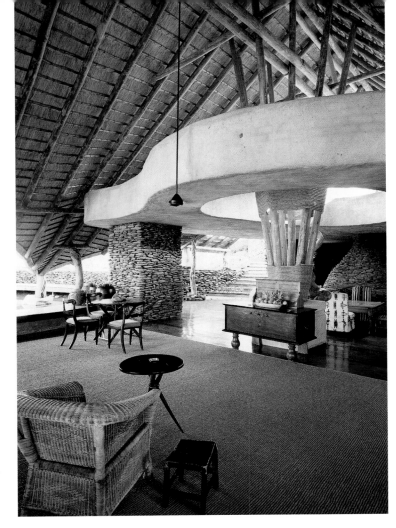

❋ **PREVIOUS PAGES, LEFT AND BELOW** Stone walls and wicker furniture of combined English and African styles. The space marries futurist shapes and traditional concepts, with raffia skirts from Mali used to make the cushions. **FACING PAGE** This dinner service is decorated with traditional motifs from the province of Mpumalanga. ❋ **VORHERGEHENDE DOPPELSEITE, LINKS UND UNTEN** Geschichtete Steinmauern, die wie irische Schornsteine anmuten, Korbmöbel, die stilistisch England mit Afrika verbinden – die Anlage kombiniert futuristische Formen mit traditionellen Elementen wie den mit Raffiabast aus Mali bezogenen Polstern. **RECHTE SEITE** Das Service im Ethno-Chic spielt mit Mustern aus der Provinz Mpumalanga. ❋ **DOUBLE PAGE PRECEDENTE, A GAUCHE ET CI-DESSOUS** Murs en pierres superposées qui évoquent les chemins d'Irlande, meubles en osier combinant les styles africain et anglais, l'espace marie les formes futuristes et les concepts traditionnels avec ses anciens pagnes du Mali en raffia qui habillent les coussins. **PAGE DE DROITE** Le service ethno-chic reprend les motifs de la province du Mpumalanga.

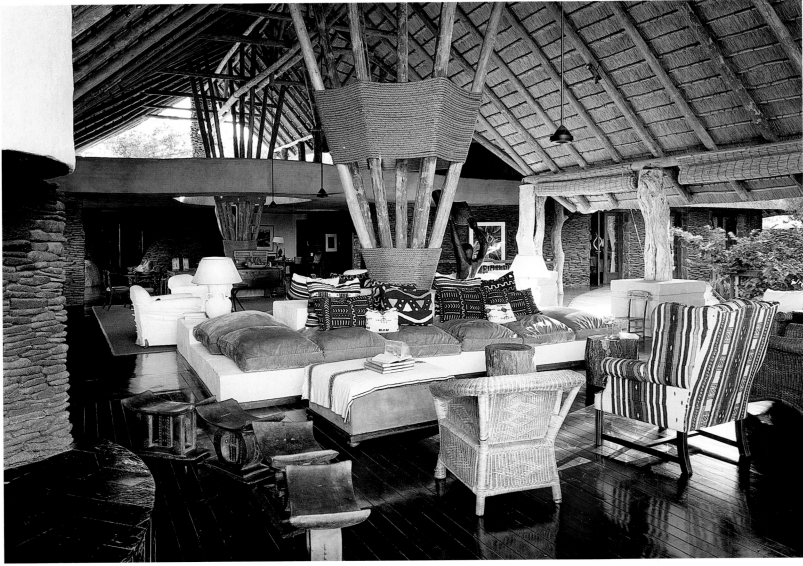

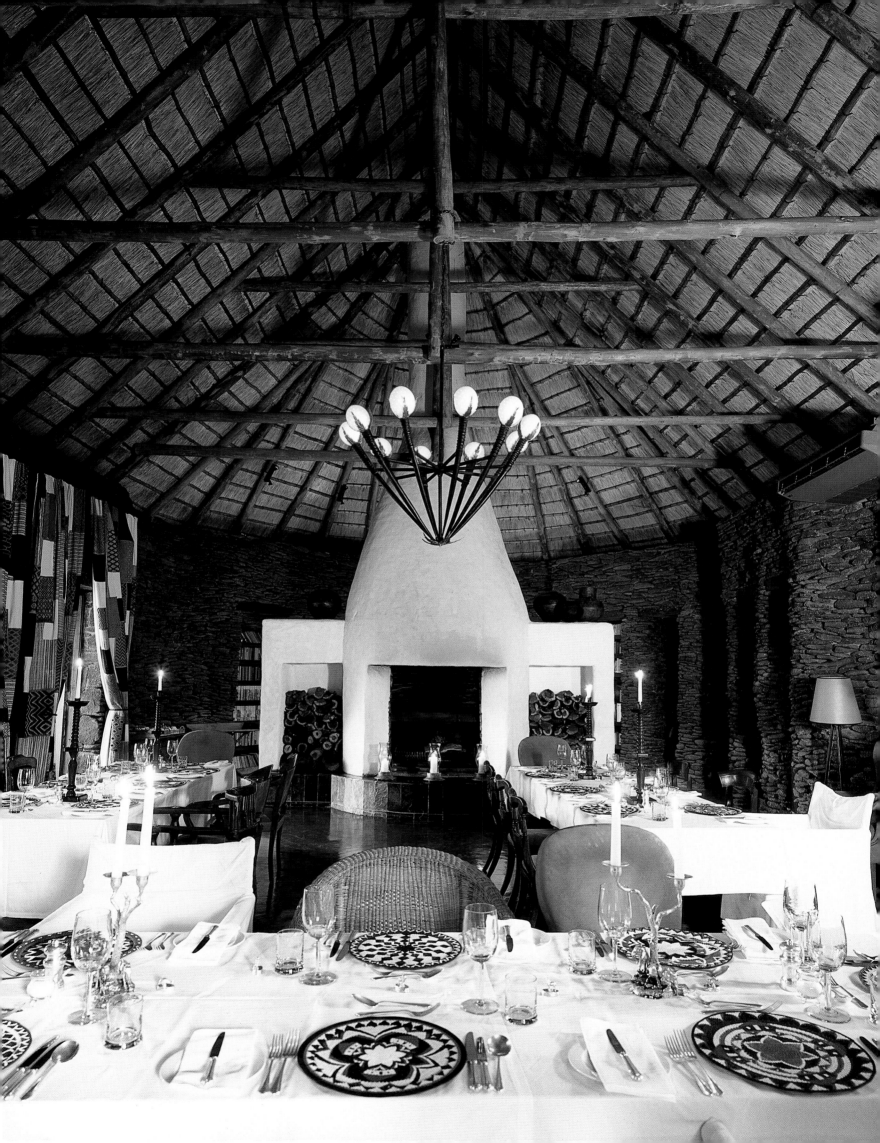

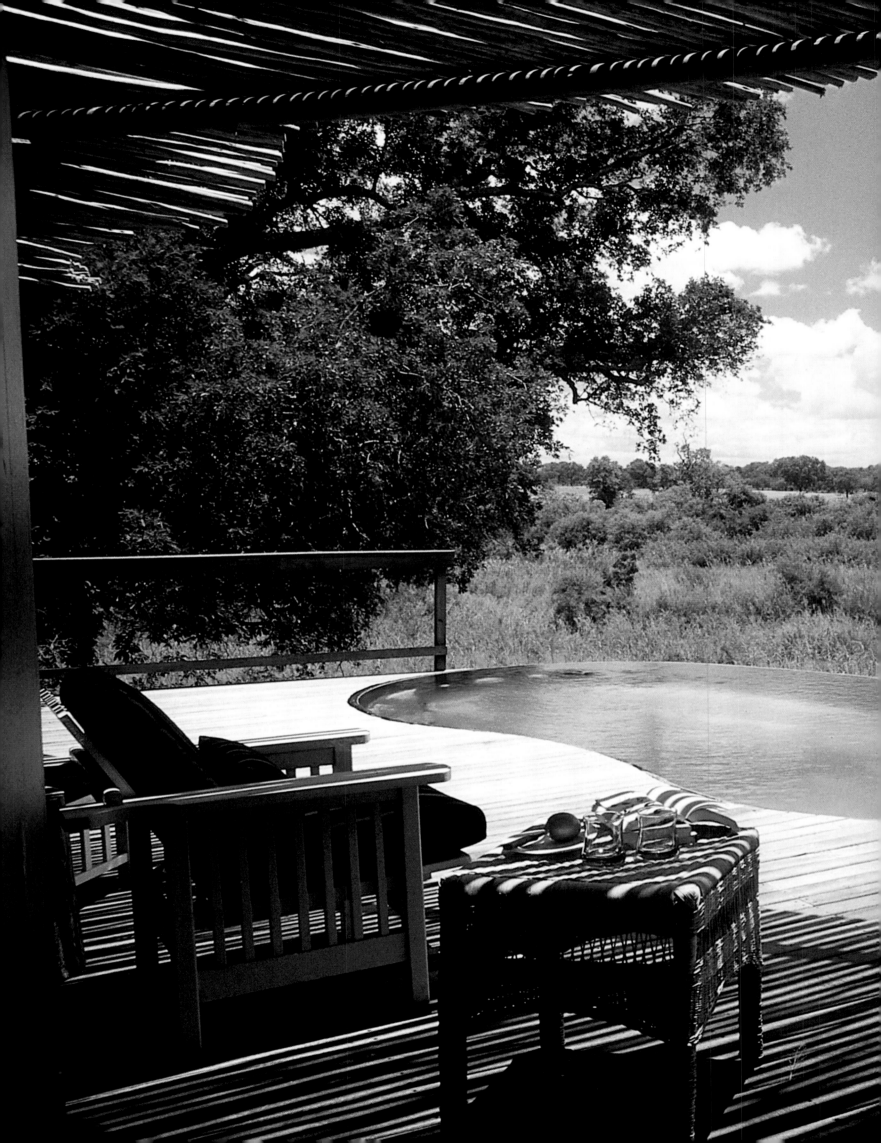

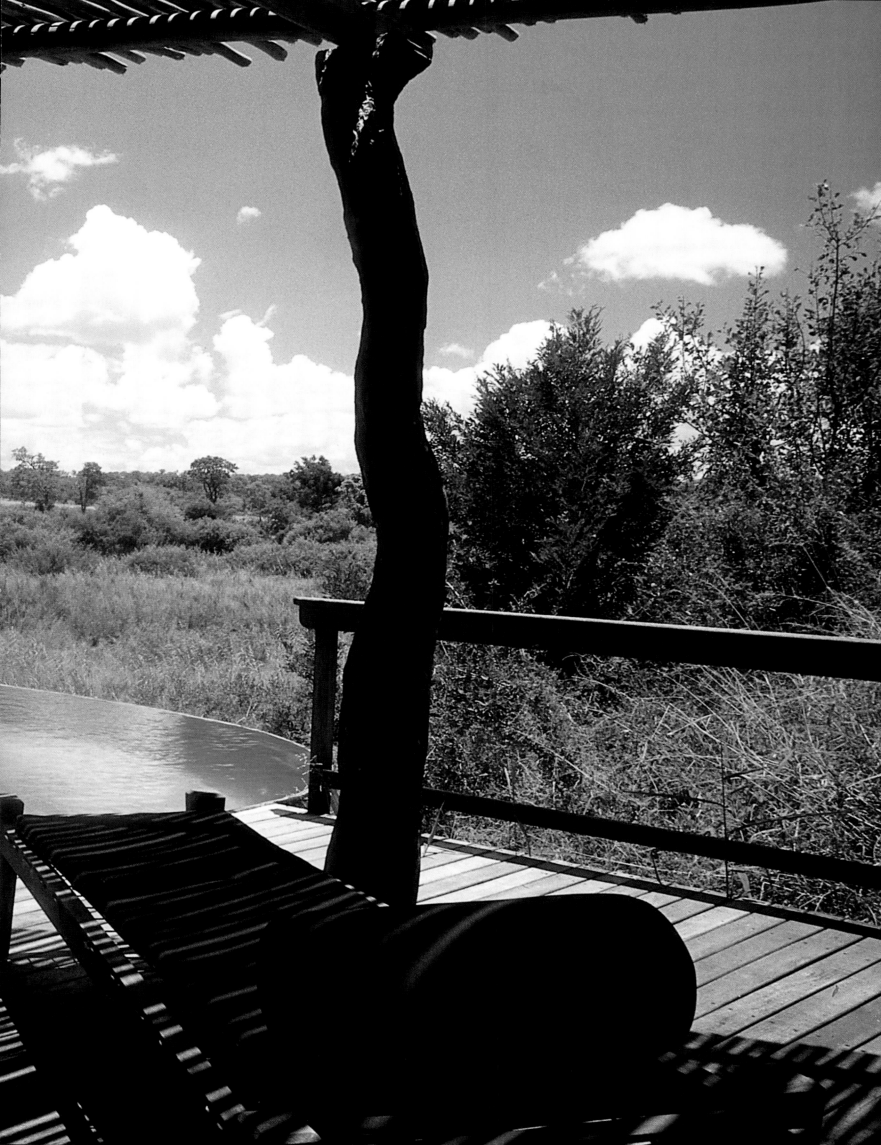

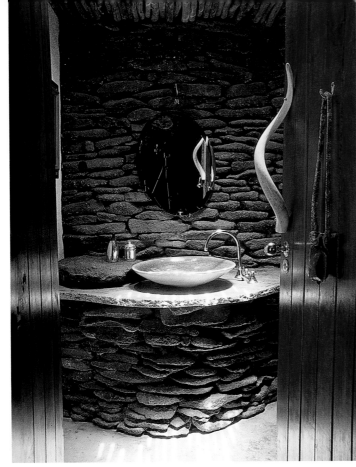

❋ **PREVIOUS PAGES** The plate glass window of a suite looking across a private pool. **LEFT** Off the reception area, a stone-walled cloakroom, with an antelope horn handle on the door. **FACING PAGE** Each bedroom has its own solid jacaranda wood bed. The sisal on the floor and the green English bedcover bring a touch of strength and rigour to the romantically-draped mosquito net and the ceiling fan. In the background, the bathroom and its outside shower. ❋ **VORHERGEHENDE DOPPELSEITE** Die Suite verfügt über ein Panoramafenster und einen Privatpool. **LINKS** Ein kleiner gemauerter Waschraum an der Rezeption – der Griff an der Tür ist aus Antilopenhorn. **RECHTE SEITE** Die großen Betten in den Zimmern sind aus Palisanderholz. Der Sisalteppich und die grüne englische Tagesdecke mildern in ihrer Strenge den eher romantischen Eindruck, den das Moskitonetz und der Ventilator vermitteln. Im Hintergrund liegen das Badezimmer und die Freiluftdusche. ❋ **DOUBLE PAGE PRECEDENTE** Dotée d'une baie vitrée, cette suite donne sur une piscine privée. **A GAUCHE** À la réception, un cabinet de toilette en pierre et sa poignée en corne d'antilope. **PAGE DE DROITE** Les chambres disposent d'un lit massif en bois de jacaranda. Le sisal sur le sol et la couverture verte anglaise apportent une touche de force et de rigueur au romantisme déjà vu de la moustiquaire et du ventilateur. Au fond, la salle de bains et sa douche extérieure.

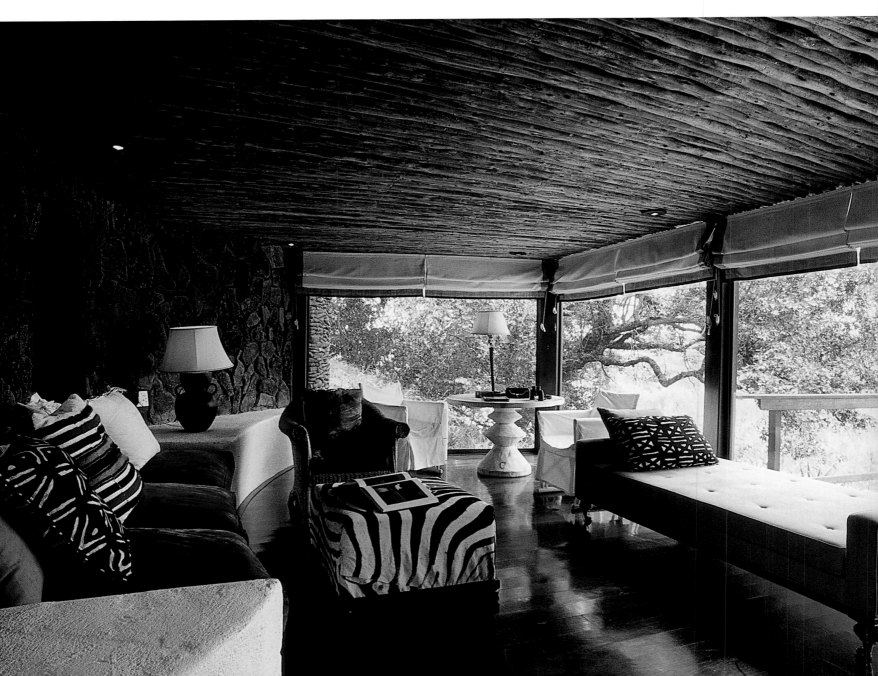

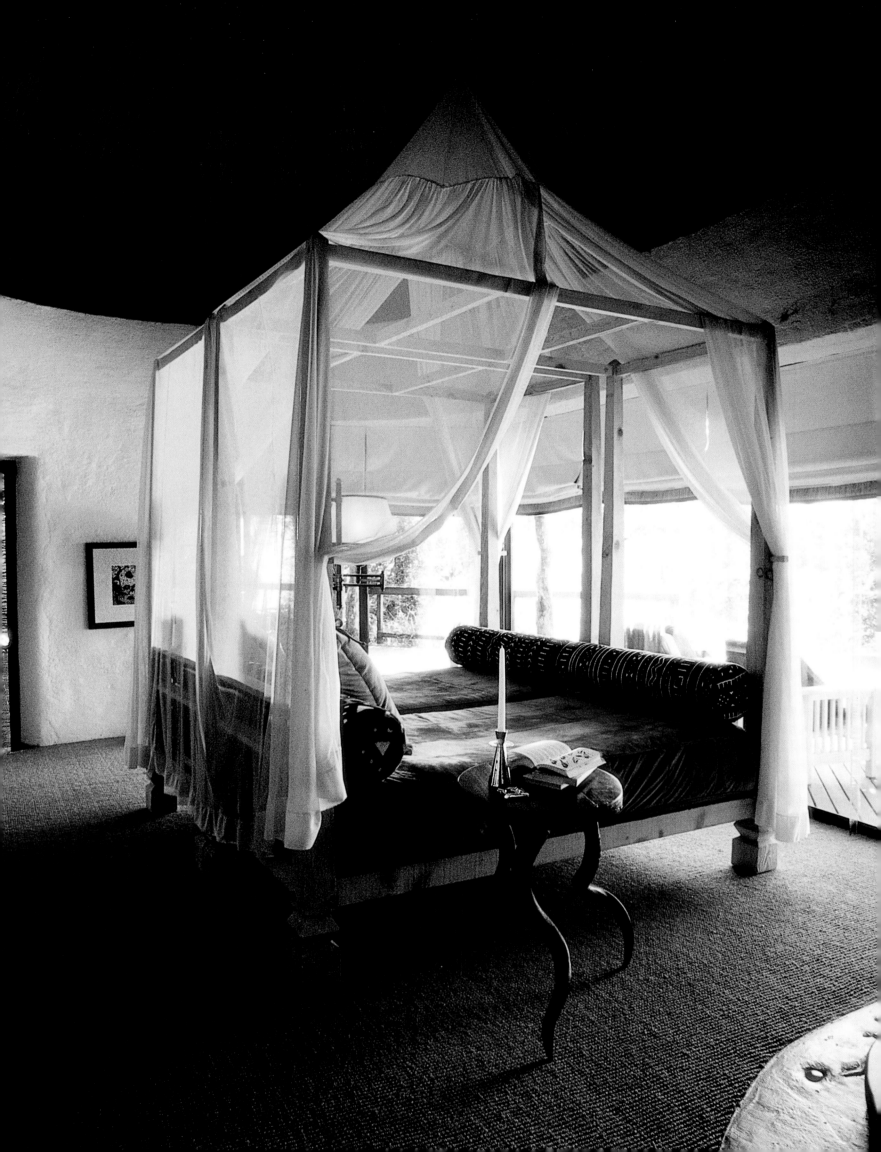

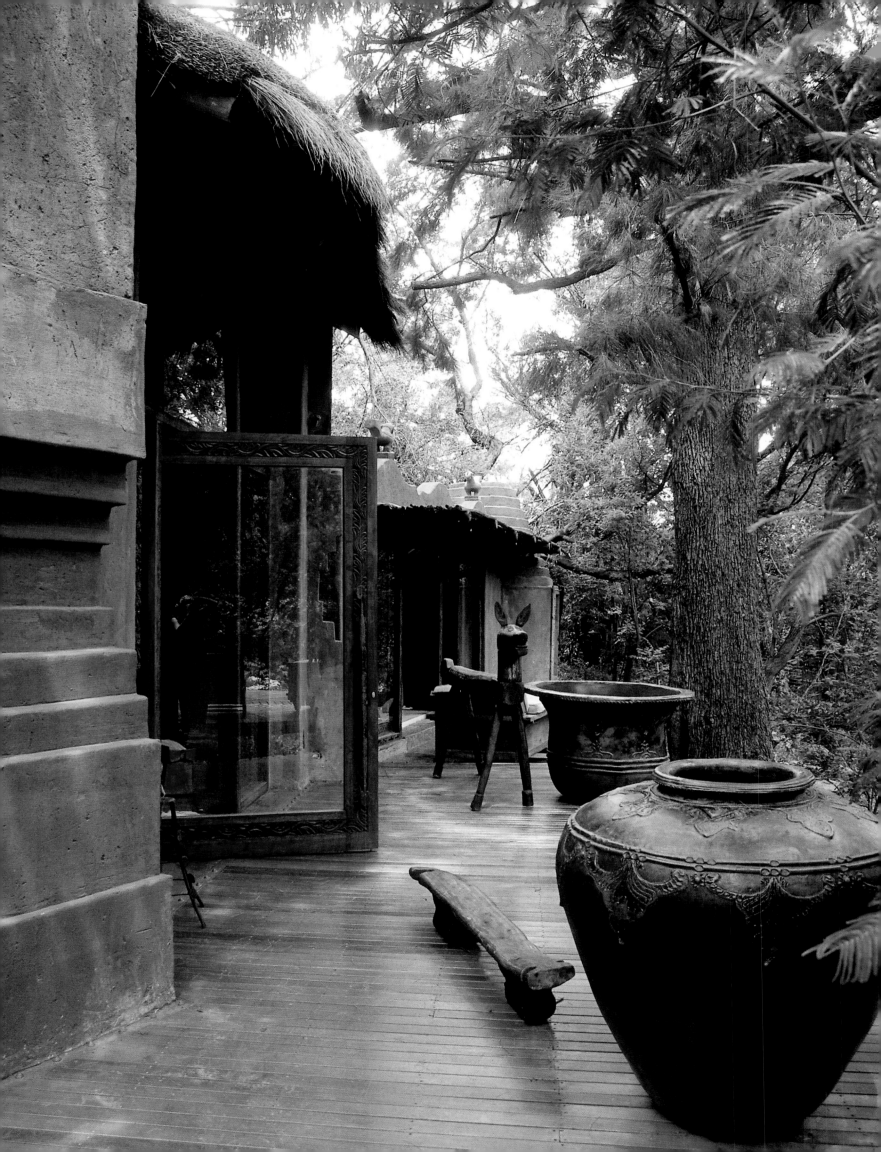

# CASA RECH

# JOHANNESBURG

Opting for a novel kind of ecological art de vivre, the celebrated architect Silvio Rech and his wife Lesley Carstens have built themselves a house of earth, stone and thatch.

Silvio Rech's house is a surprising thing to come across in a major South African city. In this fashionable quarter, the orderly American-style lines of villas seem to have turned away from indigenous Africa.

Silvio Rech has taken a totally different road. His entrance is hidden by a thick screen of vegetation; and when you enter his house you are literally stunned. Rech is a daring artist who has already built a raft of follies. His own home is a scale model, if you like, of many of the other things he has built and decorated. There are walls of brown earth supporting a thatched roof and floors of stained and varnished concrete; in short, Rech has built himself an authentic African dwelling equipped with every modern convenience. It has a wooden deck all round it, giving access to every room. By way of one of the glass doors framed by hand-carved wooden jambs, you can go into the bedroom with its bunk beds (little Gio and his sister Luna sleep below under a goatskin and their parents above). In the same way you can wander into the dining room, the kitchen, the hanging closet or the bathroom. The spaces all communicate with each other, and everywhere there are benches moulded from earth and simple cushions to lie on. This is a totally imaginary idea of Africa, say Rech's detractors. Not so – it's a transposition, or at the very least, a version of "reality corrected by style", in the words of Albert Camus .

Spaziergängern in der großen afrikanischen Stadt bietet sich ein erstaunlicher Anblick, denn die Villen in diesem Nobelviertel sind dermaßen amerikanisiert, dass man vergessen könnte, in Afrika zu sein.

Silvio Rech entschied sich für das genaue Gegenteil. Der Wohnsitz des interessanten Künstlers, unter dessen Federführung bereits viele andere »Verrücktheiten« entstanden, ist fulminant in seiner Andersartigkeit. Als wäre es ein Modell, erkennt man hier in allem und jedem die Inspiration des Chefs. Die Wände aus brauner Erde tragen ein Strohdach, der Boden besteht aus Zement, der mit Pigmenten und Lack marmoriert wurde – eine echte Hütte mit allem erdenklichen modernen Komfort. Ein Holzdeck verläuft einmal um das gesamte Haus, das man durch eine Glastür mit handgeschnitztem Rahmen betritt. Im Schlafzimmer stehen die Betten übereinander – oben schlafen die Eltern, unten der kleine Gio und seine Schwester Luna, unter einer Ziegenfelldecke. Weiter geht's ins Esszimmer, in die Küche, den eingebauten Kleiderschrank und das Badezimmer. Die Räume kommunizieren miteinander und überall laden die im Boden verankerten Bänke und schlichten Kissen zur Meditation ein. Kritiker sehen in dieser Architektur ein Bild von Afrika, das mit der Realität angeblich nichts zu tun hat. Dabei handelt es sich um eine Transposition oder zumindest um eine »durch Stil verbesserte Wirklichkeit«, wie sie schon von Albert Camus beschrieben wurde.

C'est une découverte inattendue pour qui se balade dans la grande ville sud-africaine. Dans ce quartier chic, les villas ordonnées à l'américaine semblent oublier la terre d'Afrique.

Silvio Rech a pris le chemin résolument inverse. Ici, une végétation épaisse dissimule l'entrée. On reste stupéfait devant la demeure de l'artiste un peu allumé et déjà coupable de multiples folies. En modèle réduit, toute l'inspiration du chef est là. Soutenue par des murs en terre brune, protégée par un toit de chaume, posée sur un sol en ciment marbré de pigments et de vernis, l'habitation est une véritable hutte équipée du confort moderne. Sa galerie de circulation en bois, le deck, tourne autour de chaque pièce. Par une porte vitrée encadrée de bois sculptés à la main, on entre, au choix, dans la chambre avec ses lits superposés (les parents en hauteur, le petit Gio et sa sœur Luna, en bas, sous une peau de chèvre), dans la salle à manger, la cuisine, la penderie ou la salle de bains. Les espaces communiquent entre eux et partout des bancs moulés dans la terre ou de simples coussins invitent à la méditation. Voilà une Afrique imaginaire diront les détracteurs. On leur répliquera qu'il s'agit là d'une transposition ou, tout au moins, du «réel corrigé par le style» dont parlait l'écrivain Albert Camus.

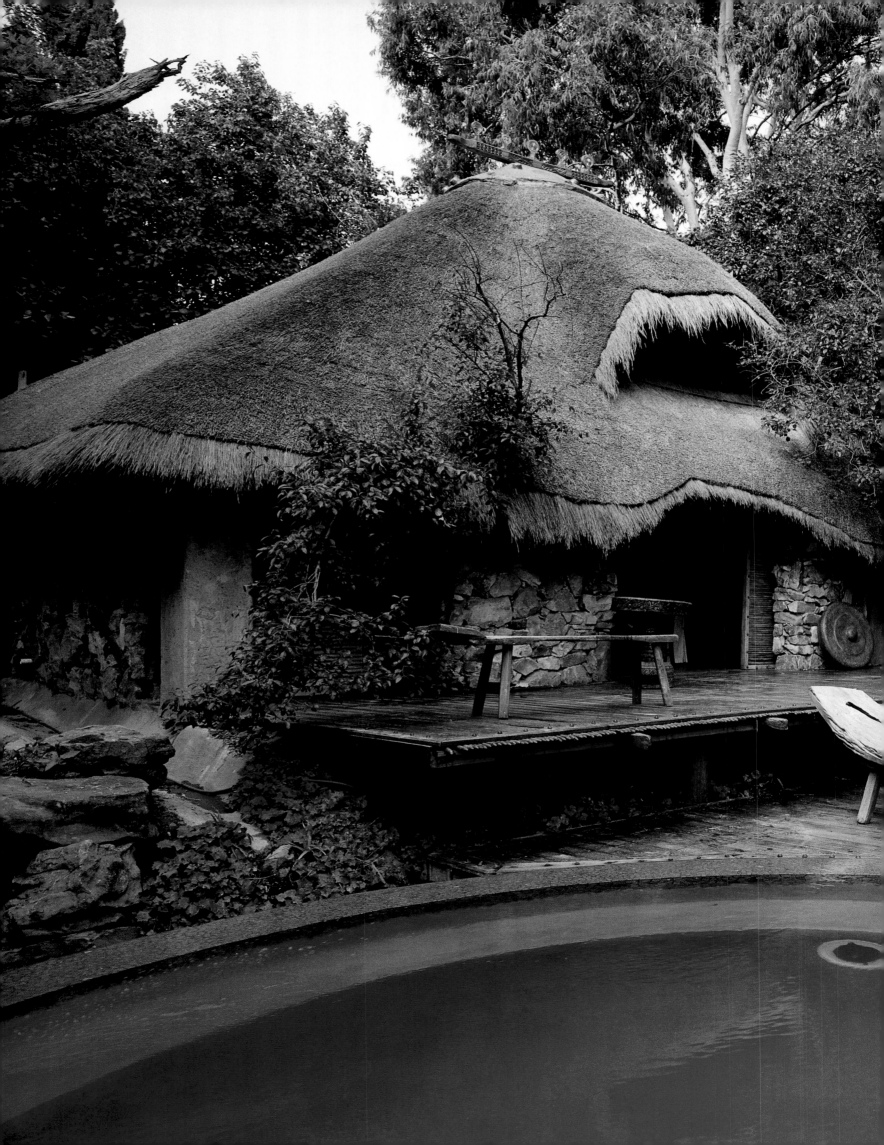

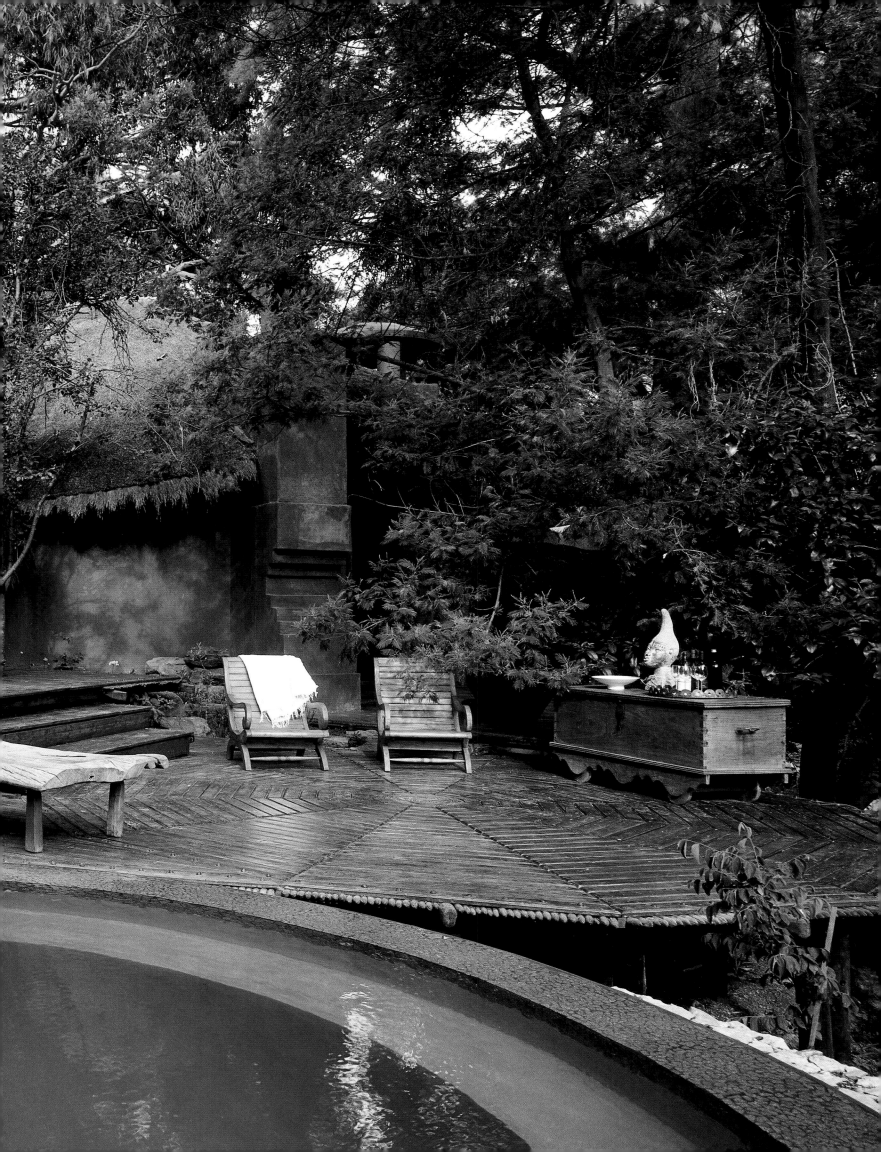

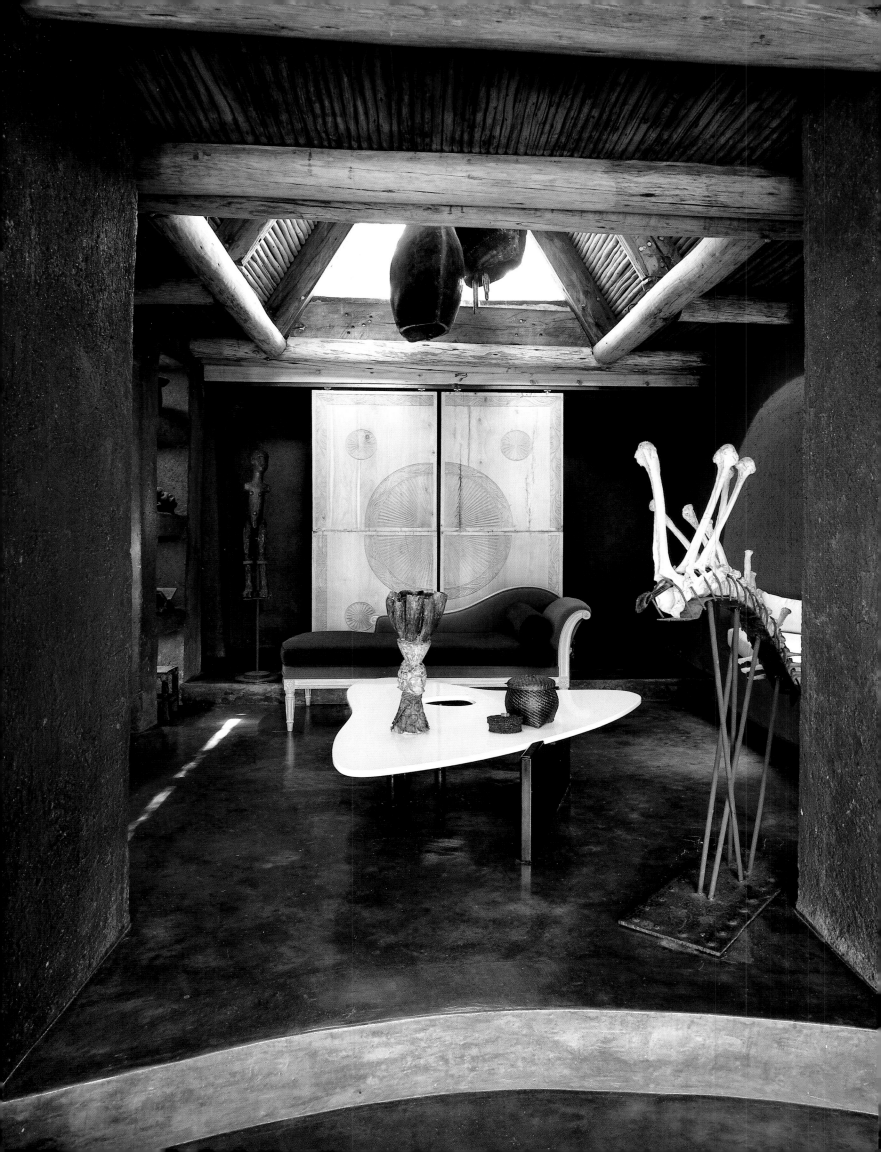

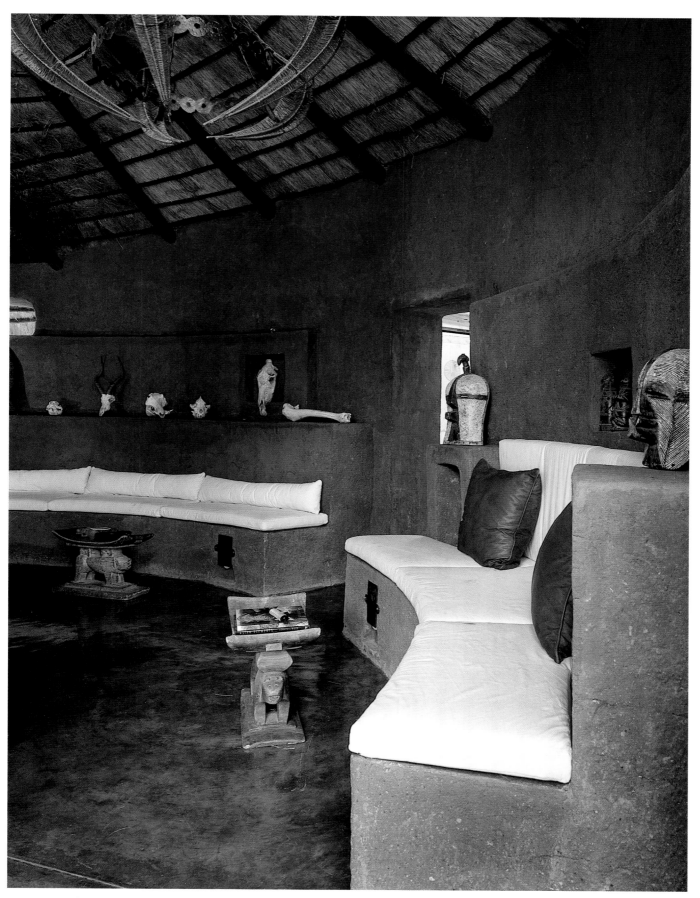

✻ **FACING PAGE** This room with its two traditional bells is positioned between the bedroom and the bathroom. It serves as both antechamber and living room.
**ABOVE** In the bedroom, the circular bench moulded out of clay is surmounted by a shelf. African masks and Asante-style stools provide basic furniture.
✻ **LINKE SEITE** Dieser Ruheraum zwischen Schlafzimmer und Bad, der gleichzeitig als Vorzimmer und Salon dient, steht ganz im Zeichen der beiden großen Glocken. **OBEN** Über der runden in die Erde eingelassenen Bank hängt ein Regal. Afrikanische Masken und Hocker nach Aschanti-Art – das ist auch schon die gesamte Einrichtung. ✻ **PAGE DE GAUCHE** À la fois antichambre et salon, cette pièce de repos que dominent deux cloches traditionnelles est située entre la chambre et la salle de bains. **CI-DESSUS** Dans la chambre, la banquette circulaire moulée dans la terre est surmontée d'une étagère. Masques africains et tabourets d'inspiration Ashanti meublent sommairement l'espace.

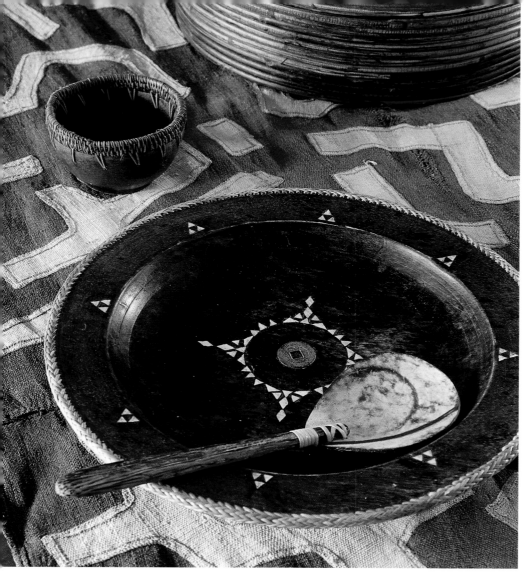

* ABOVE, RIGHT, AND FACING PAGE In the dining room, the wooden dishes are placed on a *kuba* raffia piece. The chandelier by Silvio Rech is inspired by the shape of an elephant's tusk and woven from brass wire. The furniture and the stone fireplace cohabit with contemporary lamps. * OBEN, RECHTS UND RECHTE SEITE Das Geschirr im Esszimmer steht auf *kuba*-Bast. Elefantenstoßzähne inspirierten Silvio Rech zu dem Kronleuchter aus geflochtenem Messingdraht. Die Möbel und der gemauerte Kamin passen gut zu den Lampen, die dem Raum einen moderneren Anstrich geben. * CI-DESSUS, A DROITE ET PAGE DE DROITE Dans la salle à manger, la vaisselle en bois est posée sur un raphia *kuba*. Le lustre réalisé par Silvio Rech est inspiré d'une défense d'éléphant et tressé en fil de laiton. Meubles et cheminée en pierre cohabitent avec des luminaires qui affirment un accent plus contemporain.

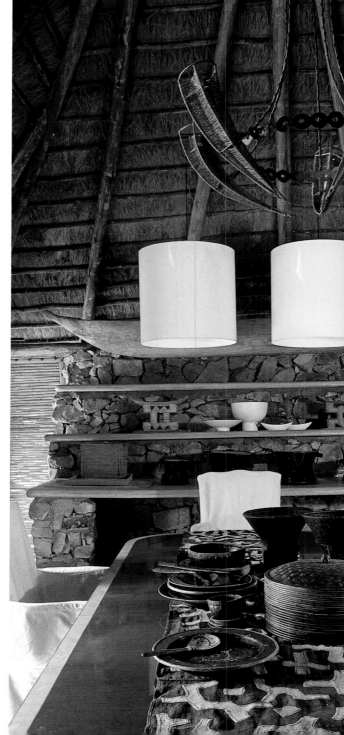

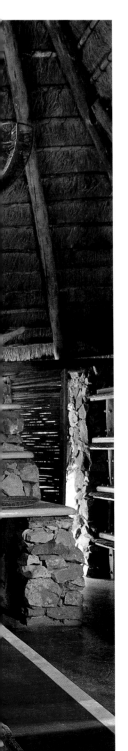
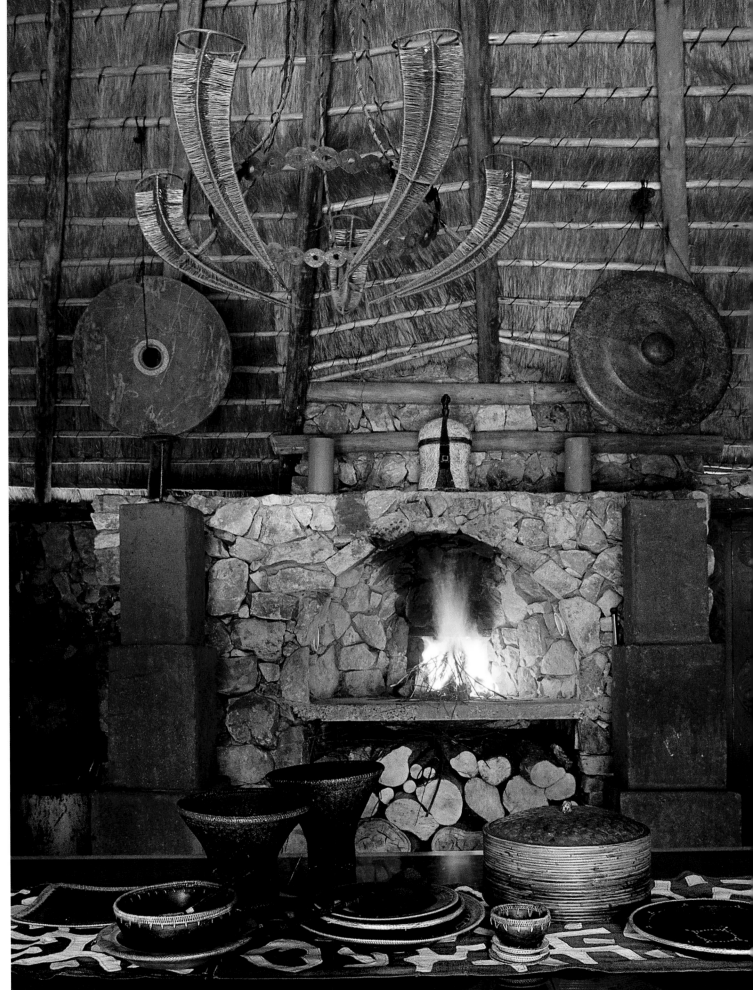

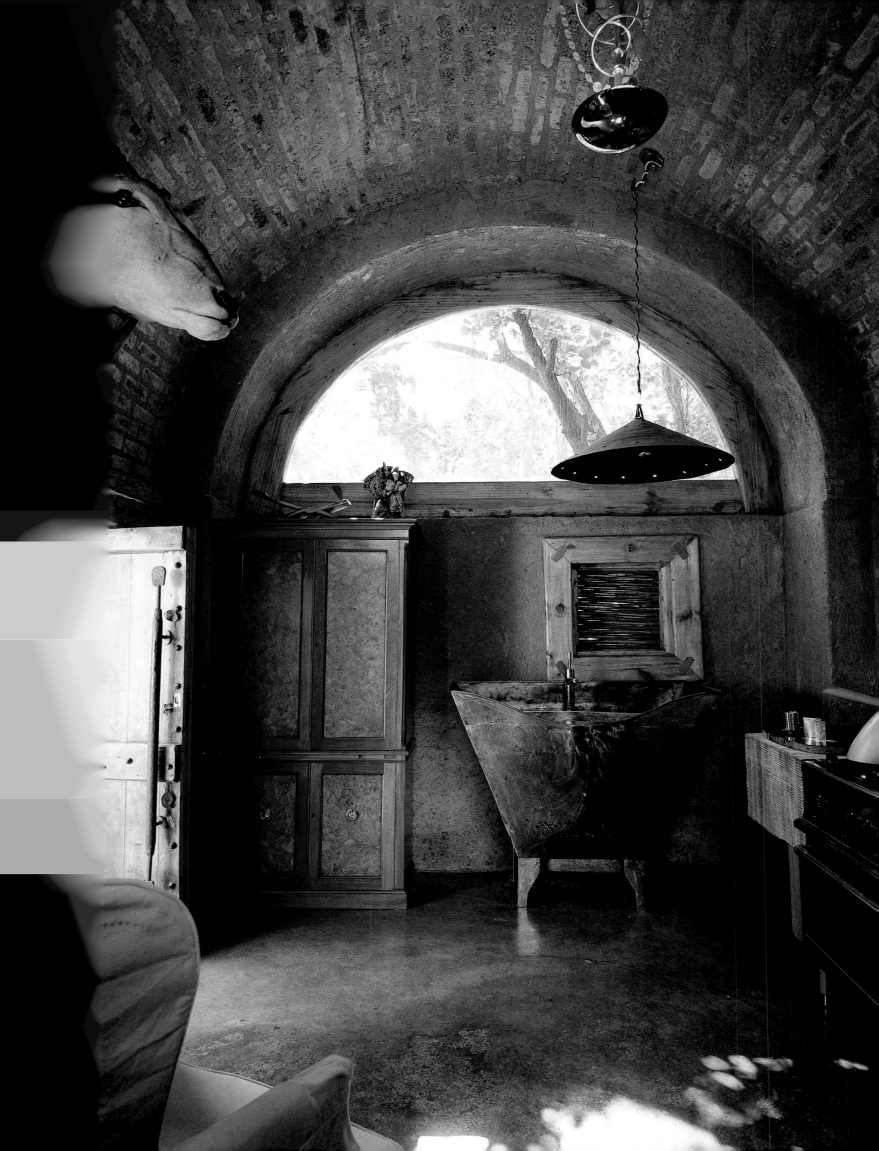

※ **FACING PAGE AND BELOW** Thatch, wicker and brick give a gentle ambiance to the kitchen, along with metal utensils and a Philippe Starck lemon squeezer. In the background, a zinc basin. **RIGHT** Like a column, a living tree grows straight from the marbled cement floor. ※ **LINKE SEITE UND UNTEN** Ziegelwände und geflochtene Körbe sorgen für eine warme Atmosphäre in der Küche. Neben Küchengerätschaften aus Metall steht die Zitronenpresse von Philippe Starck. Im Hintergrund das Spülbecken aus Zink. **RECHTS** Wie eine Säule ragt der Baum aus dem Zementboden mit dem marmorierten Finish. ※ **PAGE DE GAUCHE ET EN BAS** Le chaume et l'osier mêlés à la brique assurent une douce ambiance dans la cuisine dont les ustensiles en métal côtoient le presse-citron de Philippe Starck. Au fond, lavabo en zinc. **A DROITE** Tel une colonne, l'arbre vivant surgit du sol en ciment au fini marbré.

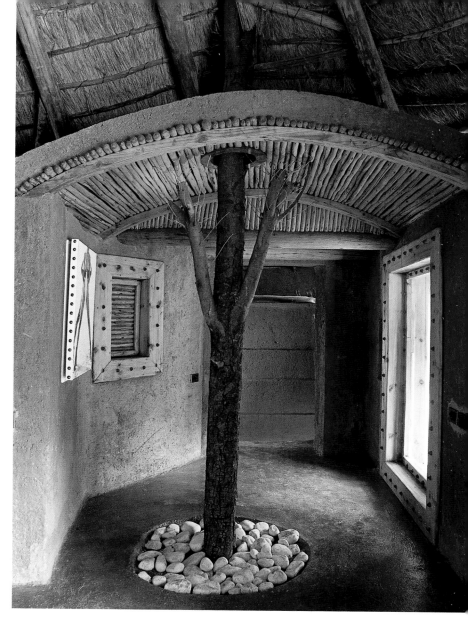

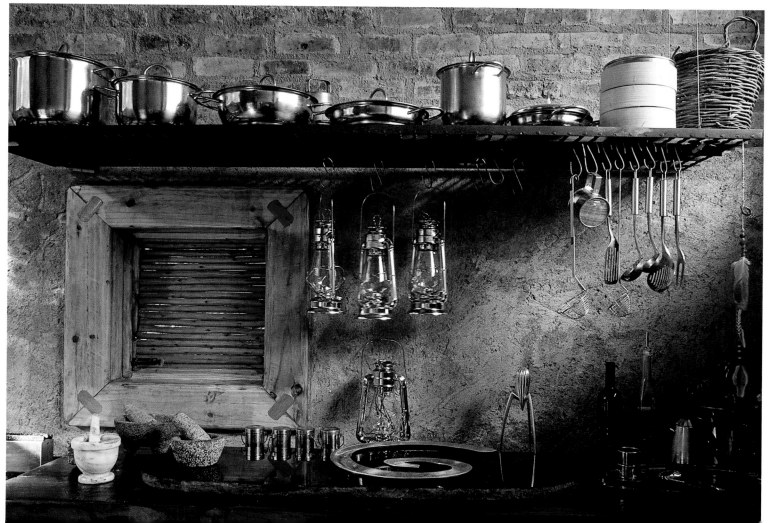

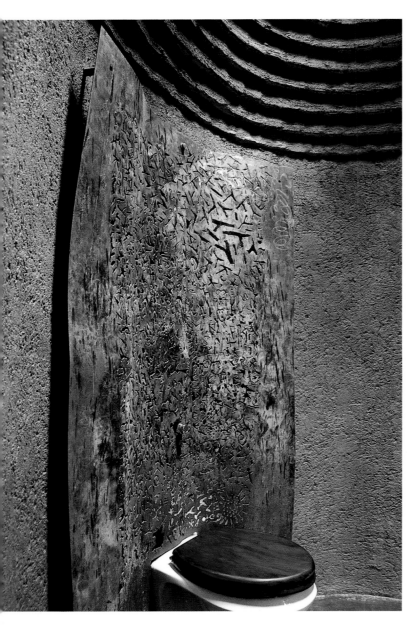

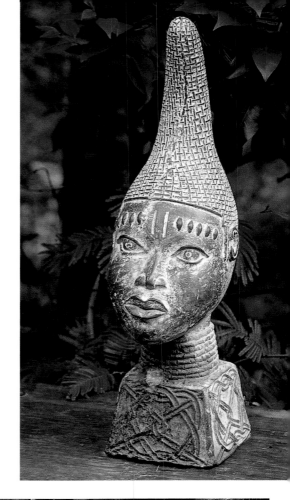

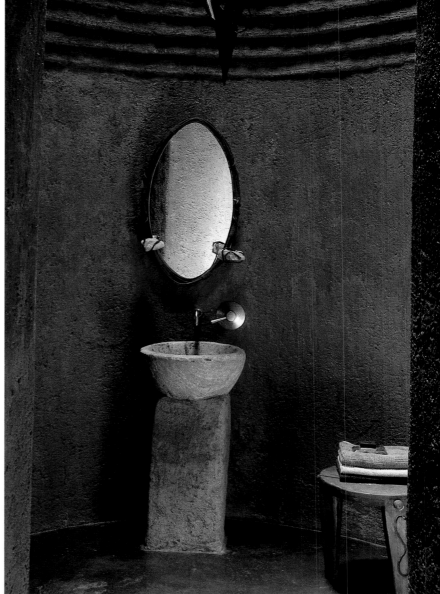

※ **ABOVE** The lavatory beside the bathroom is topped by a metal plaque and a conical ceiling with corbelled brickwork. **RIGHT** A basin designed by Silvio Rech. **FACING PAGE** The massive bathtub is on a level with the surroundings outside. The French windows give on to the circular deck. ※ **OBEN** Hinter der Toilette, die neben dem Badezimmer liegt, hängt eine Metallplatte, über der sich die kegelförmige Decke wölbt. **RECHTS** Das Waschbecken hat Silvio Rech entworfen. **RECHTE SEITE** Die riesige Badewanne wurde ebenerdig eingelassen. Die Fenstertüren führen auf die Terrasse. ※ **CI-DESSUS** Le cabinet de toilette qui jouxte la salle de bains est surmonté d'une plaque de métal et d'un plafond conique strié de briques en encorbellement. **A DROITE** Une vasque dessinée par Silvio Rech. **PAGE DE DROITE** L'immense baignoire encastrée est à hauteur du paysage. Les portes-fenêtres donnent sur le deck circulaire.

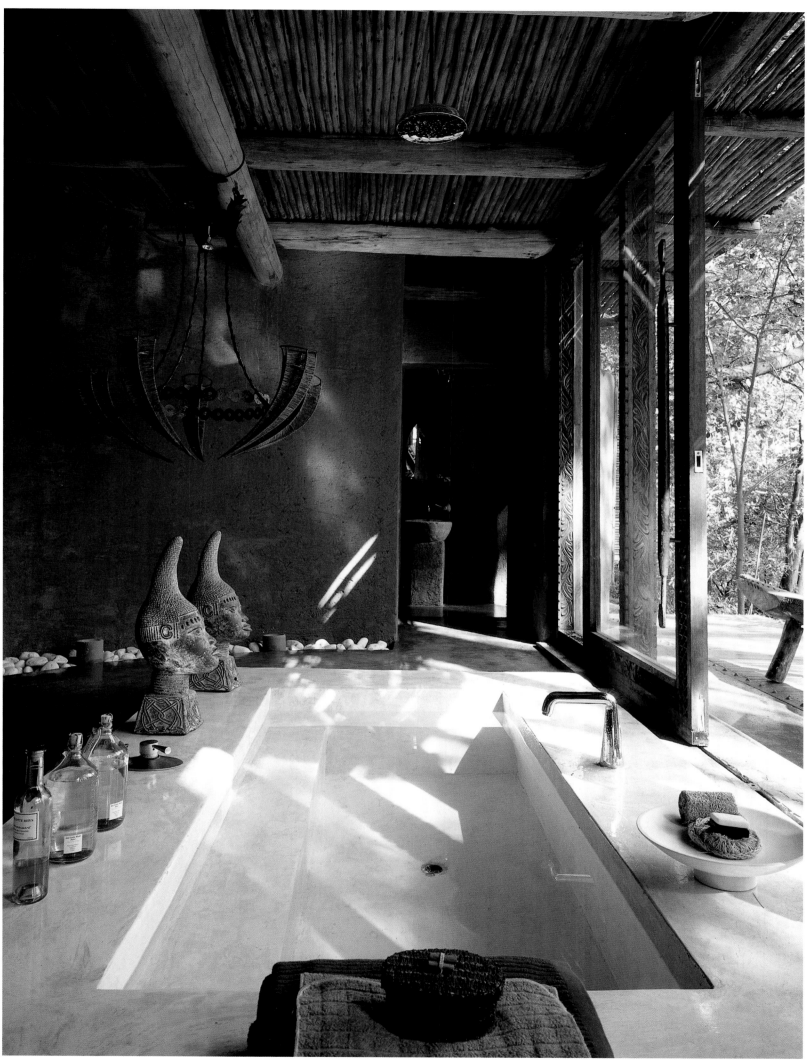

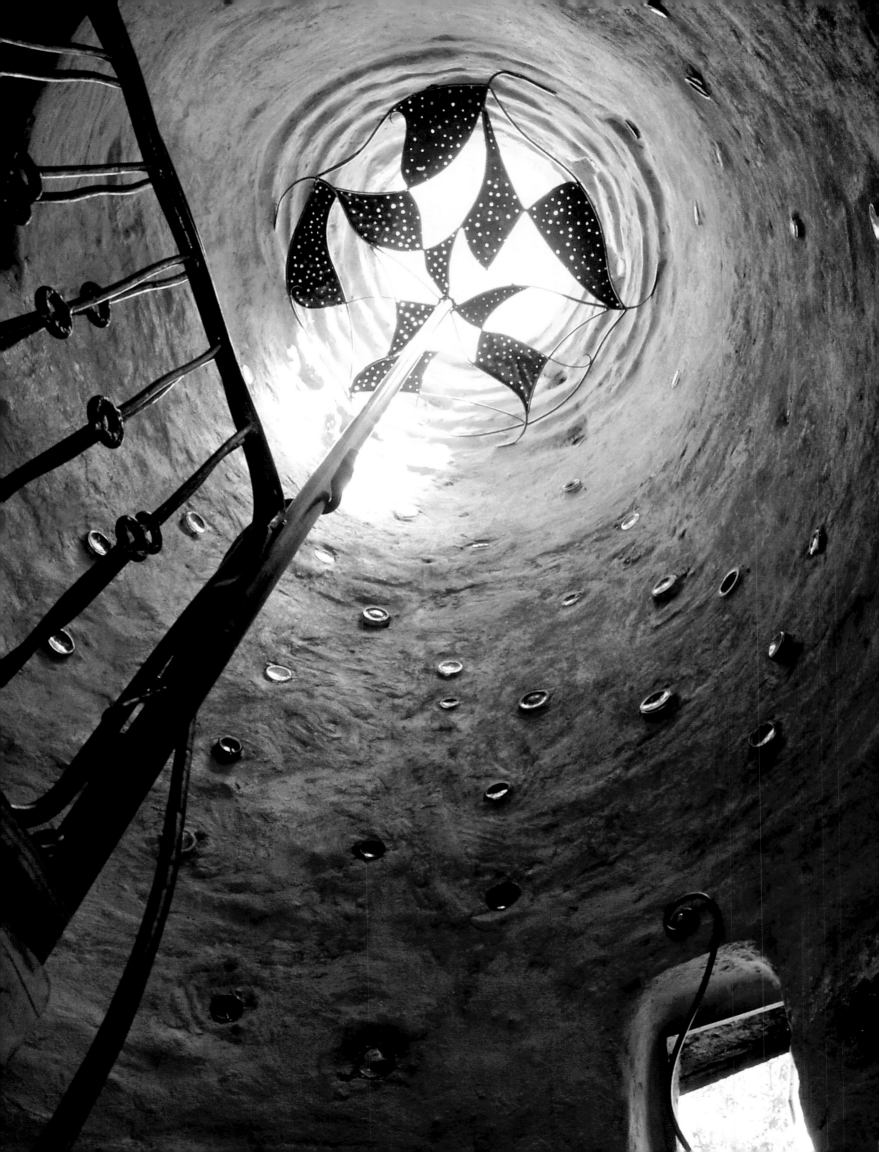

# SHAHN & ALICE ROWE

# JOHANNESBURG

This house incorporates some of the most beautiful features of the African village –
no easy task in a residential district of Johannesburg

With its brown earth walls and surrounding exotic vegetation, the building so strongly resembles a mud dwelling that the neighbours call it "Rowes' Village".

To create it, Shahn and Alice Rowe worked as a team with the architect Kate Otten, whose master is the great Egyptian architect Hassan Fathy. All his life, Fathy proclaimed his goal of rehabilitating African functionalism by bringing back earth as a primary material. African-style, the Rowes' house was born of several different recyclings. The doors and windows come from a now-vanished house that once belonged to Shahn's parents. The massive front door is made from elements picked up at railway yards. Obsessed by the idea of adapting to Africa, and above all rejecting the dominant Californian-villa style of their district, the trio used kiaat wood, Oregon pine and Zimbabwean teak. Every object has been selected for its originality. The carpets echo the mosaics and the red floor tiles. Sun-mirrors and wrought iron lamps brighten the warm rooms, and the combination of all these things is wonderfully harmonious. In the morning, the garden is laden with the scent of flowers. Who would imagine that the big city is only a few yards away?

Die von Mauern aus brauner Erde gestützte Behausung in einer exotischen Pflanzenwelt ähnelt so sehr einer Lehmhütte, dass die Nachbarn sie schon in »Rowe-Dorf« umbenannt haben.

Beim Bau des Hauses hat das Ehepaar Rowe eng mit der Architektin Kate Otten zusammengearbeitet, die sich zur Schule Hassan Fathys zählt. Fathy hat sich als Architekt ein Leben lang dafür eingesetzt, eine Art afrikanischen Funktionalismus zu begründen, indem er die Erde als Baumaterial rehabilitierte. Auf afrikanische Art und Weise bedeutet in diesem Zusammenhang, dass das Bauwerk aus einer Menge von wieder verwertbaren Materialien besteht. Die Fenster und die Türen stammen aus Shahns inzwischen abgerissenem Elternhaus. In der mächtigen Eingangstür wurde Material verwertet, das auf Eisenbahnbaustellen gesammelt wurde. Das Trio, das sich mit dem Haus an die afrikanische Umgebung anpassen und keinesfalls den Stil kalifornischer Villen nachahmen wollte, entschied sich für Kiaatholz, Oregon-Kiefer und Teakholz aus Simbabwe. Jeder Gegenstand wurde einzeln ausgesucht. Die Teppichmuster beziehen sich auf die Mosaike und Terrakottafliesen. Spiegel in Form der Sonne und schmiedeeiserne Lampen beleuchten die in warmen Tönen gehaltenen Räume. Alles strahlt Harmonie aus. Morgens verströmt der Garten seinen betörenden Duft. Kaum vorstellbar, dass die Großstadt ganz in der Nähe liegt …

Soutenue par des murs en terre brune, protégée par une végétation exotique, l'habitation ressemble à une hutte en terre au point que le voisinage la nomme le «village des Rowe».

Pour édifier son «village», donc, le couple a véritablement travaillé en équipe avec l'architecte, Kate Otten. Celle-ci revendique comme influence principale le maître égyptien Hassan Fathy. Sa vie durant, cet homme a affiché sa volonté de décliner un fonctionnalisme à l'africaine, c'est-à-dire en réhabilitant la terre. À l'africaine, cette construction est né de nombreux recyclages. Portes et fenêtres proviennent de la maison, disparue aujourd'hui, des parents de Shahn. La porte d'entrée, monumentale, mêle des éléments glanés sur les chantiers ferroviaires. Obnubilé par l'idée de s'adapter à l'Afrique, de ne surtout pas singer les villas californiennes, le trio a utilisé les bois de kiaat, le pin d'Oregon, un teck du Zimbabwe. Chaque objet a été choisi pour son originalité. Des tapis répondent aux mosaïques et aux tomettes. Des miroirs en soleil, des lampes en fer forgé illuminent les pièces chaudes. L'ensemble est très harmonieux. Au matin, le jardin embaume. Comment imaginer que la grande ville n'est qu'à quelques minutes?

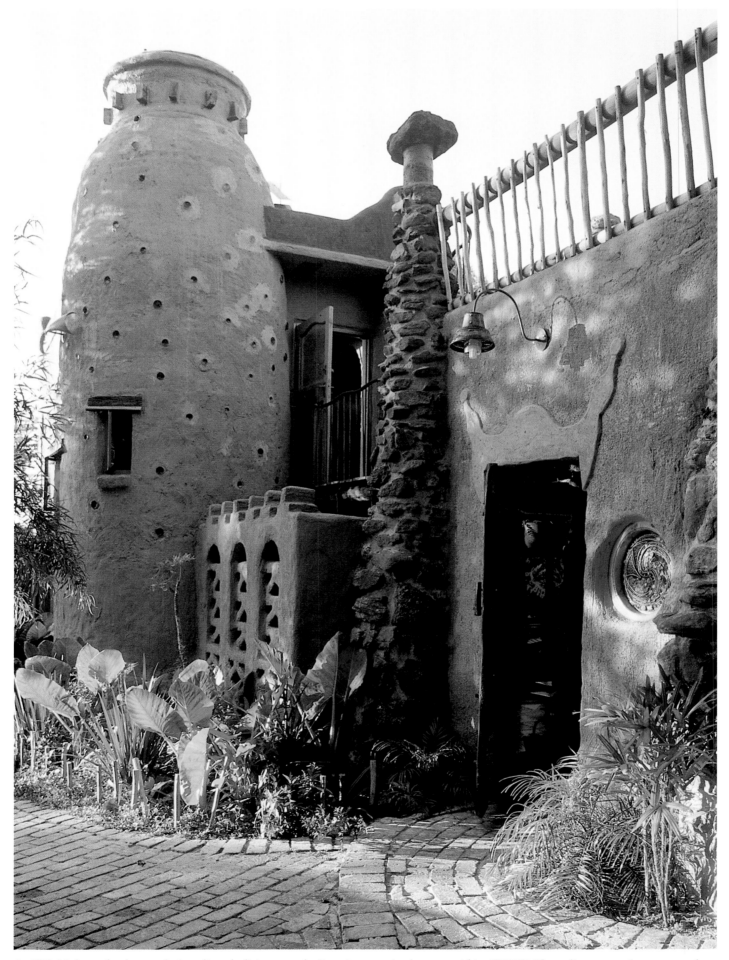

❋ **ABOVE** Made up of a photographer's studio and a living space, the Rowes' property is a homage to Africa. **FACING PAGE** The studio entrance gives on to a make-up room. ❋ **OBEN** Das Haus der Rowes – ein Teil wird als Fotostudio, der andere zum Wohnen genutzt – ist eine Hommage an Afrika. **RECHTE SEITE** Der Eingang des Studios führt zu einem Schminkzimmer. ❋ **CI-DESSUS** Formée d'un studio de photographe et d'une habitation, la propriété du couple Rowe est un hommage aux concessions d'Afrique. **PAGE DE DROITE** L'entrée du studio donne sur une salle de maquillage.

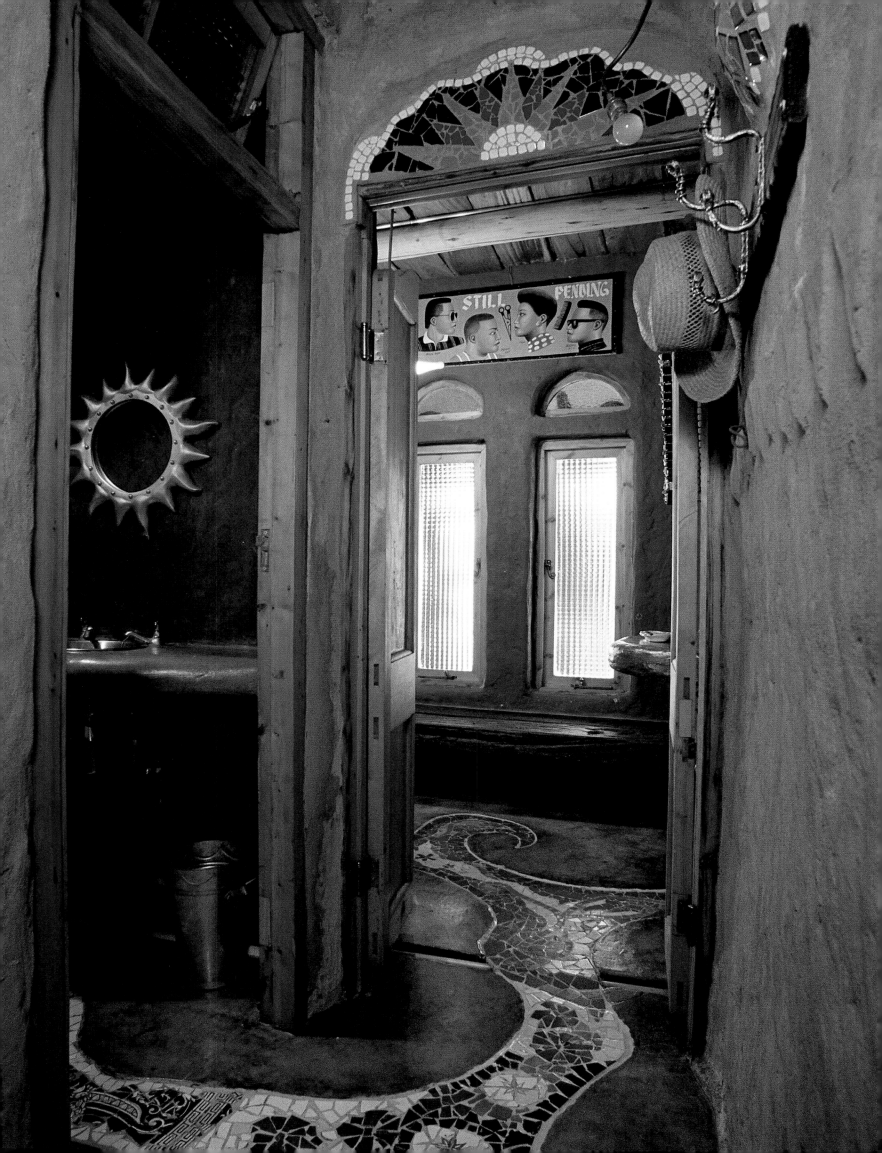

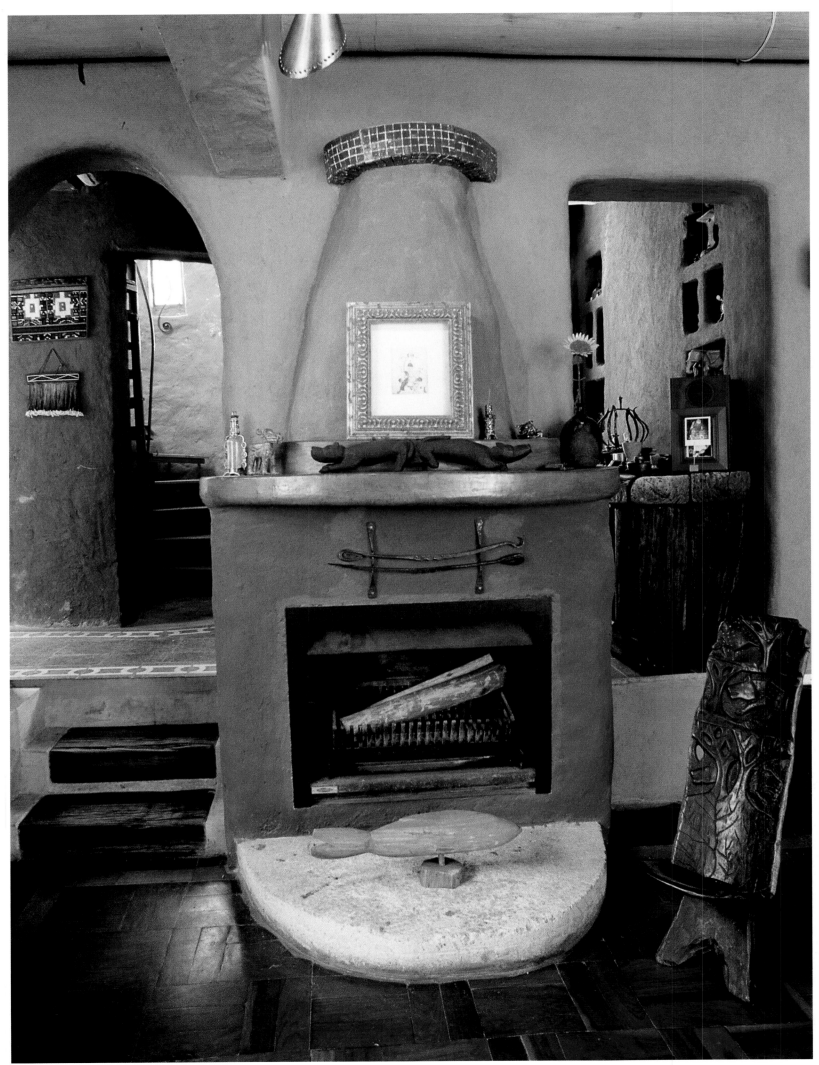

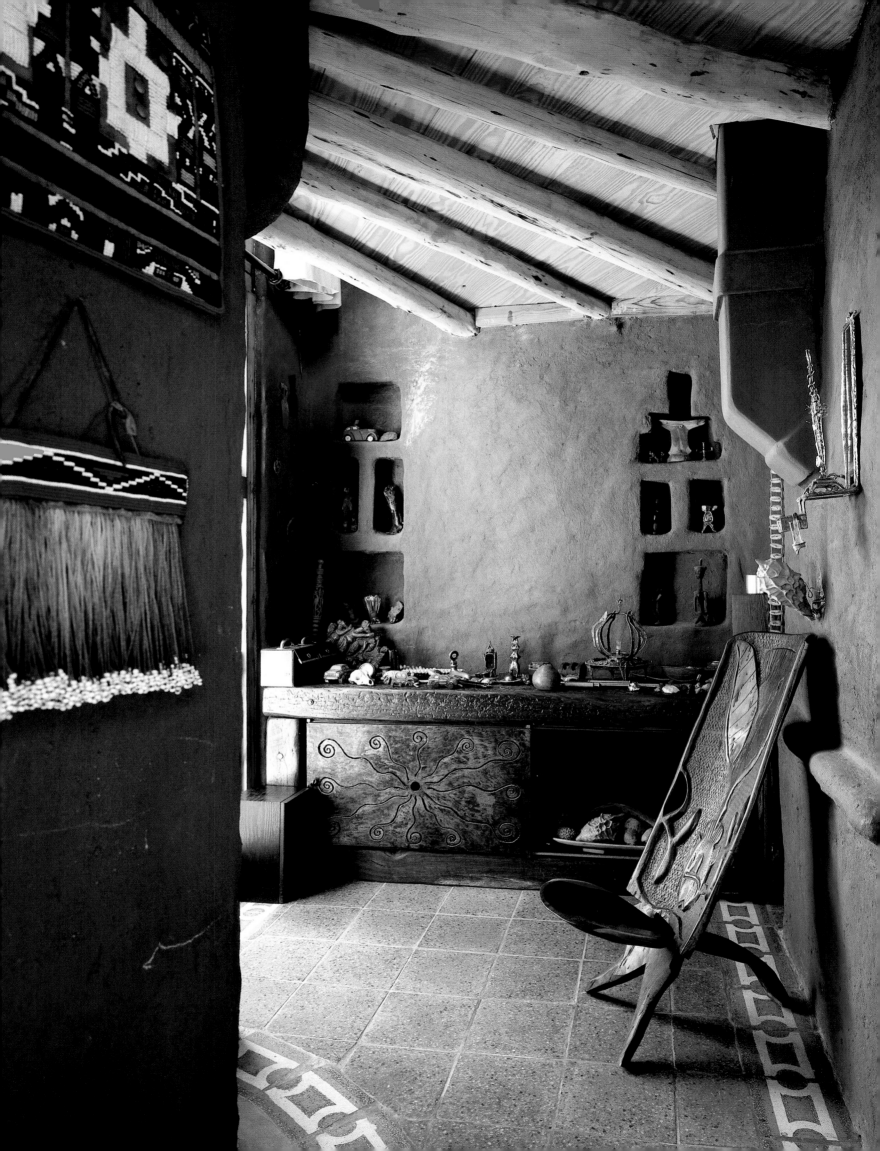

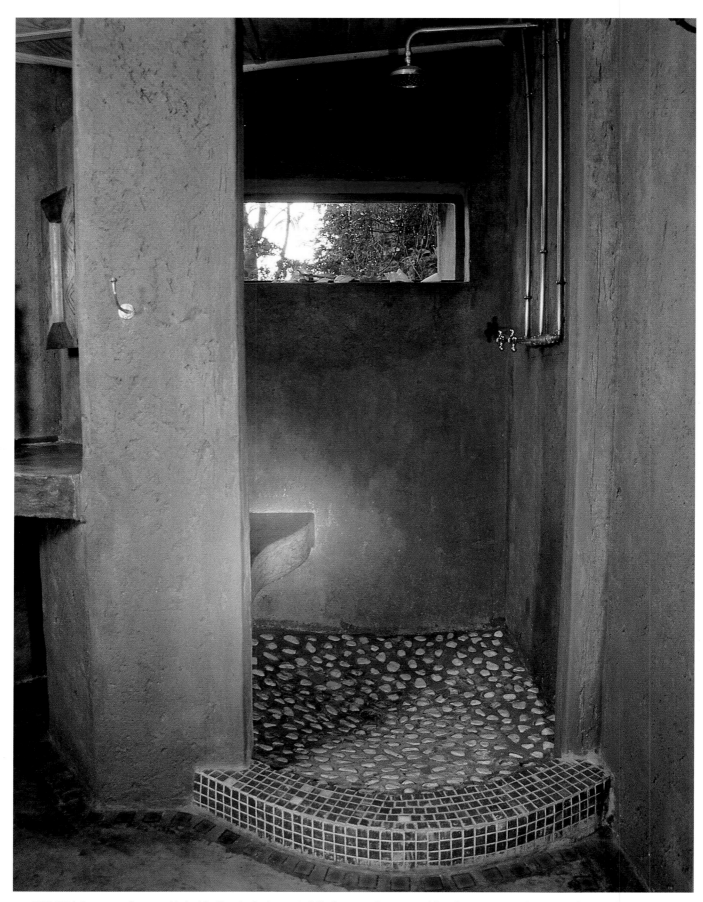

❋ **ABOVE** With its cement floor marbled with tiles, the bathroom is full of warm colours created by Alice Rowe. "We have a good spiritual environment here," they both say. **FACING PAGE** The wrought iron and wood bed is ethnically inspired. ❋ **OBEN** Das Badezimmer ist mit marmoriertem Zementboden ausgelegt; die warmen Farben hat Alice Rowe ausgewählt. »Wir leben hier in einer besonders spirituellen Umgebung«, betonen die beiden Besitzer unisono. **RECHTE SEITE** Das fein gearbeitete Bett aus Holz und Schmiedeeisen passt gut zum ethnischen Stil des Hauses. ❋ **CI-DESSUS** Posée sur un sol en ciment marbré de carreaux, la salle de bains déploie ses couleurs chaudes créées par Alice Rowe. «Nous vivons ici dans un environnement spirituel exceptionnel», répètent en chœur les propriétaires. **PAGE DE DROITE** Le lit ouvragé marie bois et fer forgé dans un concept ethnique.

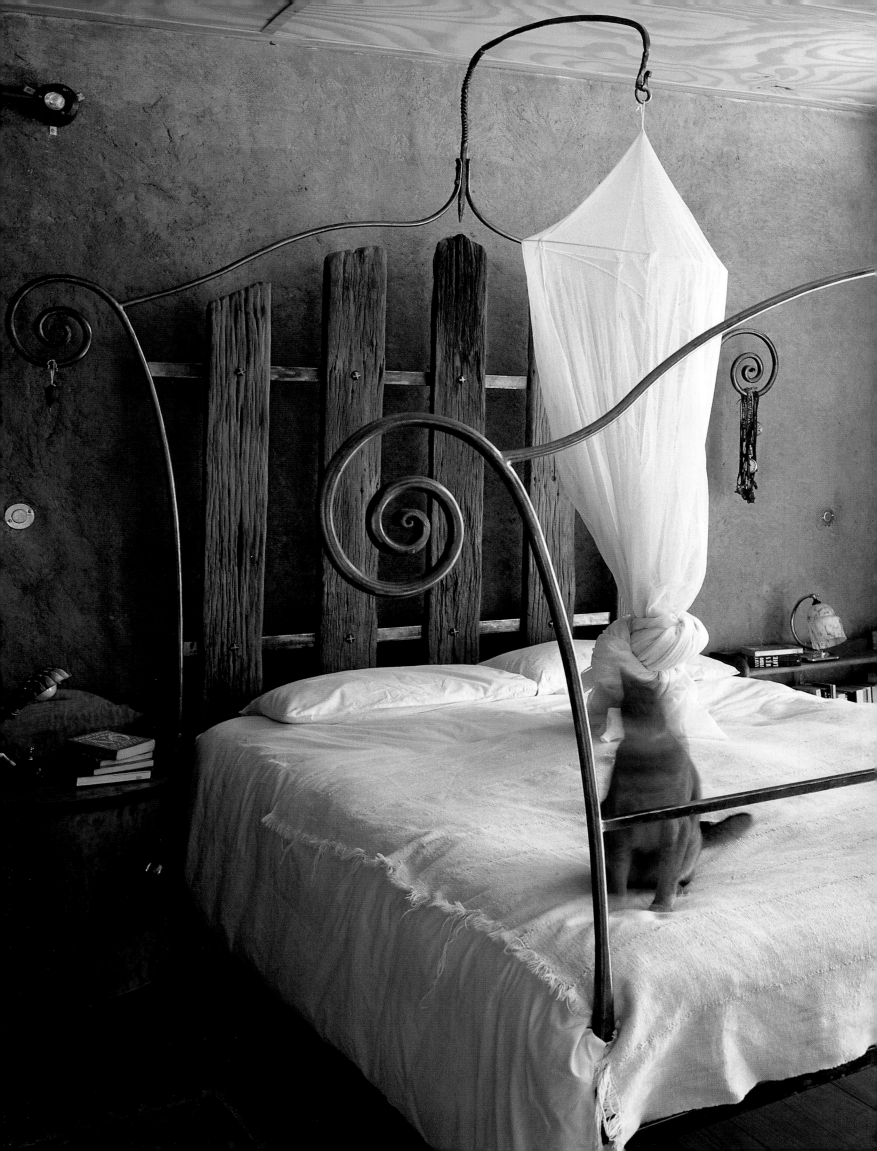

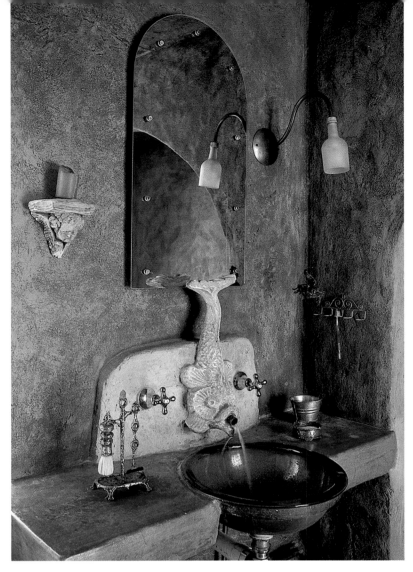

❋ **LEFT** A warm and intimate water closet, unconcerned with modern comforts. **BELOW AND FACING PAGE** A pool of light around the cement bathtub. Using traditional techniques, the Rowes and their architect Kate Otten have gleefully upset all the canons of their white residential area. ❋ **LINKS** Die kleine Toilette betont mit den warmen Farben den Charakter eines stillen Örtchens. **UNTEN UND RECHTS** Ein Lichtschacht beleuchtet die Betonbadewanne. Gelassen stellen die Rowes und ihre Architektin Kate Otten den Stilkanon der weißen Viertel Johannesburgs auf den Kopf, indem sie sich von althergebrachten Techniken inspirieren lassen. ❋ **A GAUCHE** Renforcée de teintes chaudes, le coin toilette joue la carte de l'intime en s'affranchissant du confort moderne. **CI-DESSOUS ET PAGE DE DROITE** Un puits de lumière illumine la baignoire en béton. En s'inspirant des techniques traditionnelles, le couple Rowe et son architecte Kate Otten bousculent sans états d'âme les canons en vigueur dans les quartiers blancs de Johannesburg.

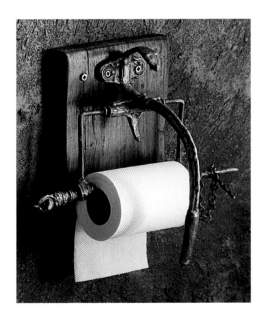

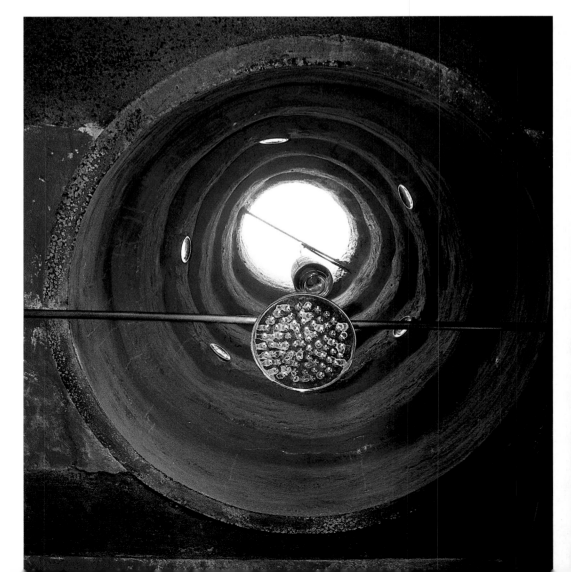

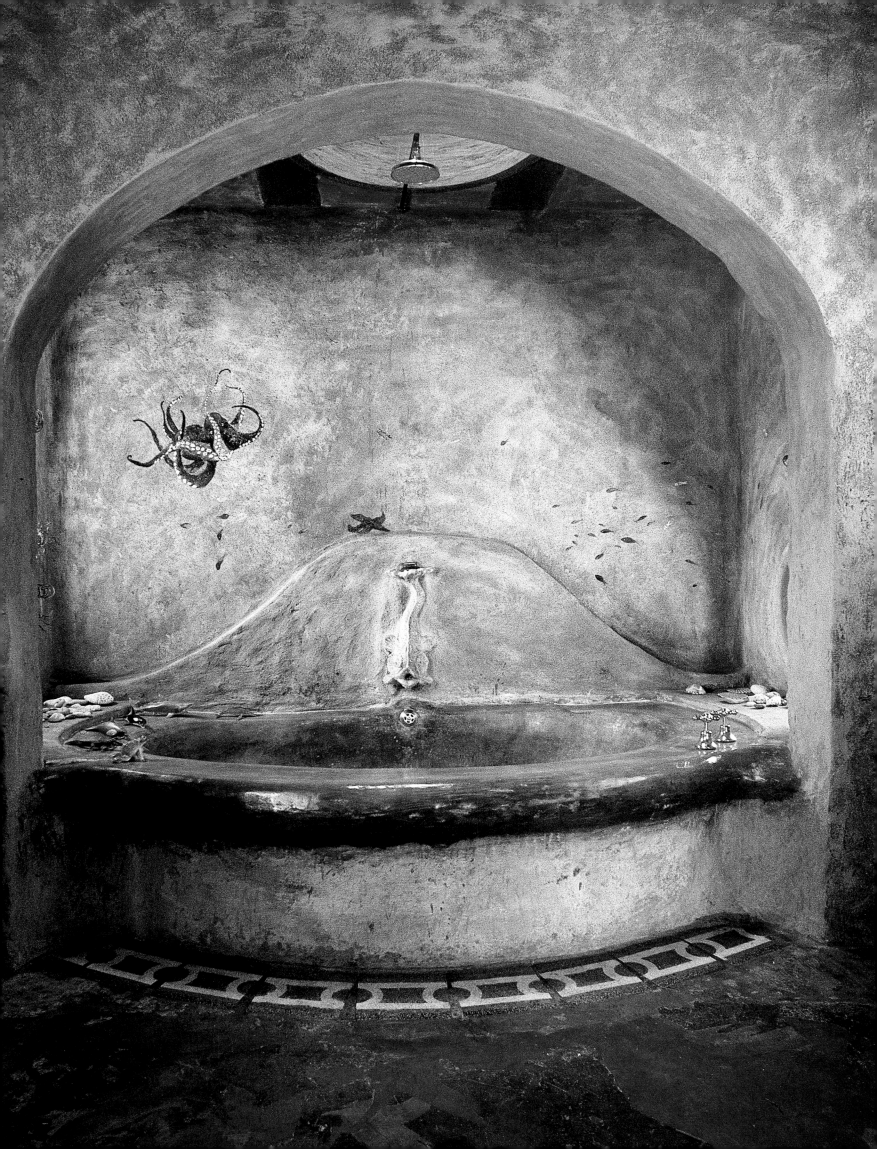

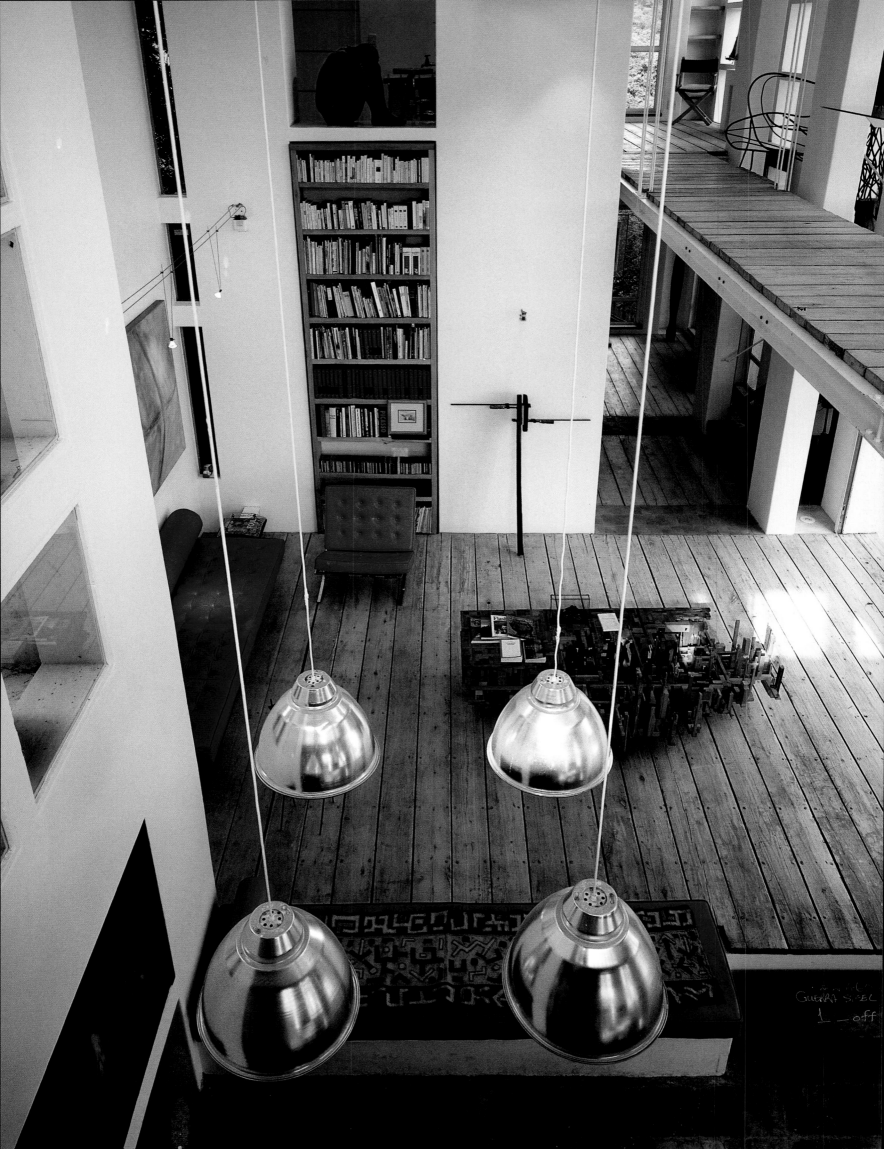

# Pierre Lombart
## JOHANNESBURG

Secure in its treetop solitude,
this house of platforms and split-levels surveys a broad vista of sky.

This is an architect's island, shot through with light and open to all manner of inspiration. It's no mean accomplishment to dominate vast spaces such as these. You can arrive, observe, sift, appropriate what you need from this place, and come away with your life permanently enriched. "We exist in forgetfulness of all our metamorphoses," says a French poet.

Pierre Lombart, himself a Belgian architect who has lived in South Africa for fifteen years, feels that it's important to keep his memories intact. How can one not be clear and straightforward, living in a house so airy and light, with architecture so easily comprehensible? The absolute requirement here was truthfulness, confronting things full on, whereas down below in the other villas the doors and shutters are all bolted for mortal fear of a country that is going through a period of profound change. The simplicity of Lombart's materials reaffirms his need to be part of his environment. He has gone back to the basics of his craft. As a sculptor of space, he sets out to celebrate every moment of daylight. His collection of contemporary art, begun fifteen years ago, includes paintings by Patrick Mautloa, Willem Boshoff and Jane Alexander – another proof, if it were needed, of Lombard's veneration for pure creativity. And everything else is confirmed by some lines by Gérard de Nerval he keeps framed in the bedroom: "May each soul go where its fancy leads it, and shut the door behind."

Auf der kleinen lichtdurchfluteten Insel des Architekten sind Inspirationen aller Art willkommen. Der Umgang mit großen Räumen ist alles andere als einfach. Man beobachtet, sondiert und nimmt mit, was das Leben bereichert. »Wir leben im Vergessen unserer Verwandlungen«, erklärte ein französischer Dichter.

Pierre Lombart, der belgische Architekt, der bereits seit 15 Jahren in Südafrika lebt, scheint dagegen ein gutes Gedächtnis zu haben. Wie sollte man in so einer luftigen Behausung nicht auf Transparenz setzen, auf eine allgemein verständliche Lesbarkeit der Architektur? Hier gibt es eine Fülle von Wahrheiten, eine Art und Weise, den Dingen ins Auge zu sehen, anders als in den Villen weiter unten, deren Türen und Fensterläden geschlossen bleiben, nicht zuletzt aufgrund der Angst in einem Land, das genau das gerade erlebt: seine Verwandlung. Die Auswahl einfacher Baumaterialien betont ebenfalls die Tendenz mit der Umgebung zu verschmelzen. Pierre Lombart hat sich auf die Grundsätze seines Berufes besonnen. Als »Bildhauer des Raums« möchte er jeden Augenblick genießen. In der Welt der Kunst kennt er sich aus: Seine vor 15 Jahren begonnene Sammlung zeitgenössischer Kunst umfasst Werke von Patrick Mautloa, Willem Boshoff und Jane Alexander. Im Schlafzimmer hängt ein Gedicht von Gérard de Nerval: »Jede Seele soll allein nach Lust und Laune leben, und bei geschloss'ner Tür nach Erfüllung streben.«

Transpercé de lumière, l'îlot de l'architecte est ouvert aux inspirations en tout genre. Ce n'est pas rien de dominer les grands espaces. On observe, et puis on peut trier, mine de rien, faire ses provisions, avant de poursuivre son chemin dans la vie. «Nous vivons dans l'oubli de nos métamorphoses», scandait un poète Français.

Pierre Lombart, architecte Belge installé en Afrique du Sud depuis 15 ans, tient à garder bonne mémoire. Comment ne pas faire vœu de transparence dans cette habitation si aérienne, à l'architecture d'une parfaite lisibilité? Il y a ici une exigence de vérité, une manière de voir les choses en face, alors qu'en bas, dans les autres villas, les portes et les volets sont clos, dans la crainte d'un pays qui, précisément, vit sa métamorphose. La simplicité des matériaux utilisés affirme encore la double volonté de se fondre dans l'environnement. Pierre Lombart s'en est remis aux fondamentaux de son métier. «Sculpteur d'espace», il a voulu célébrer chaque instant de la journée. Sa collection d'art contemporain commencée il y a 15 ans (on retrouve Patrick Mautloa, Willem Boshoff et Jane Alexander) hisse encore le drapeau de la création. Dans la chambre, c'est un poème de Gérard de Nerval qui intime: «Allez, que le caprice emporte / Chaque âme selon son désir / Et que close après vous la porte.»

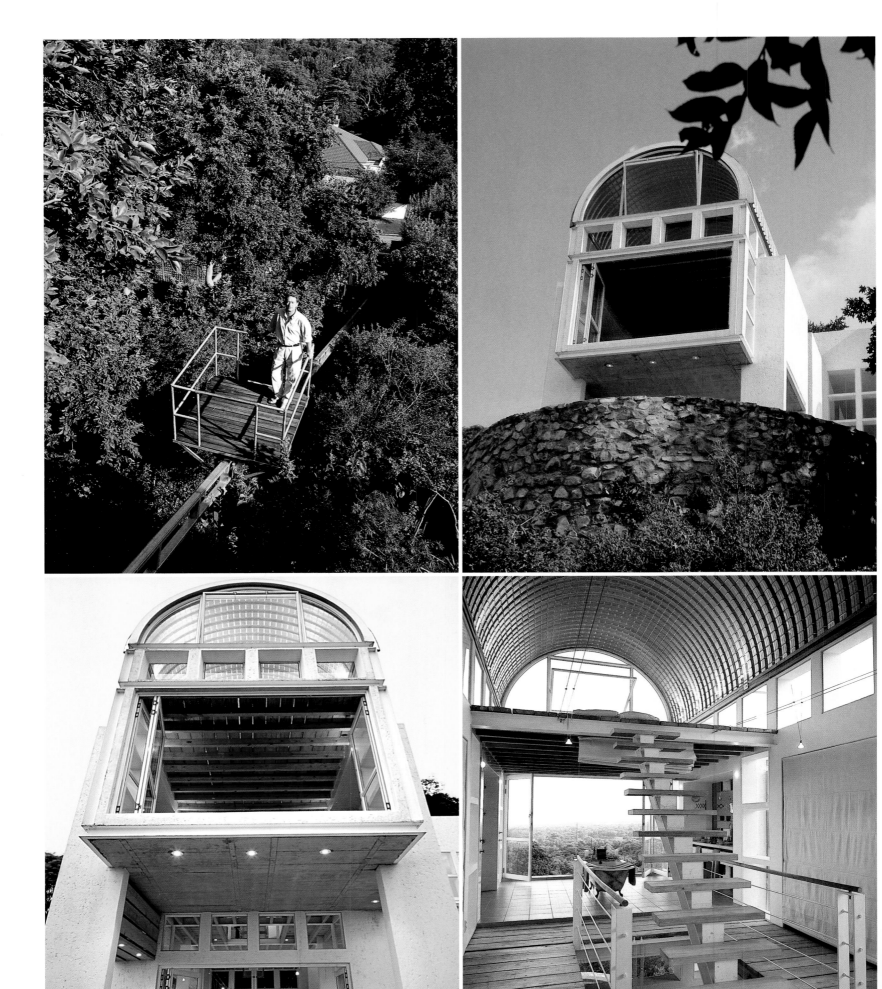

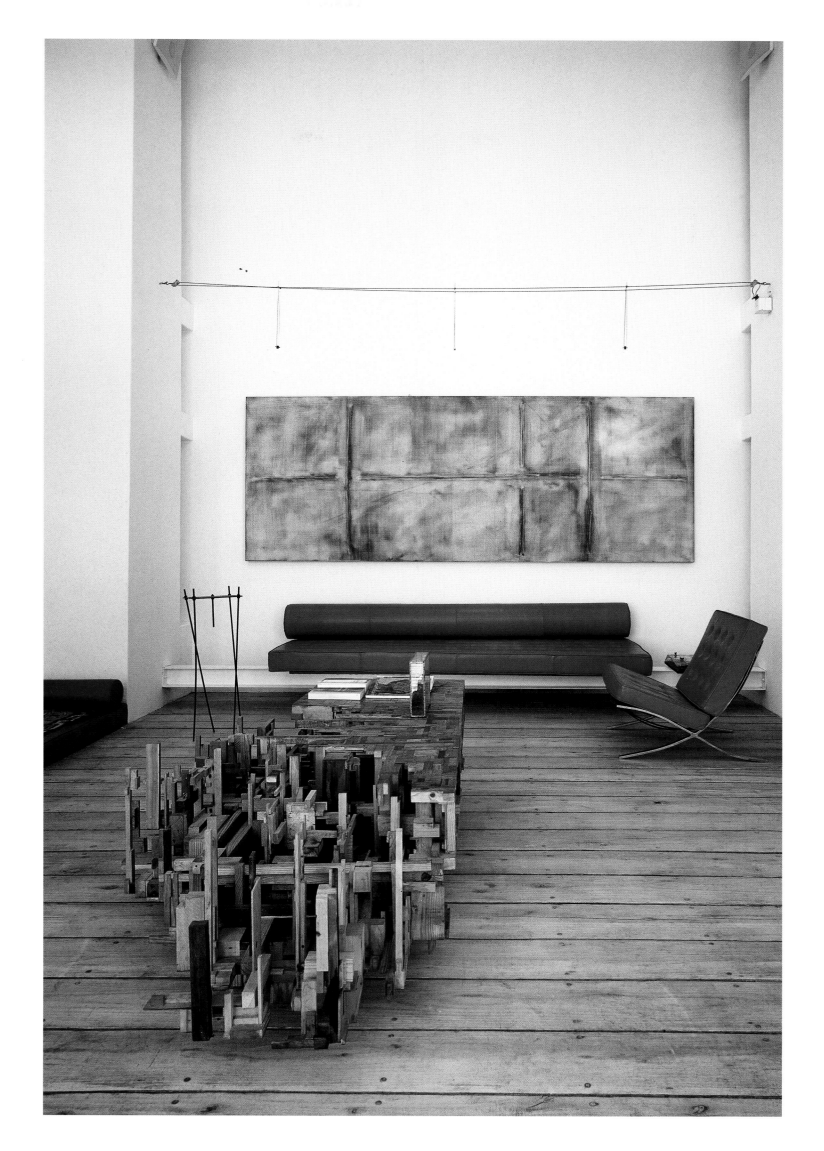

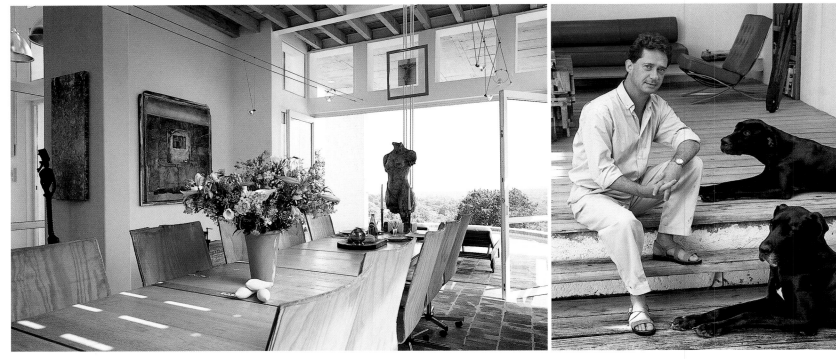

✳ **PAGE 62** An eagle's nest indeed – Overlooking a thousand square metres of garden, the house consists of three platform levels, each flooded with light. **PREVIOUS PAGE** The salon leading through to the kitchen dining room, with "Barcelona" armchairs by Ludwig Mies van der Rohe and a coffee table designed 25 years ago by the South African Willem Boshoff. **ABOVE** Brick floors and chairs around the table, designed by Pierre Lombart. **BELOW RIGHT** The staircase leading to the bedroom was made by Guy du Toit and David Rousseau out of an aeroplane wing and sundry recycled ingredients, to celebrate earth, air, fire, and water. **FACING PAGE** The footbridge leading to the study echoes the platform leading up from the roadway. Everything here is a viaduct through a world that knows no limitations. ✳ **SEITE 62** Ein Adlernest? Könnte man meinen. Oberhalb des 1000 Quadratmeter großen Gartens wird das Haus auf drei Plattformetagen von Licht durchflutet. **VORHERGEHENDE SEITE** Im Salon stehen ein »Barcelona«-Sessel von Ludwig Mies van der Rohe und der dazugehörige niedrige Tisch, den Willem Boshoff vor 25 Jahren gebaut hat. Der Raum geht in die Küche über, die gleichzeitig als Esszimmer dient. **OBEN** Die von Pierre Lombart entworfenen Stühle rollen über den Ziegelboden. **UNTEN RECHTS** Guy de Toit und David Rousseau bauten die Treppe zum Schlafzimmer aus dem Tragflügel eines Flugzeugs und anderen recycelten Dingen. Das Kunstwerk feiert die vier Elemente Feuer, Erde, Luft und Wasser. **RECHTE SEITE** Der luftige Steg führt genau bis zum Schreibtisch und betont die Idee der Plattform. Hier ist alles Viadukt, eine Welt ohne Grenzen. ✳ **PAGE 62** Nid d'aigle? Il y a de ça. Au-dessus de mille mètres carrés de jardin, la maison vit sur des plates-formes de trois étages baignées de lumière. **PAGE PRECEDENTE** Le salon avec son fauteuil «Barcelona» de Ludwig Mies van der Rohe et sa table basse crée il y a 25 ans par le Sud-Africain Willem Boshoff communique avec la cuisine-salle à manger. **CI-DESSUS** Autour de la table, les chaises créées par Pierre Lombart roulent sur les sols en brique. **CI-DESSOUS A DROITE** L'escalier qui mène à la chambre a été créé par Guy de Toit et David Rousseau à partir d'une aile d'avion et d'autres pièces recyclées, pour célébrer le feu, l'air, la terre et l'eau. **PAGE DE DROITE** La passerelle aérienne qui court jusqu'au bureau évoque la plate-forme qui grimpe depuis la route. Tout ici est viaduc, monde sans frontières.

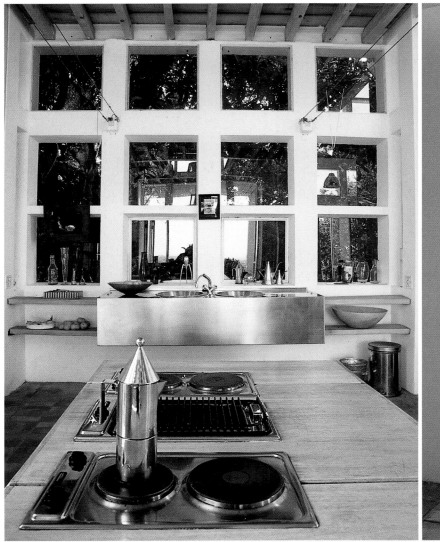

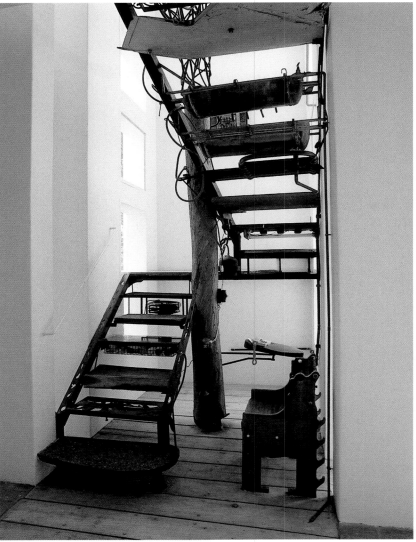

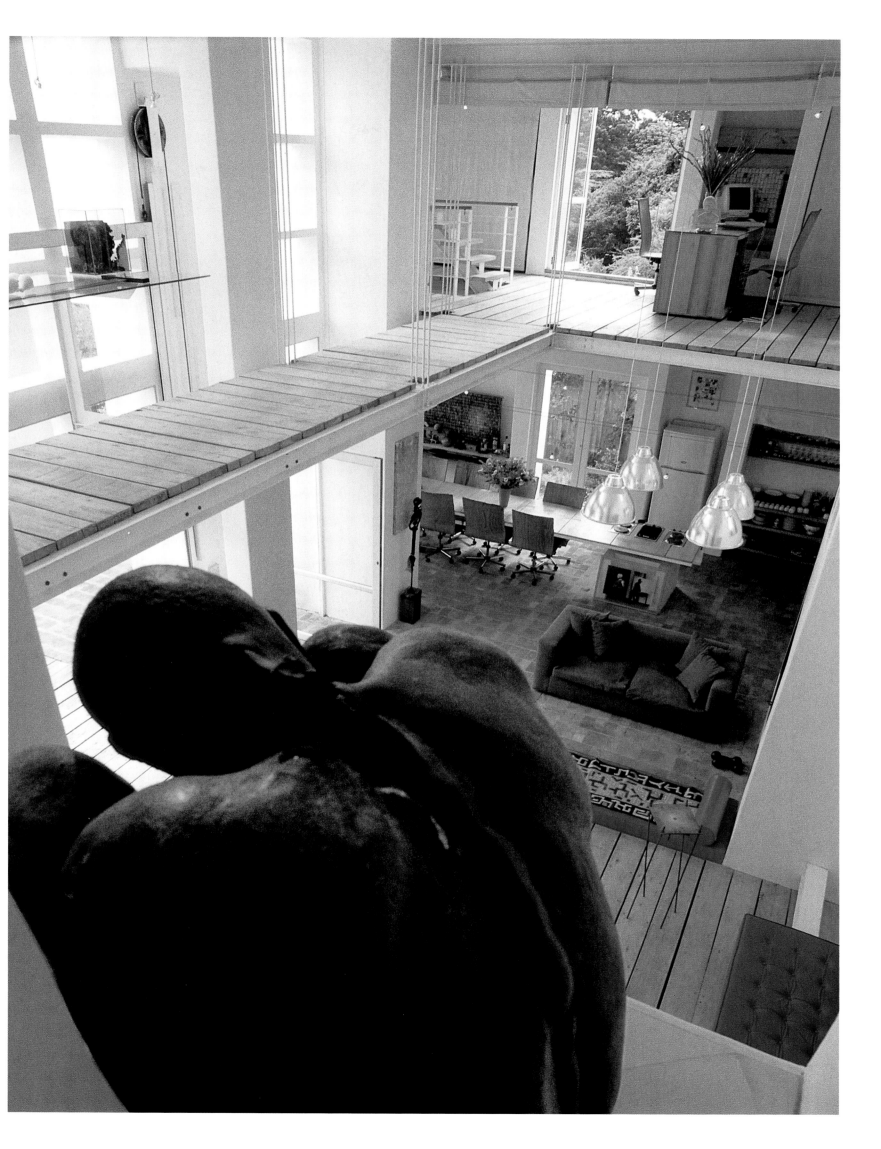

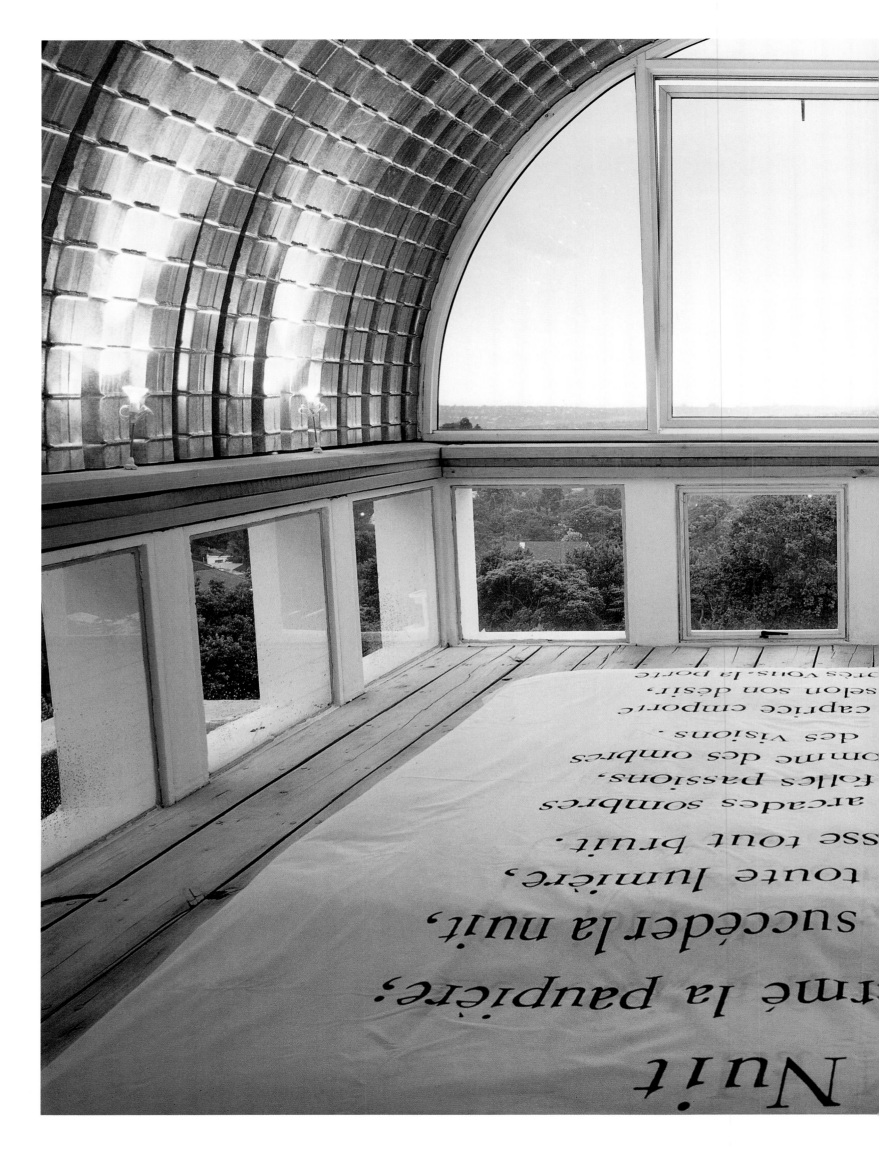

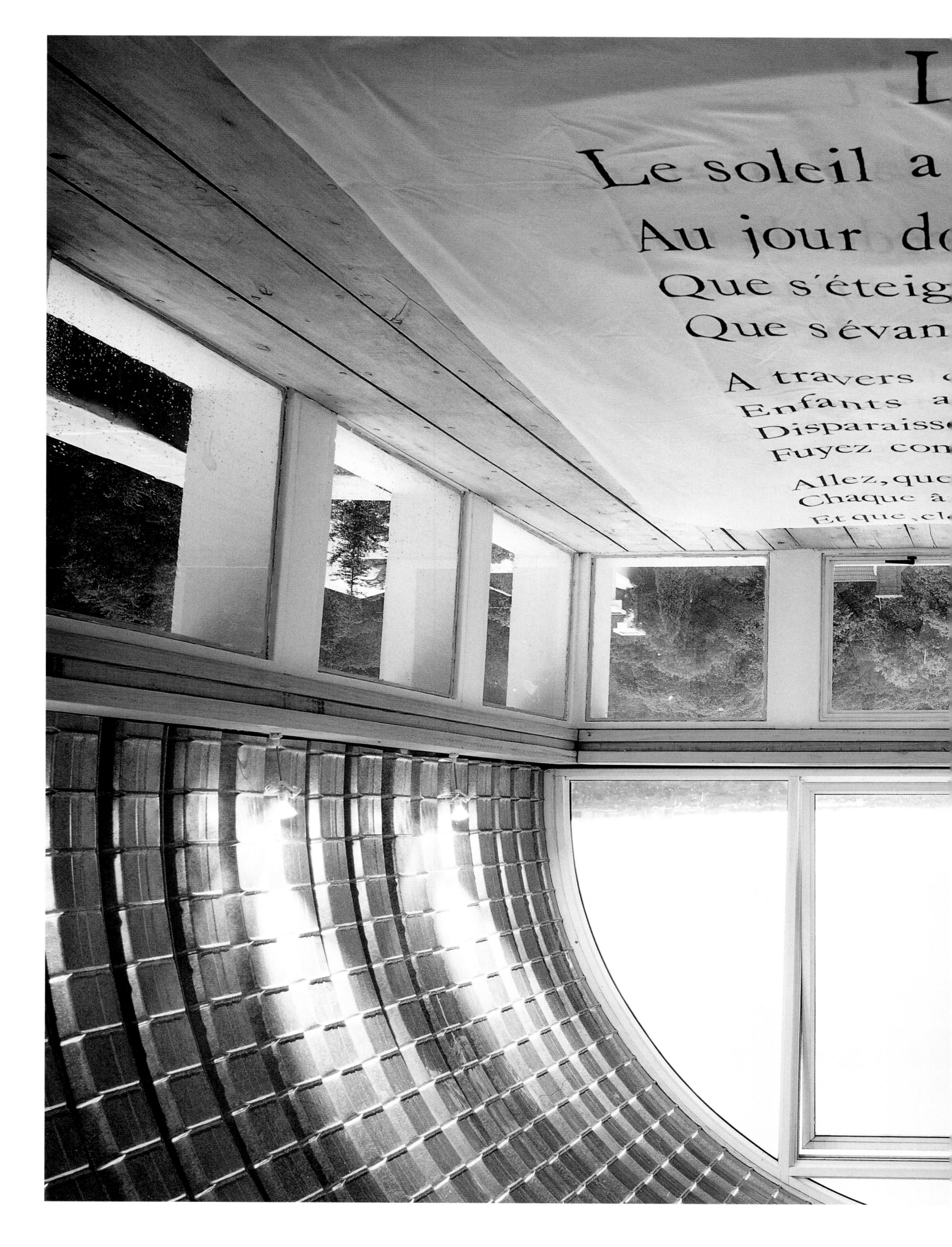

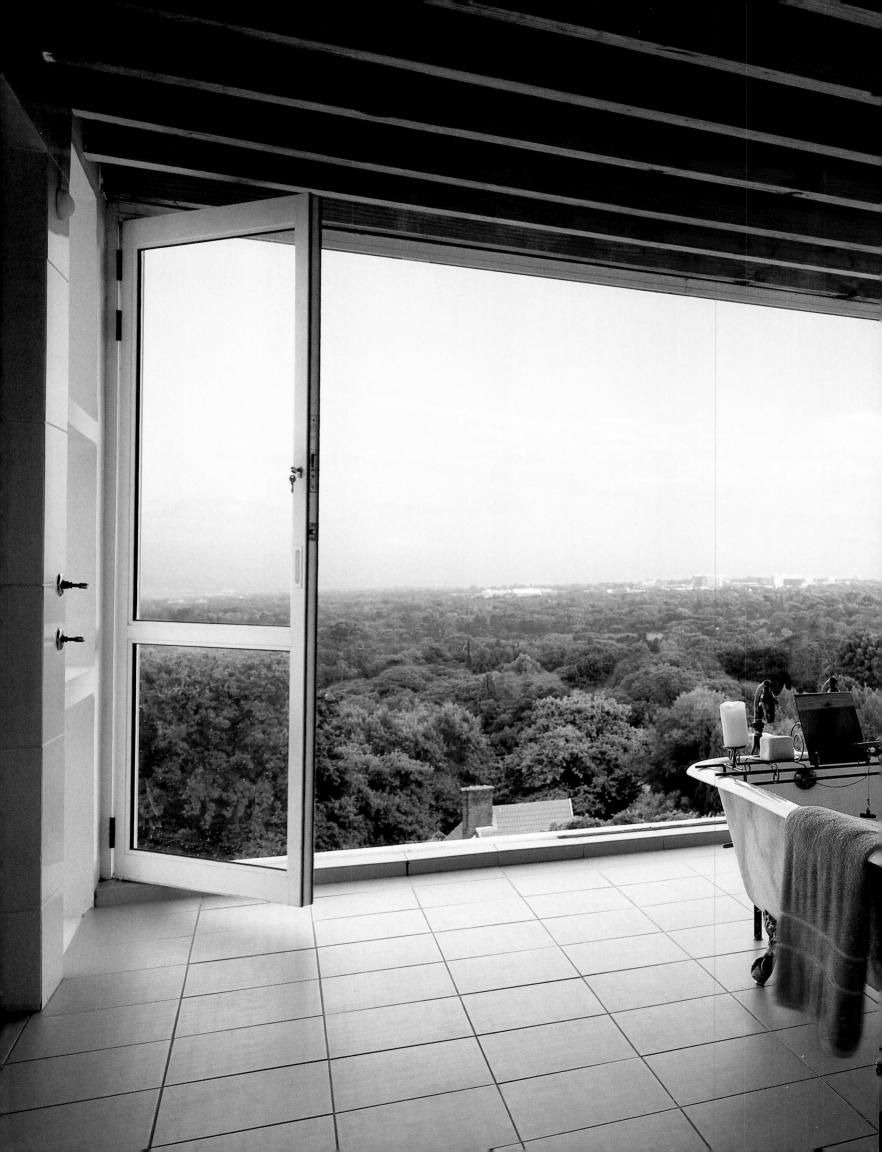

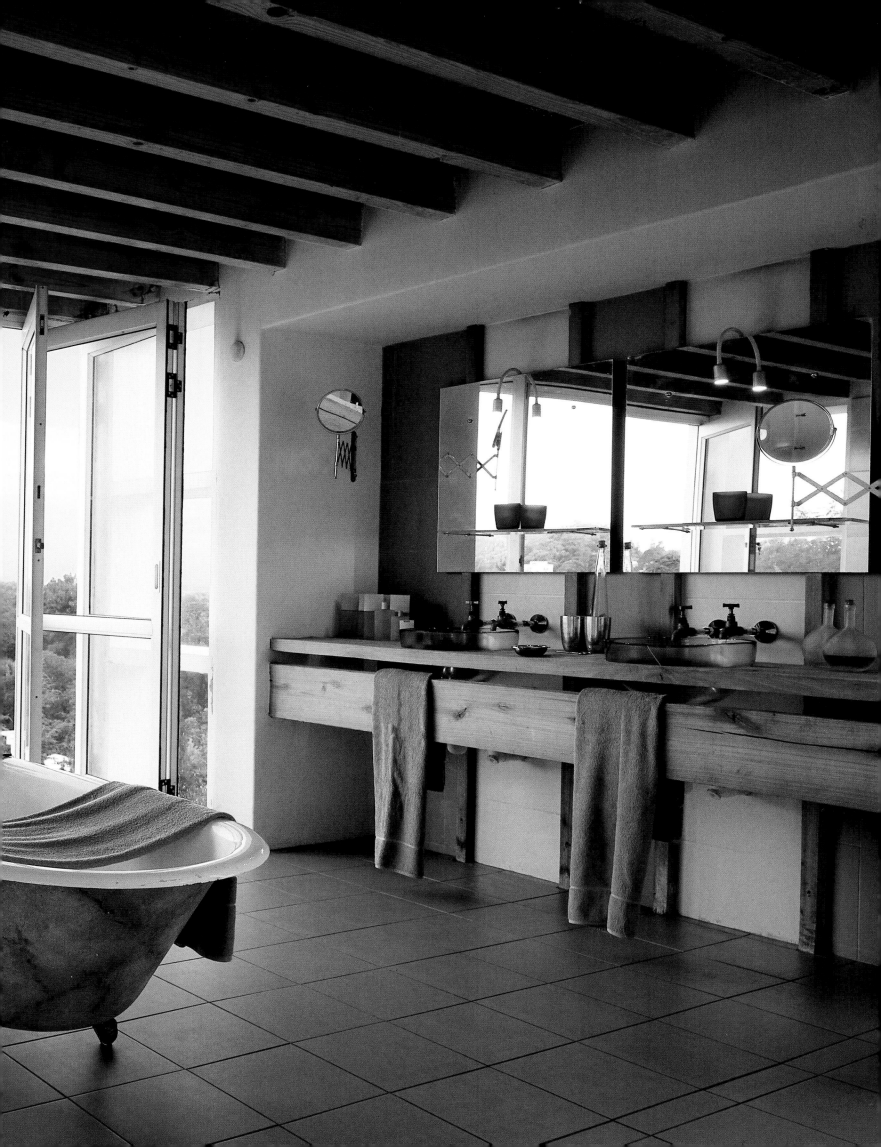

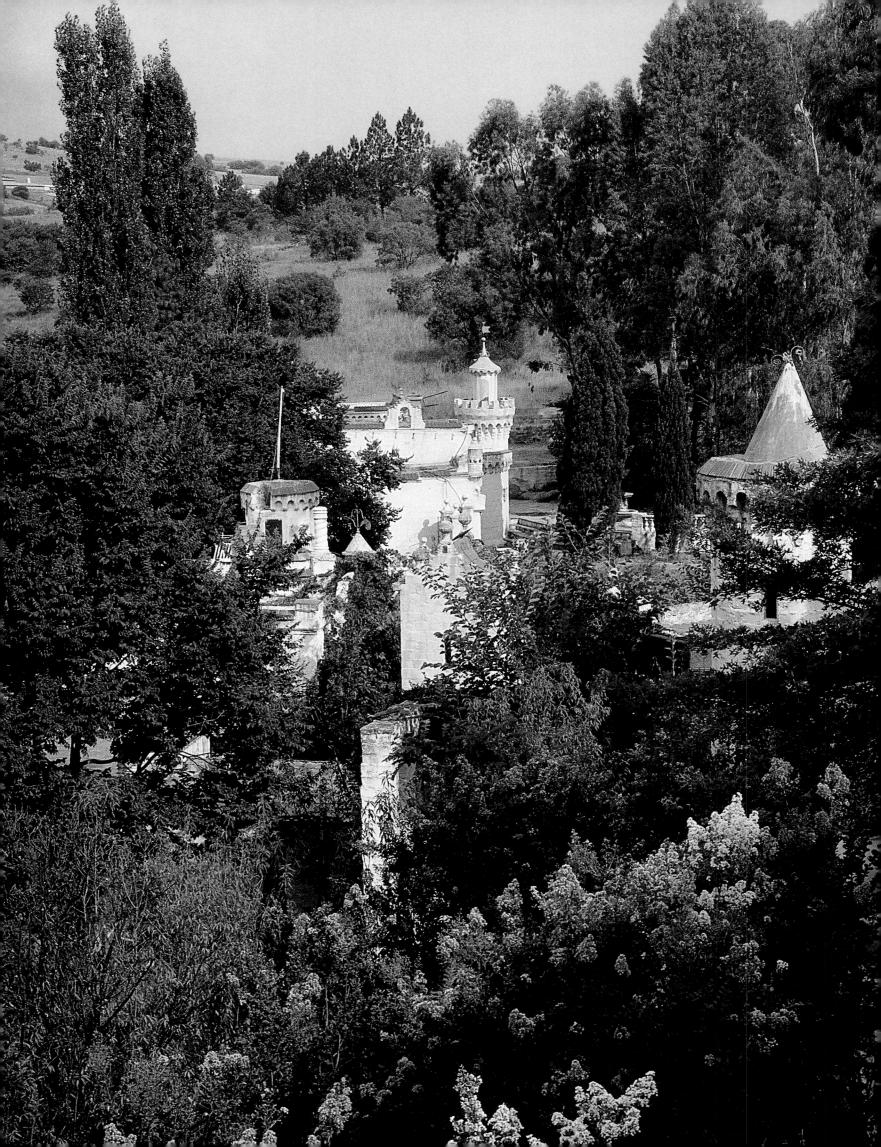

# BATHAFARH Farm
# near JOHANNESBURG

Disneyland horror or folly with a touch of genius?
Opinions are divided on this "home sweet home" with ghostly overtones.

The house has the quality of a mirage – as if the size, site and architecture of Joseph Kerham's castle didn't already make it unique in South Africa.

Overlooking a residential suburb, it's the kind of high walled citadel you'd expect to see in a fairy-tale picture book. With its formal French garden and its colonnaded Trianon pool, Castle Bathafarm represents another time, one that it exists to protect from the alien rhythms of modern life. What does its tower conceal? Whatever the reason, Joseph Kerham, its provincial builder, made a decision to bring the charm of the good old days right into the city. All that was needed was a little silence, masses of old doors, windows, wardrobes, old church pews and burnt terracotta tiles to reconstitute the era of the *ancien régime*. Kerham winds up his venerable grandfather clock beneath the incredulous gaze of a row of ancestors in gilt frames. The figurative scenes in the main drawing room evoke an old house somewhere in Europe. In the master bedroom there's a profusely-draped bed with columns at each corner and a luxurious counterpane. Here's living proof that the term *ancien régime* no longer defines an epoch, but a ready-made ambiance.

Ein Wunder? Von der schieren Größe, der Lage und erst recht der Architektur her sucht das Schloss von Joseph Kerham in Südafrika seinesgleichen.

Die Zitadelle mit den hohen abweisenden Mauern thront über einem Wohnviertel – eine Atmosphäre wie in *Dornröschen*. Der Garten im französischen Stil, das Wasserbecken mit den »Trianon«-Säulen à la Versailles, alles hier brüstet sich mit einem vergangenen Lebensstil, der sich mit Händen und Füßen gegen die Moderne wehrt. Was verbirgt sich wohl hinter dem Bergfried? Joseph Kerham rechnet in typischer Provinzlermanier die Nachteile der Großstadt gegen den Zauber der »guten alten Zeiten« auf. Um das »Ancien Régime« wiederzubeleben, bedurfte es vieler Türen, ein wenig Stille, dazu kamen Fenster, antike Schränke, alte Kirchenbänke und Terrakottafliesen. Unter den ungläubigen Blicken seiner Ahnen in den goldenen Bilderrahmen zieht der Hausherr die alte Uhr auf. Selbst die gegenständliche Malerei im großen Salon zeigt eine Besitzung im alten Europa. Das von hohen Säulen umgebene Bett im Schlafzimmer des Schlossbesitzers strahlt mit den Kissen und der verführerisch weichen Tagesdecke eine zeitlose Wehmut aus. Dabei bezeichnet der Begriff »Ancien Régime« schon lange weniger eine bestimmte Epoche, als vielmehr eine häusliche Atmosphäre.

Un mirage? De par sa taille, son emplacement et son architecture, le château de Joseph Kerham est unique en Afrique du Sud.

Surplombant une banlieue résidentielle, la citadelle, avec ses hauts murs de soutènement, génère une vision fantastique digne de la *Belle au Bois dormant*. Avec son jardin à la française, son bassin à colonnes «Trianon», elle vante un art de vivre révolu tout en se protégeant du rythme de la vie moderne. Alors, que dissimule le donjon? De manière provinciale, Joseph Kerham a choisi de conjuguer les inconvénients de la grande ville et les charmes du «bon vieux temps». Il a suffi d'un peu de silence, de lots de portes, de fenêtres, d'antiques armoires, de vieux bancs d'église et de carreaux de terre cuite brûlée pour reconstituer l'époque de l'Ancien Régime. Monsieur remonte la vieille horloge sous le regard incrédule des ancêtres dans leurs cadres dorés. Même les scènes figuratives du grand salon évoquent une demeure de la vieille Europe. Dans la chambre du maître de maison, un lit bordé de larges colonnes, agrémenté d'étoffes et d'un langoureux dessus-de-lit, parle encore une langueur hors du temps. Mais il y a belle lurette que le terme d'Ancien Régime désigne davantage une ambiance qu'une époque.

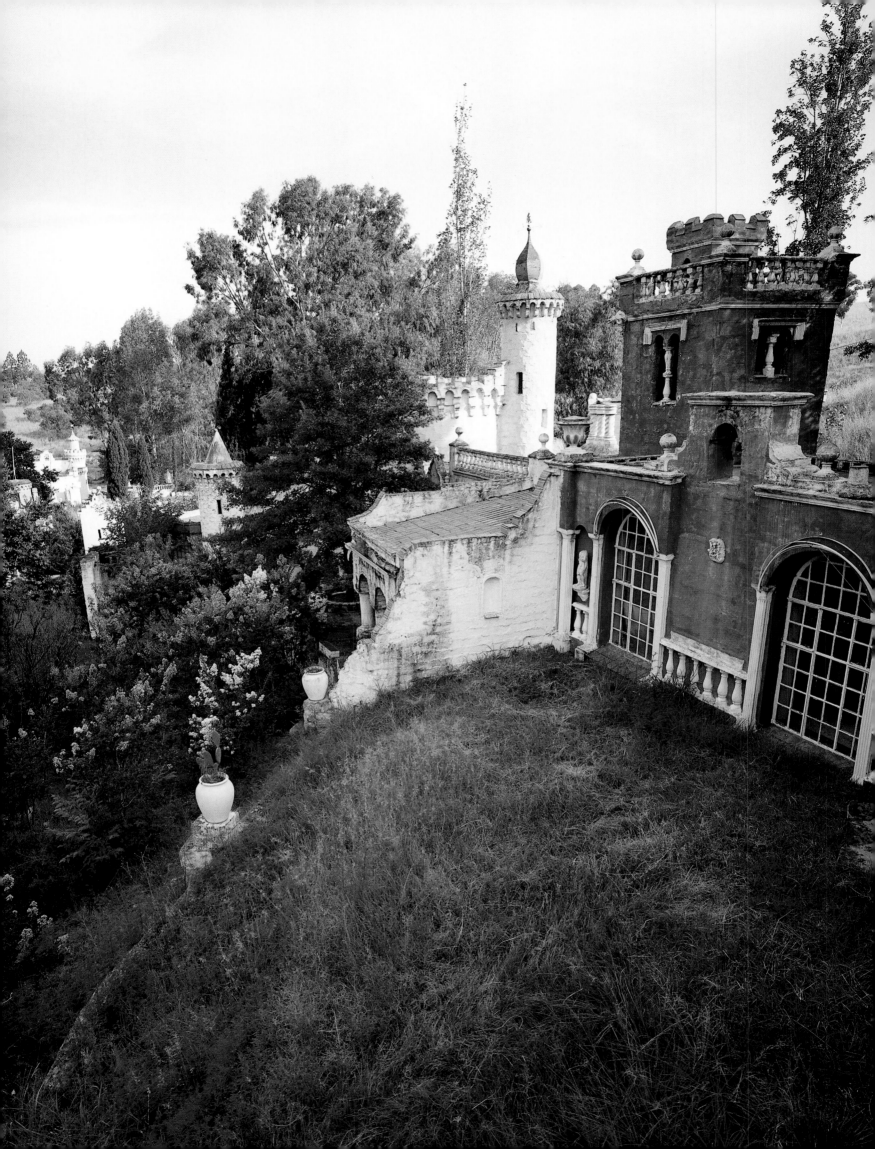

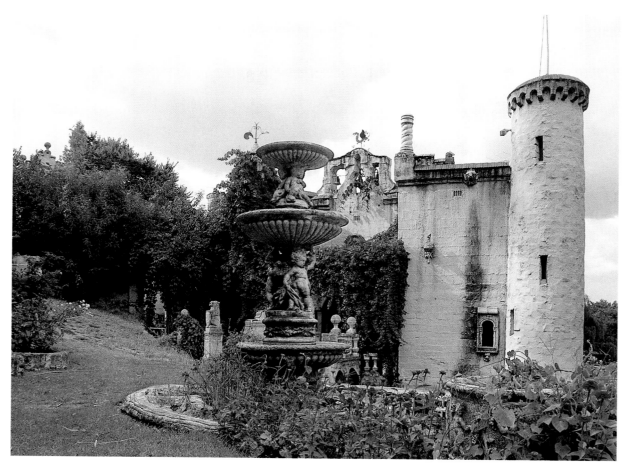

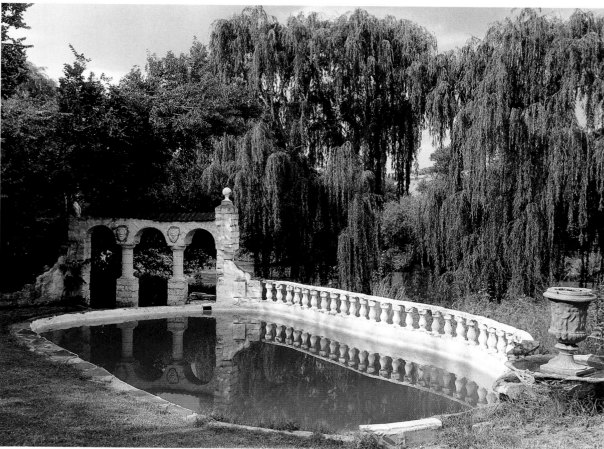

✻ **FACING PAGE AND ABOVE** Joseph Kerham's Trianon-style park. **FOLLOWING PAGES** An effervescence of styles in the living room – copies of 18th century chairs and an antique kilim. ✻ **LINKE SEITE UND OBEN** Joseph Kerhams Park im Anklang an das »Petit Trianon« in Versailles. **FOLGENDE DOPPELSEITE** Eine Fülle verschiedener Stile wird im Salon kombiniert. Die Stühle auf dem alten Kelim imitieren den Stil des 18. Jahrhunderts. ✻ **PAGE DE GAUCHE ET CI-DESSUS** Joseph Kerham a aménagé un parc aux accents «petit Trianon». **DOUBLE PAGE SUIVANTE** Foisonnement de styles dans ce salon; les chaises imitent le 18e siècle sur un kilim ancien.

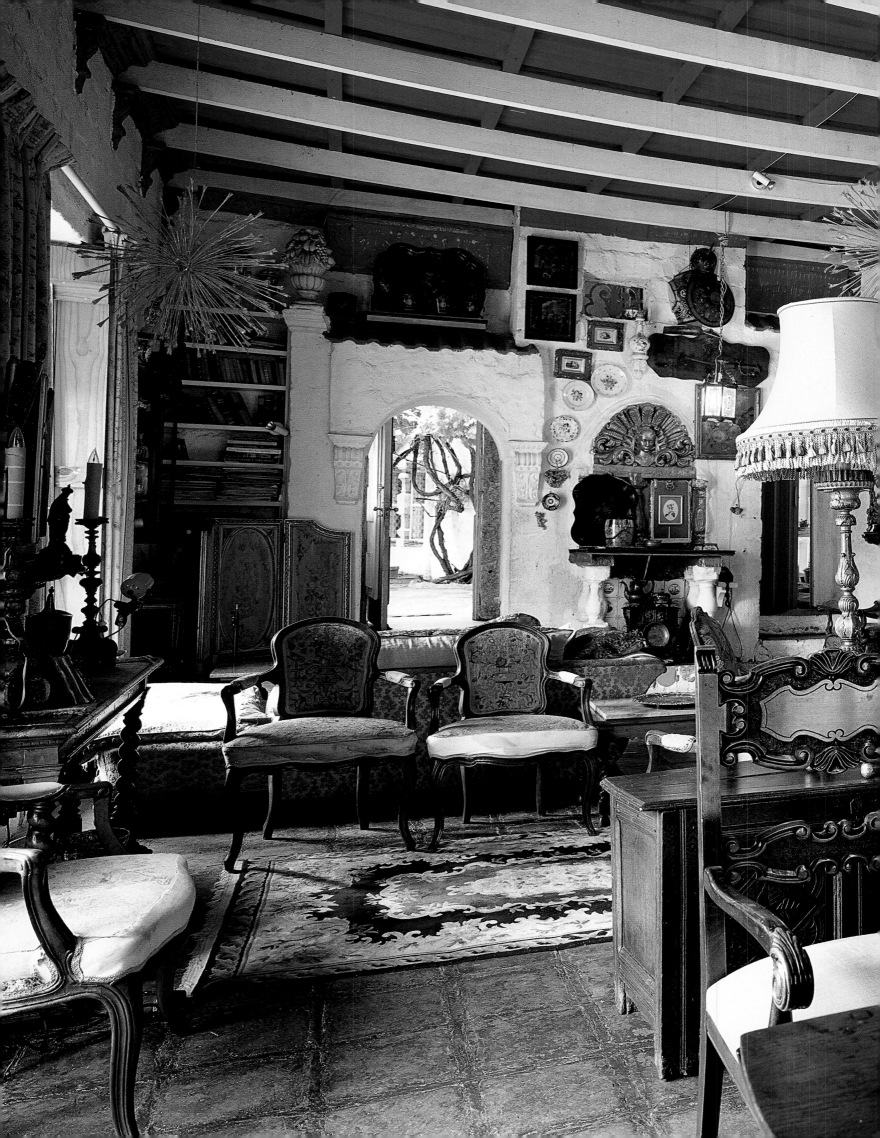

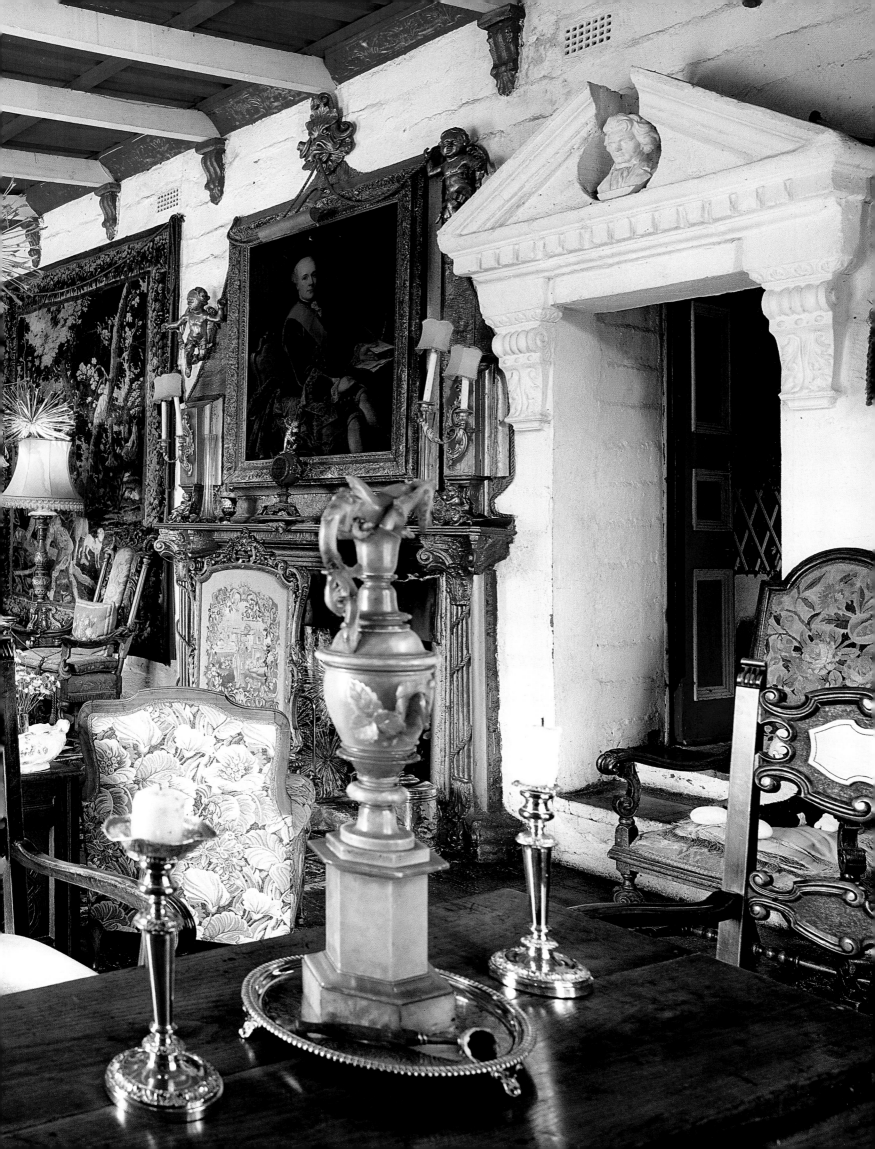

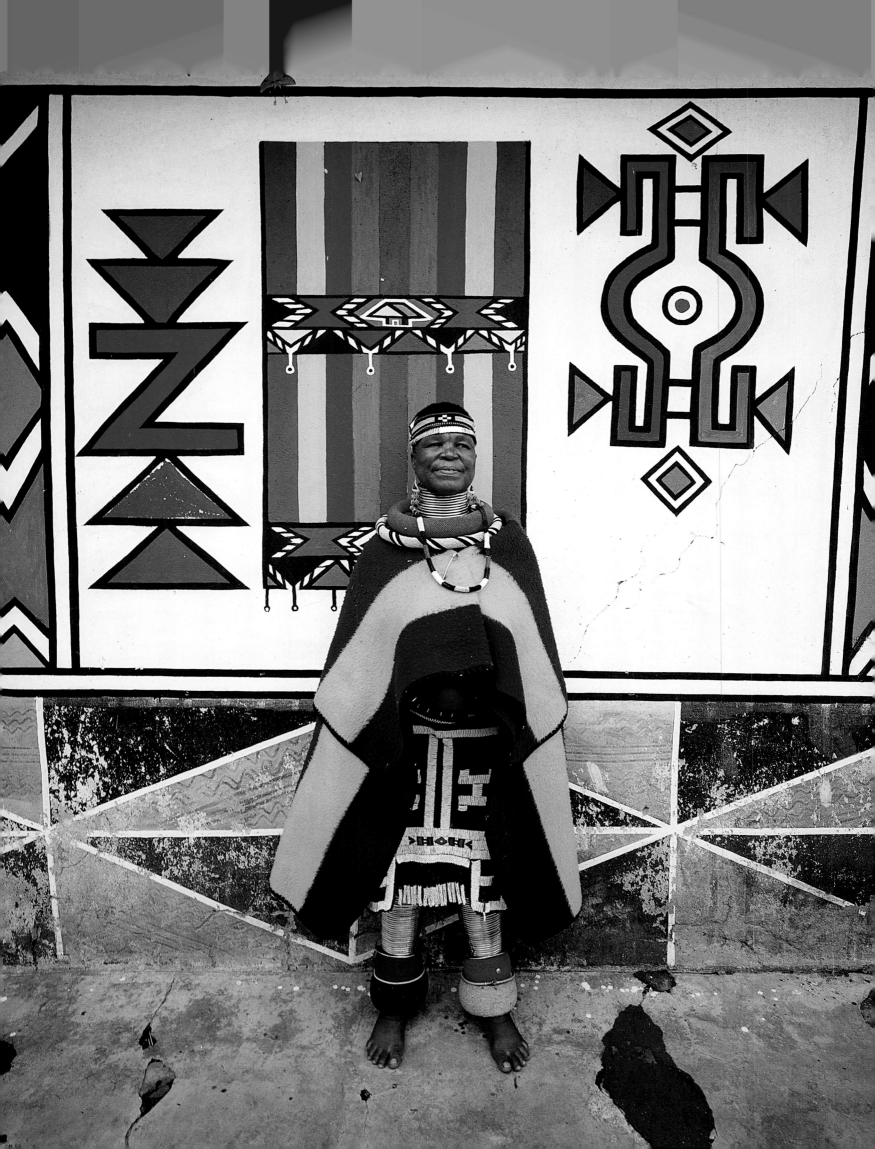

# NDEBELE
## MPUMALANGA PROVINCE

The renowned Ndebele wall frescoes reflect the evolution of the world.

In the mid-19th century, when the Ndebele people of South Africa forsook their straw huts for houses made of earth, they discovered not only a new form of architecture but also a finger-painting technique handed down by their Sotho neighbours.

As time went by, their iconography grew richer and when in 1923 a white farmer had the bright idea of asking his agricultural workers to paint his house in bright colours against a white background, the result was a revelation. Colour replaced the patterns painted with mud and natural oxides. Later, the original geometrical shapes were influenced by the urban experiences of Ndebele artists working in industry. Today, Esther Mahlangu has become a virtuoso in the art of bridging the gulf between tradition and the new motifs linked to latter day urban development. Her frescoes show not only the beaded skirts worn by young brides, but also such ordinary modern things as sloping roofs, ladders, windows, and double-edged razor blades. She paints with feather brushes and uses traditional calabashes instead of pots for her colours. Although these paintings have no magic powers according to the Ndebele, they are nevertheless thought to protect houses against the evil eye – a belief that is widespread in Africa.

Als die Ndebele in Südafrika Mitte des 19. Jahrhunderts aus ihren Strohhütten in Häuser aus Lehm zogen, entdeckten sie gleichzeitig mit dieser neuen Architekturform die Technik der Fingermalerei bei ihren Nachbarn, den Sotho.

Im Laufe der Zeit entwickelten die Ndebele diese Technik immer weiter und als 1923 ein weißer Farmer eine seiner Landarbeiterinnen bat, die weißen Wände seines Hauses in bunten Farben zu bemalen, war die Sensation perfekt. Die früher mit Erdfarben und natürlichen Oxiden gemalten Muster waren farblich eher gedämpft. Wieder einige Zeit später veränderten sich die geometrischen Muster durch die Erfahrungen, die Ndebele-Künstlerinnen in der Stadt und bei der Arbeit in der Industrie machten. Esther Mahlangu verbindet virtuos die althergebrachte Kunst mit neuen Motiven, die mit der Verstädterung zusammenhängen. Die Wandmalerei zeigt so unterschiedliche Motive wie die mit Perlen bestickten Schürzen verheirateter Frauen, geneigte Dächer, Leitern, Fenster oder zweischneidige Rasierklingen. Zum Malen benutzt die Künstlerin Federpinsel, als Farbtopf traditionelle Kalebassen. Wenngleich diese Bilder den Ndebele zufolge keinerlei Zauberkraft haben, sollen sie doch wie in vielen afrikanischen Ländern die Häuser vor Unglück schützen.

Au milieu du 19e siècle, quand le peuple Ndebele d'Afrique du Sud abandonne ses huttes en paille pour des habitations en terre, il découvre en même temps qu'une nouvelle forme d'architecture une technique de peinture au doigt léguée par ses voisins, les Sothos.

Au fil du temps, l'iconographie gagne en richesse et, en 1923, quand un fermier blanc demande à une de ses ouvrières agricoles de peindre sa maison de couleurs vives sur fond blanc, c'est une révélation. La couleur remplace les motifs peints à la boue avec des oxydes naturels. Plus tard encore, les formes géométriques sont influencées par l'expérience urbaine de nombreux artistes Ndebele qui travaillent dans l'industrie. Aujourd'hui Esther Mahlangu est virtuose dans l'art de jeter un pont entre la tradition et les nouveaux motifs liés à l'urbanisation. Ces fresques représentent aussi bien les motifs des pagnes de perle que portent les jeunes femmes mariées que des toits en pente, des échelles, des fenêtres, ou encore des lames de rasoir à double tranchant. Pour peindre, elle utilise des pinceaux en plume et, en guise de pots, des calebasses traditionnelles. Si ces peintures n'ont aucun pouvoir magique selon les Ndebele, elles contribuent néanmoins, comme dans de nombreux pays d'Afrique, à protéger les maisons du mauvais sort.

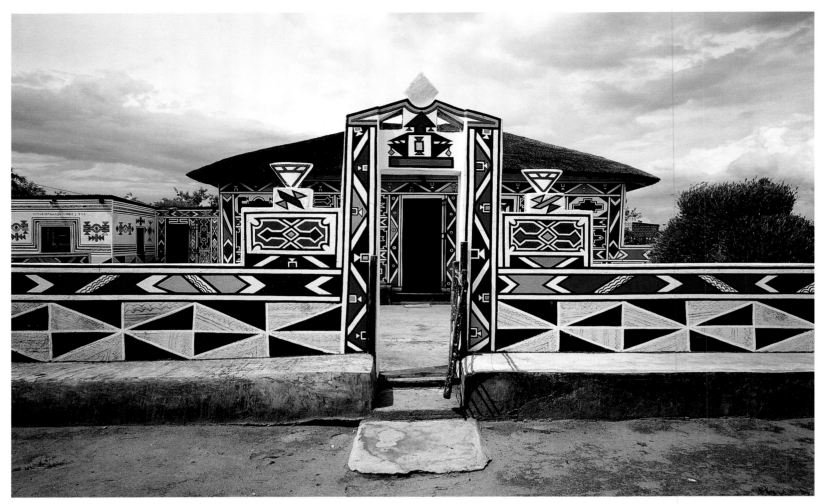

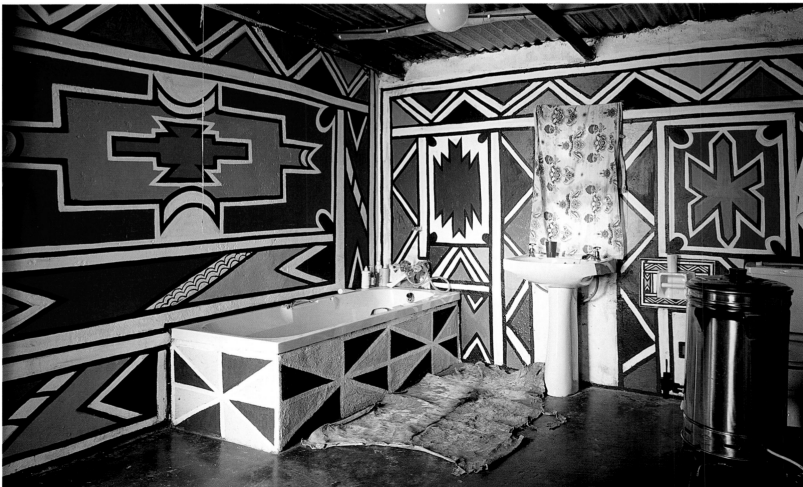

✳ **PAGE 76** Esther Mahlangu is the most famous living Ndebele artist. Her geometrical drawings are known all over the world. **ABOVE** Her house is a blend of brightly coloured symmetrical motifs and modern equipment. ✳ **SEITE 76** Esther Mahlangu ist die berühmteste Malerin der Ndebele. Ihre symmetrischen Zeichnungen gehen um die Welt. **OBEN** In ihrem Haus verbindet sie geometrische Muster mit lebhaften Farben und einer modernen Einrichtung. ✳ **PAGE 76** Esther Mahlangu est l'artiste Ndebele la plus célèbre. Réalisés dans la symétrie, ses dessins ont fait le tour du monde. **CI-DESSUS** Sa maison mêle les motifs géométriques de couleurs vives et l'équipement moderne.

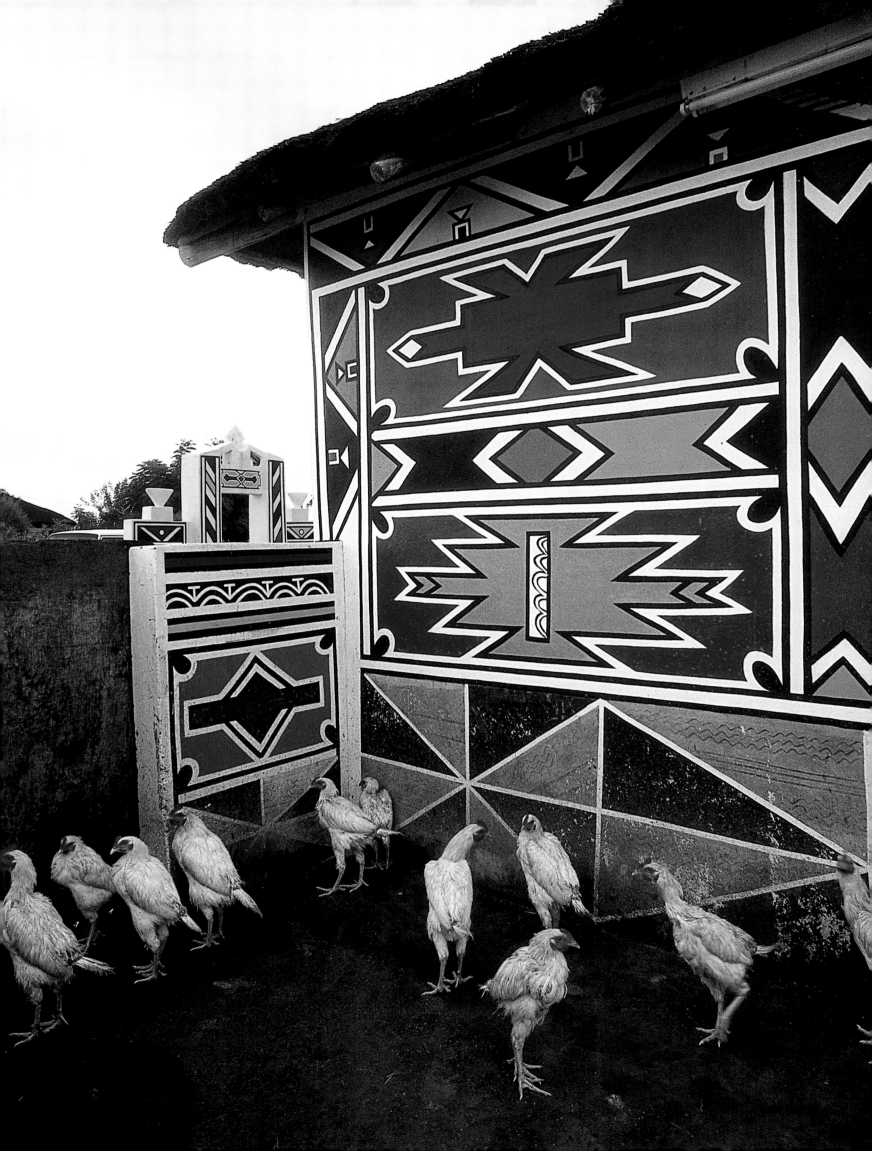

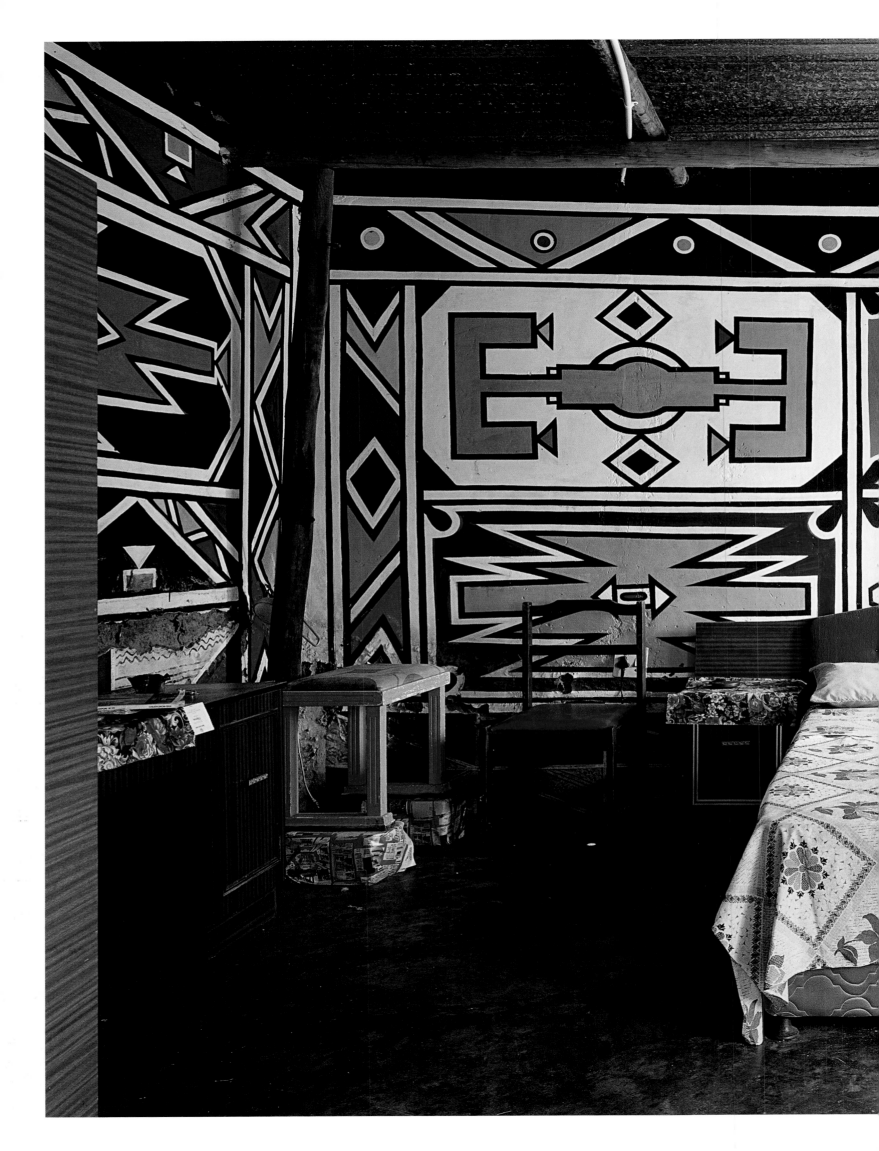

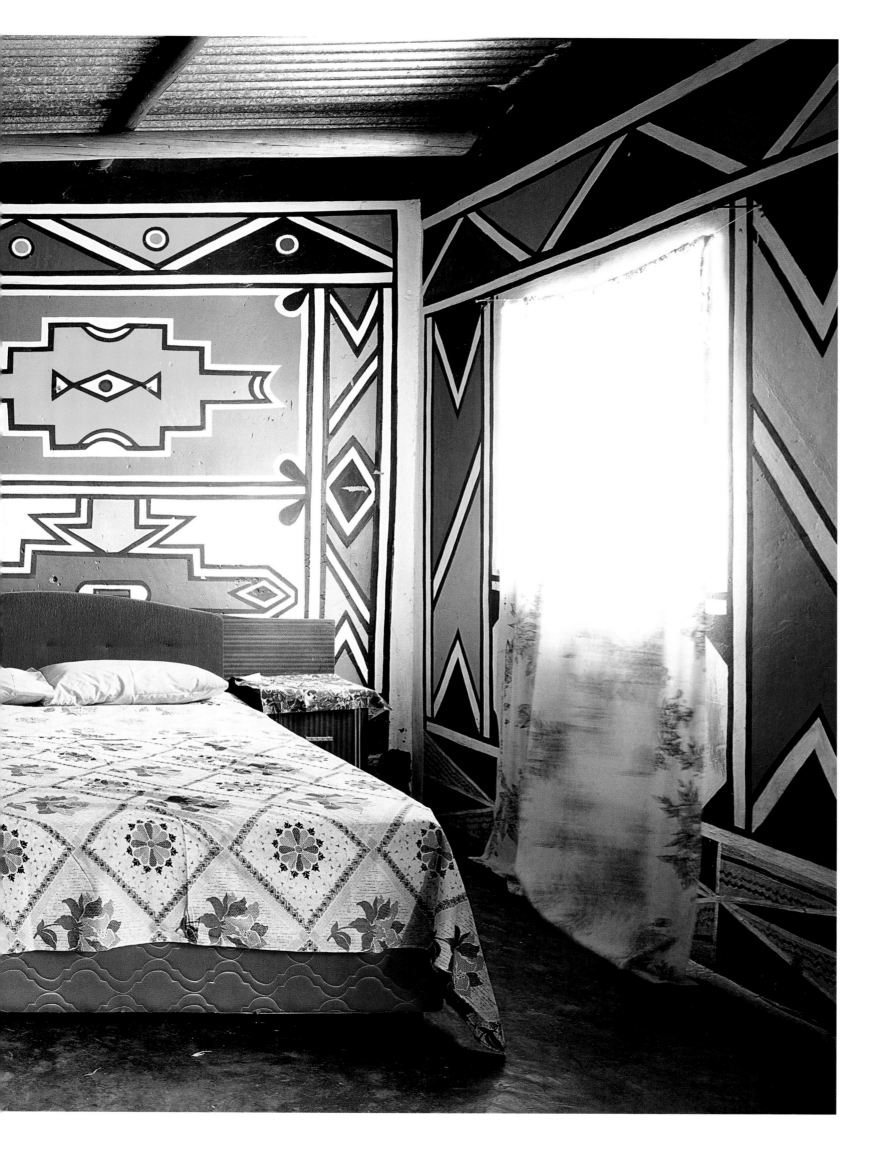

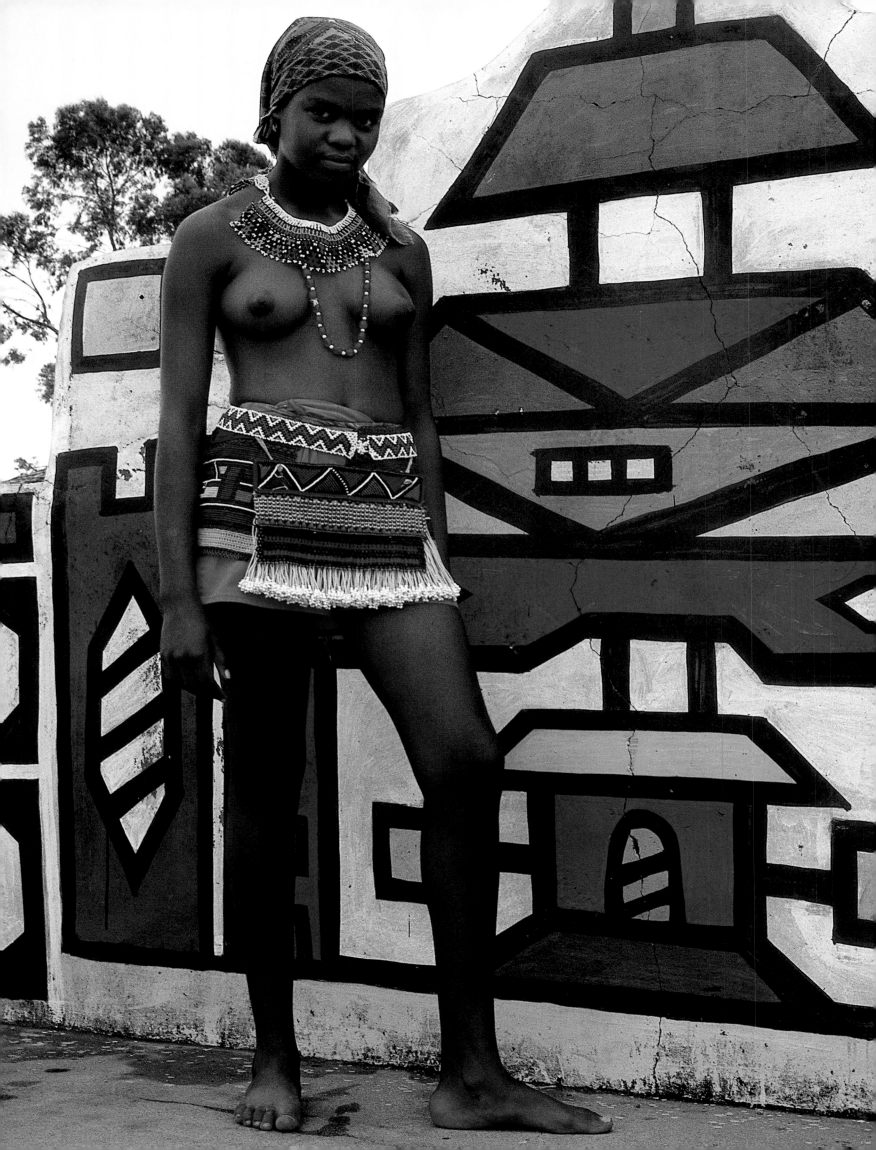

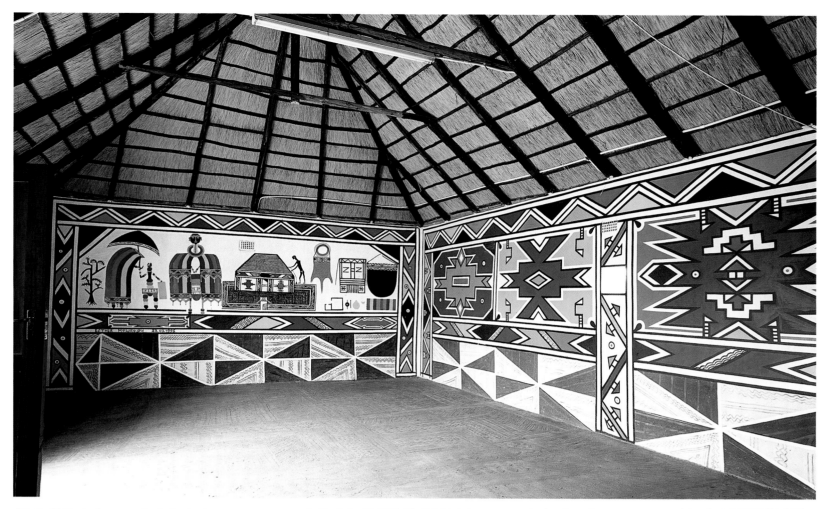

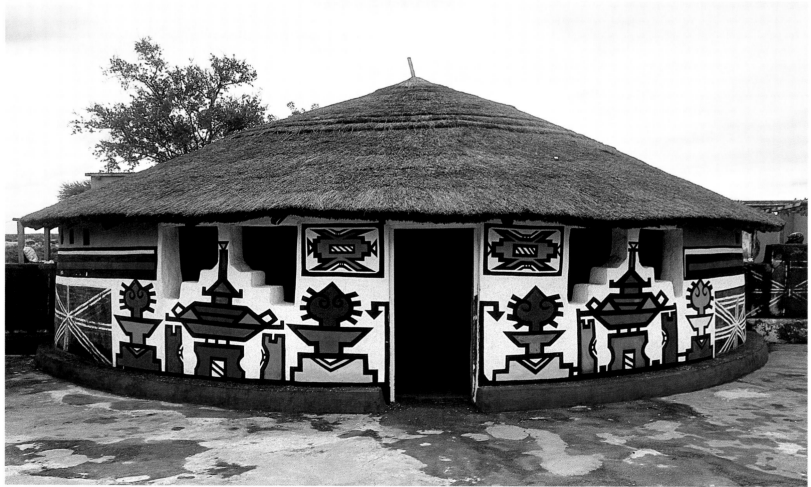

※ **FOLLOWING PAGES** In the KwaNdebele region, there are still two or three villages where traditional brown motifs are mixed with bright acrylic colours representing aeroplanes, transistors and televisions. ※ **FOLGENDE DOPPELSEITE** In der Gegend von KwaNdebele mischen sich in einigen Dörfern noch die althergebrachten braunen Muster mit denen in bunten Acrylfarben, die Flugzeuge, Radios und Fernseher darstellen. ※ **DOUBLE PAGE SUIVANTE** Dans la région de KwaNdebele, il existe encore deux ou trois autres villages où les motifs traditionnels bruns se mêlent aux couleurs vives acryliques représentant des avions, des transistors et des téléviseurs.

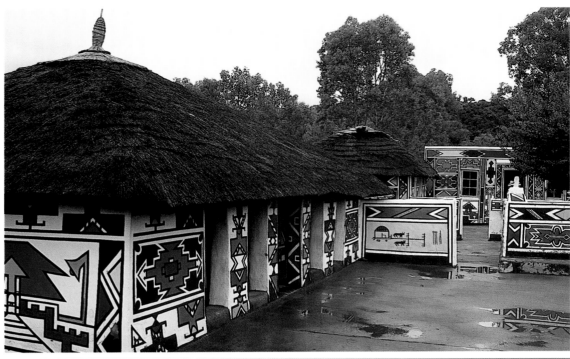
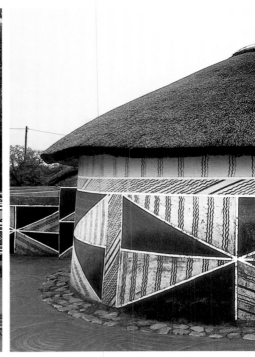
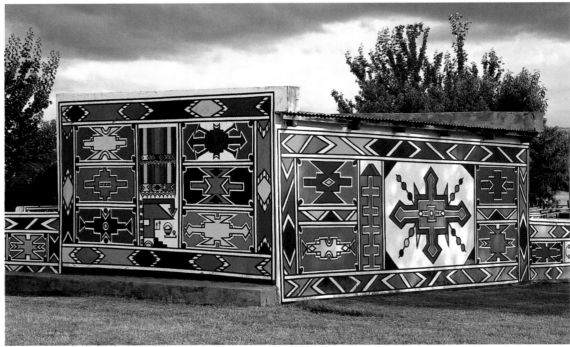
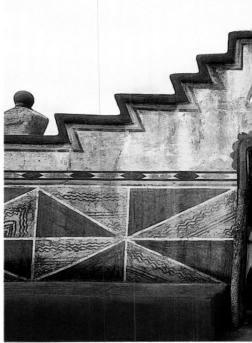
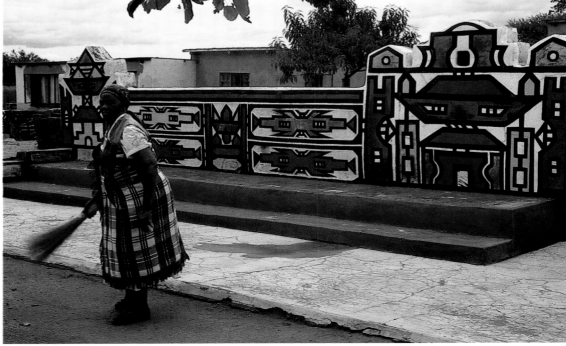
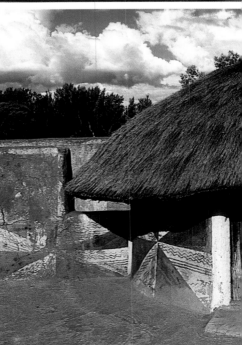

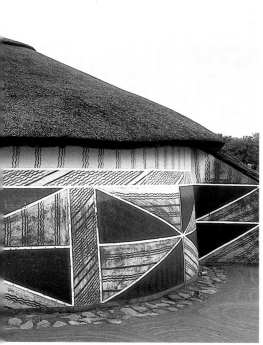
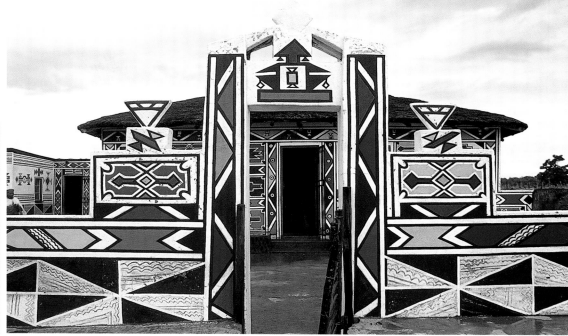
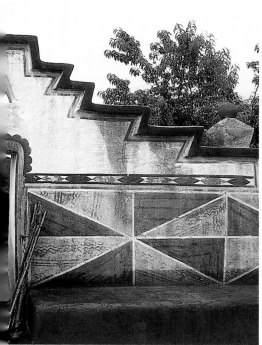
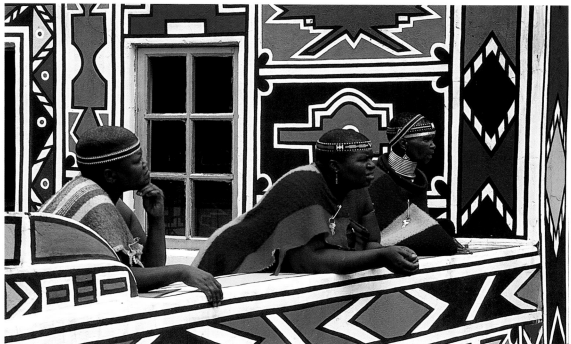
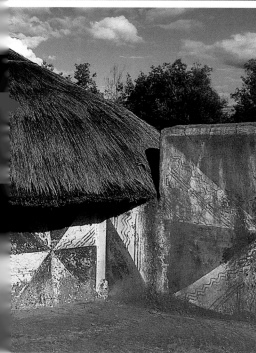
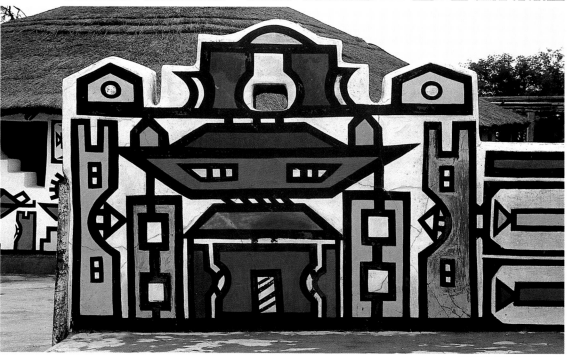

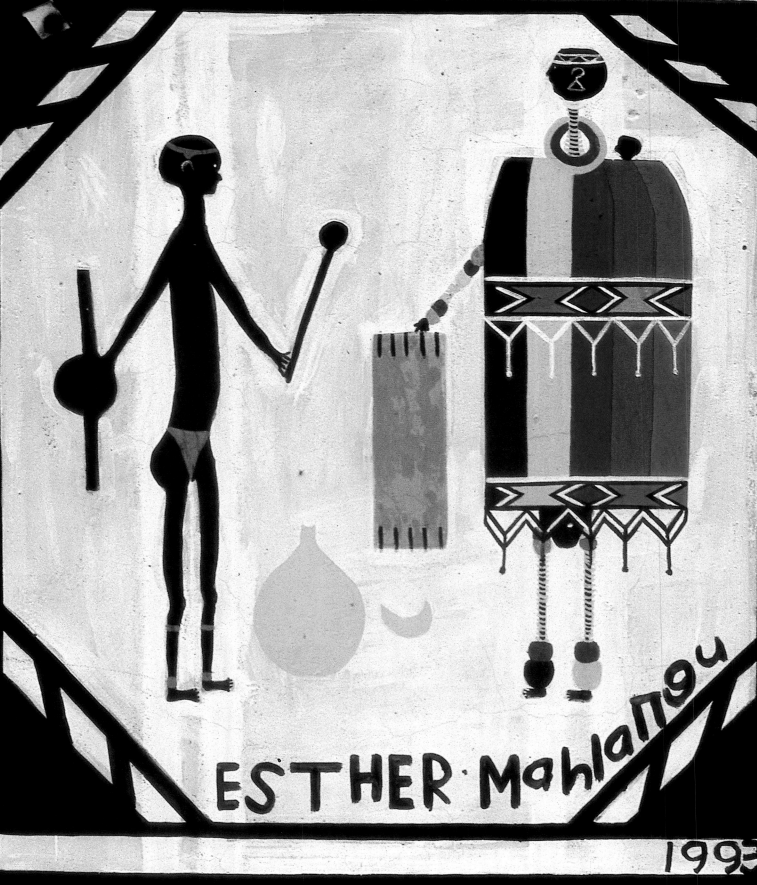

ESTHER Mahlangu

1993

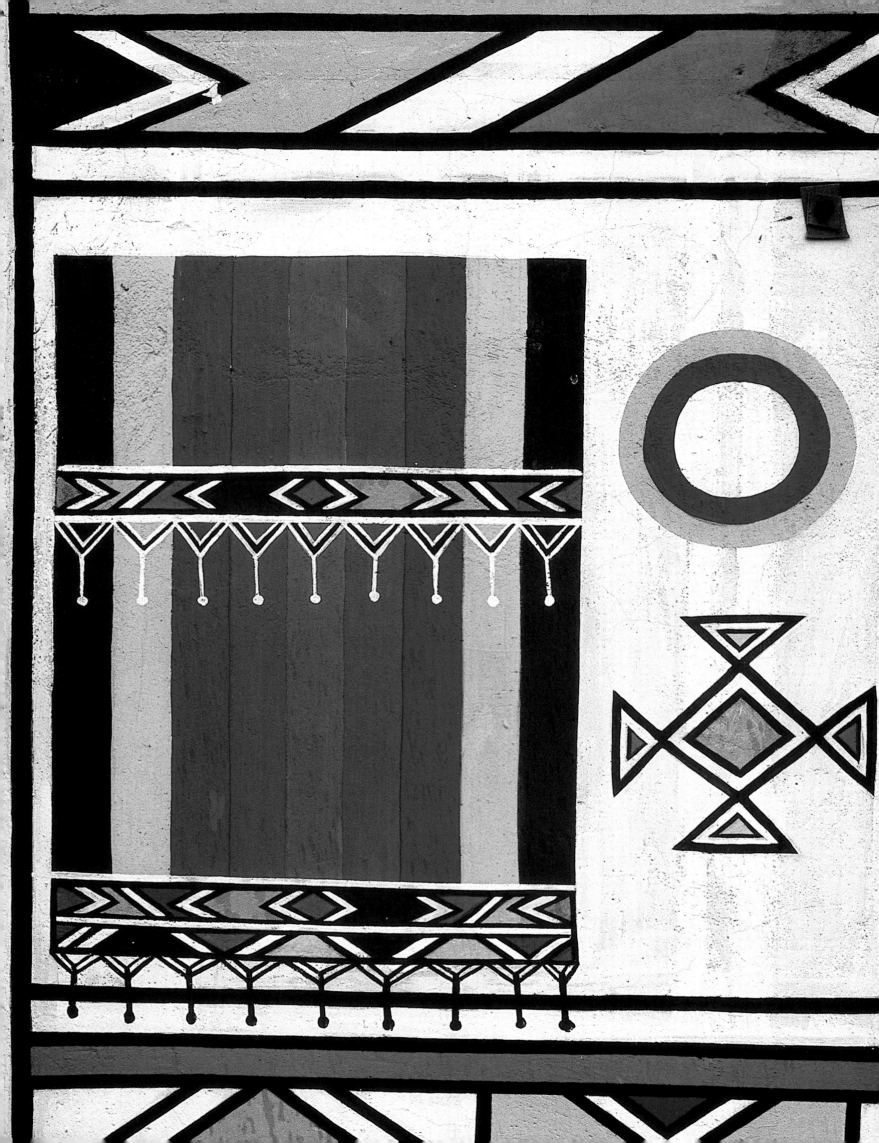

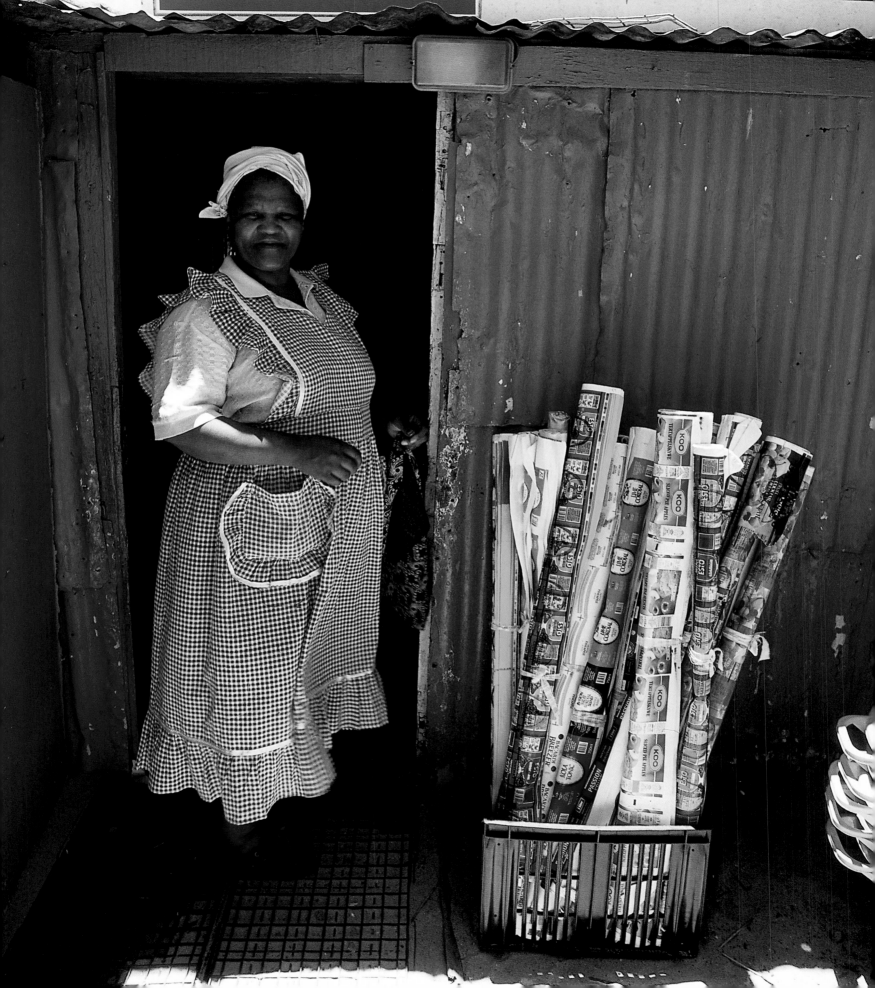

# TOWNSHIPS
## Cape Town

The slum dwellers around the airport struggle perpetually against the encroaching sand – and do what they can to make their homes attractive.

**Black or white** – before Nelson Mandela and freedom, the simplistic horror of South Africa applied to everything from skin colour to the walls of houses.

White villas against bright African facades, as in the Malay quarter which still exists today; for years the mad theorists of apartheid imposed the difference, forcing people who didn't meet their racial criteria to move out of the central part of the Cape area. This brought about the creation of the townships. According to the prevailing wisdom, these districts were expected to separate the races, while supplying visual proof in downtown Cape Town that the myth of white South Africa was really true. The "Cape Flats" (so called to distinguish them from the residential quarters on the slopes of Table Mountain) today have a population of nearly two million, hovering just outside the city. What could be more natural today than the celebration of colour, in honour of a country that calls itself the Rainbow Nation? More often than not, the walls inside the houses are covered with advertisements for consumer products, which serve as wallpaper of a kind. Food cartons and cans are recycled, too. In summer, the tin shacks are furnace-hot, and in the winter they're so cold that entire families go to bed at six, as soon as they get home from school or work. So a touch of colour on the walls is more than welcome.

**Schwarz oder Weiß** – bis zu Nelson Mandelas Befreiung lief es in Südafrika schrecklicherweise stets auf die Frage nach der Hautfarbe hinaus. Für Häuser galt das Gleiche.

Weiße Villen gegen die bunten Fassaden in afrikanischem Patchwork wie in dem noch immer existierenden Viertel Malay. Über lange Zeit siedelten die fanatischen Vertreter einer Menschen verachtenden Apartheidpolitik unerwünschte Bürger nach rassischen Kriterien aus den Stadtzentren um. So entstanden die Elendsviertel am Stadtrand. Die Stadtteile sollten nach Rassen getrennt werden, auch um in der Innenstadt die Illusion eines weißen Südafrika aufrecht erhalten zu können. Die »Cape Flats« (Bezeichnung, um sie von den Wohnvierteln am Hang des Tafelbergs zu unterscheiden) am Stadtrand beherbergen heutzutage fast zwei Millionen Einwohner. Hier steht die Farbe im Mittelpunkt, wie ein Echo darauf, dass sich das südafrikanische Volk den Beinamen »Regenbogen-Nation« gegeben hat. An den Wänden hängen statt Tapeten bunte Papierrollen mit Anzeigen, die für Güter des täglichen Bedarfs werben. Dosen aller Art werden ebenfalls wieder verwertet. Im Sommer ist eine Wellblechhütte der reinste Backofen, im Winter dagegen ein Kühlschrank. Zu dieser Jahreszeit gehen manche Familien schon um sechs Uhr abends schlafen, sobald sie von der Arbeit oder von der Schule nach Hause kommen. So gestalten sie wenigstens ihre Wände ein wenig fröhlicher …

**Noir ou blanc** – avant la libération de Nelson Mandela, l'effroyable simplisme de l'Afrique du Sud se déclinait du pigment des peaux aux murs des maisons.

Villas blanches contre façades bariolées de patchworks africains, à l'exemple du quartier Malay qui existe encore; longtemps, les savants fous de l'apartheid ont accompli leur sale besogne, déplaçant du centre de Cape Town les populations rejetées par les critères raciaux. Ainsi sont nés les bidonvilles. Dans la mythologie d'alors, ces quartiers avaient pour vocation de séparer les races, mais aussi d'entretenir visuellement, là-bas en ville, le mythe d'une Afrique du Sud blanche. Les «Cape Flats» (ainsi désignés en opposition aux quartiers résidentiels à flanc de la Montagne de la Table) abritent aujourd'hui près de deux millions d'habitants en périphérie de la ville. Quoi de plus naturel que d'y célébrer aujourd'hui les couleurs, en écho à cette nation autoproclamée «Arc en ciel»? Les murs sont le plus souvent bariolés de rouleaux de papier à la gloire de produits de consommation courante tenant lieu de papier peint. On recycle également toutes sortes de boîtes de conserve. L'été, la cabane en tôle est une fournaise. L'hiver, c'est un frigo au point que, sitôt revenues du travail et de l'école, les familles se couchent dès six heures. Alors, un peu de gaieté aux murs…

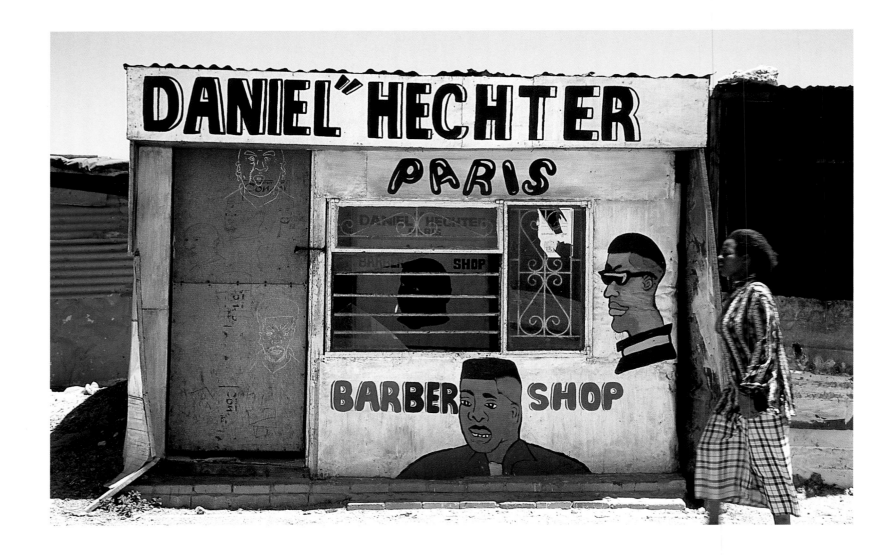

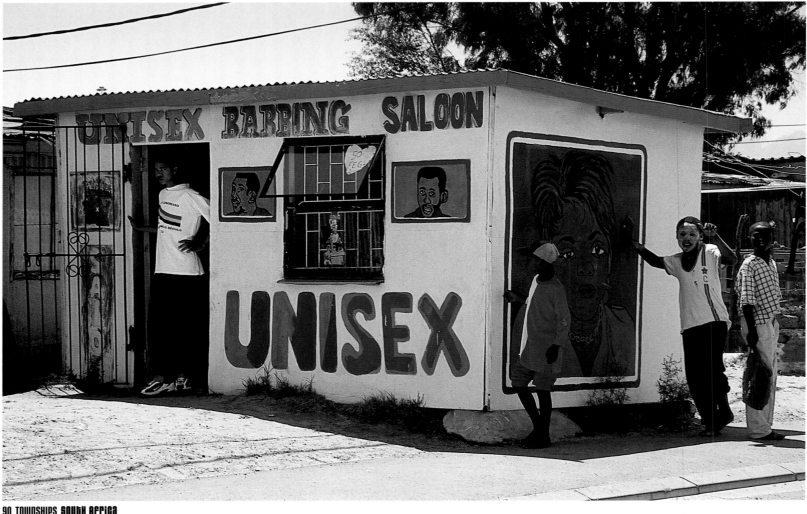

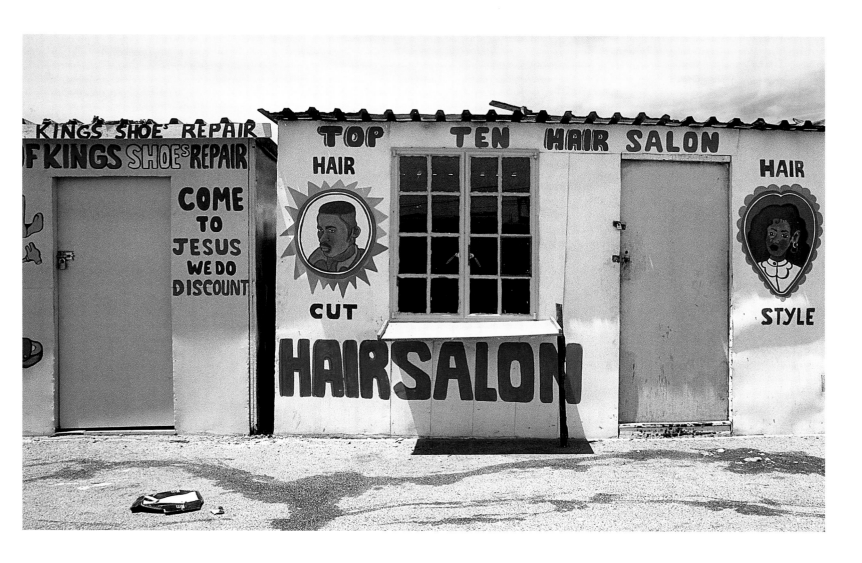

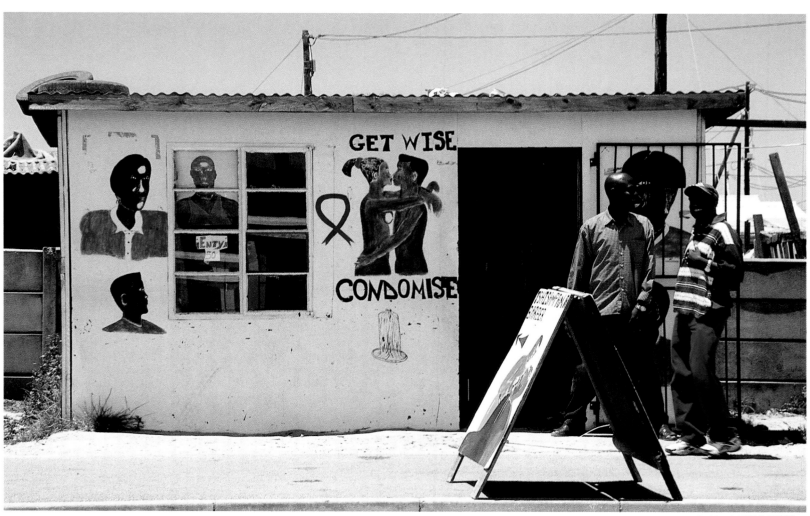

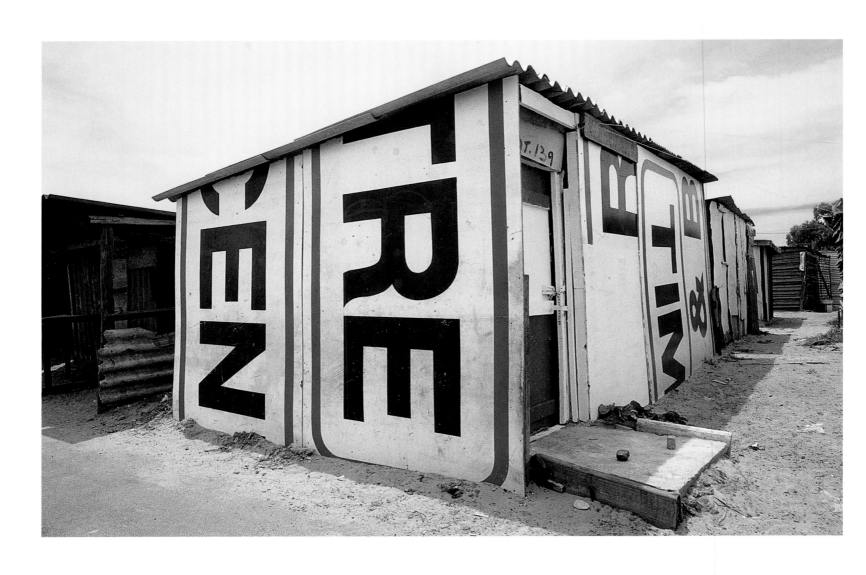

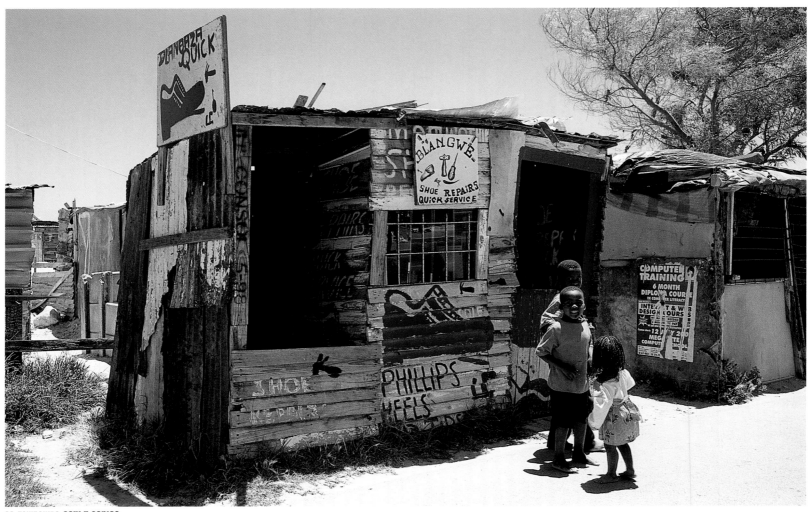

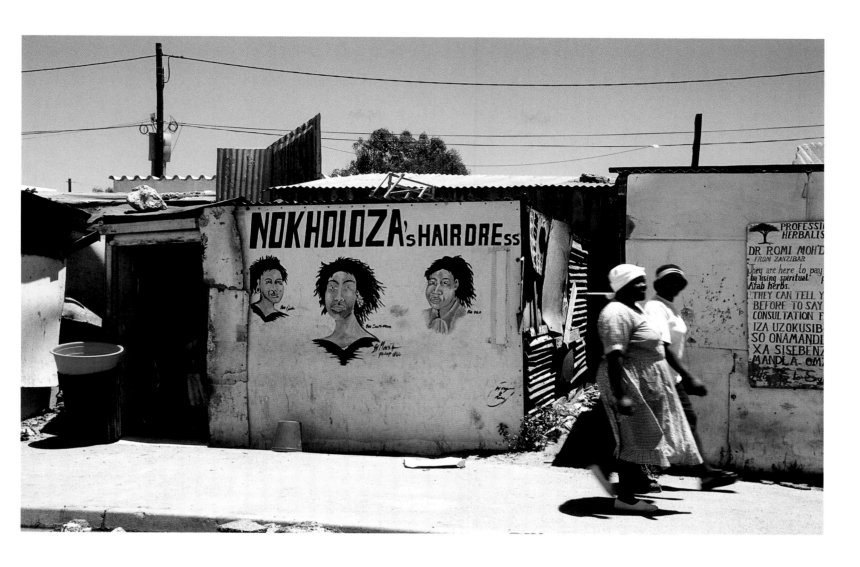

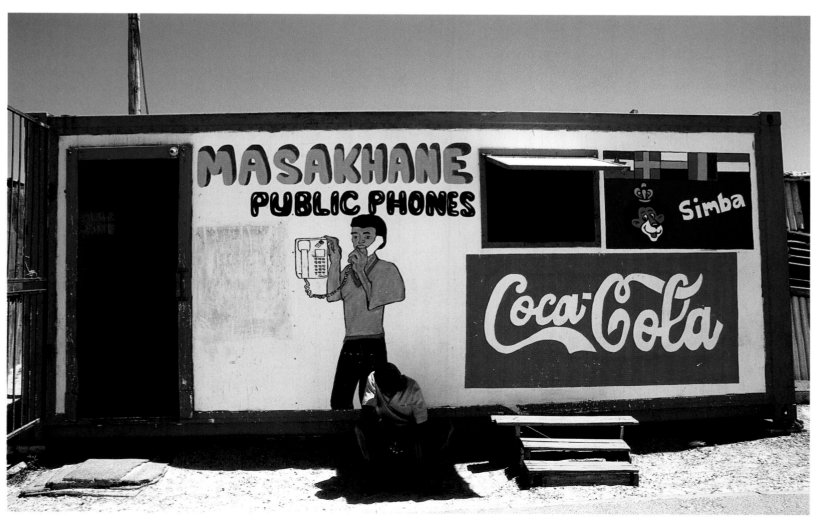

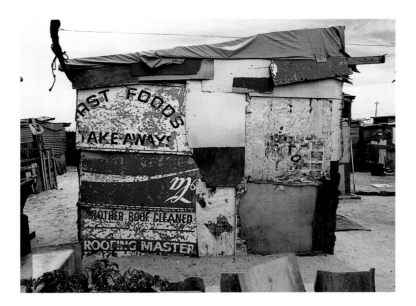
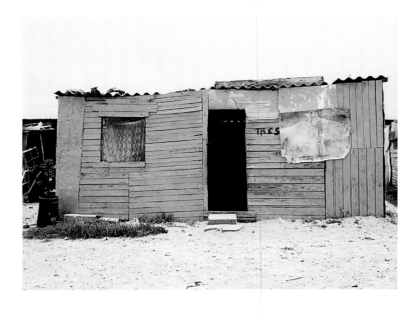
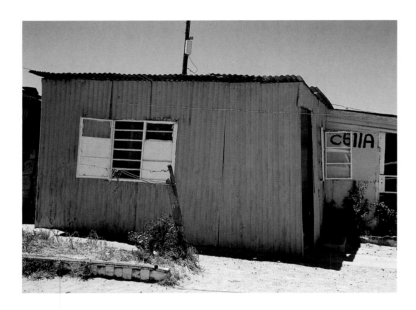
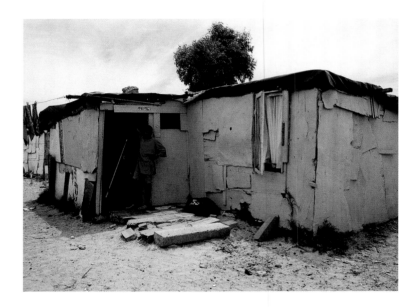
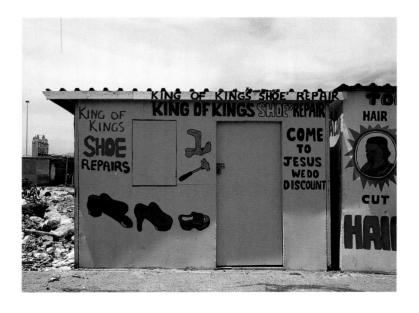
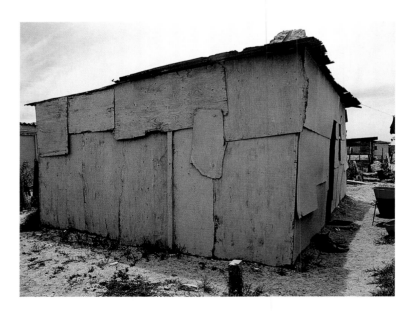

❋ **ABOVE** The corrugated iron shacks are built on a dusty, windswept plain. Amid this scene of dire poverty, people signify their sense of belonging with brightly decorated walls. In winter, the houses are heated with paraffin, at the mortal risk of starting a general conflagration. ❋ **OBEN** Die Wellblechhütten stehen im sandigen, windigen Flachland. In diesem extremen Elend gestaltet man seine Wände höchstens mit bunten Werbeplakaten. Im Winter wird mit Paraffin geheizt – nicht selten kommt es zu verheerenden Bränden. ❋ **CI-DESSUS** Les cabanes en tôle ondulée sont édifiées sur une plaine sablonneuse battue par les vents. Dans cette misère extrême, on marque l'appartenance par des murs bariolés. L'hiver, on se chauffe à la paraffine au risque de terribles incendies.

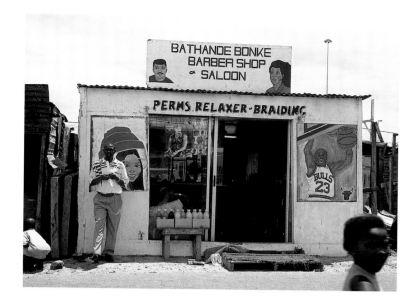
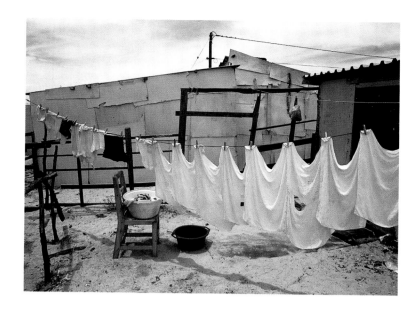
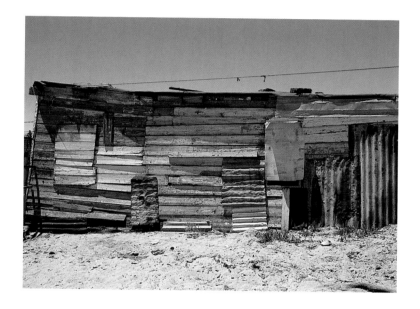
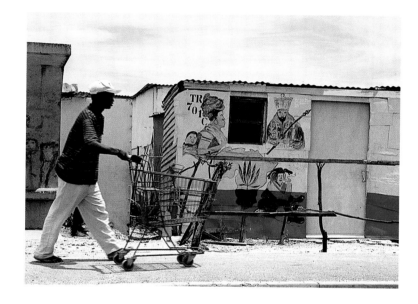
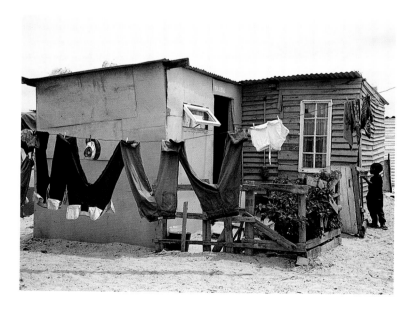
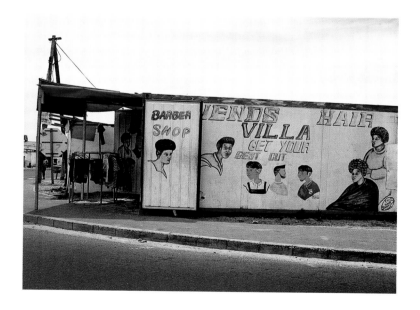

❋ **ABOVE** Every year, the rural exodus brings hundreds of thousands more people to the capital of Cape Province. Huge construction programmes are under way to replace shanties without water or electricity. ❋ **OBEN** Jährlich führt die Landflucht dazu, dass Hunderttausende von Neuankömmlingen in die Hauptstadt am Kap strömen. Umfassende Bauvorhaben sollen dafür sorgen, dass die Menschen nicht länger in Baracken ohne Wasser und Strom hausen müssen. ❋ **CI-DESSUS** Chaque année, l'exode rural provoque l'arrivée de centaines de milliers de nouveaux habitants dans la ville du Cap. D'immenses programmes de construction visent à remplacer ces baraques sans eau ni électricité par des maisons en dur.

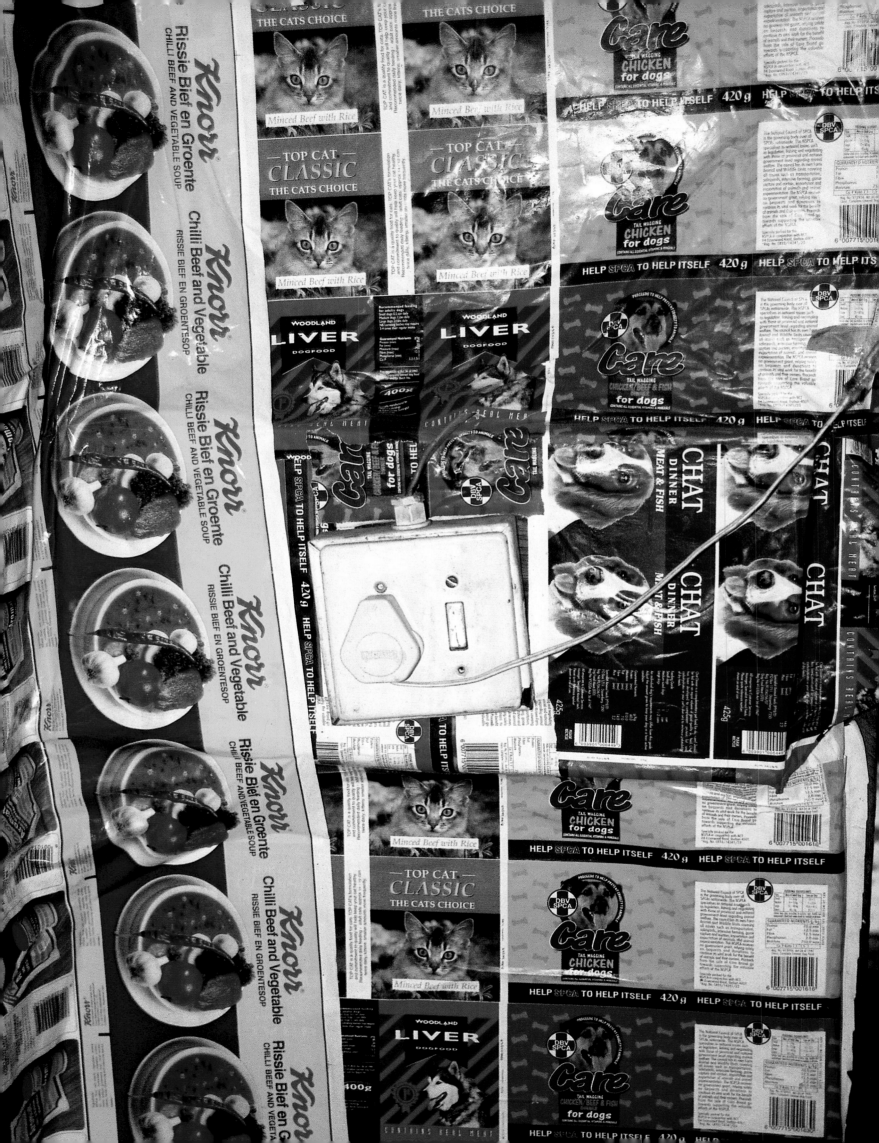

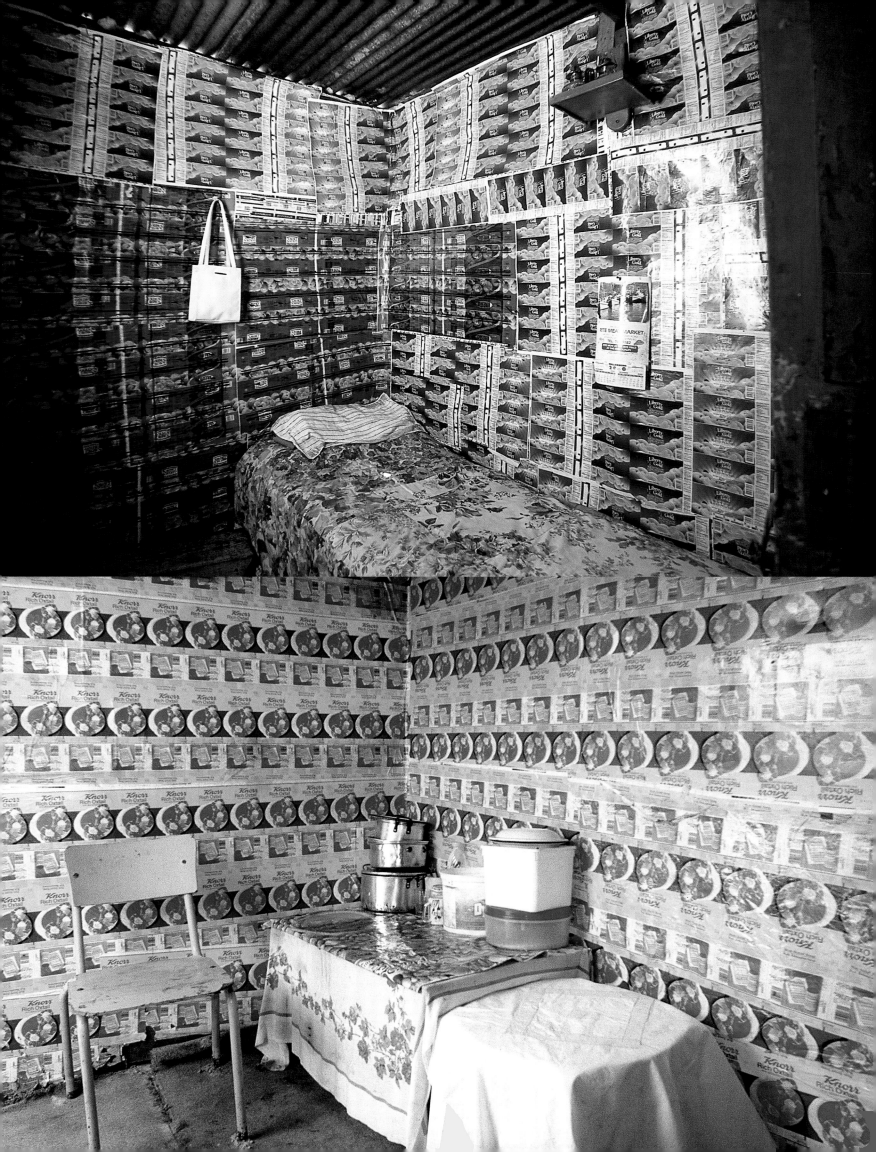

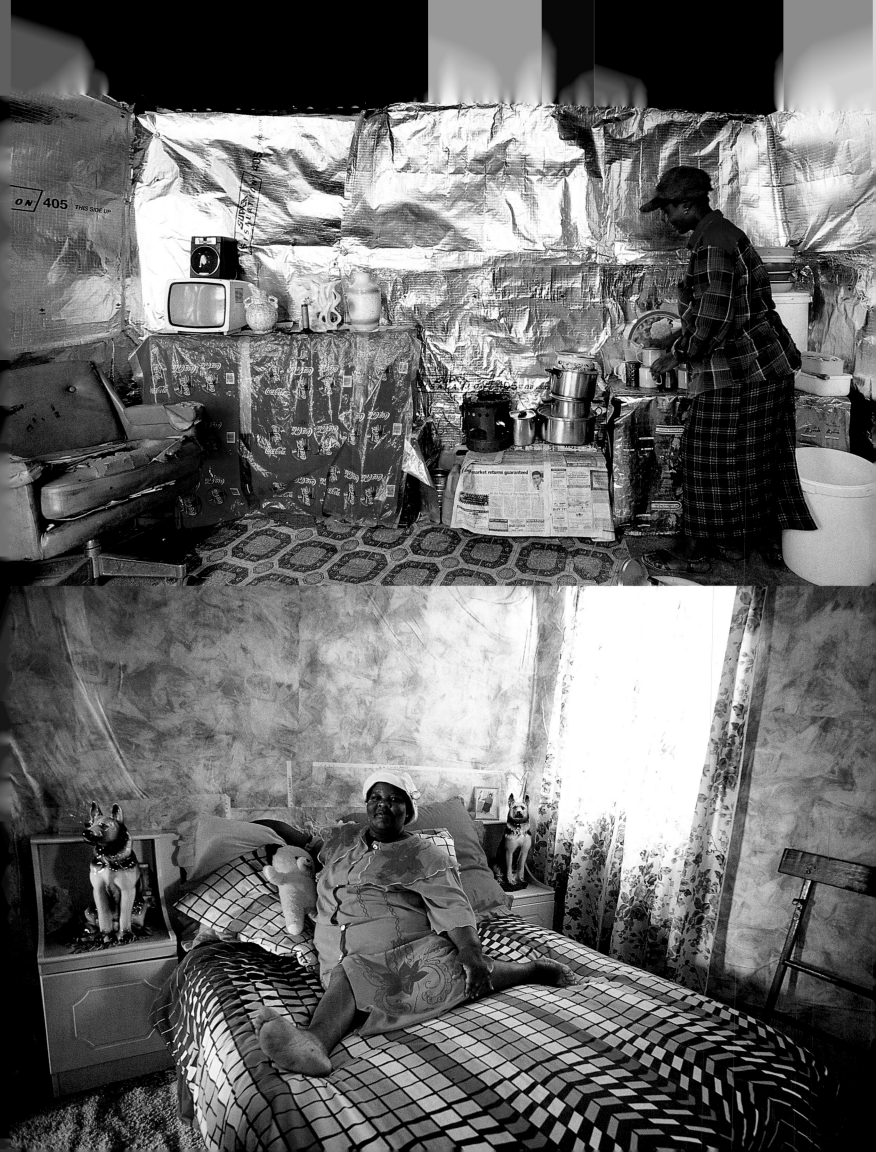

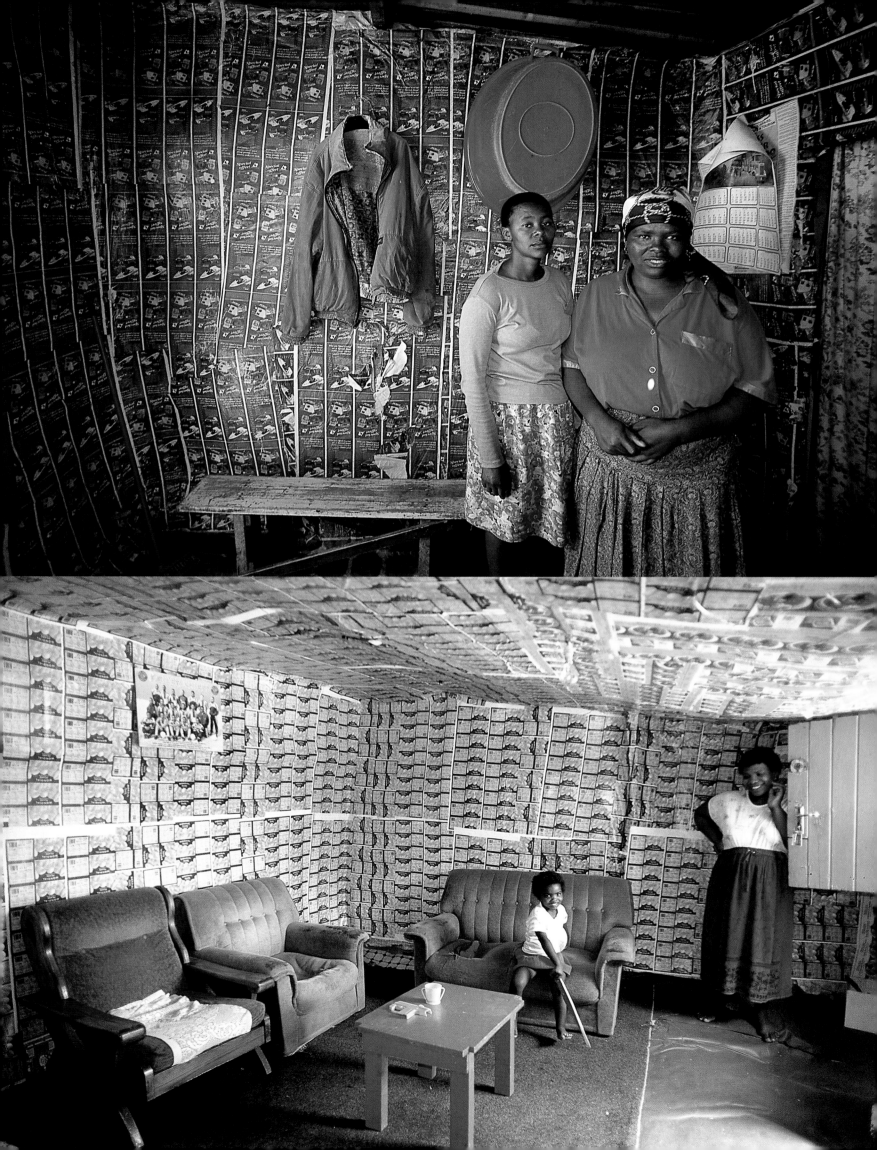

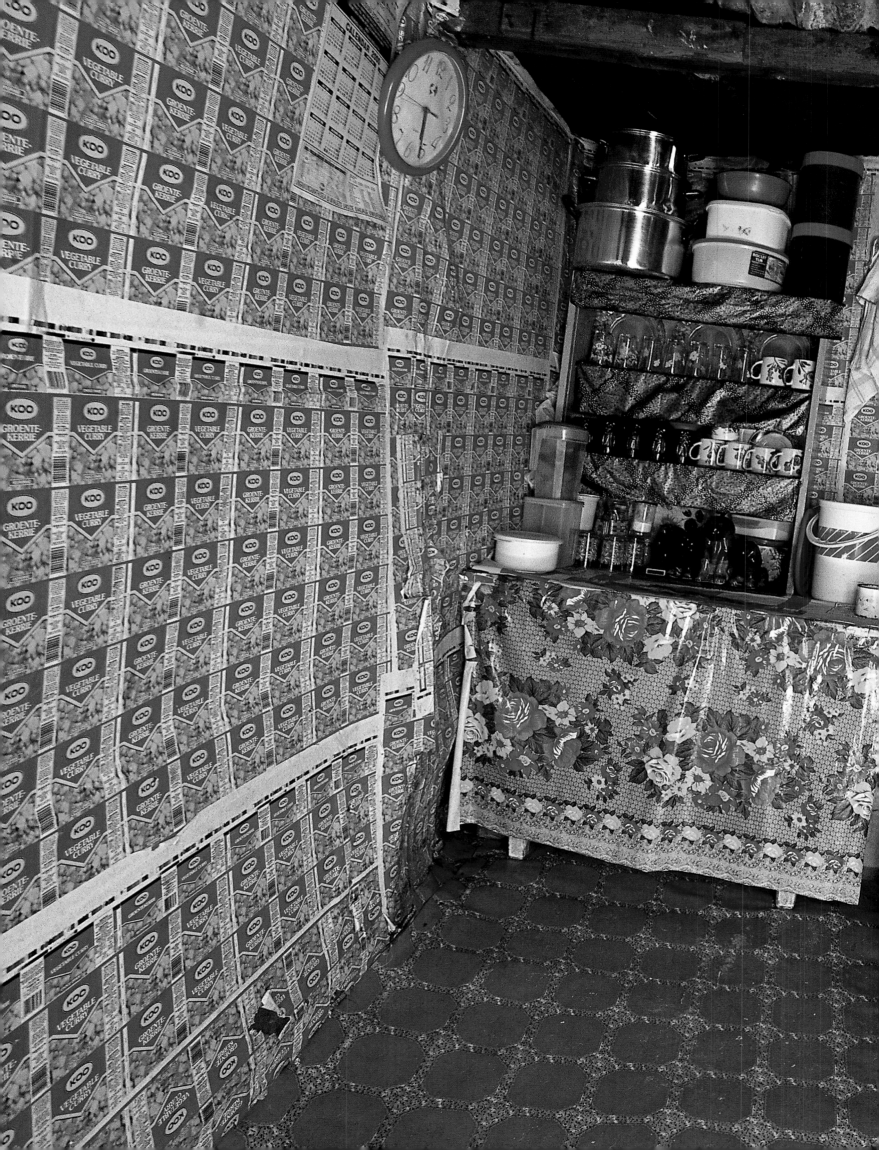

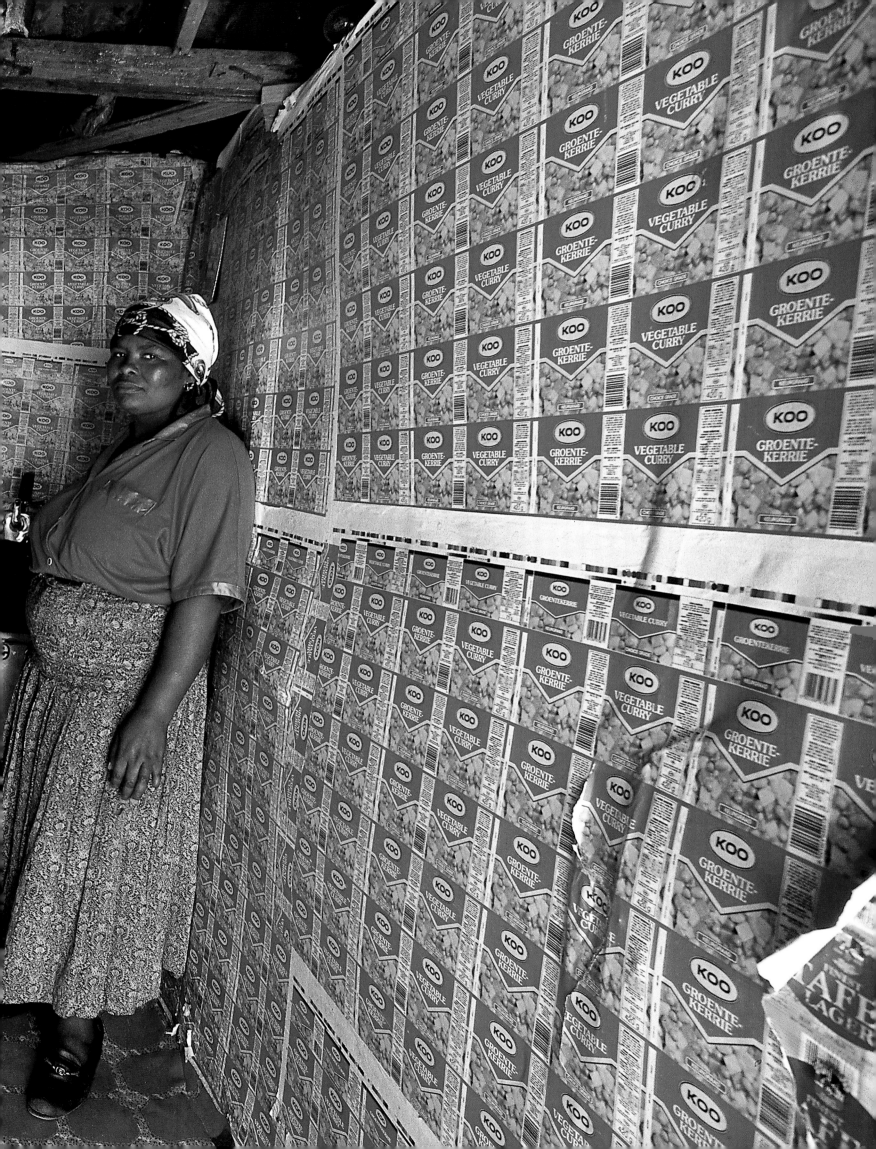

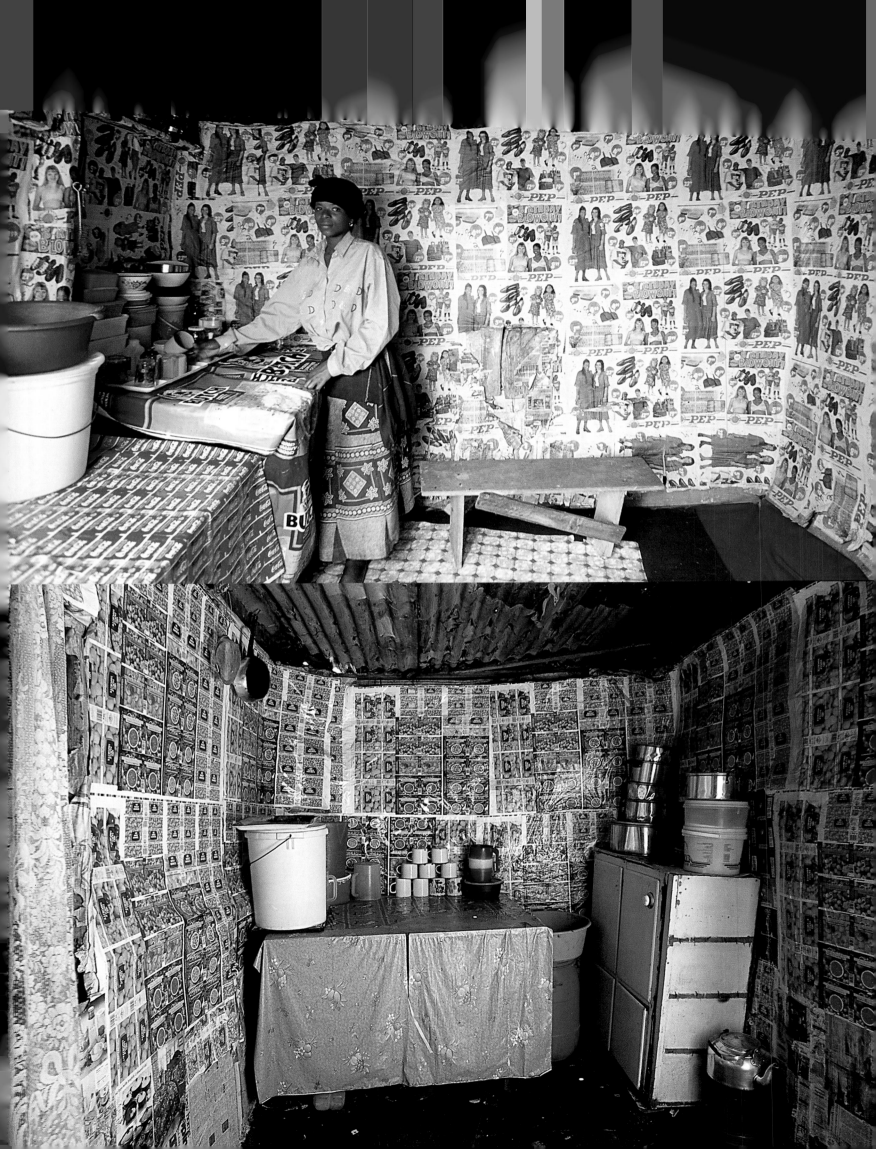

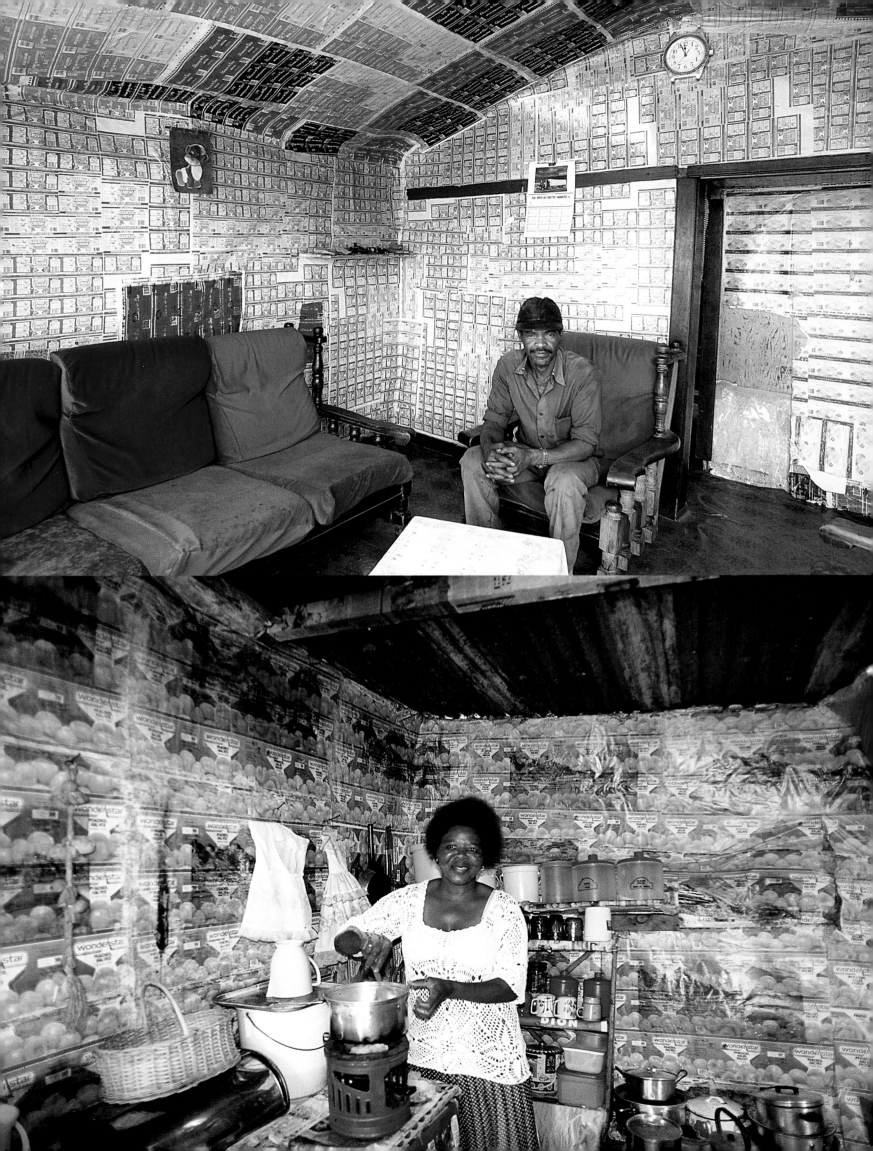

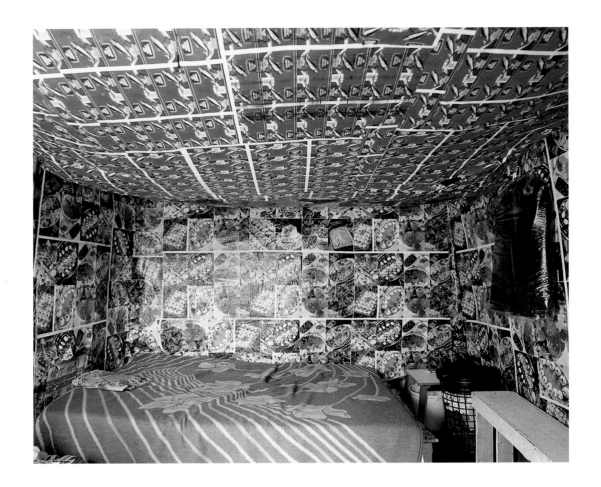
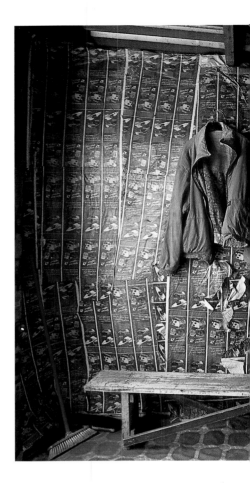
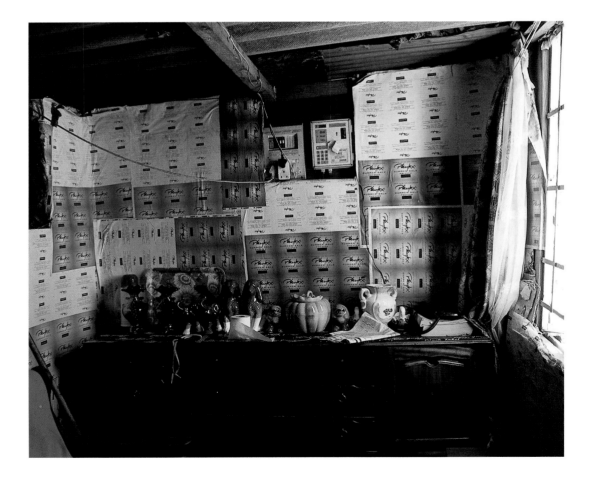
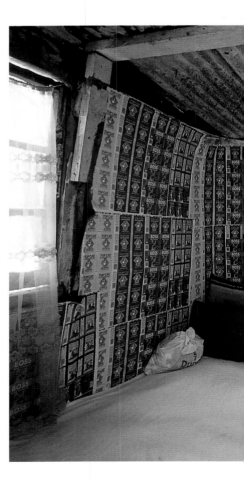

✳ **ABOVE** Township-style, the partitions are covered with wrapping paper advertising soap, chocolate, wine; there are also recycled cigarette cartons and small match-boxes adorned with lions' heads. ✳ **OBEN** Die Trennwände sind wie in den Townships üblich mit Werbung oder Verpackungen von Seife, Schokolade oder Wein beklebt. Ein Löwenkopf schmückt Zigarettenstangen und Streichholzpackungen. ✳ **CI-DESSUS** À la mode des bidonvilles, les cloisons des pièces sont recouvertes de papier d'emballage récupéré à la gloire de savons, de marques de chocolat, de vin, de cartouches de cigarettes ou encore de petites boîtes d'allumettes arborant la tête d'un lion.

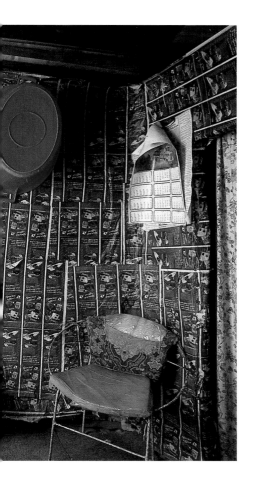
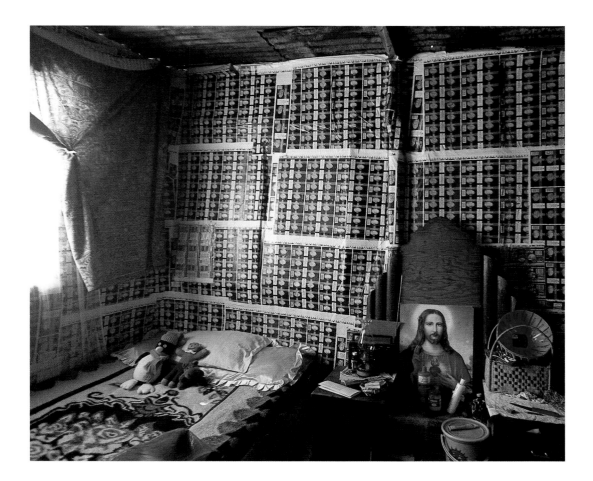
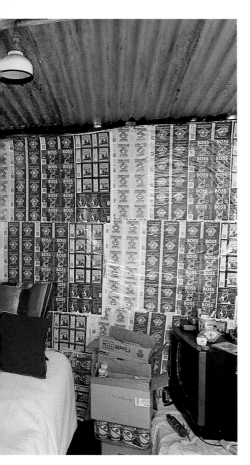
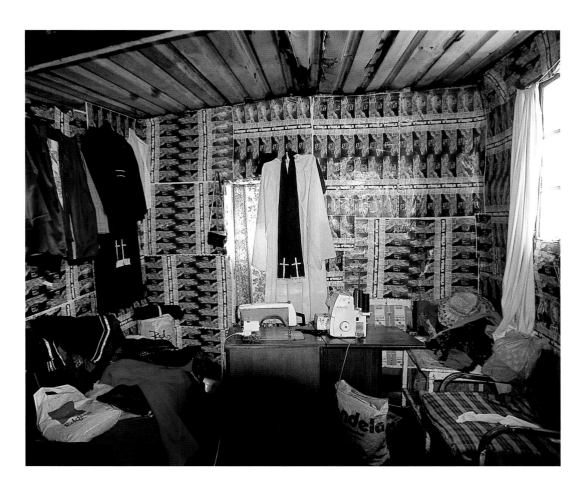

※ **ABOVE** The art of survival in the townships – floors are covered with pieces of carpet and linoleum picked up in the residential areas. Things abandoned by other people are brought back into use, and religious belief is very strong. ※ **OBEN** Überlebenskunst in den Townships: Auf den Böden liegen Teppich- oder Linoleumreste, die die Bewohner in den vornehmen Wohnvierteln aufgetrieben haben. Man richtet sich mit weggeworfenen Dingen ein. Dabei sind die Bewohner der Elendsviertel sehr gläubig. ※ **CI-DESSUS** L'art de (sur)vivre des habitants des townships: on couvre les sols de bouts de moquette ou de lino, récupérés dans les quartiers résidentiels; on s'équipe d'objets abandonnés. Et on est très croyant.

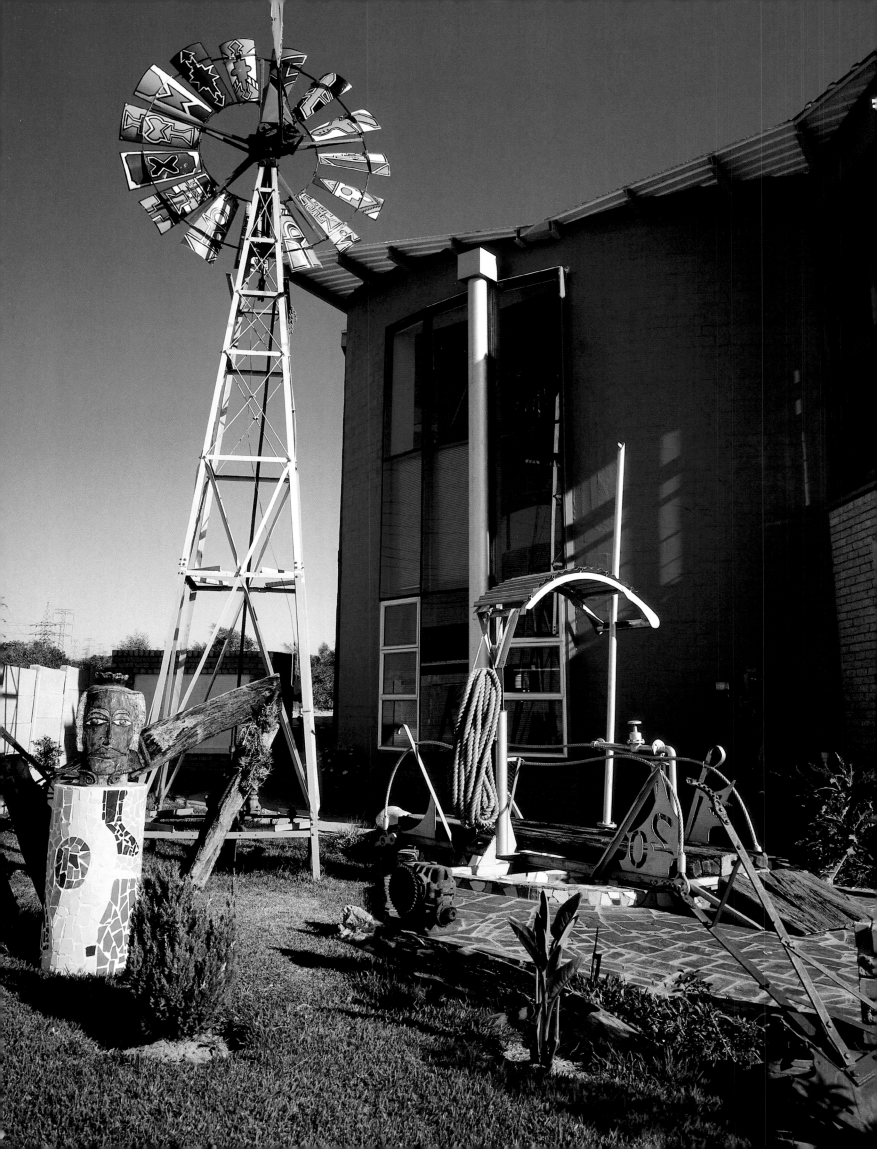

# WiLLie BeSter
## cape town

This artist has invited the industrial world to his house – and the result is a miniature Beaubourg on the southern tip of Africa.

It used to be a "Whites Only" suburb – a sinister label if ever there was one. The anathema applied not only to its inhabitants but also to their homes, which were all drearily alike. When the mixed-race artist Willie Bester arrived, colour arrived in his slipstream.

His house is a promising blue on the outside. Around it, a décor typical of a Karoo desert farm (the Karoo is close by) flirts with mosaics and objects salvaged and reinvented in new roles. Willie Bester himself drew up the plans for his circular house, with no corner crannies where bad thoughts could lurk. The first thing you see inside it is a steel structure strongly resembling a hot water boiler, and setting the tone for the whole house. Actually it's a column, supporting the staircase. A giant portrait of Nelson Mandela, with his eyes turned to heaven, overlooks the living room. Loftwise, the kitchen and dining room are one; the bedrooms are on the first floor, with a wing for the three children; and the studio is adjacent. Willie Bester's work has won considerable recognition in Europe, and he is now embarked on a series of new experiments. As the months go by, his 'industrial park' steadily fills with fresh creations. Viewed as life sources, his factory pipes and tubes are like so many arteries attached to an imaginary pumping heart. The organism is alive. It quivers with inspiration. One day it's a house; the next, it's a museum.

Es war einmal ein »White-only«-Vorort – was für eine finstere Bezeichnung. Der Bann bezog sich auf die Menschen, aber auch auf die Häuser mit ihren fahlen Fassaden. Als sich der Künstler Willie Bester hier einkaufte, brachte er die Farbe gleich mit.

Schon die bläuliche Fassade ist ein gutes Zeichen. Das Dekor wie von einer Farm in der nahe gelegenen Wüste Karoo harmoniert mit Mosaiken und neu zusammengesetzten Objekten vom Trödel. Willie Bester selbst zeichnete die Pläne für das runde Haus, wo sich böse Gedanken gar nicht erst einnisten können. Zunächst stolpert man über eine Stahlkonstruktion, die auf den ersten Blick einem Heizkessel ähnelt. Tatsächlich dient sie als Stützpfeiler für die Treppe. Im Salon hängt als Ausdruck der Verehrung ein Porträt Nelson Mandelas (mit Blick zum Himmel). Wie in einem Loft gehen Küche und Esszimmer ineinander über. Die Zimmer liegen im ersten Stock, ein separater Flügel ist den Kindern vorbehalten. Im Atelier nebenan widmet sich Willie Bester, der inzwischen auch in Europa bekannt wurde, neuen Experimenten. Nach und nach füllt sich sein »Industriepark« mit neuen Kreationen. Als eine Quelle des Lebens führen die Fabrikrohre wie Arterien zu einem imaginären Herzen – ein lebendiger Organismus im Einklang mit der Inspiration. Heute ist dies ein Haus, morgen vielleicht schon ein Museum.

C'était une banlieue «White only» – sinistre appellation s'il en est. L'anathème s'appliquait aux habitants mais aussi aux demeures, toutes semblables avec leur façade blafarde. Quand l'artiste métis Willie Bester a investi les lieux, la couleur se devait d'être au rendez-vous.

C'est un extérieur bleuté de bon augure qui accueille le visiteur. Autour, un décor de ferme du Karoo (le désert voisin) flirte avec les mosaïques et des objets de récupération réinventés. Willie Bester a lui-même dessiné les plans d'une maison circulaire, sans recoins pour les mauvaises pensées. On tombe alors sur une structure en acier semblable à une chaudière. Le ton est donné. C'est en vérité un pilier qui soutient l'escalier. Révérence oblige, un grand portrait de Nelson Mandela, yeux au ciel, fait face au salon. À la manière d'un loft, cuisine et salle à manger se relayent; les chambres sont à l'étage, avec une aile pour les trois enfants; l'atelier est contigu. Reconnu désormais en Europe, Willie Bester s'y livre à de nouvelles expérimentations. Mois après mois, ce «parc industriel» s'enrichit de nouvelles créations. Source de vie, les tuyaux d'usine sont des artères reliées à un cœur imaginaire. L'organisme est vivant. Il bat au gré des inspirations. Un jour, c'est une maison, un autre c'est un musée.

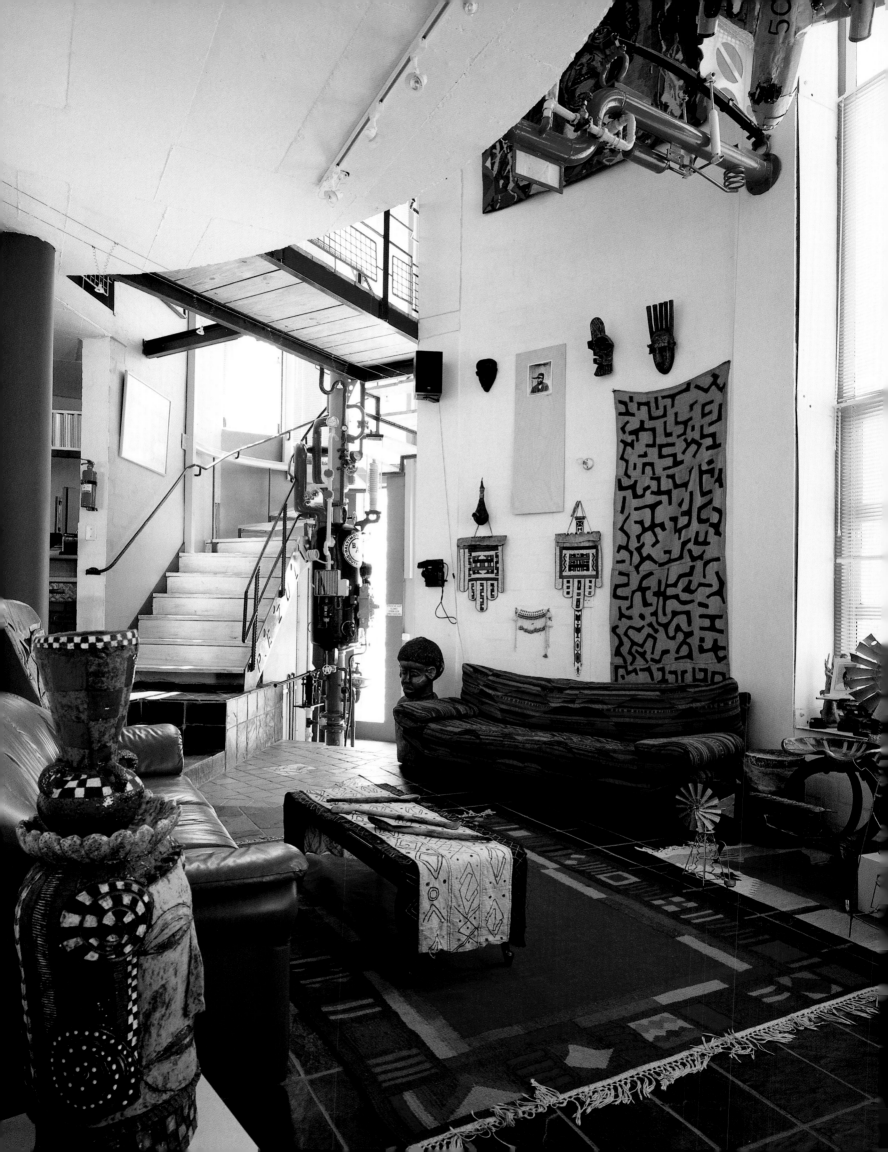

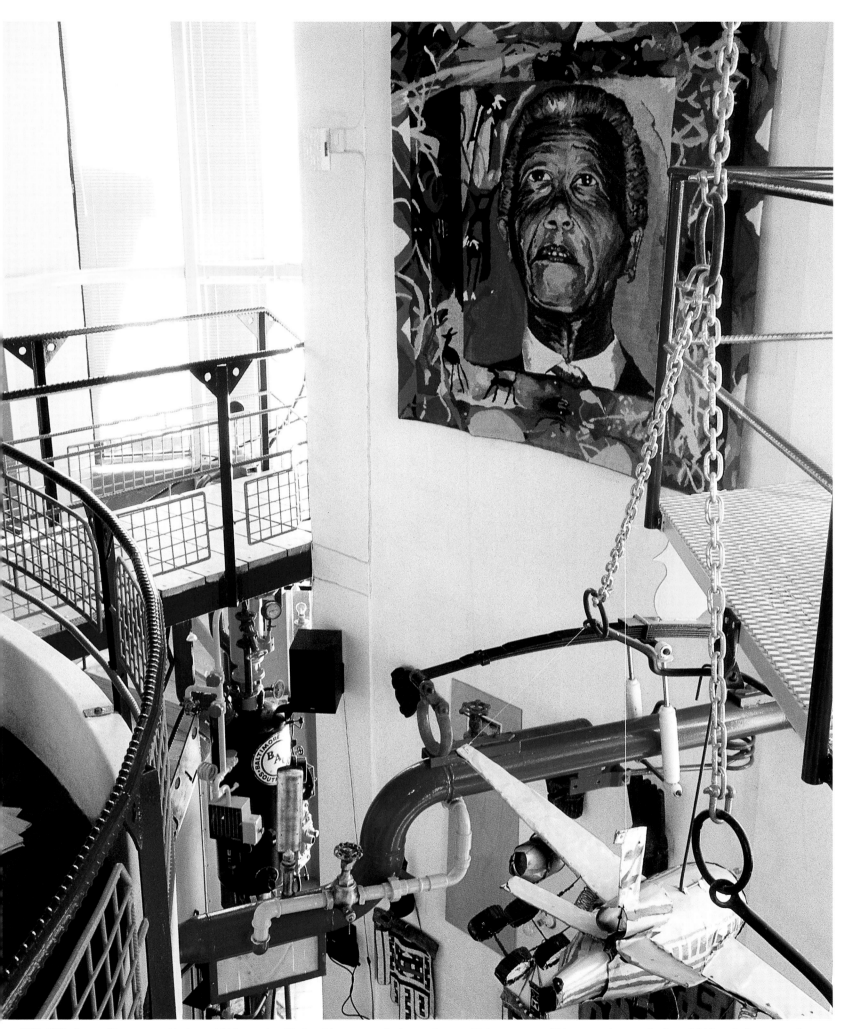

❋ **ABOVE** Willie Bester, 47, grew up with the prohibition against Blacks taking any part in the creative arts. He has represented his country in many foreign exhibitions. In homage to the great man, a portrait of Nelson Mandela dominates his "industrial park". ❋ **OBEN** Der 47-jährige Willie Bester erlebte noch mit, dass Schwarze vom Kunstbetrieb ausgeschlossen waren. Heute vertritt er sein Land auf zahlreichen Ausstellungen. Als Hommage hängt ein Porträt Nelson Mandelas in seinem »Industriepark«. ❋ **CI-DESSUS** Willie Bester, 47 ans, a grandi avec l'interdiction faite aux Noirs de toucher aux arts. Il a représenté son pays dans de nombreuses expositions. En hommage, un portrait de Nelson Mandela domine son «parc industriel».

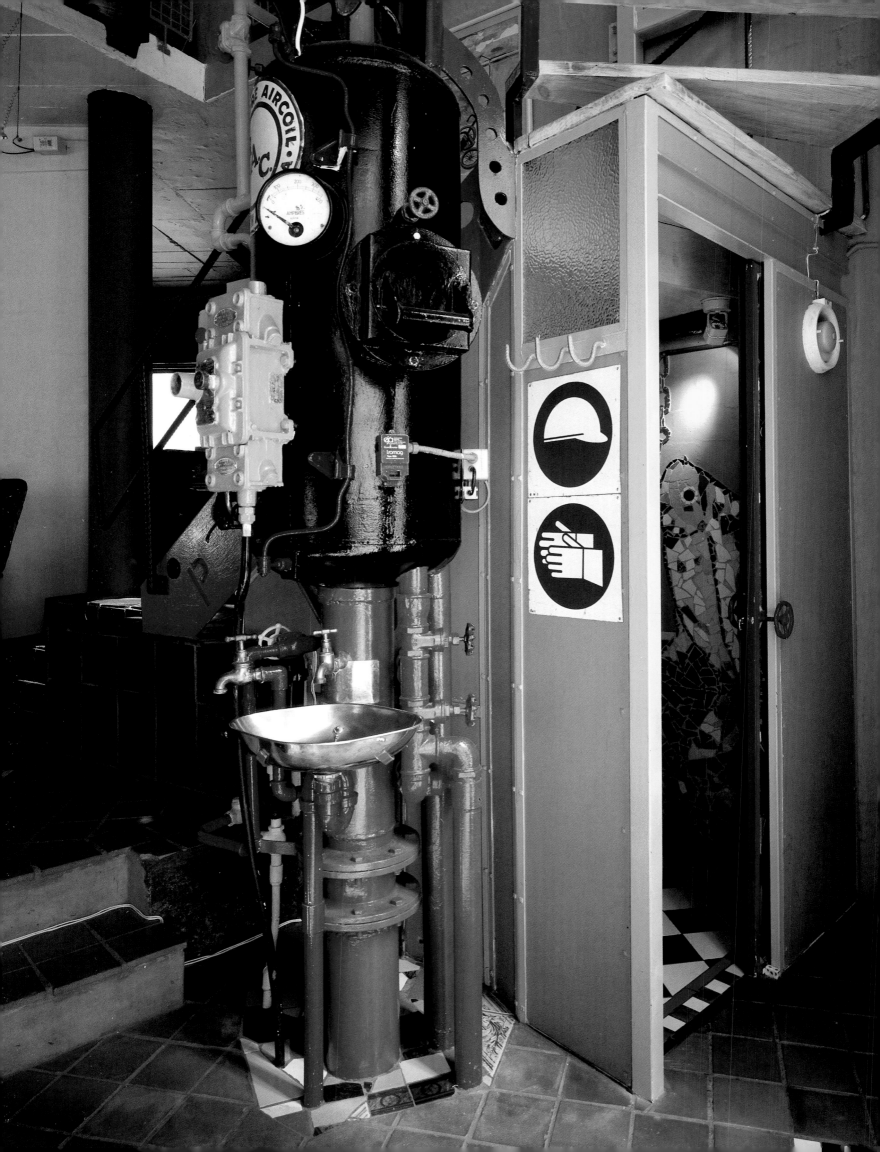

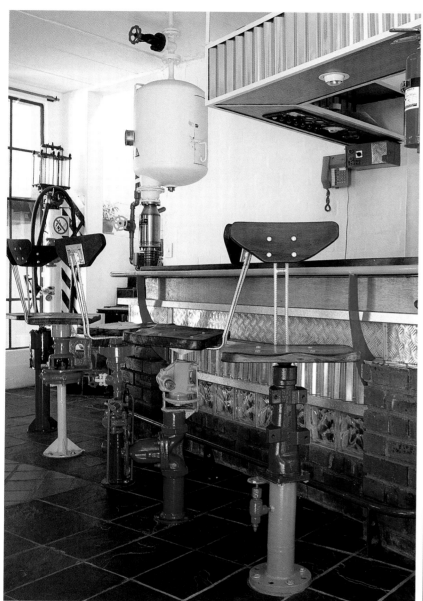

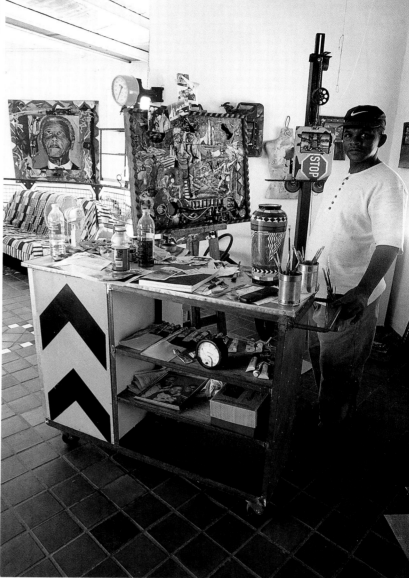

※ **FACING PAGE** The boiler recycled as a column for the staircase is emblematic of the work of this artist, who places industrial society at the centre of his creative work. **ABOVE** The chairs at his bar are recycled drains; in general, his raw materials are pieces of wood, tin cans, squashed paint tubes and other objects picked up on the streets of the townships. ※ **LINKE SEITE** Ein als Treppenpfeiler zweckentfremdeter recycelter Heizkessel ist sinnbildlich für die Arbeiten des Künstlers, der die Industrie in den Mittelpunkt seines Schaffens stellt. **OBEN** Ausrangierte Wasserrohre bilden die Füße der Barhocker. Ausgangsmaterial für Besters Kunstwerke sind oft Holzstücke, Konservendosen, ausgedrückte Farbtuben und verschiedene andere Dinge, die er auf den Straßen der Elendsviertel sammelt. ※ **PAGE DE GAUCHE** La chaudière recyclée en pilier pour l'escalier est emblématique du travail de l'artiste qui place la société industrielle au centre de sa création. **CI-DESSUS** Les fauteuils de son bar sont des conduites d'eau revisitées; de manière générale, ses matières premières sont des bouts de bois, des conserves, des tubes de peinture écrasés et divers objets ramassés dans les rues des bidonvilles.

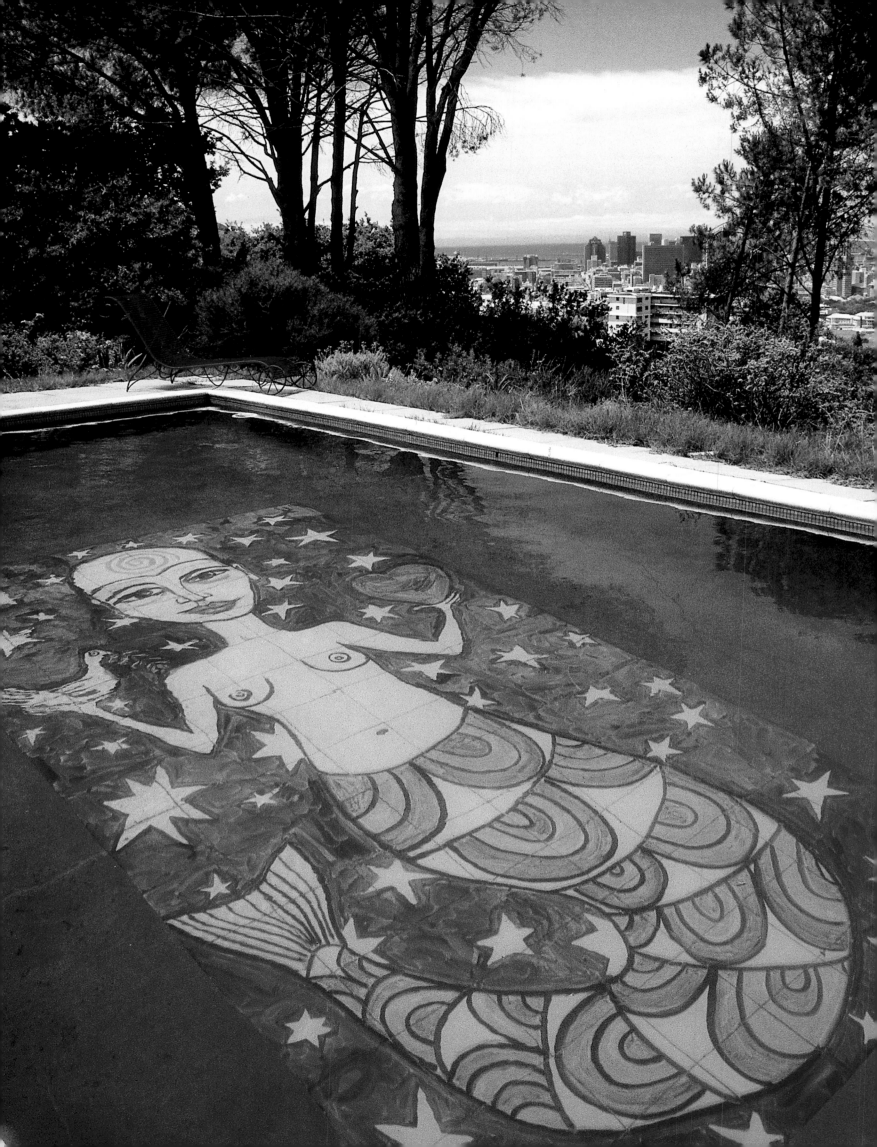

# BEEZY BAILEY
## CAPE TOWN

The home of an iconoclastic painter who salvages furniture
in the shadow of Table Mountain.

"There's a wild sexy garden around it, outrageously spacious," is how David Bowie, who often goes there to paint, describes the house of his South African friend.

Overlooking the city, under the lip of Table Mountain, this reinvented bungalow doesn't look much like a haunt of celebrities. Beezy Bailey appropriated the family plot, colouring and transforming it into something entirely his own. The original space didn't alter, but the interior has lost its innocence somewhat, in the image of the staircase rearing up and out of the living room. The furniture is something of a cocktail, mixed with a strong dose of humour. Beezy is an eccentric painter and he juggles irony and double-take in his "Bleu Yves Klein salon". There are all kinds of influences here. The sense of belonging to several different cultures is one that Beezy plays with, just as he has played with the institutions and their infatuation with Black art. For example, he only needed to adopt the pseudonym of Joyce Ntobe, a *soi-disant* African woman artist, to gain admittance to the collections of the South African National Gallery. There's a siren picked out in mosaic at the bottom of his swimming pool, and she's the emblem of his house. Exhibitionist that he is, the man known to all as "Busy-Bee-Beezy" stoutly resists the wiles of such women every day of his life – and that alone is a tall order.

»Umgeben von einem wilden sexy Garten, schrecklich groß«, so beschrieb David Bowie das Haus seines südafrikanischen Freundes, wohin er sich gern zum Malen zurückzieht.

Oberhalb der Stadt, im Schatten des Tafelbergs liegt der neu gestaltete Bungalow, in dem niemand ein Refugium ruhebedürftiger Berühmtheiten vermuten würde. Beezy Bailey investierte in das Familiengrundstück, weil er einen eigenen Raum bunt gestalten und verändern wollte. Die ursprüngliche Raumaufteilung wurde zwar nicht verändert, aber das Hausinnere hat seine Unschuld verloren, wie man an der Treppe erkennen kann, die den Raum zerschneidet und aussieht, als wäre sie bereit zum Abheben. Die Einrichtung ähnelt einem köstlichen Cocktail mit einer guten Dosis Humor. Als exzentrischer Maler geht Beezy mit einer gehörigen Portion (Selbst-) Ironie an seinen Salon in Yves-Klein-Blau heran, in dem er allerlei Stilrichtungen kombiniert. Der Künstler spielt nicht nur mit dem Multikulti-Gefühl sondern auch mit den Institutionen und der plötzlichen Begeisterung für die Kunst der Schwarzen. Unter dem Pseudonym Joyce Ntobe gab er vor, eine schwarze Afrikanerin zu sein, woraufhin er eingeladen wurde, seine Bilder in der South African National Gallery auszustellen. Auf dem Grund des Swimmingpools wacht eine Sirene als Mosaik – sie ist das Wahrzeichen des Hauses. Der exhibitionistische Busy-Bee-Beezy, wie er genannt wird, widersteht täglich von neuem ihren Sirenengesängen. Zweifellos eine bedeutende Aufgabe.

«Bordée d'un jardin sauvage et sexy, outrageusement spacieuse»: c'est ainsi que David Bowie décrit la maison du copain sud-africain chez qui il aime peindre.

Dominant la ville, sous la Montagne de la Table, le bungalow réinventé n'a pourtant rien d'un repaire de célébrités. Beezy Bailey a investi le terrain familial pour colorer et transformer un espace bien à lui. Le volume original n'a pas tremblé, mais l'intérieur a perdu de son innocence, tel cet escalier qui perce le salon et dont les lignes tentent un envol. Le mobilier est un savoureux cocktail, mélangé avec une bonne dose d'humour. Peintre excentrique, Beezy manie l'ironie et le second degré dans son salon Bleu Yves Klein. Toutes les influences cohabitent ici. Ce sentiment d'appartenance à de multiples cultures, l'artiste en joue comme il a joué avec les institutions et l'engouement pour l'art Noir: il lui a suffi de prendre le pseudonyme de Joyce Ntobe, soi-disant femme africaine, pour entrer dans les collections de la South African National Gallery. Au fond de la piscine, veille une sirène en mosaïque. C'est l'emblème de la maison. Exhibitionniste, Busy-Bee-Beezy comme on le surnomme, résiste chaque jour à ces chants de démon femelle. Ce qui en soi est tout un programme.

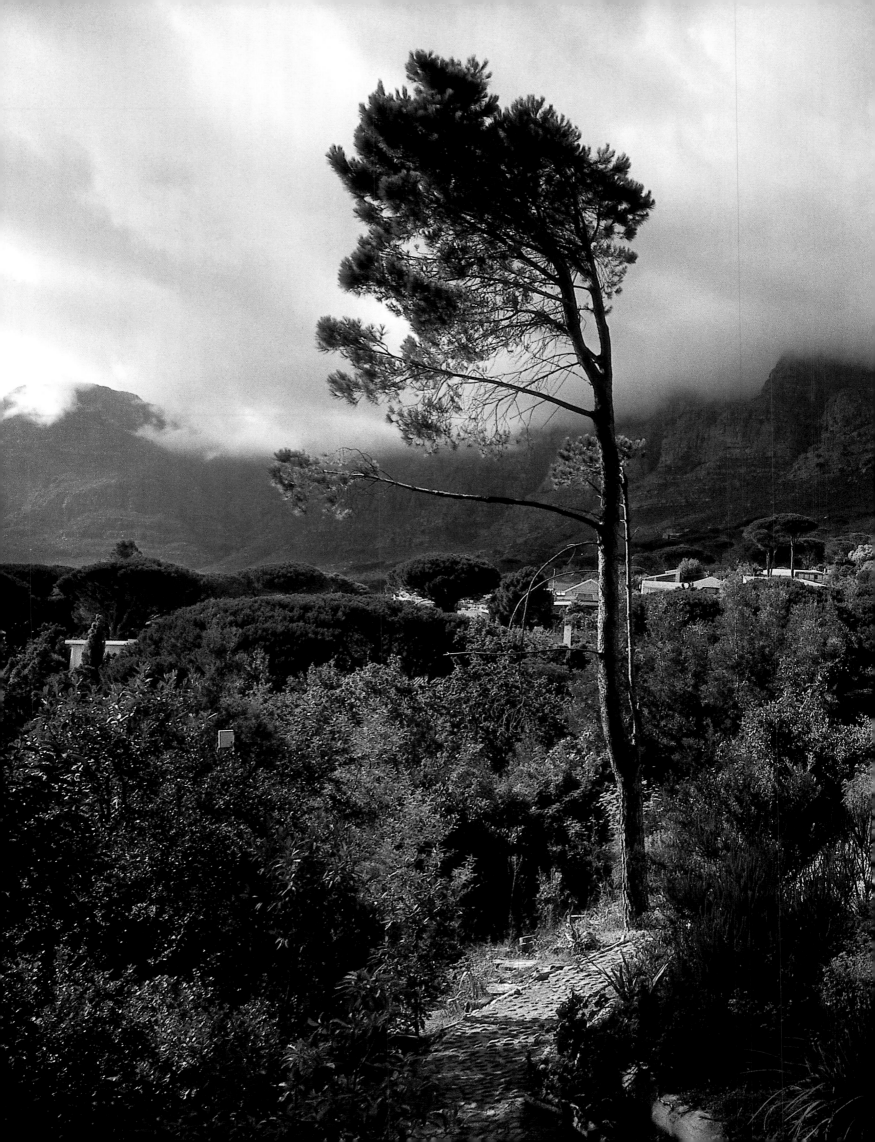

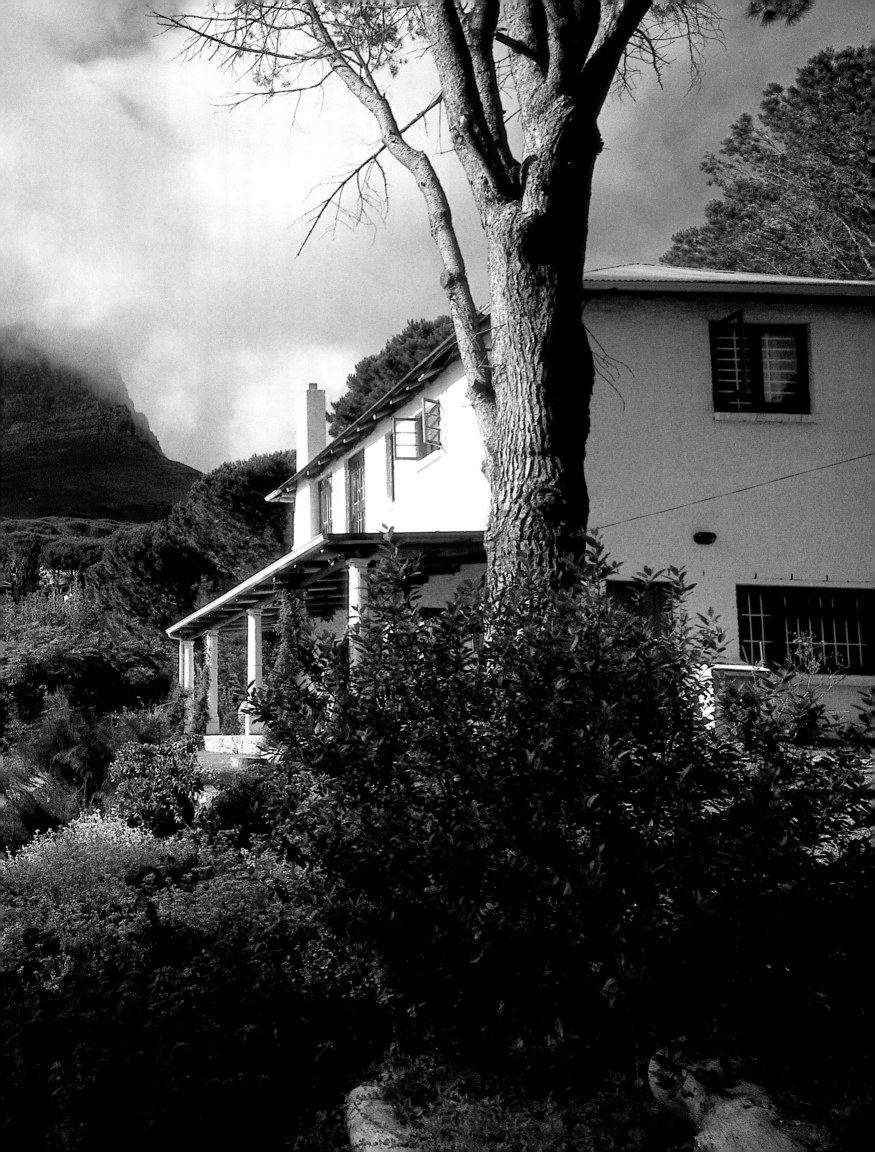

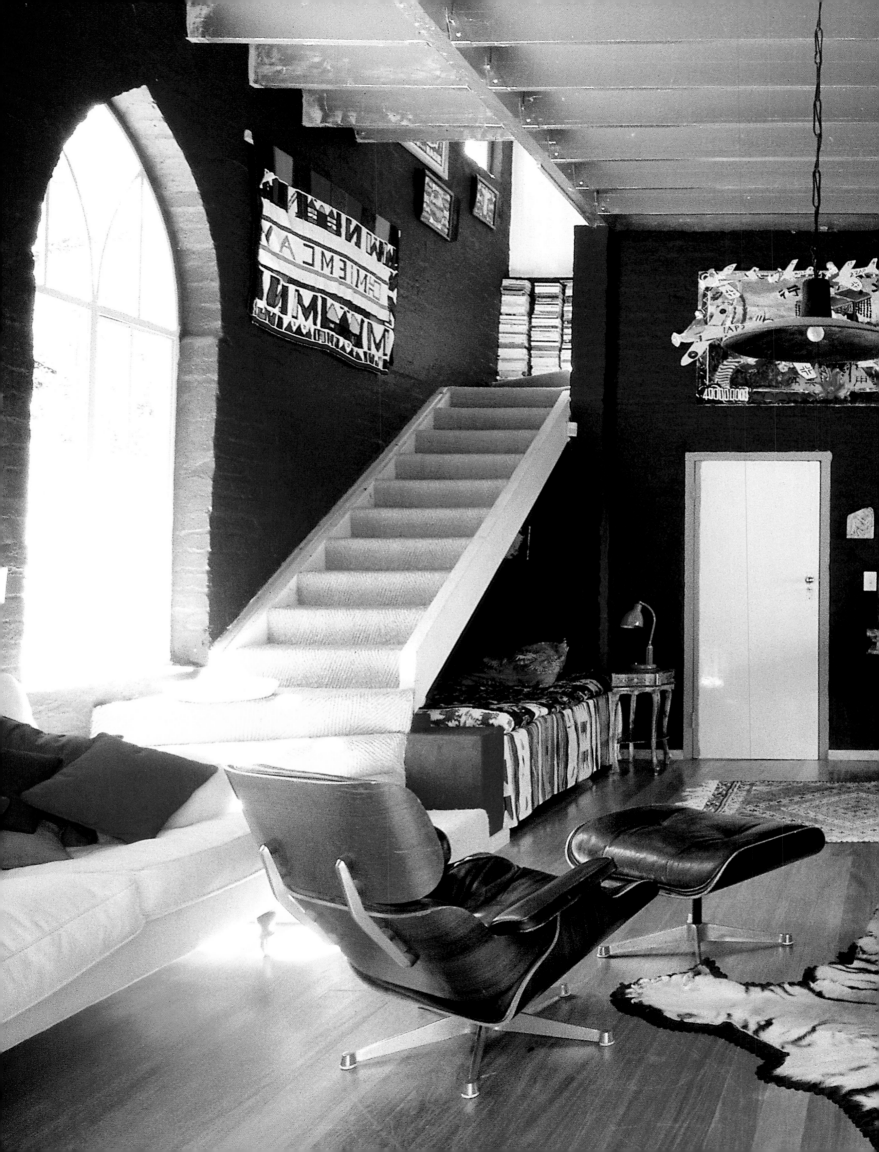

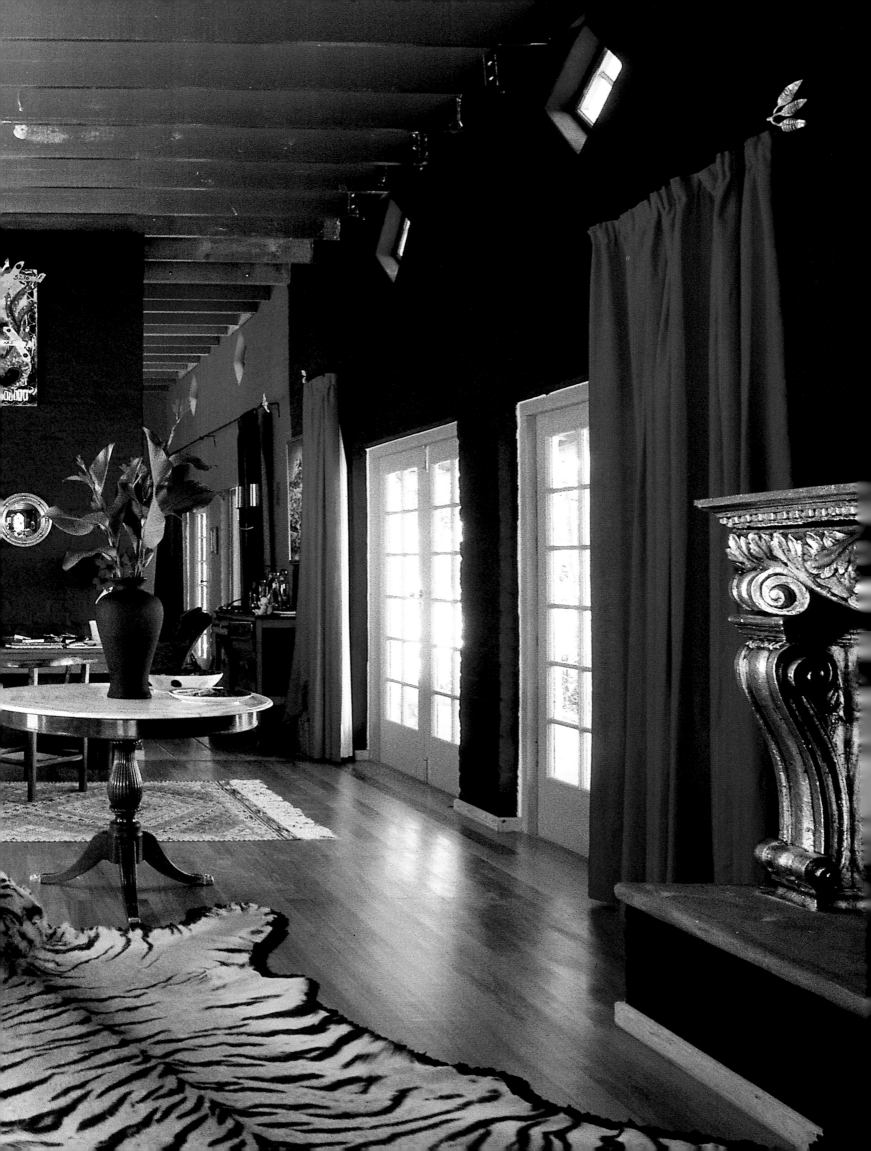

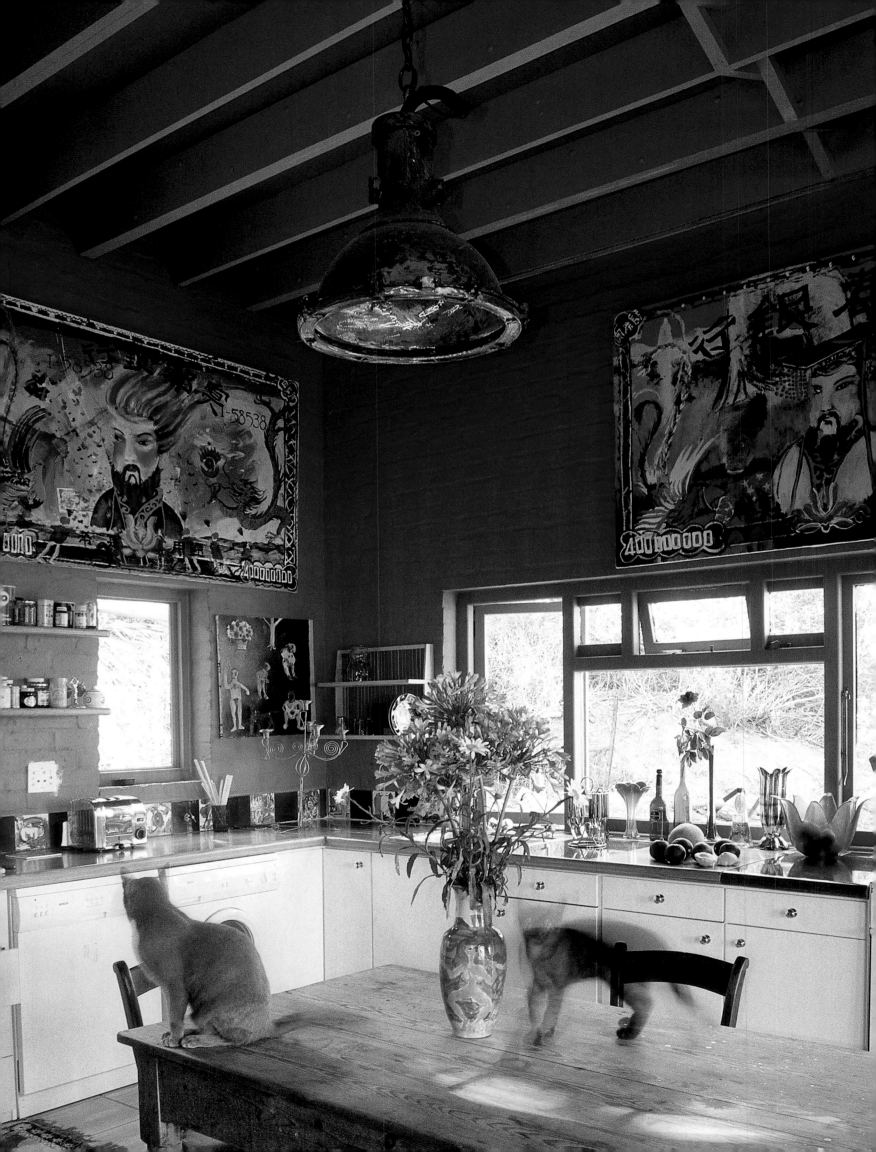

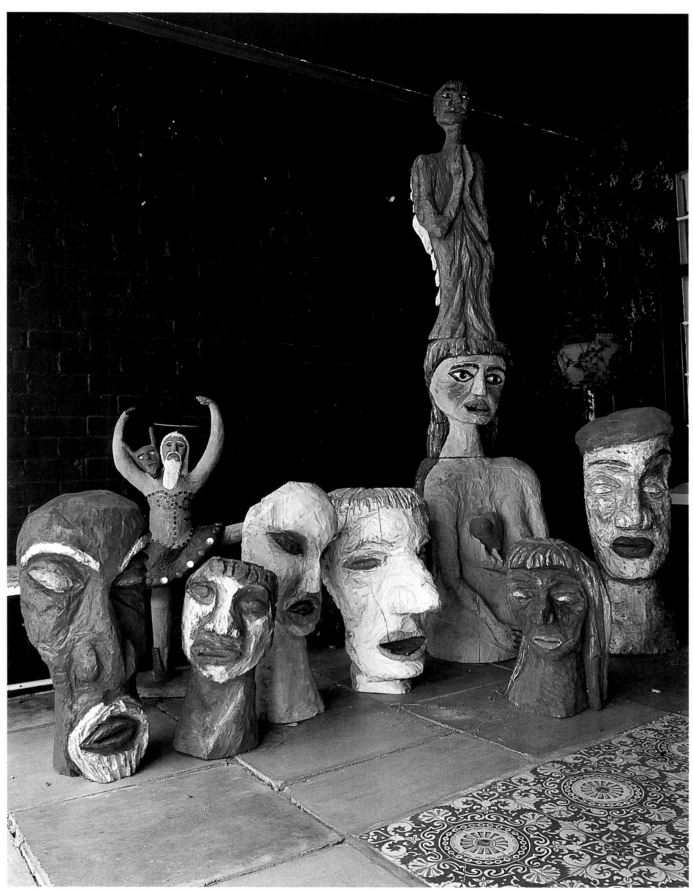

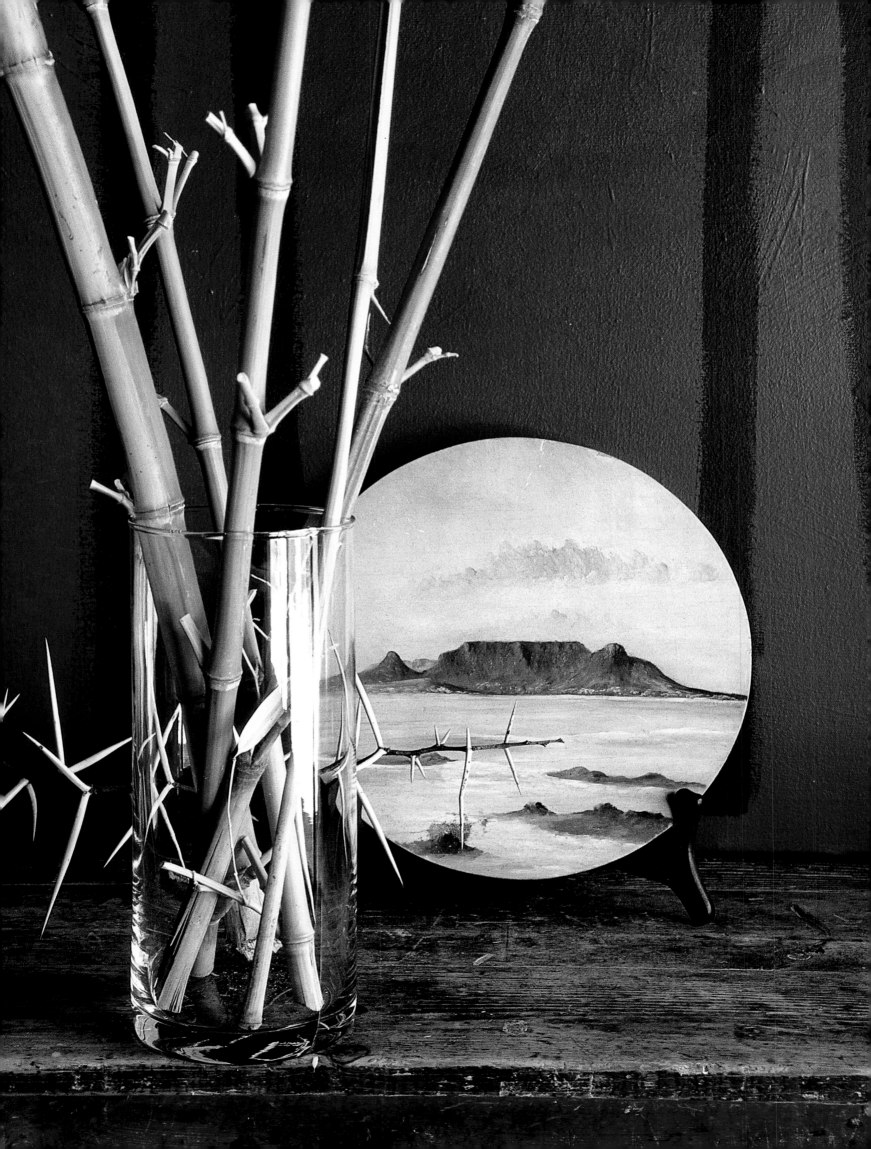

# MALCOLM KLUK

# Cape Town

This navy-blue house in the trendy Greenpoint district
is a reflection of sky and glittering sea.

The sun beats down and the wind blows. The
Cape climate is pure and violent. In imitation of the
open sea, the designer Malcolm Kluk has clothed his
house in blue.

Outside, it hangs over the ocean; inside it's as if
one were under the surface. "My guests find this very
intimate and soothing," he says. "Not surprisingly, in
aurasoma therapy dark blue represents the third eye
of protection and providence." The house is also a
physical expression of its owner's moods. Words have
been scrawled on the walls – Hope, Dreams, Desire –
to form a triptych, a kind of reassuring background
murmur. A line by Dylan Thomas encapsulates the
attitude of Malcolm Kluk: "Rage, rage against the
dying of the light." Dreams are there to come true for
us, if we can only do our best. The designer draws
inspiration for his art from the place in which he lives.
His secret, he says, is that he "… just brings everything together; the assembled effect becomes right,
because I make no effort to superimpose some kind
of preordained look." Malcolm Kluk was born in
Durban and knows England well, having lived there
for eight years. He carries within himself a mix of
influences which he seeks to express in his interior. In
the future other desires will come, along with other
passions, fires and colours.

Kapstadt funkelt in einem Klima, das, mit viel Wind
und Sonne gesegnet, klar und brutal zugleich ist. Der
Designer Malcolm Kluk hat sein Haus ganz in Blau
eingerichtet, als wollte er auf die hohe See hinaus.

Das Haus selbst ragt über dem Meer empor, innen
hat man dagegen eher das Gefühl, unter Wasser zu
leben. »Meinen Gästen gefällt die neue Gemütlichkeit
des Navy Blue. In der Aura-Soma-Therapie steht diese
Farbnuance für das Dritte Auge, das für Schutz und
Vorsehung zuständig ist«, erklärt der Hausherr lächelnd.
Das unter solchem Schutz stehende Haus spiegelt die
Stimmungen seines Bewohners wider. Wie Hinweise
stehen hingekritzelt Wörter an den Wänden. »Hoffnung«, »Träume« und »Lust« bilden ein Triptychon, das
die Menschen glücklich machen soll. Ein Gedicht von
Dylan Thomas veranschaulicht ebenfalls Malcolm
Kluks Philosophie: »Wüte, wüte gegen das Sterben
des Lichts«. Es fordert dazu auf, den Träumen nach-
zuspüren und sie zu verwirklichen. Hirngespinste?
Keineswegs. Der Designer zieht die schöpferische
Kraft für seine Arbeit aus diesem Haus. Verrät er sein
Geheimnis? »Ich bringe alles zusammen, so entsteht
genau die richtige Wirkung, weil eben kein gewollter
›Look‹ aufgesetzt wird.« Malcolm Kluk, der in Durban
geboren wurde und acht Jahre in England gelebt hat,
schöpft aus den Erfahrungen mit verschiedenen Stilrichtungen, die er in seinem Haus zum Ausdruck bringen will. Später werden dann andere Wünsche, Fie-
berträume, Verbrennungen und andere Farben hinzu-
kommen.

Vent et soleil intenses, Cape Town étincelle sous
un climat pur et violent à la fois. Comme pour prendre le large, le styliste Malcolm Kluk a habillé sa maison de bleu.

À l'extérieur, on est suspendu au-dessus de la mer;
à l'intérieur, c'est au contraire comme si on vivait sous
la mer. «Mes invités se réjouissent d'une intimité re-
trouvée grâce au Navy blue. Dans la thérapie aurasoma, cette nuance représente le troisième œil, celui de
la protection et de la providence», sourit-il. Placé sous
un tel patronage, l'habitat est une représentation des
humeurs de son propriétaire. Aux murs, sous forme
d'avertissements, des mots ont été griffonnés. Espoir,
Rêves et Désir forment un triptyque, un «mur-murs»
pour rendre les gens heureux. Un poème de Dylan
Thomas illustre encore la philosophie de Malcolm
Kluk: «Rage, rage contre la lumière mourante», invite à
poursuivre la quête des rêves et de leur accomplisse-
ment. Chimères? Pas le moins du monde. Le styliste
puise l'inspiration de son art dans sa maison. Son
secret? «Je pose tout ensemble et l'effet d'assemble-
ment est juste, car il n'y a pas d'effort pour imposer
un look.» Originaire de Durban, familier de l'Angle-
terre où il a passé huit années, Malcolm Kluk porte en
lui un mélange d'influences qu'il veut reproduire dans
son intérieur. Plus tard, viendront d'autres désirs,
d'autres fièvres, d'autres brûlures, d'autres couleurs.

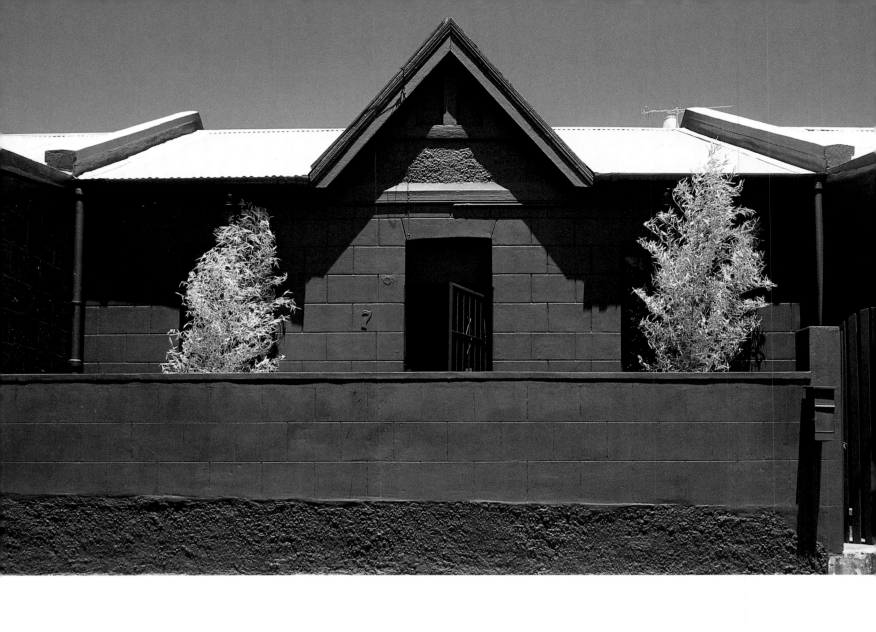

※ **ABOVE** Corrugated iron roof, party walls, terrace on the street, balcony and small yard: the house is typical of this formerly working class Cape area, now fashionable. ※
**OBEN** Wellblechdach, Brandwände, eine Terrasse zur Straße, ein Balkon und ein kleiner Hof – ein völlig normales Haus in dem früheren Arbeiterviertel, wo sich jetzt die Schickimicki-Szene von Kapstadt einnistet. ※ **CI-DESSUS** Toit en tôle ondulée, murs mitoyens, terrasse sur la rue, balcon et petite cour, la maison est typique de cet habitat autrefois populaire, aujourd'hui investi par les bobos de Cape Town.

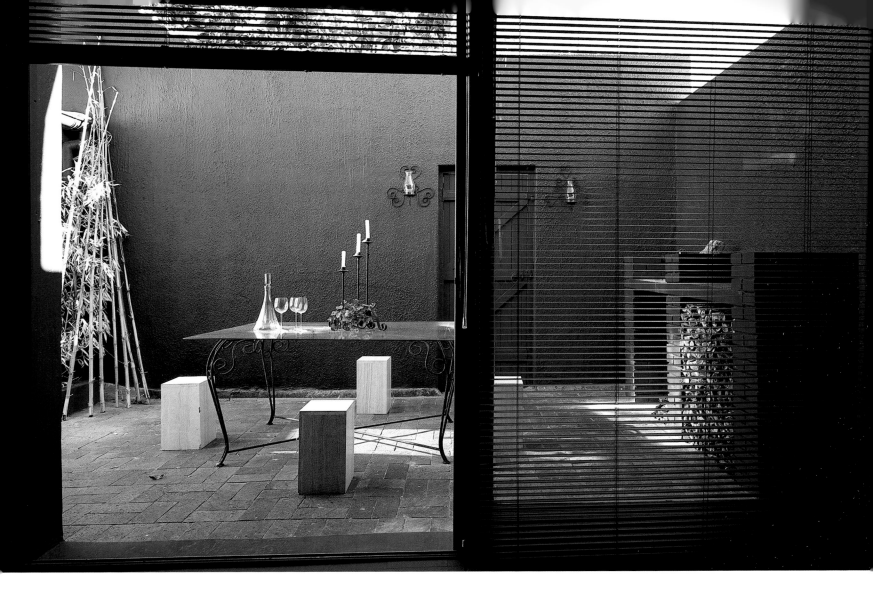

※ **ABOVE** The houses of the Cape all have a small yard contiguous to the living room, which is sheltered from the wind and used for open air dining. **FOLLOWING PAGES** The long table comes from a garage, where it was used as a work bench. Malcolm Kluk came across it when he was buying his car. ※ **OBEN** Die meisten Häuser in Kapstadt haben als Verlängerung des Salons einen kleinen windgeschützten Hof, in dem man unter freiem Himmel essen kann. Als Sitzgelegenheiten dienen Malcolm Kluk weiß lackierte hohe Holzzylinder. **FOLGENDE DOPPELSEITE** Der lange Tisch stammt aus einer Garage, wo er als Werkbank benutzt wurde. Malcolm Kluk entdeckte ihn, als er sein Auto kaufte. ※ **CI-DESSUS** Les maisons de Cape Town mettent toutes en valeur la petite cour à l'abri du vent qui prolonge le salon et sert de salle à manger à ciel ouvert. En guise de sièges, Malcolm Kluk a redécouvert ces plots de bois peints en blanc. **DOUBLE PAGE SUIVANTE** La longue table provient d'un garage où elle servait d'établi. Malcom Kluk l'a découverte en achetant sa voiture.

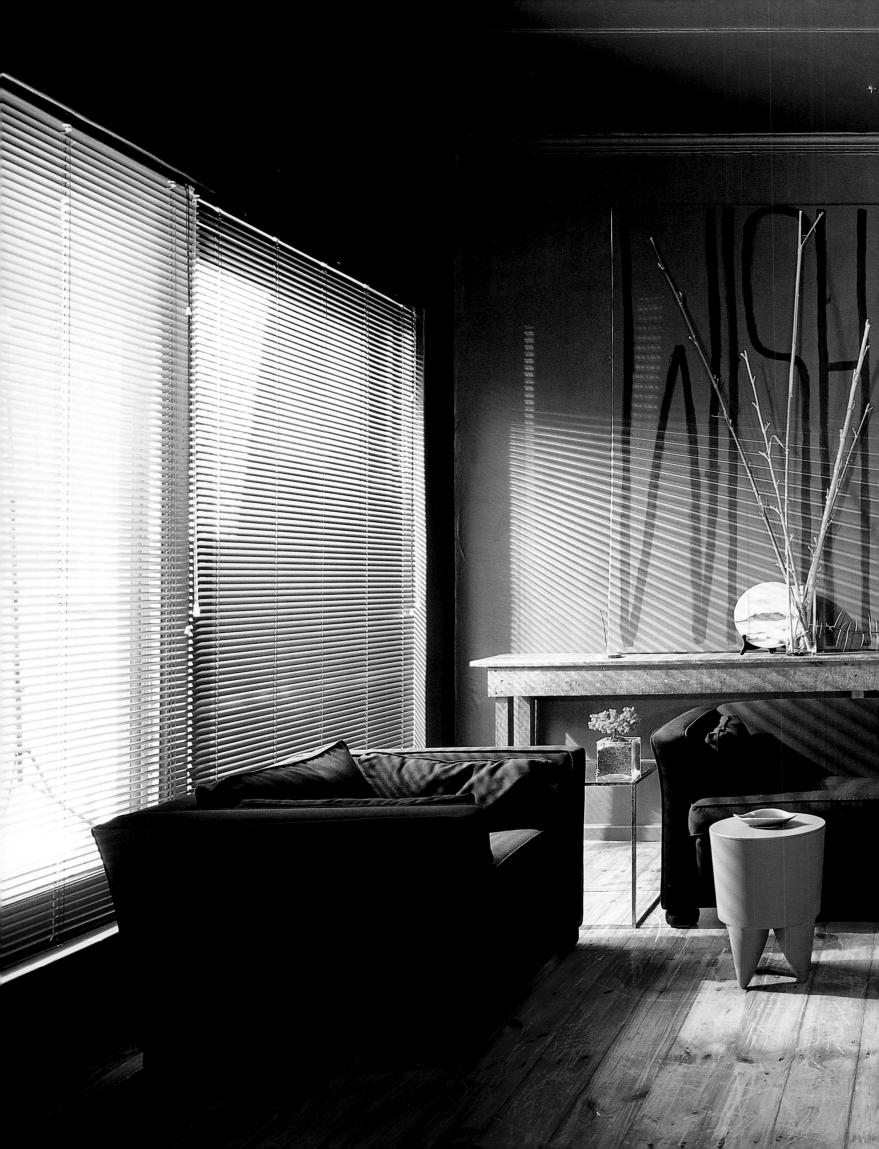

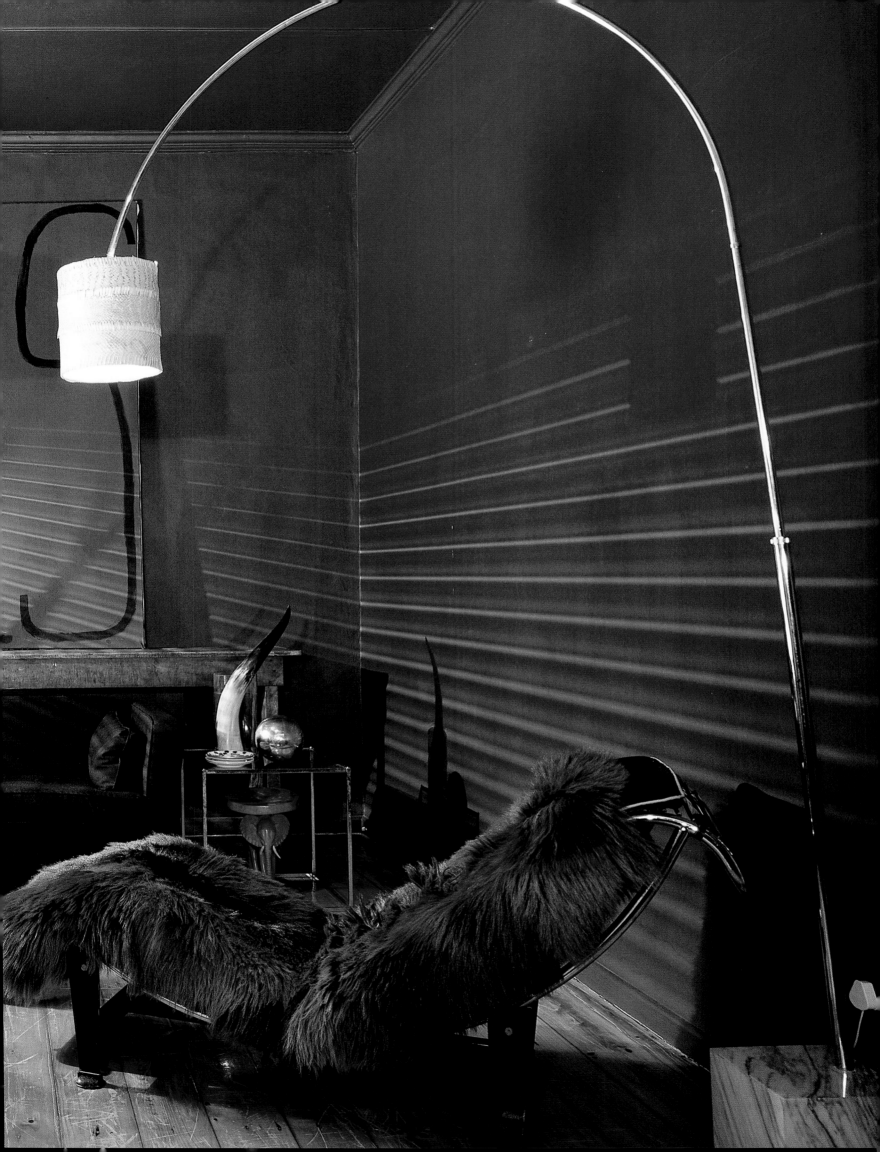

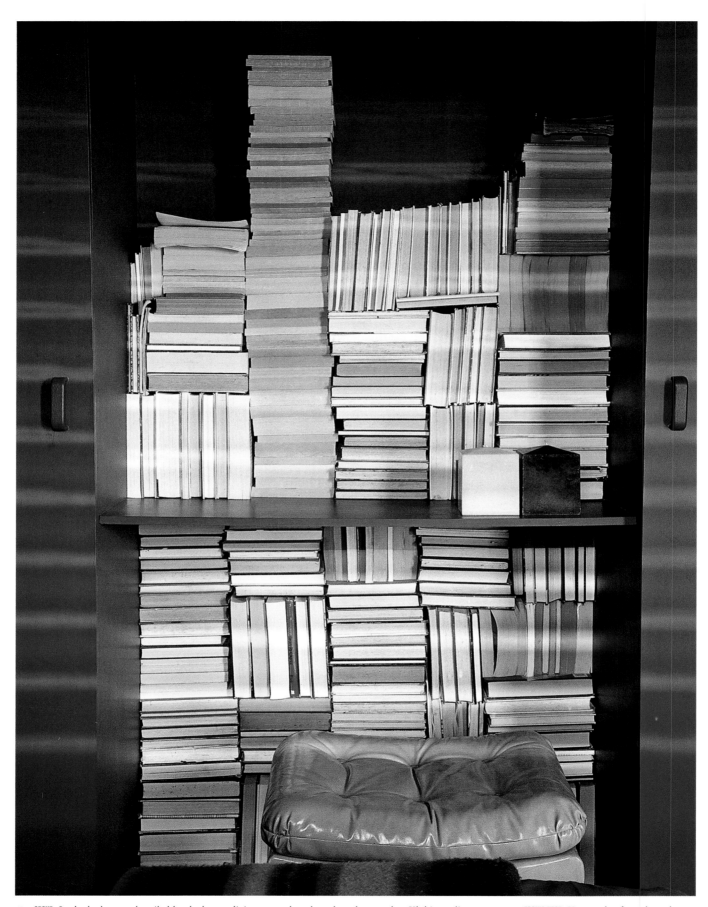

✷ **ABOVE** In the bedroom, the piled books have a living curve, lengthened or shortened as Kluk's reading progresses. **FACING PAGE** Keywords of good conduct on the blue-painted walls. ✷ **OBEN** Die Bücherstapel im Schlafzimmer weisen darauf hin, dass die Bibliothek stets mit Neuzugängen versorgt wird. **RECHTE SEITE** Die Worte an den blau getünchten Wänden fordern uns auf, das Richtige zu tun. ✷ **CI-DESSUS** Dans la chambre à coucher, l'empilement de livres assure à la bibliothèque une courbe vivante, rétrécie ou allongée au fil des lectures. **PAGE DE DROITE** Aux murs badigeonnés de bleus des mots soufflent un code de bonne conduite.

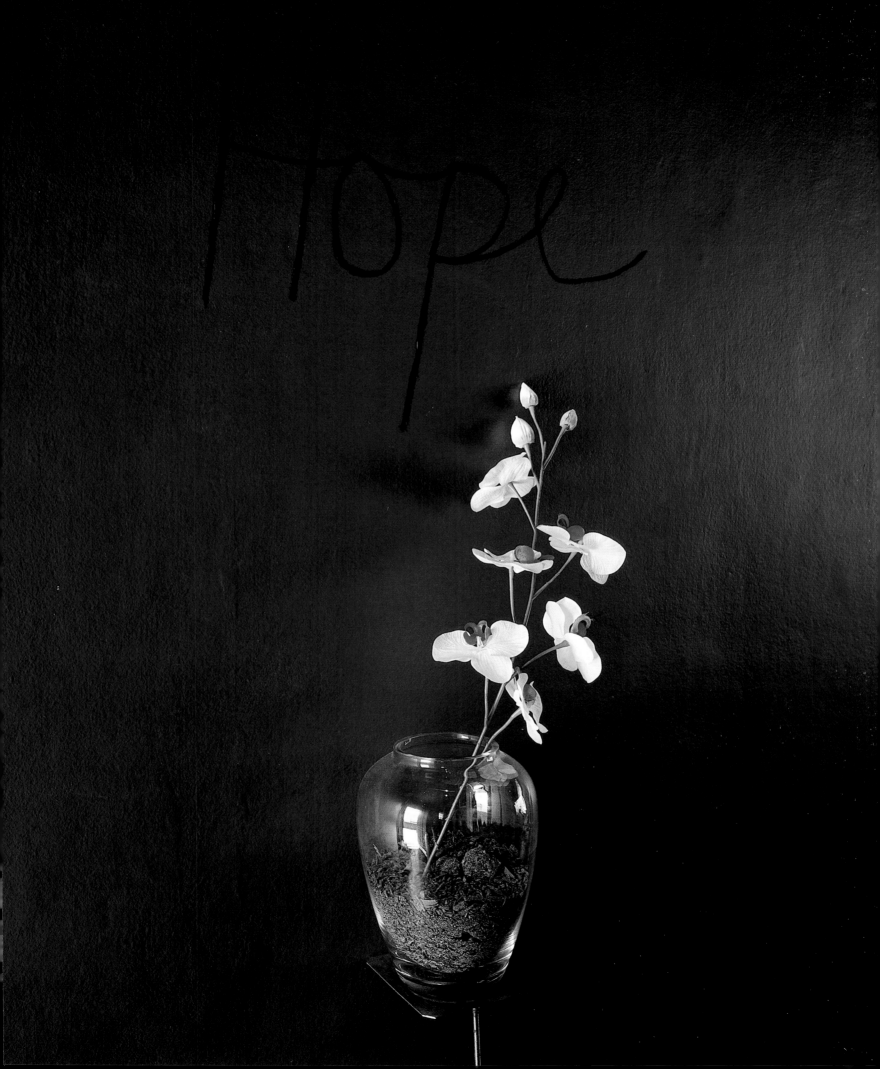

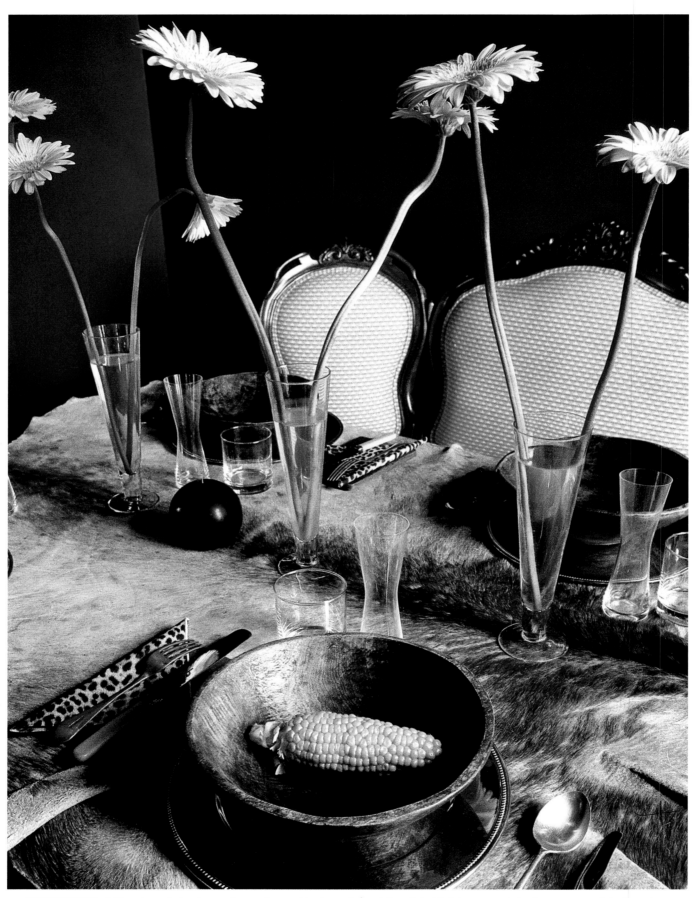

❋ **ABOVE AND FACING PAGE** A Victorian sofa for three and an ordinary table. A metal chandelier, of the kind that are made in the streets round the Cape, hangs from the ceiling. The furniture was patiently assembled from antique shops, markets and friends' houses. ❋ **OBEN UND RECHTE SEITE** Ein dreisitziges viktorianisches Sofa lädt dazu ein, sich an diesem klassischen Tisch niederzulassen. Von der Decke hängt einer der Metalllüster, wie sie auf den Straßen von Kapstadt hergestellt werden. Geduldig hat der Hausherr die Möbel in Antikläden, auf dem Flohmarkt oder bei Freunden gesammelt. ❋ **CI-DESSUS ET PAGE DE DROITE** Un sofa trois places victorien sert d'assise à une table des plus classique. Au plafond, un lustre en métal comme on en fabrique dans les rues de Cape Town. Le mobilier a été patiemment rassemblé auprès d'antiquaires, dans des foires ou chez des amis.

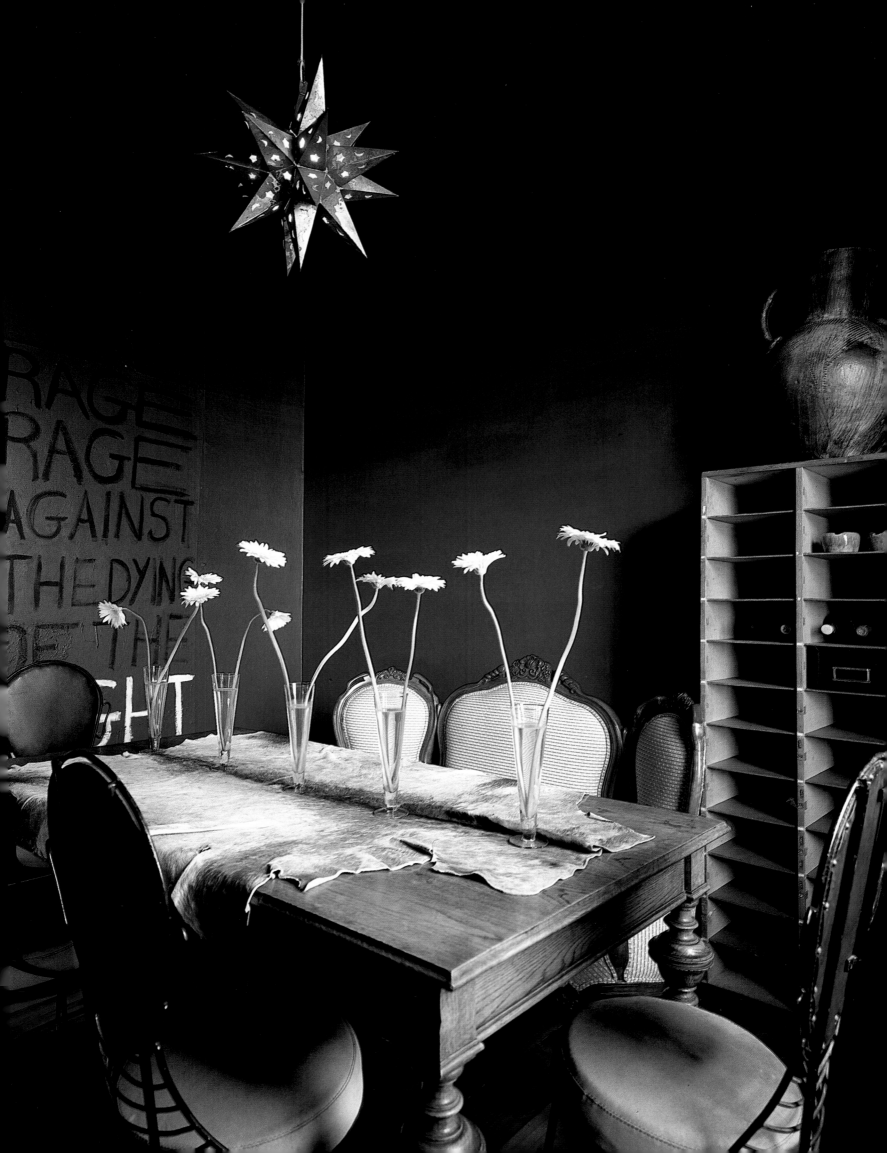

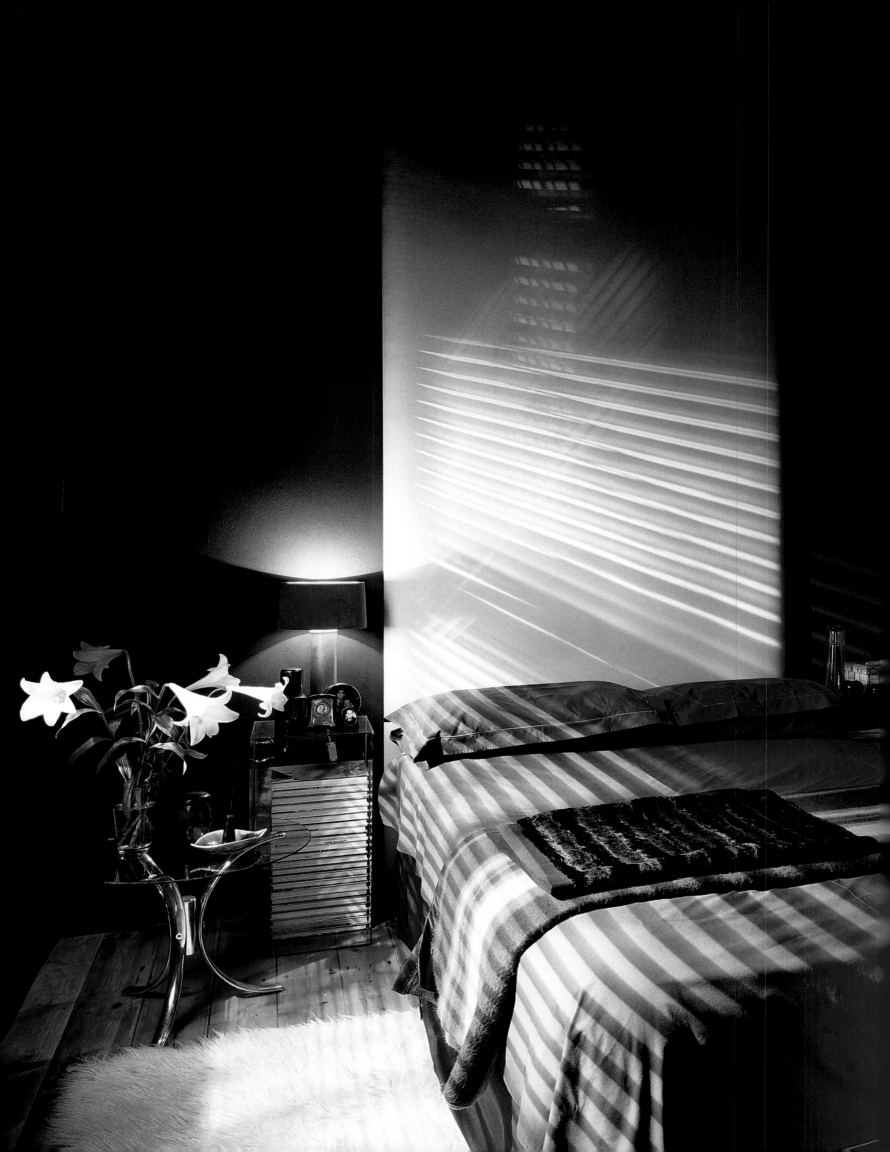

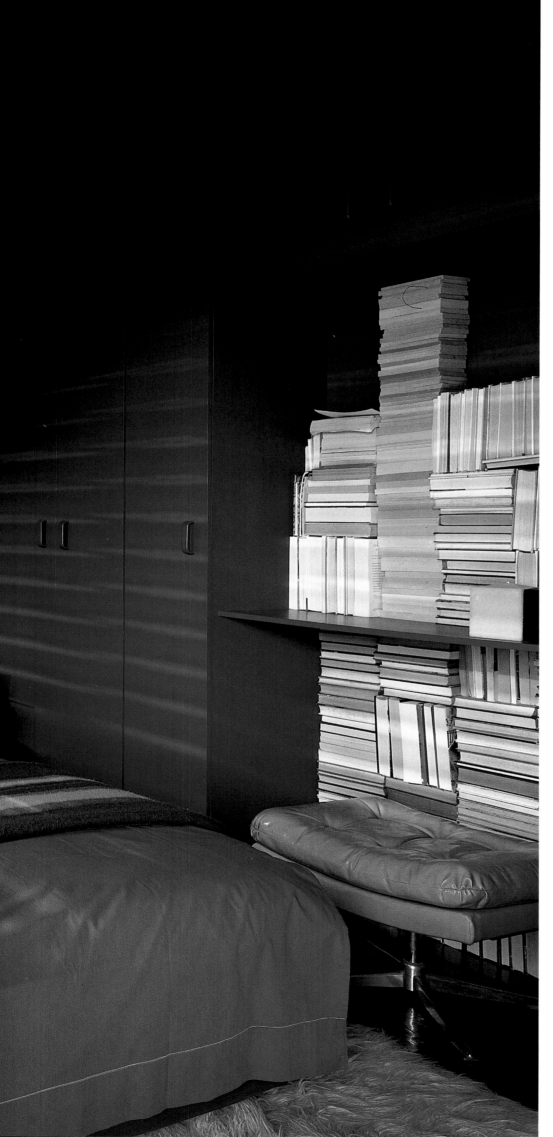

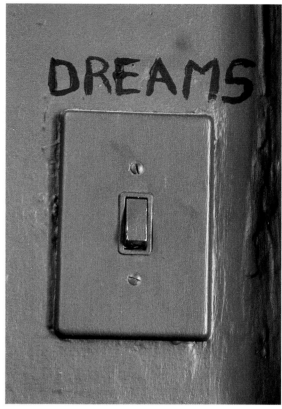

❊ **LEFT** The bedroom is a mix of styles, with books and personal objects. The owner views his furniture as so many photographs that precisely evoke moments in time, or people. Dream or reality? ❊ **LINKS** Im Schlafzimmer gehen die verschiedenen Stilrichtungen eine harmonische Verbindung mit den Büchern und anderen persönlichen Dingen ein. Der Hausherr betrachtet seine Möbel wie Fotografien, die punktgenau Momente und Personen heraufbeschwören können. Traum oder Wirklichkeit? ❊ **A GAUCHE** La chambre marie les styles avec des livres et des objets personnels. Le propriétaire considère ses meubles comme des photographies qui évoquent avec précision des moments ou des personnes. Rêve ou réalité?

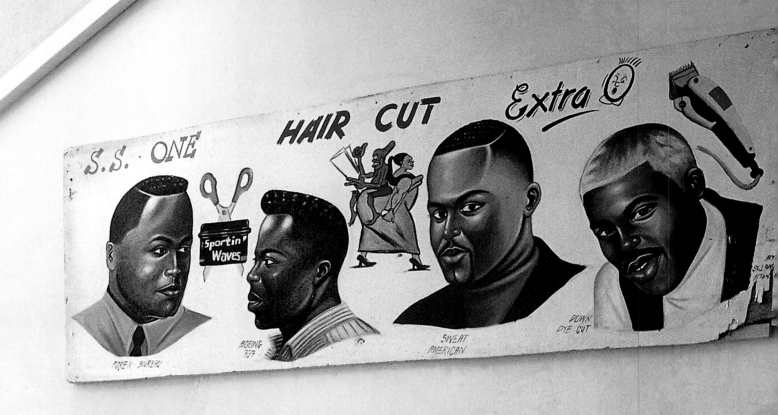

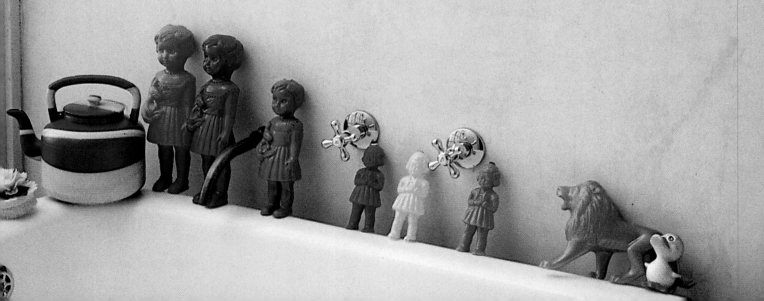

# TRACY RUSHMERE & PETER MALTBIE
## CAPE TOWN

Here the influences of many continents co-exist, though Africa predominates.

**An Indian spear on one side of the bed, African statues on the other – such is the norm for the owners of this house in the centre of the Cape.**

The need to combine various genres is a natural one in an interior developed by Tracy Rushmere, who runs a well-known shop in town called African Image, and Peter Maltbie, a photographer of Amerindian origin. All roads intersect here, with a kilim from Turkey on the pale wood floor, a robe from the Nigerian Hausa tribe on the wall, a Ghanaian bedcover on the bed, and an ivory lion from Mozambique. While there's African art everywhere – even the sound system is kept in a Zulu meat cabinet – there are touches of the Orient and South America to complete the picture, with Indian tables, decorative stones from the Far East, and above the bed a traditional Indian shield with medicinal virtues made by Peter Maltbie. Being open to the world means not being blind to one's surroundings, and Tracy Rushmere, a South African, hasn't neglected antiques made by the Boer settlers who reached the Cape three centuries ago. An example is her 19th century wooden chair, known locally as a *boerstoel*. The space is regularly enriched with finds like this.

**Auf der einen Seite des Kopfendes eine indische Lanze, auf der anderen afrikanische Statuen – deutlicher kann man den Geschmack des Hausbesitzerpaares mitten in Kapstadt nicht auf den Punkt bringen.**

Beide haben das Bedürfnis, Genregrenzen zu überwinden – Tracy Rushmere, berühmt für ihr Geschäft African Image und Peter Maltbie, Fotograf indianischer Abstammung. Von Norden nach Süden kreuzen sich die Stile, wie bei dem türkischen Kelim auf hellem Holzboden oder der Robe vom Stamm der Hausa aus Nigeria an der Wand, der Tagesdecke aus Ghana oder auch den elfenbeinernen Löwen aus Mosambik. Die allgegenwärtige afrikanische Kunst (sogar die Musikanlage steckt in einem Vorratsschrank der Zulu) wird ergänzt durch östliche oder südamerikanische Einrichtungsgegenstände, durch indische Tische, Schmucksteine aus Fernost oder den über dem Bett angebrachten indianisch anmutenden Schild, der Heilkräfte besitzen soll – selbst gemacht von Peter Maltbie. Wer weltoffen ist, richtet seinen scharfen Blick auch auf die eigene Umgebung. Die Südafrikanerin Tracy Rushmere interessiert sich jedenfalls für die Antiquitäten der Buren (jener holländischstämmigen Bevölkerung, die seit über 300 Jahren am Kap siedelt), beispielsweise für diesen *boerstoel*, einen Holzstuhl aus dem 19. Jahrhundert. Nach und nach tragen die beiden Hausbesitzer immer neue Funde zusammen.

**Une lance indienne d'un côté de la tête de lit, des statues africaines de l'autre, comment mieux résumer le parti pris des propriétaires de cette maison située au centre de Cape Town?**

Ce besoin de marier les genres s'exprime naturellement dans l'intérieur de Tracy Rushmere, célèbre en ville pour sa boutique African Image, et de Peter Maltbie, photographe aux origines amérindiennes. Du Nord au Sud, les routes se croisent avec ce kilim de Turquie sur le sol en bois blond, cette robe de la tribu Hausa du Nigeria sur un mur, ce dessus-de-lit du Ghana, ou encore ce lion en ivoire mozambicain. Si l'art africain est partout (même la chaîne hi-fi est placée dans un garde-manger zoulou), des touches orientalistes ou sud-américaines complètent le tableau, avec les tables indiennes, les pierres décoratives d'Extrême-Orient, et toujours au-dessus du lit, ce bouclier aux vertus médicinales dans la tradition indienne fabriqué par Peter Maltbie. Être ouvert au monde ne signifie pas pour autant être aveugle à ce qui les entoure, et Tracy Rushmere, Sud-Africaine, ne néglige pas les antiquités des Boers (Hollandais ayant débarqué il y a trois siècles), avec, notamment, cette chaise en bois du 19e siècle appelée *boerstoel*. L'espace s'enrichit régulièrement de trouvailles à l'occasion d'une nouvelle pêche aux trésors.

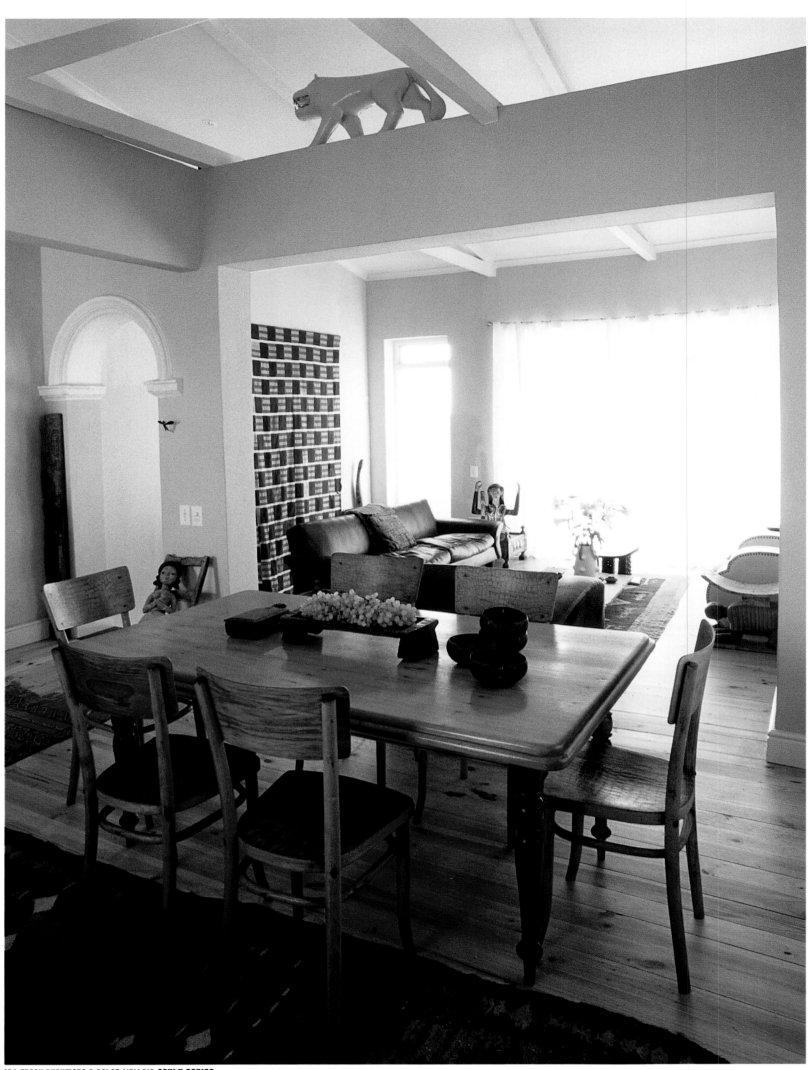

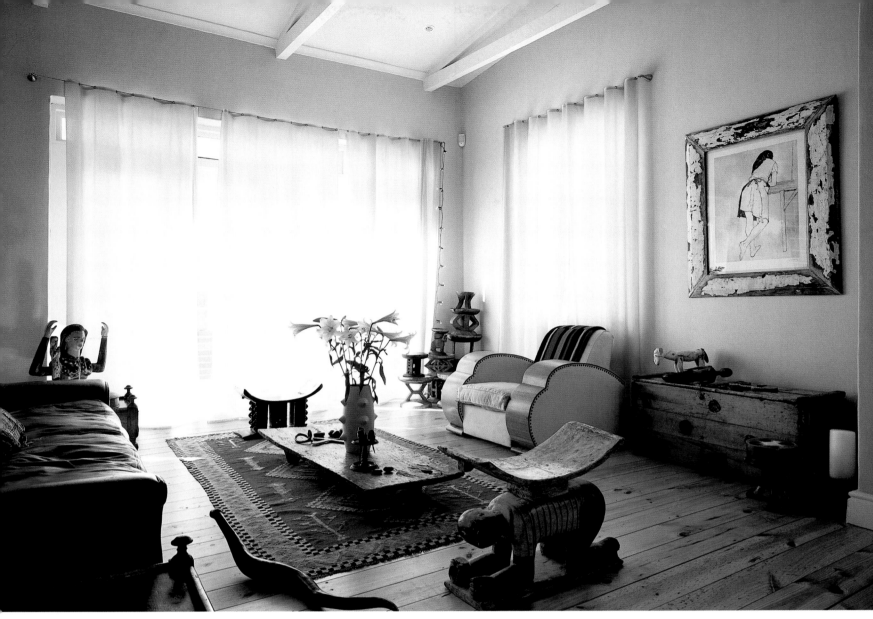

✳ **FACING PAGE AND ABOVE** The living room, like the rest of the house, is a fine mix of African artifacts (statues and stools) and Art Deco furniture, always reference for Tracy Rushmere.
**BELOW** The bedroom symbolizes the double culture of the owners, with its African influences (note the Ghanaian bedcover) and American Indian religious objects. ✳ **LINKE SEITE UND OBEN**
Wie das Haus insgesamt bildet auch der Salon eine geschmackvolle Mischung aus afrikanischen Raritäten (Statuen und Schemel) und Art-déco-Möbeln, Tracy Rushmeres Spezialität.
**UNTEN** Das Schlafzimmer spiegelt die beiden kulturellen Welten der Hausbesitzer wider – die Tagesdecke kommt aus Ghana, die Kultgegenstände stammen von amerikanischen Indianern. ✳ **PAGE DE GAUCHE ET CI-DESSUS** Le salon, à l'image de la maison, est un savoureux mélange de curiosités africaines (statues et tabourets) et de meubles Art Déco, période de référence pour Tracy Rushmere. **CI-DESSOUS** La chambre à coucher symbolise la double culture des propriétaires avec ses influences africaines (dessus-de-lit du Ghana) et ces objets cultuels des Indiens d'Amérique.

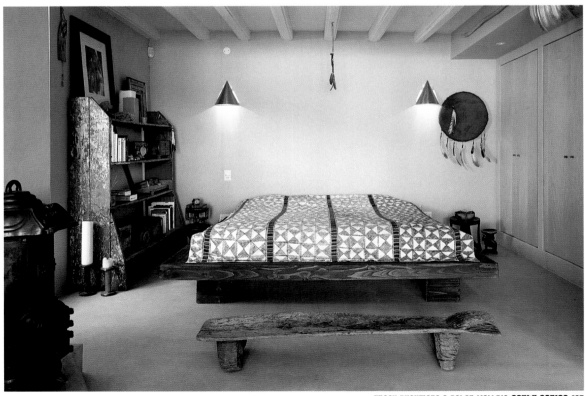

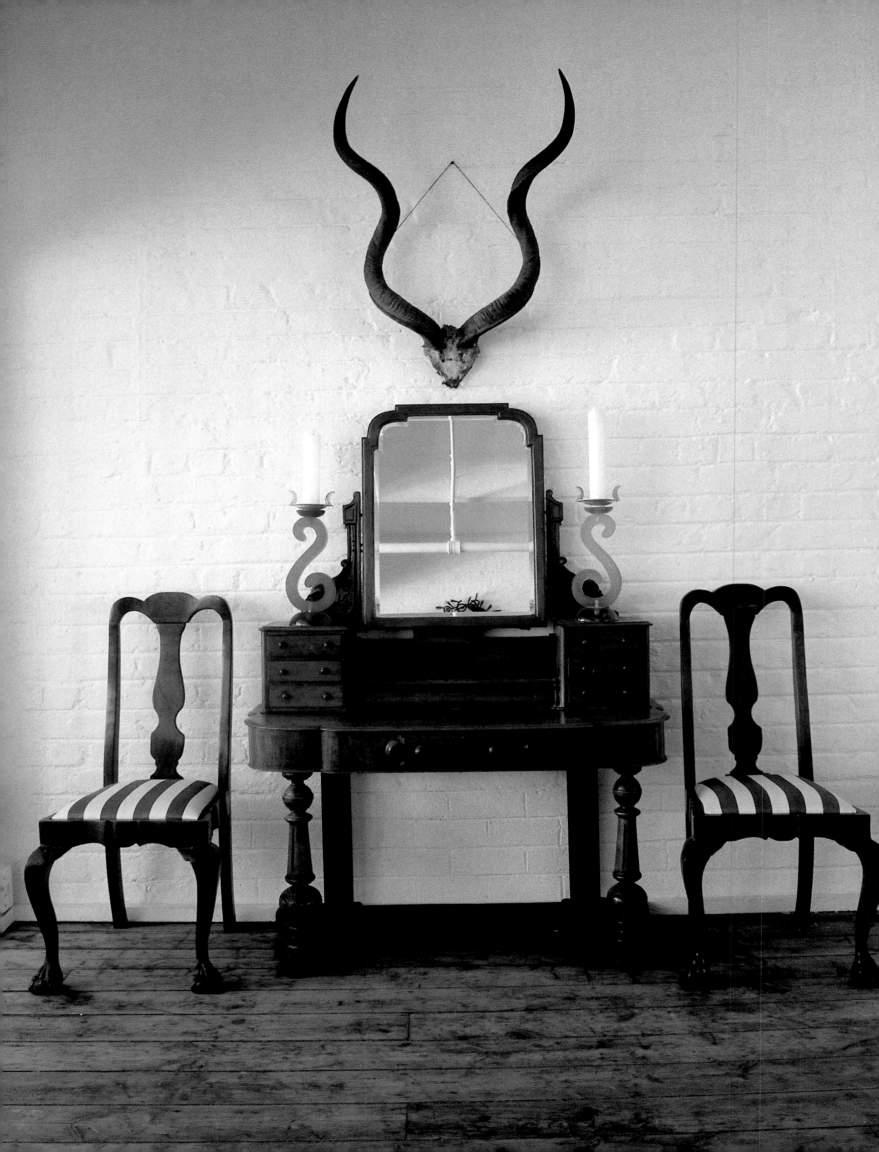

# DE OUDE SCHUUR
## Cape Town

A city centre loft,
high above the celebrated Malay quarter.

When apartheid was still functioning in South Africa, the heart of Cape Town was pretty much out of bounds. Today all that's changed. The area around Long Street, Bree Street and up to Kloof Street is full of people, galleries and crowded bars. Craig Port's loft is in the middle of all this.

Like its forerunners in New York, London and Paris, the space preserves its original shape as a warehouse, though the ambience is softened by subtle decoration. At all times of day, sunshine floods across the pale wood floors. Light is the cardinal element: there are windows everywhere, looking out towards Table Mountain and the town. The walls are of brick, covered in white: they exemplify the approach of Craig Port, which has been to preserve the authenticity of the place and only to give it the thinnest veneer of covering. There's no veranda, no walkway and no unnecessary effects: this is relentless industrial chic, completely austere. All the purchases for the loft were made in Long Street, at auctions or in Cape Town second hand shops. There's nothing ostentatious, only the occasional small luxury, such as the Art Deco table picked up at Groot Schuur Hospital, the HQ of the celebrated Dr. Christian Barnard.

Zu Zeiten der Apartheid wollte niemand so recht in die Innenstadt – das ist heute anders. In der Umgebung der Long Street, der Bree Street und weiter oben zur Kloof Street hin sind Galerien und Bars stets gut besucht. Das Loft liegt mittendrin.

Wie in New York, London oder Paris wahrt es seine Lageratmosphäre, die jedoch mit Hilfe einer wohl überlegten Dekoration wohnlich gestaltet wurde. Den ganzen Tag lang wirft die Sonne ein Streifenmuster auf das helle Parkett. Helligkeit wird hier insgesamt groß geschrieben: Es gibt überall Fenster zum Tafelberg oder zum Stadtzentrum. Die weiß getünchten Ziegelwände verraten viel über Craig Ports Methode, die Ursprünglichkeit des Ortes zu wahren, indem er seine eigenen Vorstellungen kaum wahrnehmbar einbringt. Veranden, komfortable Übergänge, platzraubende Kunstsammlungen oder überflüssige Effekte sucht man hier vergebens. Der Hausherr setzt auf Industrie-Chic, auf karge, eher nüchterne Akzente. Die Einrichtung stammt aus der Umgebung der Long Street, von Auktionen, Versteigerungen oder aus vereinzelten Trödelläden. Angeben ist verpönt, aber ein wenig Luxus darf sein, wie dieser Art-déco-Tisch, den Craig Port in der Groot-Schuur-Klinik aufgetrieben hat, wo der berühmte Professor Christian Barnard einst operierte. Eine gute Wahl. Wer schlicht und einfach lebt, muss keine Herzkrankheiten fürchten …

Au temps de l'apartheid, le cœur de la cité était un lieu infréquentable. Aujourd'hui, tout a changé. C'est autour de Long Street, Bree Street et en remontant sur Kloof Street, que la ville étale sa liberté avec ses galeries et ses bars. Ce loft est au milieu de la centrifugeuse.

Comme ses modèles de New York, Londres ou de Paris, il préserve sa forme d'entrepôt et adoucit l'ambiance à l'aide d'une décoration pointue. À tout instant de la journée, les rayons du soleil strient le parquet en bois clair. La luminosité est d'ailleurs un élément essentiel: partout des fenêtres sont percées en direction de la Montagne de la Table ou du centre-ville. Les murs de briques recouverts de blanc témoignent de la démarche de Craig Port: préserver l'authenticité du lieu, ne revêtir l'ensemble que d'une fine pellicule. Point de véranda, de passerelles, d'encombrantes collections ou d'effets superfétatoires: on la joue industriel chic, dans la sobriété assumée. Le shopping a été réalisé autour de Long Street, aux enchères ou chez les quelques brocanteurs de la ville. Rien d'ostentatoire, juste de petits luxes, comme cette table Art Déco chinée au Groot Schuur Hospital où officiait le célèbre professeur Christian Barnard. Un bon choix. À vivre ainsi dans la simplicité, on limite les risques cardiaques…

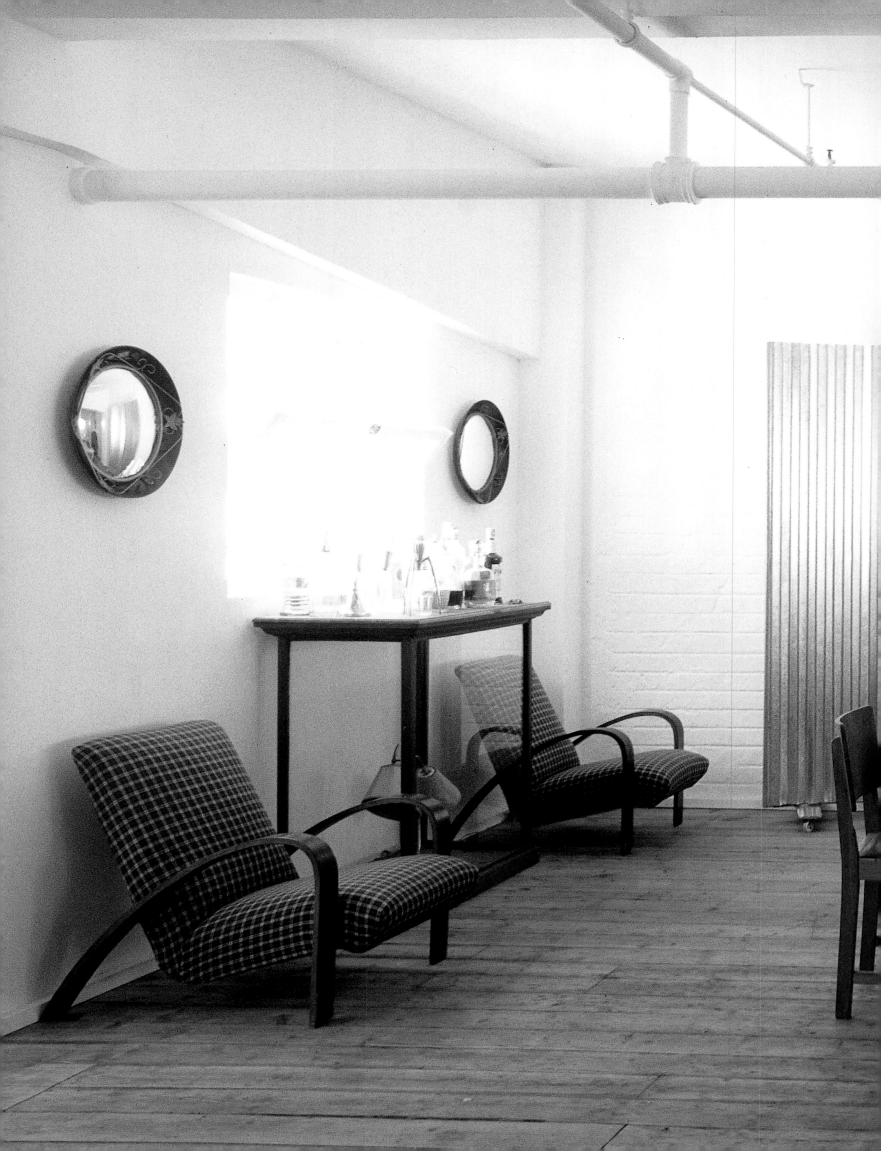

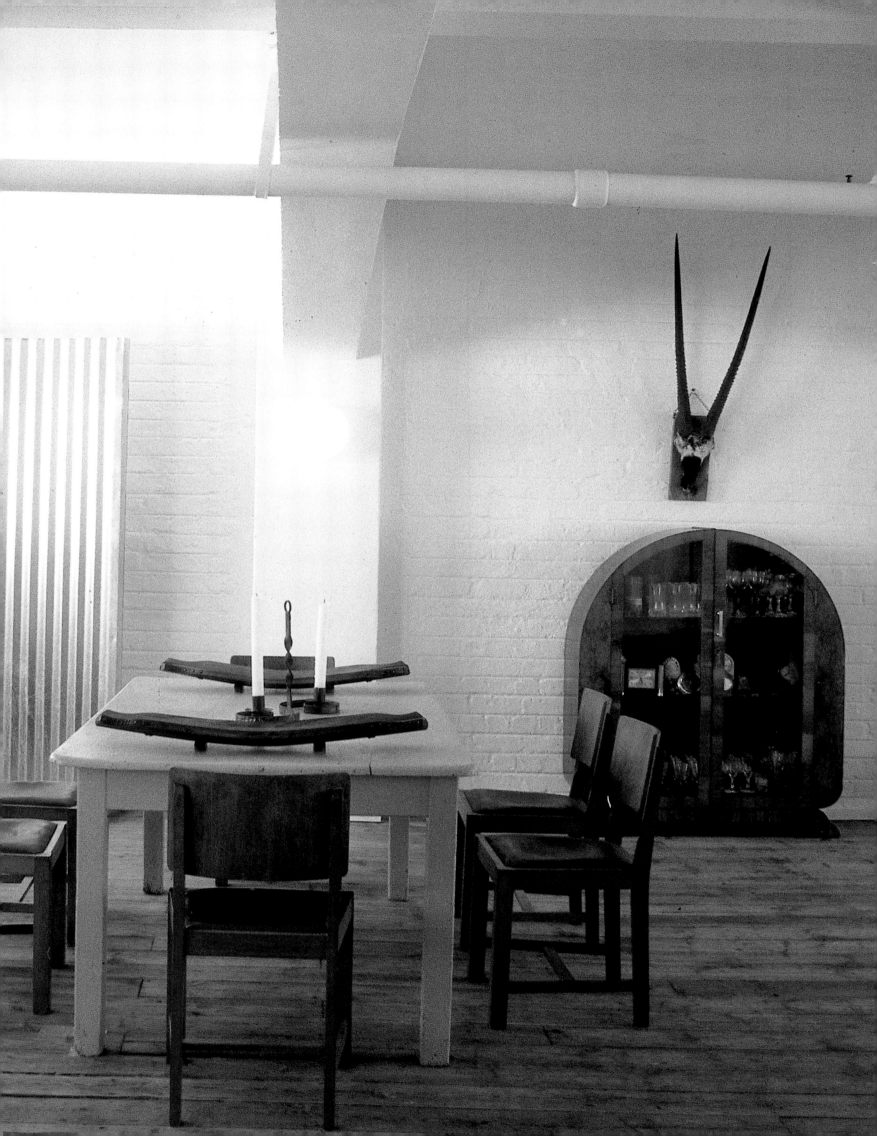

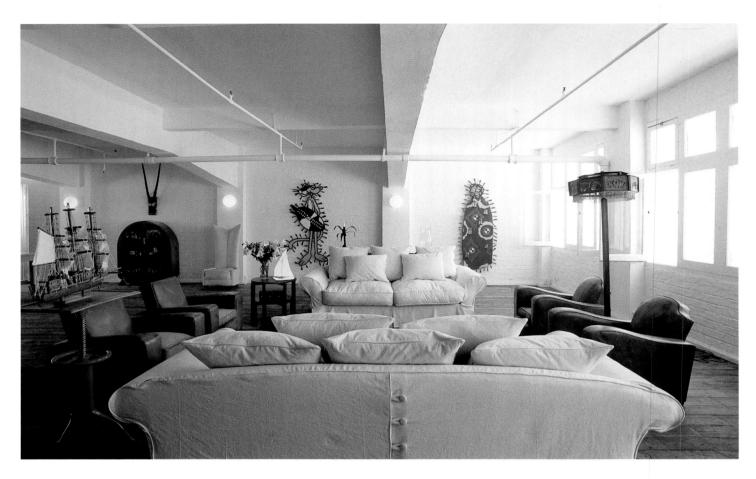

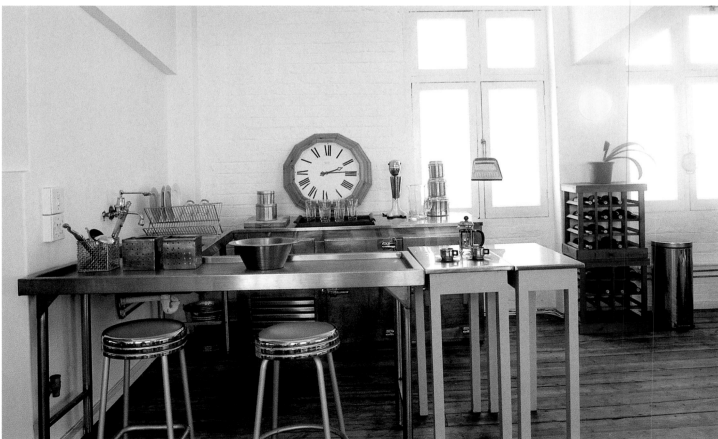

❋ **ABOVE** The square living room with its re-upholstered sofas and club chairs purchased in the city. The sculptures on the walls are by Brett Murray, an artist from the Cape. **BELOW** The thoroughly functional kitchen has a three-door refrigerator and metal everywhere. The 1950s stools came from a Cape milk bar. ❋ **OBEN** Der viereckige Salon mit neu bezogenen Kanapees und Klubsesseln, die Craig Port in der Stadt entdeckt hat. An den Wänden Skulpturen von Brett Murray, einer Künstlerin aus Kapstadt. **UNTEN** Die Küche ist vorwiegend funktionell eingerichtet, hier dominiert Metall. Nicht zu übersehen ist der dreitürige Kühlschrank. Die Barhocker aus den 1950er Jahren stammen aus einer Milchbar in Kapstadt. ❋ **CI-DESSUS** Le salon carré avec ses canapés rehoussés et ses clubs chinés en ville. Aux murs, les sculptures sont de Brett Murray, un artiste de Cape Town. **CI-DESSOUS** Fonctionnelle avant tout, la cuisine où domine le métal est équipée d'un réfrigérateur «Déli» à trois portes. Les tabourets des années 1950 proviennent d'un milk-bar de Cape Town.

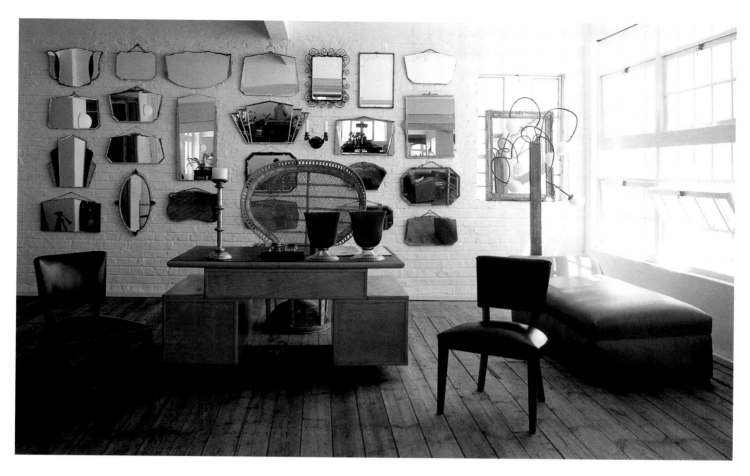

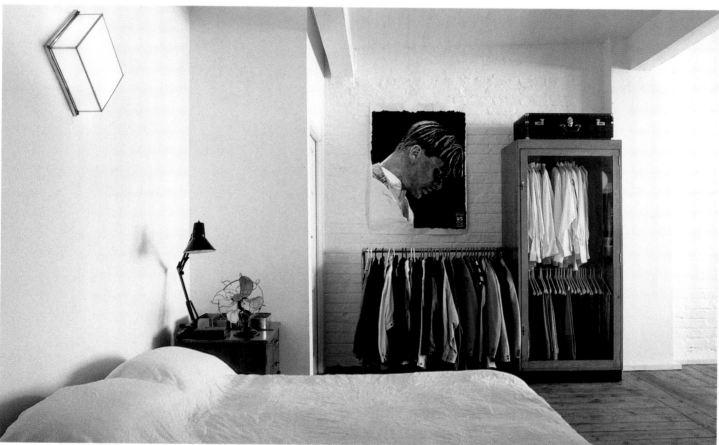

✳ **ABOVE** Under a collection of mirrors, the owner's study – with an Art Deco table from Groot Schuur Hospital and an ostrich egg lamp designed by Trevor Dykman. **FOLLOWING PAGES** A bed found at a sale in Groote Schuur Hospital. The hanging frame was once a cake trolley. ✳ **OBEN** Viele Spiegel zieren das Büro des Hausherrn. Der Art-déco-Tisch stammt aus der Groot-Schuur-Klinik, während die medusenhäuptige Straußeneier-Lampe von Trevor Dykman entworfen wurde. **FOLGENDE DOPPELSEITE** Auch das Bett stammt aus den Beständen der Groot-Schuur-Klinik. Als Kleiderschrank dient ein ehemals für den Transport von Backwaren benutztes fahrbares Regal. ✳ **EN HAUT** Sous une collection de miroirs, le bureau du propriétaire, avec sa table Art Déco chinée au Groot Schuur Hospital, et sa lampe méduse en œufs d'autruche signée Trevor Dykman. **DOUBLE PAGE SUIVANTE** Un lit trouvé dans une vente du Groot Shuur Hospital. En guise de penderie, un trolley utilisé autrefois pour les pâtisseries.

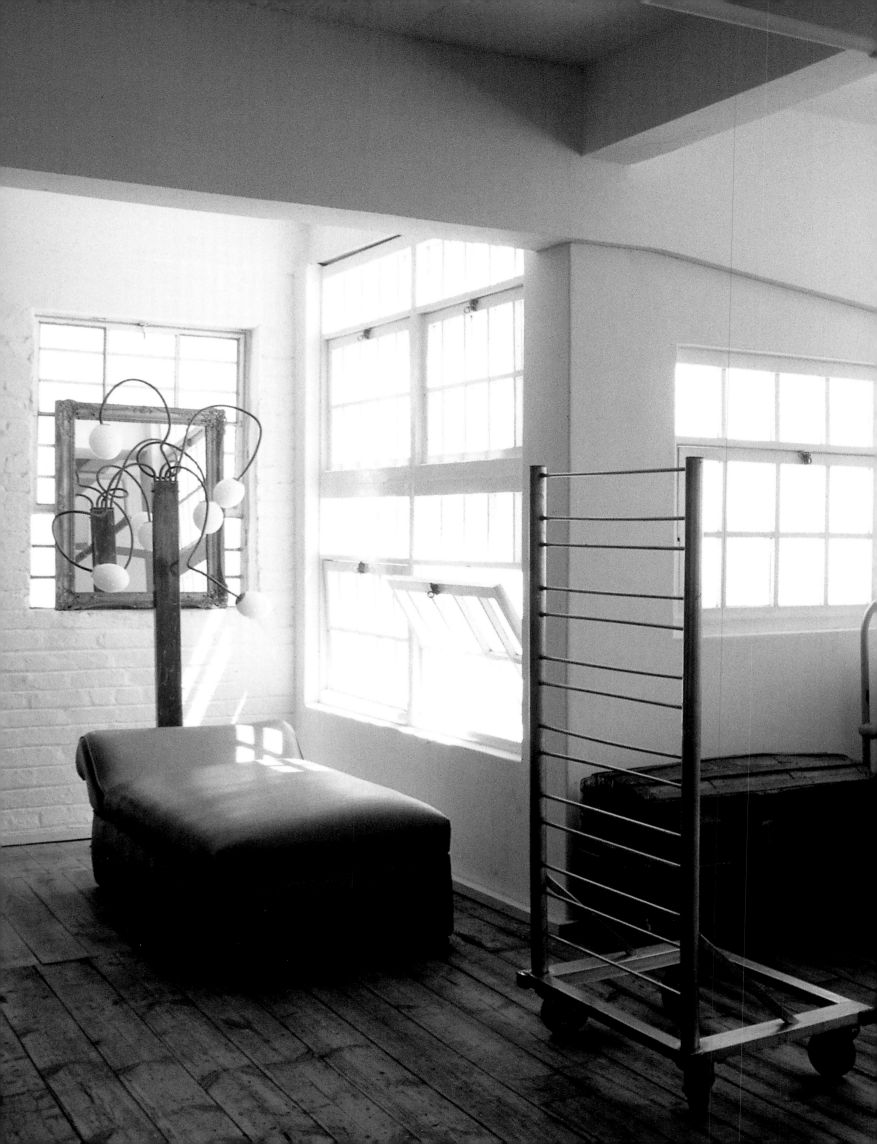

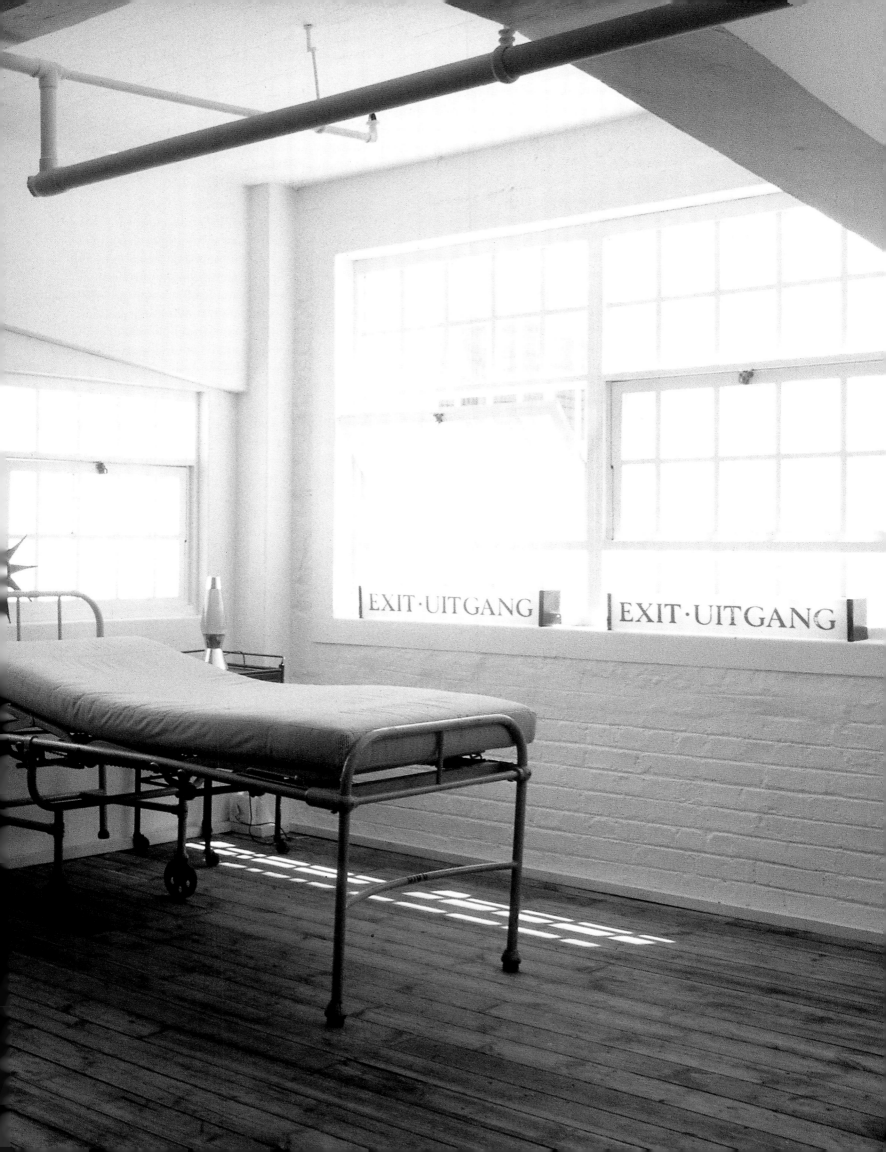

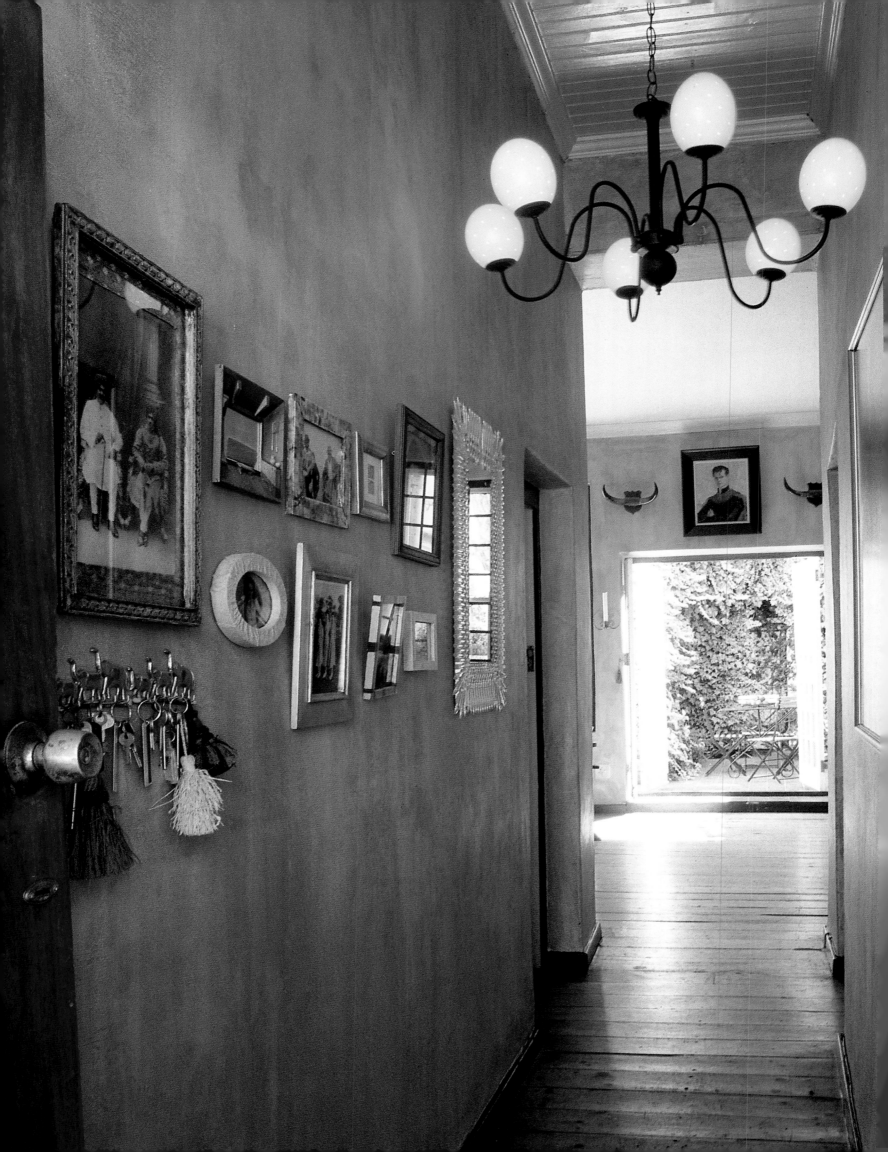

# Louise Hennigs
## Cape Town

A muffled atmosphere pervades this discreet Victorian house in the beautifully restored De Waterkant quarter.

The paved streets give the impression that you are walking up to a cottage, and when you step into the house, the pale wood floorboards seem to chime with the earthy ochre of the walls.

One of the great delights of the Cape is that it reminds you of its Englishness all the time, from the more distant districts of Mowbray and Observatory right up to the slopes of Table Mountain and the Lion's Head. In every house, a long hallway separates the various rooms and leads through to the living room and the small inner courtyard, and Louise Hennigs's home doesn't stray far from the norm. Perhaps, though, it has an extra dose of soul: Louise is an artist, and so her house contains a studio and every corner of it harbours another piece of her work. She used to spend her time doing wall paintings and creating decorative paper; today she works primarily with leather. Being sensitive to the materials she uses and to the truth that nakedness can reveal, she hasn't ventured to alter the place where she lives in any radical way. The floors were stripped and the walls were covered in white and ochre, in an attempt to bring out the essence of the house, but that was as far as she went. Time has stopped in the big, high-ceilinged bedrooms with their pre-war furnishings. Only the bathroom is surprisingly elegant, with African objects mixed with raffia. There are framed photographs everywhere – mementoes of Louise's childhood in the former Rhodesia.

Bereits am Eingang bringt das helle Parkett die ockerfarbenen Wände hervorragend zur Geltung. Vor der Tür verstärkt das Kopfsteinpflaster den Eindruck, eher ein Cottage als ein Stadthaus zu entdecken.

Typisch für den Charme Kapstadts, so an den Einfluss der Engländer zu erinnern, der sich ja auch in den entfernteren Vierteln von Mowbray und Observatory bis zum Tafelberg selbst und dem Löwenkopf zeigt. In diesen Häusern gehen die Zimmer von einem langen Flur ab, der erst in den Salon und dann weiter in den kleinen Innenhof führt. Auch Louise Hennigs' Haus weicht nicht von diesem innenarchitektonischen Prinzip ab und doch gestaltet sie es als Künstlerin auf ihre Art, sodass ihre Kunst an jeder Ecke zu spüren ist. Ihr Atelier liegt ebenfalls im Haus. Inzwischen arbeitet Louise Hennigs mit Leder, früher widmete sie sich in Sun City der Wandmalerei oder entwarf Geschenkpapier. Die Künstlerin, die ein Gefühl für das Baumaterial entwickelte, für die Wahrheit, die sich im Nackten zeigt, hat nur wenige Änderungen vorgenommen. Die Böden wurden gebeizt, die Wände weiß oder ockerfarben gestrichen – alles im Bestreben, das »Wesen« des Hauses zu Tage zu fördern. In diesen hohen weiten Räumen mit ihrer Vorkriegseinrichtung ist die Zeit stehen geblieben. Im Gegensatz dazu strahlt das Badezimmer in erstaunlicher Eleganz – afrikanische Objekte harmonieren mit Einrichtungsgegenständen aus Bast. Alte Fotos in Bilderrahmen wecken Erinnerungen, vielleicht an die lang vergangene Kindheit im ehemaligen Rhodesien.

Dès l'entrée, le bois blond du parquet renvoie à des murs ocre aux nuances de terre. Aux alentours, la rue pavée renforce l'impression de découvrir un cottage.

C'est tout le charme de Cape Town que d'offrir cette réminiscence de l'identité anglaise de la ville, et ce des quartiers éloignés de Mowbray ou Observatory jusqu'aux flancs de la montagne de la Table et de la Tête du Lion. Dans chaque maison, un long couloir d'entrée répartit les pièces et débouche sur le salon puis sur la petite cour intérieure. Celle de Louise Hennigs ne déroge pas à la règle mais elle offre un supplément d'âme: la dame est artiste, chaque recoin dissimule un témoignage de son travail, et l'habitation abrite un atelier. Louise Hennigs applique aujourd'hui son art au cuir. Autrefois, elle peignait les murs de Sun City ou créait du papier décoratif. Sensible à la matière, à la vérité qui peut se dégager de sa nudité, l'artiste n'a pas modifié son habitat. Décapant les sols, recouvrant simplement les murs de blanc ou d'ocre, elle n'a fait que mettre au jour l'«essence» des lieux. Le temps s'est arrêté dans les chambres hautes et vastes, avec leur ameublement d'avant-guerre. La salle de bains surprend par l'élégance d'objets africains mêlés au raphia. Partout dans les cadres, des photos anciennes raniment des souvenirs. La nostalgie, peut-être, d'une enfance passée dans l'ex-Rhodésie.

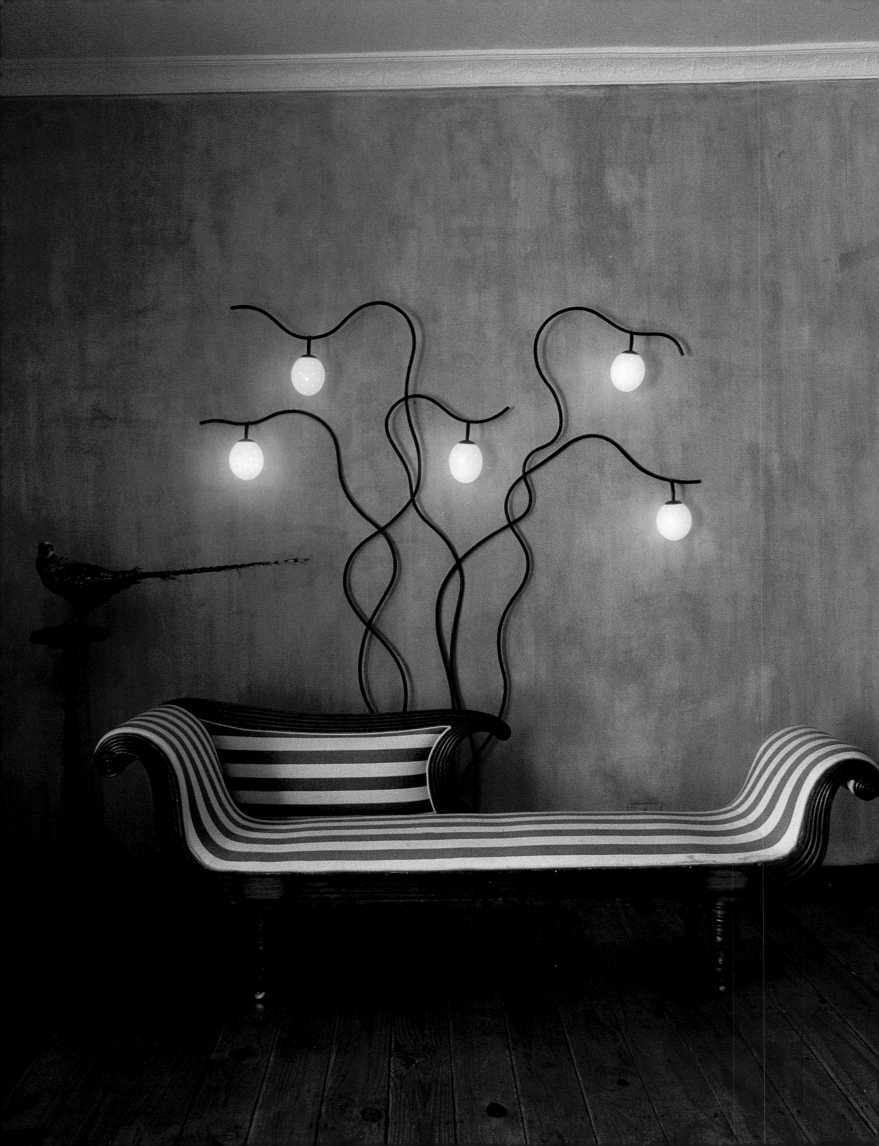

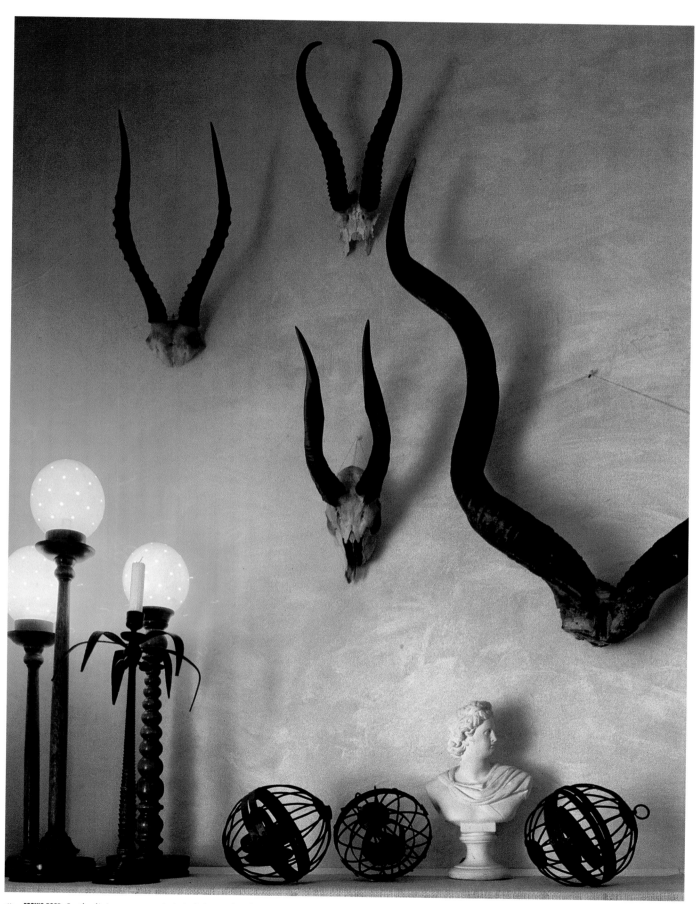

✳ **FADING PAGE** In the living room, a deckchair beneath a lamp designed by Trevor Dykman. **ABOVE** Trophy antelope horns (there are buffalo horns too) are a reminder of the bush and of a happy childhood spent in the former Rhodesia. ✳ **LINKE SEITE** Ein geschwungenes Kanapee unter einer Leuchte von Trevor Dykman. **OBEN** Antilopengeweihe als Trophäen (woanders sind es Büffelgeweihe) beschwören den Busch und die glückliche Kindheit der Dame des Hauses im ehemaligen Rhodesien herauf. ✳ **PAGE DE GAUCHE** Dans le salon, une méridienne déploie ses courbes sous un luminaire de Trevor Dykman. **CI-DESSUS** Les cornes d'antilopes en trophée (ailleurs ce sont des buffles), raniment les souvenirs du bush et de cette enfance heureuse passée dans l'ex-Rhodésie.

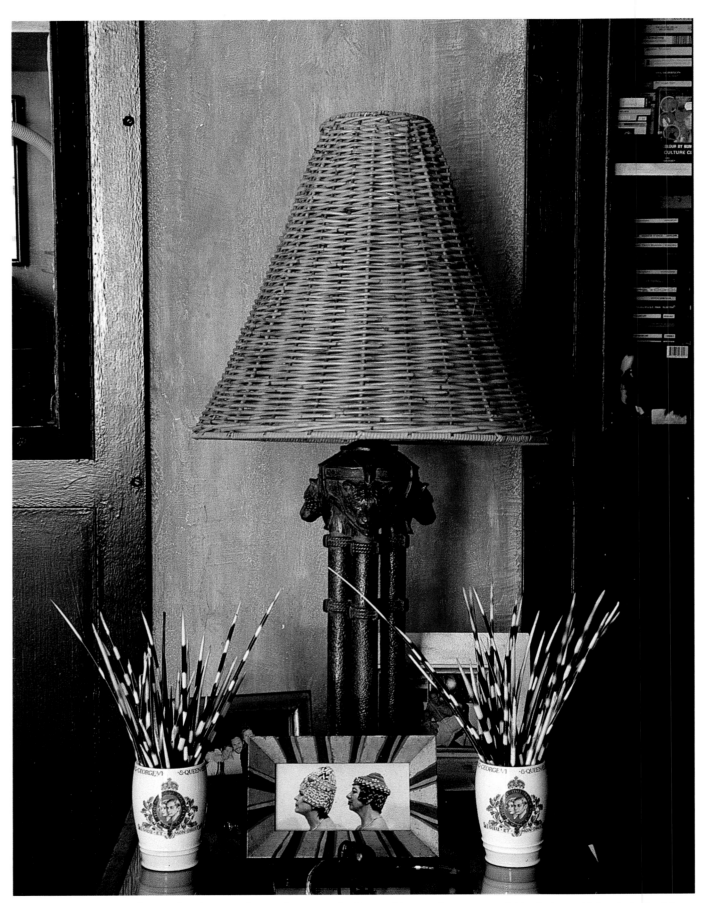

✳ **ABOVE** The porcupine quills remind us that nature is never far away at the Cape, and it seems the most natural thing in the world that the body of the lamp stand is adorned with the heads of lions. **FACING PAGE** Beyond the living room is the little courtyard, with a shower surrounded by trellised roses. ✳ **OBEN** Die Stacheln des Stachelschweins und der mit Löwenköpfen verzierte Lampenfuß erinnern daran, dass die Wildnis nicht weit ist. **RECHTE SEITE** Vom Salon aus gelangt man in den kleinen Innenhof mit Freiluftdusche und Rosenspalier. ✳ **CI-DESSOUS** Les piquants de porc-épic rappellent que la nature n'est jamais loin à Cape Town, et c'est tout naturellement qu'un pied de lampe affiche ses têtes de lionne. **PAGE DE DROITE** Au-delà du salon, la petite cour accueille une douche d'été entourée d'un treillage de roseaux.

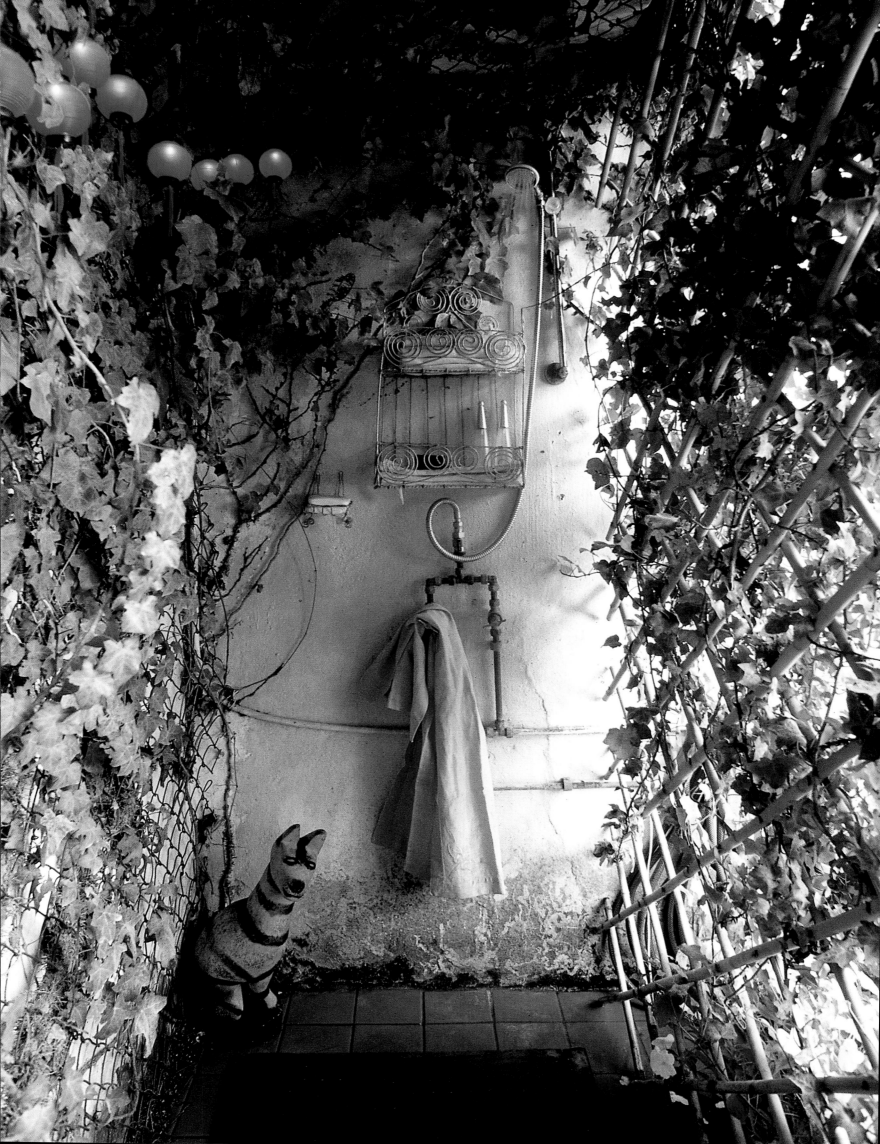

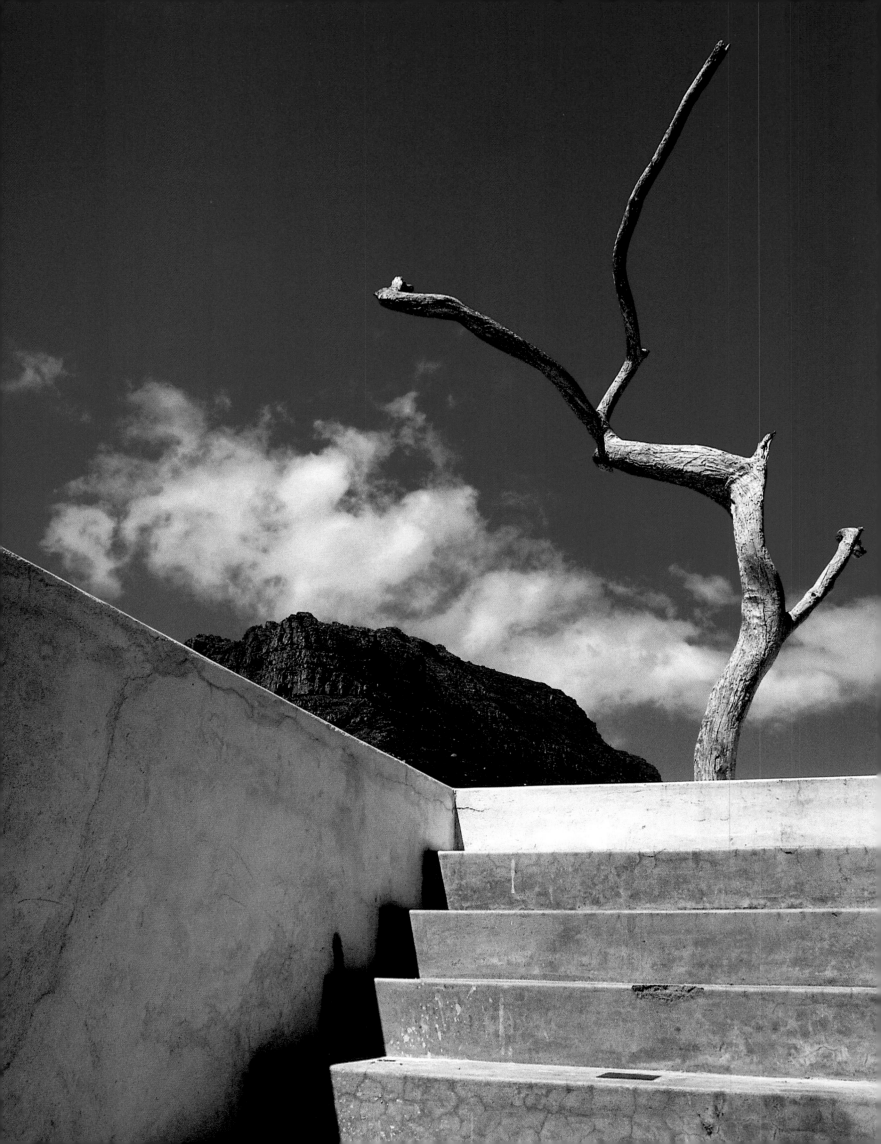

# Jean-Marc Lederman

# LLandudno

Near the Cape,
a house of glass and concrete high above the Atlantic.

Beneath a sky of pigeon's egg blue, the outline of Jean-Marc Lederman's house stands above its protected site, one of South Africa's most famous swimming places. The sea is icy cold here, but its emerald hues and the white sandy beach that rims it attract the happy few from every corner of the globe.

Building sites are rare in the vicinity and it was only the combination of obstinacy and good luck that enabled Jean-Marc Lederman to buy one. A Frenchman who has lived at the Cape since 1994, his idea was to duplicate the simplicity and sense of space perfected by the architect Frank Lloyd Wright. After two years of work, the result is a piece of architecture remarkable for its purity, its clean lines and its open aspect, designed for living between the sky and the ocean. The walls are rough-surfaced and high metal guardrails stand between the main living room and the rest of the house. Otherwise the space is virtually unadorned, with nothing but the occasional touch of bright colour to enliven it. There are Moroccan poufs, rugs and carpets, harmonizing perfectly with pieces of furniture imported from Bali and their more modern counterparts from Paris and New York. And of course the view is breathtaking. There's nothing missing from this natural décor, so reminiscent of the Côte d'Azur in the time of Claude Monet and Paul Cézanne. But that headland a few miles to the south is the Cape of Good Hope, no less.

Die Silhouette des Hauses zeichnet sich scharf vor dem meerblauen Himmel über dem geschützten südafrikanischen Badeort ab. Das Wasser ist eiskalt, aber die Happy Few der großen weiten Welt wissen die smaragdgrünen Wellen und den weißen Sandstrand zu schätzen.

Es mangelt an bebaubaren Grundstücken und nur Glück und eine gewisse Sturheit konnten Jean-Marc Lederman dazu verhelfen. Der Franzose, der seit 1994 in Kapstadt lebt, hatte es sich in den Kopf gesetzt, ein großes und dennoch schlichtes Haus im Sinne des Architekten Frank Lloyd Wright zu bauen. Nach zwei Jahren Bauzeit konnte sich das Ergebnis sehen lassen: eine glasklare Architektur mit geraden Linien und vielen Fenstern, wie geschaffen für ein Leben zwischen Himmel und Ozean. Keine Tapeten an den Wänden; eine hohe Reling aus Metall trennt den großen Salon von den anderen Räumen. Er wirkt beinahe jungfräulich, nur hier und da leuchten sparsam eingesetzt lebhafte Farben auf. Marokkanische Teppiche, Kissen und gepolsterte Hocker harmonieren mit den aus Bali importierten Möbeln sowie moderneren Stücken aus Paris oder New York. Die Aussicht auf das Meer durch die Panoramafenster ist atemberaubend. Der Natur mangelt es an nichts, hier denkt man unwillkürlich an die Côte d'Azur zu Zeiten Claude Monets oder Paul Cézannes. Dabei ragt nur wenige Kilometer südlich das Kap der Guten Hoffnung aus den eisigen Fluten.

Sous un ciel bleu marine, la silhouette se détache sur un site protégé, haut lieu balnéaire sud-africain. L'eau est glaciale, mais ses reflets émeraude et la plage de sable blanc attirent les happy few du monde entier.

Les terrains à bâtir sont rares et ce sont les effets conjugués de la chance et de l'obstination qui ont permis à Jean-Marc Lederman d'en dénicher un. Ce Français établi à Cape Town depuis 1994 avait une idée en tête: copier les volumes et la simplicité des œuvres de l'architecte Frank Lloyd Wright. Après deux années de travaux, le résultat s'impose: une architecture très pure en lignes droites avec des ouvertures partout, pour vivre entre le ciel et l'océan. Les murs sont à l'état brut et de hautes rambardes métalliques séparent le grand salon du reste de la maison. L'espace est resté pratiquement vierge avec, ici et là, des touches de couleurs vives pour rehausser l'ensemble. Poufs, tapis et coussins marocains s'harmonisent parfaitement aux meubles importés de Bali et à ceux, plus modernes, achetés à Paris ou New York. Depuis les baies vitrées qui font face à la mer, le panorama est à couper le souffle. Rien ne manque à ce décor naturel évoquant si souvent la Côte d'Azur au temps de Claude Monet et Paul Cézanne. Et pourtant, à quelques kilomètres au Sud, c'est bien le Cap de Bonne-Espérance qui pointe son museau.

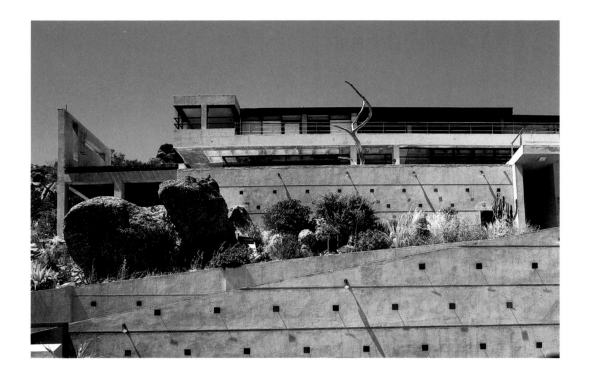

✳ **ABOVE** The gardens and terraces add a touch of green to the play of sunshine, blue sky and sea. **BELOW** The plate glass windows, as here in the bathroom, are an invitation to contemplate the view – the owner's favourite pastime, as it happens. ✳ **FACING PAGE AND FOLLOWING PAGES** Overlooking the icy sea-water is a swimming pool, suspended between ocean and sky. **PAGE 156** Here the philosophy is entirely minimalist, dominated by grey and white. The whole house is decorated with sculptures and paintings by South African artists discovered by Jean-Marc Lederman in the JOAO gallery in Cape Town. ✳ **OBEN** Die terrassenförmig angelegten Gärten legen einen Hauch von Grün über die blau getönten Licht- und Schattenspiele. **UNTEN** Wie hier im Badezimmer laden die Panoramafenster dazu ein, die Landschaft zu betrachten, eine der Lieblingsbeschäftigungen des Hausherrn. **RECHTE SEITE UND FOLGENDE DOPPELSEITE** Das lang gestreckte Schwimmbad mit Blick auf das eiskalte Meer scheint zwischen Himmel und Erde zu schweben. **SEITE 156** Minimalismus als Philosophie – Weiß und Grau dominieren. Skulpturen und Gemälde südafrikanischer Künstler, die Jean-Marc Lederman in der Galerie JOAO im Zentrum von Kapstadt entdeckt hat, vervollständigen das Bild. ✳ **CI-DESSUS** Les jardins en terrasses ajoutent une touche verte à ces jeux d'ombre et de lumière où domine le bleu. **CI-DESSOUS** Les baies vitrées, comme ici dans la salle de bains, invitent à contempler le paysage, l'exercice favori du propriétaire. **PAGE DE DROITE ET DOUBLE PAGE SUIVANTE** Face à l'eau glacée, une piscine tout en longueur joue la suspension entre le ciel et la terre. **PAGE 156** Philosophie minimaliste où dominent le gris et blanc. L'ensemble est décoré de sculptures et de peintures d'artistes sud-africains que Jean-Marc Lederman a découvert dans la galerie d'art JOAO située au cœur de Cape Town.

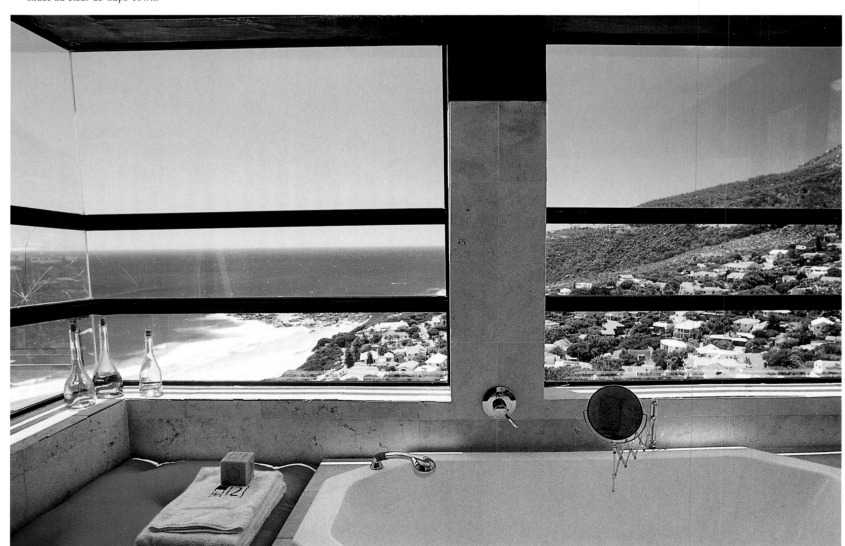

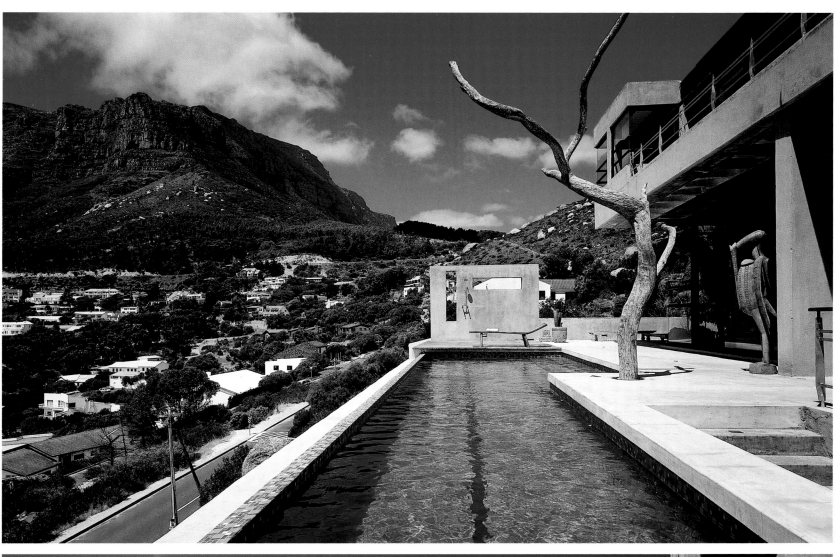

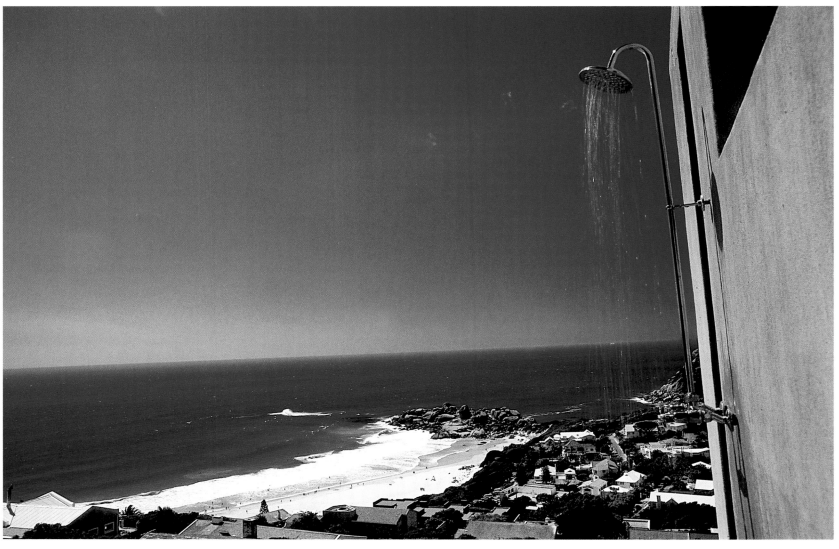

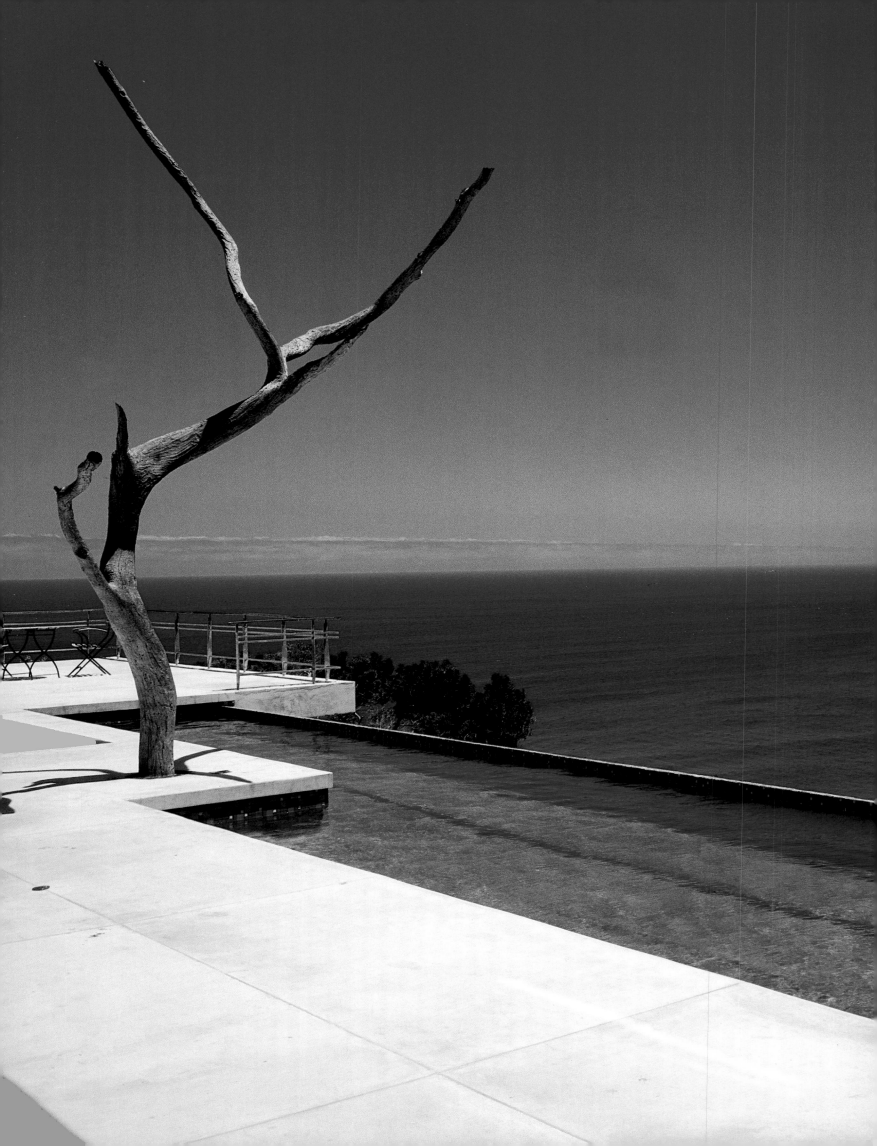

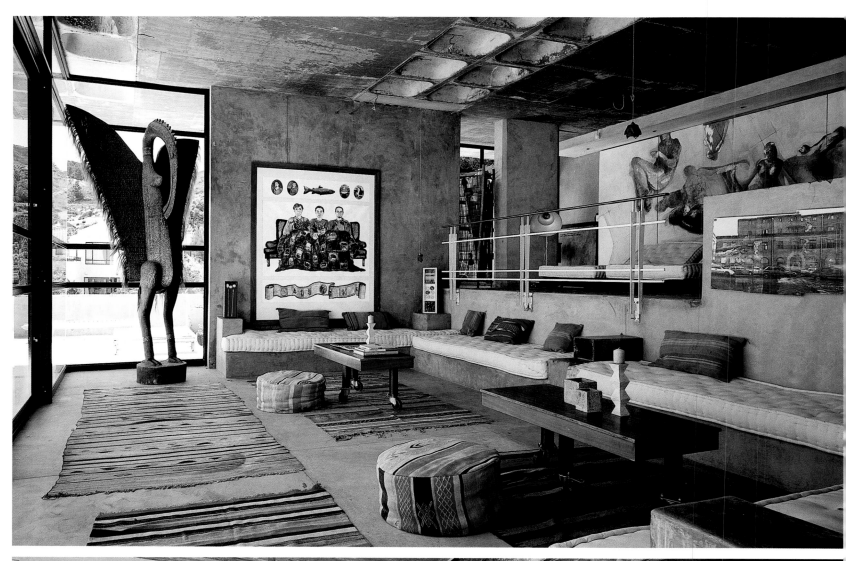
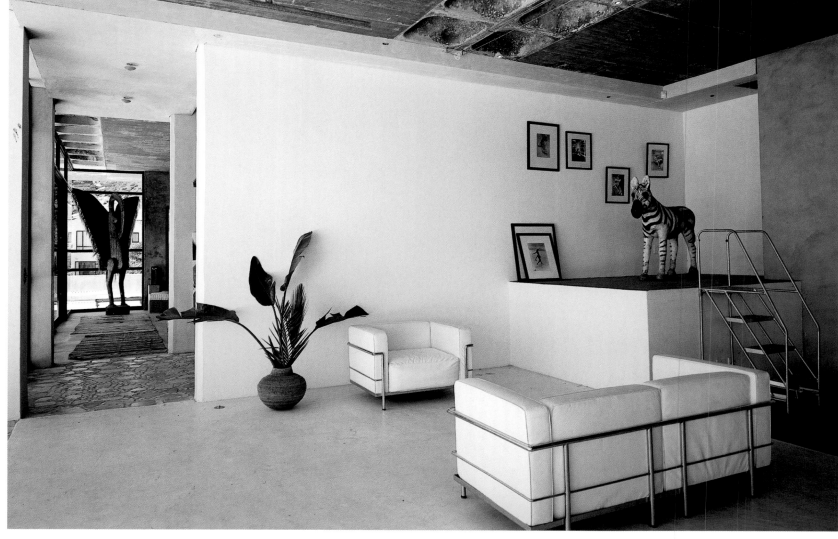

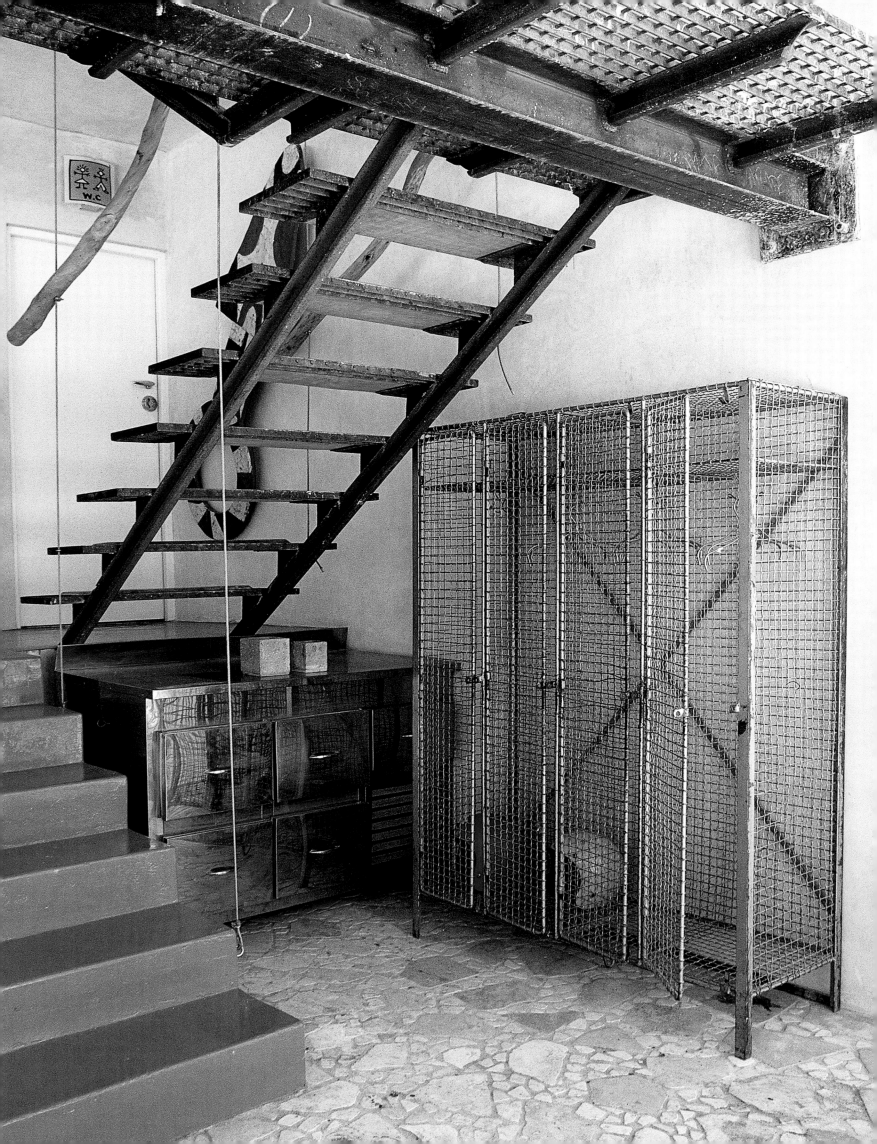

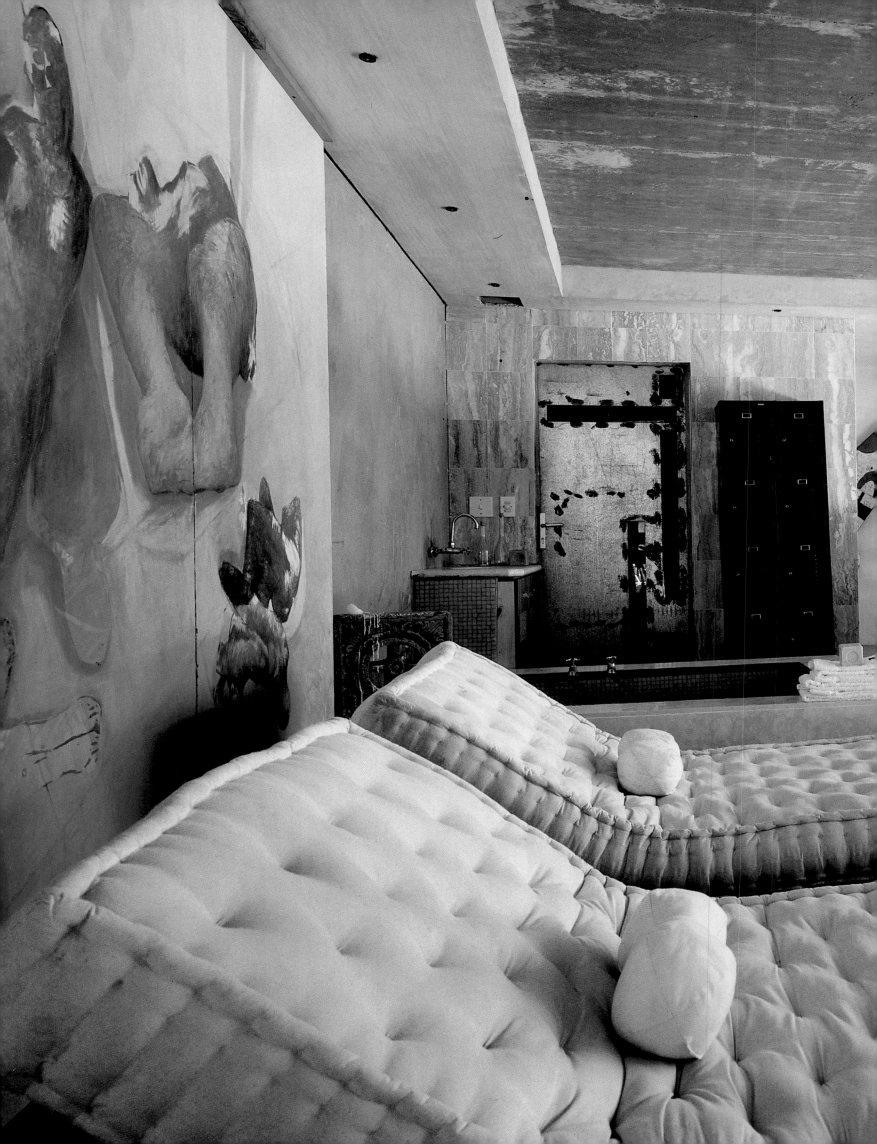

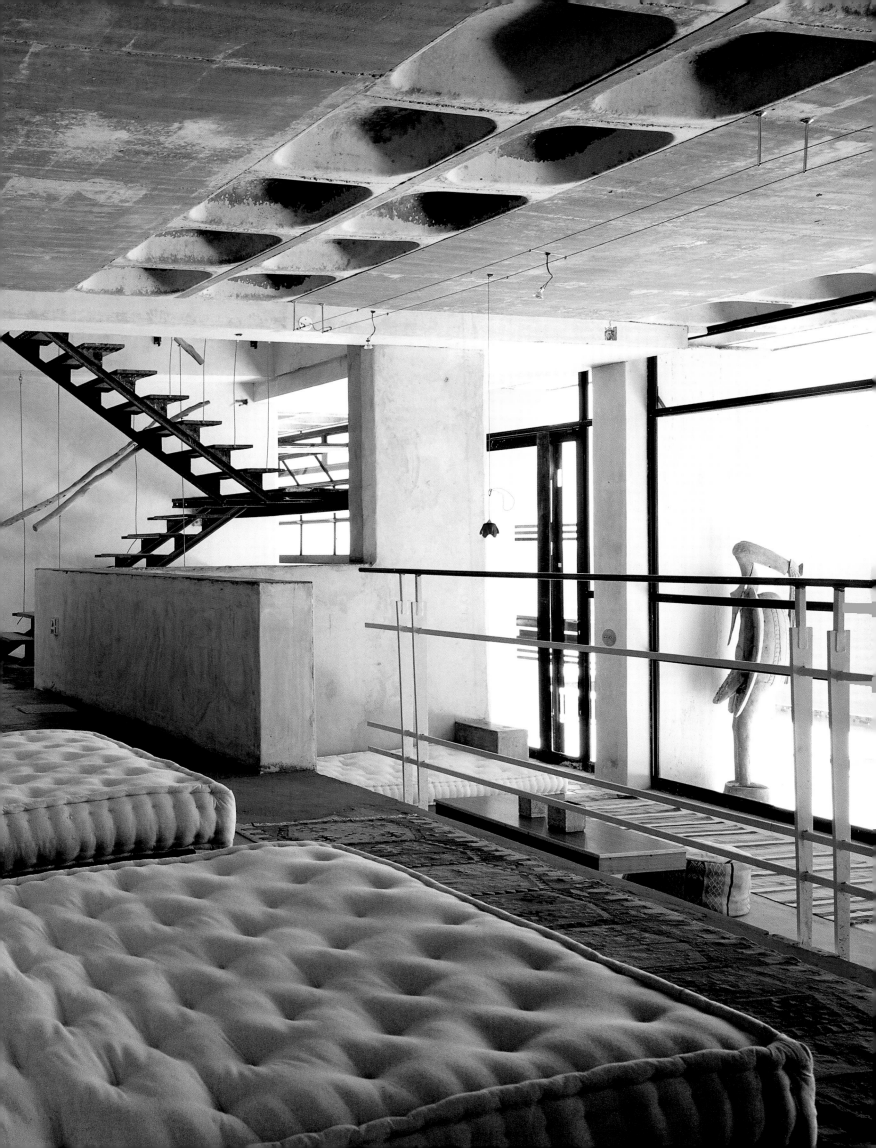

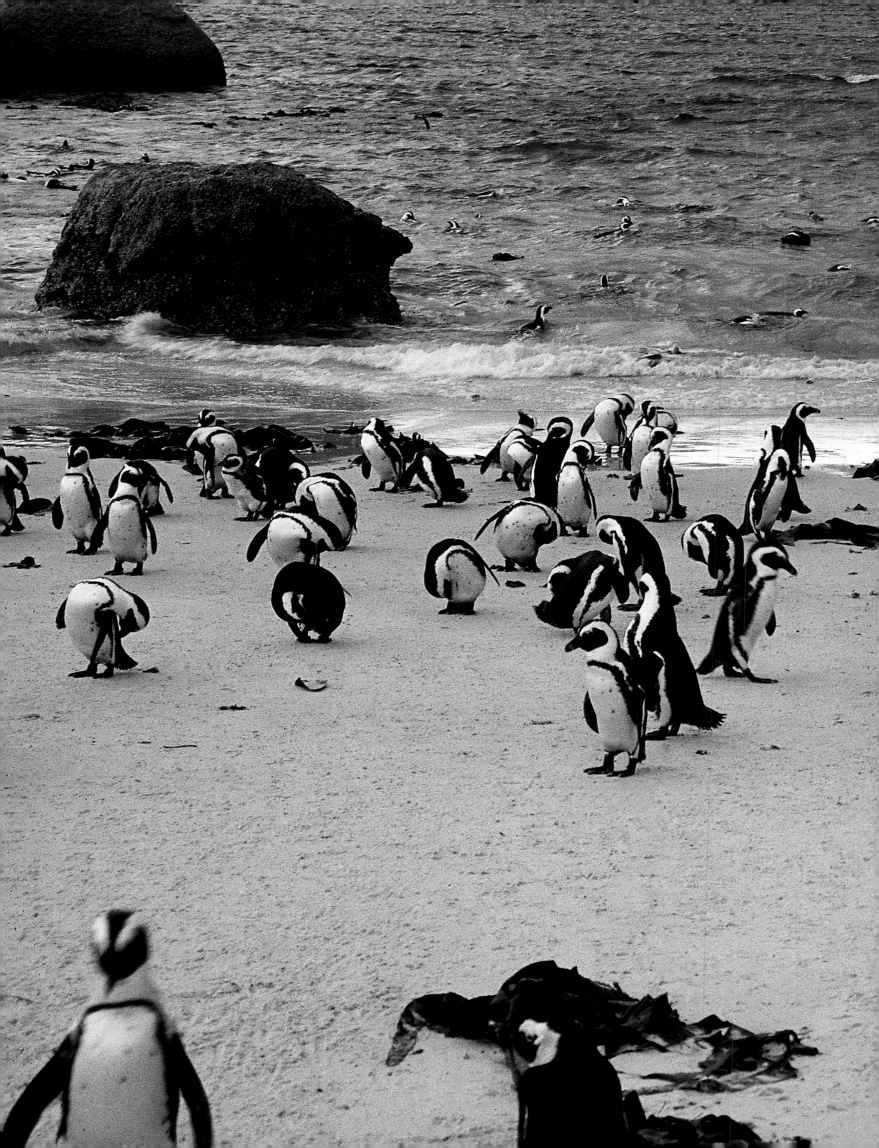

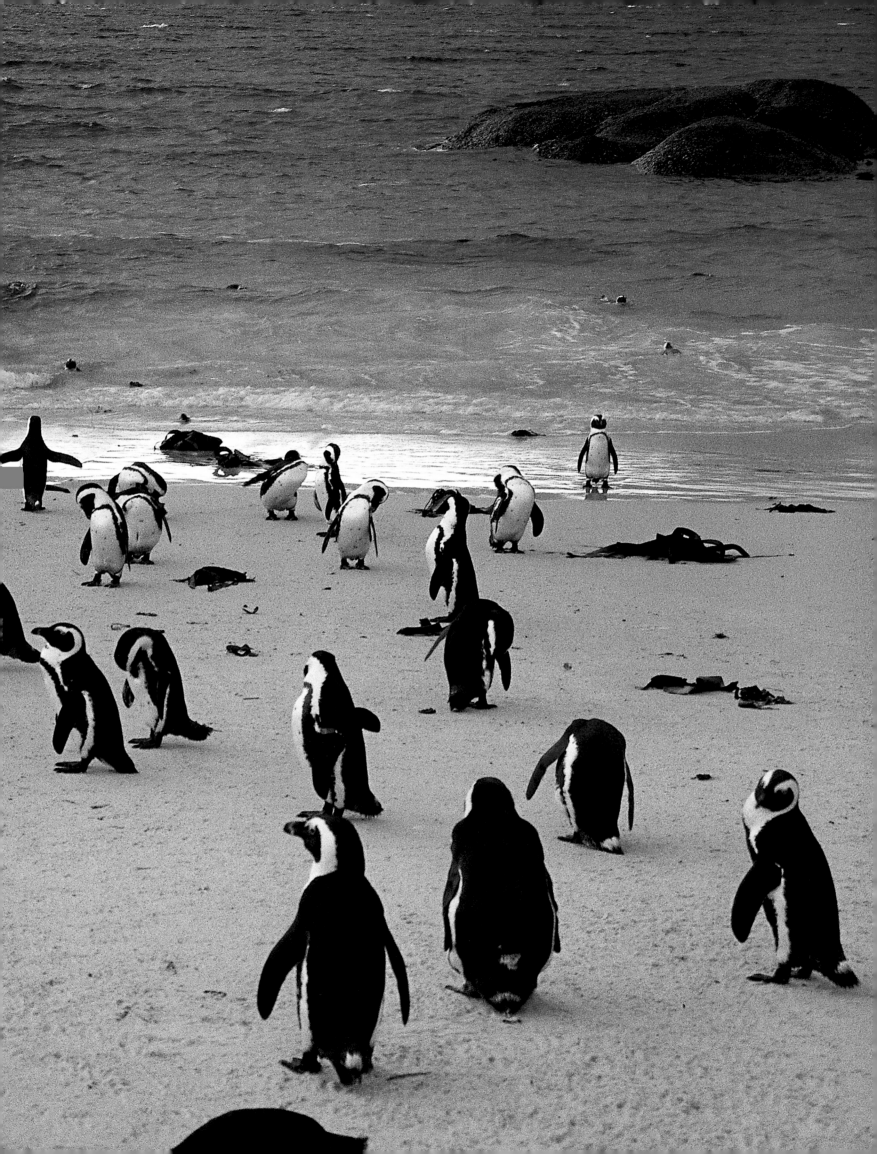

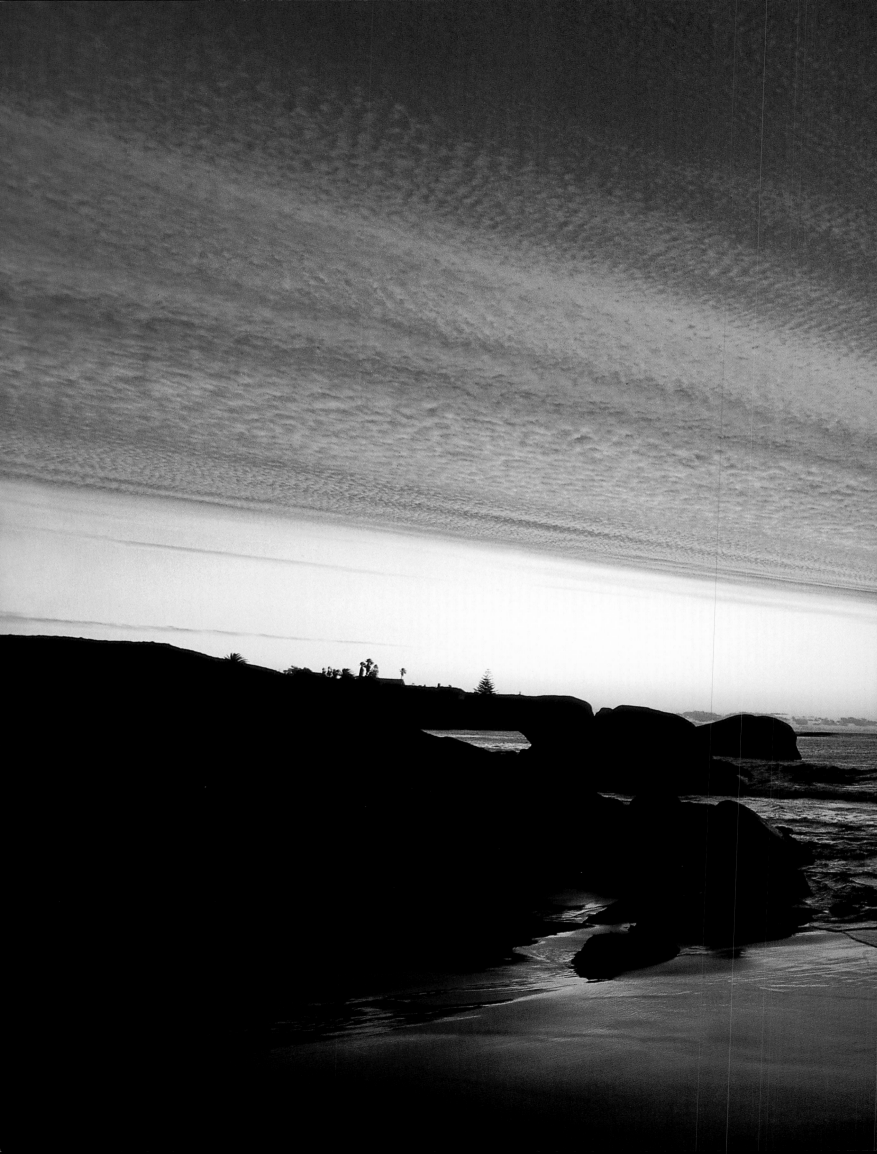

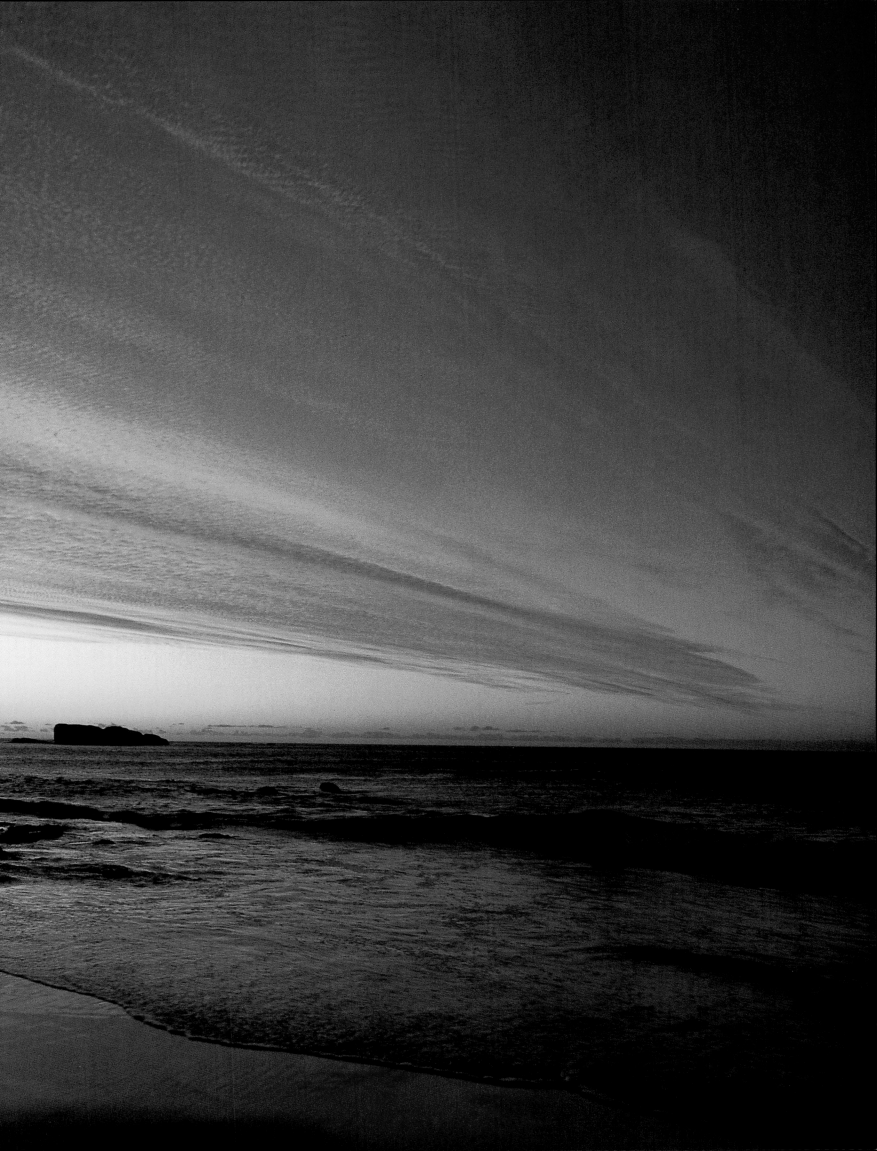

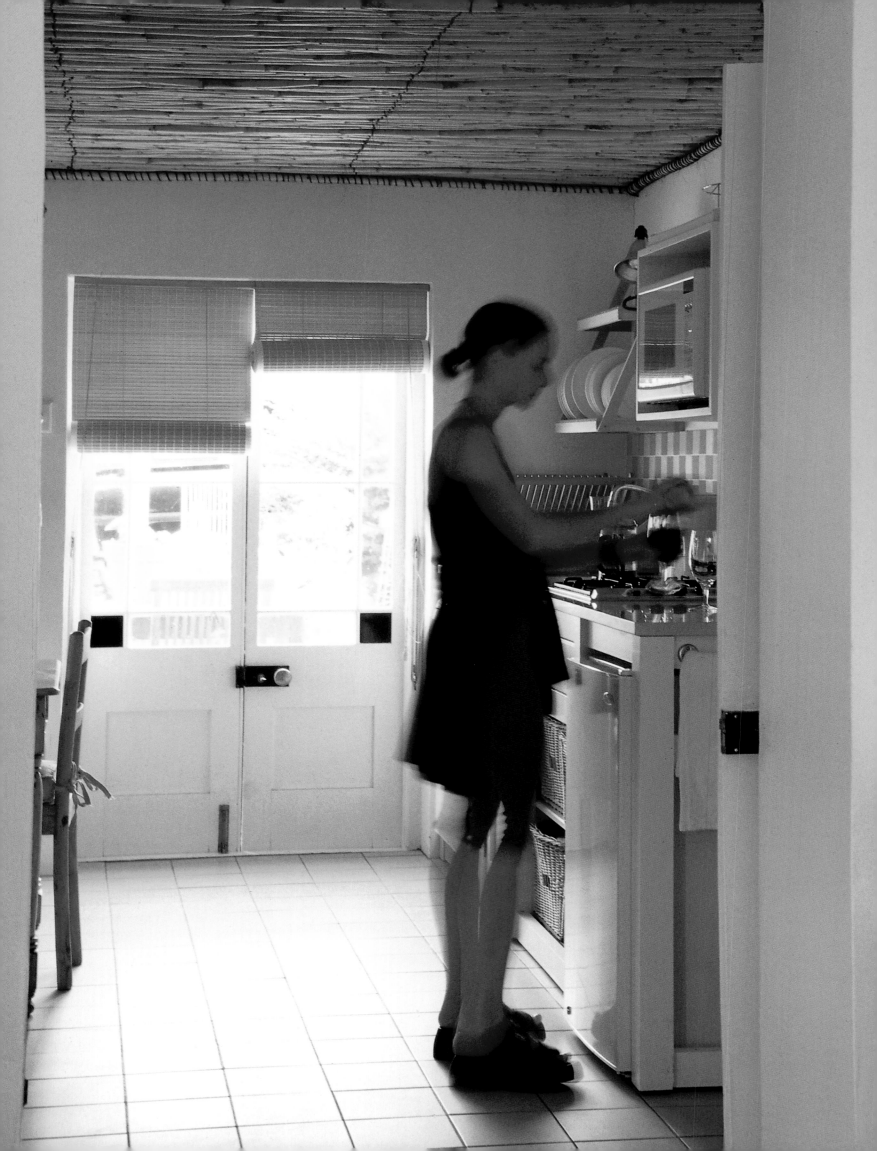

# JONATHAN GREEN & MARINA PRETORIUS
# Greyton

Two architects worked together to renovate this simple, restful house.

Far from the vineyards and the tourist circuits is Greyton, a small village well known to the intellectuals and artists of South Africa. It's a bit like a town in France's Lubéron, suddenly transported to an area only two hours from Cape Town.

There's no sea – that would be overdoing it – only the countryside and a network of rivulets. Nothing's really changed here for about 120 years: "Greyton was a poor village which eked out a hard living selling vegetables to the missionary settlements nearby," explain Jonathan Green and Marina Pretorius. "The cottages were pretty humble ones and wherever possible we did our best to preserve the historic aspect of the place." Like the efficient architects they are, they restored their house in five months. From the "happy door" of the veranda – the chosen domain of Edgar, an Irish terrier, and Emma, a Schnauzer – there's a view of the dining and living rooms inside, then of the kitchen with its pergola off to the side. The loftiness of the ceiling, which extends right to the corrugated iron roof, is a surprise. The walls are painted a rich butter yellow whose warmth is reinforced by unpretentious wooden furniture, with only a few fittings in wrought iron to add a touch of black. The owners, who like things minimalist, seem to fear nothing but garishness and slavery to fashion.

Abseits der Weinberge und Touristenpfade, aber nur zwei Autostunden von Kapstadt entfernt, liegt das kleine Dorf Greyton, das unter südafrikanischen Intellektuellen und Künstlern sehr beliebt ist.

Kein Meer – viel zu vulgär – stattdessen ist man auf dem Land, wo viele kleine Bäche den Städter erfreuen. In den letzten 120 Jahren hat sich hier nur wenig verändert. »Greyton war ein armes Dorf, in dem sich die Menschen mühsam durch den Verkauf von Gemüse an die benachbarten Missionare über Wasser hielten«, erzählen Jonathan Green und Marina Pretorius. »Die Bauweise der Cottages war bescheiden. Wir haben uns dafür entschieden, den historischen Charakter beizubehalten.« Innerhalb von fünf Monaten restaurierte das Architektenpaar respektvoll das Haus. Durch die Verandatür, wo uns Edgar, der Irische Terrier, und Emma, die Schnauzerhündin, fröhlich kläffend begrüßen, gelangt man ins Esszimmer und in den Salon, an den sich die Küche und eine Pergola anschließen. Die beeindruckend hohen Decken reichen bis zum Wellblechdach. Die buttergelb getünchten Wände strahlen Ruhe und Gelassenheit aus, ein Eindruck, der durch die Holzmöbel noch unterstrichen wird. Nur die schmiedeeisernen Elemente tragen einen Hauch von Schwarz bei. Als leidenschaftliche Minimalisten lehnen die Hausbesitzer alles Vulgäre oder krampfhaft Moderne ab.

Bien loin des vignobles et des circuits touristiques, il y a Greyton, petit village très réputé chez les intellectuels et artistes sud-africains, quelque chose comme le Lubéron français transposé à deux heures de Cape Town.

Pas de mer – trop vulgaire – mais la campagne et ses petits ruisseaux si prompts à détendre le citadin. Ici, rien, ou presque, n'a changé en 120 ans. «Greyton était un village pauvre qui ne vivait que des légumes vendus à des missionnaires voisins», expliquent en cœur Jonathan Green et Marina Pretorius. «Les cottages étaient modestes dans leur fabrication; nous avons voulu préserver le caractère historique des lieux.» En architectes respectueux, le couple a restauré la maison en cinq mois. De «la porte heureuse» de la véranda où glapissent joyeusement Edgar, le terrier irlandais, et Emma, le schnauzer, on aperçoit la salle à manger et le salon, puis la cuisine et sa pergola dans l'alignement. La hauteur du plafond, élevé jusqu'au toit en tôle ondulée, est impressionnante. Dictés par l'envie de calme et de tranquillité, les murs affichent une belle couleur beurre frais dont la chaleur est renforcée par des meubles en bois. Seules les installations en fer forgé apportent une touche noire. Les propriétaires férus de minimalisme ne craignent que le vulgaire ou le branché.

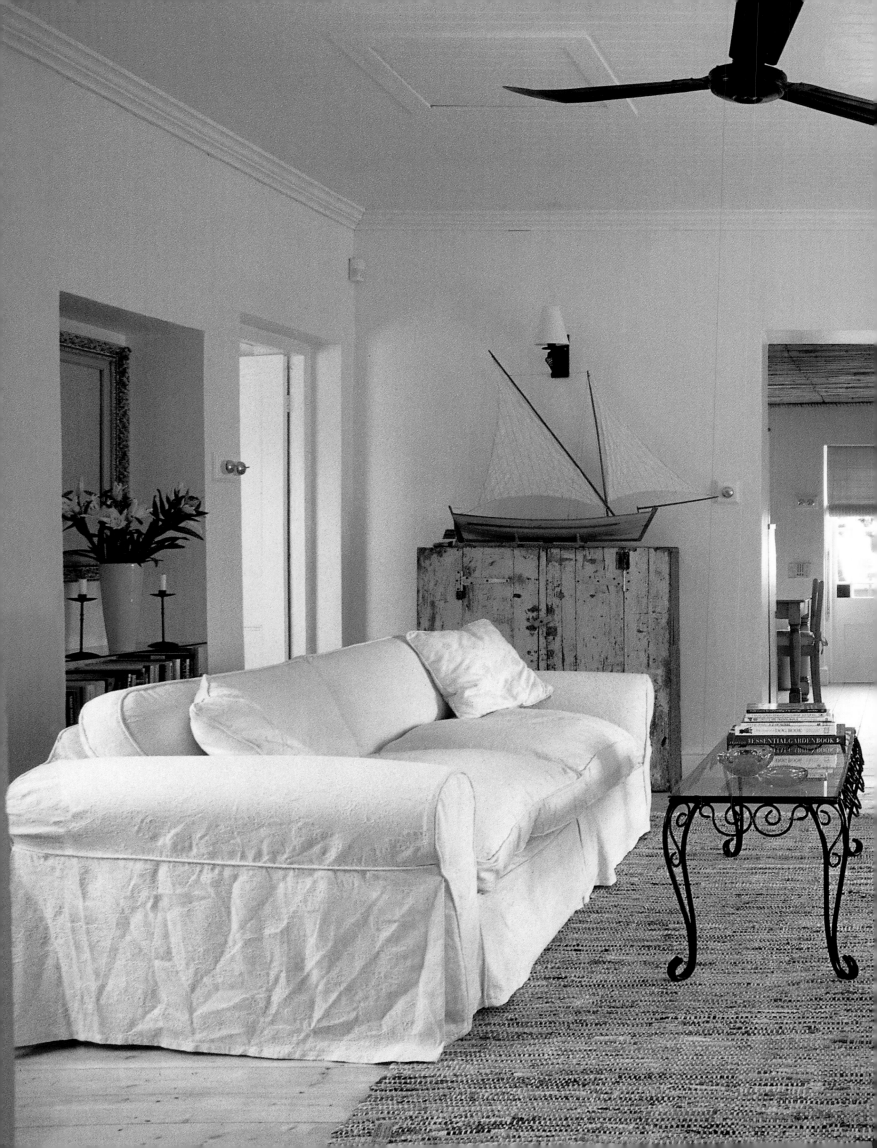

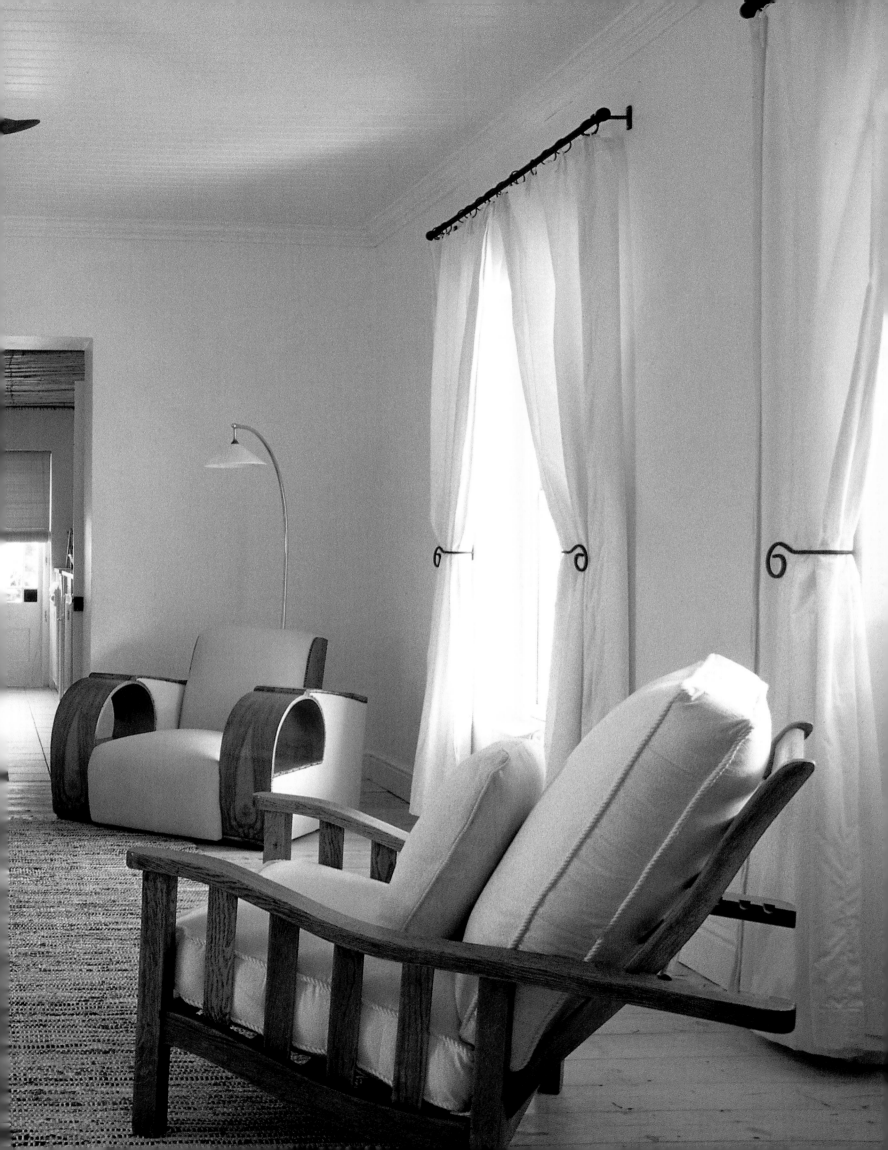

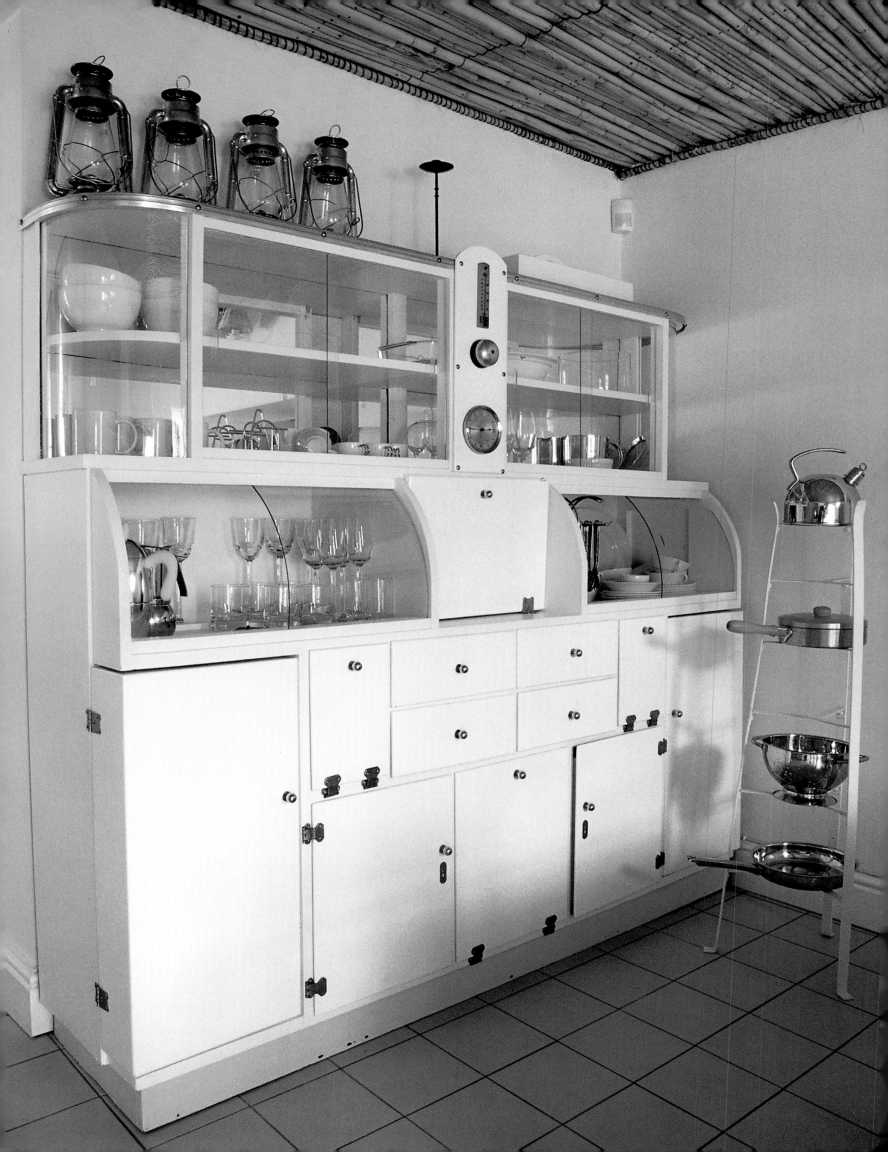

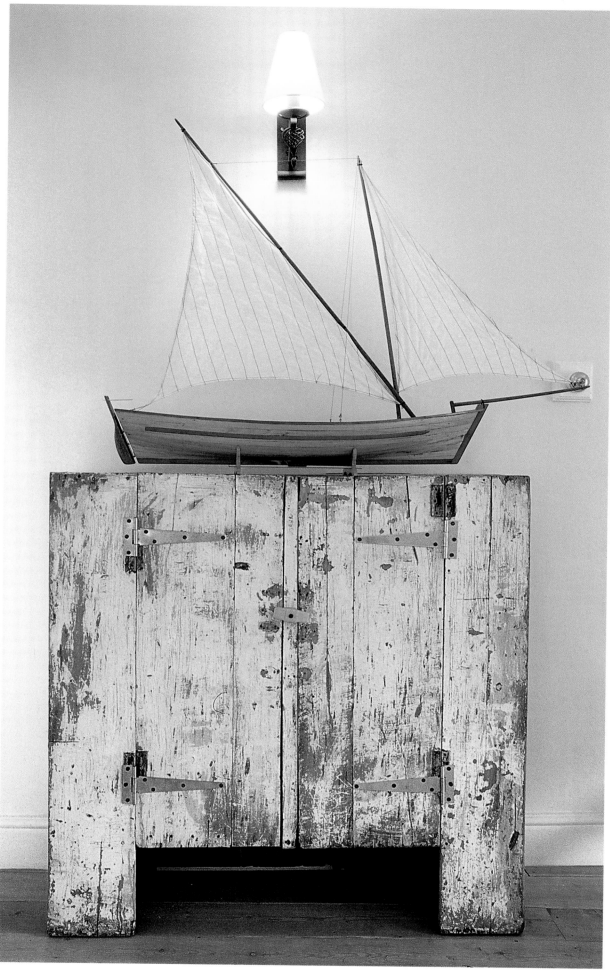

❋ **PREVIOUS PAGES** The living room was originally made up of two bedrooms. Calico curtains, Art Deco armchair and a sofa renovated by Marina Pretorius. **FACING PAGE** The kitchen is built around a 1960s sideboard found at the Cape. ❋ **VORHERGEHENDE DOPPELSEITE** Ursprünglich bestand der Salon aus zwei Räumen. Vorhänge aus Kaliko, Art-déco-Sessel und ein Kanapee, das die Dame des Hauses selbst restauriert hat. **LINKE SEITE** Das Leben in der Küche spielt sich rund um den Geschirrschrank aus den 1960er Jahren ab, den das Paar in Kapstadt aufgetrieben hat. ❋ **DOUBLE PAGE PRECEDENTE** Le salon était à l'origine composé de deux chambres. Rideaux en calicot, fauteuil Art Déco, canapé rénové par la maîtresse de maison. **PAGE DE GAUCHE** Autour du buffet des années 1960 trouvé à Cape Town s'organise l'unité cuisine.

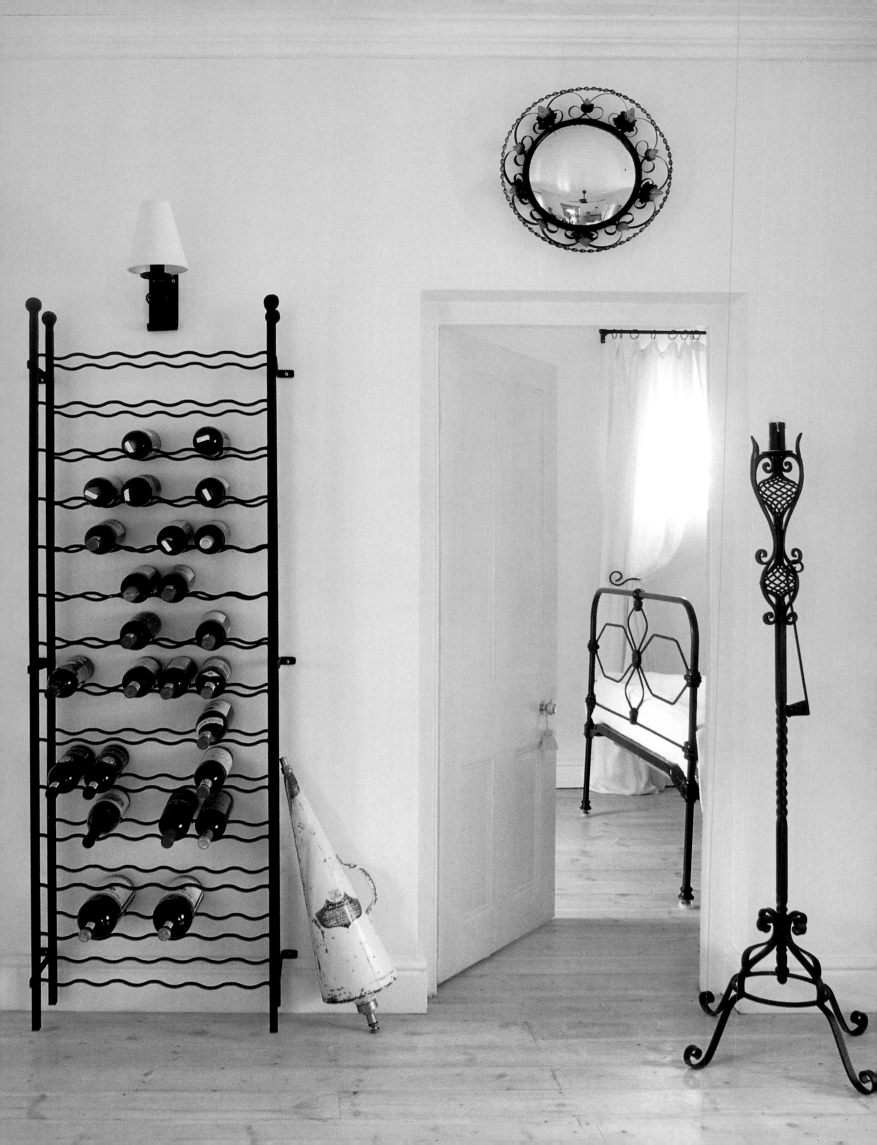

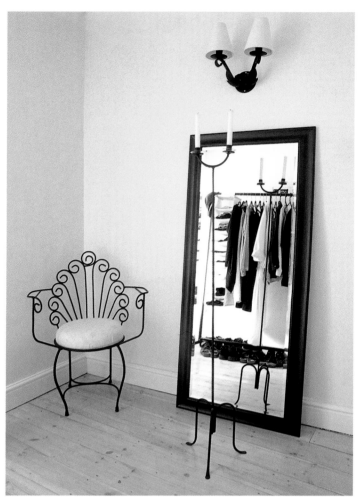

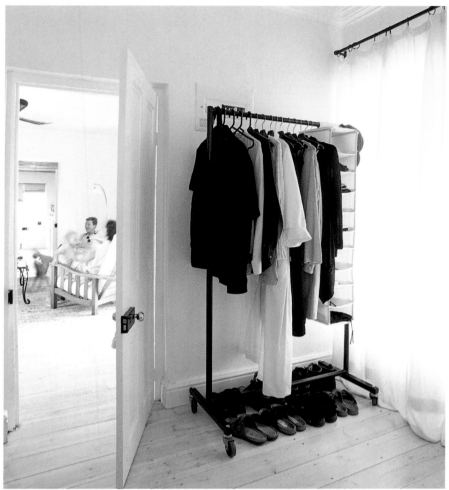

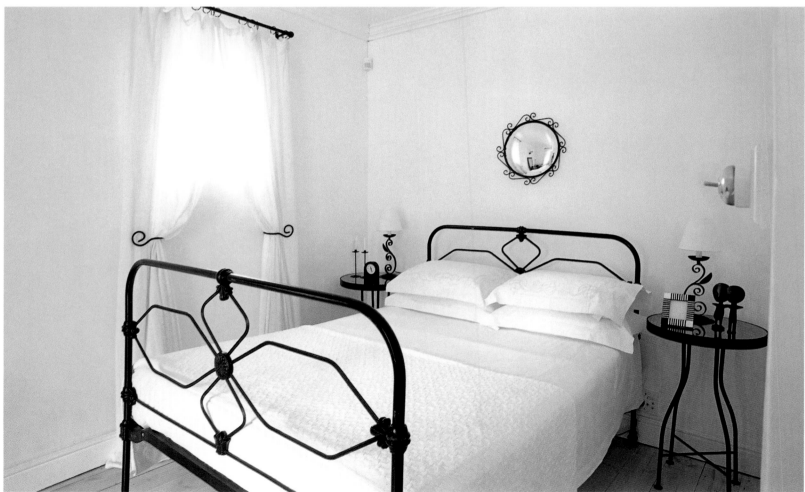

✷ **FACING PAGE AND ABOVE** The wrought iron bed in the summer bedroom was discovered by Marina Pretorius's father during the 1970s, at Prince Albert in the Karoo Desert. The couple have decorated the house throughout with objects accumulated since their student days. ✷ **LINKE SEITE UND OBEN** Marina Pretorius' Vater entdeckte das schmiedeeiserne Bett im Sommerzimmer in den 1970er Jahren in Prince Albert, einem Ort in der Wüste Karoo. Die überwiegend schlichten Einrichtungsgegenstände haben die beiden Architekten seit ihrer Studentenzeit nach und nach zusammengetragen. ✷ **PAGE DE GAUCHE ET CI-DESSUS** Le lit en fer forgé de la chambre d'été a été découvert à Prince Albert (désert du Karoo), dans les années 1970 par le père de Marina Pretorius. Le couple a sobrement décoré la maison avec les objets accumulés depuis le temps où ils étaient étudiants.

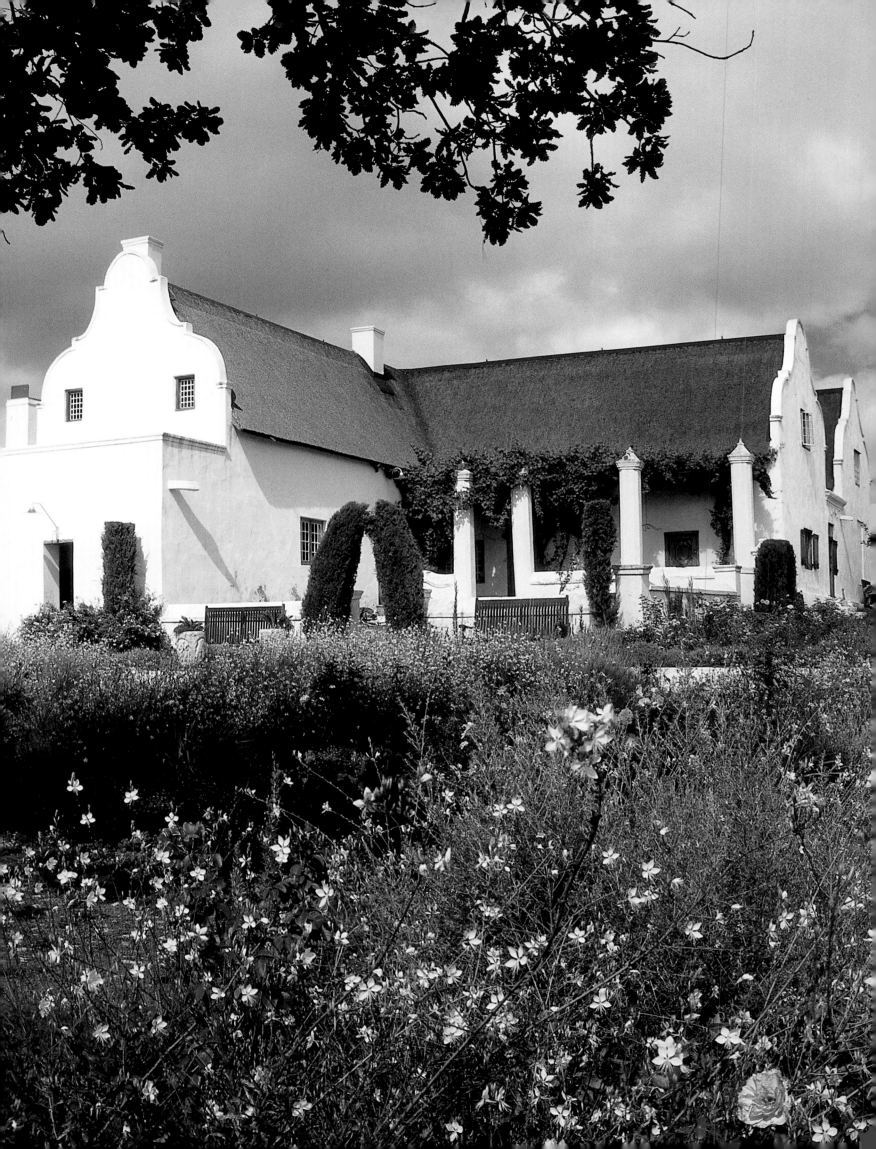

# Meerlust
## Stellenbosch

Meerlust is the most famous vineyard in South Africa,
and the Cape Dutch architecture of its historic main house is nothing short of a reference.

Seven generations of the Myburgh family have lived and died under this venerable thatched roof and the present owner, Hannes Myburgh, likes to relate how each one has left its mark ever since the first pioneers arrived in the Cape region in 1669.

Meerlust was settled and founded in 1756, and ever since then the place has gradually accumulated furniture and paintings. The house now consists of some 30 rooms, distributed over two stories. In the 1970s, before becoming a winegrower, Hannes Myburgh travelled widely in Europe. When he came home he lived in the former slave quarters adjoining the main building, before inheriting the property in 1988 and endowing the house with his own contribution of African and European furniture and objects. His first decision was to make the kitchen a more convivial area. Today this is where everyone at Meerlust gathers for meals, around a big square maple wood table with a dozen leather-upholstered chairs bought at an auction years ago. There are club armchairs or a delicately faded chintz sofa, should you be feeling too enfeebled to endure a candlelit dinner. The dogs wander about unconcerned by the family ghosts, while life in the old house moves leisurely onward.

Ein Strohdach krönt die Besitzung, auf der sieben Generationen Myburghs ihre Spuren hinterlassen haben. 1669 ging der Pionier der Familie bei Kapstadt an Land; bereits 1756 wurde Meerlust erbaut.

Doch lassen wir die Vergangenheit ruhen und öffnen die Tür zur Gegenwart. Schon im Vorraum werden Möbel und Bilder aus verschiedenen Epochen kombiniert. 30 Räume verteilen sich auf zwei Etagen. Hannes Myburgh, der heutige Besitzer, ist weit gereist und lebte Ende der 1970er Jahre in Europa, bevor er Winzer wurde. Nach seiner Rückkehr wohnte er in einem Nebengebäude, in dem früher die Sklaven untergebracht waren. Als er 1988 sein Erbe antrat, richtete er sich neu ein und arrangierte ein Miteinander von europäischen und afrikanischen Möbelstücken und Objekten. Als Erstes erklärte er die Küche zu einem Ort des Zusammenlebens. Inzwischen trifft man sich auf Meerlust hier zum Abendessen, an einem großen rechteckigen Tisch aus Ahornholz mit einem Dutzend Lederstühlen, die Myburgh auf einer Auktion erstanden hat. Wer zu erschöpft ist, lässt sich auf dem Chintzsofa mit dem ausgeblichenen Blümchenmuster oder in einem der Clubsessel nieder. Das Festmahl wird bei Kerzenlicht serviert. Hunde tollen herum – die Schatten der Vergangenheit ruhen.

Depuis l'habitation coiffée d'un toit de chaume, sept générations de Myburgh vous contemplent. L'actuel propriétaire affirme volontiers que chacune d'elle y a laissé son empreinte.

Le pionnier de la famille a débarqué dans la région du Cap en 1669; Meerlust a vu le jour en 1756. Mais chassons les spectres et poussons la porte. Dès le vestibule, les époques se confondent en meubles et tableaux. Les 30 pièces se déploient sur deux étages. Avant de devenir vigneron, Hannes Myburgh a beaucoup voyagé et vécu en Europe à la fin des années 1970. À son retour, il a habité dans la partie attenante, autrefois réservée aux esclaves. Quand l'héritage a été prononcé, en 1988, il a investi les lieux en mêlant meubles et objets africains et européens. Sa première décision fut de faire de la cuisine un lieu convivial. À Meerlust, aujourd'hui, c'est là, autour d'une grande table carrée en érable, que l'on se retrouve pour dîner, assis sur une douzaine de chaises en cuir achetées aux enchères. Les plus alanguis prennent place sur un canapé en chintz fleuri, délicatement fané, ou un fauteuil club. Le festin est servi aux chandelles. Les chiens gambadent. Sans importuner les fantômes de la famille.

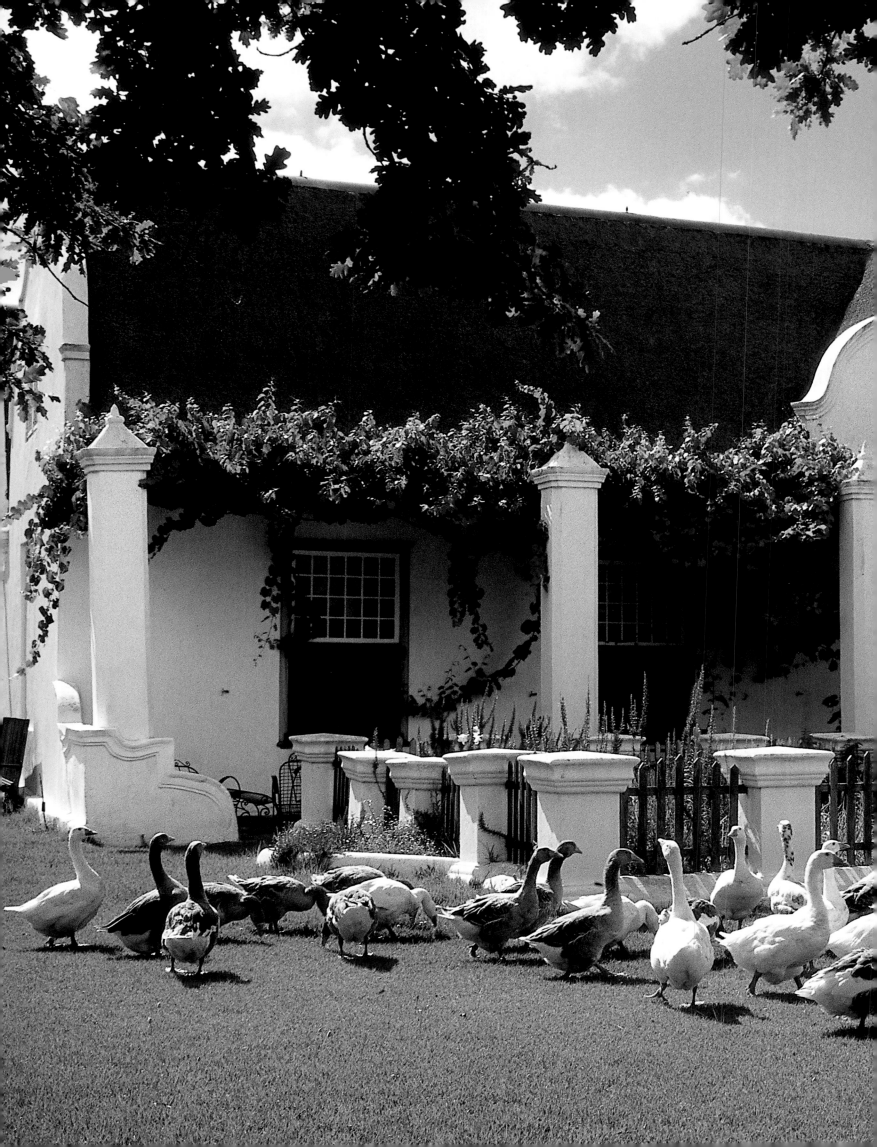

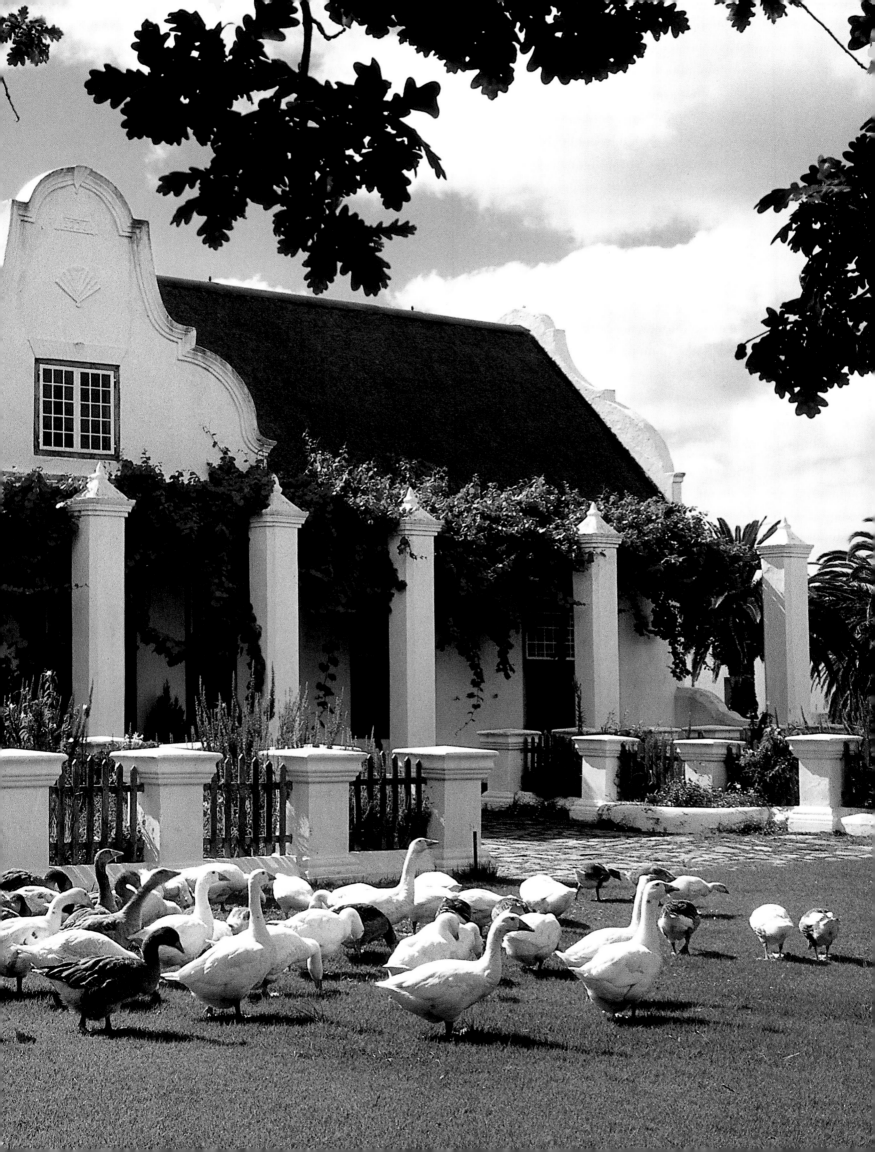

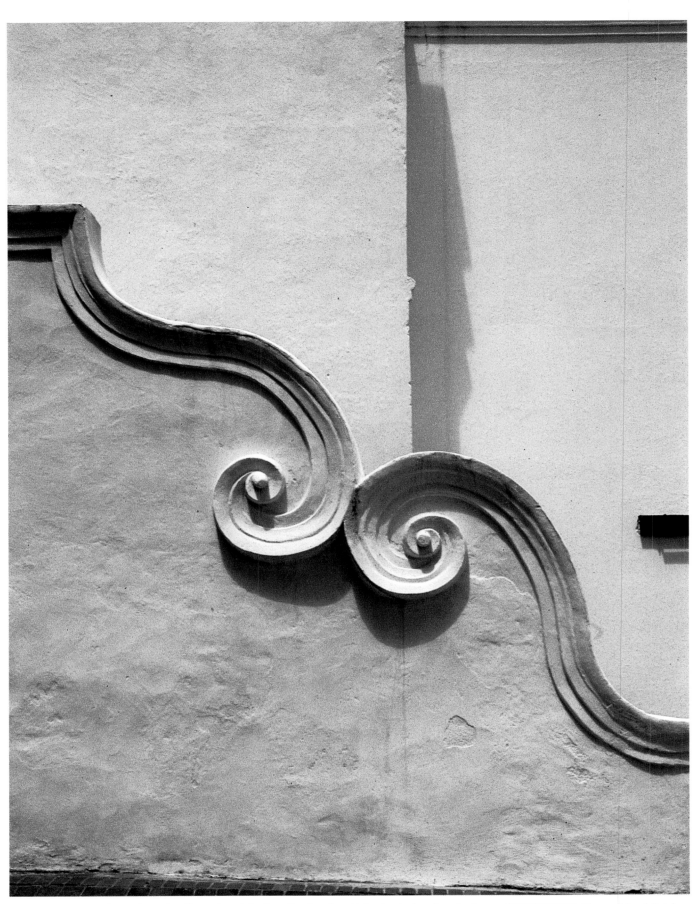

❋ **PREVIOUS PAGES** Meerlust is the perfect illustration of the Cape Dutch style, with its thatched roofs and columns. **ABOVE AND FACING PAGE** The traditional Dutch gables serve in Africa as simple decorative elements celebrating life on the farm. The walls are of brick, with a thick skin of lime wash. ❋ **VORHERGEHENDE DOPPELSEITE** Meerlust ist ein perfektes Beispiel für den Cape-Dutch-Stil: Die Strohdächer der Häuser ruhen auf Säulen. **OBEN UND RECHTE SEITE** Diese Giebelvoluten, die in der holländischen Architektur ihren festen Platz haben, dienen in Afrika nur der Zierde – die Darstellungen feiern die Arbeit in der Landwirtschaft. Die Ziegelwände sind mit einer dicken Kalkschicht rau verputzt. ❋ **DOUBLE PAGE PRECEDENTE** Meerlust est le témoignage parfait du style Cape Dutch avec ses habitations à toit de chaume, soutenues par des colonnes. **CI-DESSUS ET PAGE DE DROITE** Les pignons aux volutes traditionnelles dans l'architecture hollandaise sont en Afrique de simples éléments décoratifs célébrant les travaux de la ferme. Murs en briques, crépis d'une épaisse couche de chaux.

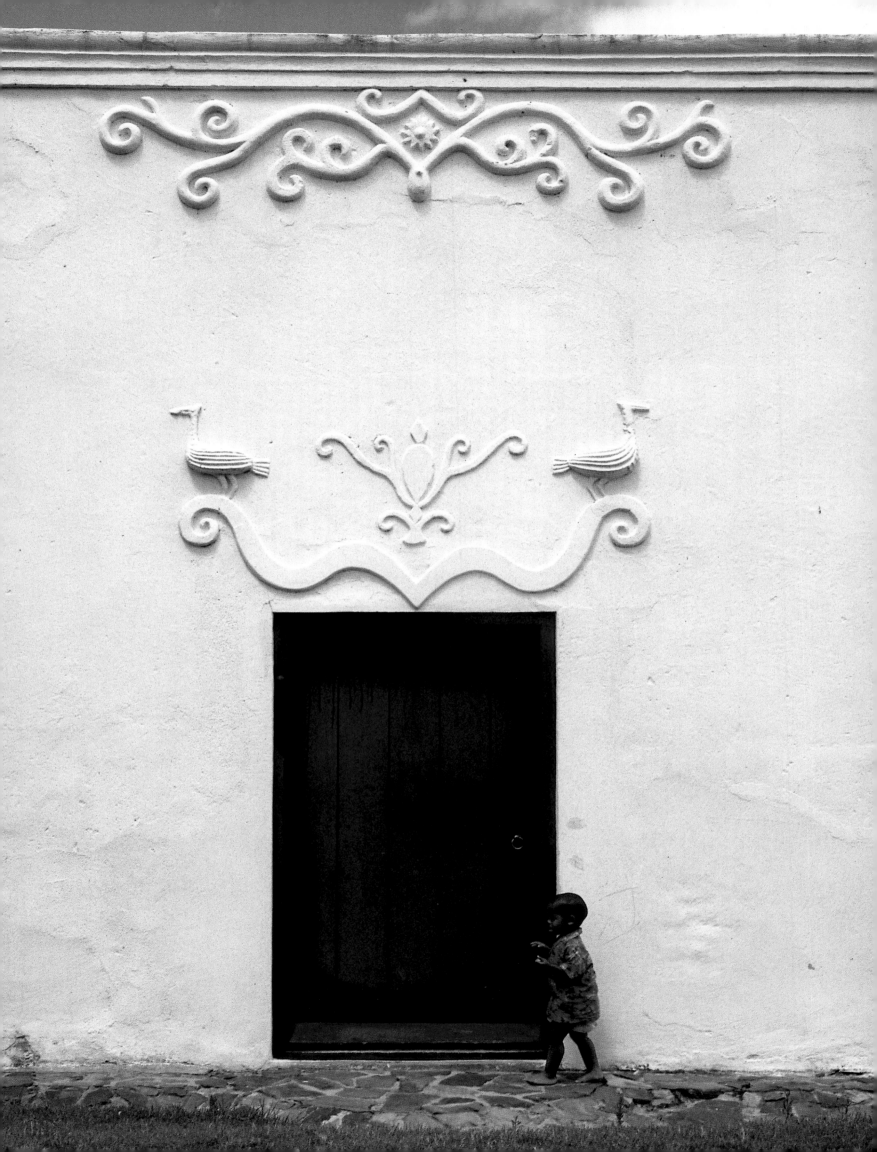

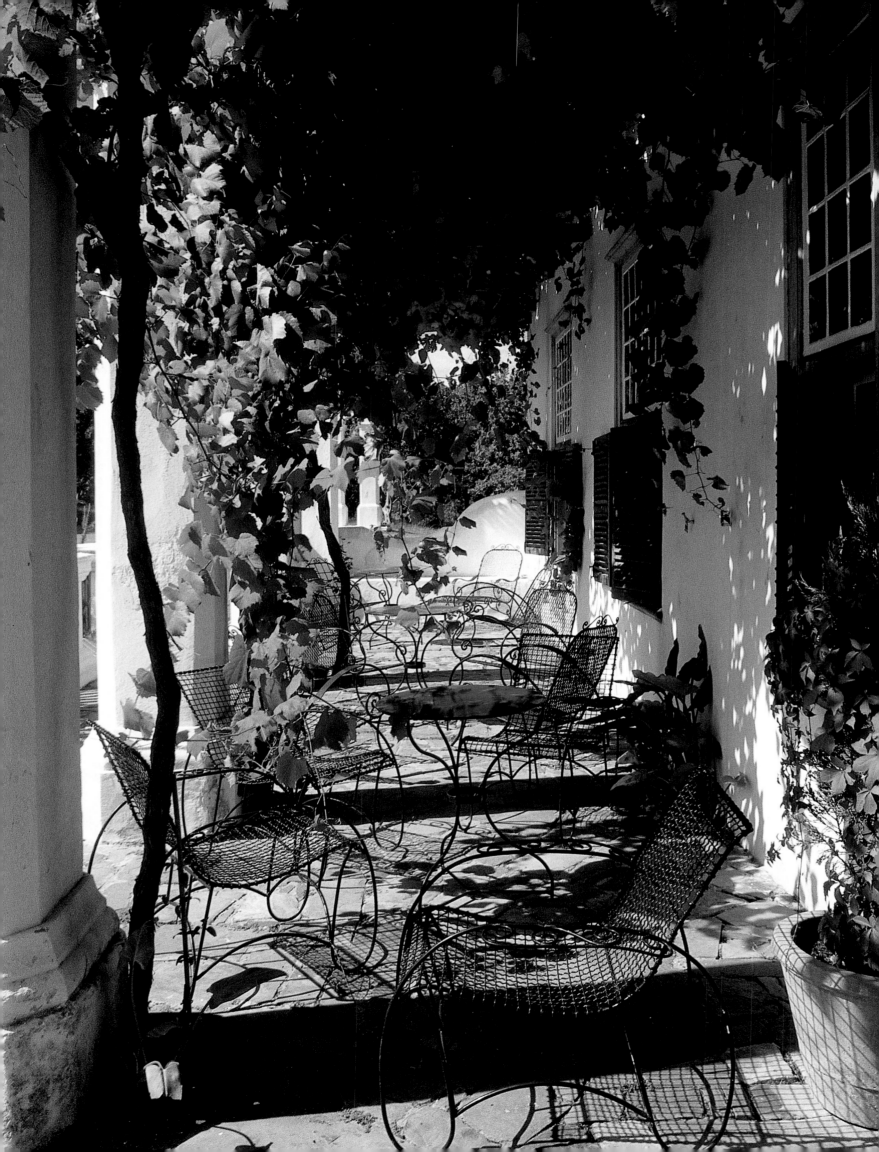

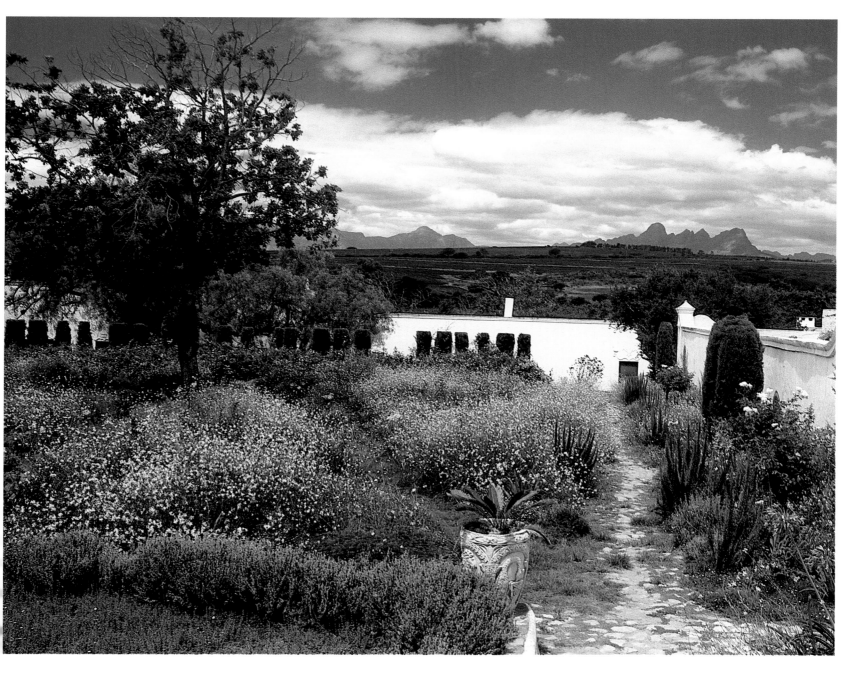

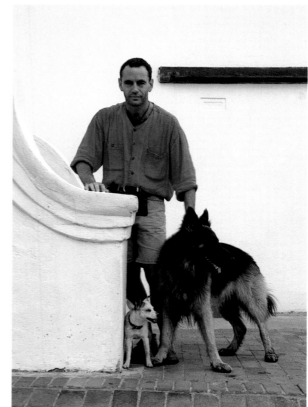

❋ **FACING PAGE** The traditional Cape Dutch veranda at the main entrance of the house. From here the view stretches as far as Table Mountain and the sea. **RIGHT** The owner, Hannes Myburgh. **FOLLOWING DOUBLE PAGE** The owner's bedroom with its comfortable armchairs, framed flags and pictures by young artists. ❋ **LINKE SEITE** Die traditionelle Veranda im Cape-Dutch-Stil ist der eigentliche Hauseingang. Die Aussicht reicht bis zum Tafelberg und übers Meer. **RECHTS** Hannes Myburgh, der Besitzer. **FOLGENDE DOPPELSEITE** In dem mit bequemen Clubsesseln möblierten Zimmer des Hausherrn hängen gerahmte Fahnen neben den Werken junger Künstler. ❋ **PAGE DE GAUCHE** La véranda traditionnelle de style Cape Dutch marque l'entrée véritable de la maison. La vue porte jusqu'à la montagne de la Table et la mer. **A DROITE** Le propriétaire, Hannes Myburgh. **DOUBLE PAGE SUIVANTE** La chambre du propriétaire avec ses clubs confortables, marie les œuvres de jeunes artistes aux drapeaux encadrés.

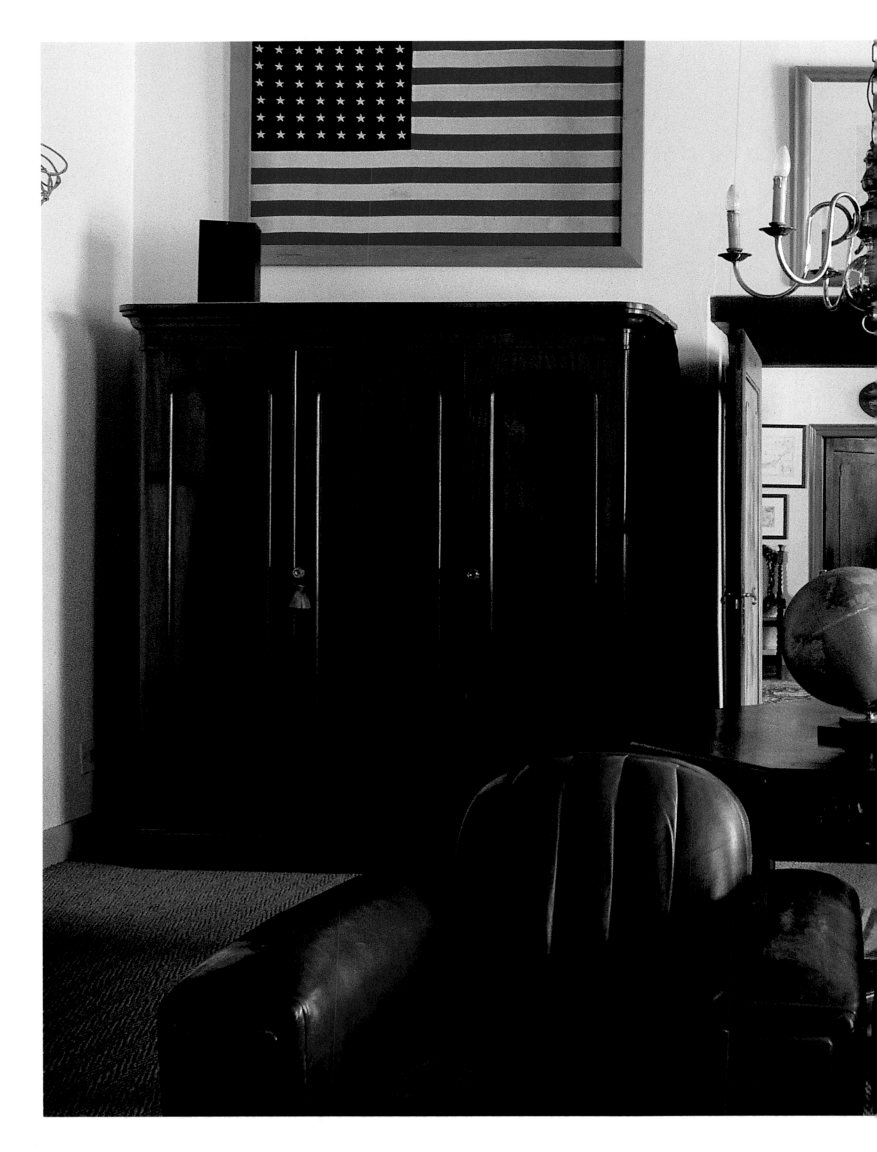

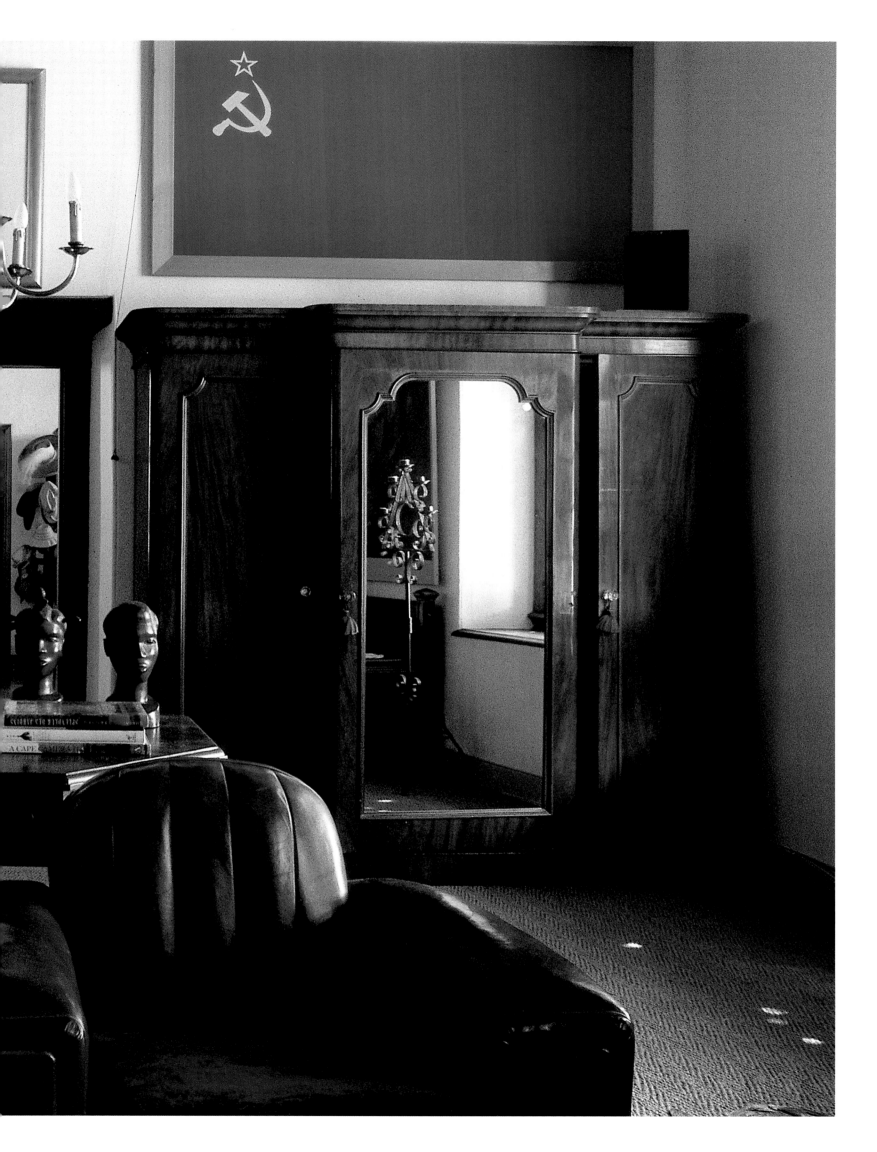

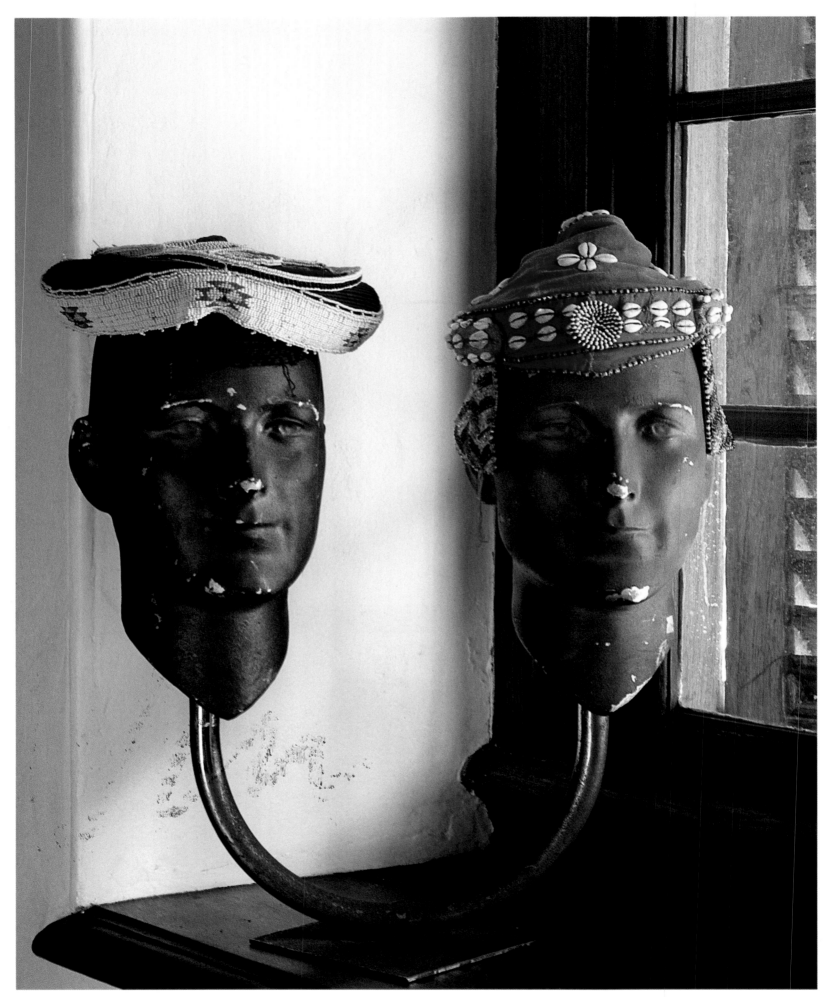

✳ **ABOVE** Austrian plaster heads dating from before the war. **FACING PAGE** The kitchen is the heart of the house, with its big maple wood table and its buffet filled with dishes, vases and farm produce put up in jars. ✳ **OBEN** Gipsköpfe aus dem Vorkriegsösterreich. **RECHTE SEITE** Die Küche ist der Mittelpunkt des Hauses – ein großer Tisch aus Ahornholz, ein Küchenschrank mit Geschirr, Vasen und Konserven aus der eigenen Produktion. ✳ **CI-DESSUS** Têtes en plâtre fabriquées avant-guerre en Autriche. **PAGE DE DROITE** La cuisine est le cœur de la maison avec sa grande table en érable et son buffet d'épicier rempli de vaisselle, de vases et de produits de la ferme en bocaux.

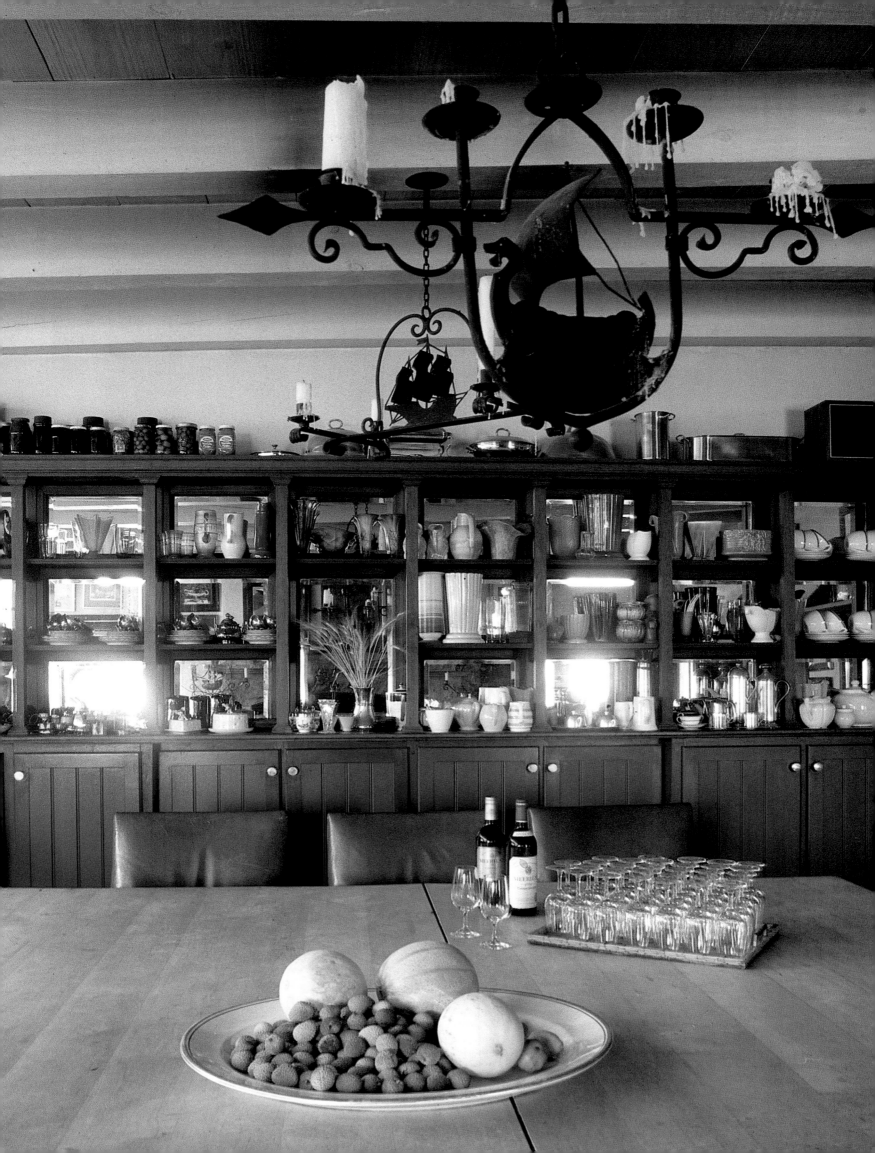

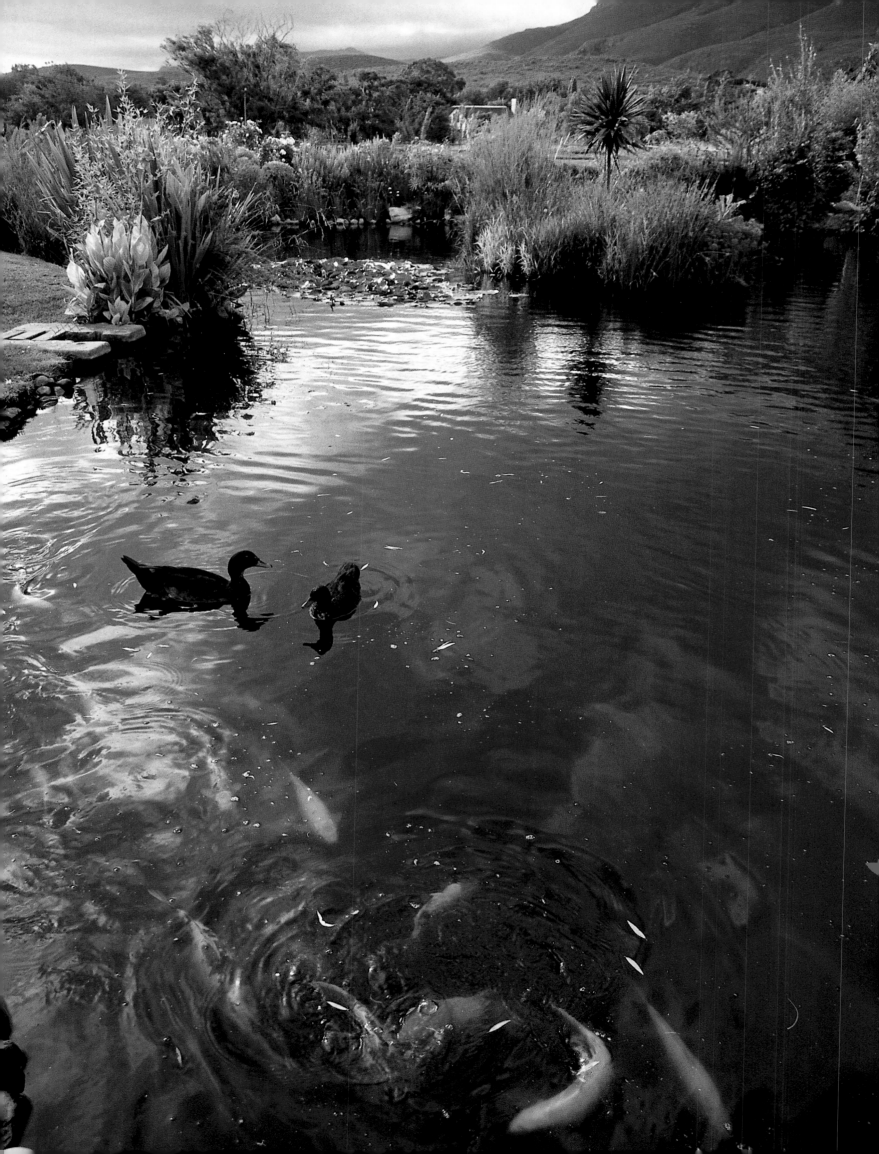

# CAPAD Cottage
## Greyton

A cottage – and a warm fireside for the cold South African winters.

Turn on your time machine, close your eyes and enter the enchanted world of Beatrix Potter's Peter Rabbit and Pigling Bland, where all the geese are distinguished-looking and pigs are clean as whistles.

There's something of this idyll in Mike Donkin's lovely cottage at Greyton. To the pure lines of the surrounding meadows and hills, he has added an interior décor that is the antithesis of his house in town. Donkin is a stout supporter of country style; his cottage has beams galore, a massive ladder leading up to the attic, old-fashioned kitchen appliances, and bare floors. Yet there's not a shred of pretension here – one of the pictures on the wall may have cost him only 25 rand (about two pounds sterling) at a local auction, but that doesn't make him any less proud of it. Similarly, elements of a watering system twine around the flamboyant candleholder on the veranda, which is dressed up with cheap glass. Old armchairs and worn cushions are always good enough for Donkin; yet if you look more closely there's a subdued theme running through the house. In every room there's some kind of reference to the sea, whether it be a candlestick with a seashell base, or a collection of model boats, or a miniature lighthouse. Maybe he misses the ocean, even though water abounds on his property, with springs, a dam and a pool. Beatrix Potter would thoroughly approve.

Ab in die Zeitmaschine, Augen schließen und schon fühlt man sich in die Zauberwelt von Beatrix Potter zurückversetzt. Wer erinnert sich nicht an Peter Hase, die Flopsi-Häschen und die bukolische Idylle mit vornehmen Gänsen und porentief sauberen Schweinen?

Mike Donkins hübsches Cottage in Greyton würde gut in diese Welt passen. Das Interieur, das in scharfem Kontrast zu Donkins ansonsten städtischem Umfeld steht, ist als Ergänzung der klaren Linien der Wiesen rundum und des sanften Schwungs der Hügel zu verstehen. Mit Snobismus hält sich Mike Donkin nicht auf, er pflegt im Gegenteil einen betont rustikalen Stil: Stolz präsentierte Holzbalkendecken, eine wuchtige Speichertreppe, veraltete Elektrogeräte im Haushalt und unbehandelte Fußböden. An der Wand hängt ein Bild, das er für 25 Rand (rund drei Euro) auf dem hiesigen Trödel gekauft hat. Der flackernde Kerzenleuchter auf der Veranda ist umgeben von Gartenschläuchen und billigen Gläsern. Alte Sessel und Kissen erfüllen ihren Zweck. In jedem Zimmer wird man auf die eine oder andere Art ans Meer erinnert, sei es durch einen Kerzenleuchter mit einem Fuß aus Muschelschalen oder eine Sammlung von Modellbooten oder einen Miniatur-Leuchtturm. Vielleicht weil der Ozean so weit entfernt ist? Das reichlich vorhandene Süßwasser lässt ihn rasch in Vergessenheit geraten, ob beim Anblick der Springbrunnen und des Stauwehrs oder im Swimmingpool. Beatrix Potter hätte es hier jedenfalls gefallen.

Mettez en route la machine à remonter le temps, fermez les yeux et retrouvez le monde enchanté de Beatrix Potter. Souvenez-vous l'histoire de Pierre Lapin, l'idylle pastorale avec ses oies distinguées et ses cochons tout propres. Vous ne voyez vraiment pas?

Alors filez à Greyton et observez le beau cottage de Mike Donkin. Aux lignes pures des prairies alentour, aux courbes douces des collines avoisinantes, il a joint une décoration intérieure aux antipodes de son habitat de la ville. Résolument attaché au style rustique avec ses poutres fièrement affichées, son échelle massive pour le grenier, ses appareils électroménagers d'un autre âge, ses sols nus, Mike Donkin ne s'encombre pas de snobisme. Telle peinture au mur a été achetée 25 rands aux enchères locales (moins de trois euros). Dans la véranda, le flamboyant chandelier est cerclé de tuyaux d'arrosage et fagoté de verreries bon marché. De vieux fauteuils et coussins usés font l'affaire. Étrangement, sous la forme d'un chandelier au pied en coquillage, d'une collection de bateaux ou d'un phare la mer est présente dans chaque pièce. Regretterait-on l'absente? L'eau douce se chargera de la faire oublier. Sur la propriété, elle abonde dans les fontaines, un barrage, et une piscine. Beatrix Potter apprécierait.

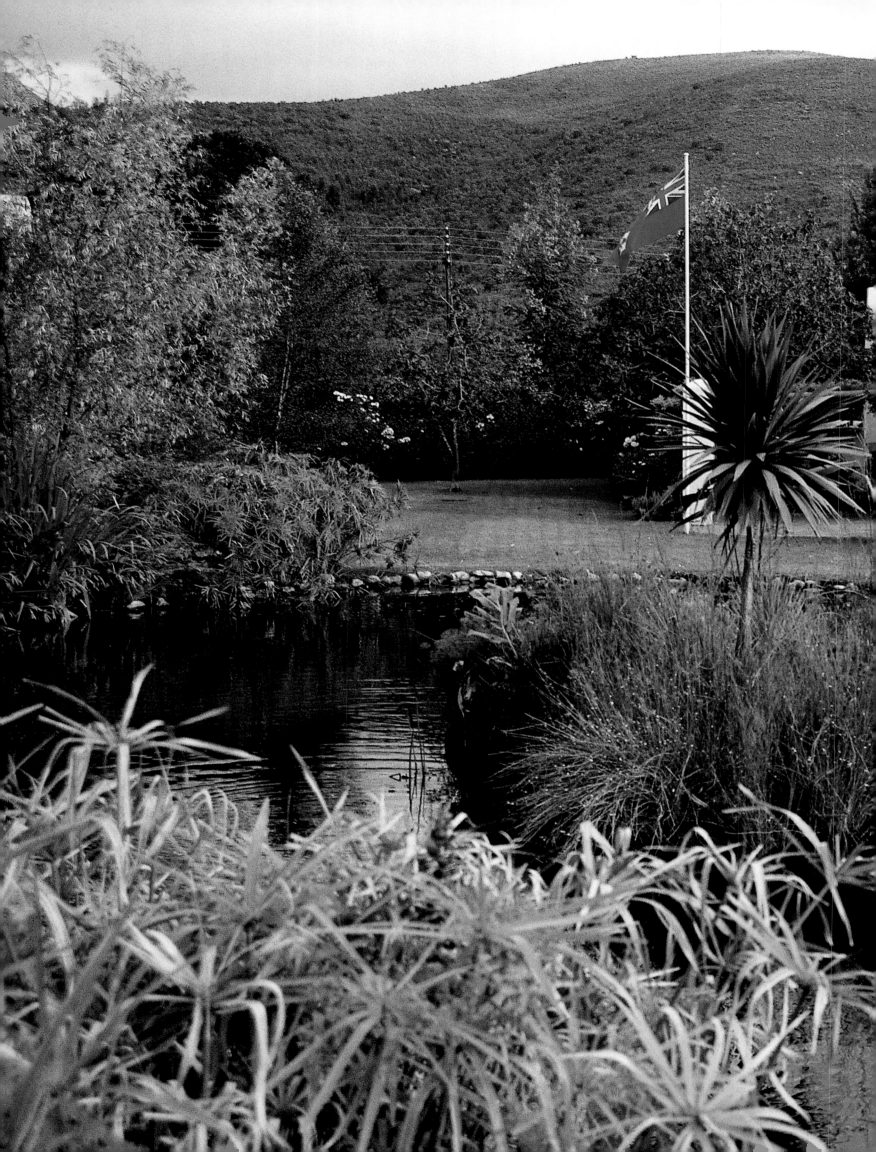

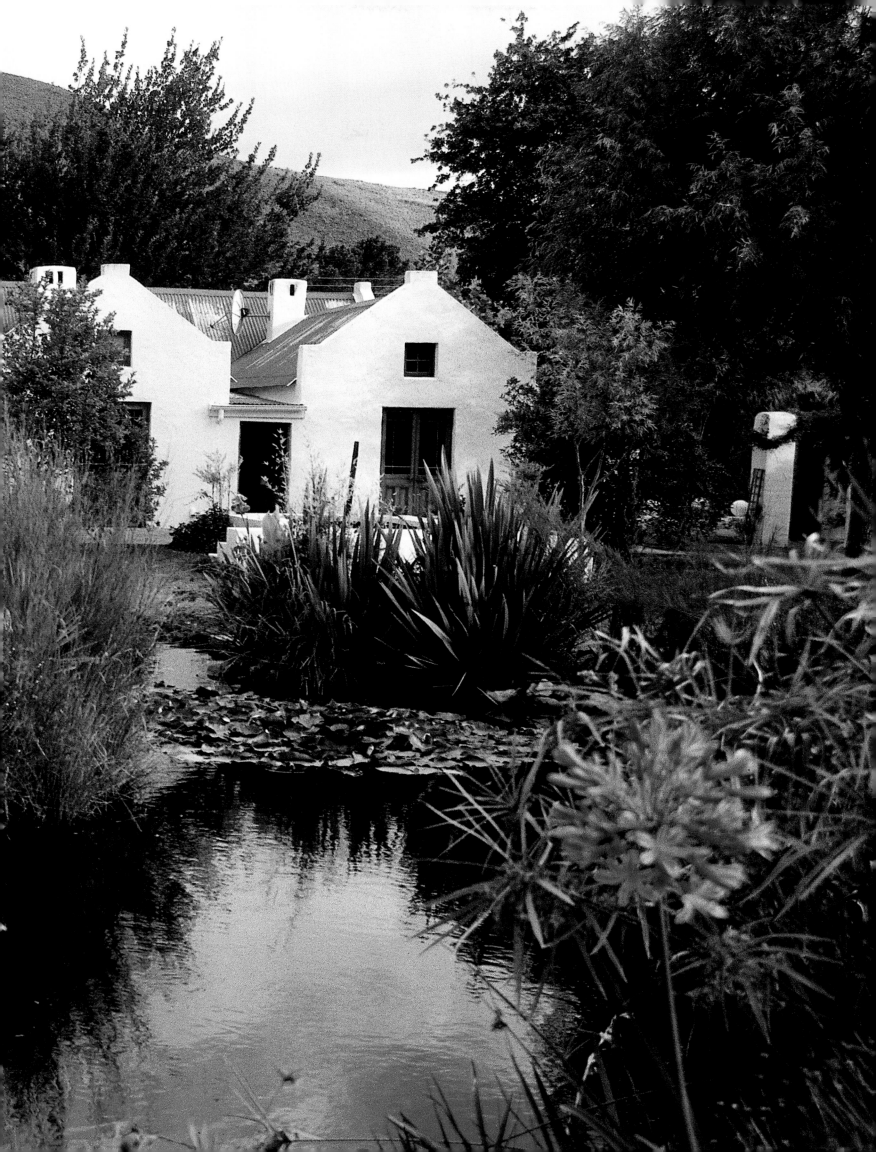

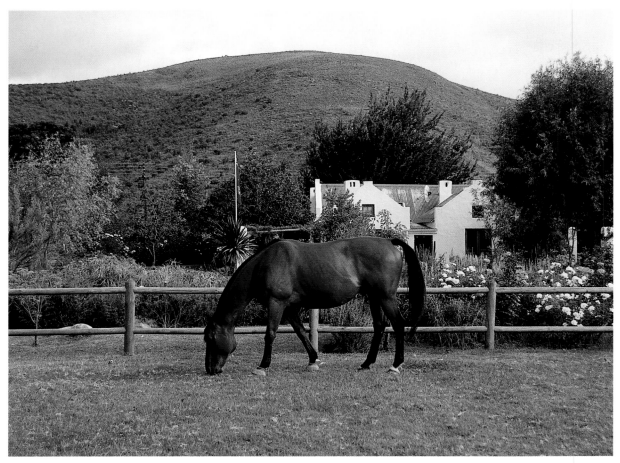

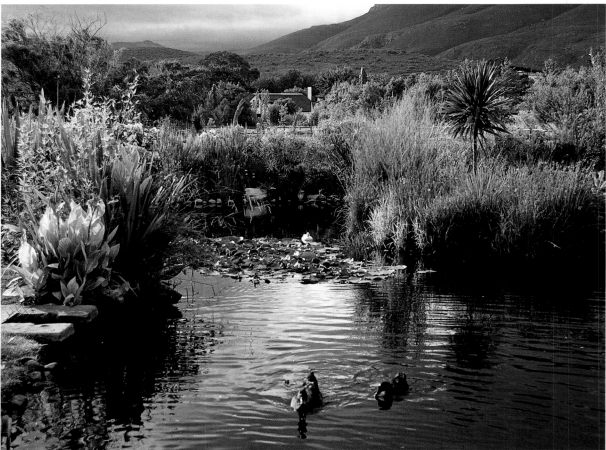

❋ **PREVIOUS PAGES AND ABOVE** Far from the demands of a career that carries him all over the world, the owner revels in the tranquillity of a weekend country house. Apple, his horse, stands silhouetted against the horizon. ❋ **VORHERGEHENDE DOPPELSEITE UND OBEN** In sicherer Entfernung von seinem Berufsleben hat der Hausherr ein ruhiges Fleckchen für die Wochenenden gefunden. Das Pferd Apple darf immer frei herum-laufen. ❋ **DOUBLE PAGE PRECEDENTE ET CI-DESSOUS** Loin de l'agitation d'une carrière qui le conduit aux quatre coins du monde, le propriétaire a choisi la tranquillité d'une maison de campagne pour les week-ends. Apple, le cheval, à l'horizon pour seule frontière.

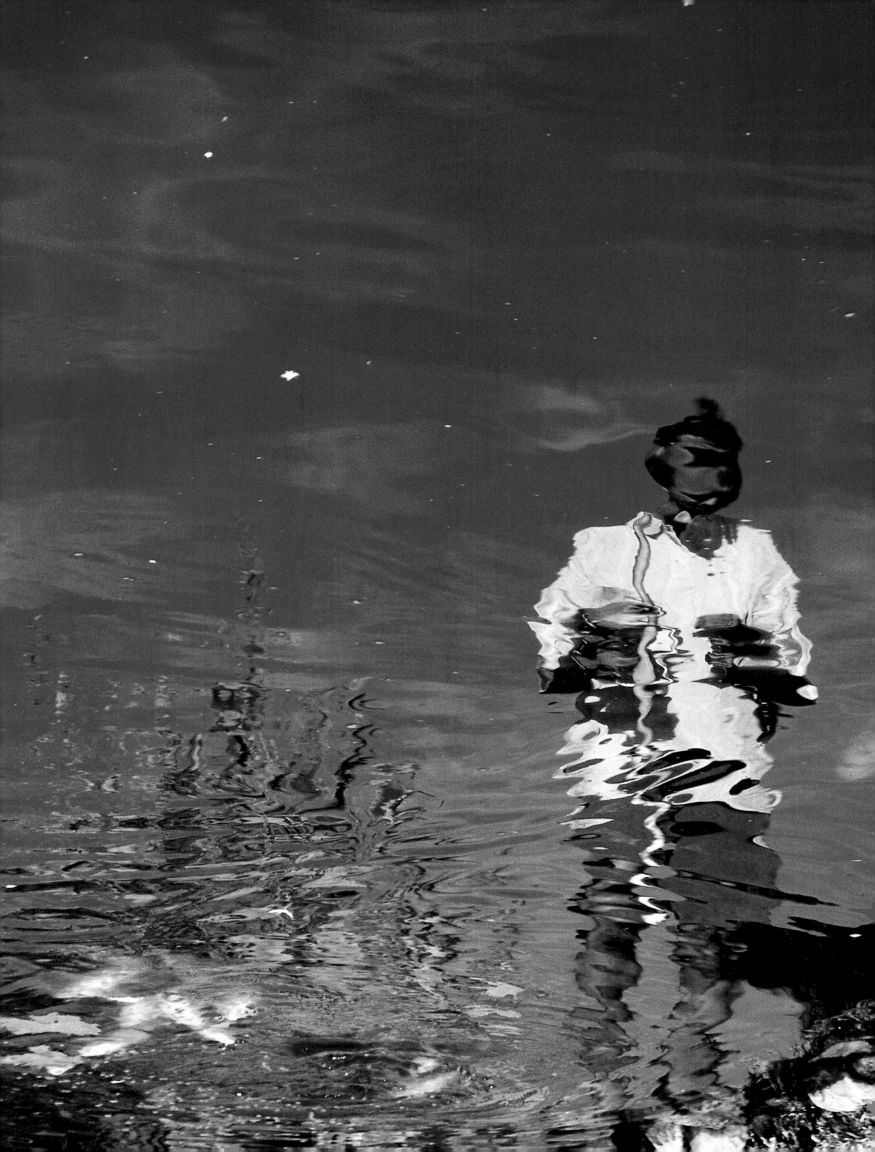

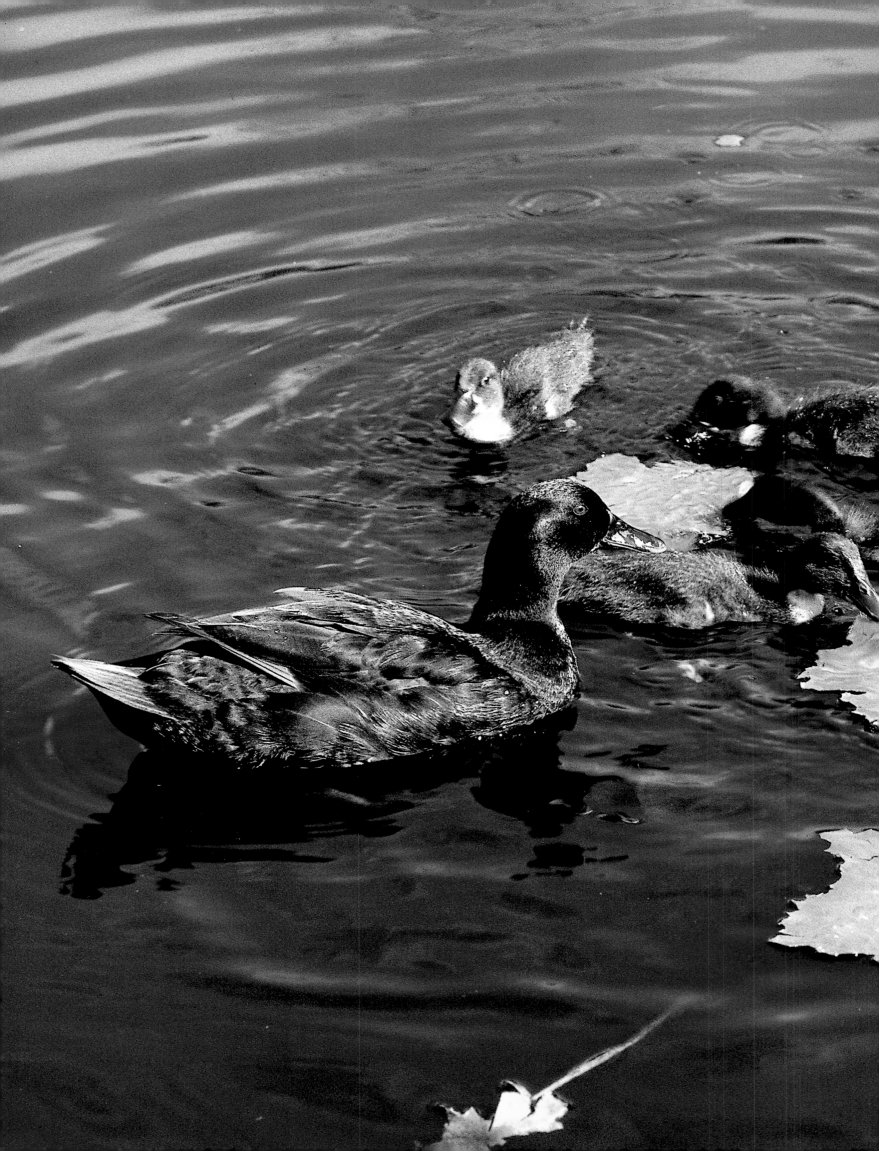

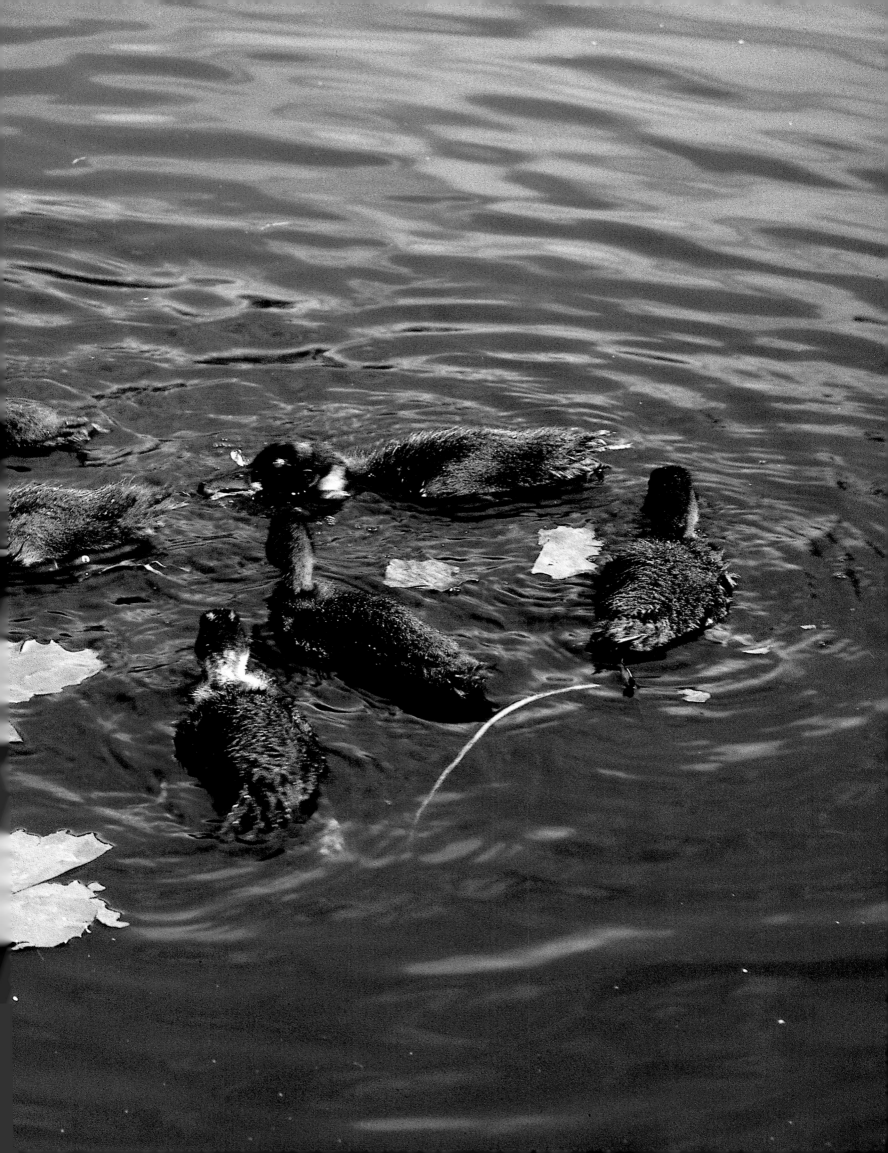

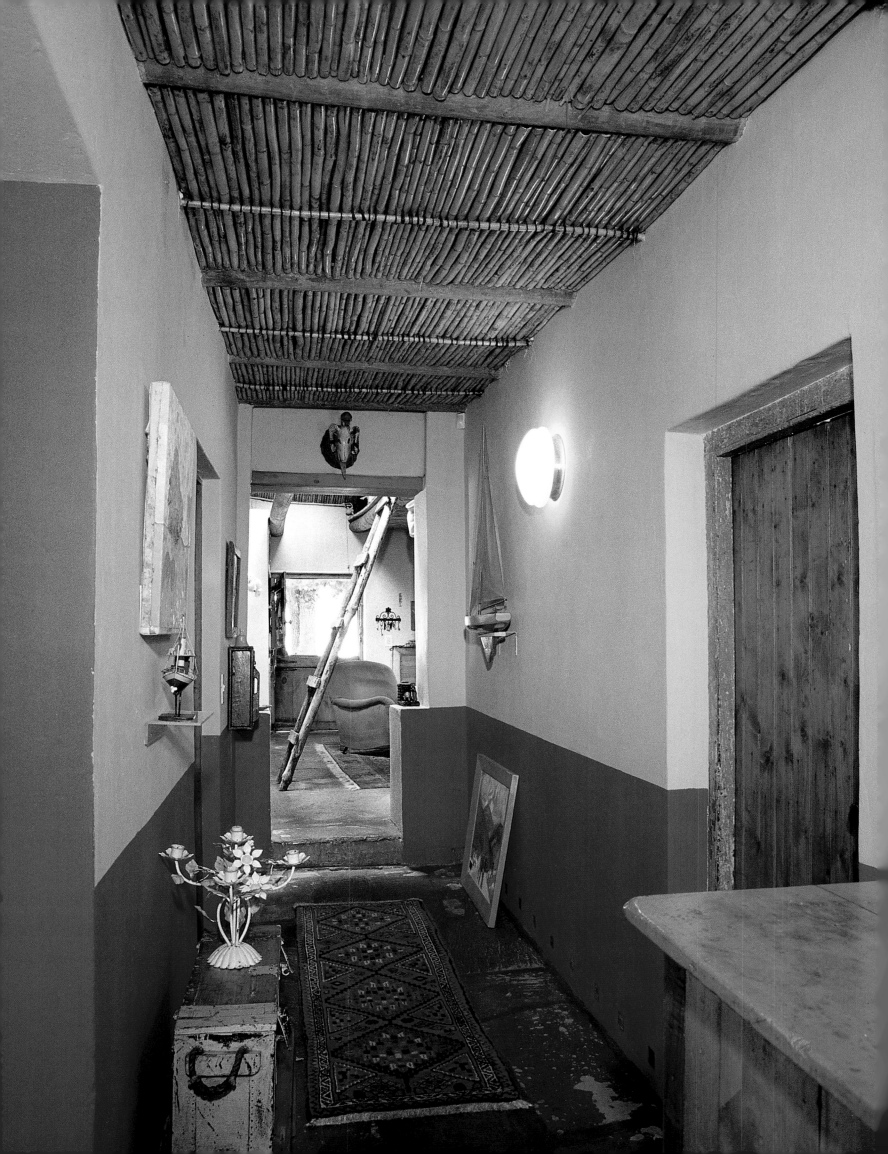

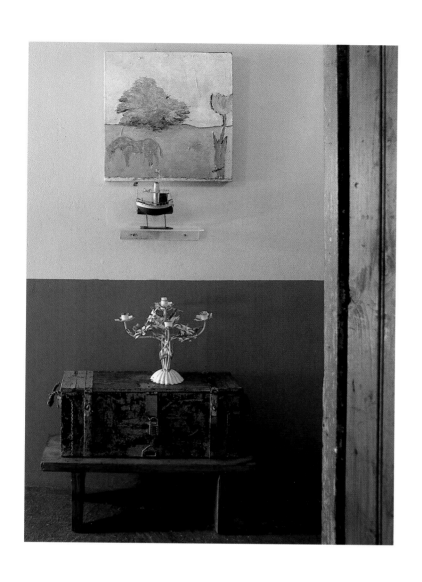

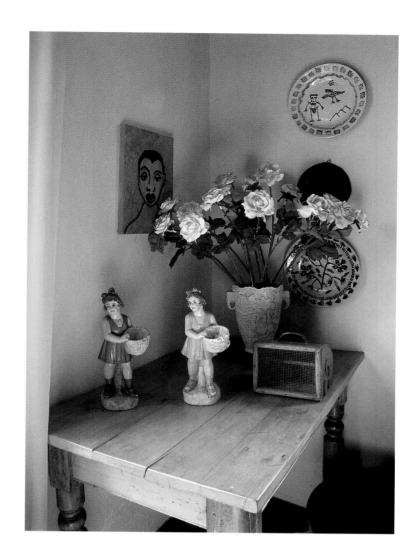

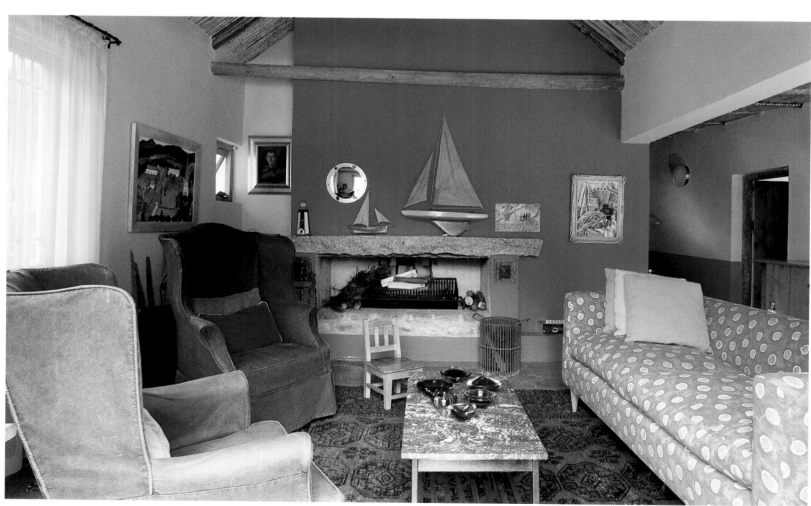

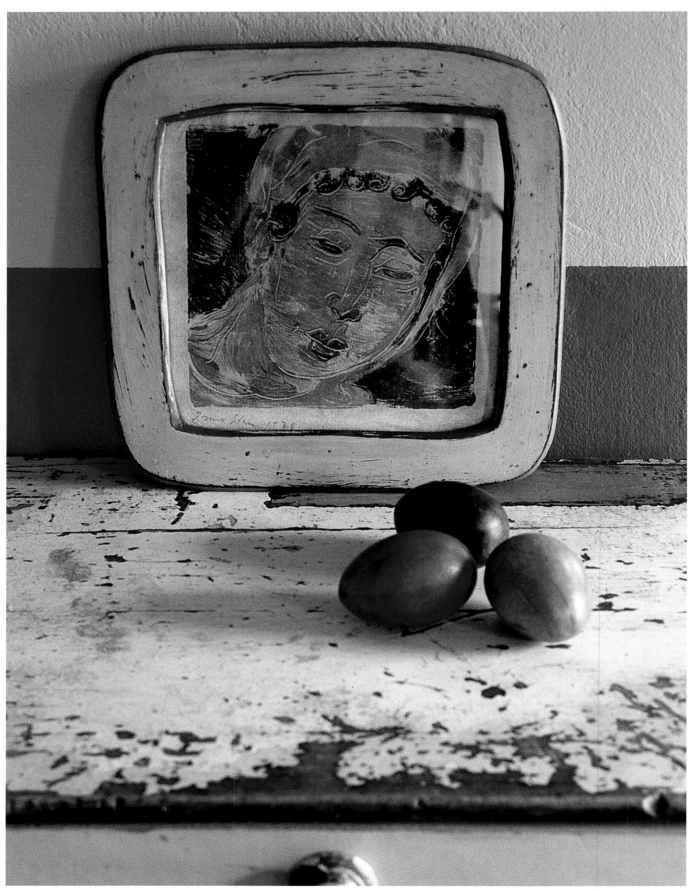

✳ **PRECEDING DOUBLE PAGE** A simple rush thatch covers the informal living room with its gay colours. The furniture, sofas and armchairs were picked up at antique shops and at auction at Sotheby's in Cape Town. **FOLLOWING PAGES** The kitchen with is massive table. Viewed as the heart of the house, it is furnished with old but indomitable electrical fittings. ✳ **VORHERGEHENDE DOPPELSEITE** Ein einfaches Rieddach deckt den formlosen, in leuchtenden Farben gestrichenen Salon. Die Möbel, Sofas und Sessel stammen aus Antiquitätenläden, vorwiegend aber von Auktionen bei Sotheby's in Kapstadt. **FOLGENDE SEITEN** Die Küche mit dem riesigen Tisch bildet den Mittelpunkt des Hauses; die Elektrogeräte sind alt aber unverwüstlich. ✳ **DOUBLE PAGE PRECEDENTE** Un simple toit de roseaux recouvre l'informel salon aux couleurs éclatantes. Les meubles, sofas et fauteuils ont été chinés chez les antiquaires et surtout achetés aux enchères de la Sotheby's à Cape Town. **DOUBLE PAGE SUIVANTE** La cuisine avec sa table monumentale est le cœur de la maison, elle se contente d'un électroménager hors d'âge mais increvable.

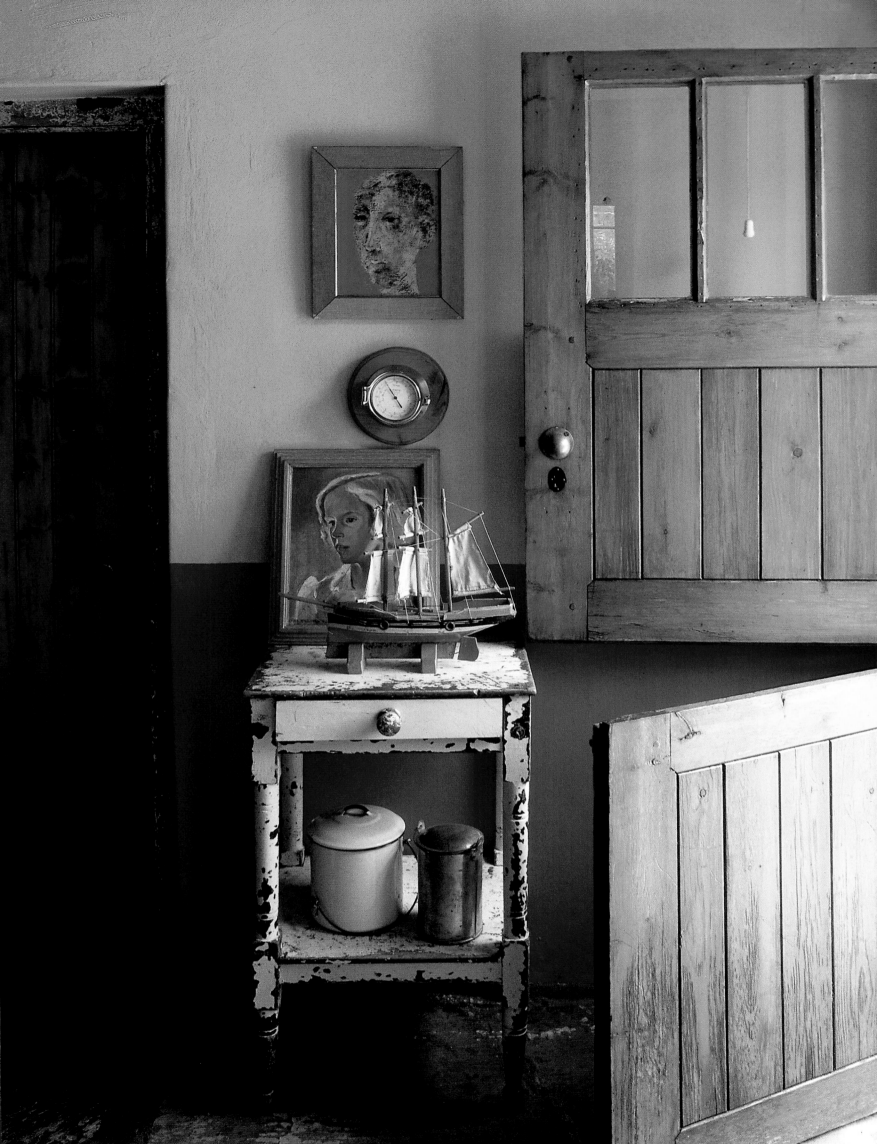

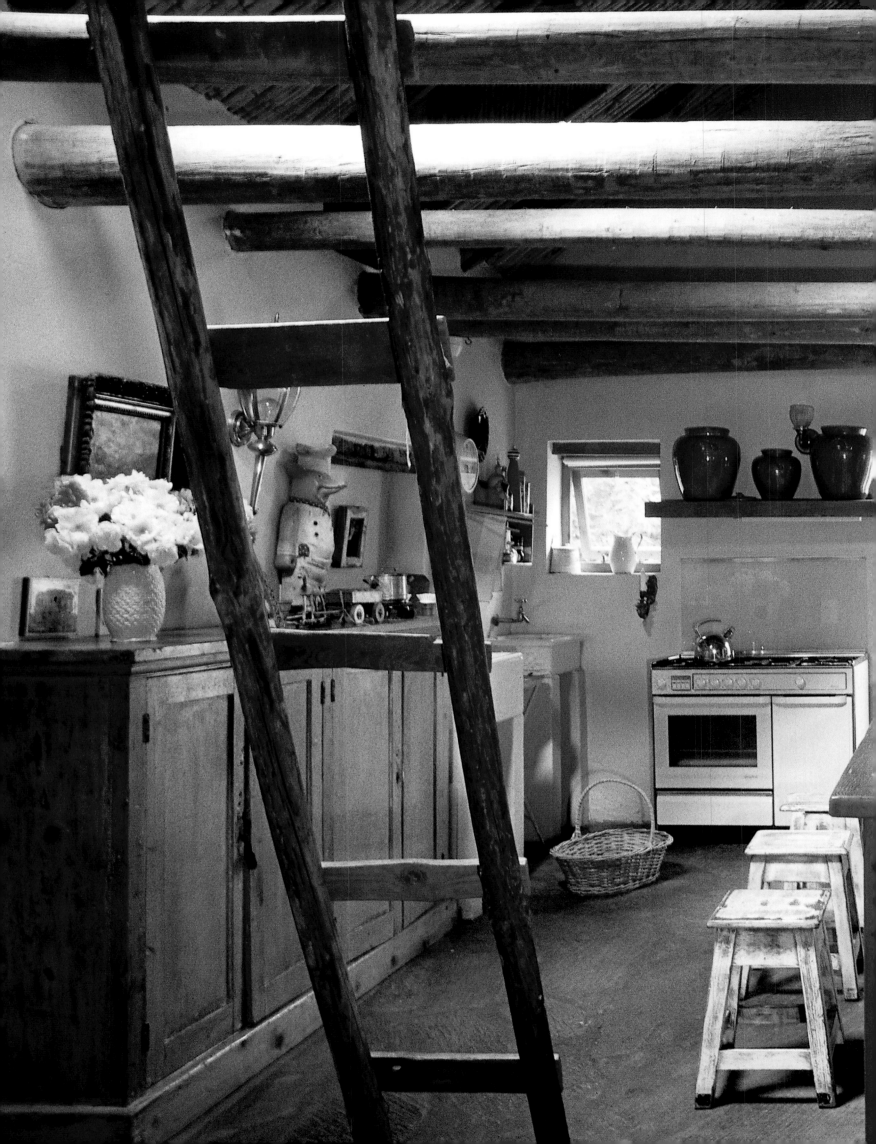

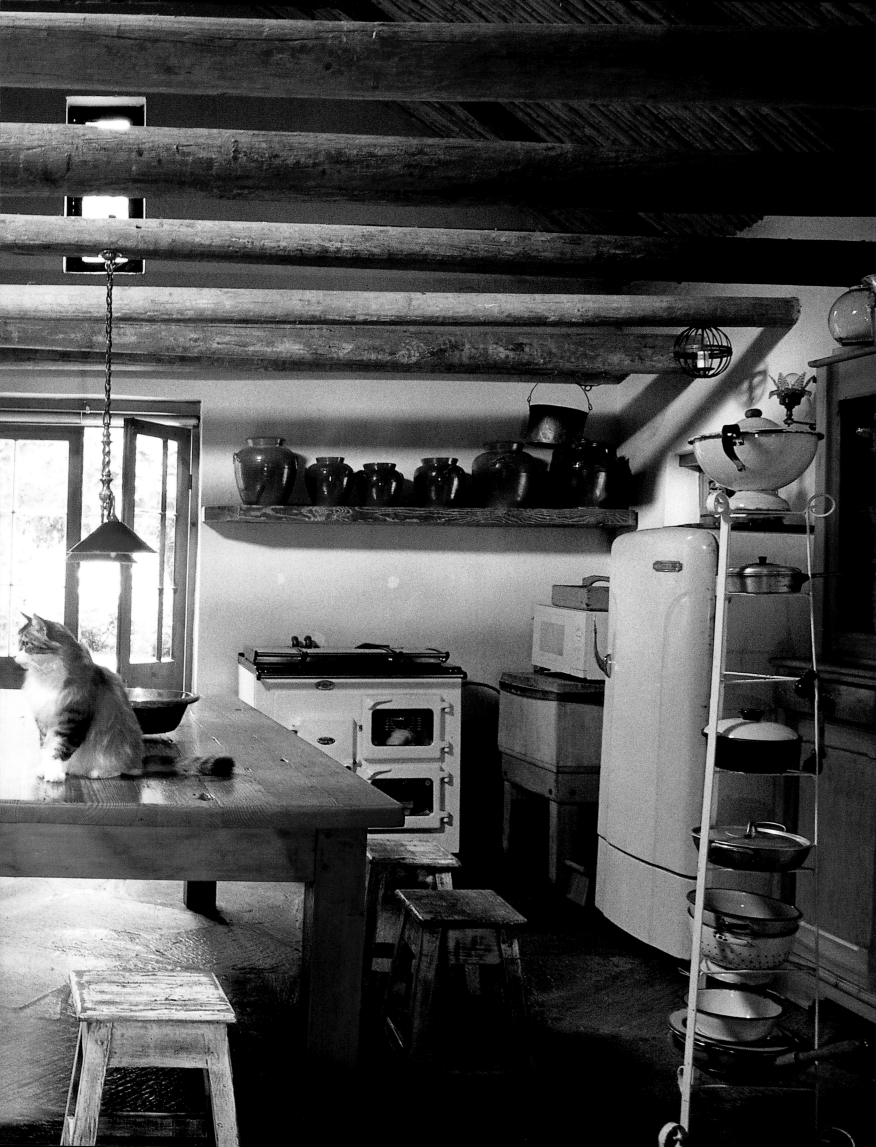

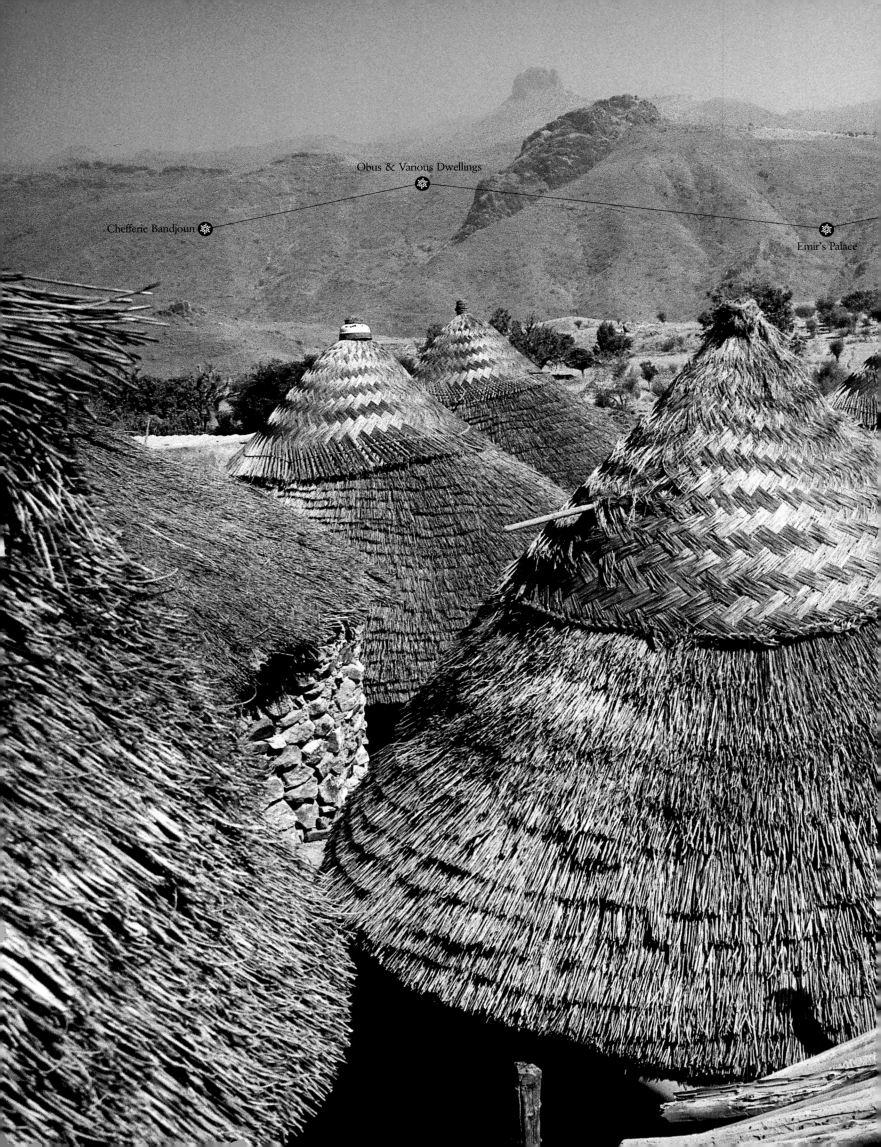

Obus & Various Dwellings ✵

Chefferie Bandjoun ✵

Emir's Palace ✵

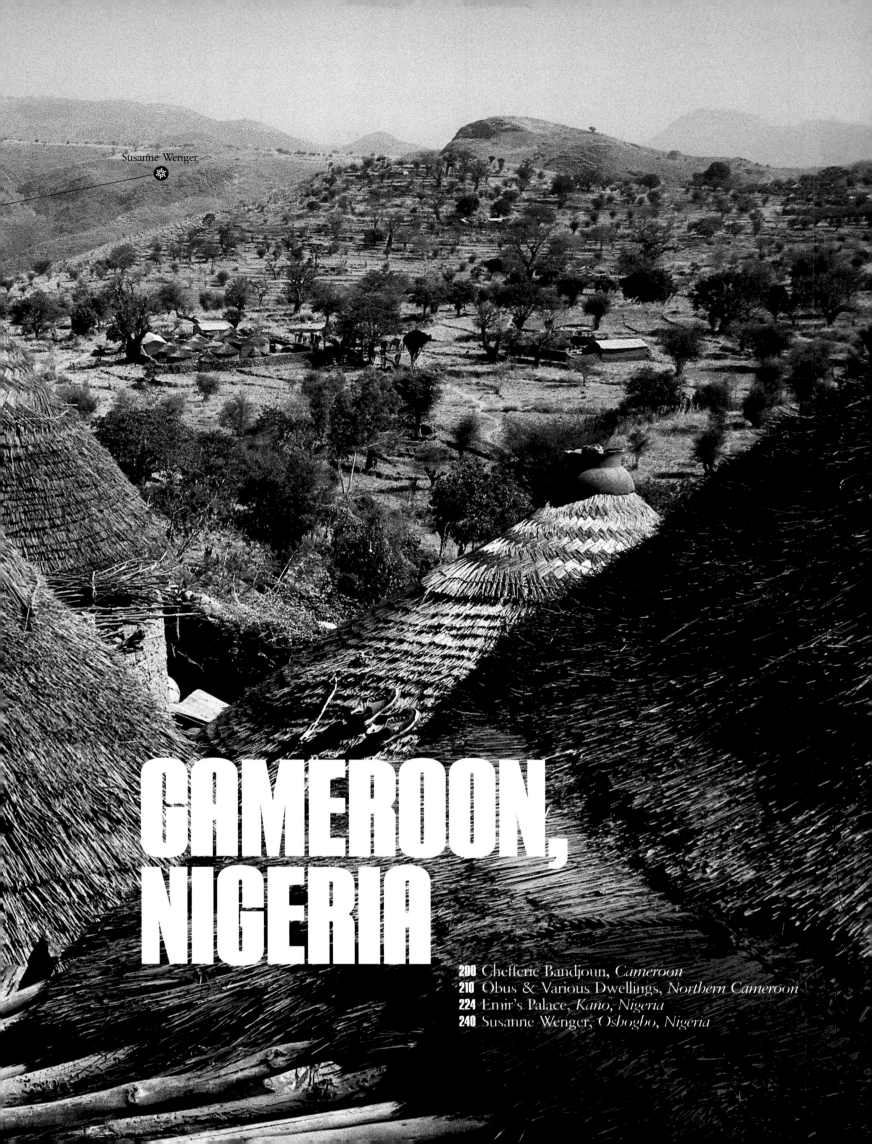

Susanne Wenger

# CAMEROON, NIGERIA

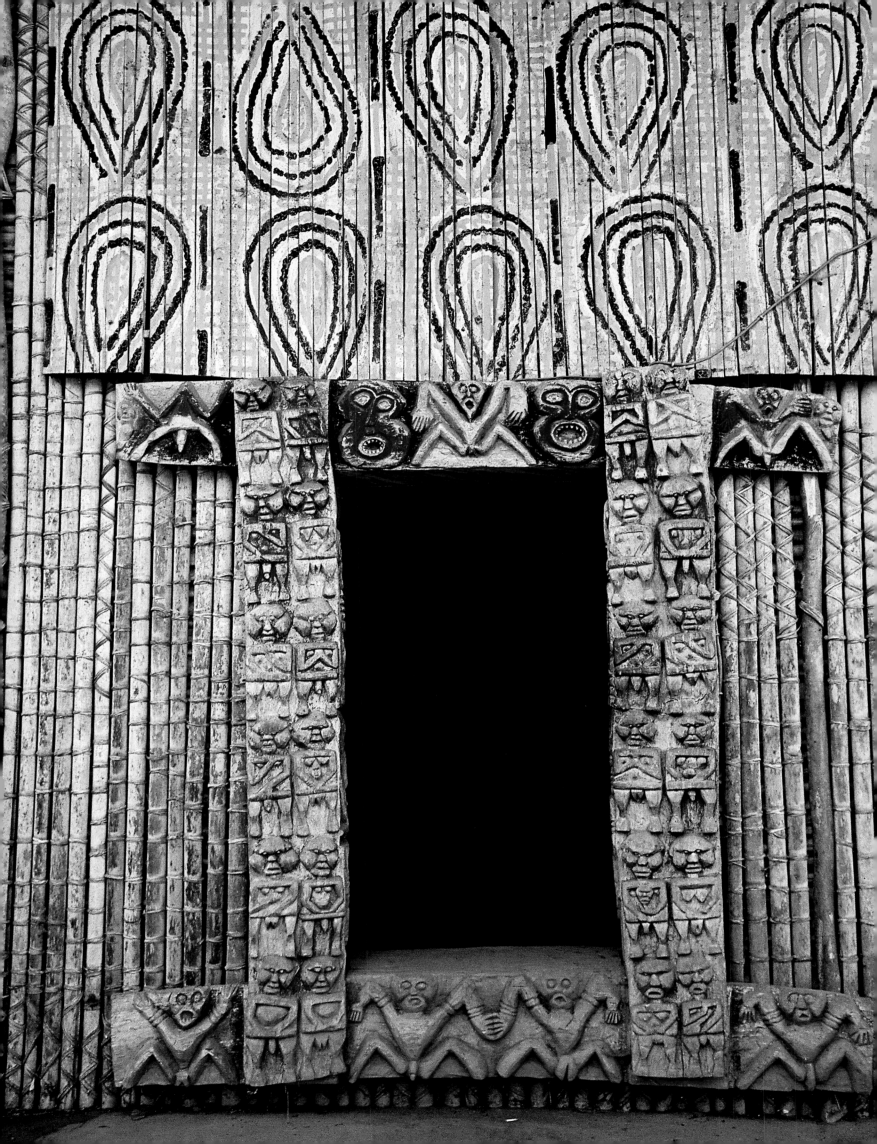

# CHEFFERIE
# BANDJOUN
# Cameroon

The Bandjoun compound is a sacred place,
a metaphor for the celestial powers.

In the Bamiléké region in western Cameroon, the people take their traditions very seriously. No power, be it colonial or central, has ever quite succeeded in dominating this remote rural area.

In the middle of it, at the end of a winding road through thick banana groves, stands a remarkable chief's compound, or *chefferie,* founded in the second half of the 17th century. Since that time, the chief in these parts has inherited all his ancestors' goods, including women and children – hence the constant necessity to find more space. The palace, decorated with sculptures, is surrounded by bamboos lashed together with raffia cord. The ceiling is held up by pillars decorated with representations of ancestors and the creation of the universe – cosmogonic art, in the scholarly definition. On either side of a central avenue, or "axis of life", are the lodgings reserved for the wives of the present chief, Joseph Ngnie Kamga, who dispenses justice from the steps of his palace. His throne stands on the lion skin which symbolizes his power. The royal chairs are adorned with cowrie shells, beads, and supporting figures in the form of leopards.

Im Gebiet der Bamiléké im Westen Kameruns wird die Tradition ernst genommen. Bereits in der Kolonialzeit ist es den Machthabern nie wirklich gelungen, diese ländliche Gegend zu unterwerfen.

Nach einer Fahrt über gewundene Straßen durch Bananenplantagen steht man erstaunt vor der Chefferie aus der zweiten Hälfte des 17. Jahrhunderts. Seitdem erbt der Häuptling alles Hab und Gut von seinem Vorfahren – inklusive Frauen und Kinder. Die Unterbringung so vieler Menschen erfordert viel Platz. Die Fassade des skulpturengeschmückten Palastes besteht aus mit Bast umwickelten Bambusstäben. Diese Pfeiler, die auch das Dach stützen, sind mit Schnitzereien verziert, die von den Ahnen und der Entstehung der Welt erzählen – so genannte kosmogonische Kunst. Auf beiden Seiten der zentralen Allee, der »Lebensachse«, stehen die Häuser der Frauen des derzeitigen Häuptlings Joseph Ngnie Kamga. Auf den Stufen seines Palastes hält er mit Hilfe eines Beraterstabes Gericht. Sein Thron steht auf einer Löwenhaut, die seine Machtfülle symbolisiert. Die königlichen Sitze sind mit Kaurimuscheln, Perlen und Stützfiguren in Form von Leoparden geschmückt.

En pays Bamiléké, à l'ouest du Cameroun, on ne plaisante pas avec les traditions. Les pouvoirs, qu'ils soient coloniaux ou centraux, n'ont jamais réellement soumis cette région rurale.

Au terme d'une route sinueuse qui progresse à travers les bananiers, on s'émerveille devant cette chefferie fondée durant la seconde moitié du 17e siècle. Depuis cette époque, le chef hérite de tous les biens de son ancêtre, femmes et enfants compris. D'où la nécessité d'étendre l'espace pour loger son monde. Le palais, décoré de sculptures, est ceint de bambous liés par des cordons de raphia. Le plafond est maintenu par des piliers décorés de représentations qui symbolisent les ancêtres et la création de l'univers, ce qu'on nomme l'art cosmogonique. De chaque côté de l'allée centrale, «l'axe de la vie», se trouve le quartier réservé aux femmes du chef actuel, Joseph Ngnie Kamga. Aux marches du «palais», tous les quatre jours, celui-ci rend la justice lors d'un conseil. Son trône est déposé sur une peau de lion symbolique de sa puissance. Les sièges royaux sont en cauris et perles avec des colonnettes de soutien en forme de panthères.

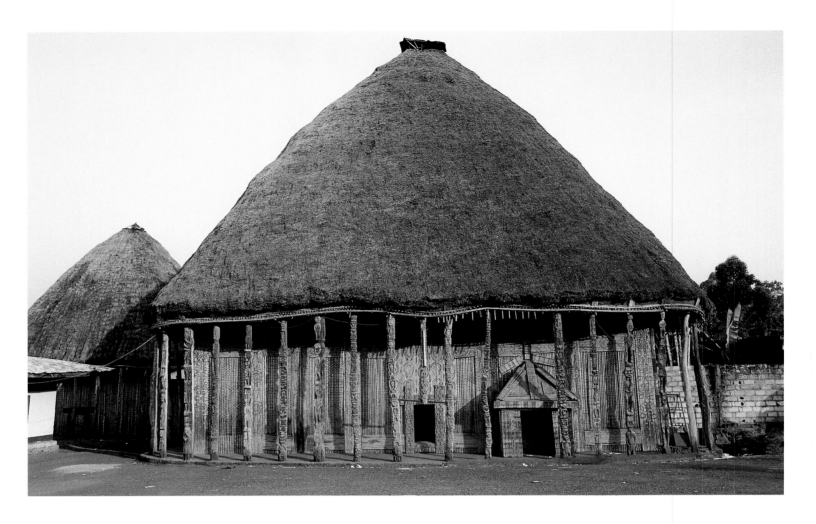

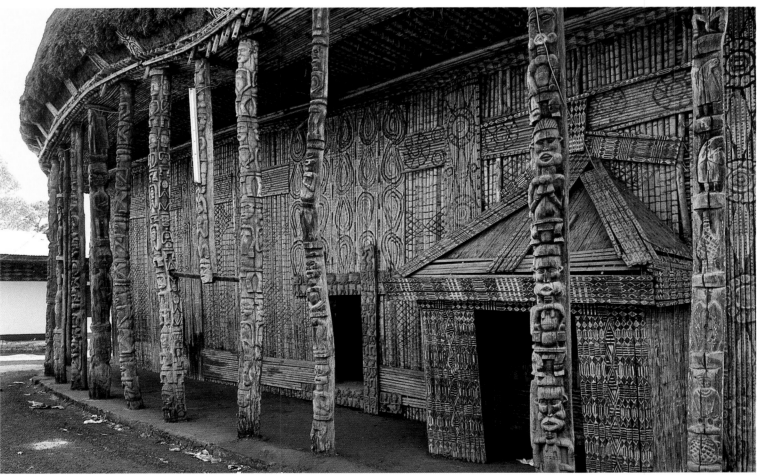

❋ **ABOVE** The building has a conical thatched roof over a loft, which formerly came in very useful. The doors are framed with carved panels. ❋ **OBEN** Über dem Palast wölbt sich ein konisches grasgedecktes Dach. Darunter liegt der Speicher, der früher eine große Rolle spielte. Die Türen sind mit skulptierten Paneelen eingefasst. ❋ **CI-DESSOUS** Le bâtiment est surmonté d'un toit conique en chaume qui abrite le grenier, espace autrefois important. Les portes sont encadrées de panneaux sculptés.

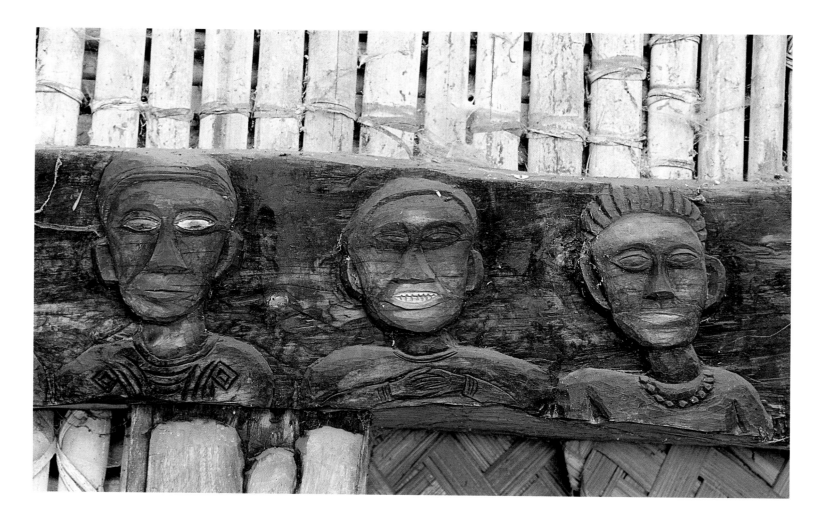

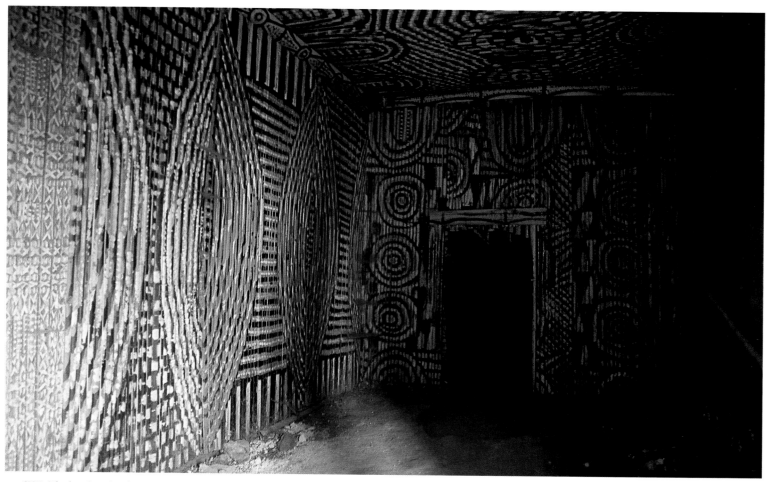

✳ **ABOVE** The bamboo facades, patiently woven together with raffia, are decorated with human forms. **BELOW** The entrance to the ceremonial house, with its geometrical patterns painted on the bamboo walls. ✳ **OBEN** Plastische Figuren zieren die Bambuspfeiler, die untereinander sorgfältig mit Bast verbunden wurden. **UNTEN** Die Eingangstür zum Haupthaus, dessen Bambuswände mit grafischen Mustern bemalt sind. ✳ **CI-DESSUS** Les façades en bambou patiemment attaché avec du raphia, sont ornées de représentations humaines. **CI-DESSOUS** À l'entrée de la maison cérémoniale ornée de dessins géométriques peints sur les murs en bambou.

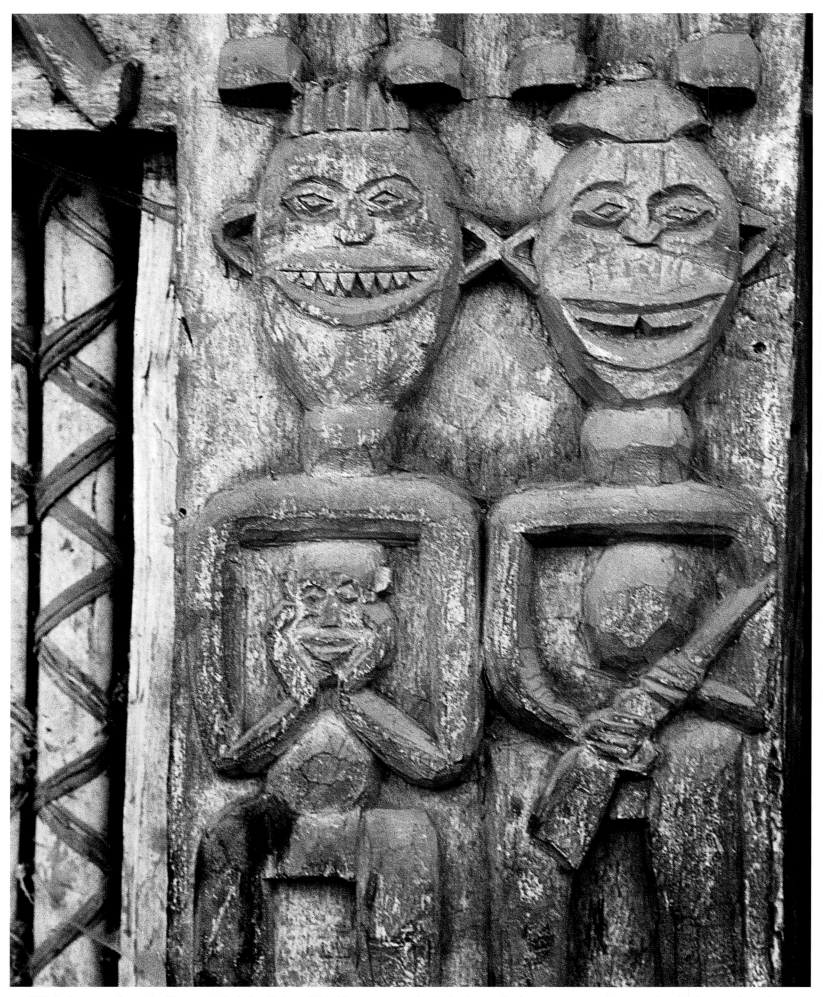

❋ **ABOVE** In the course of everyday life, a magical relationship is established between men and animals – hence what happens to one can happen to the other. In totem form, the animal serves as an alter ego used by ritual healers to drive out evil. ❋ **OBEN** Im Alltag besteht eine Verbindung zwischen Mensch und Tier. Was dem einen zustößt, kann auch dem anderen widerfahren. In Form eines Totems dient das Tier als wahres Alter Ego den Heilern bei den rituellen Austreibungen des Bösen. ❋ **CI-DESSUS** Dans la vie courante, une relation magique est établie entre les hommes et les animaux, et ce qui arrive à l'un peut arriver à l'autre. Représenté sous la forme d'un totem, l'animal, véritable alter ego, sert au guérisseur dans les rites d'expulsion du mal.

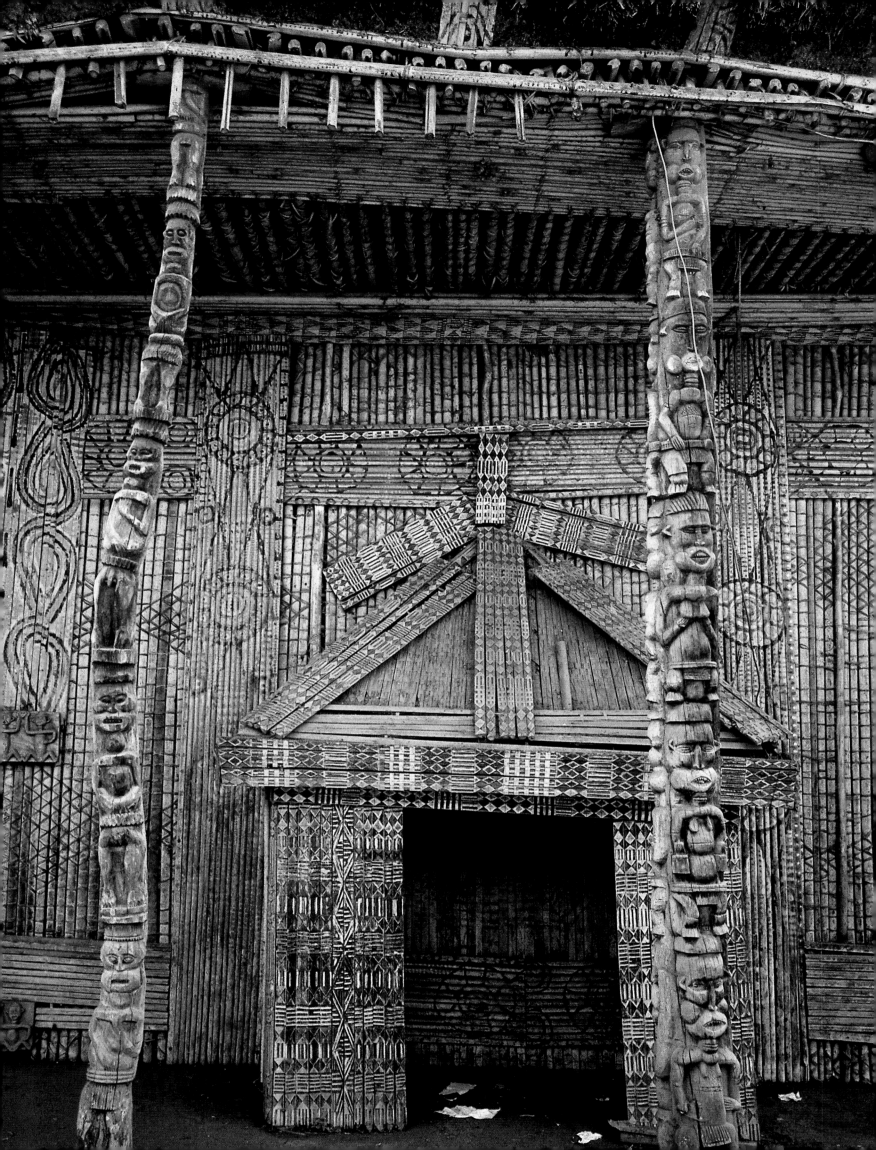

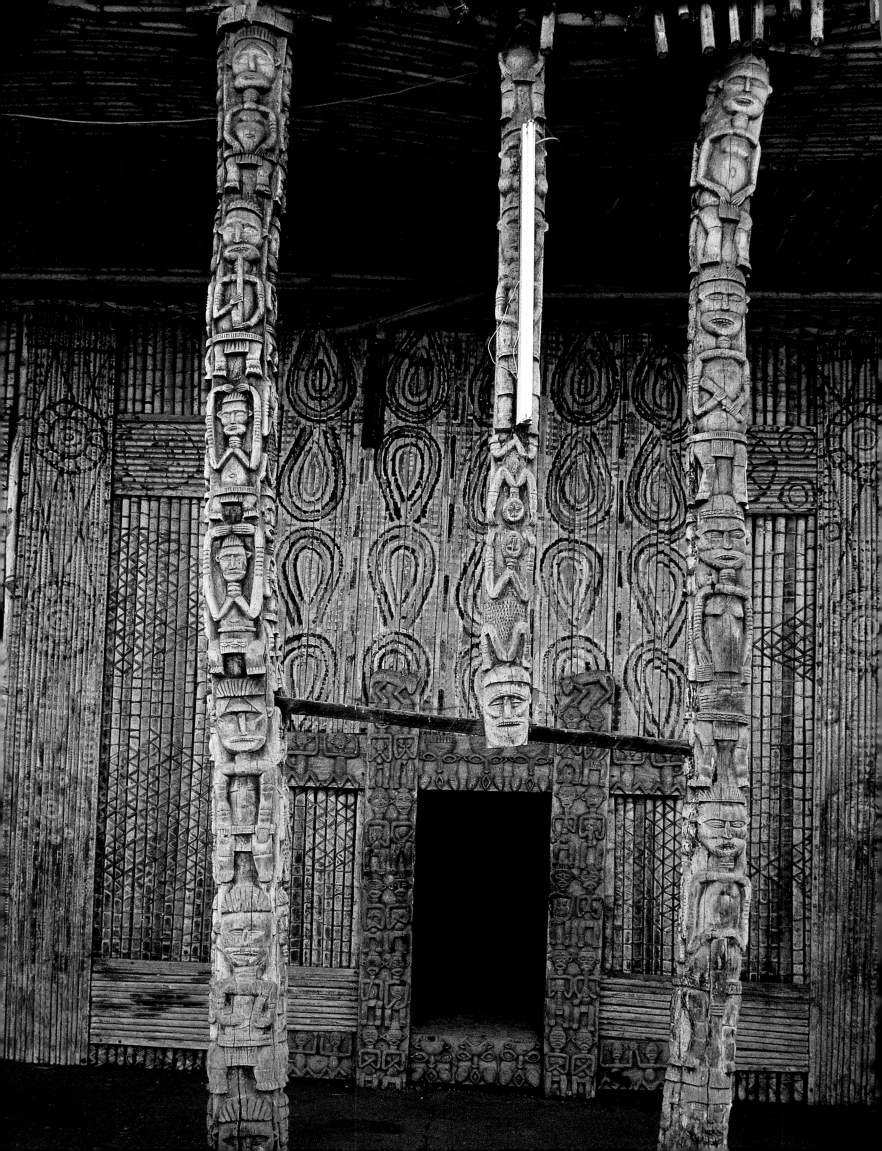

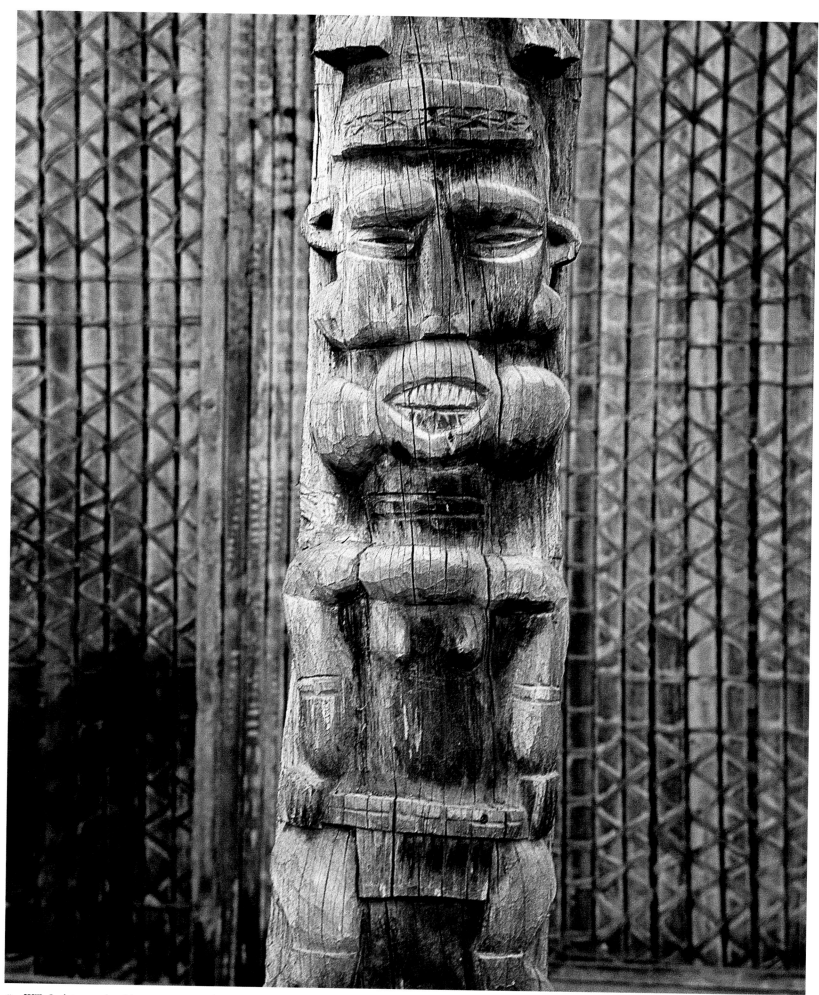

✳ **ABOVE** Sculpture and architecture come together in the pillars that hold up the tall roofs. The representations of cosmogonic art serve as icons for healers and priests. **FACING PAGE** The doors are raised 50 centimetres to keep out floodwater and animals. ✳ **OBEN** Bambuspfähle stützen die hohen Dächer. Die künstlerischen kosmogonischen Darstellungen dienen Priestern und Heilern als Ikonen. **LINKE SEITE** Die Türen sind 50 Zentimeter höher gelegt, damit weder Regen noch Tiere eindringen können. ✳ **CI-DESSUS** Sculpture et architecture unissent leur force dans les piliers soutenant les hauts toits. Les représentations de l'art cosmogonique servent d'icônes aux guérisseurs et aux prêtres. **PAGE DE GAUCHE** Les portes sont surélevées de 50 centimètres afin d'empêcher la pluie ou les animaux d'entrer.

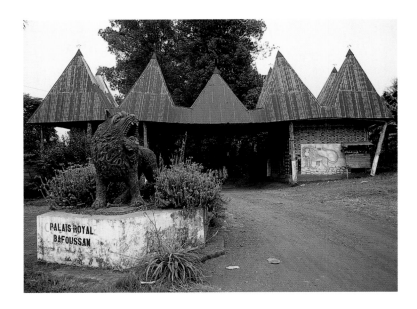
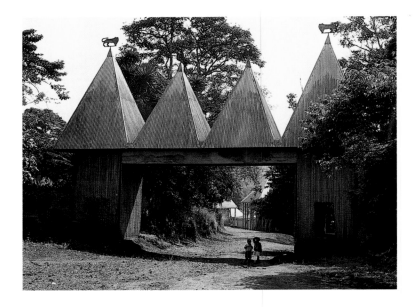
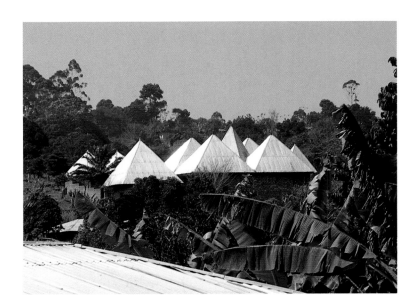
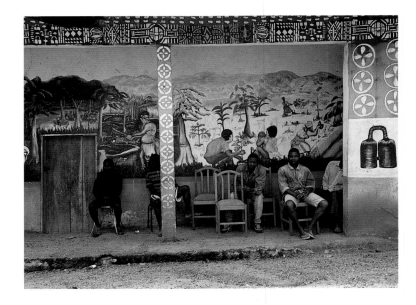
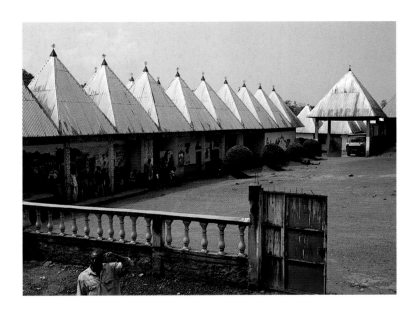
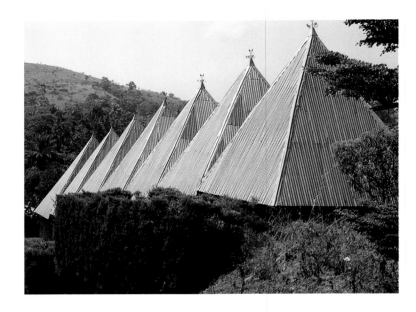

⁂ **ABOVE** In the west of Cameroon, the number of conical roofs in a chief's compound attest to his power: some of them are veritable royal households. ⁂ **OBEN** Im westlichen Teil Kameruns glitzern die Metalldächer weiterer Chefferien in der Landschaft. Je höher die Anzahl der Spitzdächer, desto bedeutender ist die Chefferie – einige haben sich zu wahren Königshöfen entwickelt. ⁂ **CI-DESSUS** Dans l'ouest du Cameroun, d'autres chefferies font briller leurs demeures métalliques dans le paysage. Le nombre des toits coniques témoigne de l'autorité de la chefferie; certaines sont de véritables cours royales.

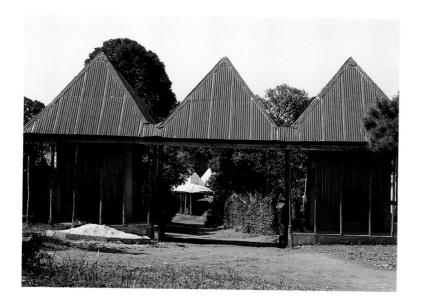
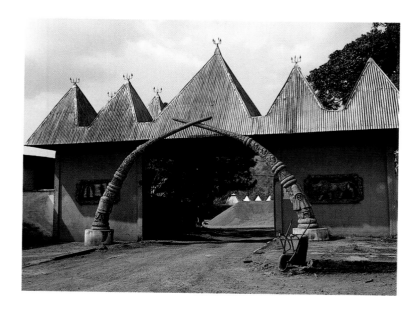
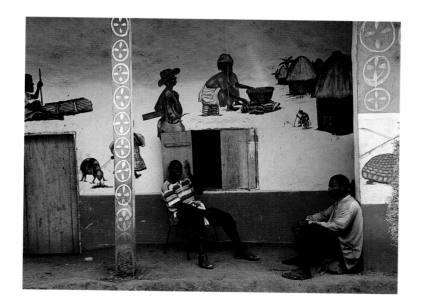
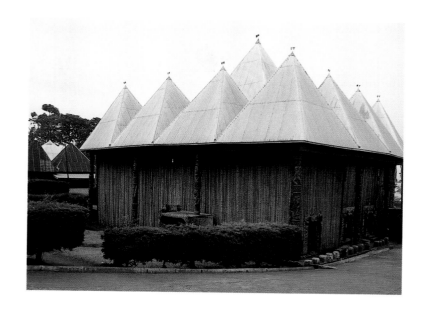
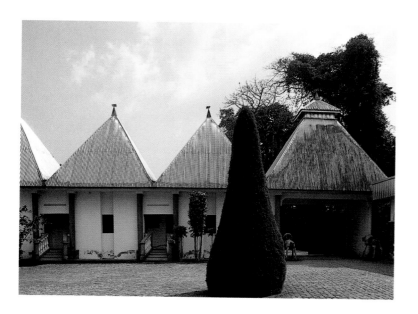
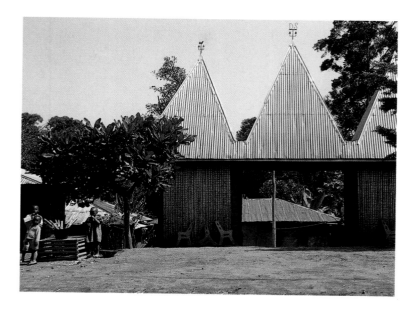

❋ **ABOVE** The chief's compound has not been spared the inroads of the modern world. The outsides of the houses are changing more and more with the advent of magnificent corrugated iron roofs overhanging their bamboo facades. ❋ **OBEN** Auch eine Chefferie bleibt von modernen Einflüssen nicht verschont. Das Äußere der Häuser ist Wandlungen unterworfen wie der Einführung von Wellblechdächern, die als neue Wahrzeichen der Macht über der Bambusfassade aufragen. ❋ **CI-DESSUS** La chefferie n'est pas épargnée par le monde moderne. L'extérieur des cases se modifie de plus en plus avec l'apparition de toits en tôle ondulée magnifiques surmontant le rideau en bambou des façades, nouvelles formes de pouvoir.

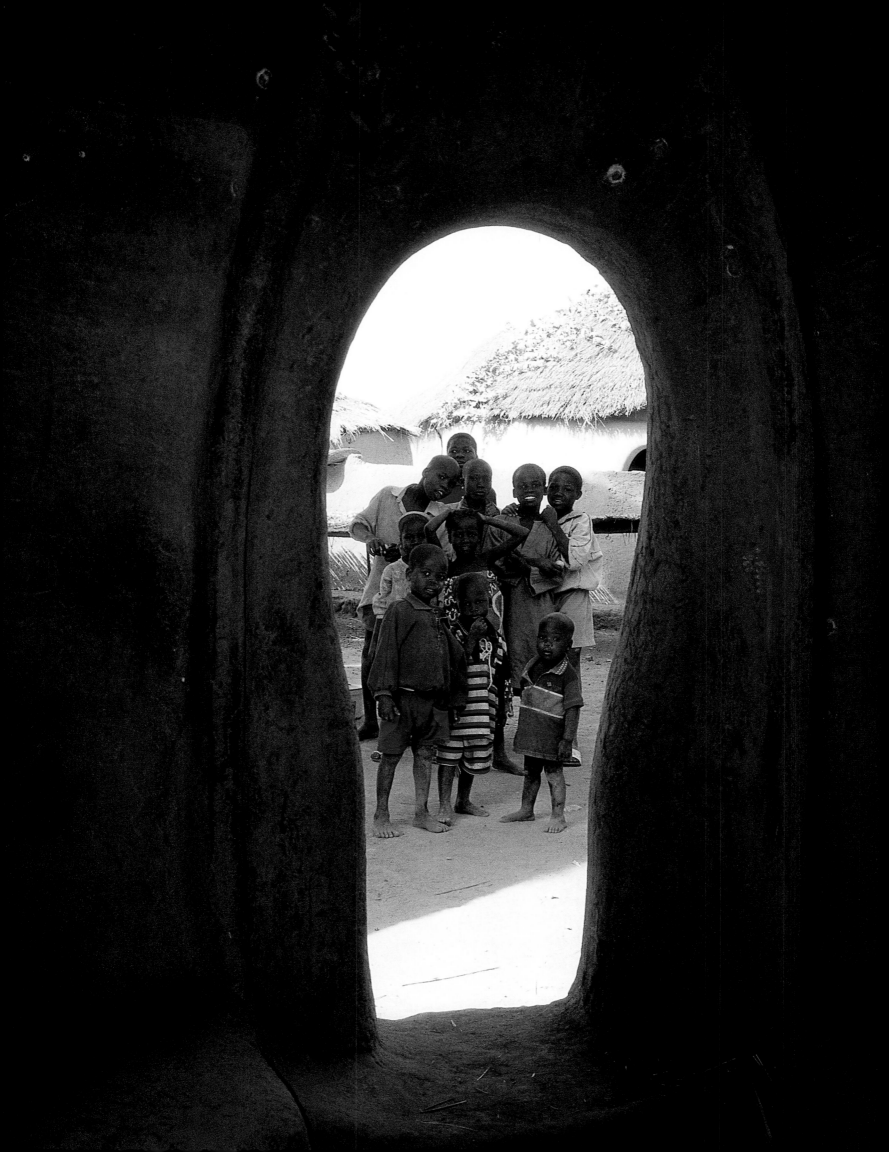

# OBUS
## & various dwellings
## northern cameroon

In this arid landscape,
people survive in the earth houses with pointed tops.

The tall *obu* dwellings, with their carefully worked, ribbed façades, are unique and famous in northern Cameroon. Elsewhere in the country, the *saré* houses, as they are called locally, are like small compounds.

The area is part of the Sahel, where the *harmattan* wind burns the landscape and dries everything to a crisp, from the scrub-covered pastureland to the village wells. Stone walls here are held together with clay. The vaulting is assembled from clay bricks, and the roof is tressed millet straw bound with raffia. There are no openings apart from a tiny door, because the main purpose here is always and forever to keep out the murderous heat. Under the thatch, there's a small grain store for the reserves of millet and ground nuts which make up the staple diet here. There's no ladder up to it, you have to pull yourself up by your arms. From a distance, the villages blend into the vegetation – the savannah and its inhabitants form an indivisible unit – and everywhere there is the same reddish colour, turning to black wherever there's been a bush fire. The herders frequently start fires to make a thin layer of short-lived grass grow under the scrub. The flames consume everything in their path, except for the *pisé* constructions which are protected by a natural barrier of undergrowth. Once the fires die down, the plain is covered in black stripes, similar to the ones on the inside walls of the dwellings.

Die einzigartigen schlanken *obu*-Hütten im Norden Kameruns sind für ihre kunstvollen Fassaden berühmt. In anderen Landesteilen stehen so genannte *saré*, mehrere Hütten in kleinen Einfriedungen.

In der Sahelzone verwischt der Harmattan die Landschaft und lässt von den mit Gestrüpp bedeckten Weideplätzen bis zu den Dorfbrunnen alles austrocknen. Die gemauerten Wände bestehen infolgedessen aus lehmiger Erde, die zuvor tüchtig geknetet wurde. Eine Lehmmischung bildet das Gewölbe, während das Dach aus Hirsehalmen besteht, die mit Pflanzenfasern umwickelt und zusammengehalten werden. Außer einer kleinen Tür gibt es keine Öffnungen – hier kommt es darauf an, die mörderisch heiße Sonne abzuhalten. Auf dem Speicher unter dem Strohdach werden die Vorräte an Hirse und Erdnüssen gelagert, die als Grundnahrungsmittel dienen. Leitern gibt es nicht, man muss sich schon selbst hochziehen, um an die Vorräte zu gelangen. Aus der Ferne verschmelzen die Dörfer mit der Vegetation – die Bewohner werden eins mit der Savanne – überall die gleiche Rotschattierung, die ins Schwarze übergeht, wenn es gebrannt hat. Denn Brandrodung ist eines der Hilfsmittel dieser Hirtenvölker, weil sie die zarten Gräser, die dann kurzzeitig unter dem abgebrannten Gestrüpp wachsen, für ihre Herden brauchen. Die Flammen vernichten alles Leben in der Landschaft, nur die Lehmhütten sind durch eine natürliche Sperre aus Astwerk geschützt. Wenn das Feuer erloschen ist, sieht die Savanne schwarzgefleckt aus. Diese Flecken finden sich auch an den Innenwänden der Hütten wieder.

Les cases-obus, élançées, caractérisées par leur façade travaillée et renforcée de nervures, sont uniques et célébrées dans le nord du Cameroun. Ailleurs dans le pays, les habitations, des *saré* selon l'appellation locale, évoquent de petites enceintes.

La zone est sahélienne, l'harmattan brouille le paysage, assèche tout, des pâturages broussailleux aux puits des villages. Ainsi, les murs en pierres cimentées sont formés de terre argileuse préalablement malaxée. Un assemblage de pain de terre structure la voûte. Le toit est une simple natte à base de tiges de mil réunies par un raphia. Pas d'ouverture sinon une petite porte, car l'enjeu, ici encore, est de se préserver d'un soleil assassin. Sous le chaume, un petit grenier abrite les réserves de mil et d'arachides qui constituent l'alimentation de base. Il n'y a pas d'échelle pour y accéder, on se hisse à la force des bras. De loin, les villages se confondent avec la végétation – la savane et ses habitants forment un tout –, partout la même teinte rousse qui vire au noir les jours d'incendie. Afin de faire pousser sous les broussailles une herbe tendre mais éphémère pour leurs troupeaux, les pasteurs pratiquent intensivement le brûlis. Les flammes attaquent tout sur leur passage, sauf les cases de pisé protégées par une barrière naturelle de branchages. Le feu éteint, la savane affiche ses marques noires. Ces teintes que l'on retrouve sur les murs intérieurs des cases.

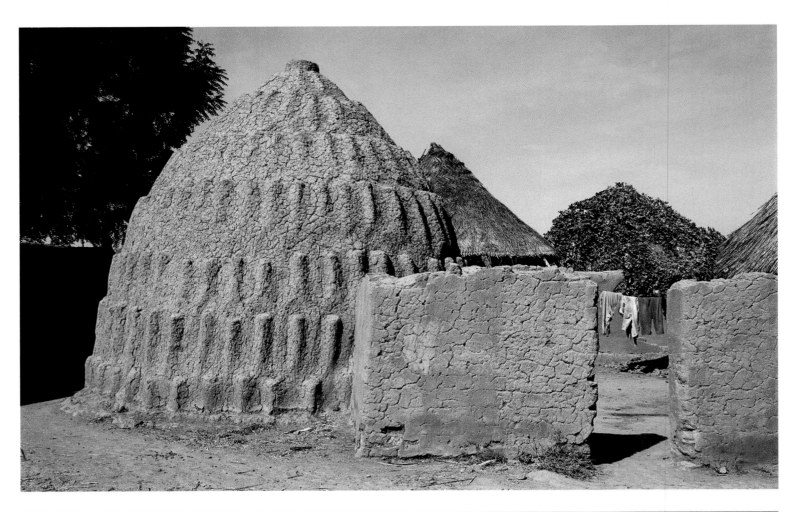

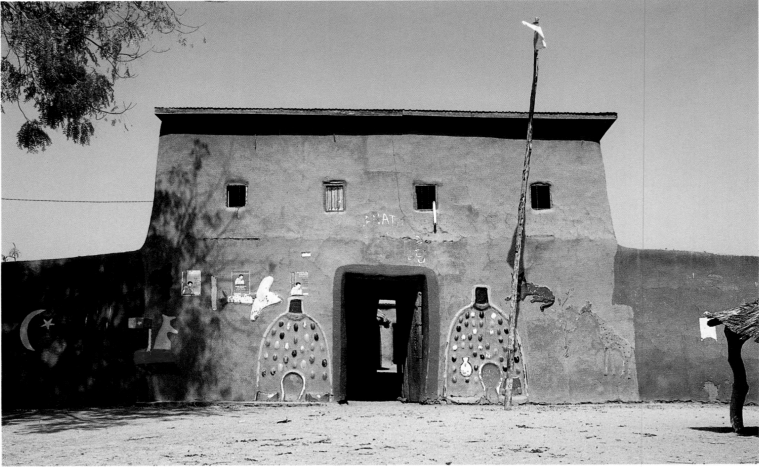

❋ **ABOVE** The technique used makes the construction of the *obu* dwellings waterproof, as well as facilitating the climb to the top when repairs are needed during the rainy season. ❋ **OBEN** Die Schichttechnik der Lehmbauweise der *obu*-Hütten verstärkt einerseits die Dichte und erleichtert andererseits den Aufstieg bis zur Spitze, damit die Hütte nach der Regenzeit besser repariert werden kann. ❋ **CI-DESSUS** Les cases-obus sont fabriquées avec de la terre. La technique en empilement permet à la fois de renforcer l'étanchéité mais aussi facilite l'escalade jusqu'au sommet lors des réfections après la saison des pluies.

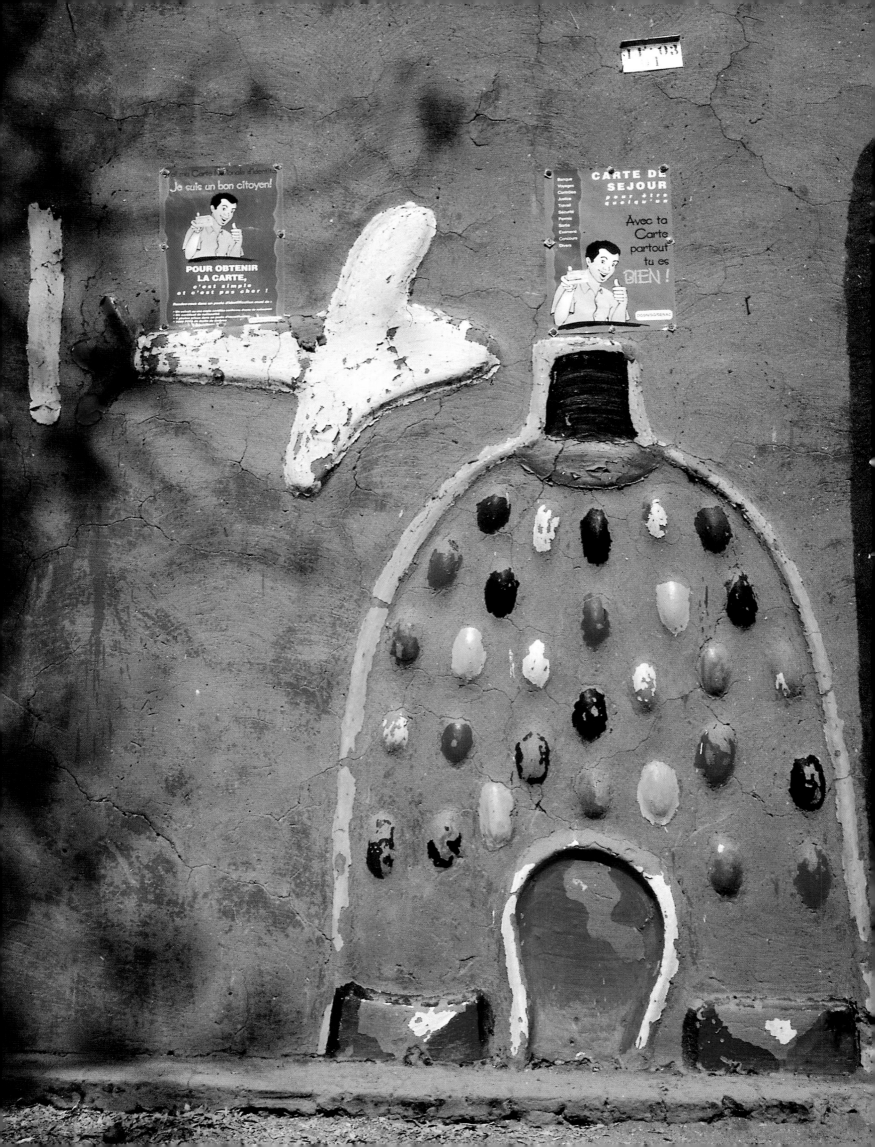

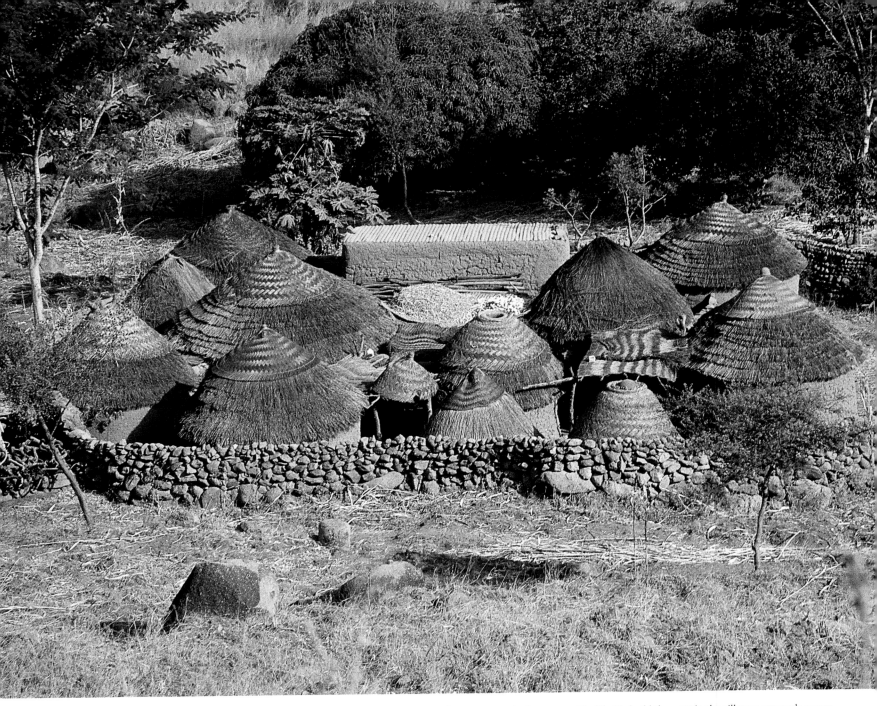

❋ **ABOVE** A *saré* in the north, nearer the mountains. Its main characteristic is that it expands or contracts in the course of its life. To build these *sarés*, the villagers use earth, a very little water, pieces of crumbling, twisted wood, stones and millet stalks. ❋ **OBEN** Weiter im Norden in der Nähe der Berge: eine *saré* genannte Ansammlung von Hütten, die im Laufe der Zeit größer wird oder schrumpft. Aus einem winzigen Wasservorrat, krummen, brüchigen Ästen, Steinen und Hirsehalmen bauen die Dorfbewohner ihre Hütten. ❋ **CI-DESSUS** Plus au nord, près des montagnes, un *saré* qui se caractérise parce qu'il prend de l'ampleur ou s'amenuise au cours d'une vie. Pour les construire, les villageois n'ont que très peu d'eau, du bois tordu et friable, des pierres et des tiges de mil.

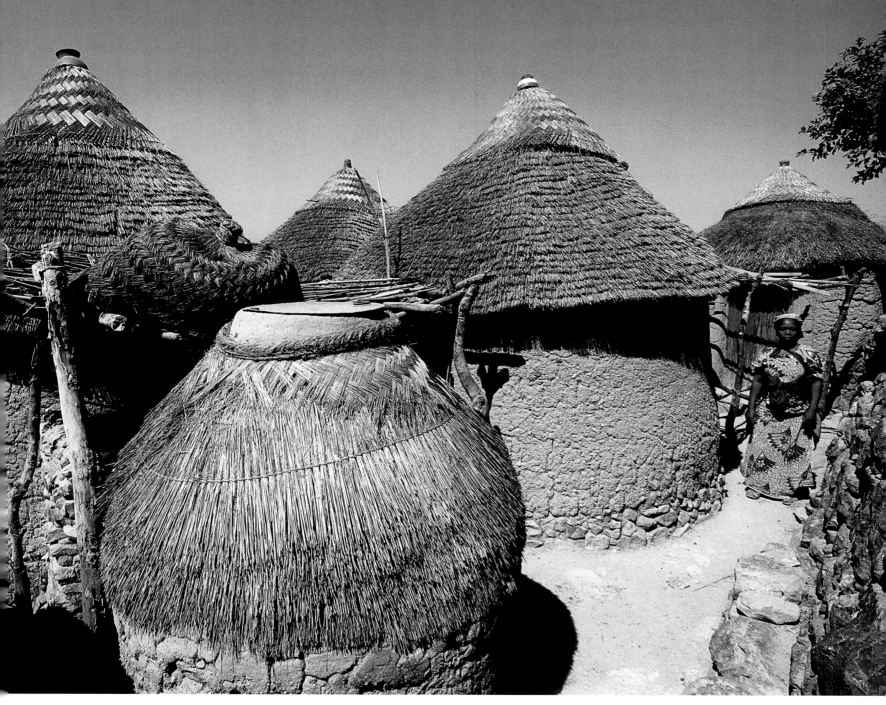

❋ **ABOVE** The head of the family controls the room facing the entrance, while his wives and children occupy the others along with the kitchen houses. To protect themselves from the sun, people spend much of their time inside or in the shade nearby. The village comes to life at the end of the day. ❋ **OBEN** Der Familienvorstand wohnt in der Hütte direkt am Eingang, während seine Frauen und Kinder in anderen Hütten leben, wo auch die Küchen untergebracht sind. Als Schutz gegen die Sonne verbringen die Menschen den ganzen Tag in ihren Hütten oder im Schatten. Erst nach Sonnenuntergang wird das Dorf lebendig. ❋ **CI-DESSUS** Le chef de famille contrôle la case qui fait face à l'entrée, ses femmes et ses enfants disposent des autres avec les cuisines. Pour se protéger du soleil, on vit beaucoup à l'intérieur ou à l'ombre, dans la cour. Le village s'anime au coucher du soleil.

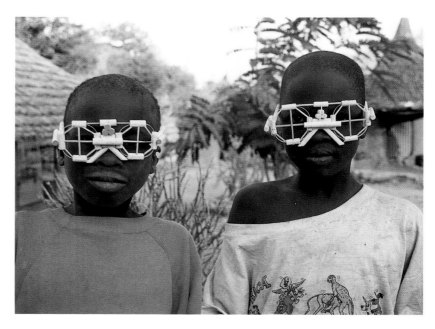

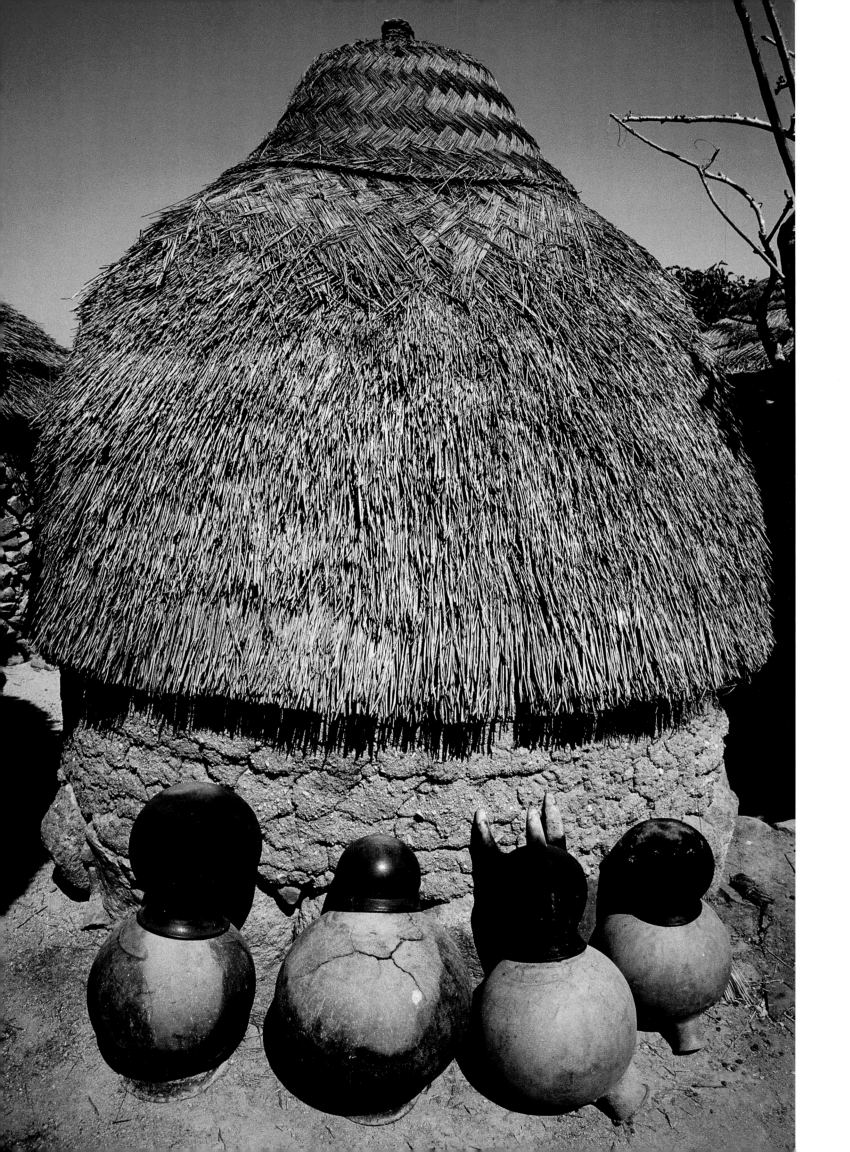

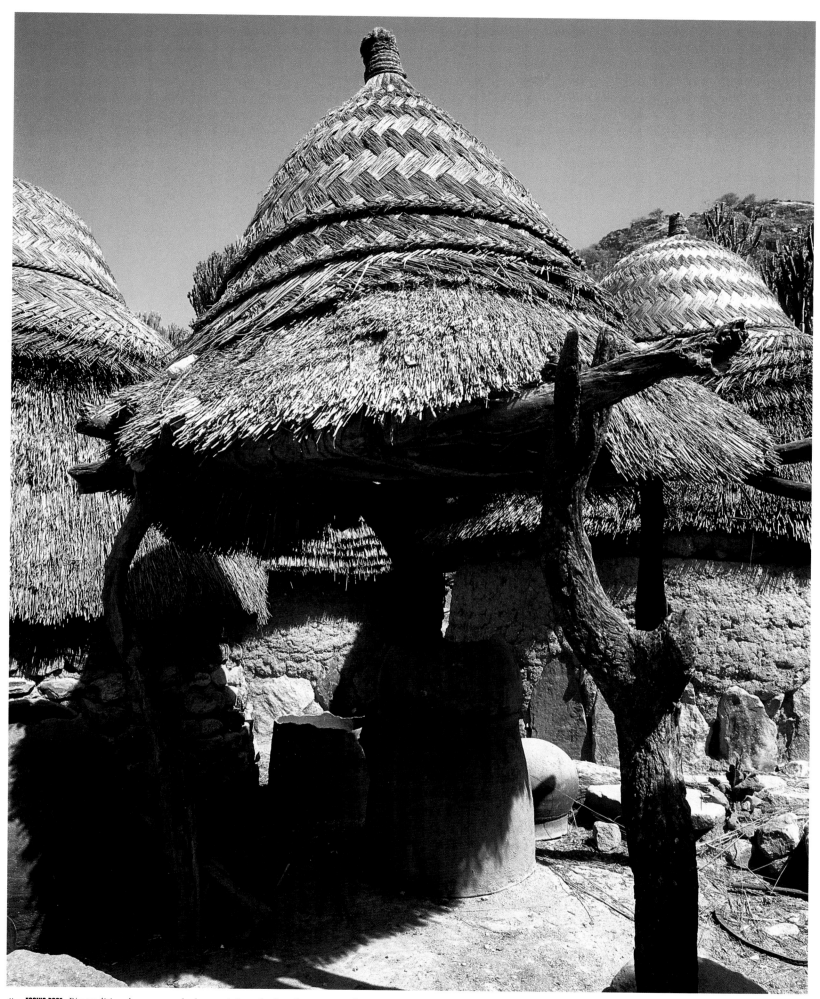

✳ **FACING PAGE** Big traditional ewers are the best recipients for keeping water cool. Drums containing millet beer and cooking pots are the other vital domestic utensils. **ABOVE** The kitchens, under a simple tress made with millet stalks held together with raffia. ✳ **LINKE SEITE** Der Hausrat besteht aus den traditionellen großen Tonkrügen für Trinkwasser, bauchigen Flaschen für Hirsebier und einigen wenigen Kochtöpfen. **OBEN** Unter von Pflanzenfasern zusammengehaltenen Matten aus Hirsehalmen befinden sich die Küchen. ✳ **PAGE DE GAUCHE** Les traditionnelles grandes jarres gardent l'eau fraîche, les bonbonnes contenant la bière de mil et les marmites constituent l'équipement domestique. **CI-DESSUS** Sous une simple natte à base de tiges de mil fixées à l'aide de raphia se trouvent les cuisines.

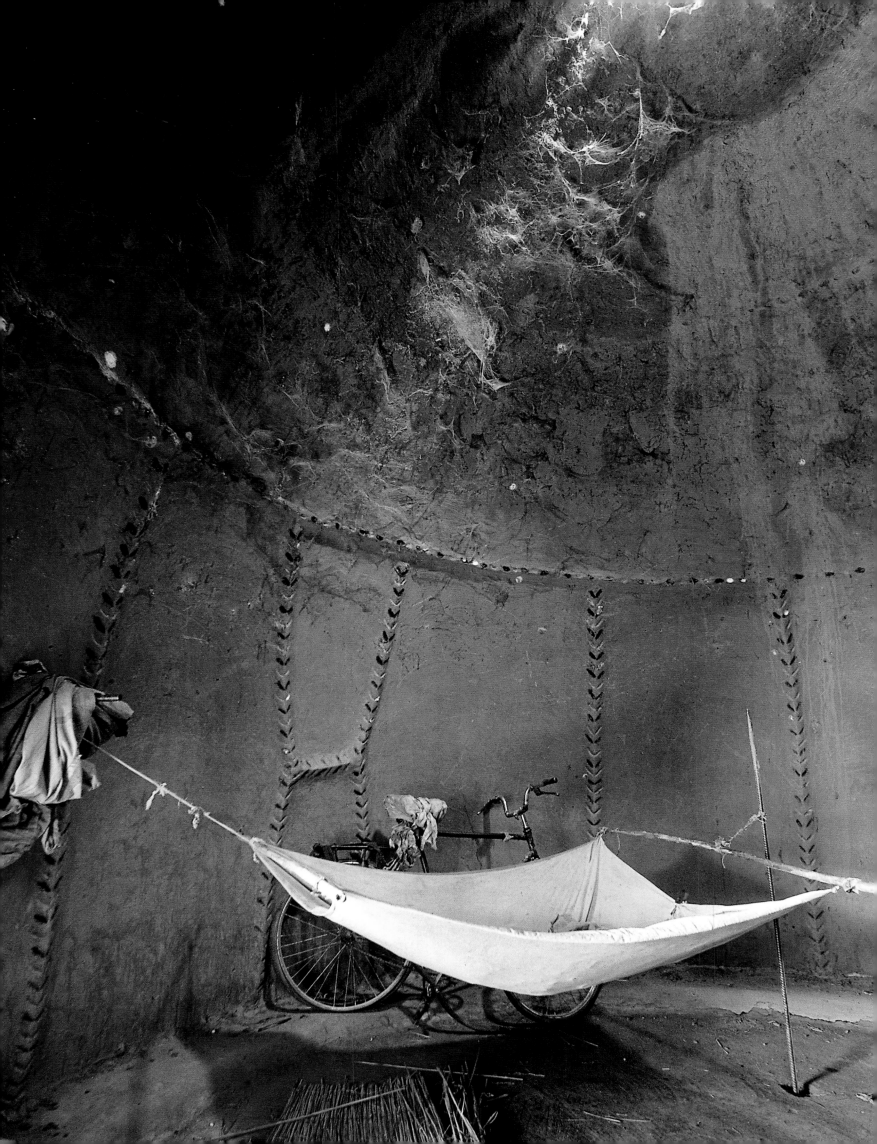

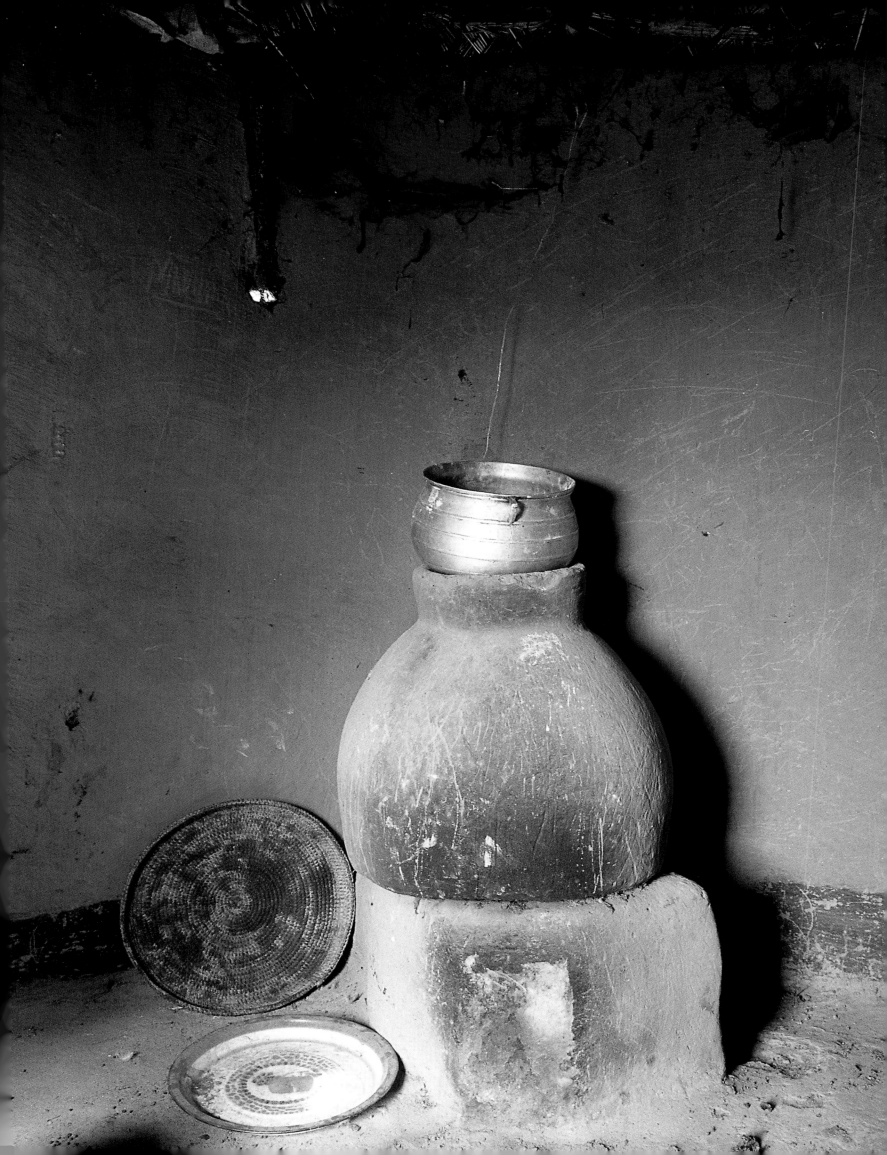

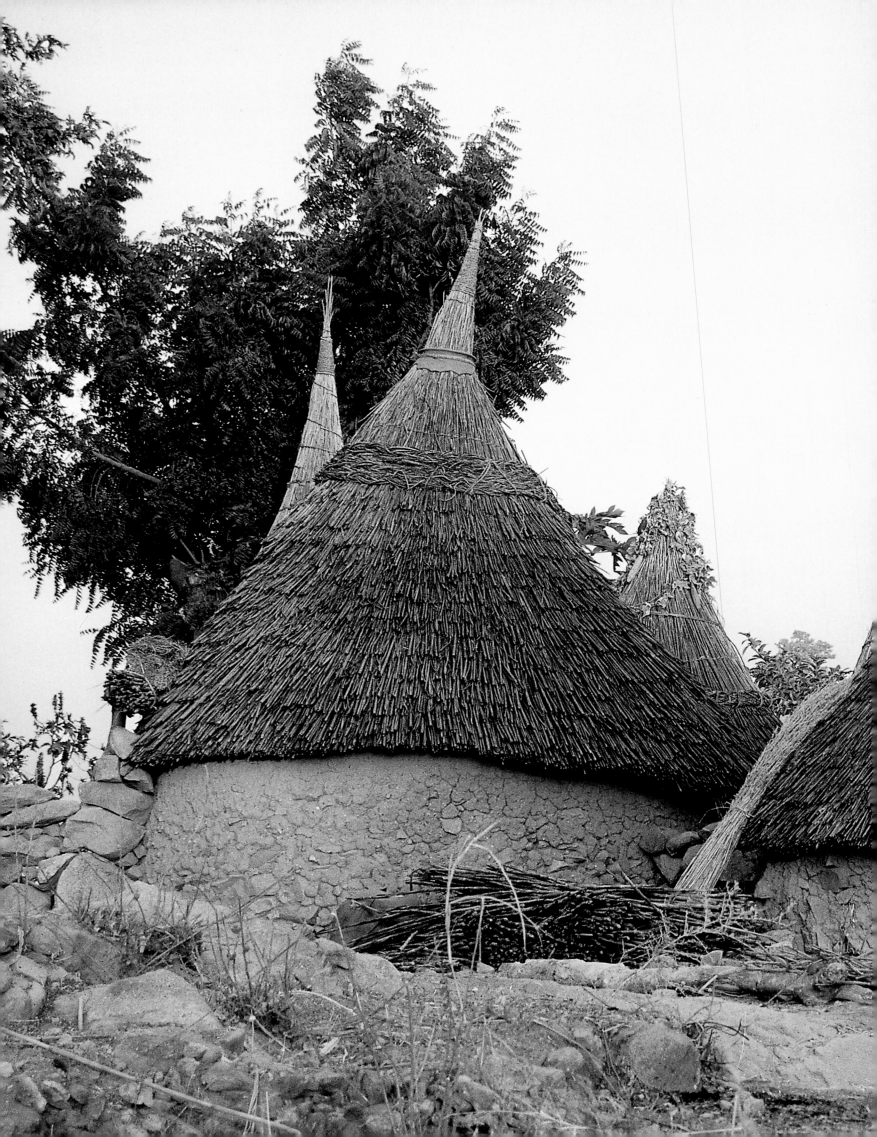

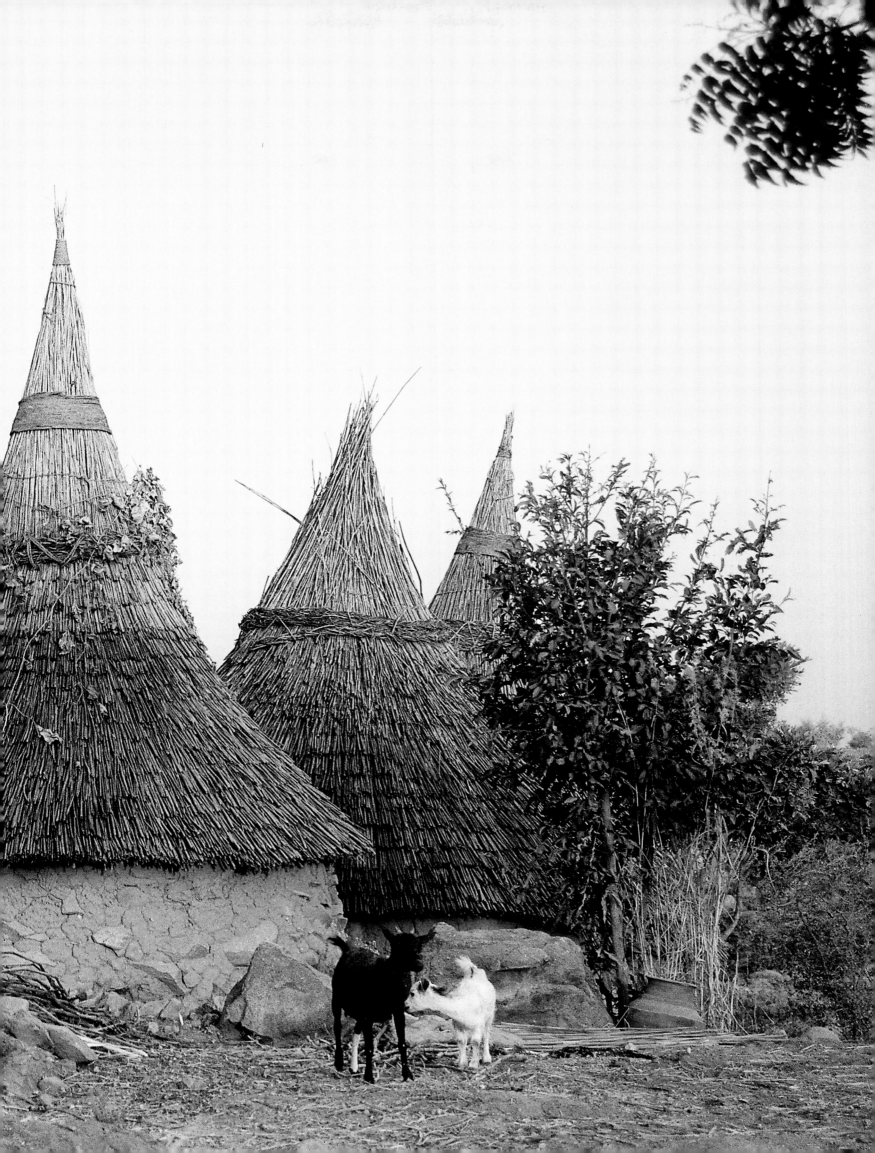

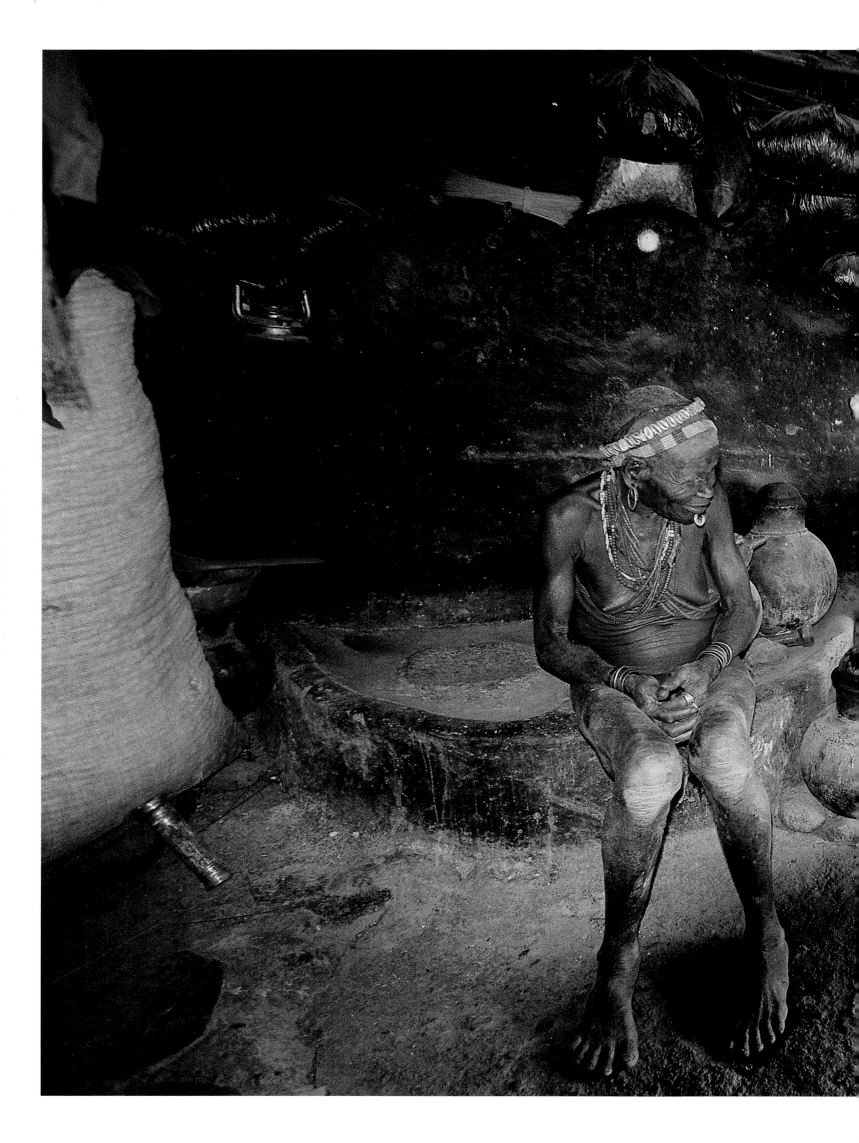

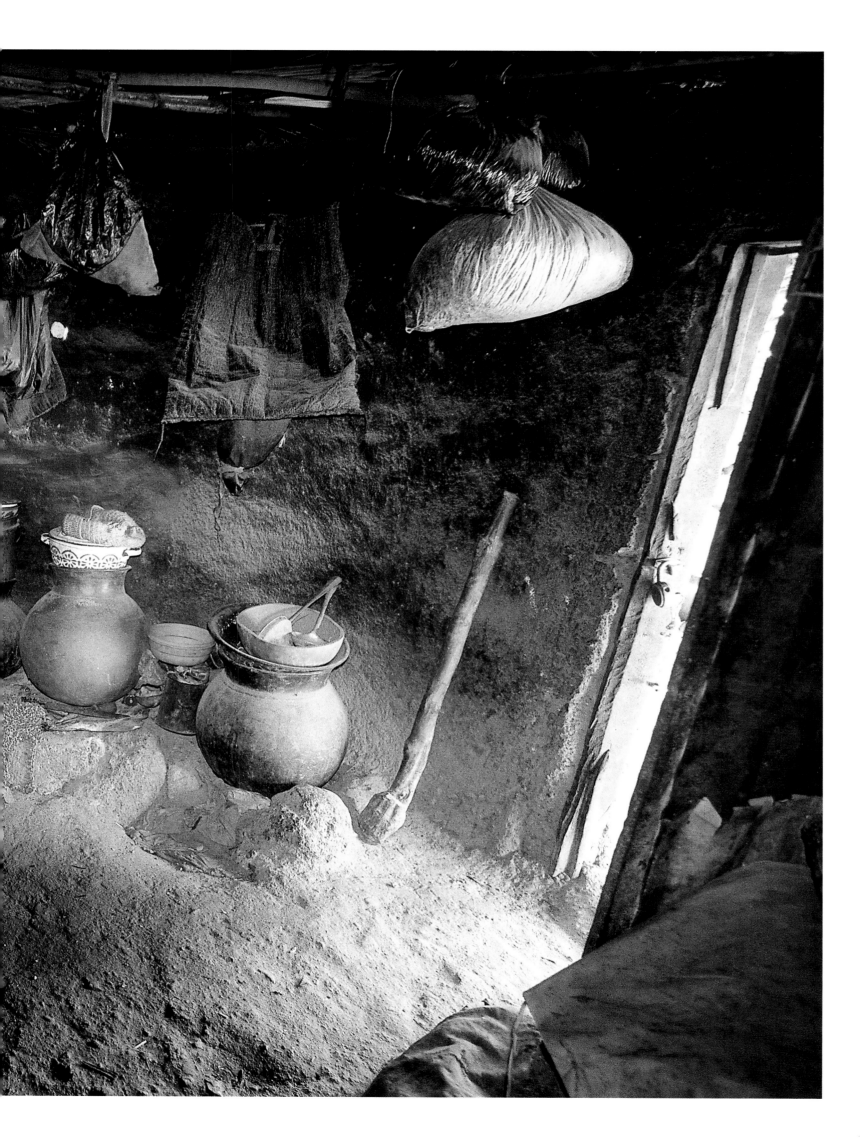

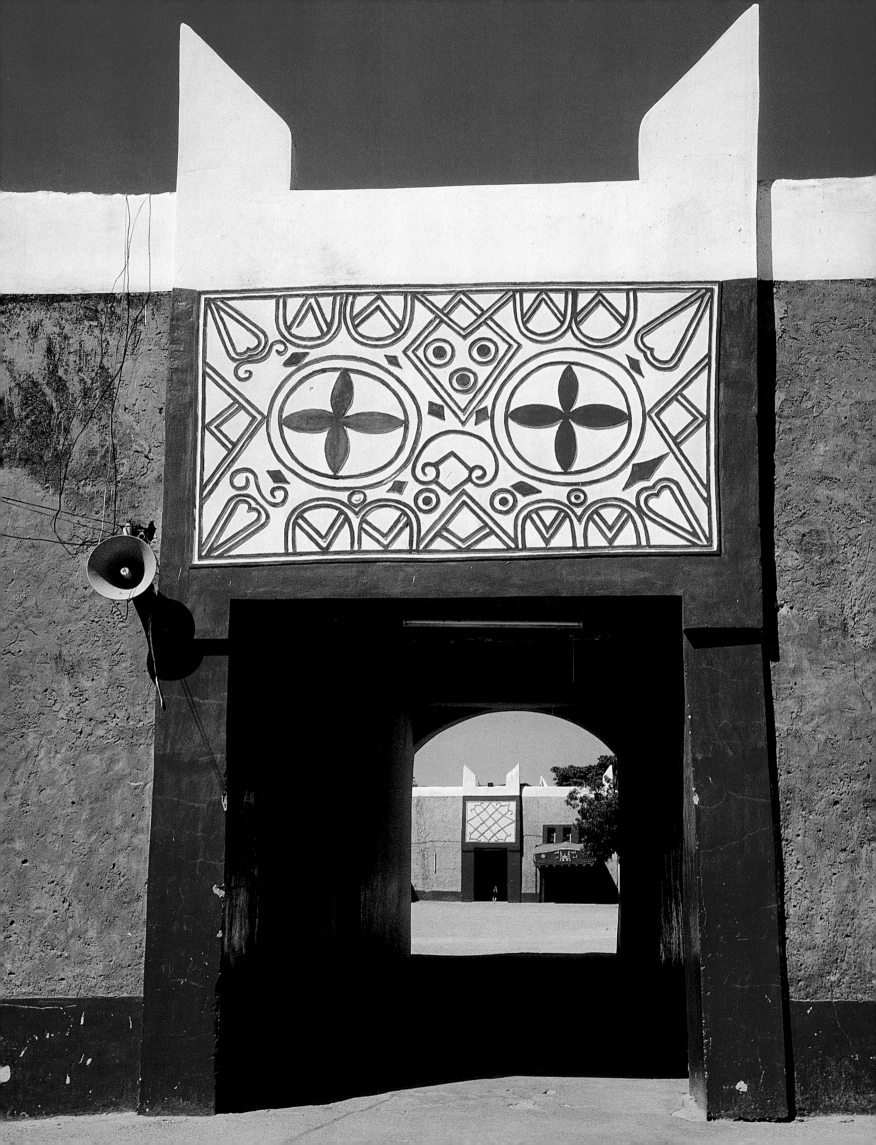

# Emir's Palace
## Kano

This is a place to be entered on tiptoe,
as if one were visiting Versailles in the time of Louis XIV.

Flashback to the 19th century: The centuries-old Hausa states are conquered and absorbed into the Fulani empire. From then on the Fulani reigned supreme, appointing emirs and, while developing great splendour, imposing a new, strictly islamic law.

Their new religious order spared no expense: the first European explorers to reach Kano in the early 20th century rhapsodized about the beauty of the arches in the audience chamber, the refinement of the decoration and the sophistication of the private apartments. Without any political mandate in modern Nigeria, to this day the emirs of the north have maintained autonomy in the transmission of cultural values and traditional ceremonials in the towns of Daura, Katsina, Kano and Zaria. So today these palaces are not museums. Inside, they have walls built in *tubali*, plastered and covered in mica – a shiny mineral that abounds in volcanic rock – to offset massive iron-bound doors. The deep black of the floors increases the gloom. Coloured geometrical motifs cover every inch of the ceilings and arches. Outside, there is a kind of citadel encircled by an eight-foot-high wall. The effect is of a great strongbox; although there is no treasure inside, it keeps intact the memory of a time when the Sahara caravans came here to trade in gold, ivory and slaves.

Rückblende ins 19. Jahrhundert: Die seit Jahrhunderten existierenden Hausastaaten werden von den Fulbe-Stämmen erobert und in deren Reich eingegliedert. Fortan herrschen in diesem Gebiet die Fulbe, die Emire einsetzen und bei gleichzeitiger großer Prachtentfaltung eine neue, strenge islamische Gesetzgebung durchsetzen.

Im 20. Jahrhundert staunen Forscher über die Schönheit der Bögen im Empfangssaal, die Feinheiten der Dekoration und die Eleganz der Privatgemächer. Auch im modernen Nigeria konnten sich die Emire im Norden des Landes ihre Autonomie bewahren. In den Städten Daura, Katsina, Kano und Zaria leben sie nach ihren kulturellen Wertvorstellungen und führen die traditionellen Zeremonien durch. Bei den Palästen handelt es sich also keineswegs um Museen. Im Inneren der Prunkbauten harmonieren die Wände aus *tubali*, die vergipst und mit Mica (einem glänzenden Mineral, das im Vulkangestein reichlich vorhanden ist) bestrichen wurden, mit den schweren Türen aus Brettern mit schmiedeeisernen Kanten. Die tiefschwarzen Böden verstärken noch die düstere Wirkung des Halbdunkels. An den Decken und Bögen entfalten sich bunte grafische Muster. Die Zitadelle selbst ist von einer zwei Meter dicken Mauer umgeben. Der Ort wirkt wie ein Tresor, der zwar keine Schätze in klingender Münze mehr bewahrt, dafür aber umso mehr historische Erinnerungen – an die Zeit, als die Karawanen aus der Sahara hier ihre Tauschgeschäfte mit Gold, Elfenbein und Sklaven abwickelten.

Flash-back au 19$^e$ siècle. Les états Haoussa qui existent depuis des temps immémoriaux sont conquis par les Fulbe et inclus dans leur empire. Dès lors, les Fulbe règnent sur ce territoire et les émirs instaurent une nouvelle lois islamique des plus strictes qui s'impose avec faste.

Les explorateurs européens du début du 20$^e$ siècle ne s'y trompent pas. Tous soulignent la beauté des arches dans la chambre d'audience, le raffinement de la décoration, la sophistication des appartements privés. Sans mandat politique dans le Nigeria moderne, les émirs du nord du pays conservent dans les villes de Daura, Katsina, Kano ou Zaria une autonomie dans la transmission des valeurs culturelles et le maintien des cérémonies traditionnelles. Les palais ne sont donc pas des musées. À l'intérieur, les murs édifiés en *tubali,* plâtrés et recouverts de mica (un minerai brillant abondant dans les roches éruptives), répondent aux portes massives en planches bordées de fer. Le noir profond des sols accentue la pénombre. Partout sur les plafonds et les arches s'enroulent des motifs géométriques colorés. Dehors, un mur de près de deux mètres limite la citadelle. L'endroit est un coffre-fort. S'il ne renferme plus de trésors en monnaies sonnantes et trébuchantes, il séquestre au moins une mémoire. Celle des temps où les caravanes sahariennes échangeaient ici de l'or, de l'ivoire et des esclaves.

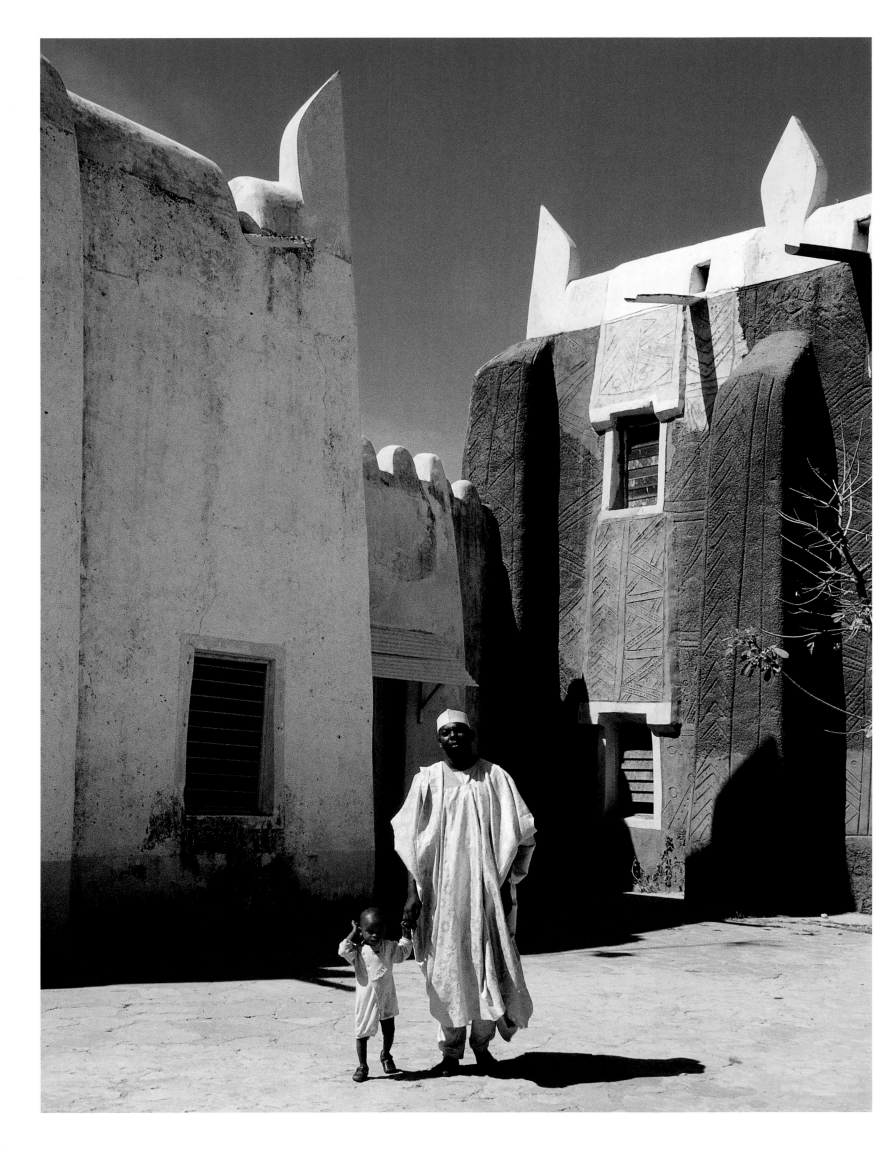

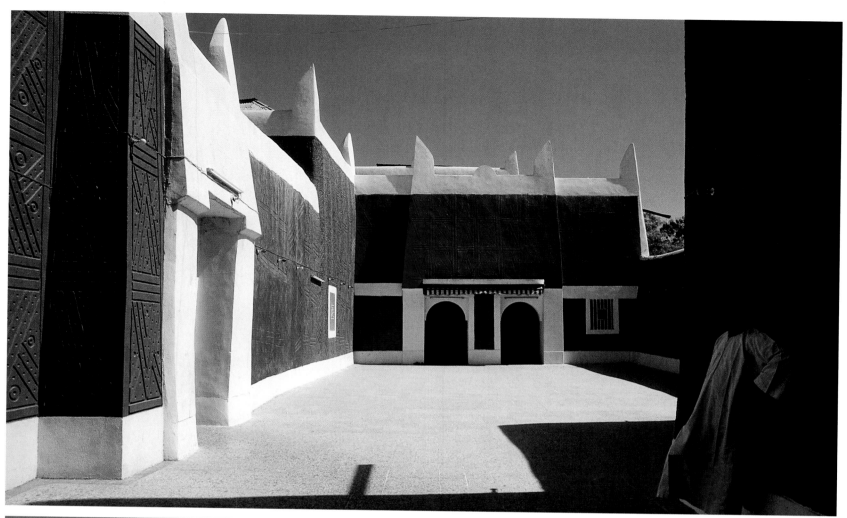

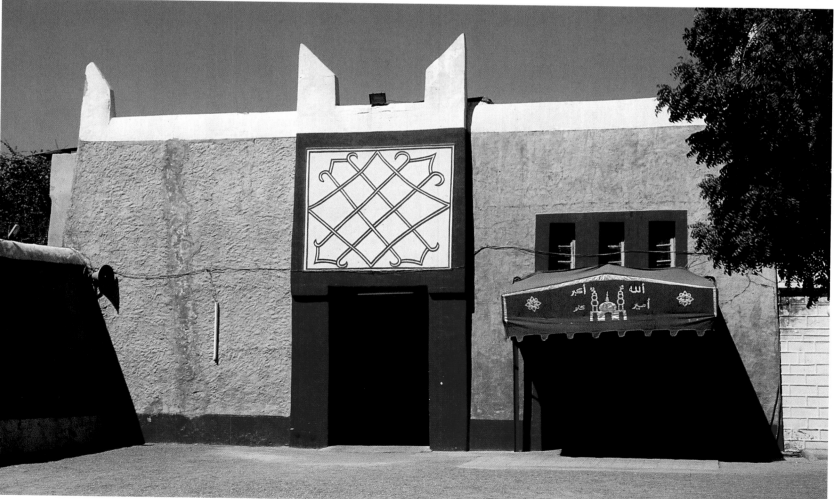

❋ **ABOVE** The inner courtyard of the Kano palace of Emir H.H. Aminu Ado Bayero. The walls are covered in a clay rendering, painted by hand with circular motifs. The palace proper is hidden behind the walls of a small citadel. ❋ **OBEN** Der Innenhof des Palastes in Kano, im Besitz des Emirs H.H. Aminu Ado Bayero. Auf die Mauern wurde per Hand mit kreisenden Bewegungen ein Lehmputz aufgetragen. Der Palast liegt fast verborgen hinter den Mauern der kleinen Zitadelle. ❋ **CI-DESSOUS** Cour intérieure du palais de Kano de l'émir H.H. Aminu Ado Bayero dont les murs sont recouverts d'un enduit d'argile peint à la main en mouvements circulaires. Le palais se dissimule derrière les murs de la petite citadelle.

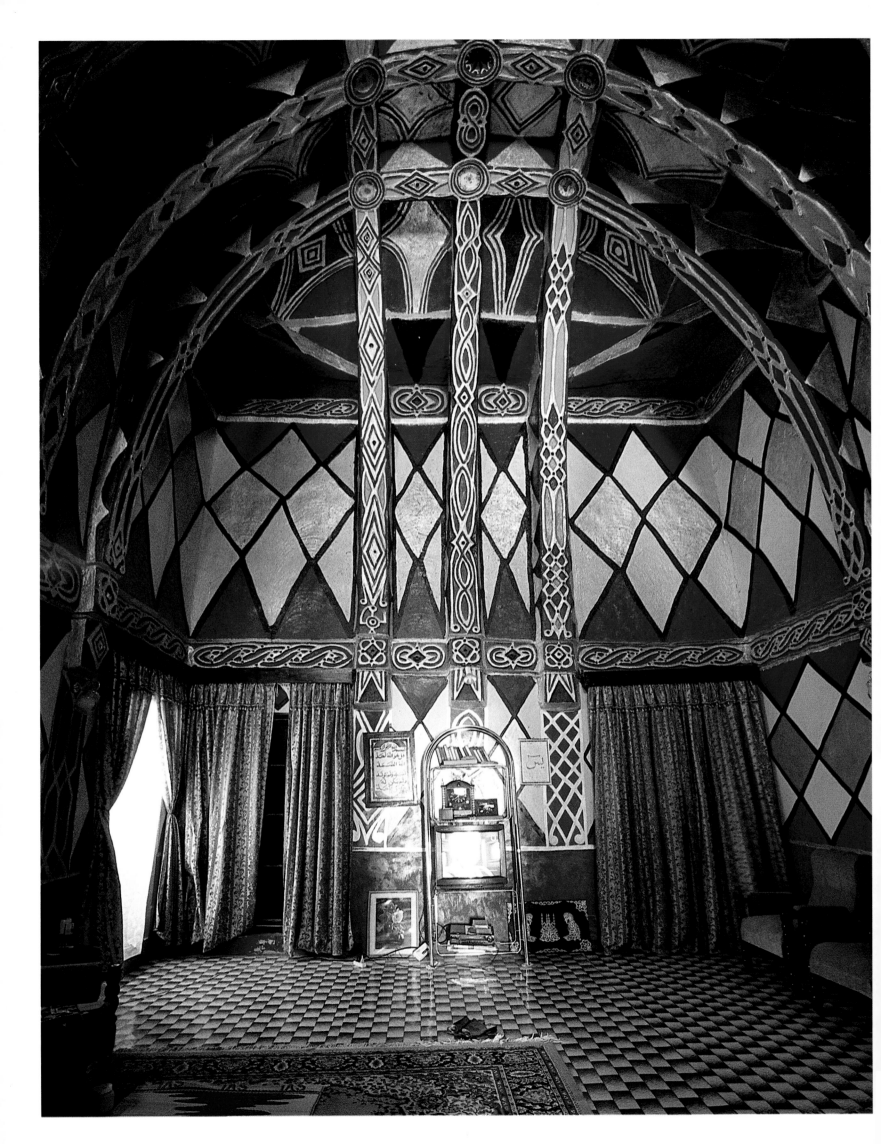

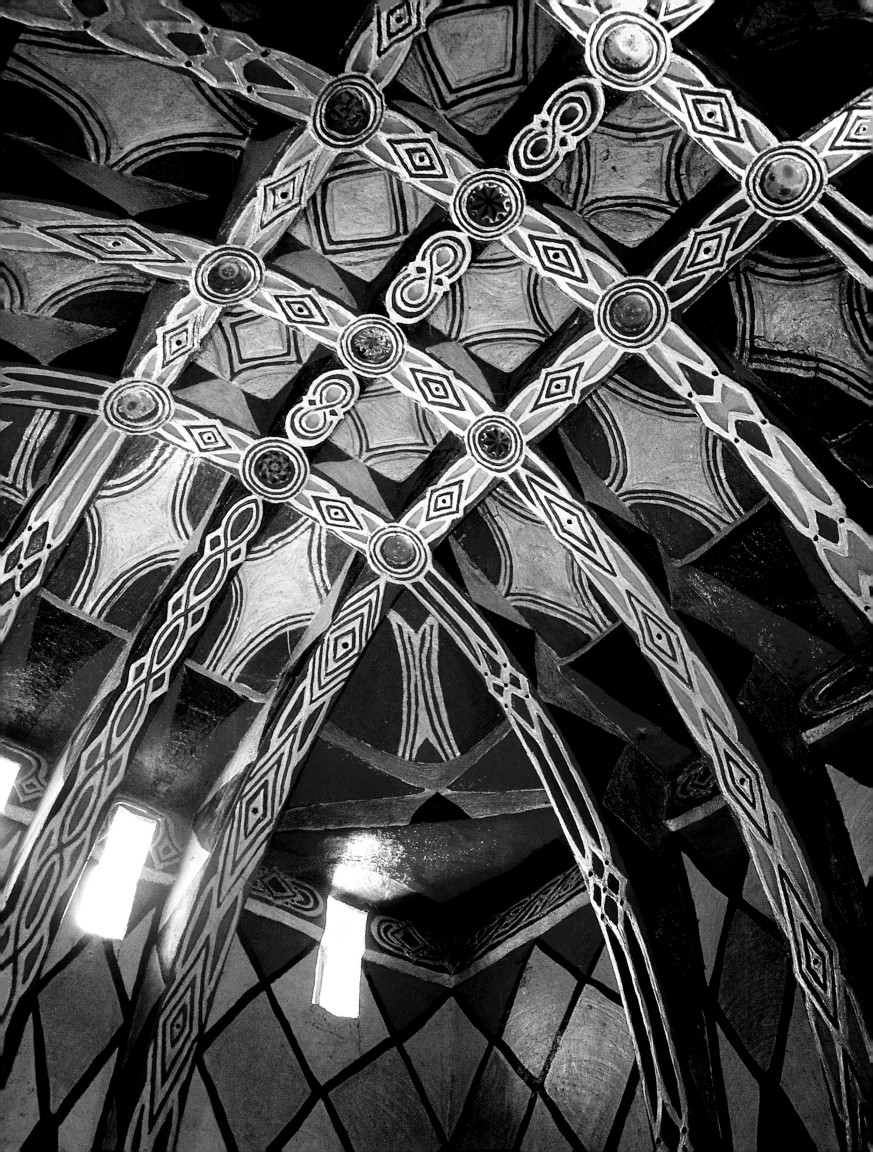

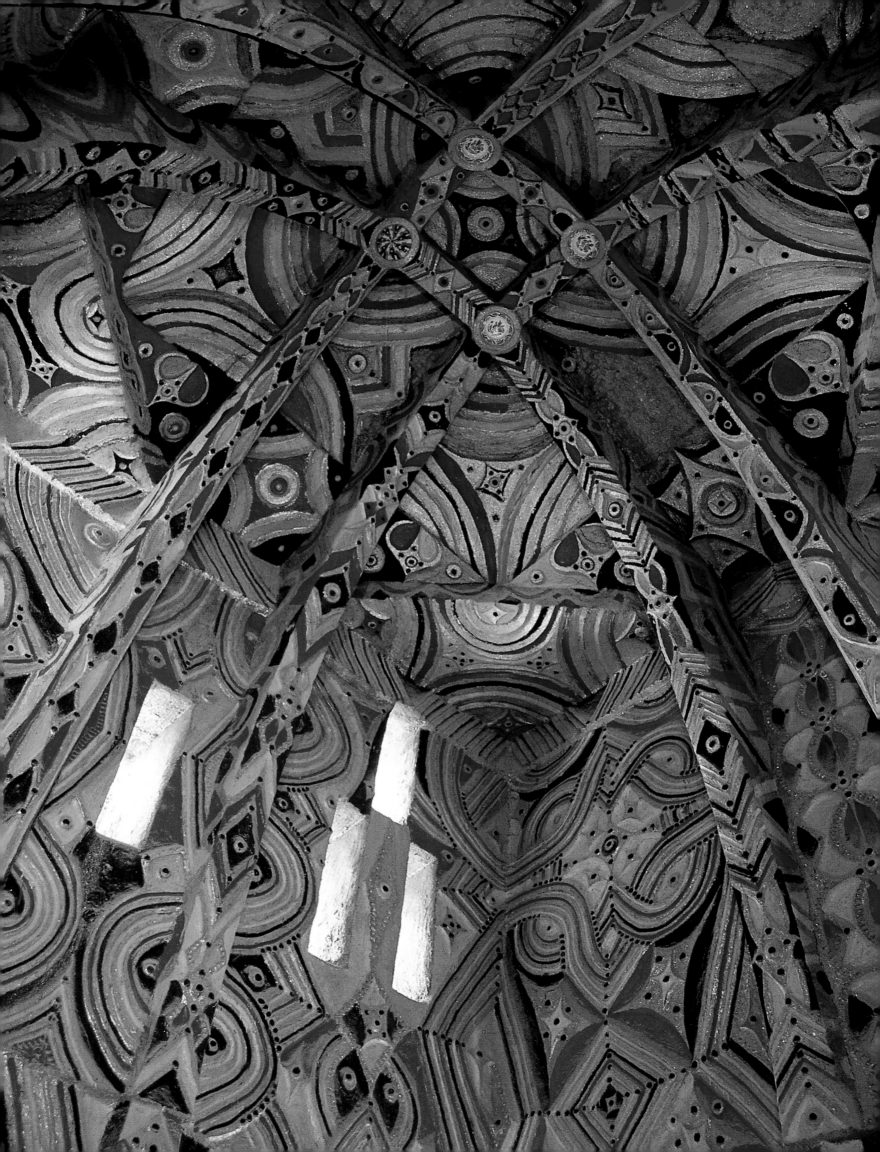

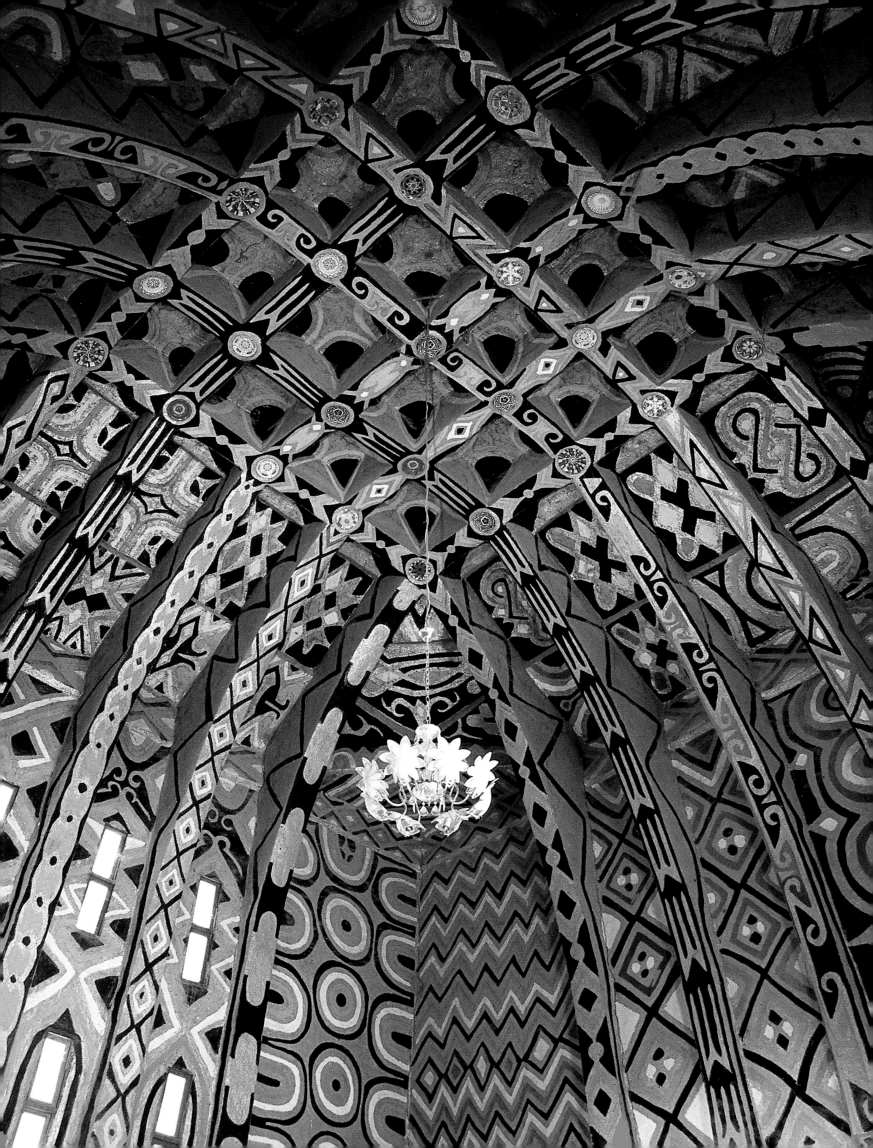

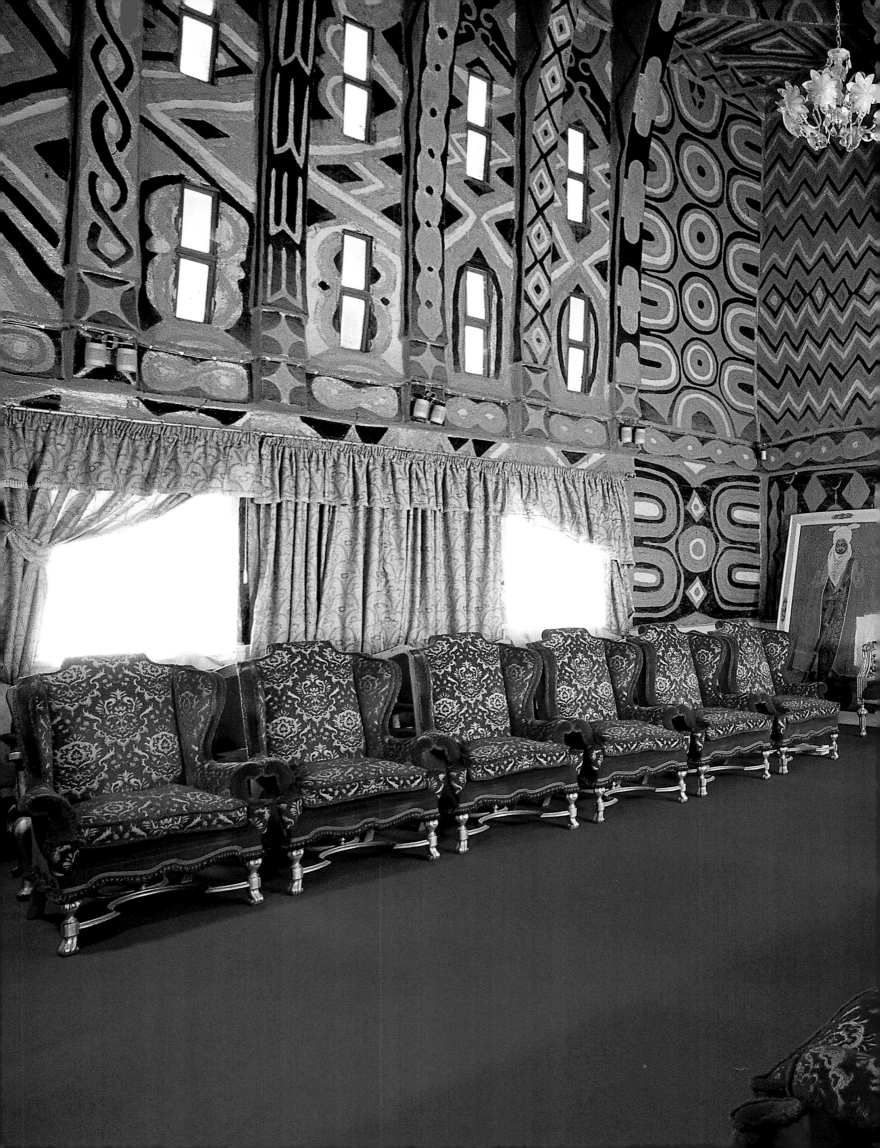

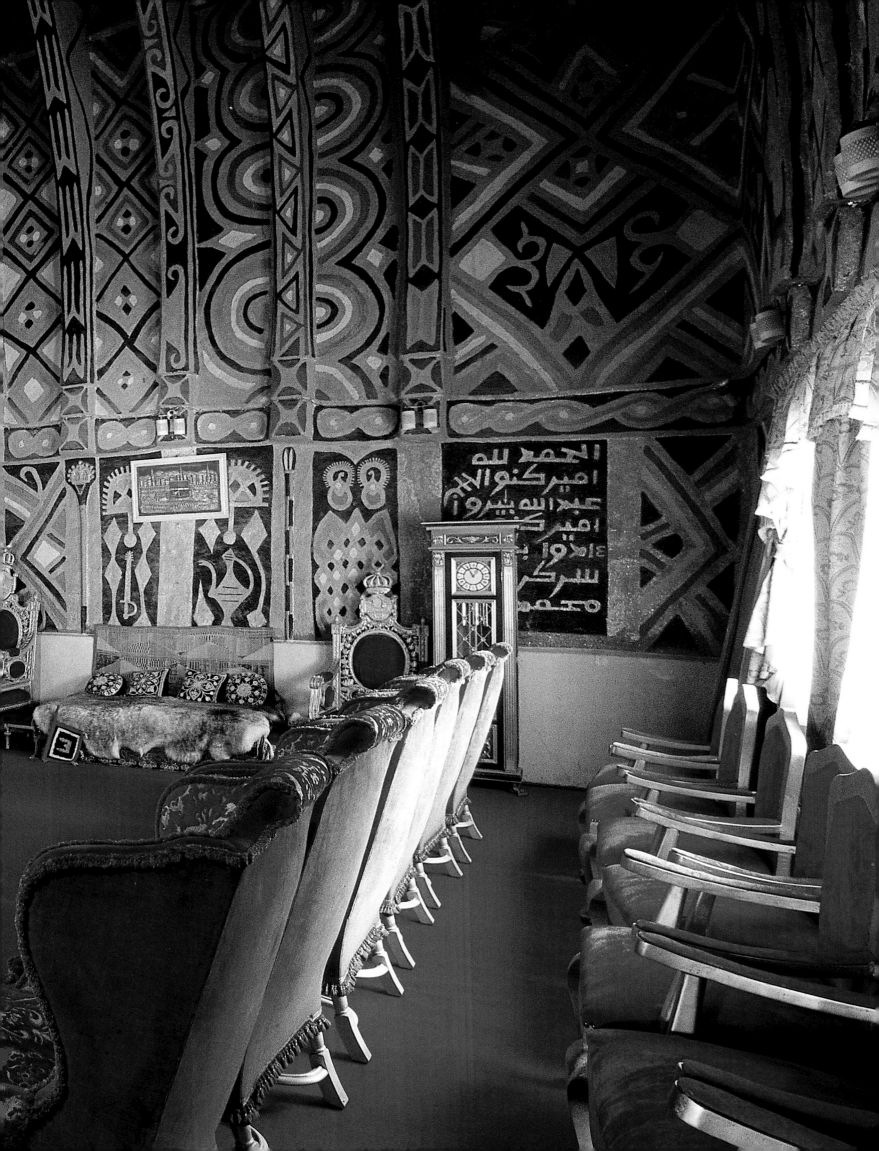

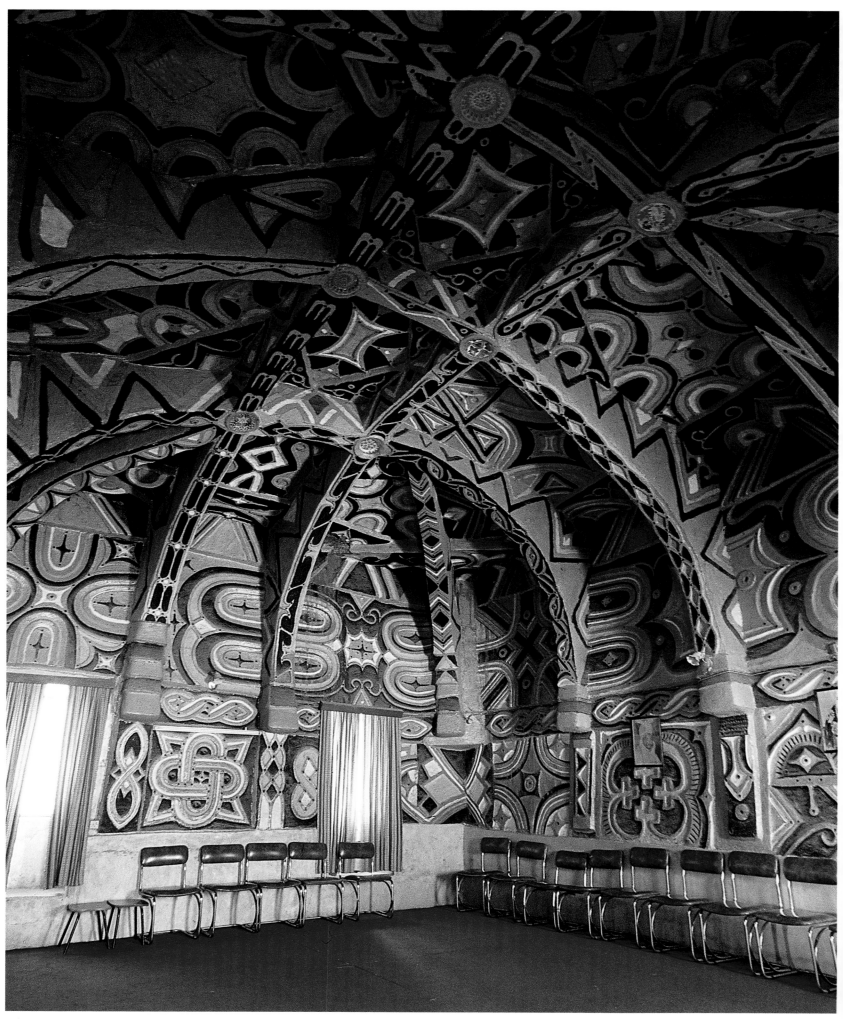

✳ **FACING PAGE AND PREVIOUS PAGES** Details of the ceilings of the emir's palace at Kano. The women's quarters, enlivened by greens, reds, and yellows. **PAGES 298-299** The entrance to the palace at Zaria. ✳ **RECHTE SEITE UND VORHERGEHENDE SEITEN** Details der Decken im Palast des Emirs von Kano. Die Frauengemächer strahlen in Grün-, Rot- und Gelbtönen. **SEITEN 298-299** Das Eingangstor zum Palast von Zaria. ✳ **PAGE DE DROITE ET PAGES PRECEDENTES** À Kano, détails des plafonds du palais de l'émir. Les quartiers des femmes, animés de couleurs vertes, rouges et jaunes. **PAGES 298-299** La porte d'entrée du palais de Zaria.

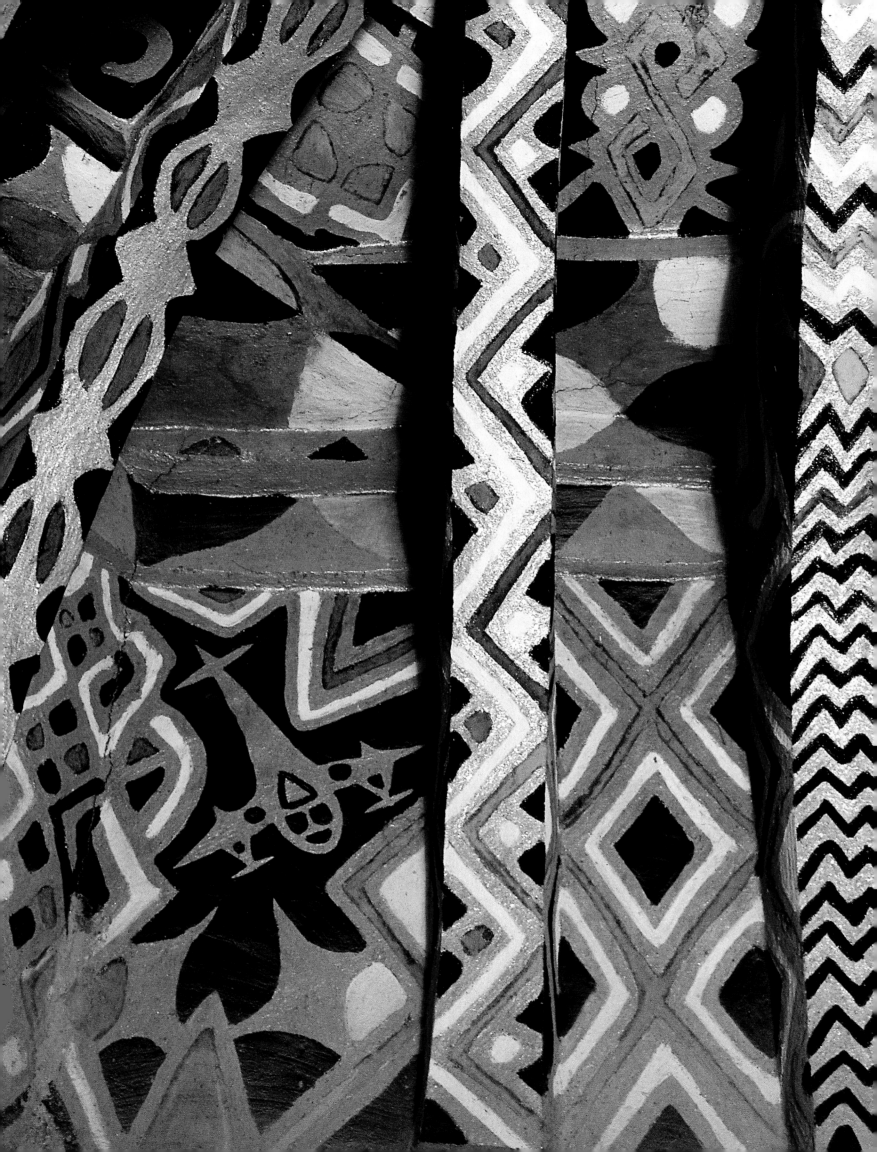

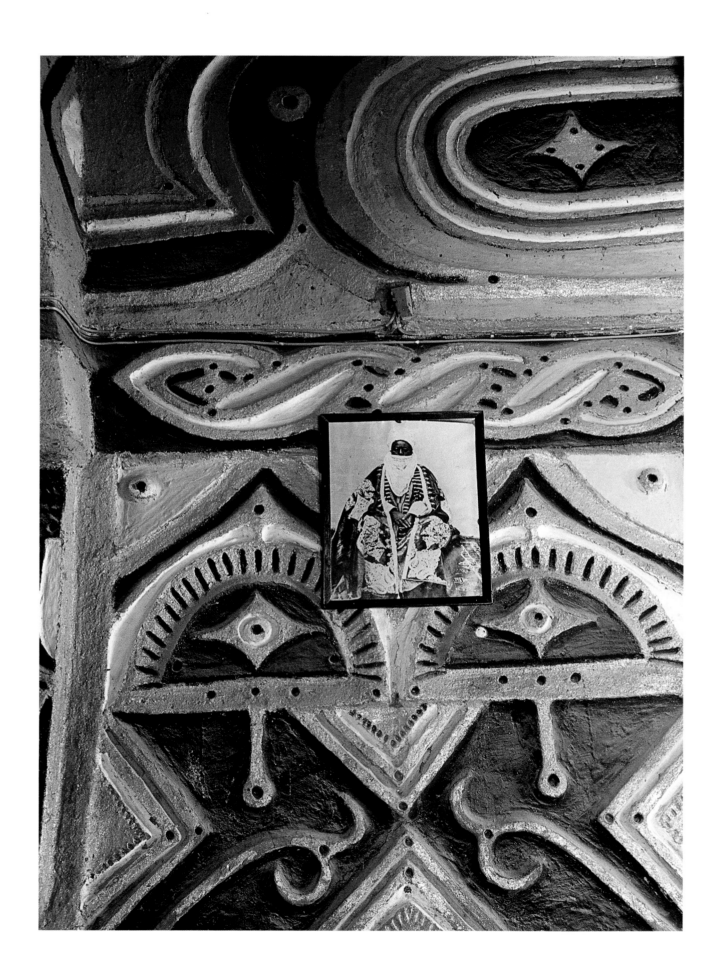

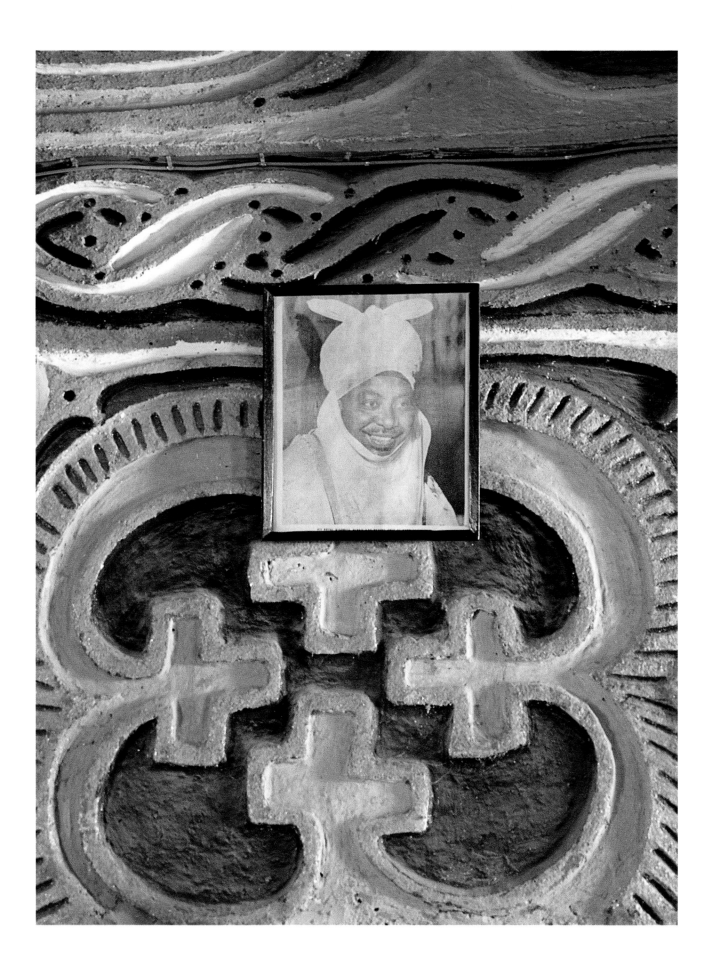

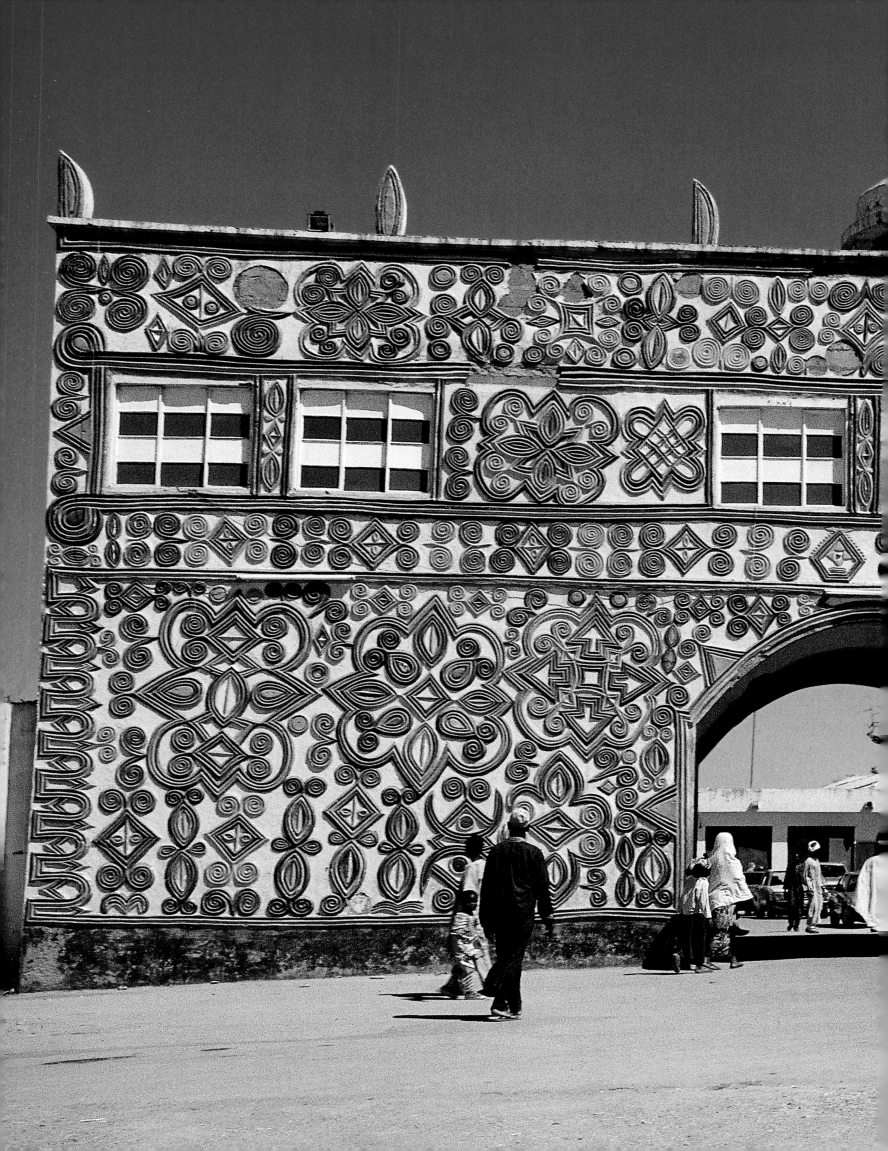

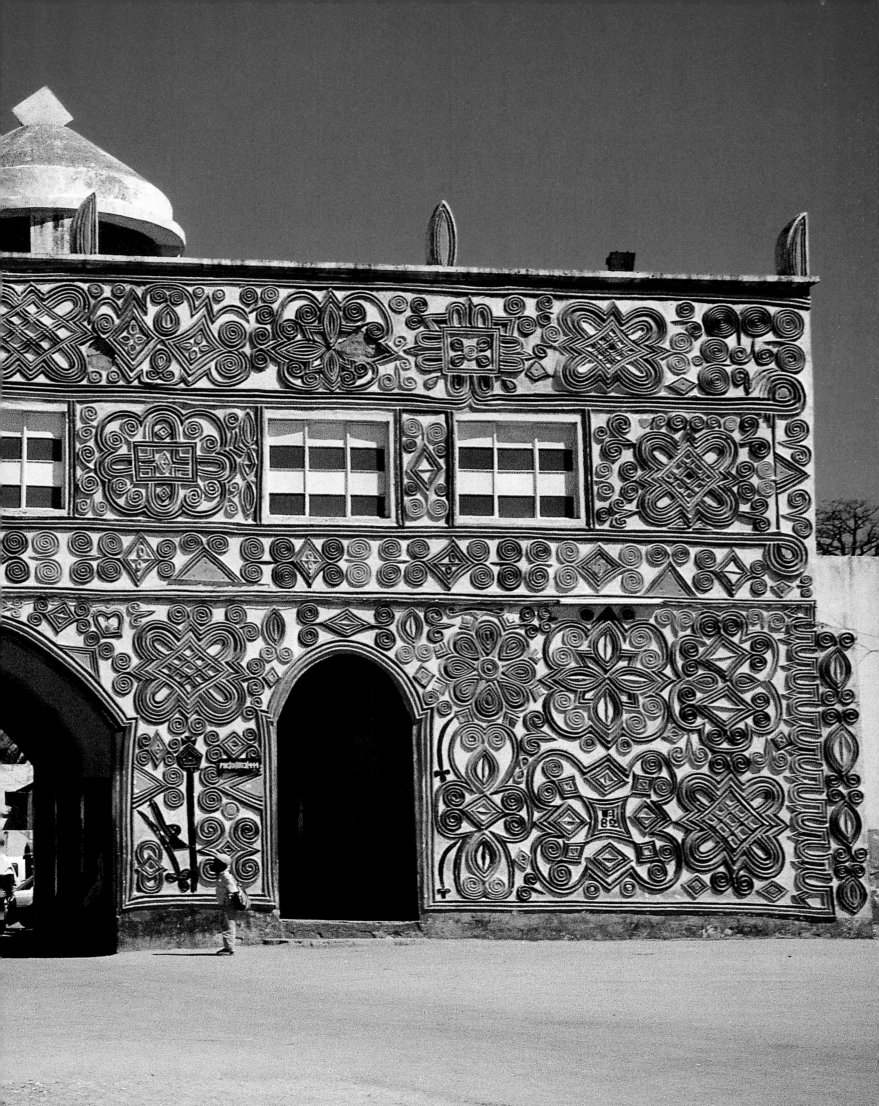

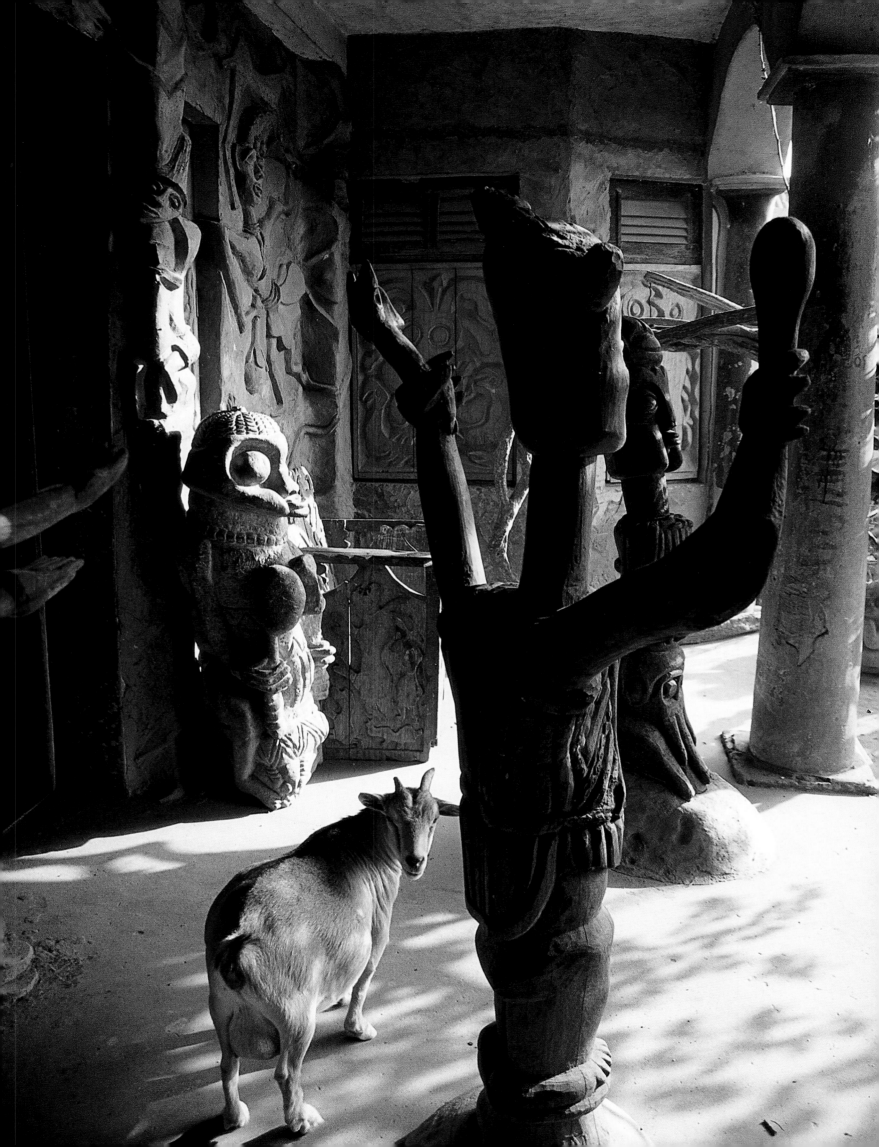

# SUSANNE WENGER

# OSHOGBO

For the last 50 years, this Austrian artist has been perpetuating the religious and philosophical foundations of the Yoruba region.

**Fantastic animals – lions, cats, and grasshoppers – form a kind of honour guard to the beautiful Brazilian-baroque townhouse of Susanne Wenger.**

For over half a century, this artist has been closely linked to the Yoruba people; with her, the sculptors and craftsmen of the city have founded a creative school, the Mbari Mbayo Club, which in the Igbo language means literally "when we see it, we're happy". The Yoruba culture, based on theatre, music, poetry and masquerade, celebrates harvests and the arrival of rain by sacred rituals that Wenger has reinterpreted in her house. "Nature is my only master," she likes to say. These works, whether they are sculptures, batiks or paintings, seem to grow around her home like rampant plants. A few miles away, beside the river, the sacred Yoruba forest is also an extension of her work. Here people come to pause reverently before the images and invoke the ancestral Yoruba ideal – that of patience and tranquillity in the face of a turbulent world. Susanne Wenger, confronted by Iya Nla, the deity who maintains order in the world at the same time as threatening its stability, has responded with a new form of sacred art.

**Fantasietiere, Löwen, Katzen und Heuschrecken bewachen wie eine Leibgarde Susanne Wengers Haus im brasilianischen Barockstil.**

Seit einem halben Jahrhundert fühlt sich die Künstlerin dem Volk der Yoruba eng verbunden. Gemeinsam mit Handwerkern und Bildhauern der Stadt hat sie eine kreative Schule gegründet, den Mbari Mbayo Club, was in der Igbosprache bedeutet: »Wenn wir es sehen, sind wir glücklich«. Die Kultur der Yoruba stützt sich auf das Theater, die Dichtung und die Maskerade. Die Künstlerin aus dem Westen interpretiert die heiligen Rituale zum Erntedank oder zum Beginn der Regenzeit auf ihre Art neu. »Ich erkenne nur die Natur als meine Meisterin an«, lautet das Credo der Dame des Hauses. Ihre Werke, seien es Skulpturen, Batikkunst oder Gemälde, sprießen wie Pflanzen in ihrem Heim. Einige Kilometer von der Künstlerresidenz entfernt setzt Susanne Wenger ihre Arbeit am Flussufer in dem so genannten »Heiligen Hain« fort. Andächtig verharrt man vor den Darstellungen, die ein altes Ideal der Yoruba beschwören: in einer turbulenten Welt, Ruhe und Gelassenheit zu bewahren. Die Österreicherin, die unter dem Schutz der mächtigen Urmutter Iya Nla steht, die für Ordnung in der Welt sorgt, indem sie ihre Stabilität bedroht, hat eine eigene Antwort gefunden: eine neue Sakralkunst.

**En ville, des animaux fantastiques, lions, chats et sauterelles forment un garde-fou à une belle maison de style baroque brésilien, celle de Susanne Wenger.**

Voilà plus d'un demi-siècle que cette artiste est étroitement liée au peuple Yoruba. Avec elle, les artisans et sculpteurs de la ville ont inventé une école de création, le Mbari Mbayo Club, littéralement en langue Igbo, «quand nous le voyons, nous sommes heureux». La culture Yoruba, fondée sur le théâtre, la poésie et la mascarade, célèbre les moissons et l'arrivée des pluies par des rituels sacrés réinterprétés dans sa maison par l'artiste occidentale. «Je n'ai pas d'autre Maître que la nature», a coutume de répéter la maîtresse des lieux. Ces œuvres, qu'elles soient sculptures, batik ou peinture, grandissent chez elle comme des plantes. À quelques kilomètres de la résidence, en bordure d'une rivière, la forêt sacrée prolonge le travail. On s'y recueille devant les représentations en invoquant l'idéal ancestral Yoruba: garder patience et tranquillité d'esprit dans un monde turbulent. Susanne Wenger, placée sous la toute puissance de la mère ancestrale, Iya Nla, laquelle assure l'ordre du monde tout en menaçant sa stabilité, a trouvé sa réponse: un nouvel art sacré.

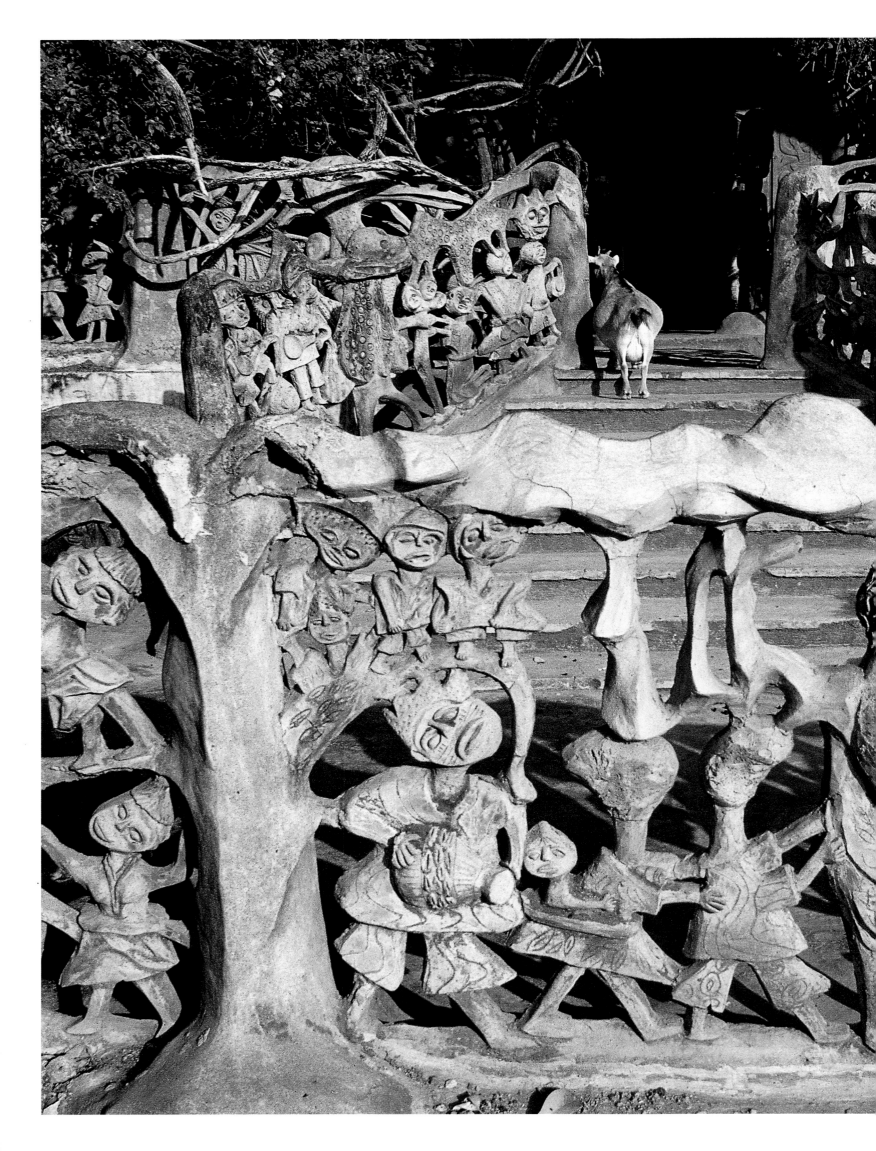

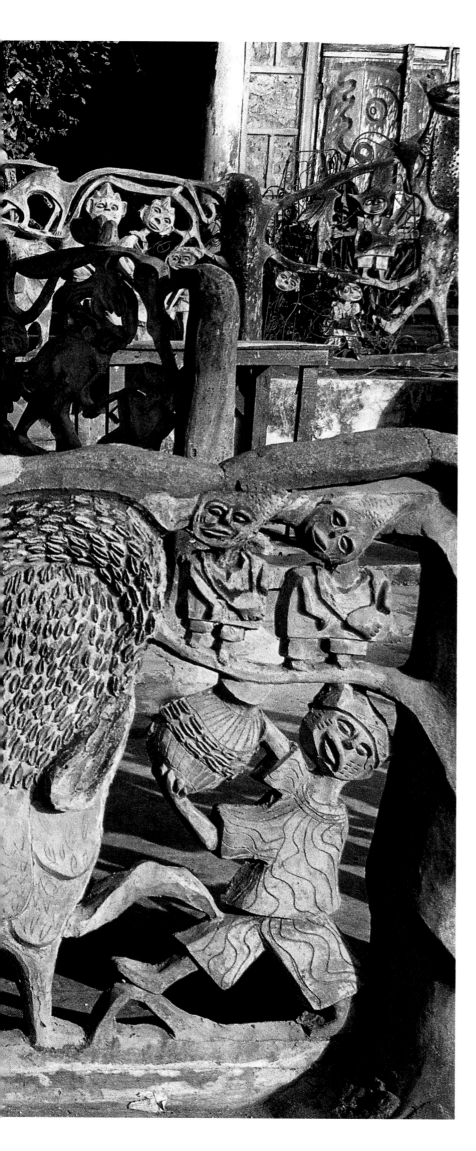

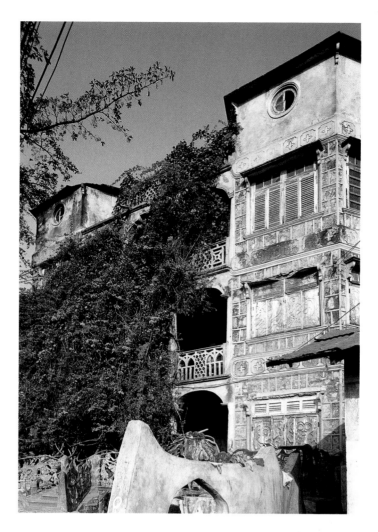

✻ **FACING PAGE** Seen from the gate, fantastic animals symbolise a view of the universe as a single entity. **ABOVE** Inspired by the Brazilian baroque style, the house of Susanne Wenger contains the results of nearly 50 years' work on the confluence between sacred art and scenes of ordinary life. ✻ **LINKE SEITE** Die Fantasietiere am Eingang symbolisieren eine Annäherung an ein Universum, das als Gesamtheit betrachtet wird. **OBEN** Susanne Wengers Haus im brasilianischen Barockstil beherbergt ihr Werk aus 50 schöpferischen Jahren. In ihrer Kunst vermischen sich sakrale Elemente mit Szenen aus dem Alltag. ✻ **PAGE DE GAUCHE** Dès le portail, des animaux fantastiques symbolisent une approche de l'univers conçu comme un tout. **CI-DESSUS** D'inspiration baroque brésilien, la maison de Susanne Wenger abrite un travail de près de 50 ans à la confluence entre l'art sacré et les scènes de la vie quotidienne.

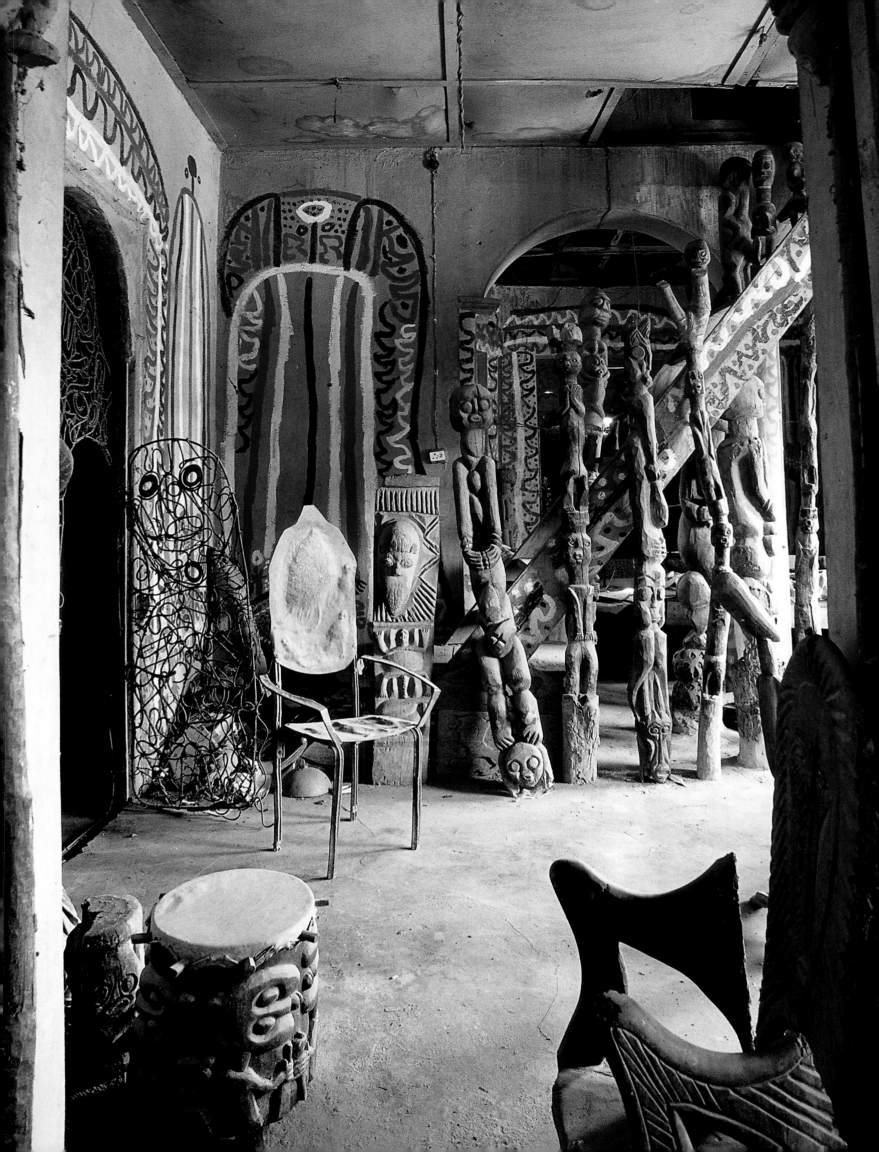

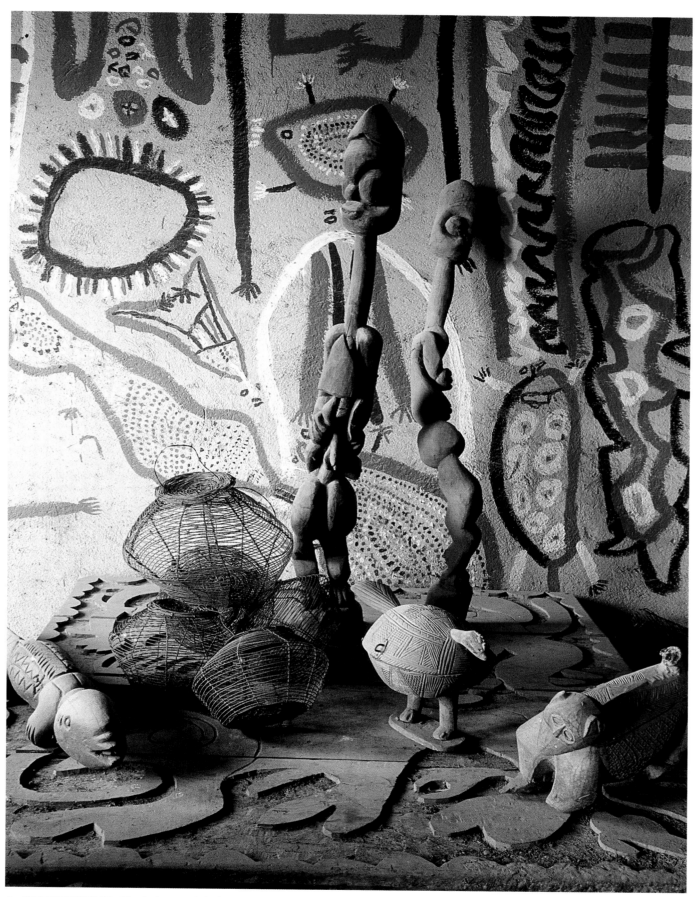

❋ **FACING PAGE AND ABOVE** The Yoruba honour their divinities with sculptures, which they place in temples of dried mud. The representations of human beings humorously illustrate traditional proverbs, while the carved figures of animals illustrate the danger run by people who fail to respect the order of the world and its social hierarchy. ❋ **LINKE SEITE UND OBEN** Die Yoruba ehren ihre Gottheiten mit Skulpturen, die sie in Tempeln aus getrocknetem Schlamm aufstellen. Die menschlichen Figuren illustrieren auf humorvolle Art die traditionellen Sprichwörter. Tierskulpturen verkörpern die Gefahr, die allen droht, die die Weltordnung und die soziale Hierarchie nicht respektieren. ❋ **PAGE DE GAUCHE ET CI-DESSUS** Les Yoruba honorent leurs divinités par des sculptures qu'ils placent dans des temples de boue séchée. Les représentations humaines illustrent avec humour les proverbes traditionnels, tandis que les figures d'animaux sculptés représentent le danger que courent ceux qui ne respectent pas l'ordre du monde et la hiérarchie sociale.

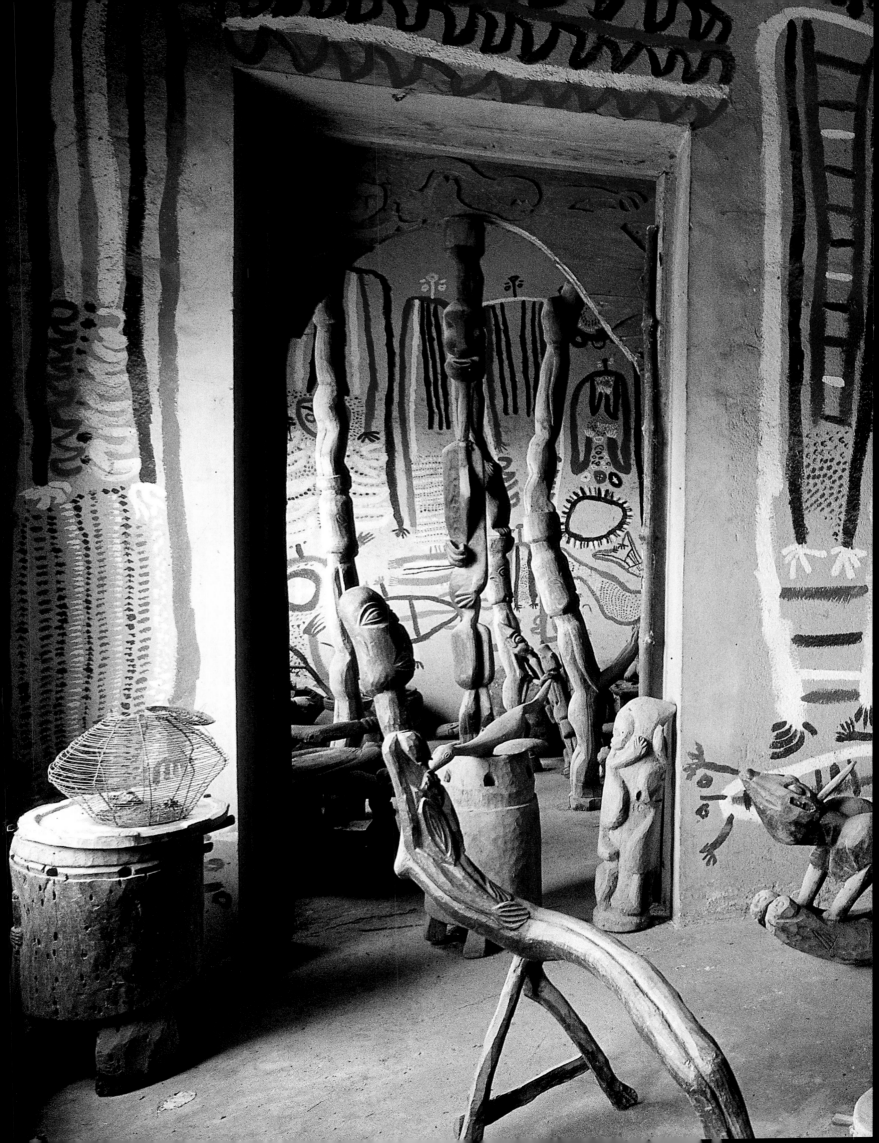

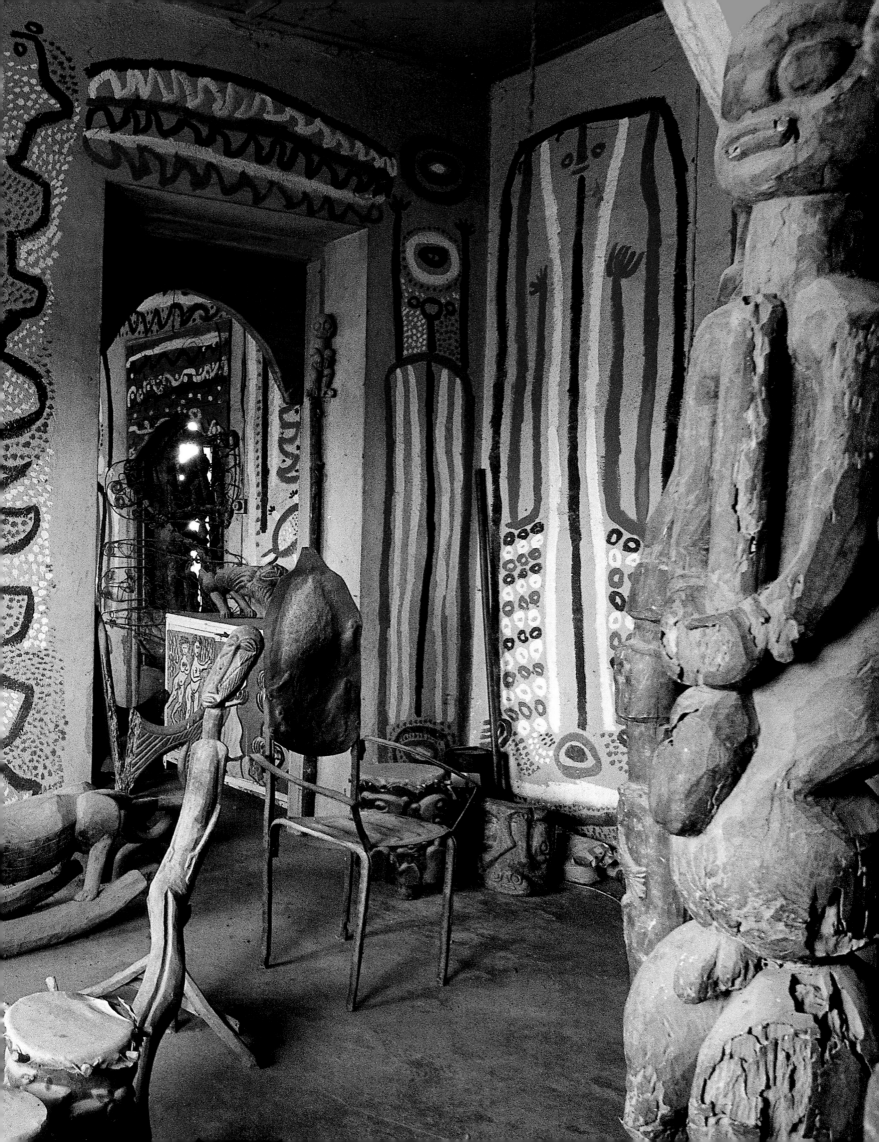

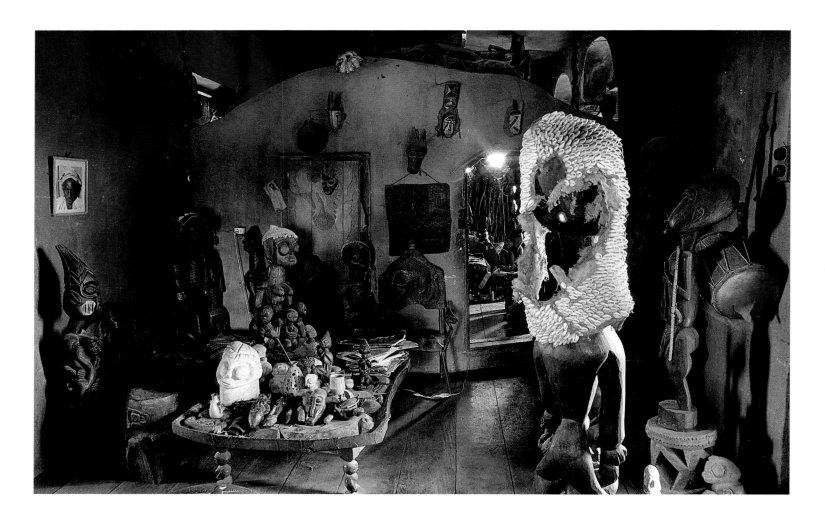

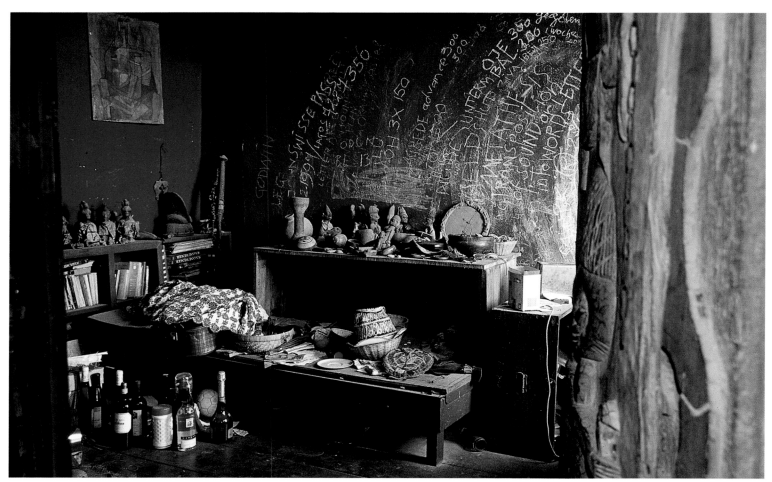

✳ **ABOVE** Oshogbo, the cradle of Yoruba art, has produced many gifted young artists. Some, like Twins Seven Seven, have won international fame. ✳ **OBEN** Oshogbo, die Wiege der Yoruba-Kunst, hat viele Künstler hervorgebracht. Einige wie der Künstler Twins Seven Seven sind international bekannt. ✳ **CI-DESSOUS** Berceau de l'art Yoruba, Oshogbo est demeurée une pépinière d'artistes. Certains, comme Twins Seven Seven, ont atteint une renommée internationale.

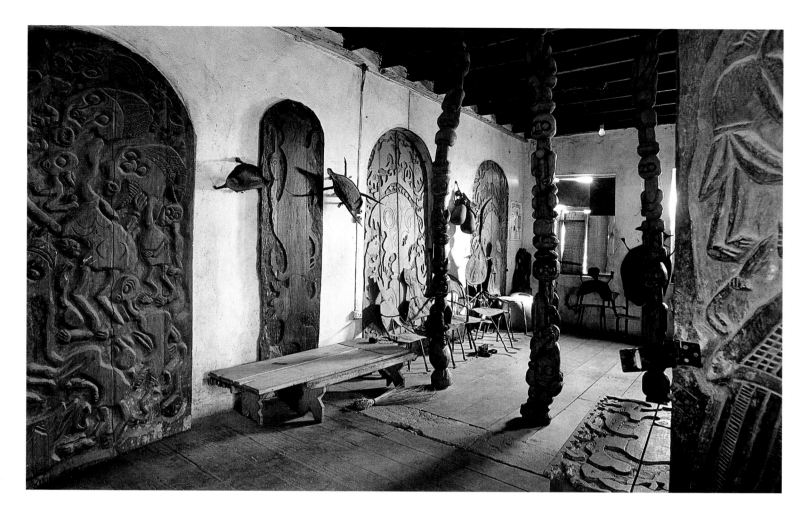

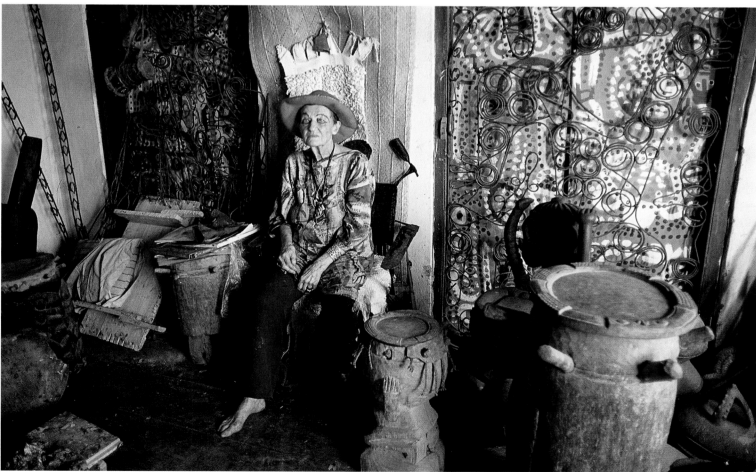

❋ **ABOVE** With her totems and sculptures, Susanne Wenger brings the religious and philosophical founding principles of the Yoruba nation both into her own house, and into the sacred forest. ❋ **OBEN** Indem sie ihre Totems und Skulpturen erschafft, verewigt Susanne Wenger in ihrem Haus und in dem »Heiligen Hain« die religiösen und philosophischen Vorstellungen der Yoruba. ❋ **CI-DESSUS** À travers la réalisation de totems et de sculptures, Susanne Wenger perpétue dans sa maison et la fôret sacrée les fondements religieux et philosophiques du pays Yoruba.

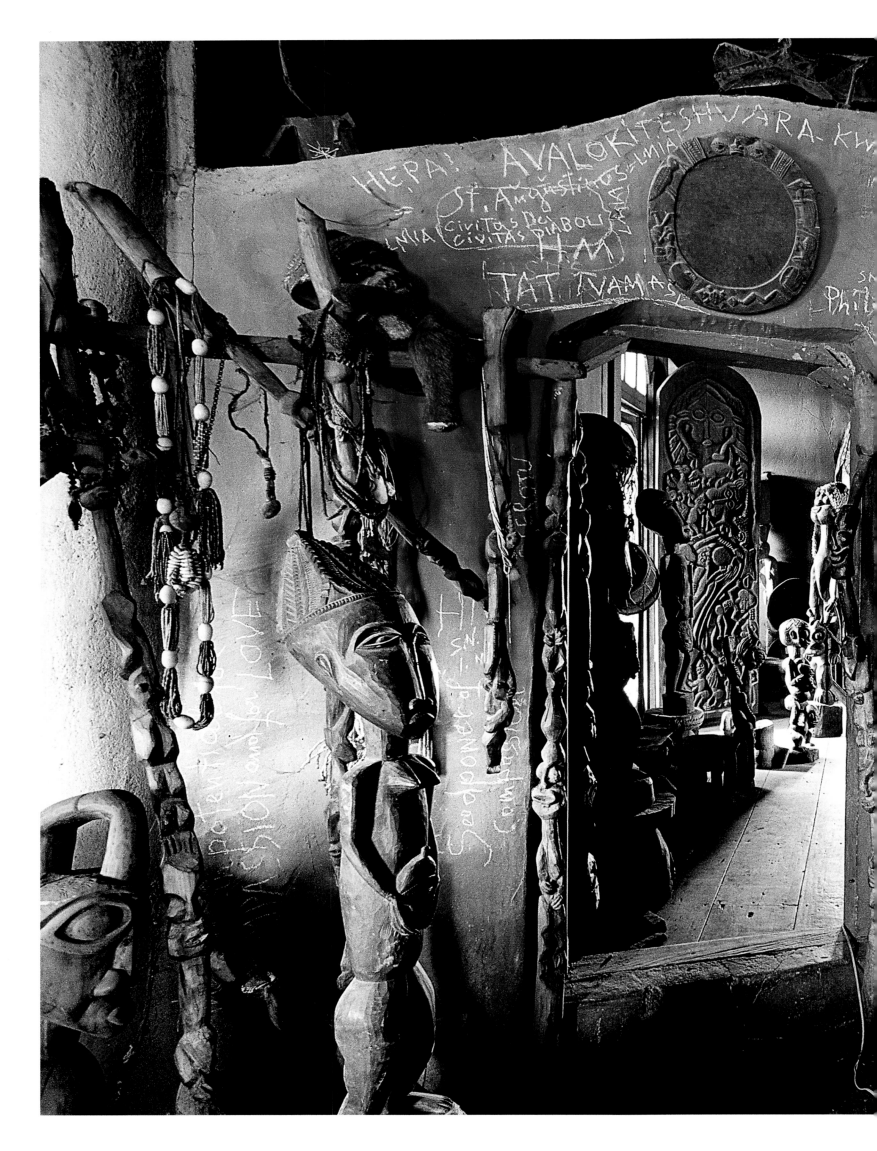

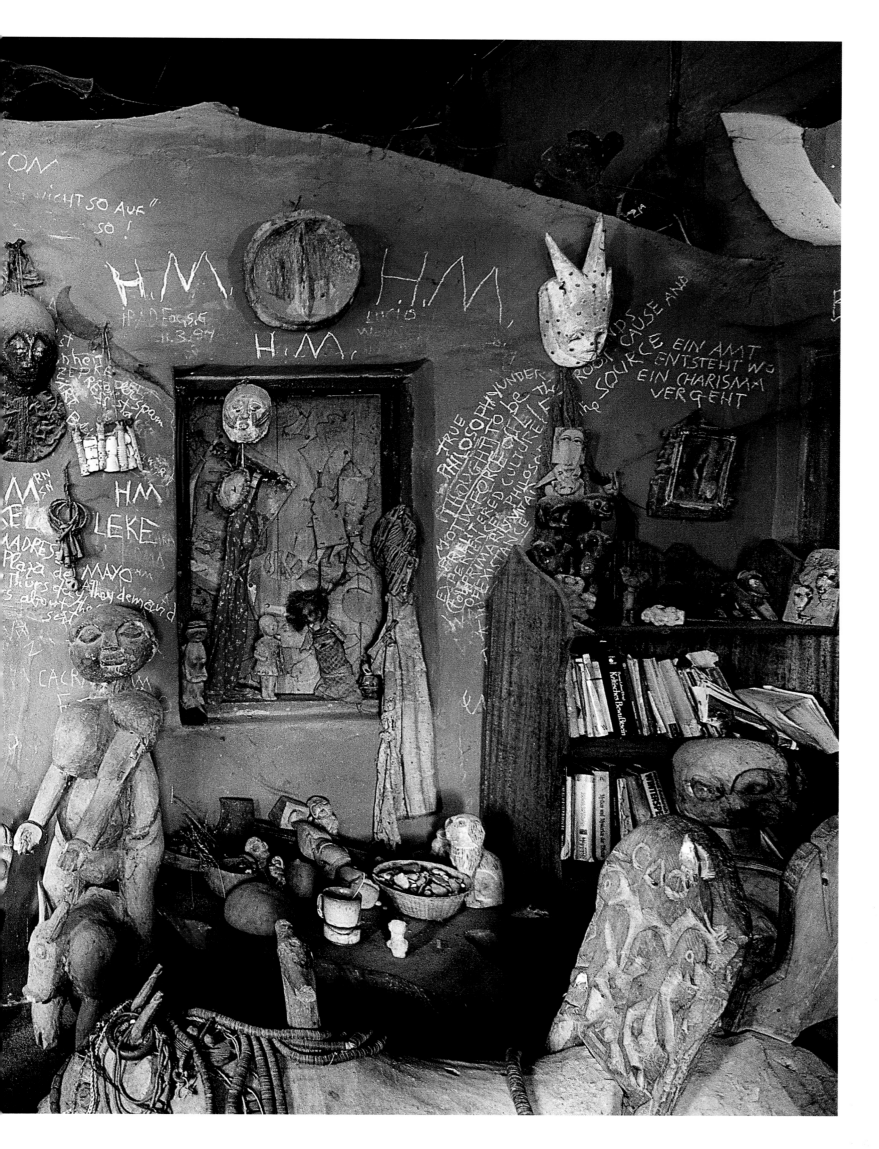

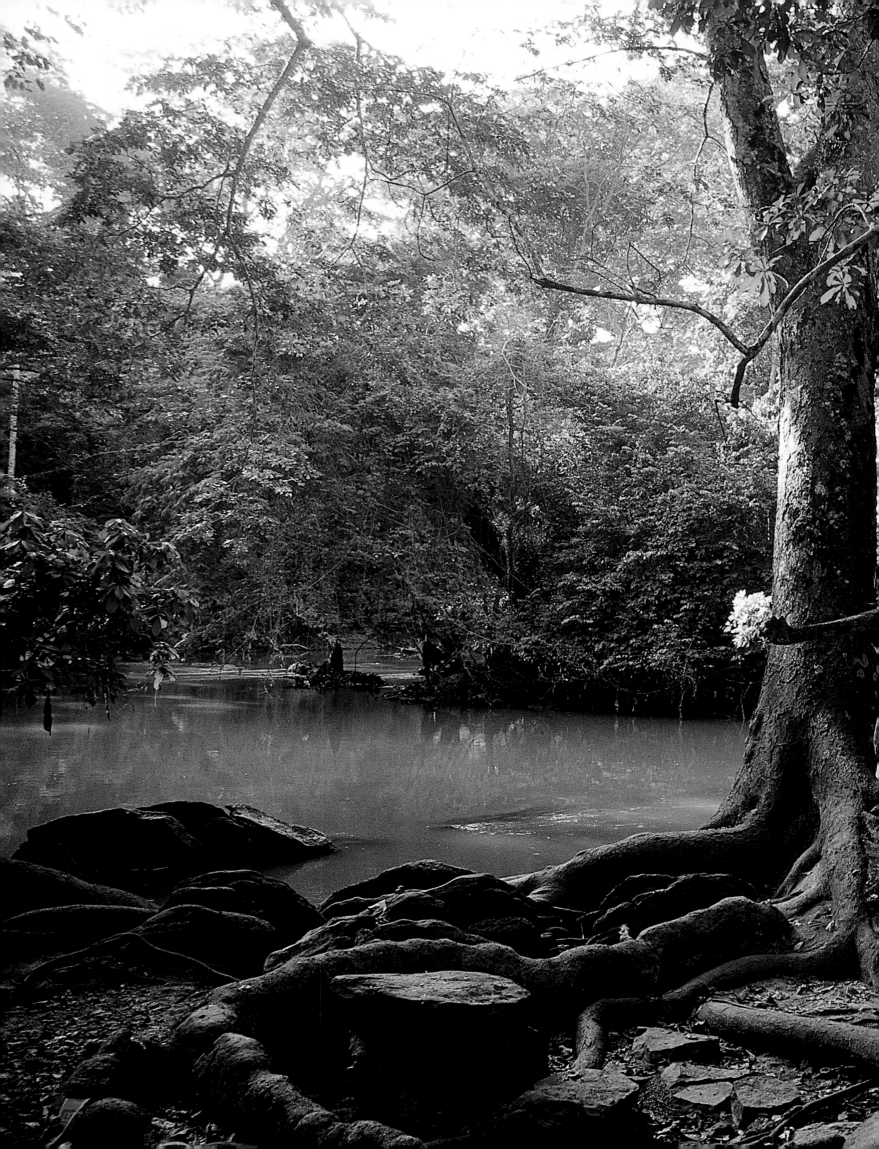

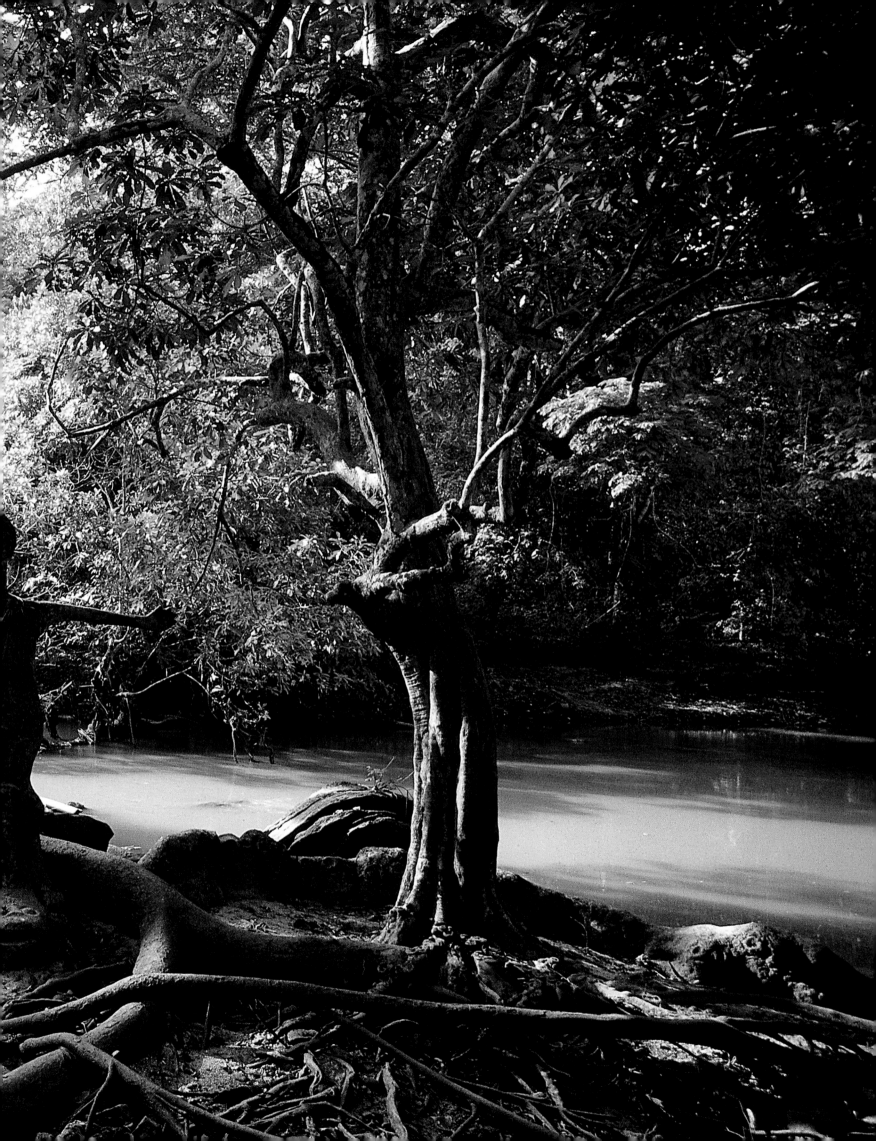

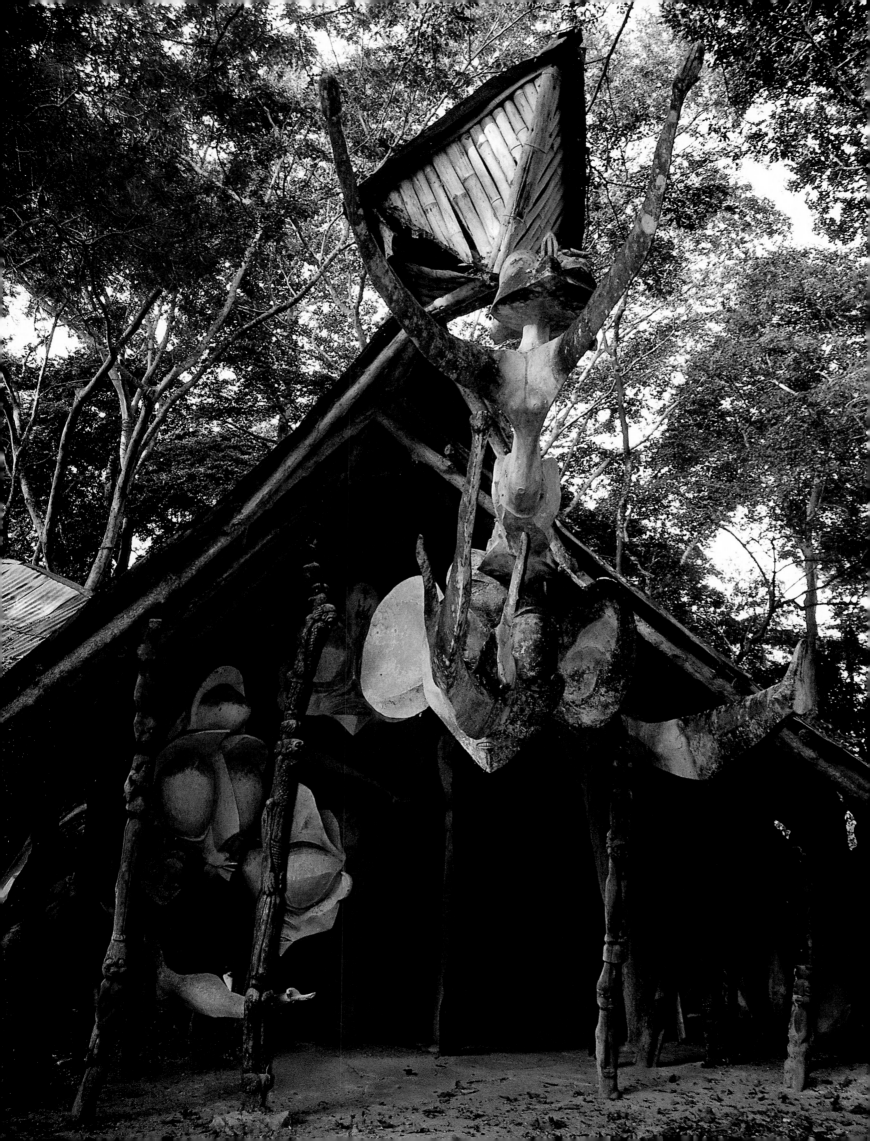

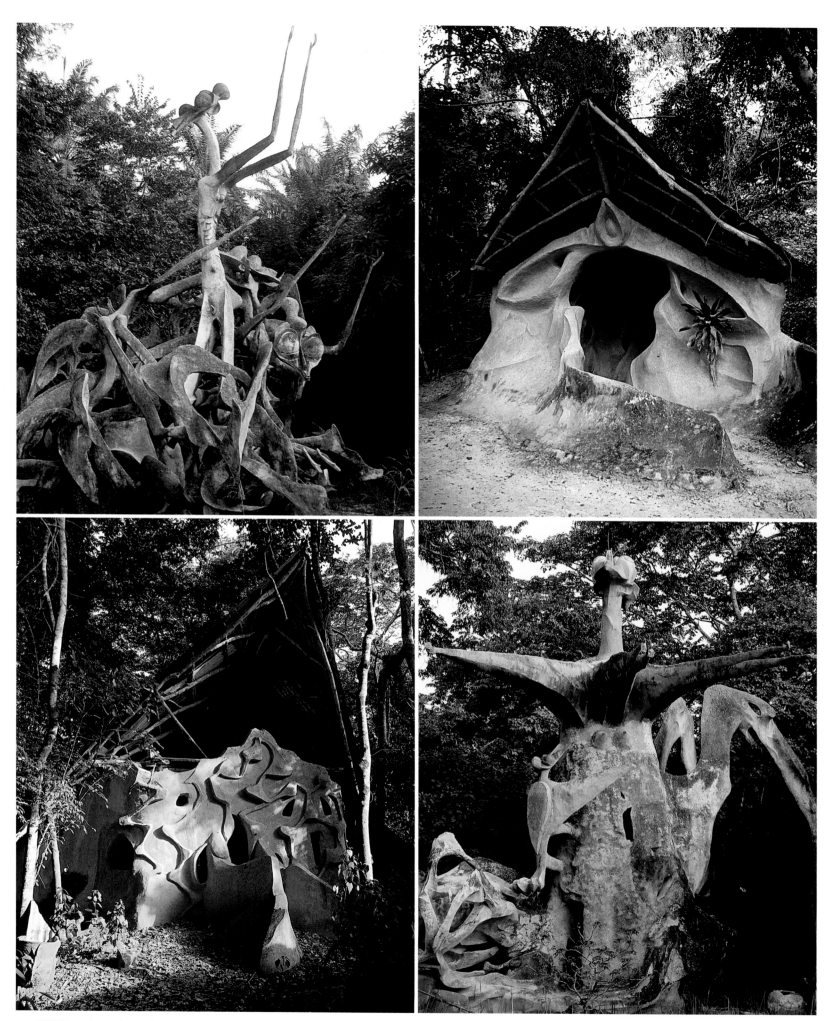

❋ **FACING PAGE AND ABOVE** The nearby sacred forest contains enormous sculptures and sanctuaries dedicated to the various Yoruba gods, notably the famous sanctuary of Osun. ❋ **LINKE SEITE UND OBEN** In dem nahe gelegenen »Heiligen Hain« stehen riesige Skulpturen und Heiligtümer, die den verschiedenen Göttern der Yoruba geweiht sind, darunter auch das Heiligtum der Göttin Osun. ❋ **PAGE DE GAUCHE ET CI-DESSUS** La forêt sacrée voisine renferme d'énormes sculptures et des sanctuaires dédiés aux différents dieux Yoruba, dont le célèbre sanctuaire d'Osun.

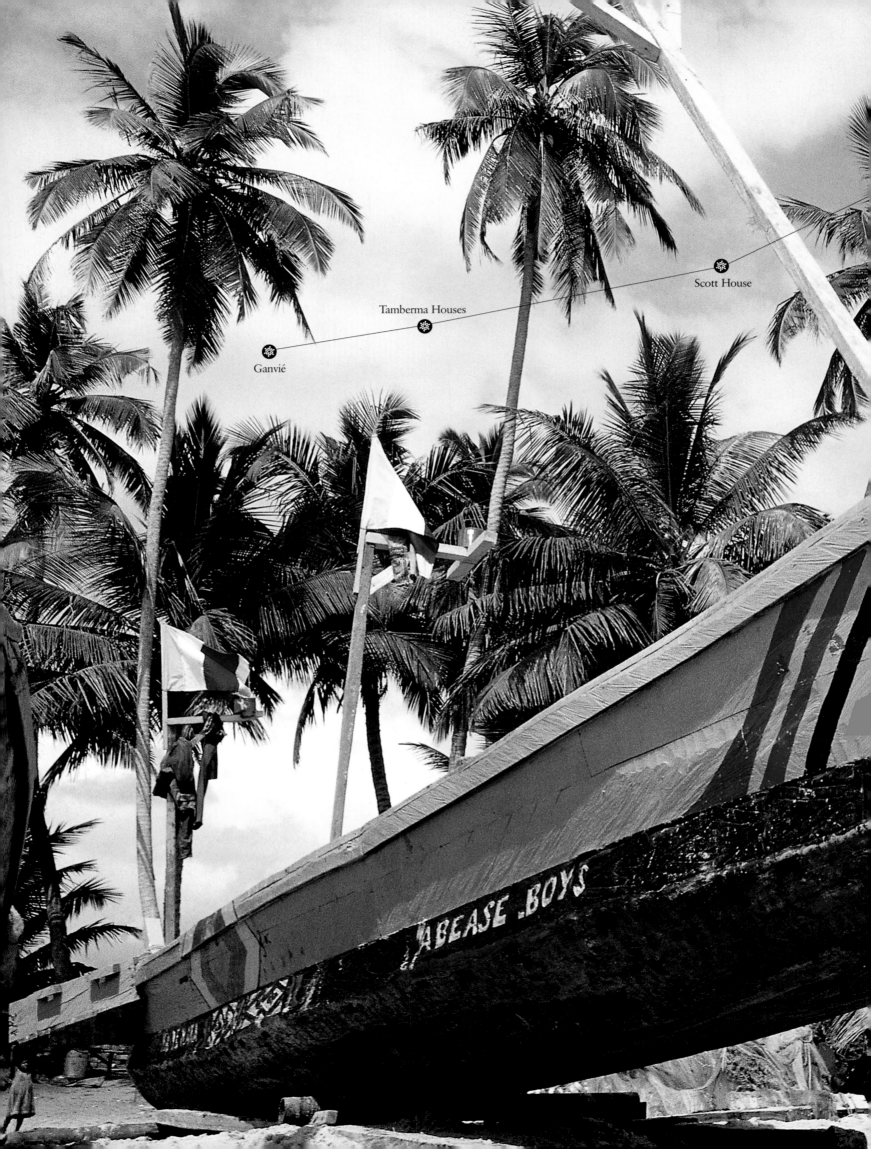

Ganvié

Tamberma Houses

Scott House

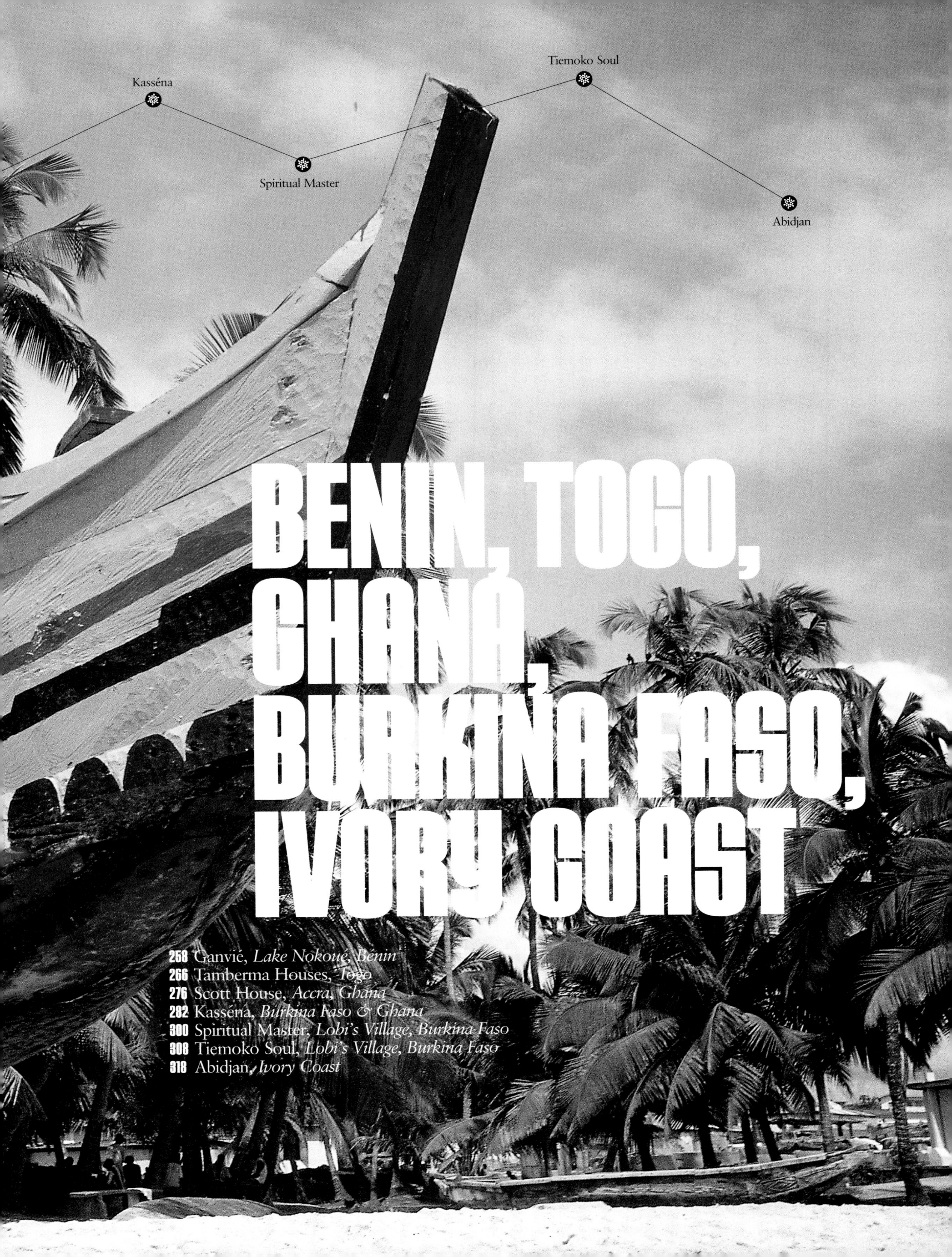

Kasséna

Tiemoko Soul

Spiritual Master

Abidjan

# BENIN, TOGO, GHANA, BURKINA FASO, IVORY COAST

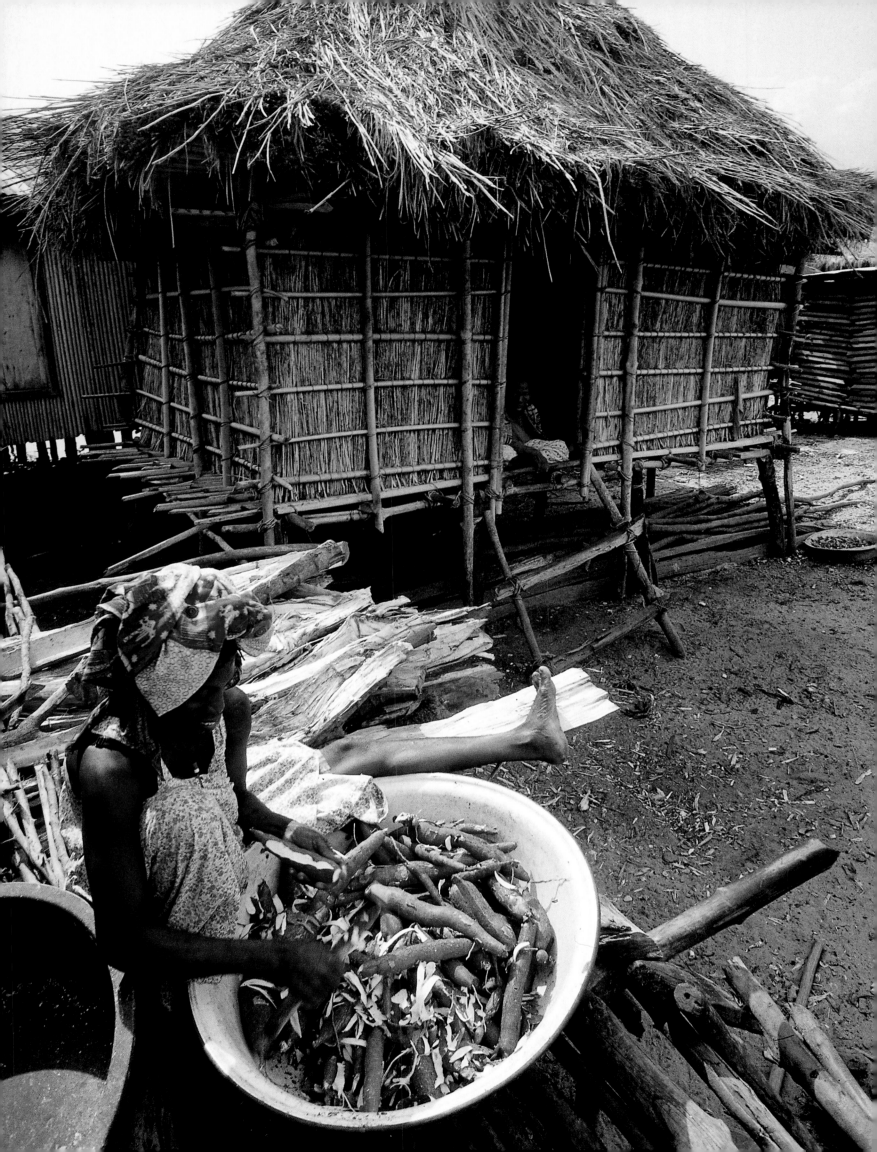

# Ganvie
# Lake Nokoue

The raised lake houses of a township
only 20 kilometres from the nation's capital Porto-Novo.

**A swarm of pirogues loaded with children, food and jerry cans of water crosses the lagoon.**

Their destination is a tangle of houses made from palm fronds, with roofs topped by a thick layer of straw, balanced on stilts standing in five feet of dull blue-green water. These rectangular huts are home to 45,000 people. Inside their houses, the surface of the water flickers through the interstices of the bamboo floors. Simple rattan furniture and basic household utensils are the only items to be seen. At the foot of each hut is its *acadja*, or cage made of branches, for raising crayfish and fish. The lake's annual yield used to be quite astounding, with a ton of fish per hectare, but now it has fallen off disastrously following the construction of a port at the sea-estuary, which has let salt water into the lake; and as a result Ganvié has lapsed into poverty of late. The Toffinous (watermen) originally came here as refugees from tribal wars and the slave-hunters sent by the king of Abomey. The word Ganvié itself means "the town of those who have found peace". For how much longer?

**Ein Schwarm von Pirogen fährt durch die Lagune, schwer beladen mit Kindern, Lebensmitteln und Wasserkanistern. Und das Dorf?**

Ein Wirrwarr von Häusern aus Palmblättern, gekrönt von dicken Strohdächern, stützt sich auf Pfähle, die in 1,50 Metern Höhe aus dem meergrünen Wasser ragen. In den rechteckigen Häusern wohnen 45000 Menschen. Durch die Spalten im Bambusboden kann man die Lagune sehen, und das Mobiliar besteht aus Rattanmöbeln und einigen wenigen Küchengerätschaften. Unter den Häusern liegen mit Astwerk abgesteckte Wasserfelder, so genannte *acadjas*, in denen Fische und Krebse gezüchtet werden. Zweimal im Jahr wird geerntet. Früher war die Ausbeute grandios (eine Tonne Fisch pro Hektar), aber seit an der Flussmündung ein Hafen gebaut wurde, sinkt der Ertrag. Das Meerwasser überschwemmt den See und wegen der Versalzung bleiben die Fische aus, sodass Ganvié in Armut versinkt. Einst waren die Toffinu (»Wassermenschen«) vor Stammeskriegen und den Sklavenjägern des Königs von Abomey hierher geflüchtet. Ganvié bedeutet »Gemeinschaft der friedlich Erretteten«. Wie lange wird das noch so sein?

**Un essaim de pirogues chargées d'enfants, de nourriture et de bidons d'eau douce traverse la lagune. Le village?**

Un enchevêtrement de maisons en nervures de palmiers, les toits coiffés d'une épaisse couche de paille, soutenues par des pilotis enfoncés dans 1,50 m d'eau glauque. Des cases rectangulaires abritant 45000 personnes. À l'intérieur, le sol en bambou à claire-voie s'ouvre par interstices sur la lagune. Des meubles en rotin et les ustensiles ménagers de base forment le mobilier. Au pied de ces cases, les *acadjas*, des bassins d'élevage faits de branchage, abritent des poissons et des écrevisses. La récolte a lieu deux fois par an. Autrefois miraculeuse (un hectare donnait une tonne de poisson), la production a fondu avec la construction d'un port à l'entrée de l'estuaire. Depuis que l'eau de mer envahit le lac et que les poissons disparaissent sous l'effet de la salinité, Ganvié s'enfonce dans la pauvreté. Les Toffinou (les «hommes de l'eau») s'étaient réfugiés ici pour échapper aux guerres tribales et aux chasseurs d'esclaves du roi d'Abomey. Ganvié signifie «la cité de ceux qui ont trouvé la paix». Pour combien de temps encore?

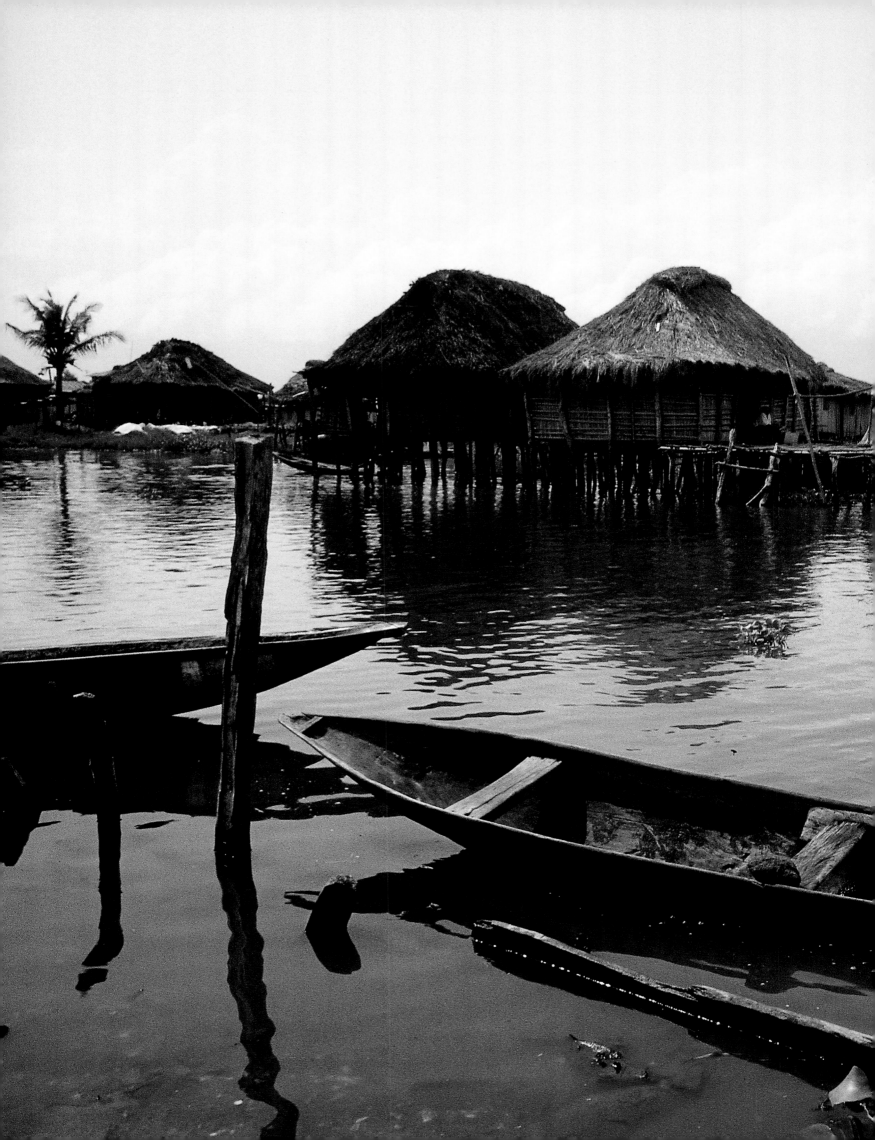

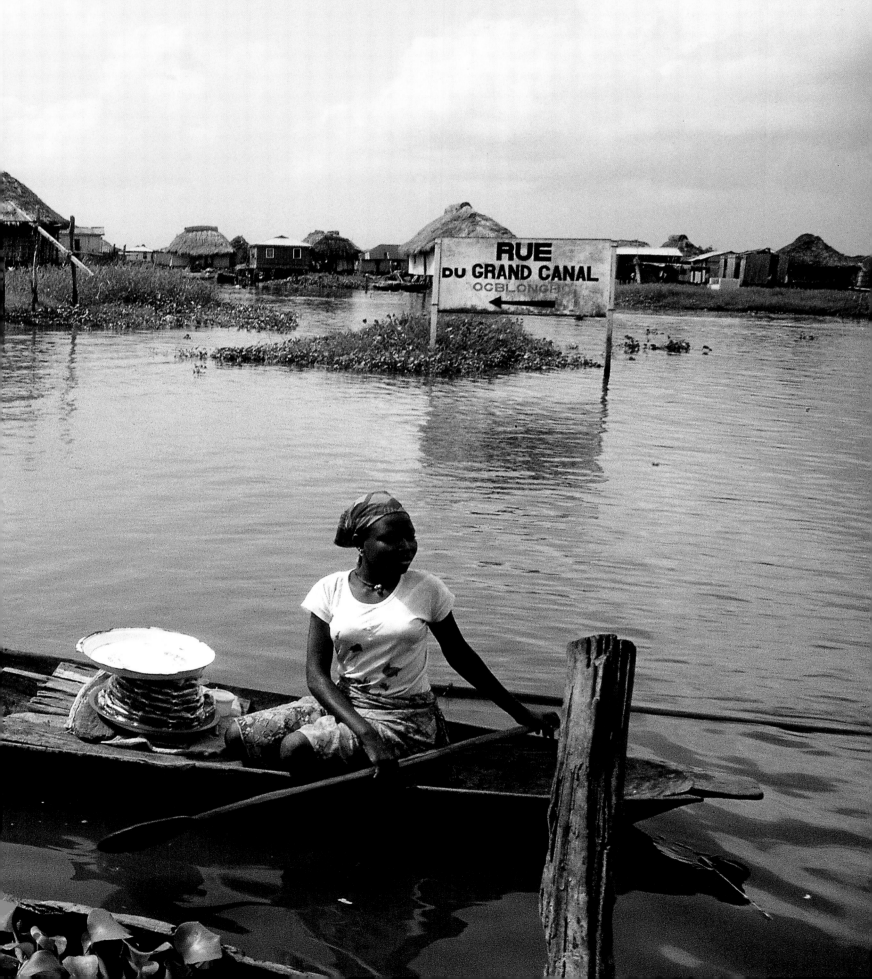

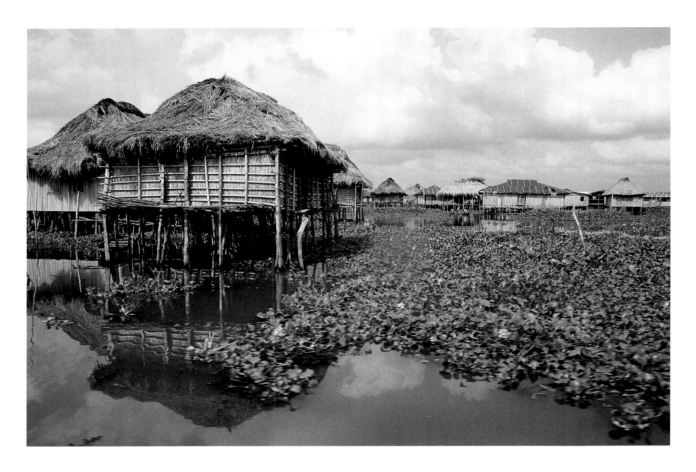

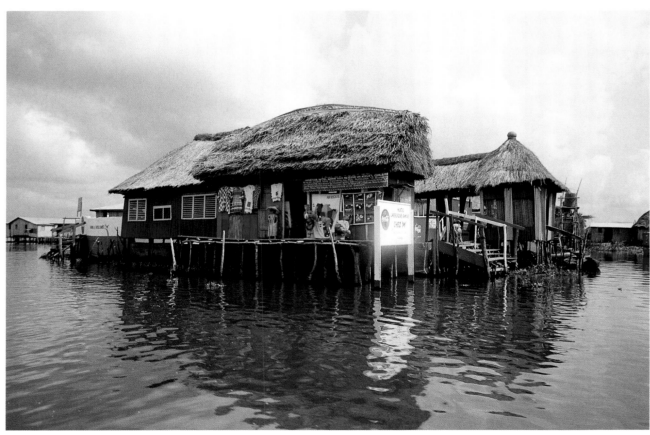

✳ **PREVIOUS PAGES AND ABOVE** Daily work is punctuated by the filling of earthenware water jugs called *canaris*. The village is criss-crossed with water-ways. Every house has its own landing stage and access ladder. ✳ **VORHERGEHENDE DOPPELSEITE UND OBEN** Das Alltagsleben wird vom Wasserholen mit großen Tontöpfen, den so genannten *canaris* bestimmt. Das Dorf ist von Wasserstraßen durchzogen. Jedes Haus hat einen Anlegeplatz, von dem eine Leiter zum Haus führt. ✳ **DOUBLE PAGE PRECEDENTE ET CI-DESSUS** L'activité quotidienne est rythmée par le remplissage d'eau douce des pots de terre appelés *canaris*. Le village est strié de voies d'eau. Chaque demeure à son ponton. Une échelle donne accès aux habitations.

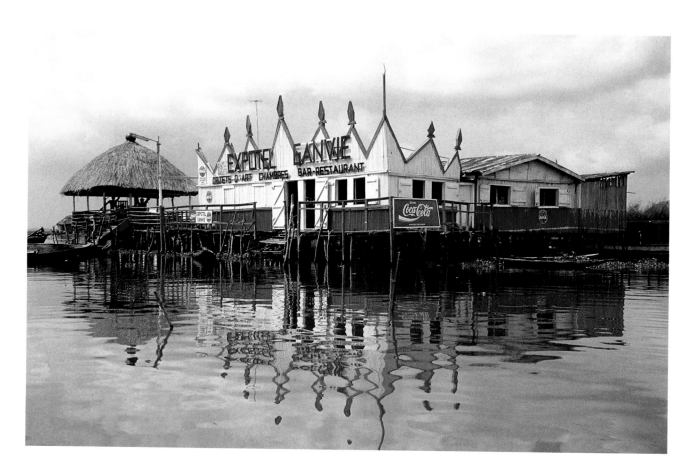

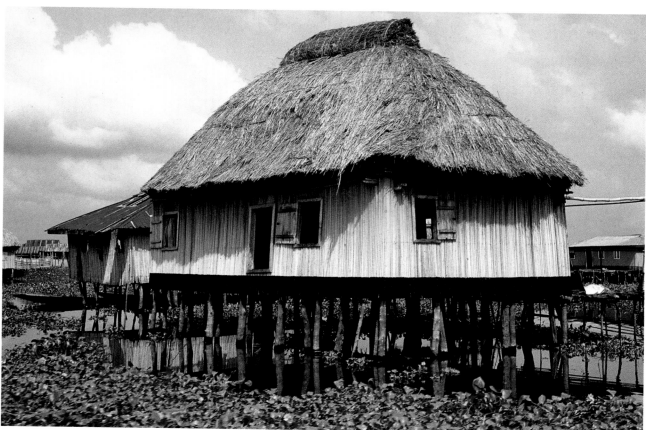

✳ **ABOVE** This bar was rebuilt in 1983 for a visit by François Mitterrand. The complex is constructed of palm fronds and bamboo on wooden stilts or imperishable teak pilings. Each year they have to survive a period of violent storms. ✳ **OBEN** Die Bar, die 1983 anlässlich des Besuches des französischen Präsidenten François Mitterrand renoviert wurde. Die Hütten aus Palmblättern oder Bambus, die erhöht auf den Pfählen oder nicht faulenden Plattformen aus Teakholz stehen, sind jedes Jahr von neuem fürchterlichen Stürmen ausgesetzt. ✳ **CI-DESSUS** La fierté du village? Son bar refait à neuf pour la visite du président français François Mitterrand en 1983. Construites en feuille de palme ou en bambou, juchées sur des pilotis de branchage ou des poteaux de teck imputrescibles, les cases subissent chaque année des tempêtes terribles.

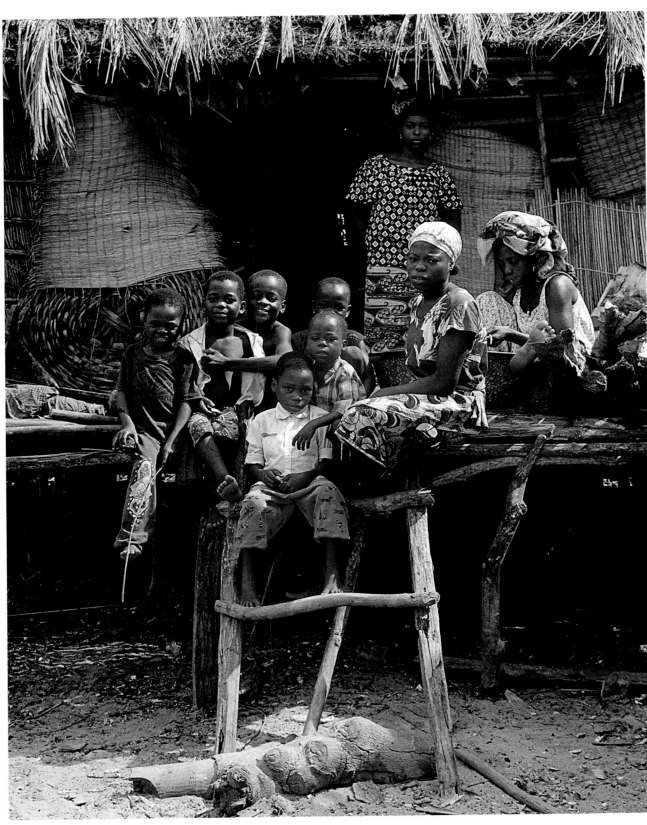

✳ **ABOVE** The residents of Ganvié live in a state of perpetual levitation, with the polluted waters of the lagoon making constant inroads upon them during the flood season. In this marsh country, the people feel protected from malevolent spirits. In fact, the germs which breed abundantly in these waters transmit typhus and tuberculosis, both of which are better under control on dry land than here. ✳ **OBEN** Die Menschen in Ganvié leben in einem permanenten Schwebezustand, denn ihre Unterkünfte werden von der Lagune und der bei Hochwasser entstehenden Umweltverschmutzung angegriffen. Die Bewohner der Sümpfe fühlen sich vor bösen Geistern geschützt. Dabei vermehren sich in diesen Gewässern die Keime rasend schnell und bringen Krankheiten wie Typhus und Tuberkulose mit sich, die auf dem Festland besser unter Kontrolle zu bringen wären. ✳ **CI-DESSUS** On vit en lévitation permanente dans ces cases rongées par la lagune et la pollution charriée pendant les crues. Dans ces marais, les habitants se sentent protégés des esprits malins. En vérité, les germes qui prolifèrent à vitesse foudroyante dans l'eau transmettent le typhus et la tuberculose, maladies mieux contrôlées à terre.

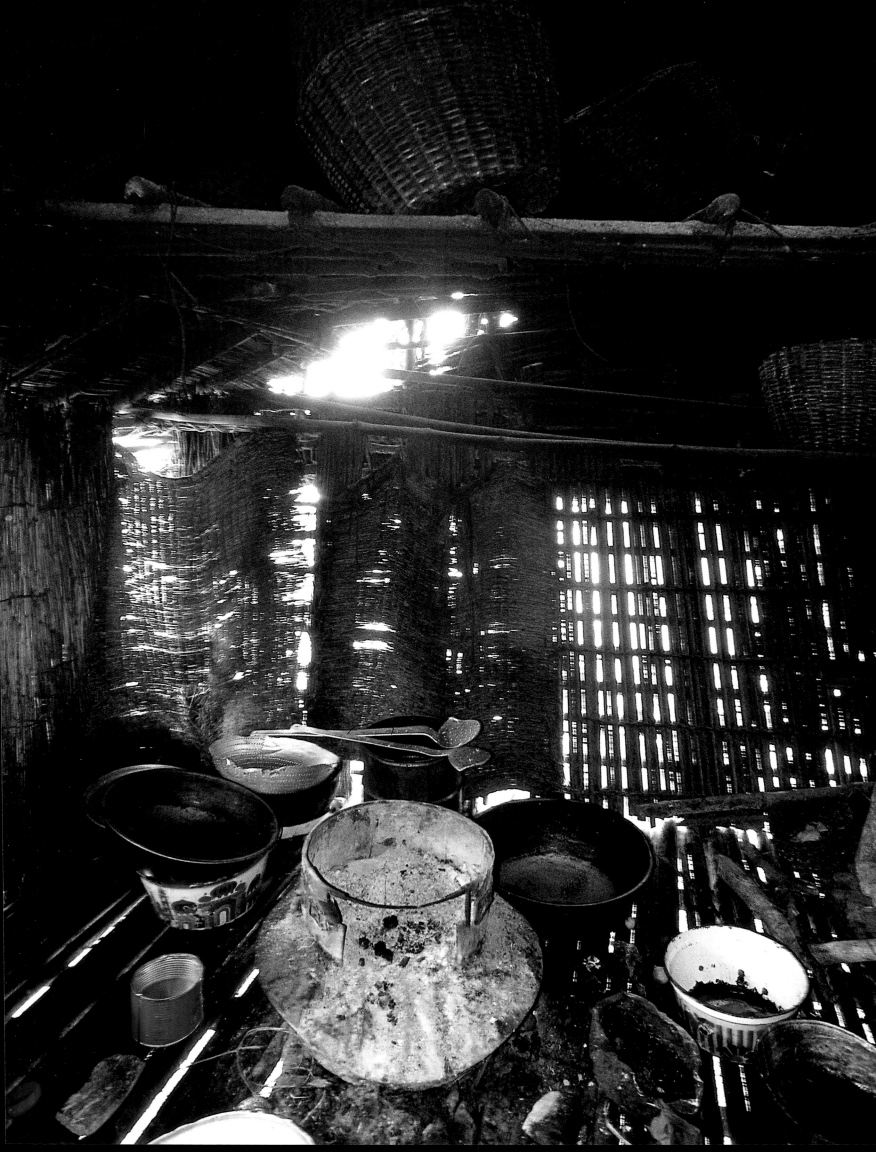

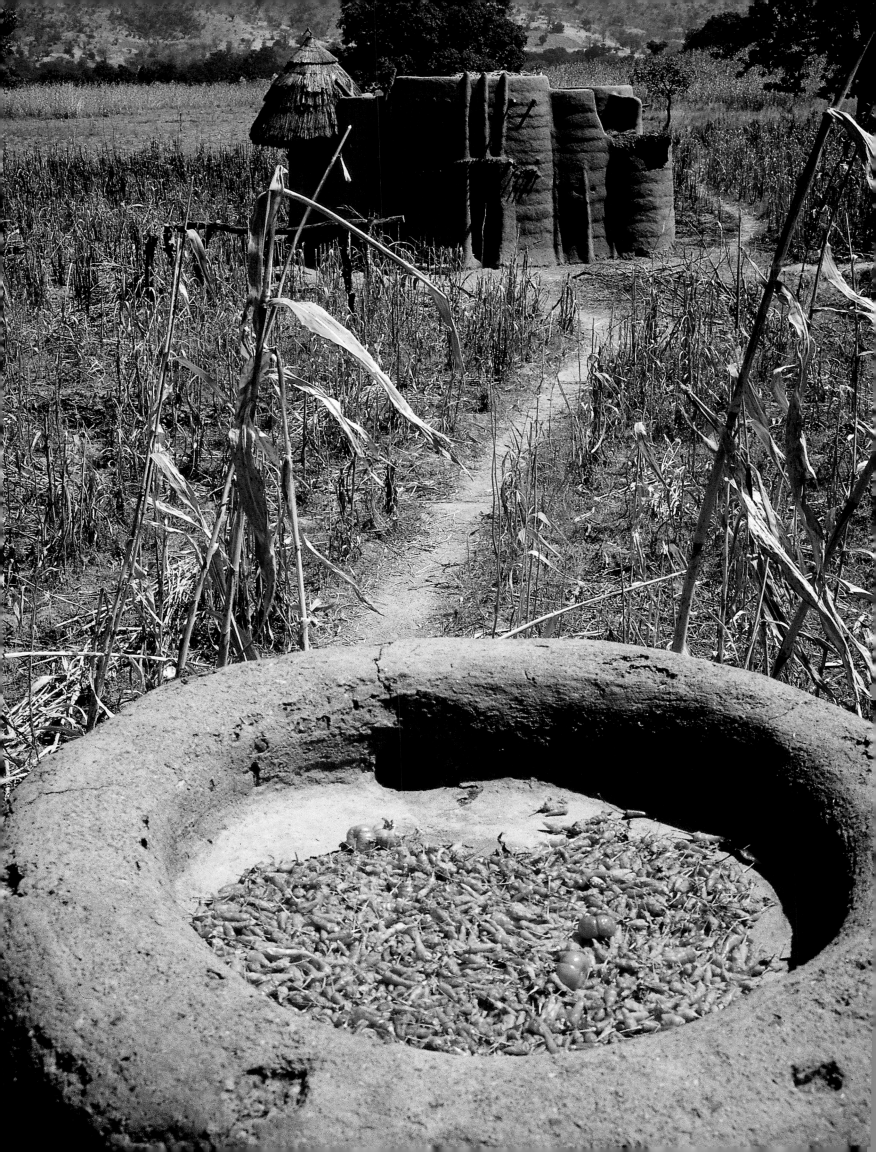

# Tamberma
# HOUSES
# TOGO

Each of these little compounds sprinkled around the millet fields contains its quota of *tatas*, round interconnected dwellings.

The name is significant: *Tamberma*, a word slightly deformed in Tamari, the local language, means "good mason". In this valley, the houses resemble the fortified farms of the Somba peoples of northern Benin.

Made up of bedrooms, a kitchen, an attic and a stable, the round Tamberma houses are linked to each other by fortress-like walls made of mud reinforced with straw. The earth insulates against the hot blast of the *harmattan* wind, but also against noise and fire. Rough or smooth, this brand of architecture – with roofs resting on forked beams – is very close to that of the houses in northern Ghana too. A single opening gives access to the ground floor. Here, on a tamped, slightly concave floor, the women pound sorghum and millet into flour. The extension includes a stable, where the animals go for shelter during the wet season. A few steps lead to an intermediate floor; this houses the indoor kitchen, the antechamber to a terrace in whose upper part are grain stores with three different sections, and (finally) small sleeping rooms you have to crawl into. A hatch reminds us that when there were raids here, the attackers would be greeted with a hail of poisoned arrows. Today, they have the more peaceful function of indicating the sites of new houses. A ceremony is traditionally held for this purpose, and the young men of the village build their *tatas* on the spot where the arrow lands.

Der Name ist Programm: Nur wenig verändert bedeutet *Tamberma* in der Tamarisprache »guter Maurer«. Die Behausungen in diesem Tal ähneln befestigten Höfen, wie man sie von den Sombastämmen im Norden Benins kennt.

Die Häuser, bestehend aus Schlafzimmern, Küche, Speicher und Stall, sind durch Mauern aus Lehm und Stroh miteinander verbunden, deren Stärke einer Festung Ehre machen würde. Der feuerfeste Lehm isoliert gegen Lärm und den heißen Atem des Harmattan. Die Architektur dieser Häuser aus glattem oder schraffiertem Lehm mit ihren von gegabelten Trägerbalken gestützten Dächern erinnert auch an den Hausbau im nördlichen Ghana. Es gibt keine Fenster, nur eine Tür führt ins Erdgeschoss, wo die Frauen Sorghum und Hirse auf dem gestampften, leicht ausgehobenen Boden stapeln. Im hinteren Teil befindet sich der Stall, in dem sich das Vieh in der Regenzeit aufhält. Stufen führen ins Zwischengeschoss mit der Küche, die als Durchgang zur Terrasse dient. Im höheren Teil dieser Terrasse ist der Speicher untergebracht, der in drei Kammern unterteilt ist. Dorthin und in die auf gleicher Höhe liegenden kleinen Zimmer gelangt man, indem man sich mit Schwung hochzieht. Eine Falltür erinnert daran, dass Angreifer früher, zu Zeiten der Raubzüge, mit Giftpfeilen empfangen wurden. Die Pfeile dienen heute friedlicheren Zwecken, so wird damit etwa der Standort neuer Häuser bestimmt. Im Rahmen einer feierlichen Zeremonie bauen die jungen Männer des Dorfes ihre *tatas* dort, wo ihre Pfeile gelandet waren. Cupido hätte nicht besser zielen können.

Le nom est tout un programme: *Tamberma*, légèrement déformé en tamari, la langue locale, signifie «le bon maçon». Dans cette vallée, les habitations ressemblent à des fermes fortifiées semblables à celles des tribus Somba du nord du Bénin.

Composées de chambres à coucher, d'une cuisine, d'un grenier et d'une étable, ces cases rondes, reliées entre elles par des murs dignes d'une forteresse, sont faites de boue renforcée de paille. La terre isole du souffle chaud de l'harmattan, mais aussi du bruit, et résiste au feu. Lissée ou hachurée, cette architecture au toit reposant sur des poutres en fourches est également proche des maisons du nord du Ghana. Une seule ouverture donne accès au rez-de-chaussée. Ici, sur un sol damé et légèrement creusé, les femmes pilent le sorgho et le mil. Dans le prolongement, se trouve l'étable, refuge du bétail en saison humide. Quelques marches mènent à l'étage intermédiaire où est située la cuisine intérieure, antichambre d'une terrasse qui, en sa partie supérieure, abrite des greniers à trois compartiments et de petites chambres que l'on gagne en rampant. Une trappe rappelle que les assaillants, au temps des razzias, étaient accueillis à coup de flèches empoisonnées. Plus pacifiquement, ces mêmes flèches servent aujourd'hui à déterminer l'emplacement des maisons. Au cours d'une cérémonie, les fils du village édifient leur *tata* à l'endroit où la flèche s'est plantée. Cupidon n'aurait pas trouvé mieux!

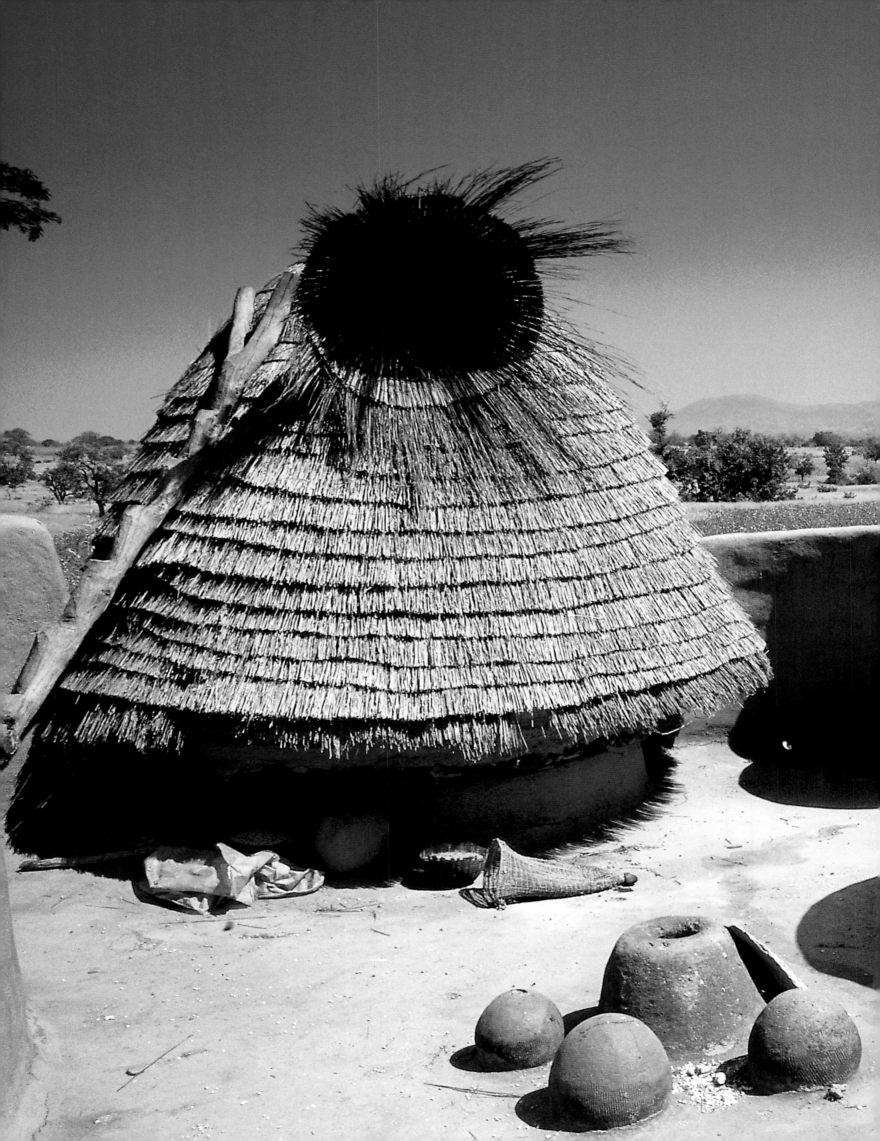

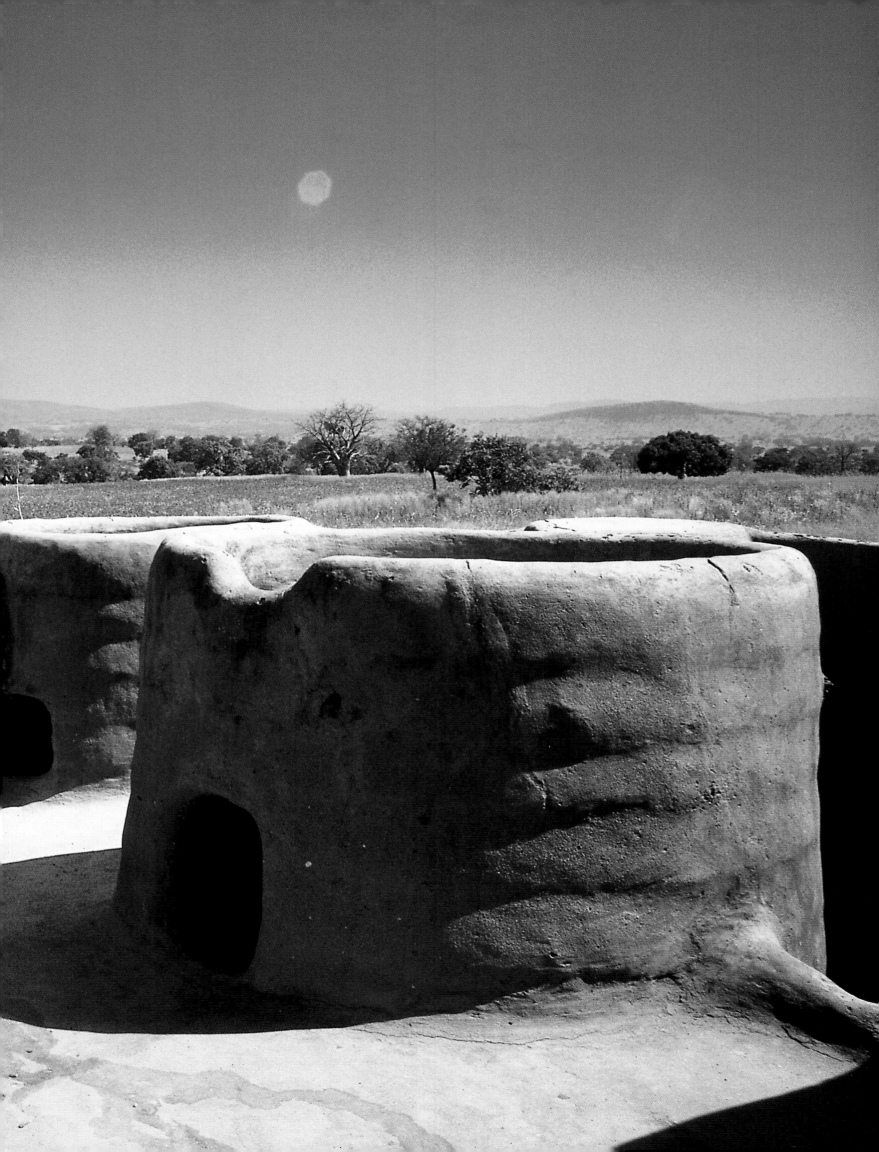

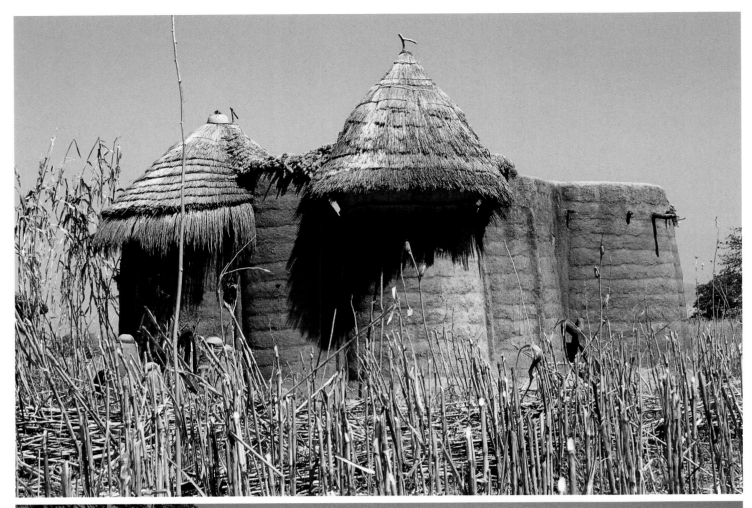

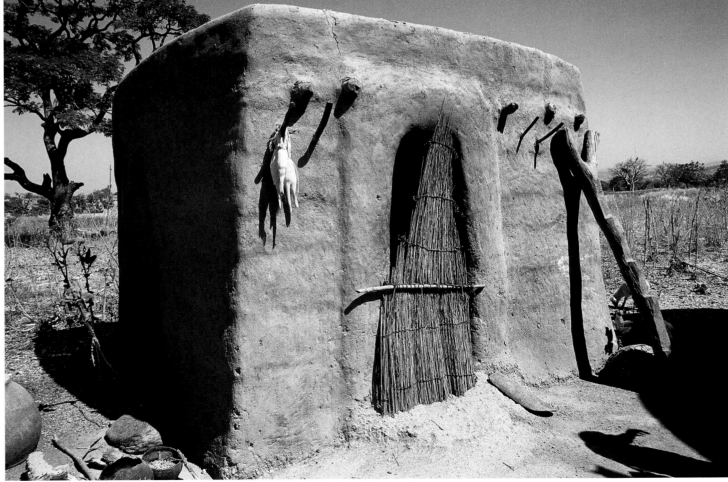

❋ **ABOVE** The use of *banco* (ochre clay) fortified with straw, cow faeces and a decoction of *néré* grain as a binding agent makes the walls completely waterproof.
❋ **OBEN** Die Häuser verdanken ihre Dichtheit dem Baumaterial *banco* (ockerfarbener Lehm), gemischt mit Stroh und Kuhfladen sowie dem Bindemittel *néré* aus einem Absud von Samenkörnern. ❋ **CI-DESSUS** L'utilisation de *banco* (terre glaise ocre) additionné de paille, de bouse de vache et d'une décoction de graines *néré* qui sert de liant assure aux murs une étanchéité parfaite.

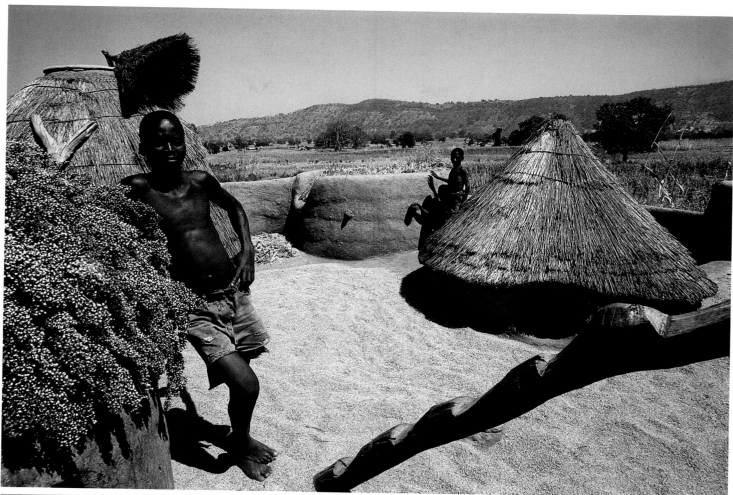

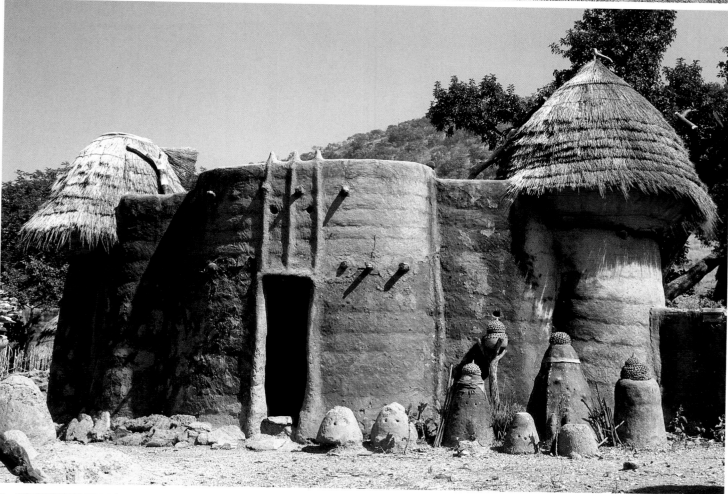

※ **ABOVE AND FOLLOWING PAGES** These houses are planned like bastions, with only one way in. In front of the main door, phallus-shaped mounds show the sites of graves. They are regularly sprinkled with millet beer and the blood of sacrificed animals. ※ **OBEN UND FOLGENDE DOPPELSEITE** Wie bei einer richtigen Festung gibt es nur einen einzigen Zugang zu den Häusern. Vor der Eingangstür markieren mehrere phallusartige Erdhügel die Lage der Gräber. Sie werden regelmäßig mit Hirsebier und dem Blut von Opfertieren begossen. ※ **CI-DESSUS ET DOUBLE PAGE SUIVANTE** Véritable bastion, ces maisons n'ont qu'une seule entrée. Devant la porte principale, plusieurs monticules de forme phallique désignent l'emplacement des tombes. Ils sont régulièrement arrosés de bière de millet et du sang des animaux sacrifiés.

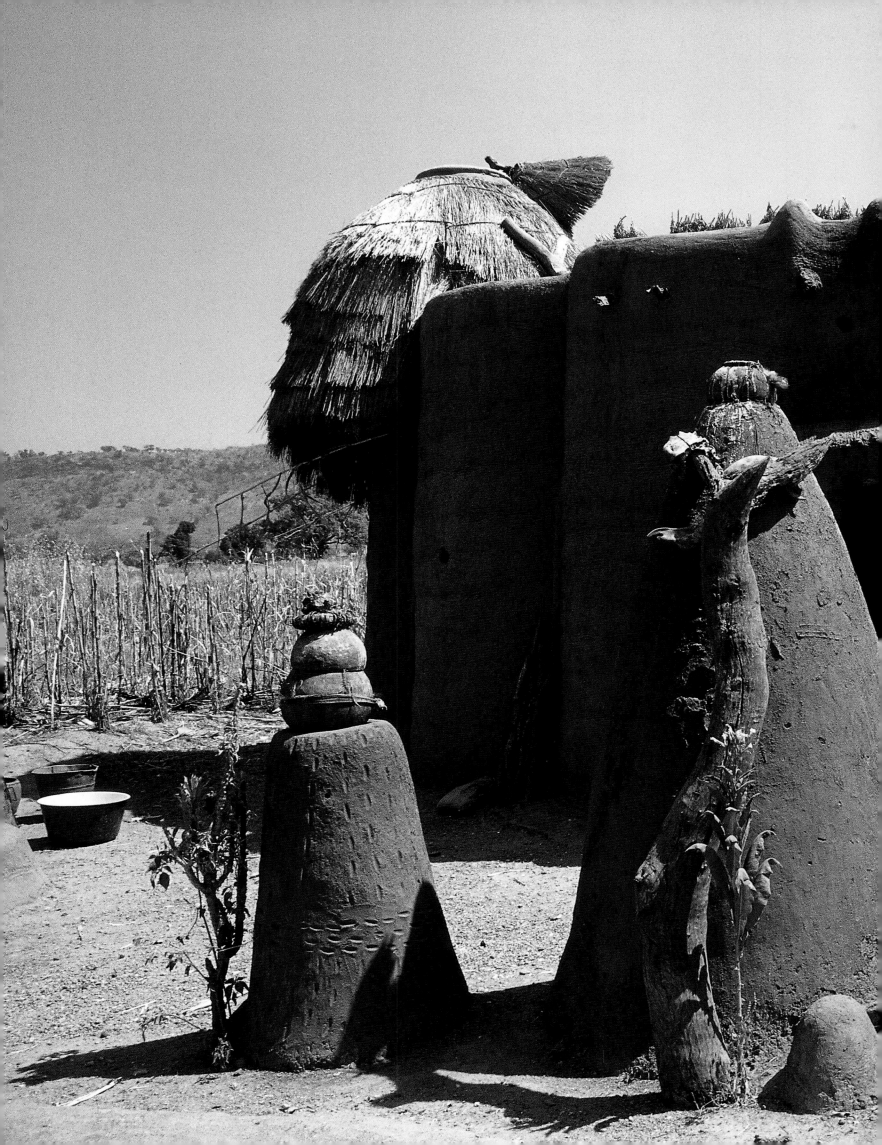

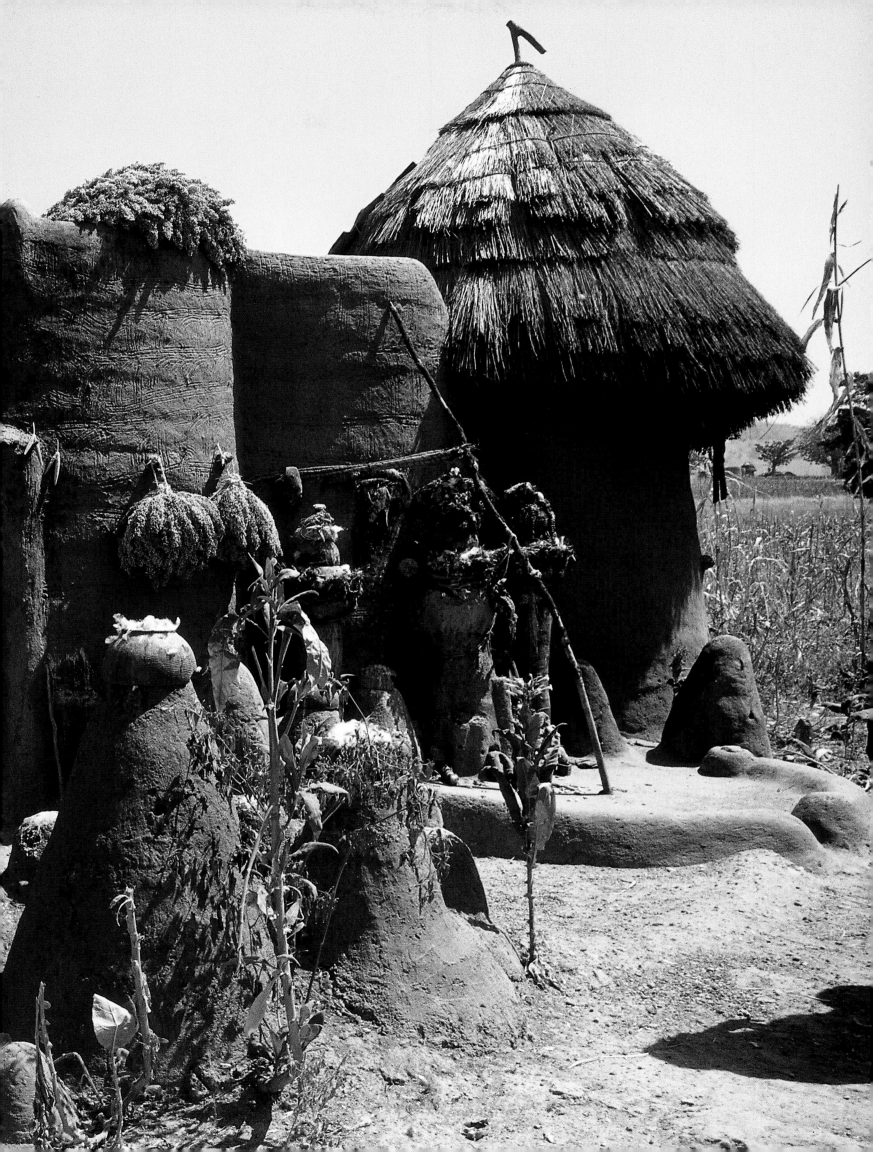

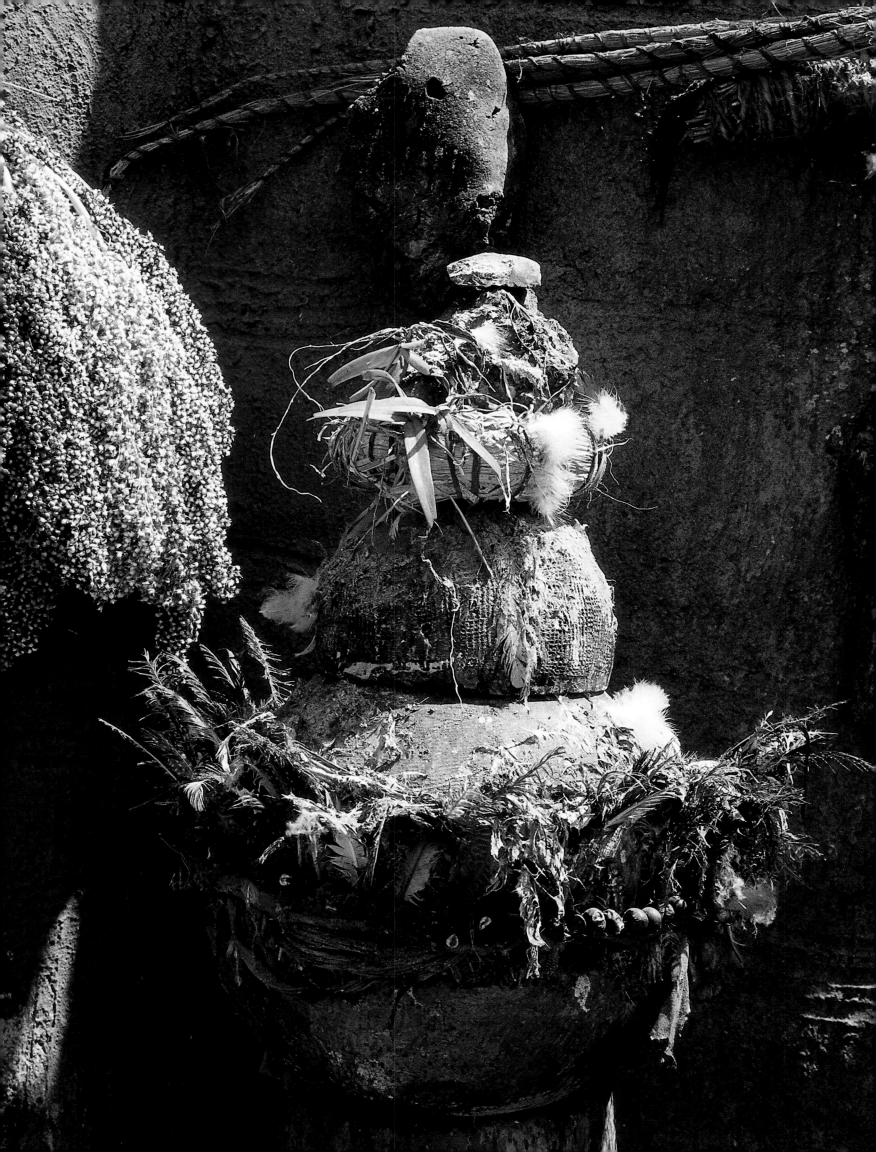

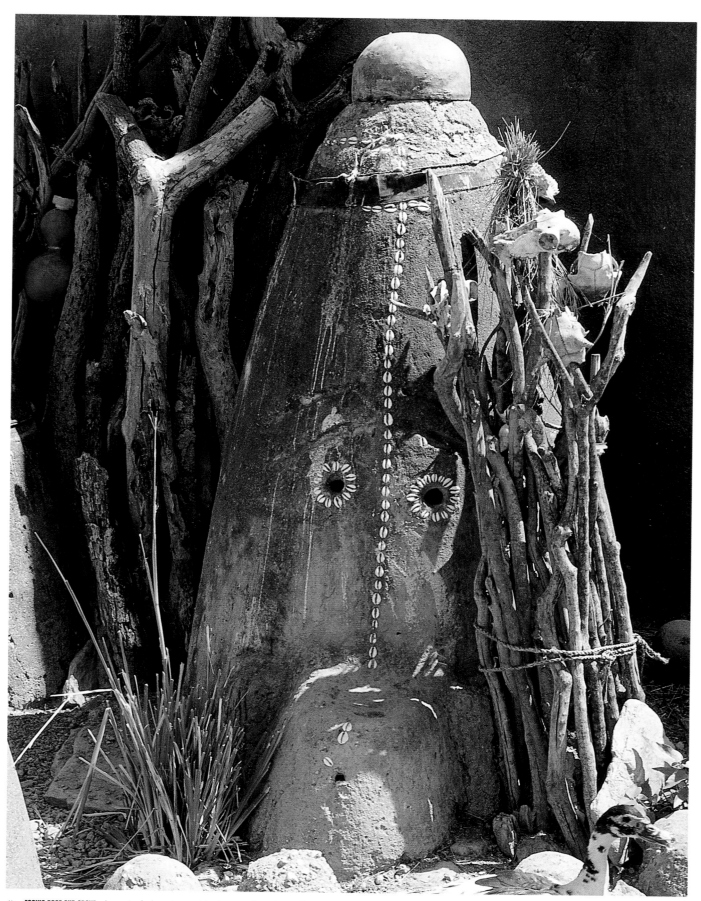

✳ **FACING PAGE AND ABOVE** A conical clay altar, with the remains of sacrifices and libations. Still loaded with necklaces of goats' skulls, goats' horns, and sticks, these altars – which are very numerous in the Tamberma country – are generally placed in front of the houses. ✳ **LINKE SEITE UND OBEN** Auf dem kegelförmigen Altar aus Lehm liegen noch Reste von (Trank-)Opfern. Altäre, die wie dieser mit Ketten aus Zickleinköpfen und Ziegenbockhörnern sowie mit Stäben und Stöcken geschmückt sind, findet man im Land der Tamberma häufig direkt vor den Häusern. ✳ **PAGE DE GAUCHE ET CI-DESSUS** Un autel de terre conique laisse apparaître des restes de sacrifices et de libations. Chargés encore de colliers de crânes de chevreaux, de cornes de boucs et de bâtons, ces autels très nombreux en pays Tamberma sont placés devant les maisons.

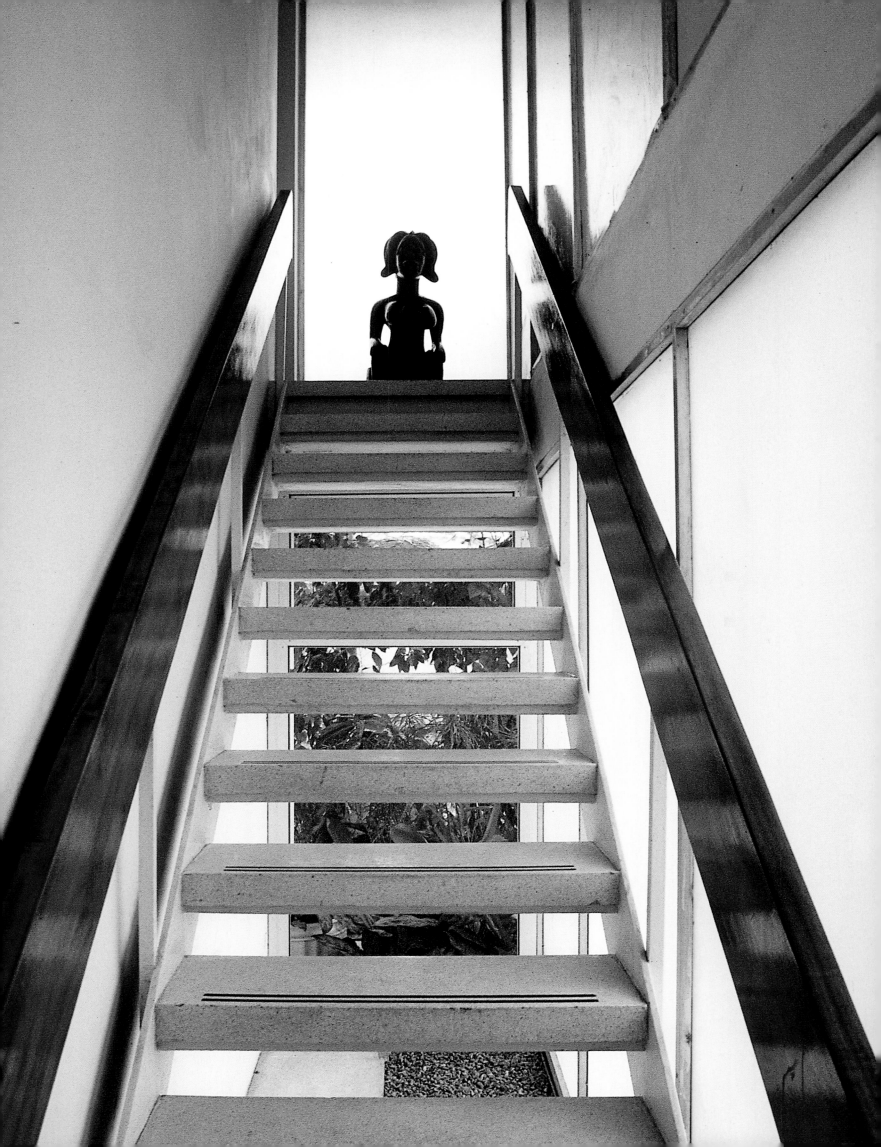

# Scott House

## Accra

A house with an eye on the past as well as the future, built by a British architect so enthralled by Ghana that he made his life there.

Some houses reflect the heart and temperament of the people who live in them. The Scott house is one of these; indeed it resembles an autobiographical account of its owner.

A lieutenant-colonel in the Royal West Africa Frontier Force during the Second World War, Kenneth Scott returned to Ghana in the late 1940s and remained there till his death in 1982. With his open-necked shirt and flowing mane of hair, Scott was a dashing president of the Accra Polo Club – but above all he was a founding member of the Ghana Institute of Architects and the archetypal post-colonial dandy. Most unusually for Accra in the 1960s and 1970s – because at that time nearly all the builders were in Lagos, Africa's New York – Kenneth Scott created an open house with no real doors, in homage to such modernist architects as Walter Gropius and Ludwig Mies van der Rohe. The angular and circular shapes he devised modulate the light and create spaces that appear to be wide open to the sky. This is the whole attraction of the building, which is both retro and futuristic, like an experimental project from the past. Kenneth Scott left his mark on many a public building in Accra, and he will long be remembered in Ghana – and what's more, his widow Thérèse Striggner Scott still lives in the house he built.

Es gibt Häuser, die die Seele und das Temperament ihrer Bewohner spiegeln. Scott House ist eins davon – es trägt regelrecht autobiographische Züge.

Kenneth Scott, der im Zweiten Weltkrieg als Oberstleutnant der Royal West Africa Frontier Force in Ghana diente, entdeckte das Land Ende der 1940er Jahre für sich und verließ es bis zu seinem Tod im Jahr 1982 nie wieder. Scott war der Inbegriff des postkolonialen Dandys: Offenes Hemd, leuchtende Mähne, Präsident des Accra Polo Clubs. Gleichzeitig gehörte er zu den Gründungsmitgliedern des Ghana Institute of Architects. Im Gegensatz zu dem, was in den 1960er, 1970er Jahren in Accra üblich war – damals zog es die Architekten, die etwas auf sich hielten, eher nach Lagos, ins »afrikanische New York« –, baute sich Kenneth Scott als Hommage an die modernen Architekten wie Walter Gropius und Ludwig Mies van der Rohe ein offenes Haus ohne richtige Tür. Eckige und runde Formen modulieren das Licht und schaffen Räume unter freiem Himmel. Die besondere Ausstrahlung dieses gleichermaßen nostalgisch und futuristisch wirkenden Hauses liegt in der Suggestion, man wohne in einem ehemals avantgardistischen Haus. An Kenneth Scott, der zahlreichen öffentlichen Gebäuden in Accra seinen Stempel aufdrückte, erinnert man sich in Ghana gern. Seine Witwe Thérèse Striggner Scott wohnt bis heute in dem Haus.

Certaines habitations reflètent l'âme et le tempérament de ceux qui les habitent. La Scott House fait partie de celles-là, tant elle se lit comme un récit autobiographique.

Lieutenant-colonel dans la Royal West Africa Frontier Force durant la Deuxième Guerre mondiale, Kenneth Scott retrouvait le Ghana à la fin des années 1940 pour ne plus quitter ce pays jusqu'à sa mort, en 1982. Chemise ouverte, crinière flamboyante, président de l'Accra Polo Club mais surtout membre fondateur du Ghana Institute of Architects, l'homme fut l'archétype du dandy post-colonial. Situation inédite à Accra dans les années 1960, 1970 – à l'époque, les bâtisseurs se pressaient plutôt à Lagos, considéré comme un New York africain –, Kenneth Scott a créé une maison ouverte, sans véritable porte, un hommage aux architectes modernistes tels que Walter Gropius et Ludwig Mies van der Rohe. Les formes angulaires et circulaires modulent la lumière et créent des espaces à ciel ouvert. C'est tout l'attrait de l'édifice, à la fois rétro et futuriste, qui donne l'impression de séjourner dans un projet expérimental du passé. Kenneth Scott, qui a marqué de son empreinte nombre de bâtiments publics d'Accra, n'est pas prêt d'être oublié au Ghana. D'ailleurs, sa veuve Thérèse Striggner Scott vit encore dans ces murs.

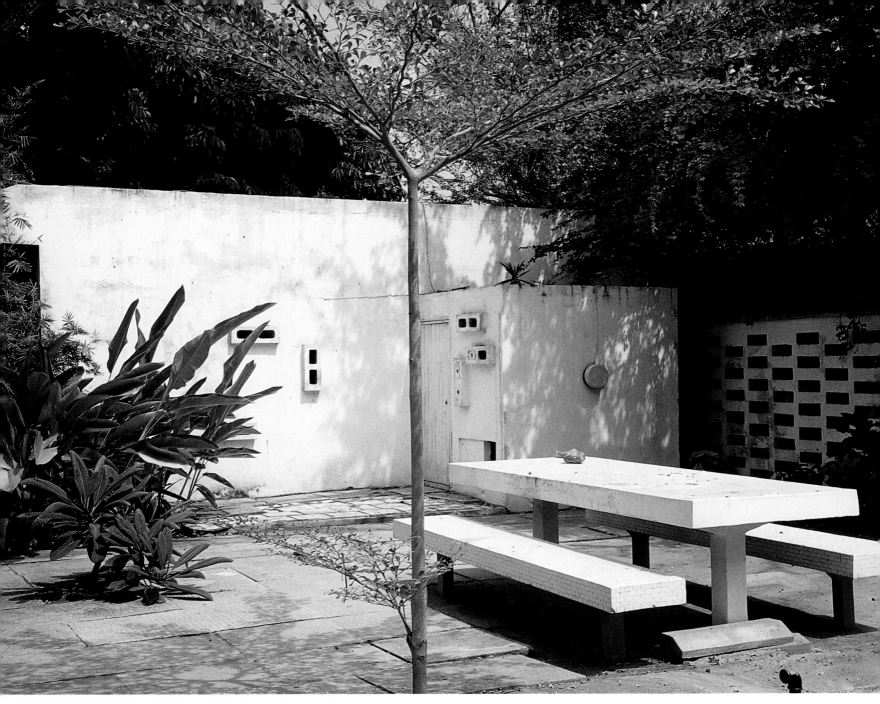

✳ **ABOVE** Faithful to Le Corbusier's dictum, "a house is a machine for living", the architect Kenneth Scott filled his house with recesses. Rather than pushing itself forward, the aesthetic of the place is quietly insinuated. Here, the outside concrete dining table and benches harmonize well with the surrounding décor. ✳ **OBEN** Getreu der Maxime von Le Corbusier »Das Haus ist eine Maschine zum Wohnen«, sorgte Kenneth Scott in seinem Haus für viele Rückzugsmöglichkeiten. Die Ästhetik des Gebäudes drängt sich nicht auf, sondern schleicht sich langsam ins Bewusstsein des Besuchers. Der Tisch und die Bänke aus Beton, an denen die Mahlzeiten im Freien eingenommen werden, passen gut in ihre Umgebung. ✳ **CI-DESSUS** Fidèle à Le Corbusier, «une maison est une machine à habiter», l'architecte Kenneth Scott a multiplié les espaces de repli. Ici, plutôt que de s'imposer, l'esthétique des lieux s'insinue doucement chez le visiteur. Pour les repas pris à l'extérieur, la table et les bancs en béton s'harmonisent avec le décor ambiant.

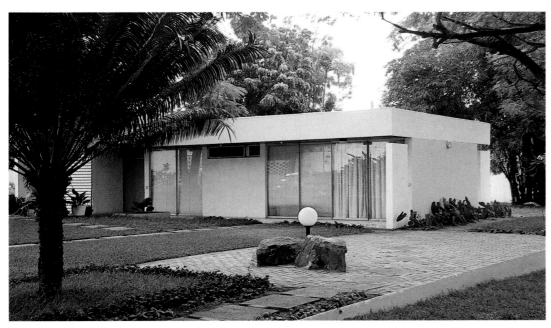

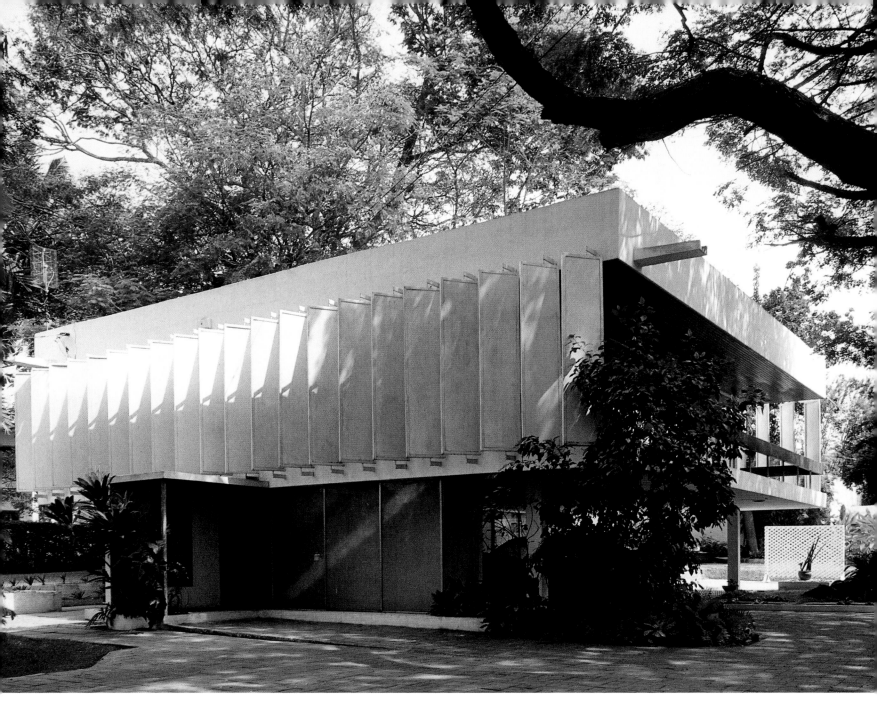

✳ **ABOVE** The raised main building overlooks the garden from behind a set of slatted concrete blinds, which protect the rooms in the back of the house from the sun. **FACING PAGE BELOW** The single storey guest building behind the main house. **BELOW** A spacious outside loggia runs along the front of the salon, giving a complete view of the garden. ✳ **OBEN** Das Hauptgebäude liegt etwas erhöht oberhalb des Gartens. Betonjalousien schützen die rückwärtigen Zimmer vor der Sonne. **LINKE SEITE UNTEN** Das Gästehaus hinter dem Hauptgebäude liegt auf gleicher Höhe wie der Garten. **UNTEN** Die weiträumige Loggia vor dem Salon bietet einen schönen Panoramablick auf den Garten. ✳ **CI-DESSUS** Surélevée, la maison principale domine le jardin avec un jeu de jalousies en béton qui protègent les pièces arrière du soleil. **PAGE DE GAUCHE EN BAS** La maison d'amis, édifiée à l'arrière de la maison principale, est construite en plain-pied. **CI-DESSOUS** La spacieuse loggia extérieure longe le salon, offrant ainsi une vue totale sur le jardin.

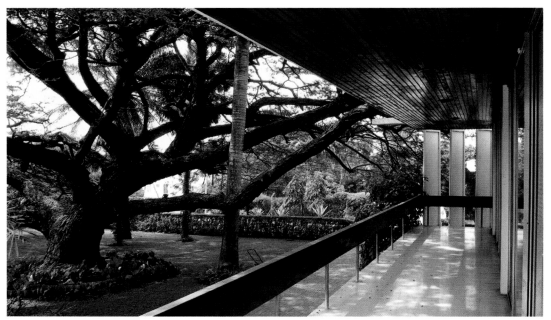

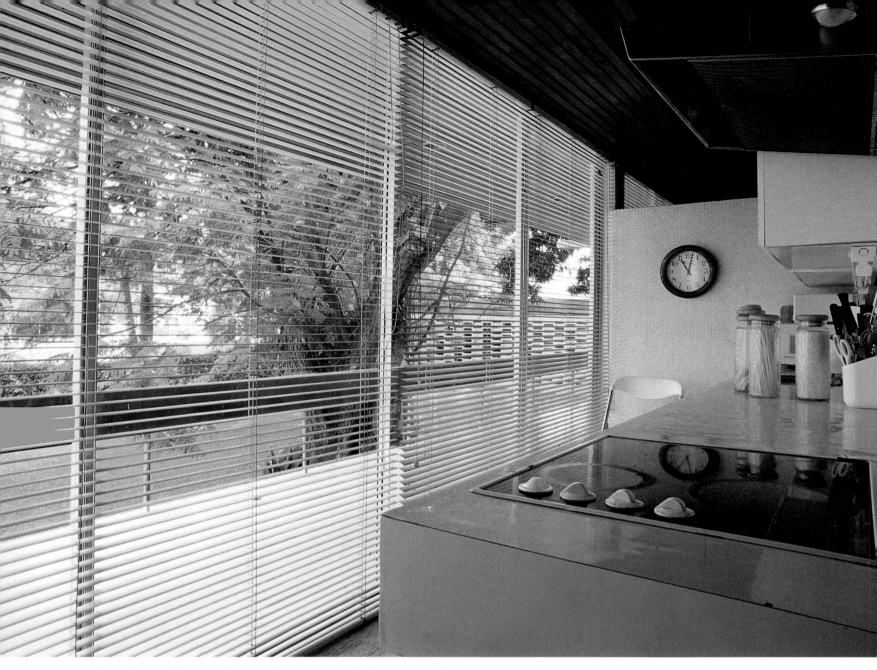

✷ **ABOVE** Seemingly part of the surrounding natural environment, the kitchen opens directly onto the garden. Here the accent is sober, contemporary and entirely minimalist. ✷ **OBEN** Als wäre sie Teil ihrer natürlichen Umgebung, geht die Küche direkt auf den Garten hinaus. In diesem Raum wirkt der Minimalismus streng, schnörkellos, nüchtern auf das Wesentliche konzentriert – ein Inbild dieses modernen Hauses. ✷ **CI-DESSUS** Comme absorbée par la nature environnante, la cuisine s'ouvre directement sur le jardin. Ici, le minimalisme est de rigueur, pas de fioritures, l'essentiel reste sobre, à l'image de cette habitation contemporaine.

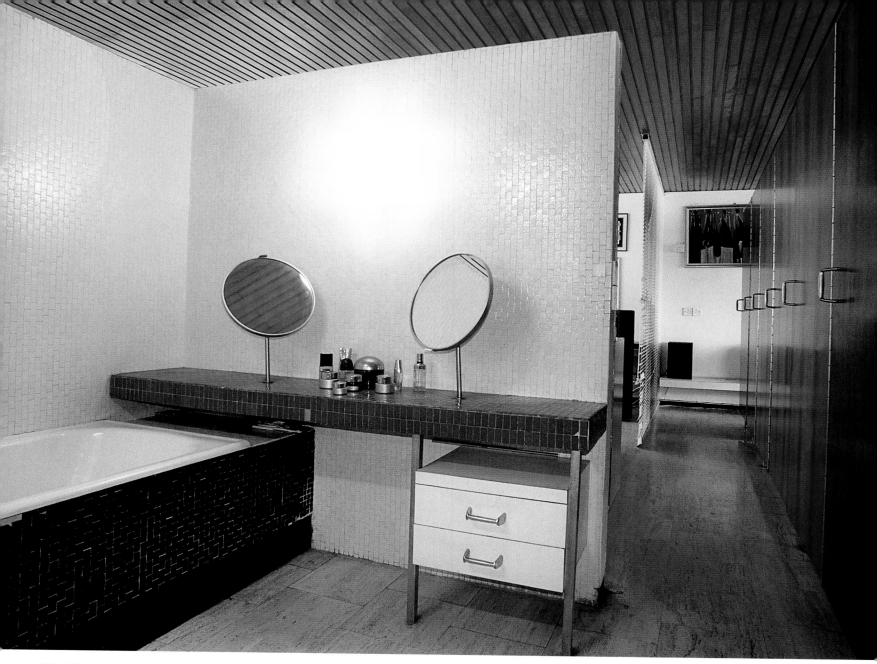

※ **ABOVE** The bathrooms are much more inward-looking, naked spaces in the spirit of Scott's ideal. Mosaics between the bathtub and the work surface, with tones of black and grey against a white background. ※ **OBEN** Die Gestaltung der Bäder wirkt ruhiger. Der blanke Raum verbindet sich mit der Atmosphäre im Haus. Die Mosaiksteinchen zwischen der Badewanne und der Ablage spielen auf weißem Grund mit den Farben Schwarz und Grau. ※ **CI-DESSUS** Les salles de bains sont plus introverties. L'espace, épuré au maximum, va de pair avec l'esprit des lieux. Le jeu des mosaïques entre la baignoire et le plan de travail s'égaie sur des tons de noir et gris sur fond blanc.

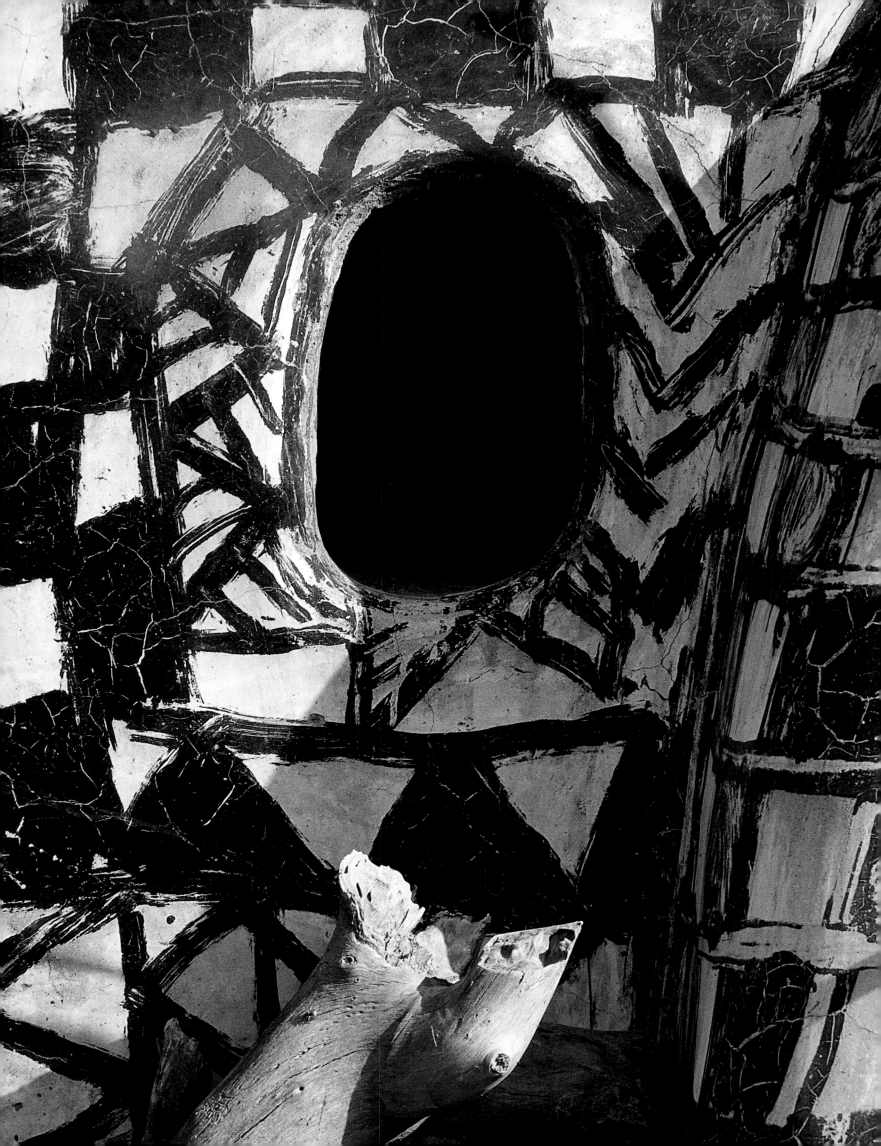

# Kassena
# Burkina Faso & Ghana

This frontier habitat is ruled by the twin concerns of functionality and aesthetic value.

The architecture of the Kassena country is the most beautiful Africa has to offer. The Kassena themselves are hunters and farmers, men and women who from time immemorial have applied their skills as potters to the building of fortified farmsteads.

Their compounds stand in fields of sorghum and millet, each with its grain stores, huts, stockyards and altars dedicated to ancestors. Walls meander between each building. These places are not so much turned in on themselves as fully geared for survival: local warfare and the slave trade made them what they are. The Kassena compounds were deliberately sited a certain distance from one another, so that when one fell into the enemy's hands, its survivors had somewhere safe to go. Originally covered in unadorned reddish clay, the walls of the houses are now painted black and white. Masonry work (*banco*) is the task of the men; the women take care of details and decoration. Kassena motifs are inspired by cosmic mythology; they can be geometrical or figurative, and they illustrate the obedience of this remarkable people to an original relationship between man and his environment. Some of the drawings depart from this pattern to represent imaginary consumer goods (TVs, cars). For the moment, in many rooms the interior furnishings are confined to shelves, chairs and beds made exclusively from clay.

Die Architektur der Kassena, so hört man, sei die schönste in ganz Afrika. Seit Menschengedenken setzen die Männer und Frauen dieses Volkes von Jägern und Feldbauern ihre Fähigkeiten als Töpfer auch beim Bau ihrer Gehöfte ein.

Die Bebauung, die aus den Hirsefeldern herausragt, besteht aus Hütten, Getreidespeichern, Altären zu Ehren der Ahnen und Einfriedungen für das Vieh. Zwischen den Häusern schlängeln sich niedrige Mauern. Diese Bauweise dient weniger der inneren Einkehr als dem Überleben. Stammeskriege und mehr noch die Jagd auf Sklaven haben die Siedlungsweise geprägt. Die Siedlungen der Kassena wurden in beträchtlicher Entfernung voneinander errichtet, damit die Überlebenden, wenn eine von ihnen in die Hände des Feindes fiel, sich in benachbarte Siedlungen flüchten konnten. Die Hausmauern, die ursprünglich mit rotbraunem Lehm bedeckt wurden, werden nun schwarz-weiß bemalt. Die Maurerarbeit mit *banco* ist den Männern vorbehalten, während die Frauen die Häuser fertig stellen und verzieren. Die sowohl geometrischen als auch gegenständlichen Motive sind der kosmischen Mythologie entlehnt und bebildern den Glauben dieses Volkes an eine tiefe Beziehung zwischen Mensch und Natur. Einige Darstellungen entfernen sich von dem traditionellen Schema und bilden imaginäre Konsumgüter wie Fernseher und Autos ab. Zur Zeit sind die Möbel in den meisten Hütten noch aus Lehm (Regale, Sitzgelegenheiten und Betten).

C'est dit: l'architecture de terre des Kasséna est peut-être la plus belle d'Afrique. Peuple de chasseurs et d'agriculteurs, ces hommes et ces femmes appliquent depuis des temps immémoriaux leurs savoir-faire de potiers à la construction de fermes fortifiées.

Émergeant des champs de mil et de sorgo, les concessions mêlent les cases, les greniers à céréales, les autels des ancêtres et l'enclos à bétail. Des murets serpentent entre chaque édifice. Repli sur soi? Question de survie plutôt. Les guerres tribales et, plus encore, la traite des Noirs, ont modelé l'habitat. Les habitations Kasséna étaient établies à bonne distance les unes des autres et lorsqu'ils voyaient qu'une concession était tombée aux mains de l'ennemi, les rescapés pouvaient s'enfuir. Couverts de glaise, à l'aspect rouge brun à l'origine, les murs des maisons sont repeints maintenant en noir et blanc. L'œuvre de maçonnerie (*banco*) est réservée aux hommes tandis que les finitions et les décorations reviennent aux femmes. Les motifs sont inspirés de la mythologie cosmique. Géométriques ou figuratifs, ils soulignent l'illustre obéissance de ce peuple à une relation originelle entre l'homme et son environnement. Quelques dessins s'éloignent du schéma pour représenter des biens de consommation imaginaires (télévision ou voiture). Pour le moment, le mobilier intérieur, dans bien des cases, est exclusivement en terre (étagères, sièges et lits).

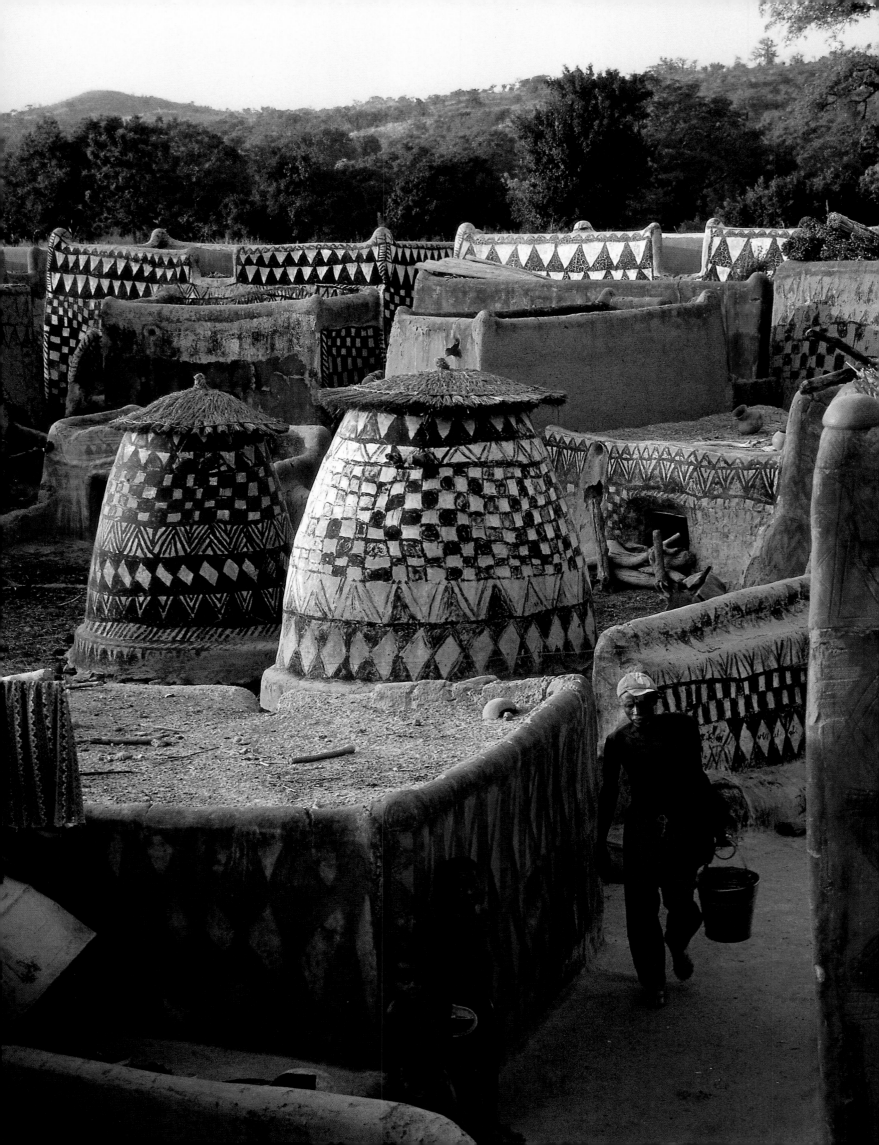

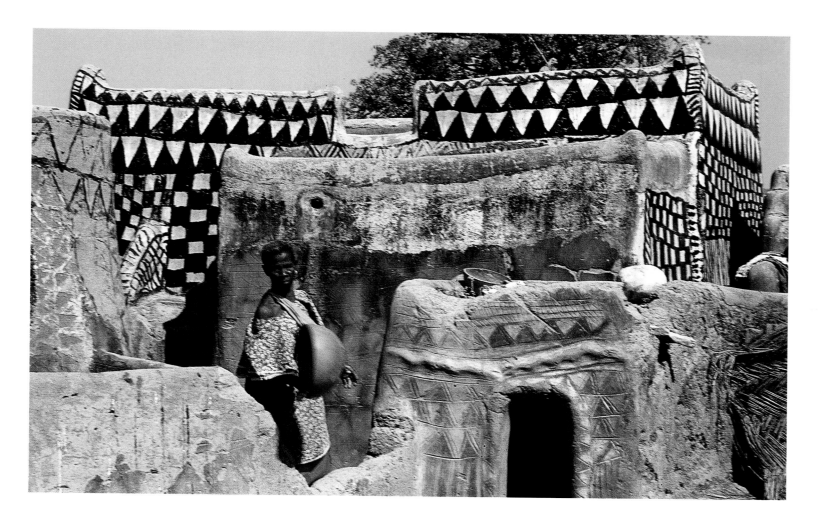

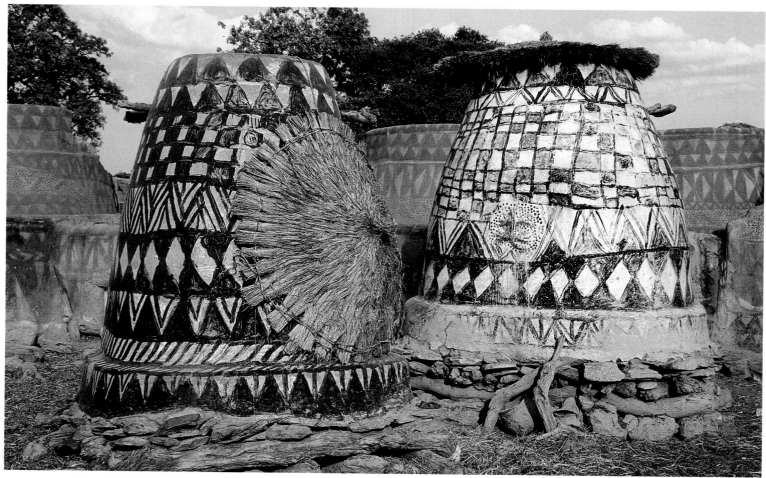

✻ **FACING PAGE AND ABOVE** Each compound is fully autonomous, beside its mango and kapok groves. The roof terraces are used for drying millet. ✻ **LINKE SEITE UND OBEN** Hinter den Mango- und Kapokbäumen beginnt das autonome Gebiet der jeweiligen Siedlung. Auf den Terrassendächern wird die Hirse zum Trocknen ausgelegt. ✻ **PAGE DE GAUCHE ET CI-DESSUS** À la lisière des manguiers et des fromagers, chaque concession a son autonomie. Les toits-terrasses assurent le séchage du millet.

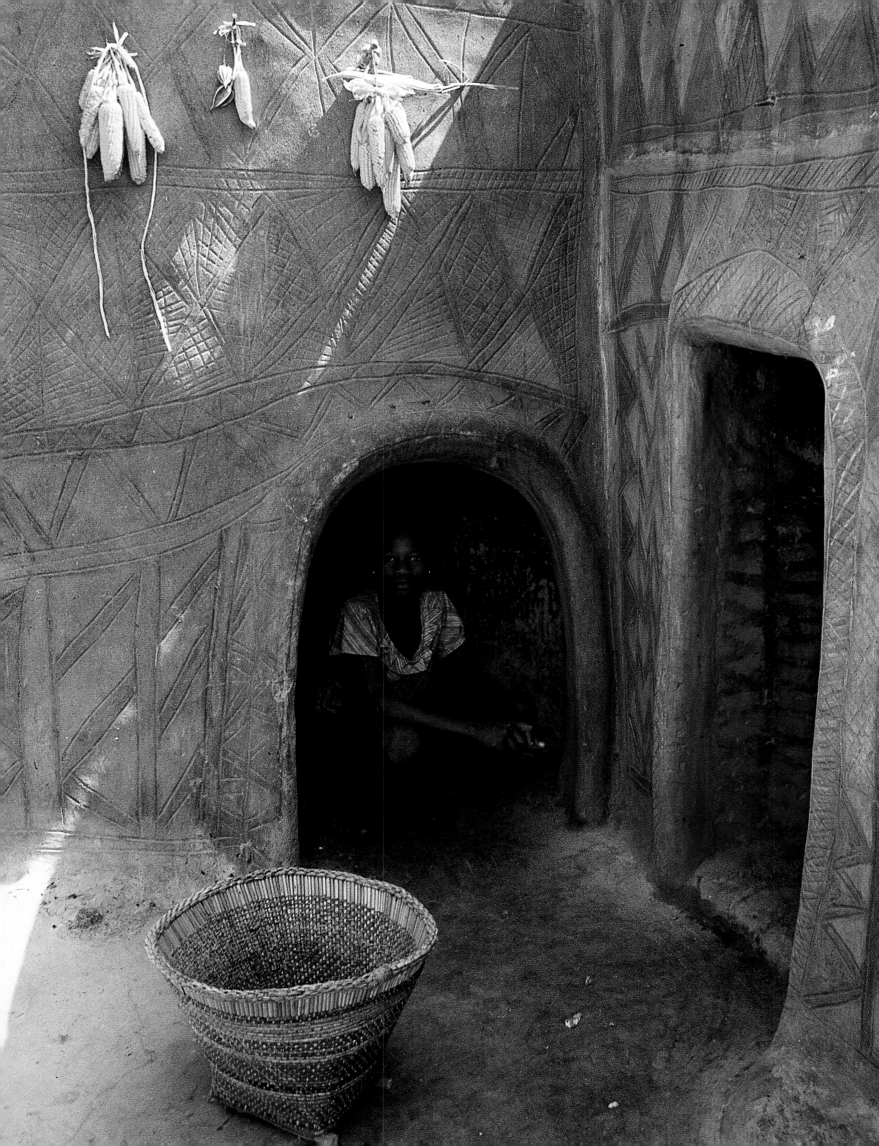

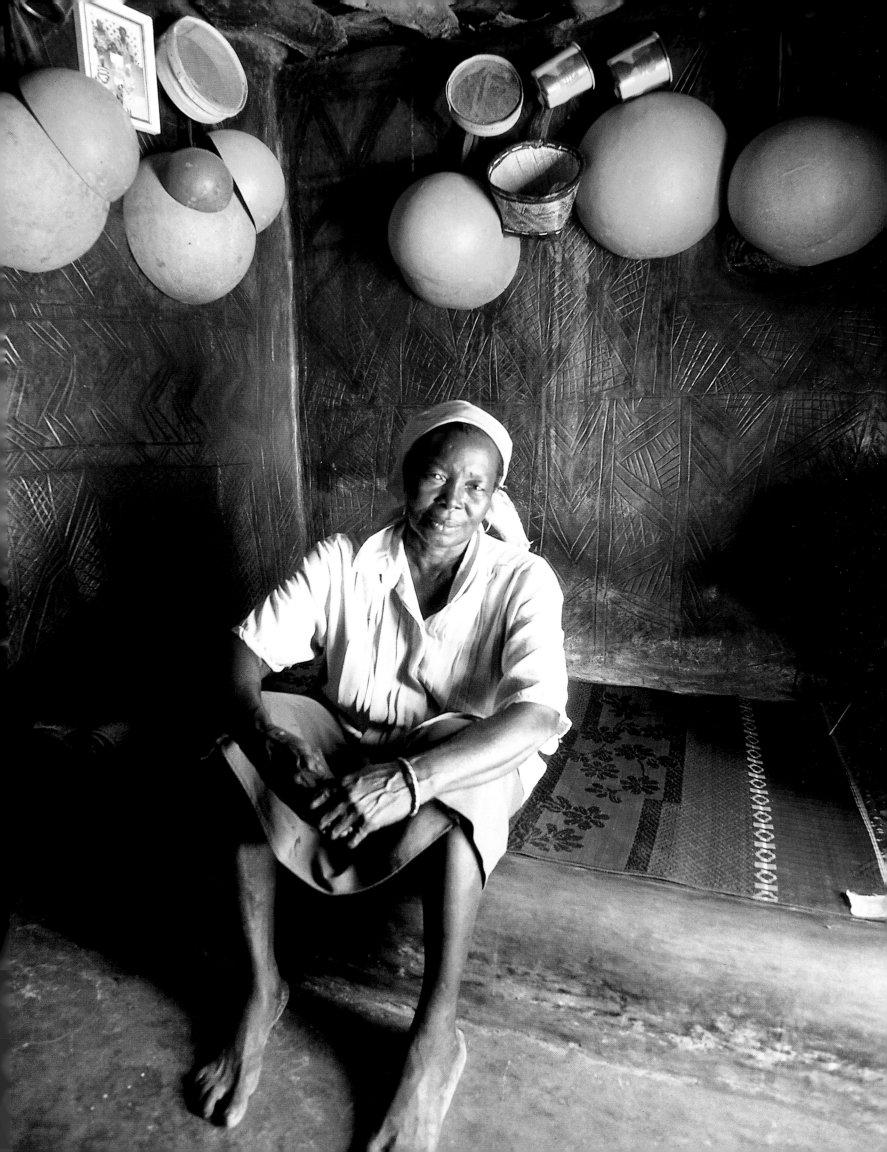

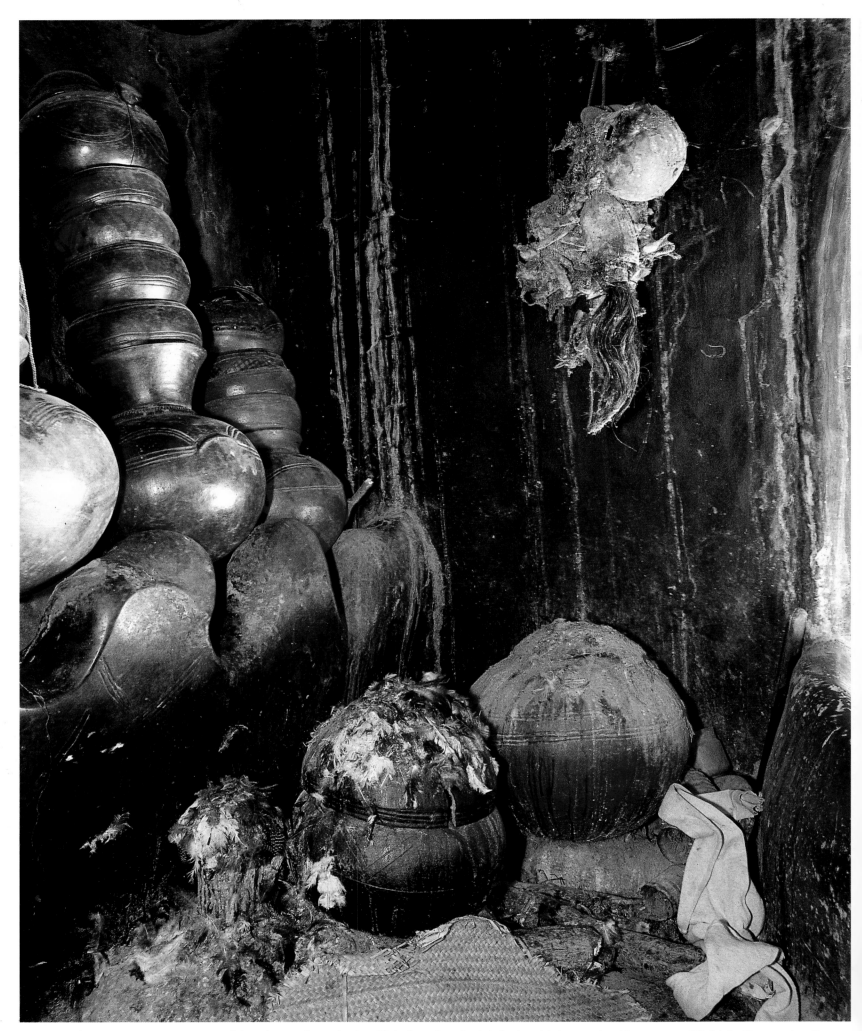

※ **ABOVE** In the Kassena country, pots are passed down from mother to daughter. Their size and number is indicative of their owners' social status. ※ **OBEN** Bei den Kassena geben die Mütter ihre Kenntnisse der Töpferkunst an die Töchter weiter. An der Zahl und Größe der Töpfe lässt sich der soziale Status ablesen. ※ **CI-DESSUS** En pays Kasséna, les poteries passent de mère en fille. Leur taille et leur nombre indiquent le statut social.

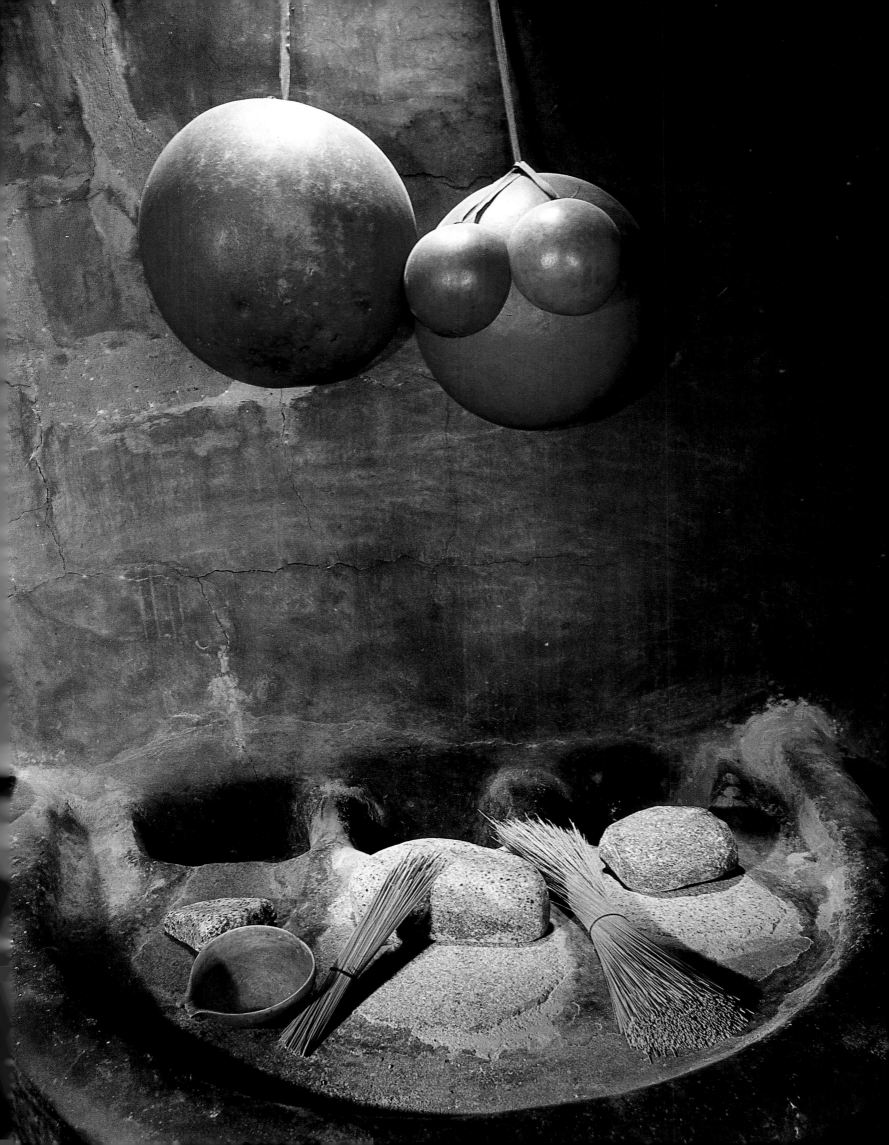

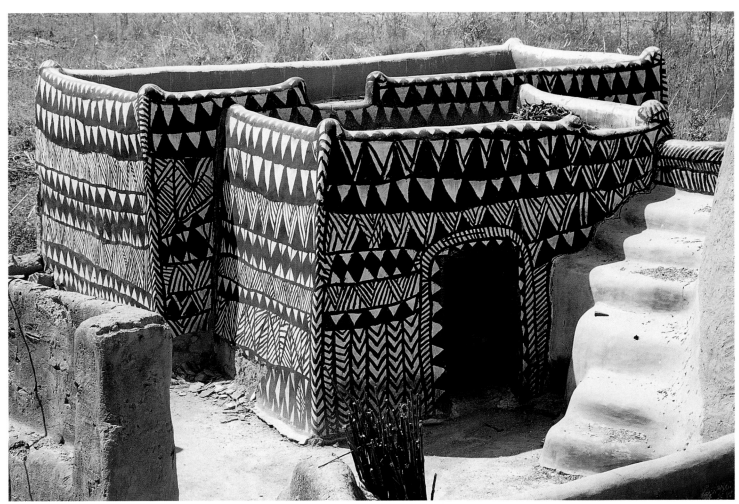

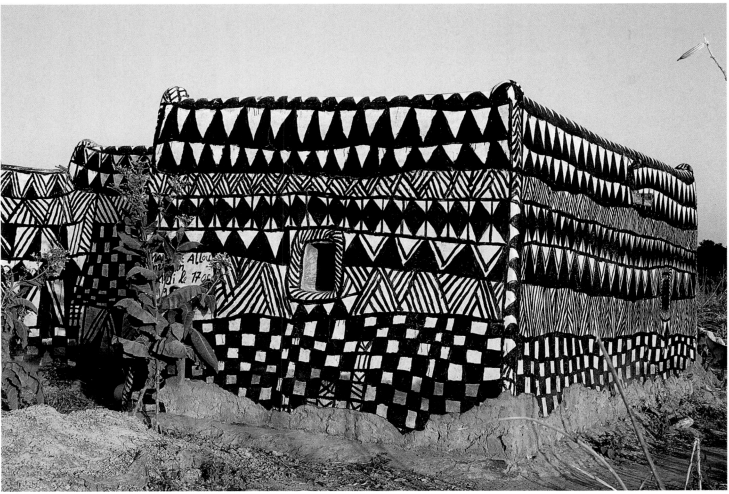

❋ **ABOVE** The motifs painted on the facades of the houses are the work of women; they usually represent the *zalenga*, a net in which calabashes are stored and the *wanzagese*, featuring pieces of crushed calabash. ❋ **OBEN** Die Frauen bemalen die Fassaden mit den Motiven des *zalenga*, einem Wurzelfasernetz, das die Kalebassen einer Frau zusammenhält und des *wanzagese*, das Scherben zerbrochener Kalebassen darstellt. ❋ **CI-DESSUS** Sur les façades des maisons, les motifs peints le plus souvent par les femmes Kasséna sont le *zalenga*, un filet végétal de rangement de calebasses, et le *wanzagese*, figurant des morceaux de calebasses brisées.

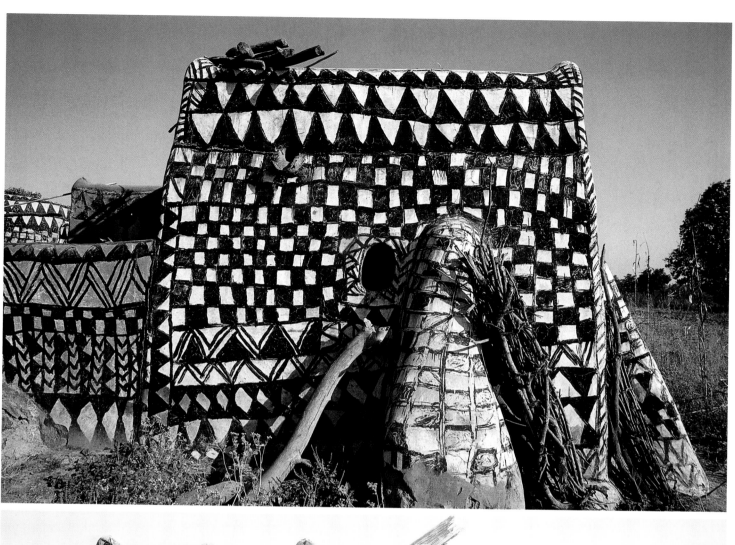

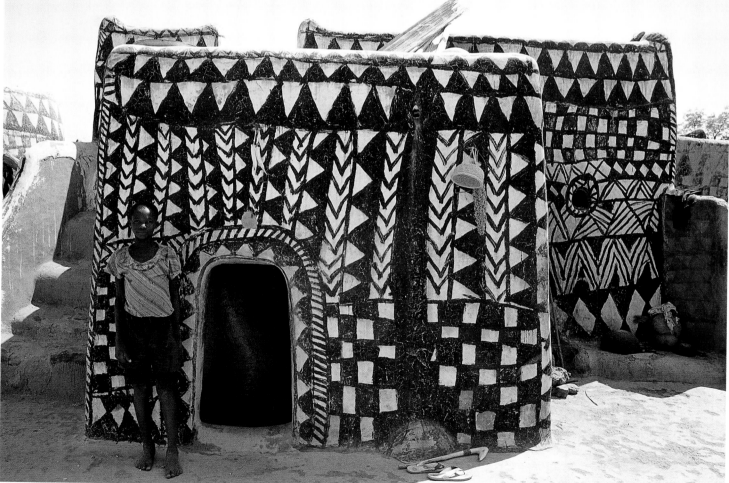

✻ **ABOVE** V-shaped compositions are a sign of welcome to visitors. **FOLLOWING PAGES** Kassena villages are laid out as small separate compounds, each run by its own family chief. ✻ **OBEN** Die gemalten V-Zeichen heißen Besucher willkommen. **FOLGENDE DOPPELSEITE** Die Kassena-Dörfer bestehen aus kleineren, voneinander getrennten Einfriedungen, in denen jeweils das Familienoberhaupt das Sagen hat. ✻ **CI-DESSUS** Les compositions en V sont un signe de bienvenue aux visiteurs. **DOUBLE PAGE SUIVANTE** Les villages Kasséna se présentent sous la forme de petites enceintes séparées les unes des autres, dont chaque maître est le chef de famille.

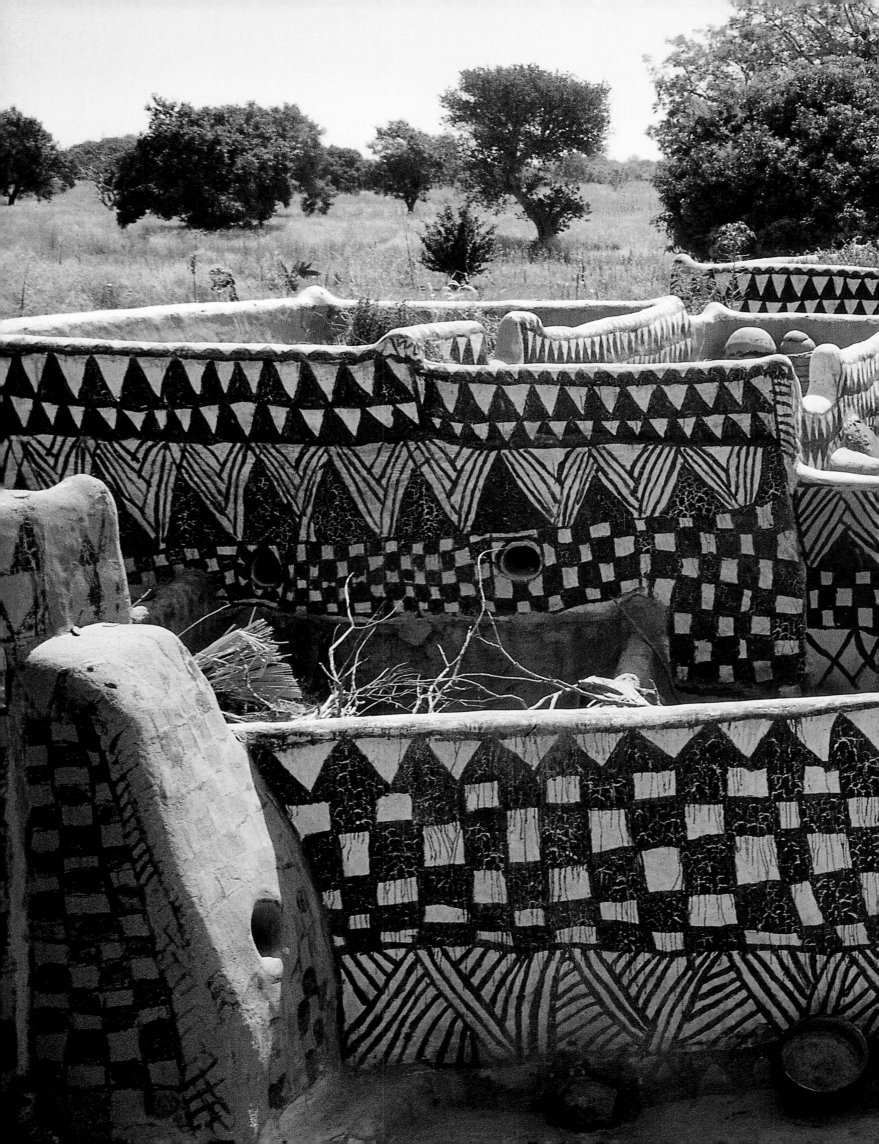

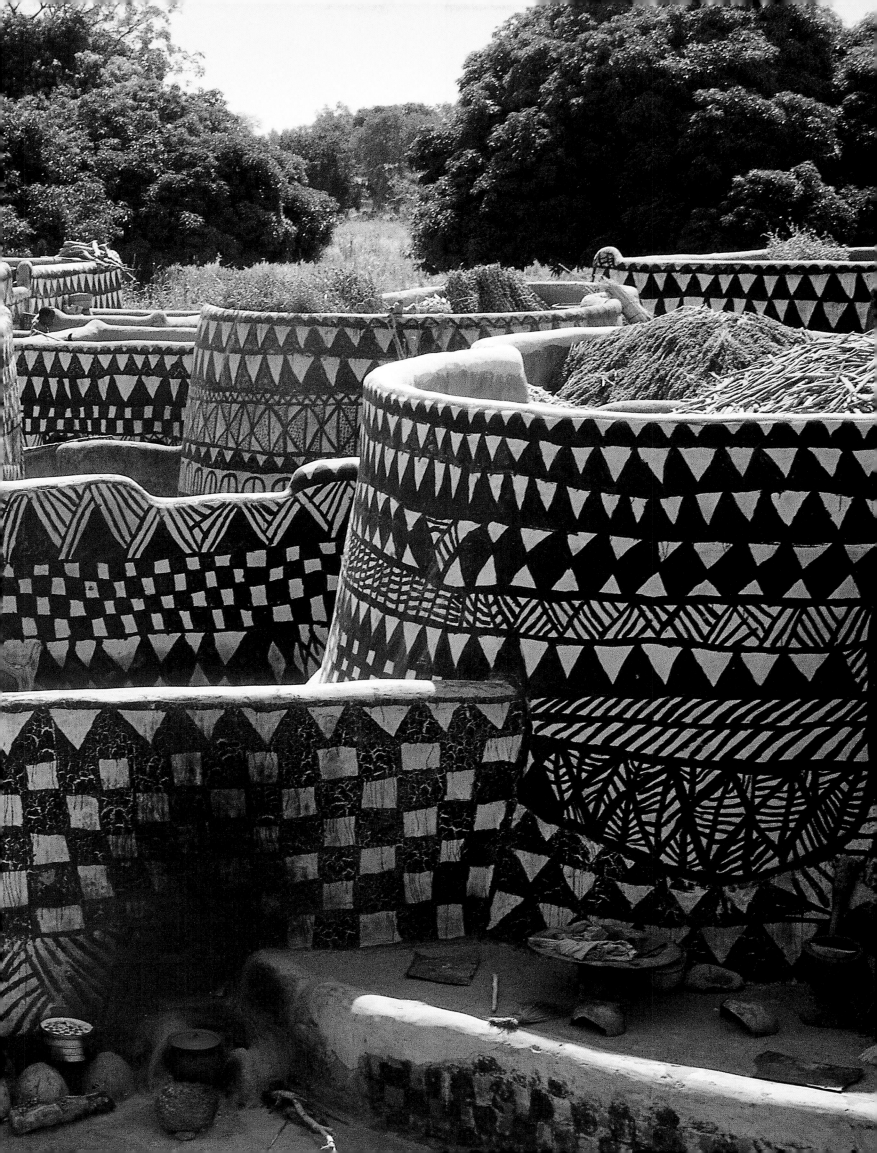

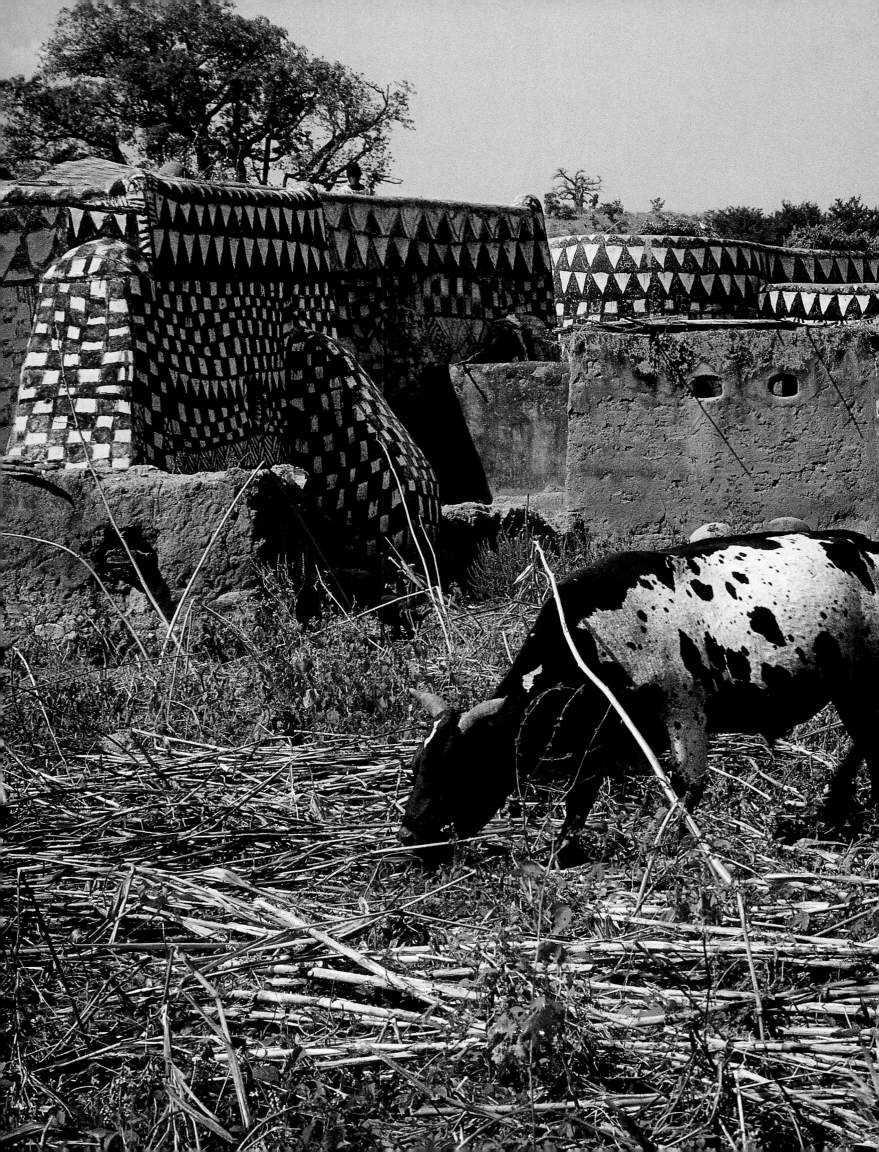

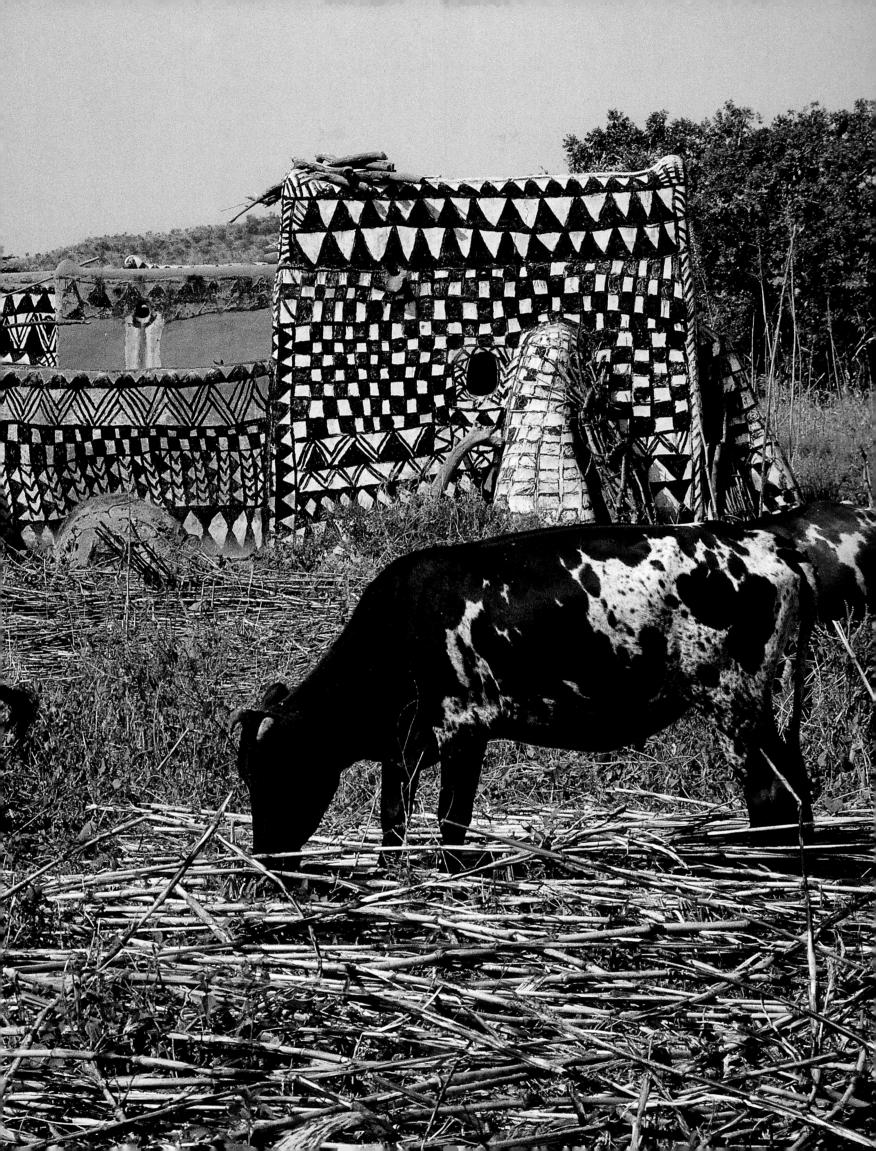

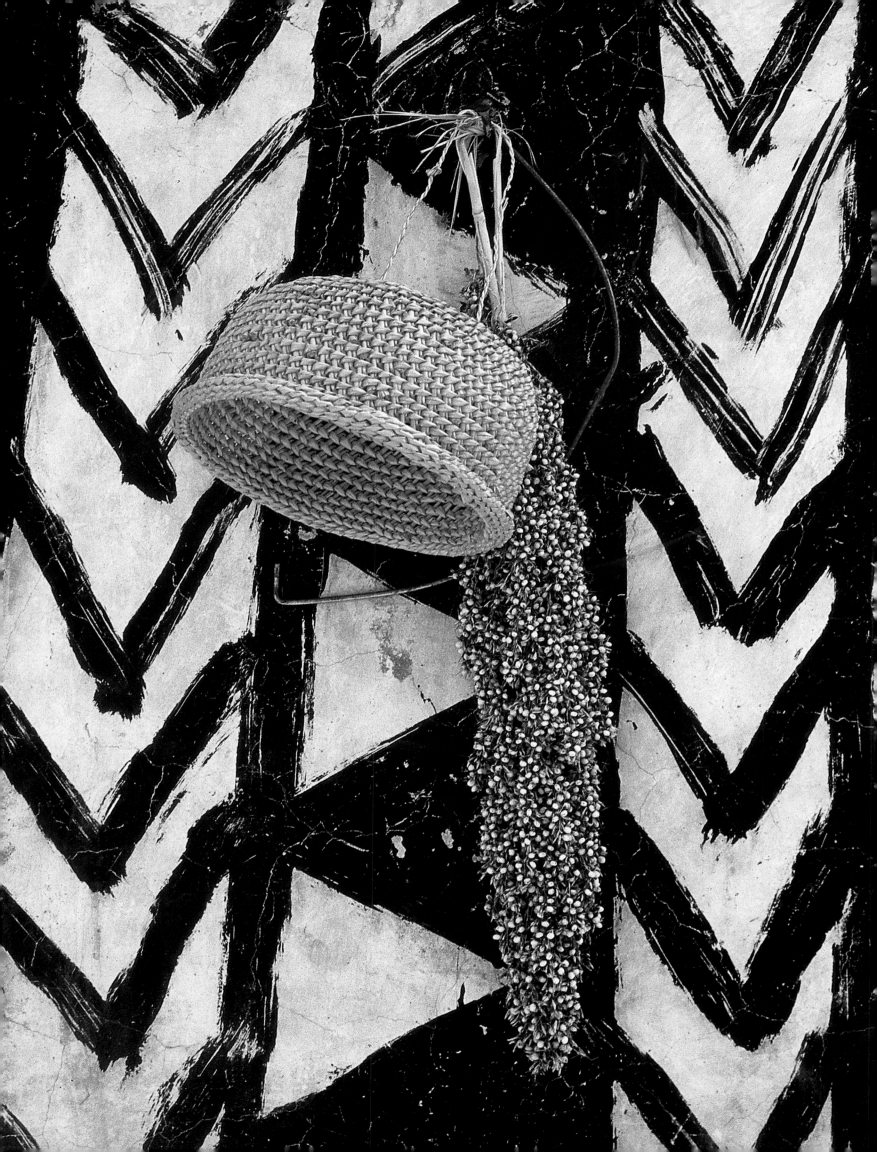

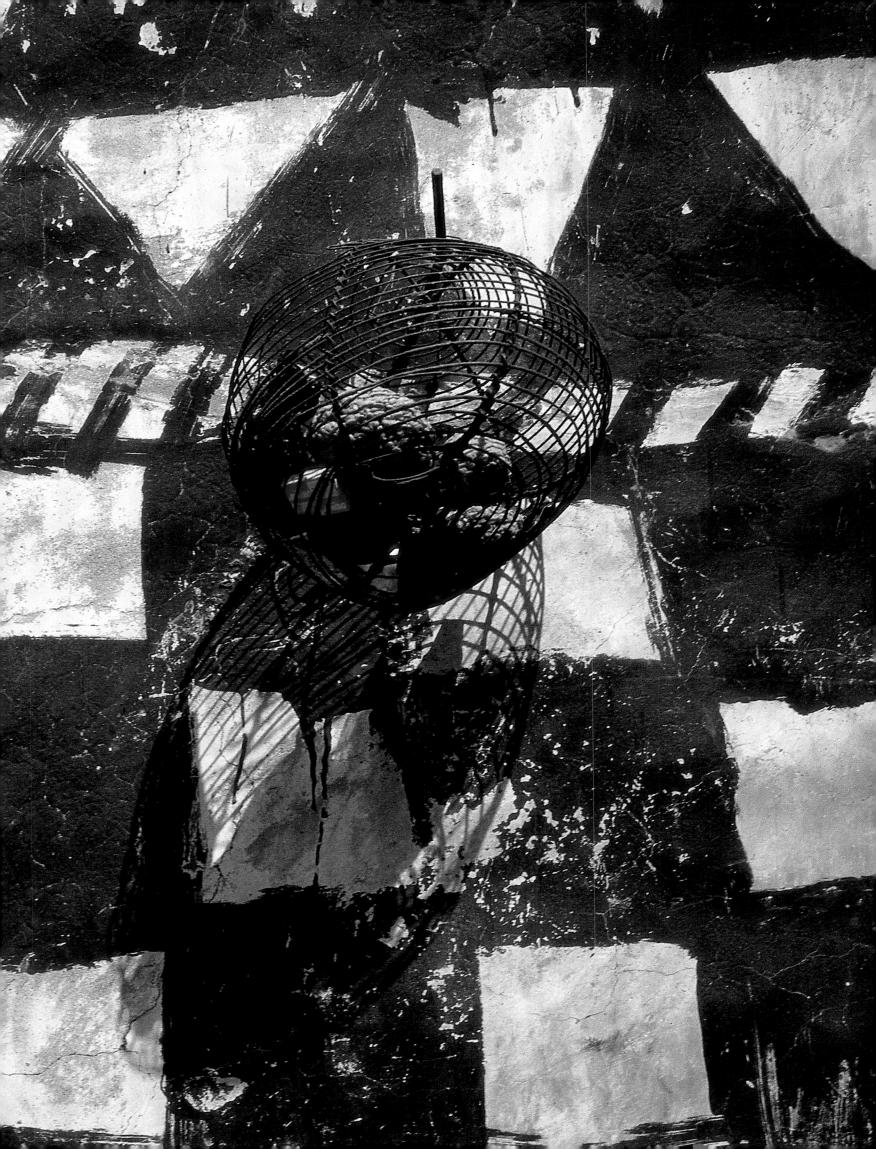

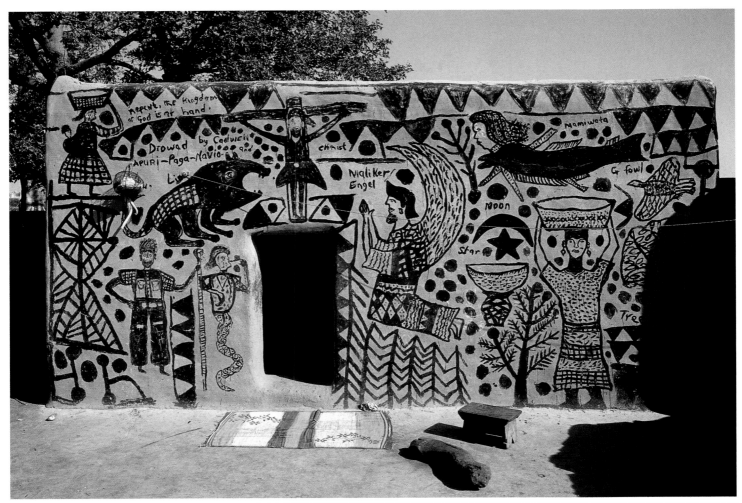

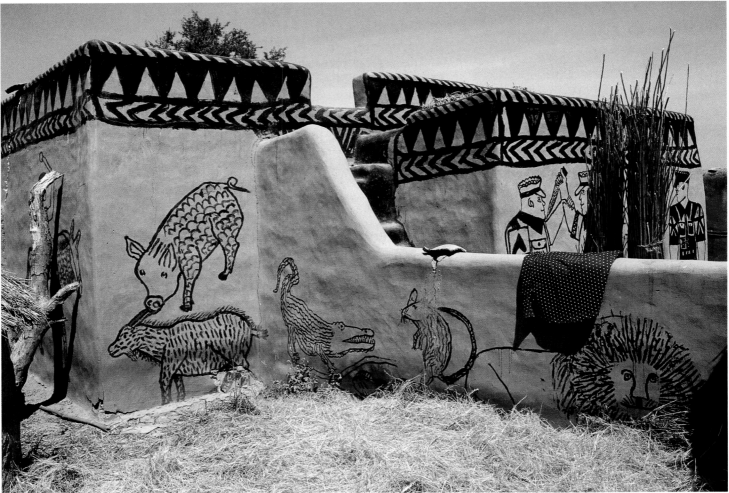

❋ **ABOVE** In Ghana, a natural rendering made with earth, ashes, cowpats, tree resin and nut butter is used as insulation against the heat. ❋ **OBEN** Als Schutz gegen die Hitze dient in Ghana ein natürlicher Rauputz aus einer Mischung aus Lehm, Asche, Kuhfladen, Baumharz und Schibutter. ❋ **CI-DESSOUS** Au Ghana, un crépi naturel fait d'un mélange de terre, de cendre, de bouse de vache, de résine d'arbre et de beurre de karité est censé isoler de la chaleur.

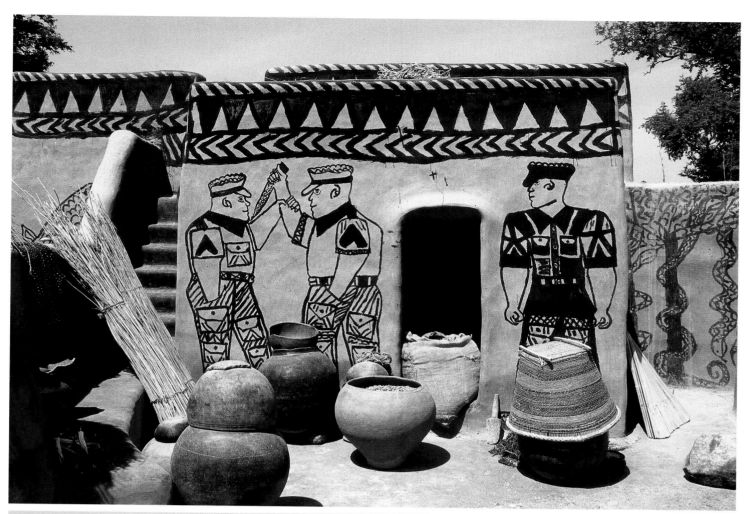

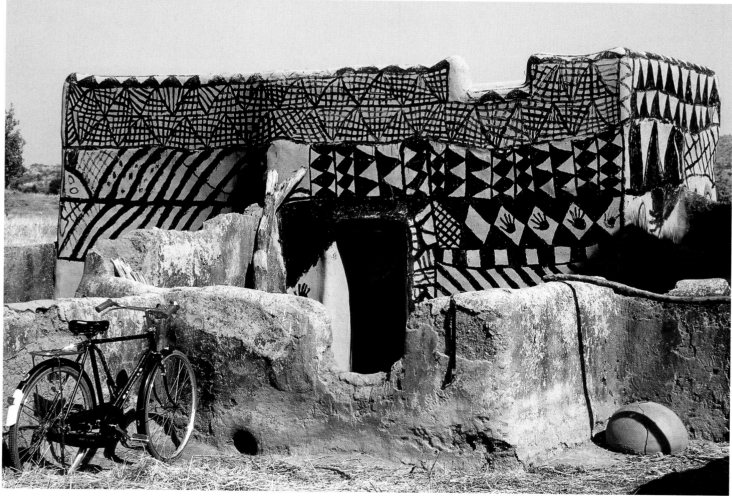

※ **ABOVE** Still in Ghana, the geometrical motifs are inspired by cosmic mythology but also by scenes of daily life – with soldier figures like these. ※ **OBEN** Die geometrischen Formen der Mauern leiten sich aus der kosmischen Mythologie her. Es gibt aber auch Alltagsszenen mit Soldatenfiguren. ※ **CI-DESSOUS** Toujours au Ghana, les motifs géométriques de ces murs sont inspirés de la mythologie cosmique mais aussi de scènes de la vie quotidienne avec ces figures de soldats.

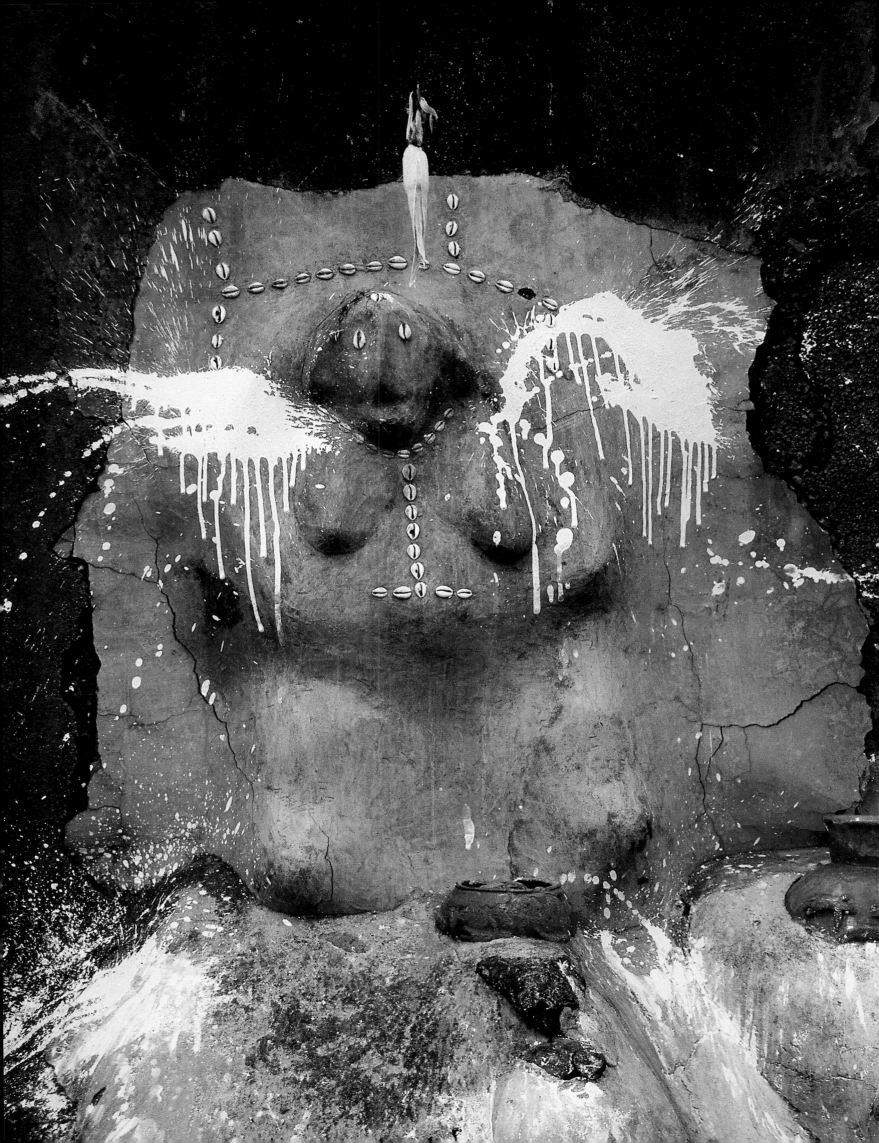

# spiritual master

# LOBI'S VILLAGE

The compound of the spiritual master Palenkité Noufe
takes its visitors to the heart of Lobi magic.

His tomb, dug in the centre of the courtyard, stands in front of the house. The statuette of a man, with a pipe in his mouth and a hat on his head, shows what he looked like. Each day, new offerings fill his dish and his glass.

In accordance with the belief that the dead live on among the living, Palenkité Noufe has been buried in his former compound since 1998. His son has taken over his duties. At the door of his thatched house, the statue of a hippo stands guard. Traces of offerings of milk and millet cover its back. The sacred chamber is just beyond: this room, built with stones chosen personally by the Master, was formerly his place of work, where he carried out his priestly and commercial functions. In animist societies, the spiritual master has the task of interpreting the will of spirits, ancestors and gods. In times of misfortune, animals are sacrificed to propitiate the souls of the dead and obtain their help. The religion involves the adoration of sacred objects made of clay or wood, which are assembled on veritable domestic altars. On the right hand side of the threshold, the altar of the Lady of the River is carved in bas-relief. She is depicted standing with her legs apart, covered in shells from her forehead to her navel. To appease the spirits, this figure is regularly sprinkled with millet beer and the blood of sacrificed animals, and the earth walls are included in this ritual. The liquid, on its way to the great beyond, licks at the roof – which is made of ashes, cowpats and straw thoroughly mixed together.

Das mitten im Innenhof ausgehobene Grab liegt direkt vor seinem Haus. Die Statue eines Mannes mit einer Pfeife im Mund und einer Mütze auf dem Kopf beschwört seine Gestalt. Sein Teller und sein Glas werden täglich mit Opfergaben gefüllt.

Getreu der Vorstellung, dass die Toten mit den Lebenden zusammenwohnen, wurde Palenkité Noufe 1998 in seiner Konzession bestattet. Sein Sohn übernahm das Amt. Vor dem Haus hält ein Flusspferd Wache, dessen Rücken Spuren von Opfergaben – Hirse oder Milch – aufweist. Direkt dahinter liegt der Raum mit den heiligen Gegenständen – die Bausteine wurden vom Priester eigens ausgewählt. Im Schutz dieses Raumes übt er seine Tätigkeit aus. In animistischen Ländern übernimmt der Priester die Aufgabe, den Willen der Geister, Ahnen und Götter zu interpretieren. In schlechten Zeiten opfert man Tiere, um die Geister der Toten zu beschwichtigen und ihre Hilfe zu erlangen. Auf den Hausaltären werden heilige Gegenstände aus Lehm und Holz platziert. Rechts an der Schwelle des Hauses befindet sich der Altar der Flussgöttin, im Relief geschnitzt. Die aufrecht stehende weibliche Figur mit den gespreizten Beinen ist von der Stirn bis zum Nabel mit Muscheln verziert. Zur Besänftigung der Geister wird sie ebenso wie die Lehmmauern regelmäßig mit Hirsebier und Tierblut begossen. Auf dem Weg ins Jenseits benetzt die Flüssigkeit auch das Dach, das aus einer Mischung aus Asche, Stroh und Kuhfladen hergestellt wurde.

Sa tombe, creusée au milieu de la cour, est située devant sa maison. La statuette d'un homme, pipe à la bouche, casquette sur la tête, évoque sa silhouette. Chaque jour, des offrandes emplissent son assiette et son verre.

Selon la croyance qui veut que les morts cohabitent avec les vivants, Palenkité Noufe est enseveli dans sa concession depuis 1998. Son fils a pris la relève. Devant l'entrée de la maison au toit de chaume, un hippopotame monte la garde. Des traces d'offrandes, mil ou lait, couvrent son dos. La chambre des fétiches apparaît juste derrière. Édifiée à l'aide de pierres choisies par le Maître, elle abritait ses activités, à mi-chemin entre le sacerdoce et le commerce. En pays animiste, le féticheur se charge d'interpréter la volonté des esprits, des ancêtres et des dieux. Dans le malheur, on procède à des sacrifices d'animaux pour apaiser les esprits des morts et obtenir le secours des disparus. Le culte s'accompagne d'une adoration des fétiches d'argile ou de bois qui sont rassemblés sur de véritables autels domestiques. Au seuil de la maison, à droite, l'autel de la Dame du fleuve est sculpté en bas-relief. Debout, les jambes écartées, la forme féminine est ornée de coquillages du front jusqu'au nombril. Pour apaiser les esprits, la belle est régulièrement arrosée de bière de millet et du sang des animaux sacrifiés. Les murs de terre n'échappent pas à ce rite. Le liquide, en chemin vers l'au-delà, lèche le toit fait de cendre et de paille mélangée à la bouse de vache.

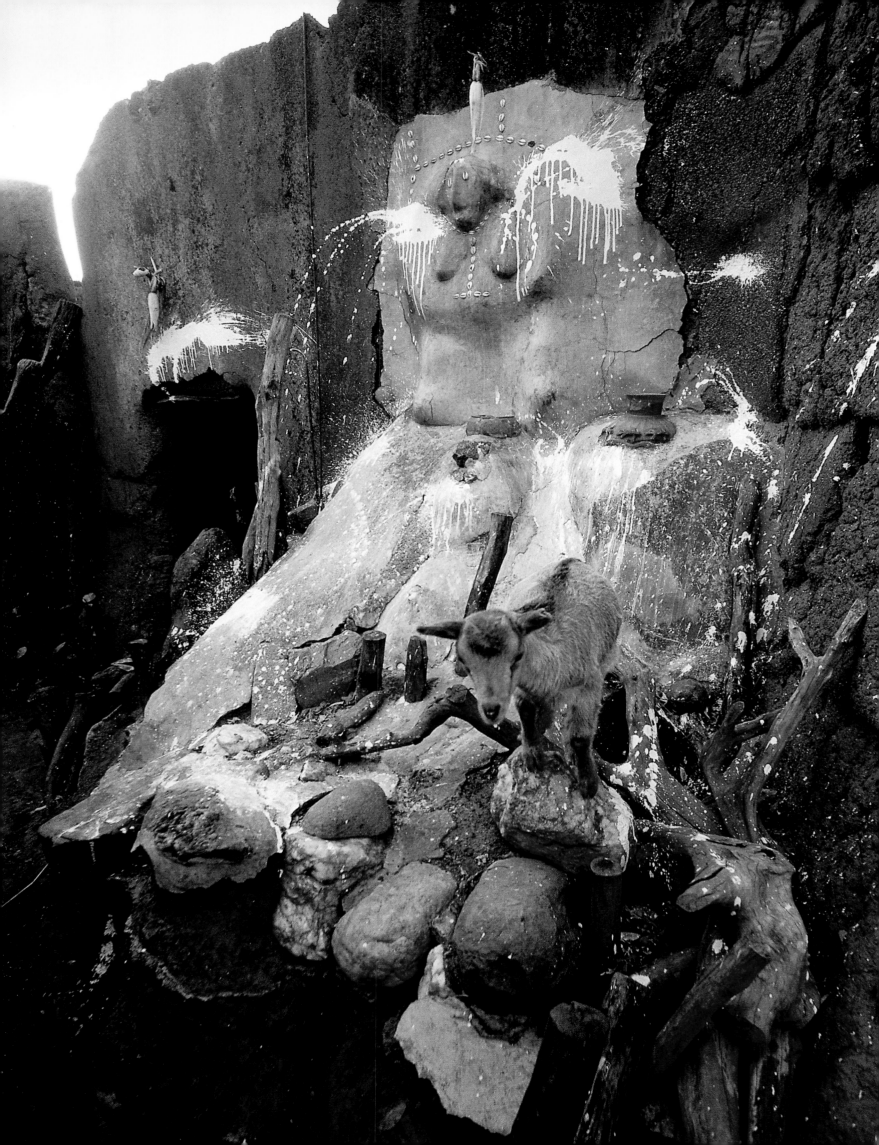

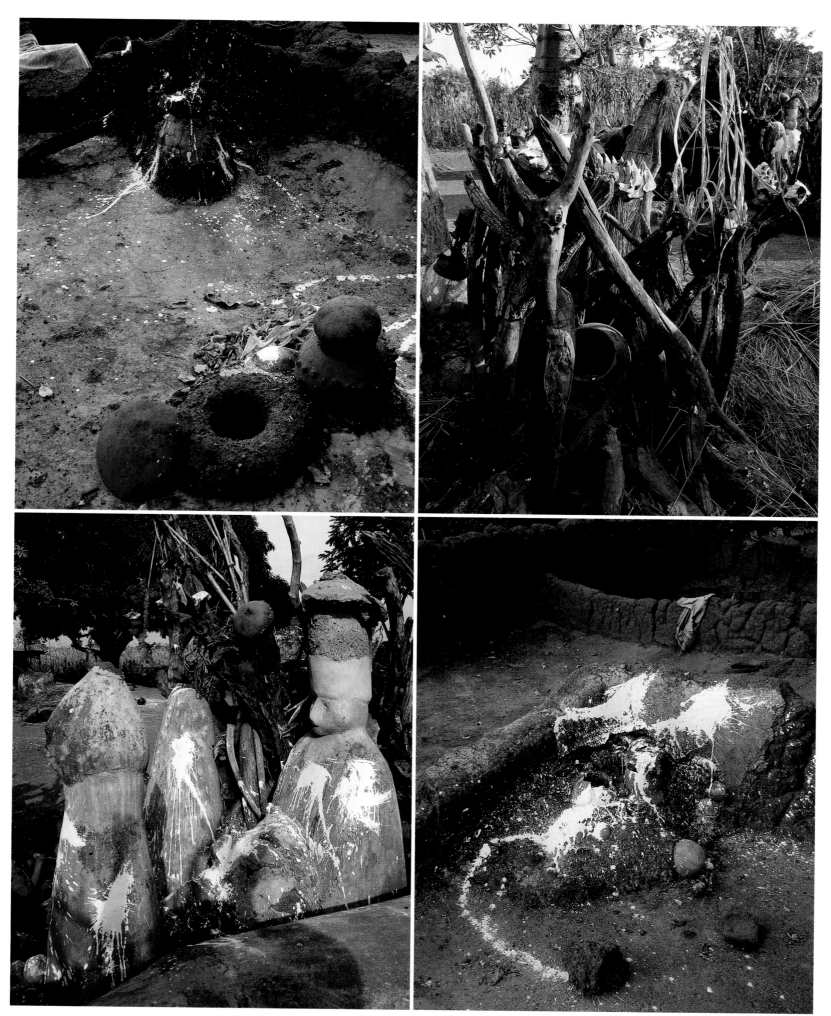

✳ **FACING PAGE** The feminine form, stained with libations and adorned with shells, evokes the black Volta, a frontier river of great mythical and religious importance to the Lobi. **ABOVE** Four traditional Lobi domestic altars. ✳ **LINKE SEITE** Die weibliche Figur, die mit Spuren der Trankopfer bedeckt und mit Muscheln verziert ist, beschwört den Schwarzen Volta, den mythisch und religiös bedeutsamen Grenzfluss. **OBEN** Vier traditionelle Hausaltäre der Lobi. ✳ **PAGE DE GAUCHE** La forme féminine, couverte de traces de libations et ornée de coquillages, évoque la Volta Noire, fleuve frontalier à l'importance mythique et religieuse. **CI-DESSUS** Quatre autels traditionnels domestiques Lobi.

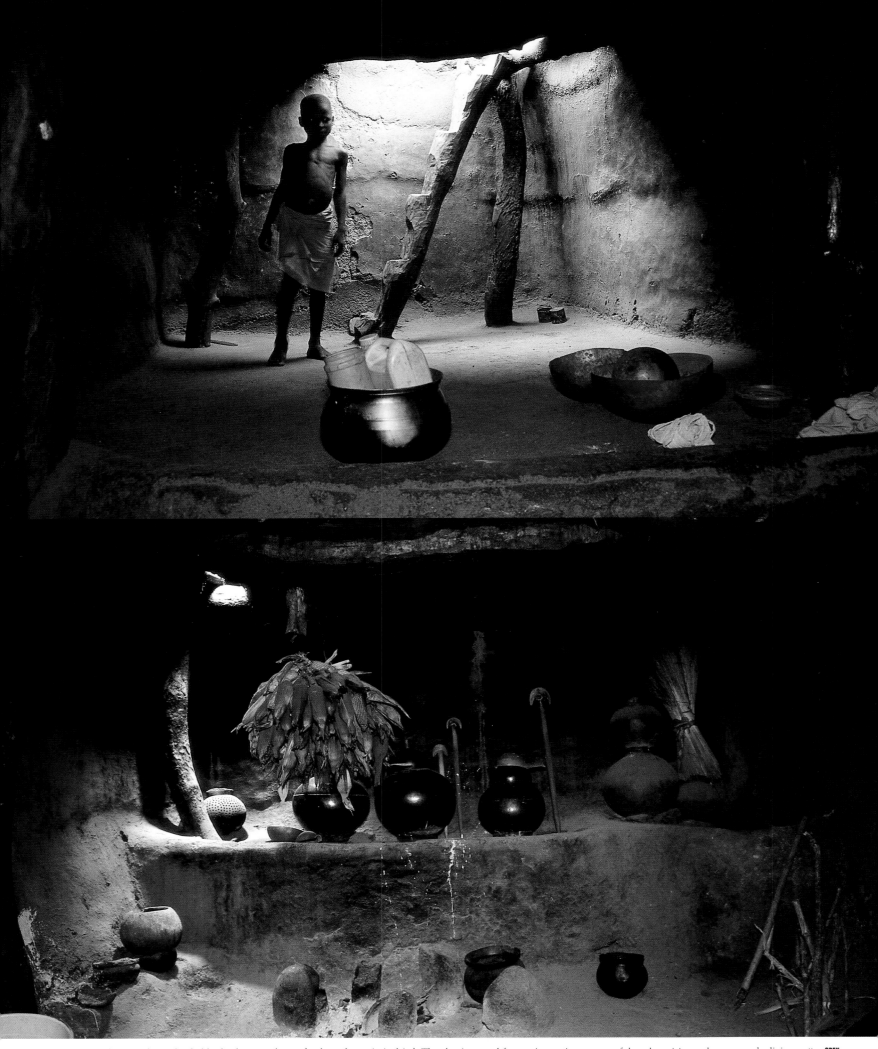

❋ **ABOVE** The carved wooden ladder leads up to the roof, where the grain is dried. The clay jars used for storing grain are as useful to the spirits as they are to the living. ❋ **OBEN** Die aus Holz geschnitzte Leiter führt aufs Dach, wo das Getreide trocknet. In Krügen aus Lehm wird das Getreide gelagert – für die Lebenden und die Geister. ❋ **CI-DESSUS** L'échelle en bois sculpté mène au toit où sèchent les céréales. Les jarres d'argile utilisées pour stocker les céréales servent aux vivants comme aux esprits.

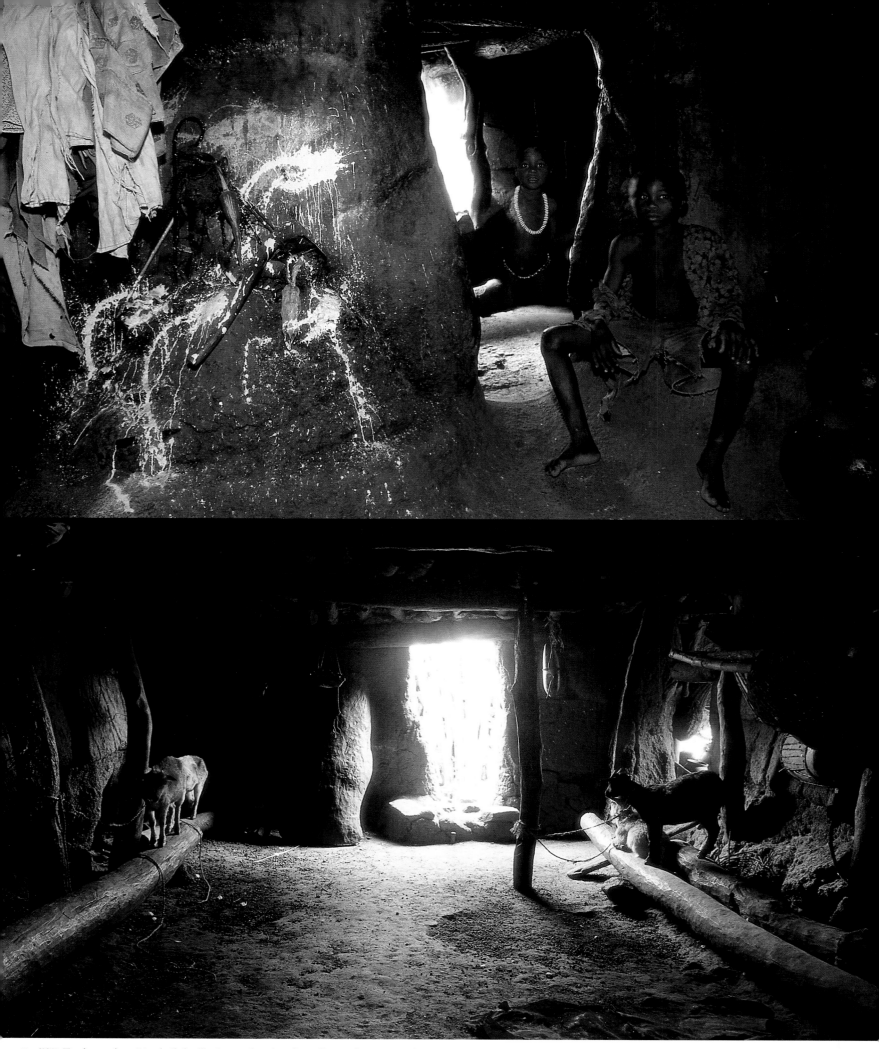

✳ **ABOVE** To placate the spirits, boiled millet is tossed against the walls. Death isn't viewed as a tragic event in these parts, because people believe the dead do not entirely depart the world of the living. ✳ **OBEN** Zur Besänftigung der Geister wird Hirsebrei auf die Mauern geschmiert. Der Tod wird hier nicht tragisch genommen, weil der Verstorbene weiter Anteil an der Welt der Lebenden hat. ✳ **CI-DESSUS** Pour apaiser les esprits, on jette de la bouillie de mil sur les murs. La mort n'a pas de caractère tragique ici car le défunt ne disparaît pas entièrement du monde des vivants.

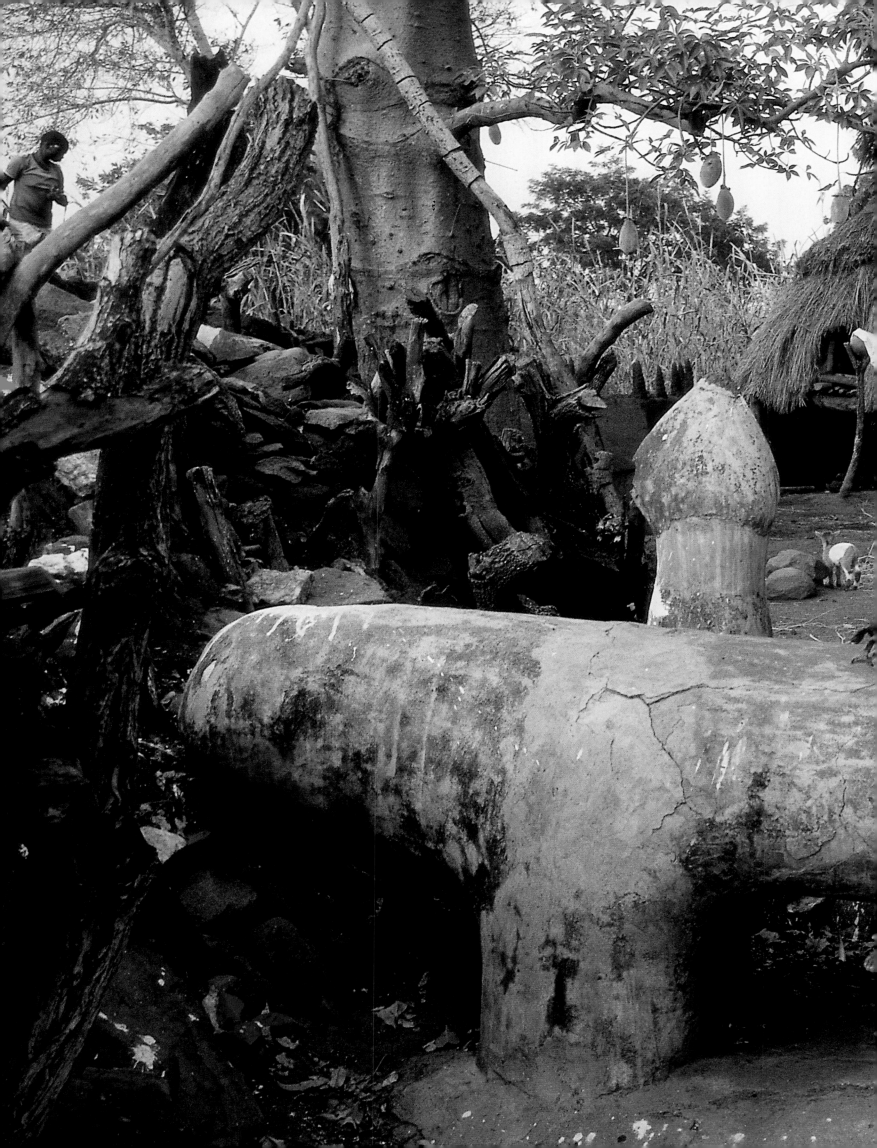

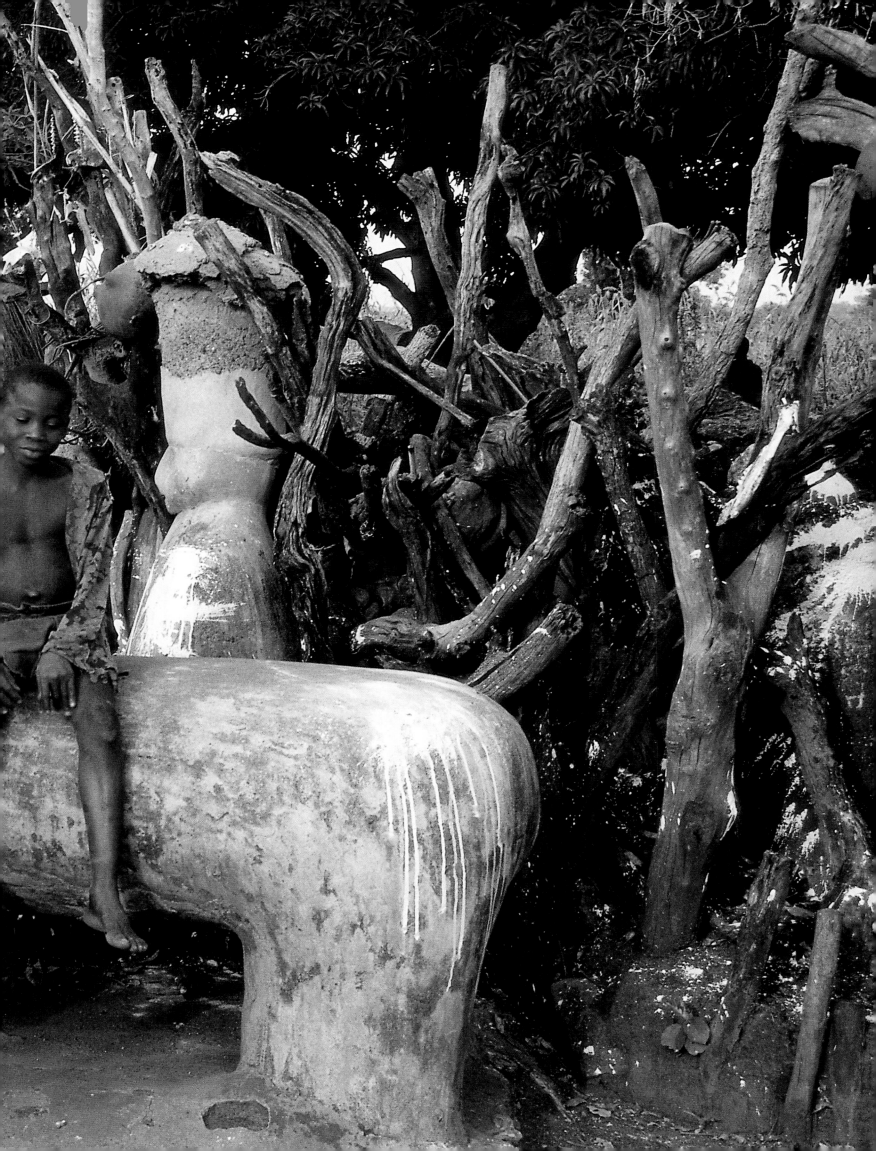

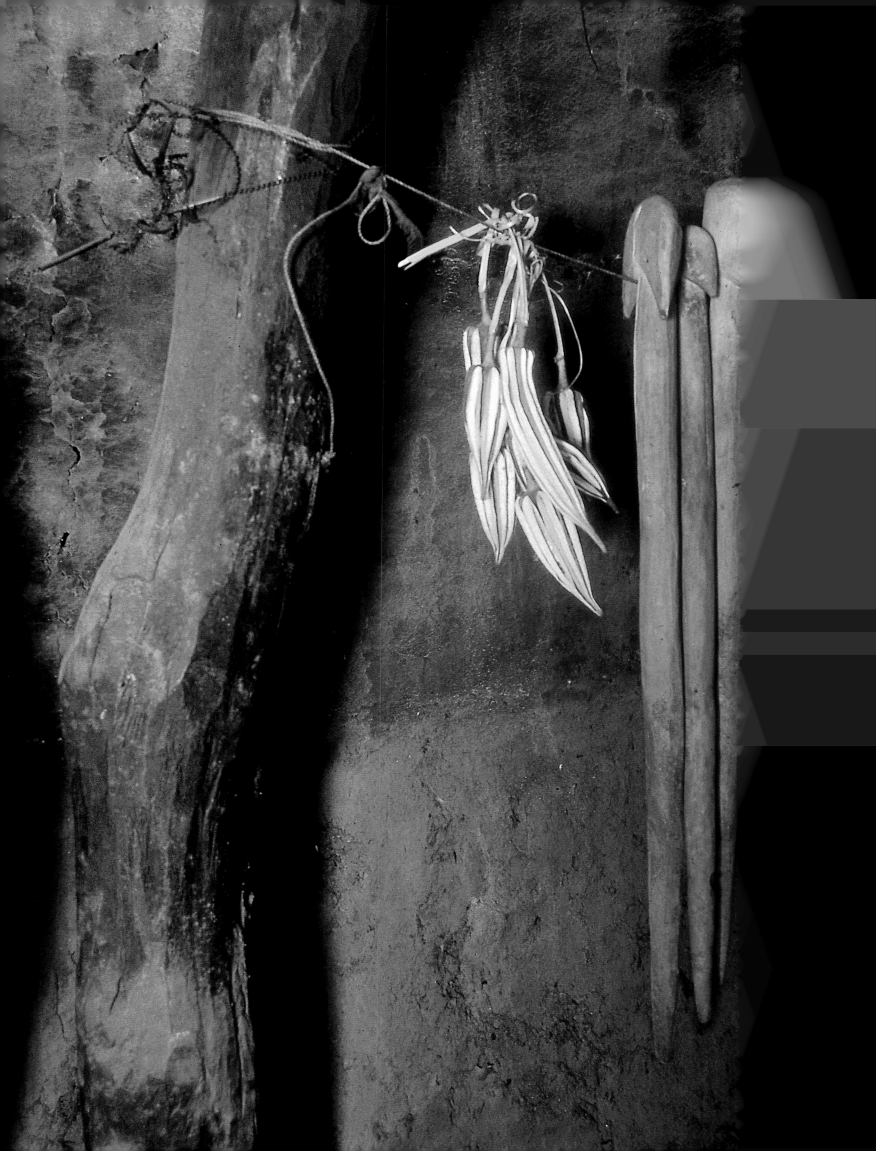

# TIEMOKO SOUL

# LOBI'S VILLAGE

The Lobi, a warrior people, built compounds they could defend, and that were well-provided with water, grain stores and stables.

As with the Kassena, and for the same reasons (to escape marauding slave traders), compounds in this part of Burkina Faso tend to be about a hundred yards apart. The *zaka* (family enclosure) brings together bedrooms, grain stores, terraces and kitchen area in an ensemble which can run to several rooms.

The Lobi have always been a fragmented group, with no system of general authority beyond each head of household; they traditionally bore the name of their home compound, and as hunters and warriors they put up a long resistance to the colonial French administration. Only recently did they renounce their central tenet as a people: "Never adopt a foreign way of life". Under the circumstances, it is small wonder that their houses are shaped as they are, turned in upon themselves. Lobi *zakas* have practically no entrances from the outside. In the old days, literally the only way in was through the roof terrace, using a Y-shaped ladder carved out of a tree trunk. Today there are doors, but the interiors of the huts are still plunged in a gloom that is scarcely relieved by light from a hatch in the ceiling. There is almost no furniture in these traditional huts: a small bench, perhaps, a mat for sleeping, a few personal items and the traditional pots and ewers for beer and food. The *zaka* is also a demonstration of the skills of the Lobi masons, who excel at both sculpture and pottery.

Aus den gleichen Gründen wie bei den Kassena (aus Furcht vor Sklavenhändlern) lagen die Besitzungen früher Hunderte von Metern auseinander. Die *zaka*, die Einfriedung einer Familienbehausung, verbindet mehrere Zimmer, Speicher, Terrassen und Küchen zu einem Ganzen.

Mehrere *zakas* können eine Einheit bilden. In dieser Form der Splittergesellschaft, in der es bis auf den Familienvater keine Führungsinstanzen gab, konnte das Volk von Jägern und Kriegern den Franzosen in der Kolonialzeit lange widerstehen. Erst vor kurzem gaben die Lobi ihre Devise »Folge niemals der Lebenseinstellung Fremder« auf. Deshalb verwundert es nicht, dass die Siedlungsweise so zurückgezogen wirkt. In einer *zaka* gibt es praktisch keine Tür- oder Fensteröffnungen. In früheren Zeiten konnte man die Häuser nur über die Dachterrassen betreten, indem man eine aus einem Baumstamm geschnitzte Y-förmige Leiter erklomm. Selbst seit Türen Einzug in diese Architektur hielten, liegen die Innenräume fast vollständig im Dunkeln – höchstens eine Falltür an der Decke lässt ein wenig Licht hinein. In den traditionellen Hütten gibt es nur wenige Möbelstücke: eine kleine Bank, eine Matte als Matratze, wenige persönliche Gegenstände sowie die herkömmlichen Töpfe und Krüge für Bier und Lebensmittel. Die *zaka* ist zudem ein gutes Beispiel für die Geschicklichkeit der Lobimaurer, die auch als Bildhauer und Töpfer arbeiten.

Comme chez les Kasséna, et pour les mêmes raisons (échapper aux chasseurs d'esclaves), les possessions étaient autrefois distantes d'une centaine de mètres les unes des autres. La *zaka* (enclos familial) relie les chambres, les greniers, les terrasses et les cuisines en un ensemble qui peut former plusieurs pièces.

Société fragmentée, sans chefferie autre que celle du père de famille (les Lobi portent le nom de leur concession), cette population de guerriers et de chasseurs a longtemps résisté aux Français à l'époque coloniale et n'a que depuis peu renoncé à son dogme: «Ne jamais suivre la devise de l'étranger.» Dans ces conditions, comment s'étonner des formes d'un habitat replié sur lui-même? La *zaka*, est presque entièrement dépourvue d'ouvertures. Autrefois, on accédait même à l'intérieur des habitations par les toits terrasses en grimpant sur ces échelles en Y sculptées à même les troncs d'arbre. Si les portes ont fait leur apparition, les intérieurs sont toujours plongés dans une obscurité à peine corrigée par une trappe au plafond. Les meubles sont rares dans ces cases traditionnelles: un petit banc, une natte en guise de matelas, de petits objets personnels, et les traditionnels pots et jarres destinés à la bière et aux aliments. La *zaka* est aussi une démonstration de l'habileté des maçons Lobi, à la fois sculpteurs et potiers.

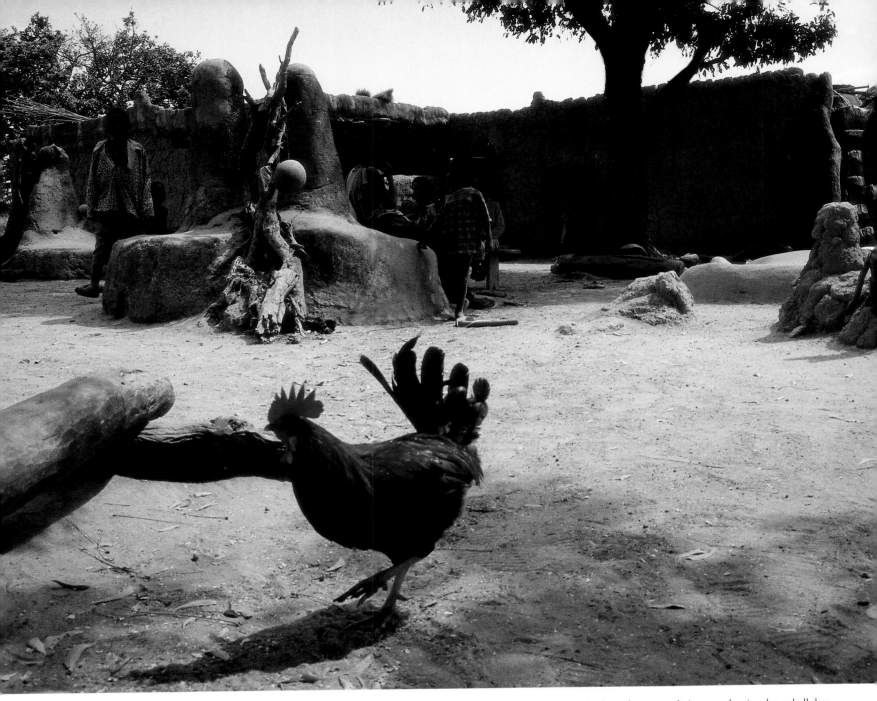

✳ **ABOVE** In the courtyard, only the chickens are allowed out to scratch around among the children. The other domestic animals are kept securely in pens, chewing the cud all day. This place of collective life is also used for the spirit-cult, with altars in front of each house. ✳ **OBEN** Im Hof ist es nur dem Federvieh erlaubt, dem geflochtenen Hühnerstall zu entfliehen und zwischen den Kindern herumzulaufen. Das übrige Vieh käut im Stall wieder. An diesem Ort des Zusammenlebens hat auch der Geisterkult seinen Platz – die Altäre stehen direkt vor dem Haus. ✳ **CI-DESSUS** Dans la cour, seule la volaille peut s'échapper du poulailler tressé et gambader au milieu des enfants. Le bétail, lui, rumine dans son enclos. Ce lieu de vie collective est aussi réservé au culte des esprits puisque des autels se dressent devant les maisons.

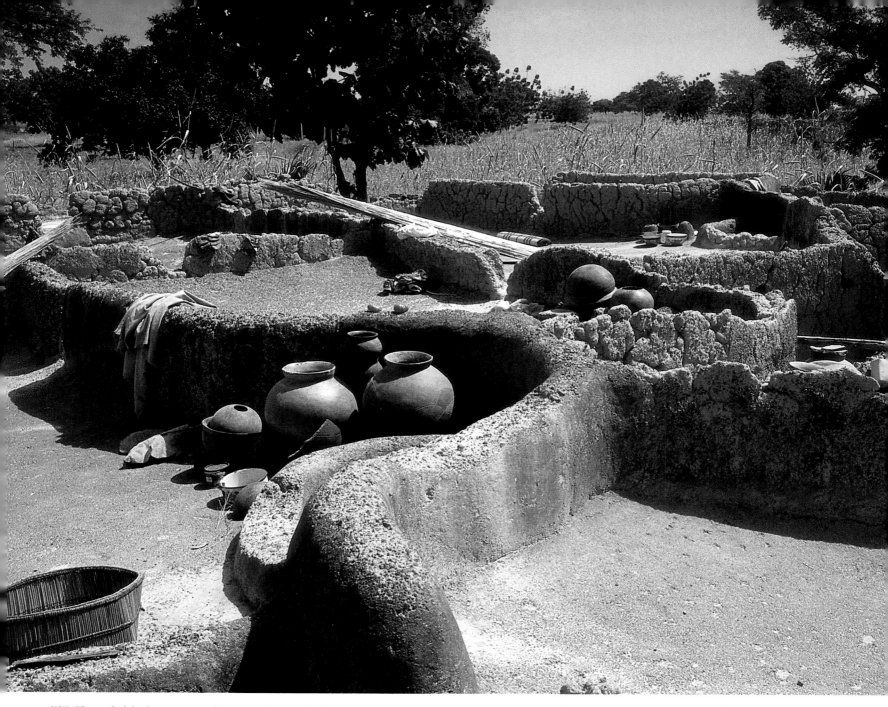

❀ **ABOVE** The roof of this house is accessible using a Y-shaped ladder, leaned against a wall built of five layers of earth. This space is used as a grain store, to dry and stock cereals.

❀ **OBEN** Auf das Dach gelangt man über eine Y-förmige Leiter, die an der Mauer aus fünf Lehmschichten Halt findet. Die Dachterrasse dient als Speicher, wo das Getreide getrocknet und gelagert wird. ❀ **CI-DESSUS** On accède au toit de cette maison à l'aide d'une échelle en forme de Y qui prend appui sur un mur formé de cinq couches de terre. Cet espace est utilisé comme un grenier, pour sécher et stocker les céréales.

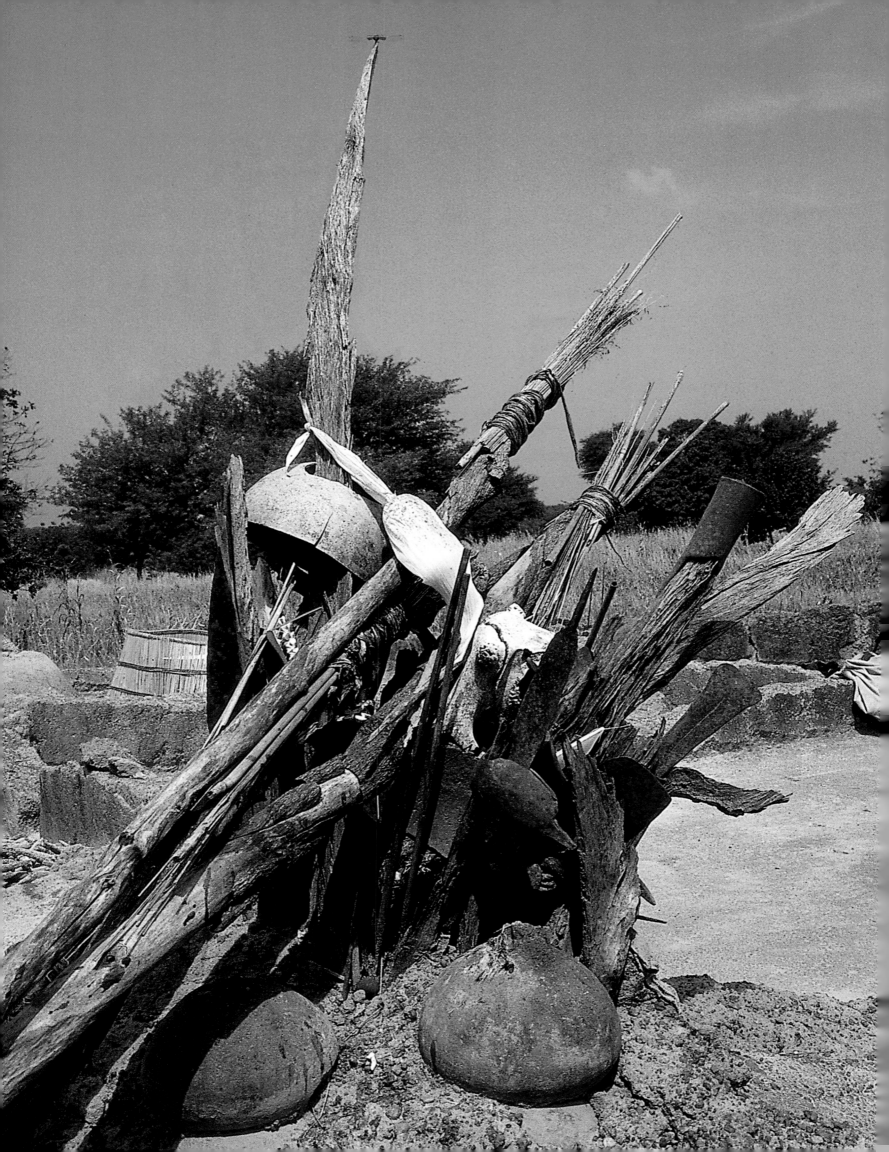

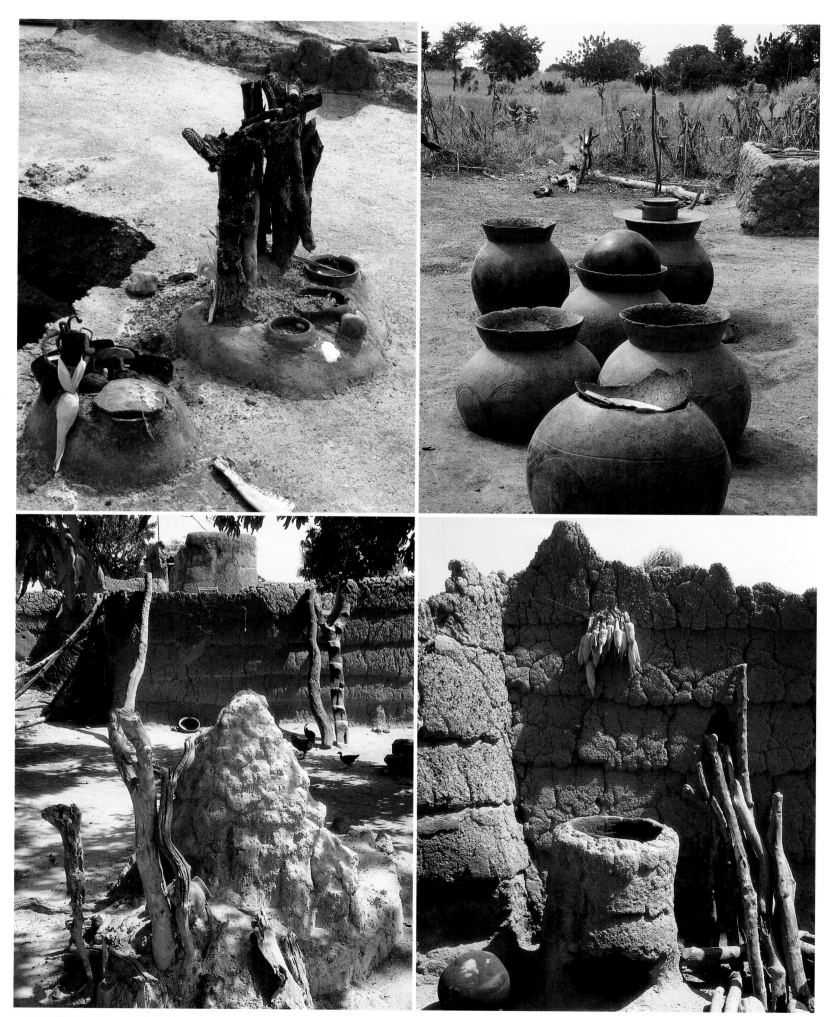

❋ **ABOVE LEFT** This altar stuck full of twigs stands beside its twin made of beaten earth, laden with figurines and iron bracelets. direkt neben einem weiteren aus gestampftem Lehm, der mit Figurinen und schmiedeeisernen Armbändern geschmückt ist. son semblable en terre damée, orné de figurines et de bracelets de fer.

❋ **OBEN LINKS** Der mit Zweigen gespickte Altar steht

❋ **CI-DESSUS A GAUCHE** Cet autel hérissé de branchages côtoie

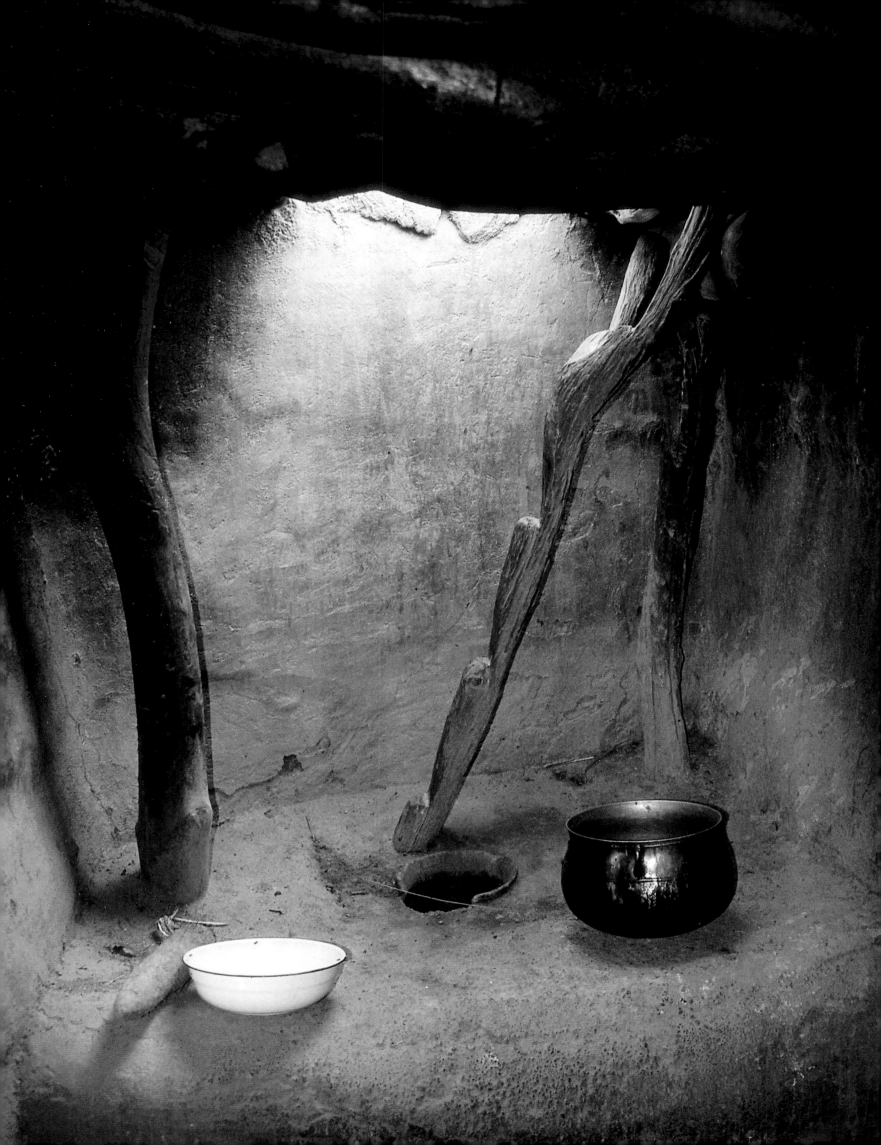

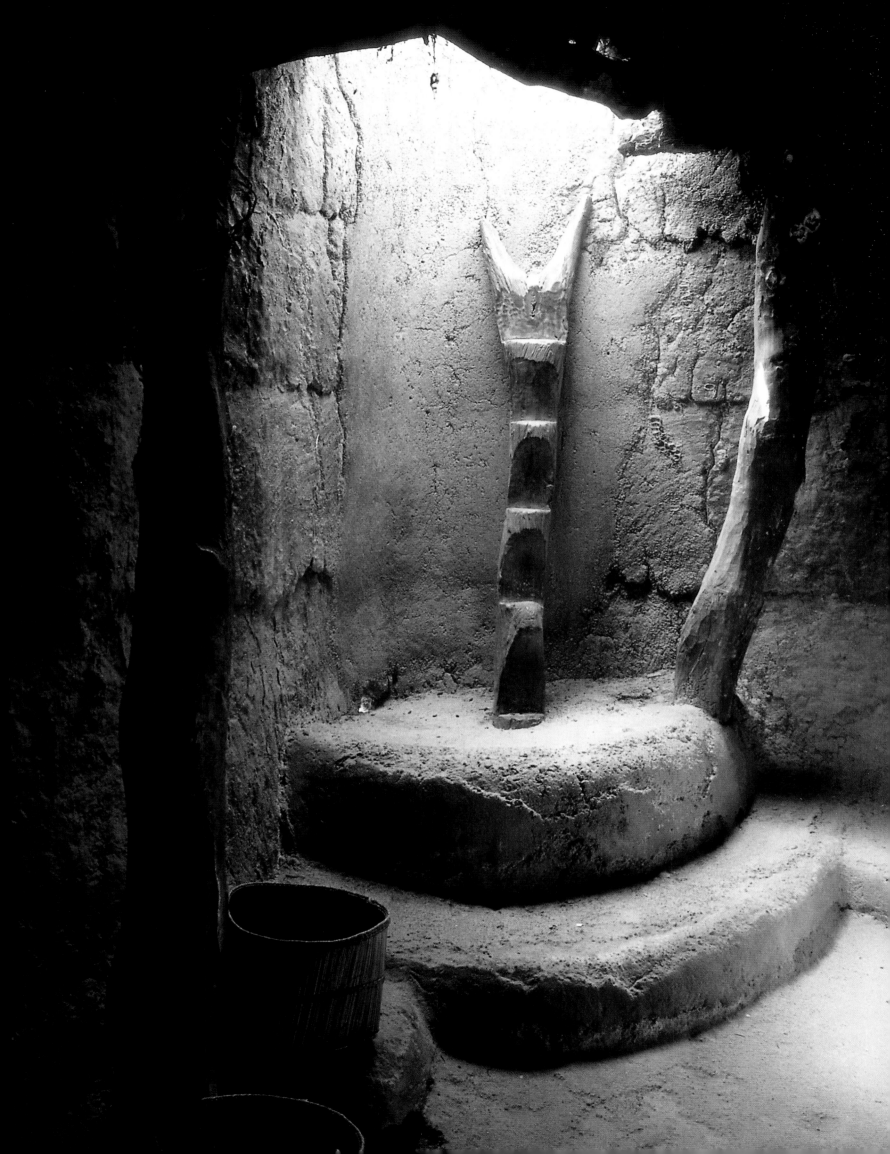

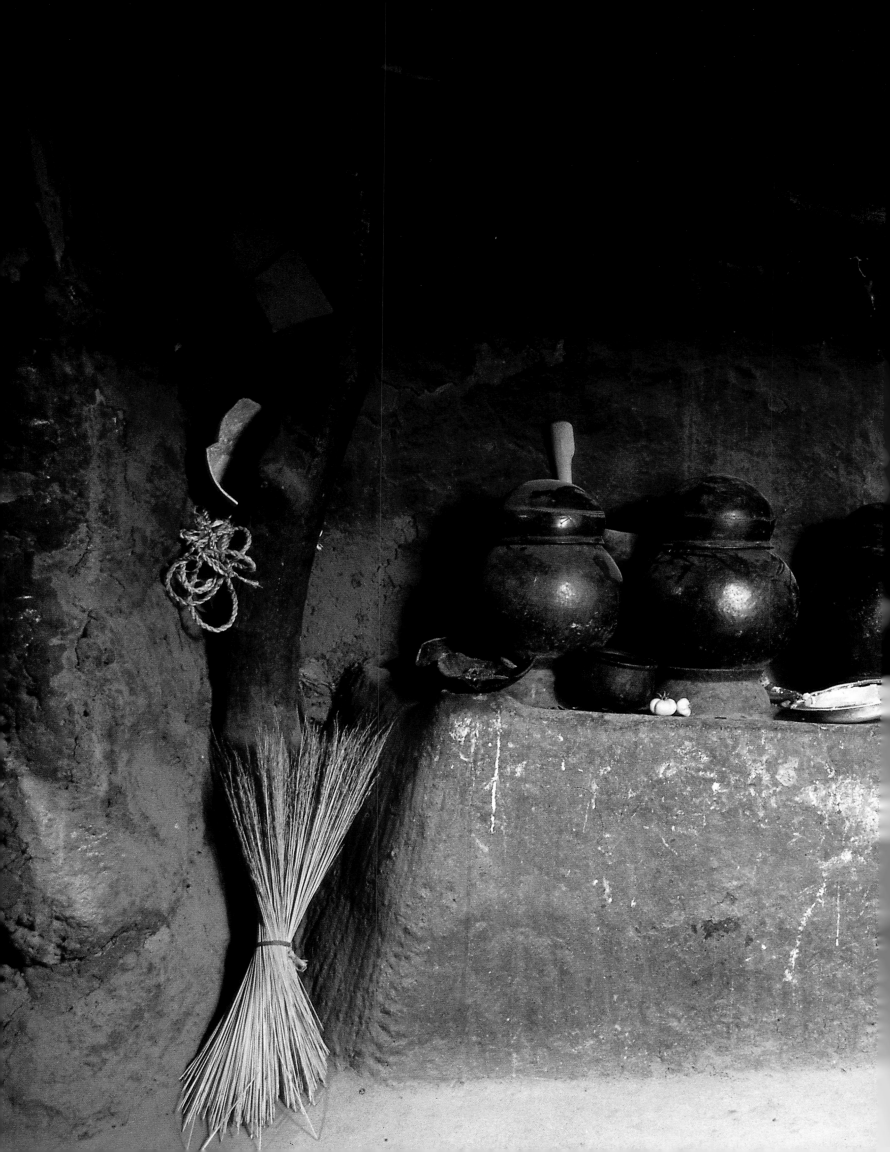

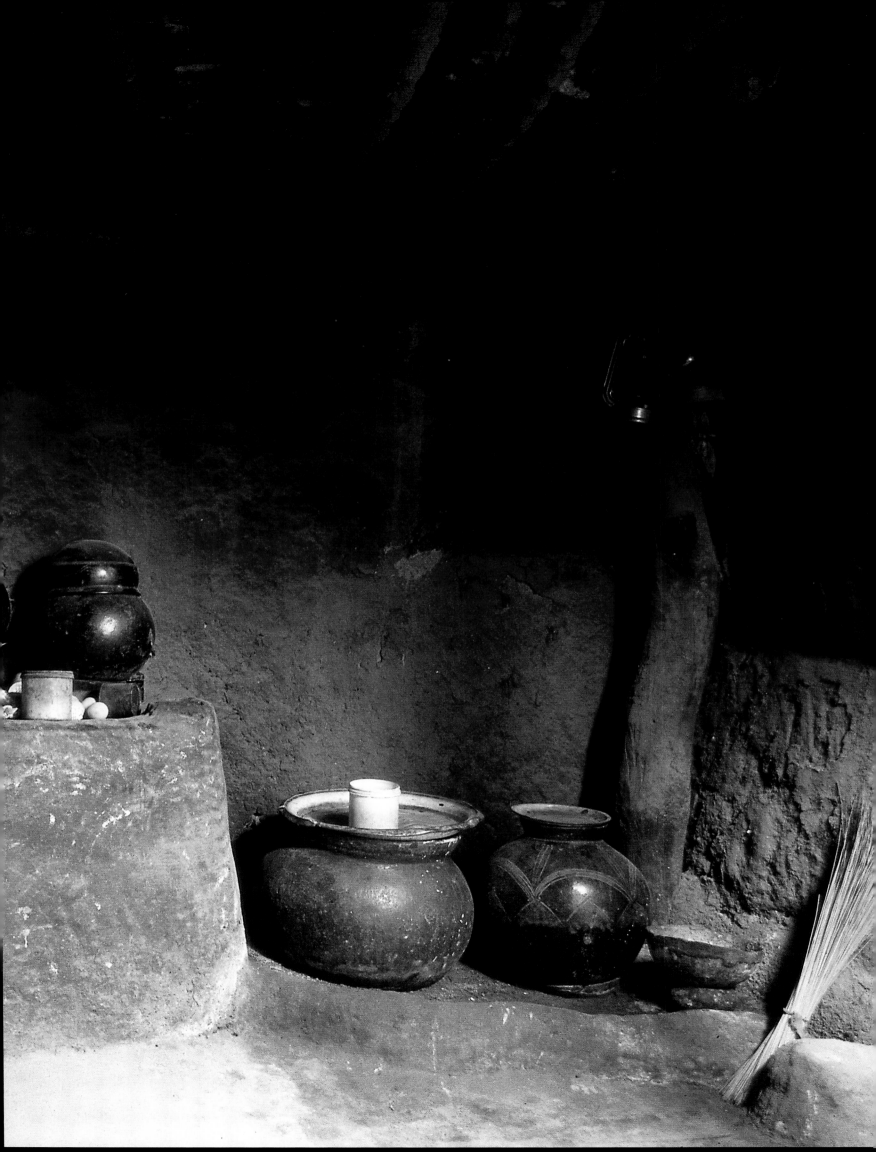

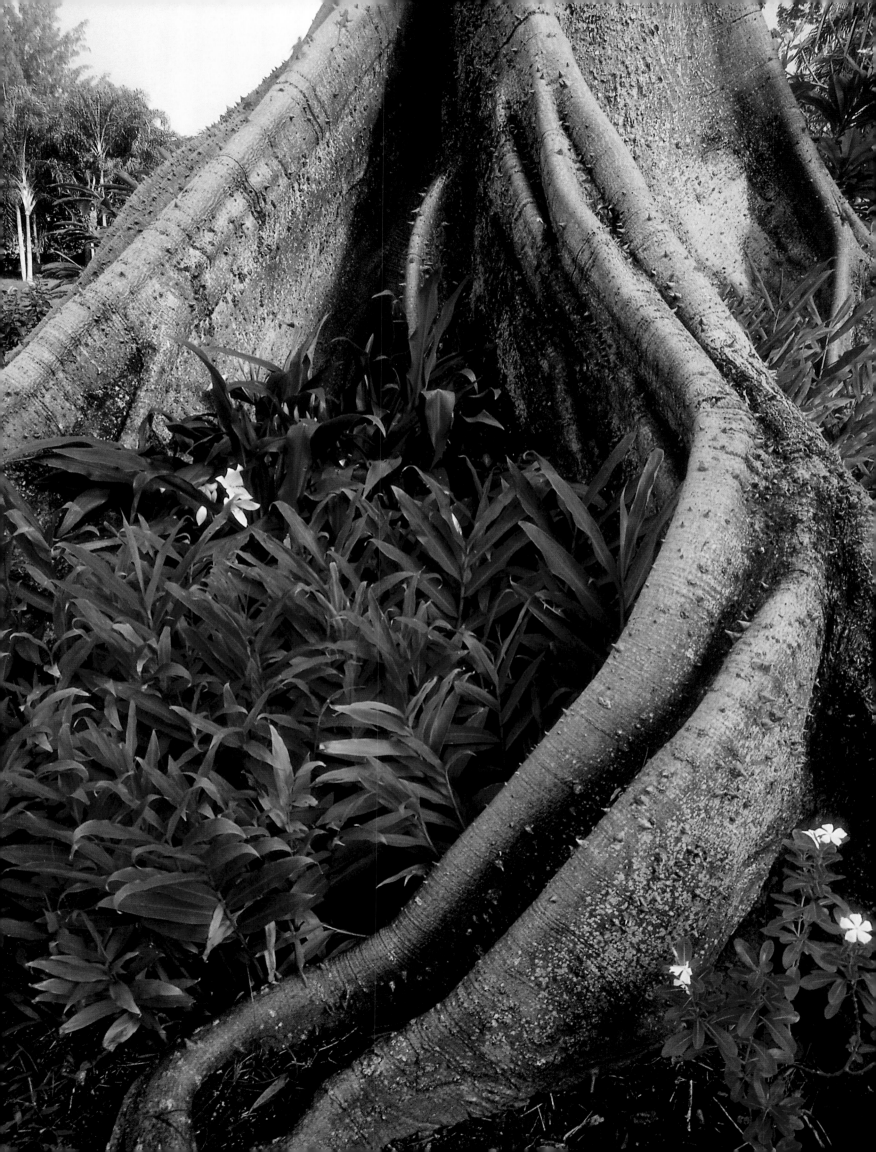

# ABiDJan
# IVOrY COast

Built with a sense of poetry and respect for local tradition, these houses are more to be apprehended than read.

We should try to create habitats that are true to local forms, and above all, not palaces. In the strength of this conviction, the architect Frédéric Thomas has developed his own unusual approach with three villas built in and around Abidjan.

The one feature they all have in common is a shell of rough clay bricks made by hand, on site. This laudable idea sprang from a practical wish to adapt to the hot and humid local climate. Thus all the Thomas houses are positioned to catch the prevailing wind and thus are as ventilated as it is possible to be, at all times. The plate glass windows may heat up the interiors, but they also keep them dry in conjunction with the draughts sweeping through. The result is that the only areas that need to be electrically air-conditioned are the bedrooms – everywhere else the heavy air is stirred by fans. Apart from their materials, the aesthetic harmony of the Thomas houses is invariably generated by their apertures. The light varies as the days go by, thanks to the bay windows and arrow-slits which cast the beams of the setting sun on the walls inside. "Today people are bold enough to confront real challenges," says the architect. Nothing clashes in his work; there are very few objects imported from Europe. One result of this rigour has been that his designs were noticed recently by some chance Japanese visitors – and now he is busy building houses in the Far East.

Eine Behausung von lokalem Zuschnitt, kein Palast jedenfalls. Der Architekt Frédéric Thomas durfte seinen Überzeugungen entsprechend drei Villen in Abidjan und Umgebung individuell gestalten.

So bekamen alle drei den gleichen »Panzer« verordnet, eine Hülle aus ungebrannten Ziegeln, die direkt auf der jeweiligen Baustelle in Handarbeit hergestellt wurden. Eine schöne Idee, die jedoch vor allem der Anpassung an das warme, feuchte Klima dient. Die Häuser sind so ausgerichtet, dass sie ständig vom Wind belüftet werden. Durch die Fenster heizen sich die Räume zwar auf, trocknen jedoch gleichzeitig besser, da ständig eine Brise hindurchweht. Aus diesem Grund sind auch nur die Schlafzimmer klimatisiert, während in den anderen Räumen Ventilatoren die stickige Luft umwälzen. Neben dem Baumaterial spielen insbesondere die Fenster eine große Rolle für die harmonische Wirkung der Häuser. Im Lauf des Tages verändert sich die Stimmung je nach Lichteinfall durch die großen Fenster und die »Schießscharten«, die bei Sonnenuntergang die Mauern beleuchten. »Inzwischen sind die Leute offener für innovative Ideen«, glaubt der Architekt. Protz und Kitsch sucht man hier jedenfalls vergebens. An Material und Möbeln wurde kaum etwas aus Europa importiert. Interessanterweise fand die Arbeit des Architekten große Zustimmung bei Japanern auf der Durchreise durch Abidjan, weshalb er inzwischen auch in Asien sehr gefragt ist.

Un habitat fidèle aux formes locales, surtout pas un palais. Fort de ses convictions, l'architecte Frédéric Thomas a développé son approche singulière à travers trois villas situées à Abidjan et dans les environs.

Elles ont en commun la même carapace, une enveloppe de briques de terre crue pressées à la main sur le chantier. L'idée est belle, mais correspond surtout à une volonté de s'adapter à un climat chaud et humide. Orientées dans le sens du vent, les maisons sont ventilées en permanence. Si les verrières provoquent un réchauffement, elles assèchent également les intérieurs balayés par les brises. Du coup, seules les chambres sont climatisées, et partout ailleurs les ventilateurs tranchent l'air épais comme du manioc. Outre les matériaux, l'harmonie des maisons est générée par les ouvertures. La lumière varie au fil des heures de la journée grâce aux baies et à des meurtrières qui illuminent certains murs au soleil couchant. «Les gens sont mûrs pour de l'audace et des défis», estime l'architecte. Point de clinquant, en effet. Très peu d'objets ou de matériaux importés d'Europe. Par ricochet, ce travail a séduit des Japonais de passage à Abidjan et, du coup, l'architecte essaime maintenant sur le continent asiatique.

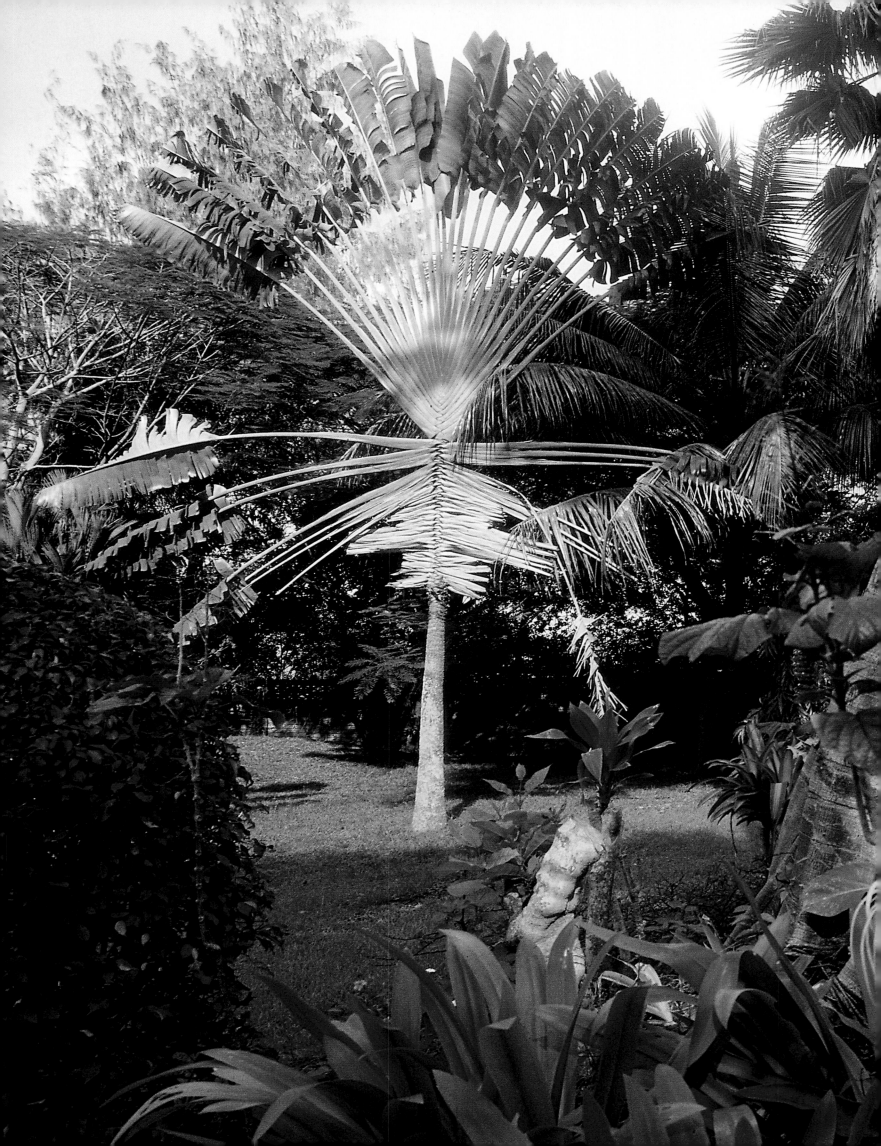

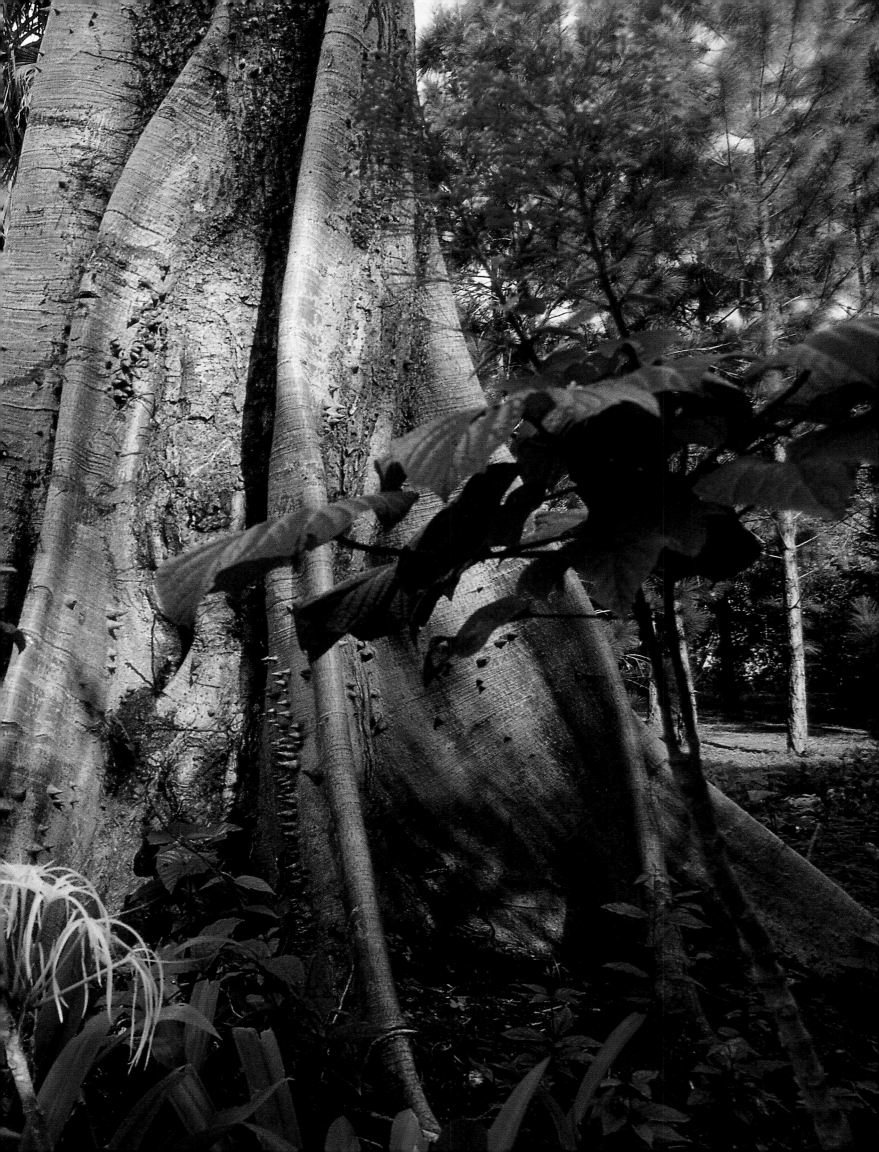

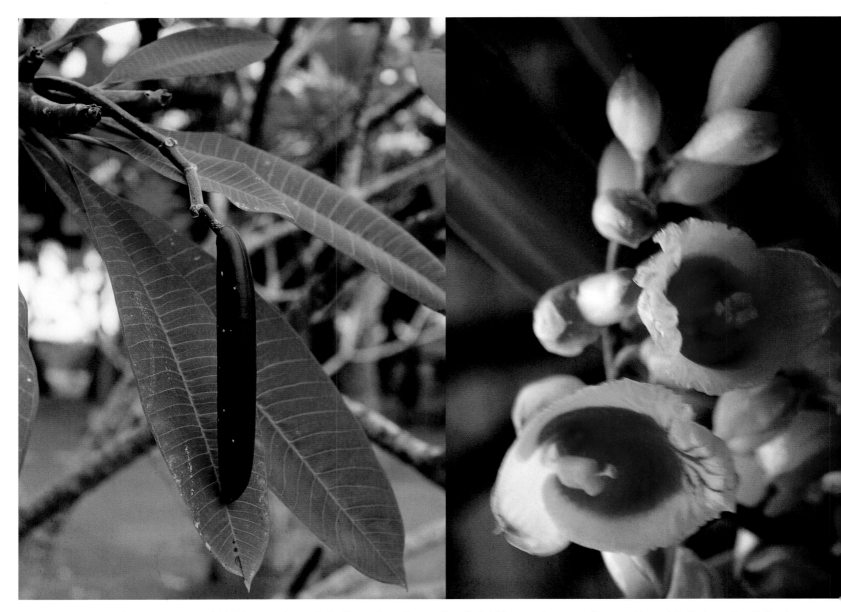

❋ **ABOVE AND FACING PAGE** The *cassia javanica*, which belongs to the acacia family, produces clusters of small pink blossoms that carpet the ground beneath it. In the garden, fleshy plants, orchids and shrubs create a symphony of colours. ❋ **OBEN UND RECHTE SEITE** Die *cassia javanica*, eine Akazienart, blüht in Trauben kleiner rosa Blüten, die einen Teppich von Blütenblättern hervorbringen. Im Garten wachsen Sukkulenten, mit Orchideen bewachsene Baumstämme und kleine Sträucher – eine wahre Symphonie der Farben. ❋ **CI-DESSUS ET PAGE DE DROITE** Le *cassia javanica*, de l'espèce des acacias, produit des grappes de petites fleurs roses qui s'étalent sur le sol comme un tapis de pétales. Dans le jardin, plantes grasses, souches d'orchidées et arbustes forment une symphonie de couleurs.

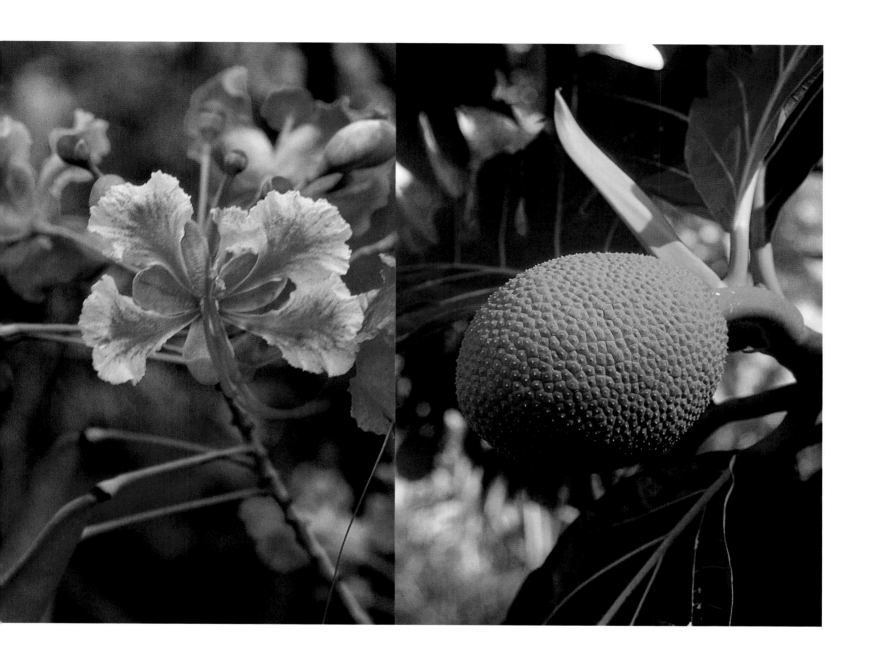

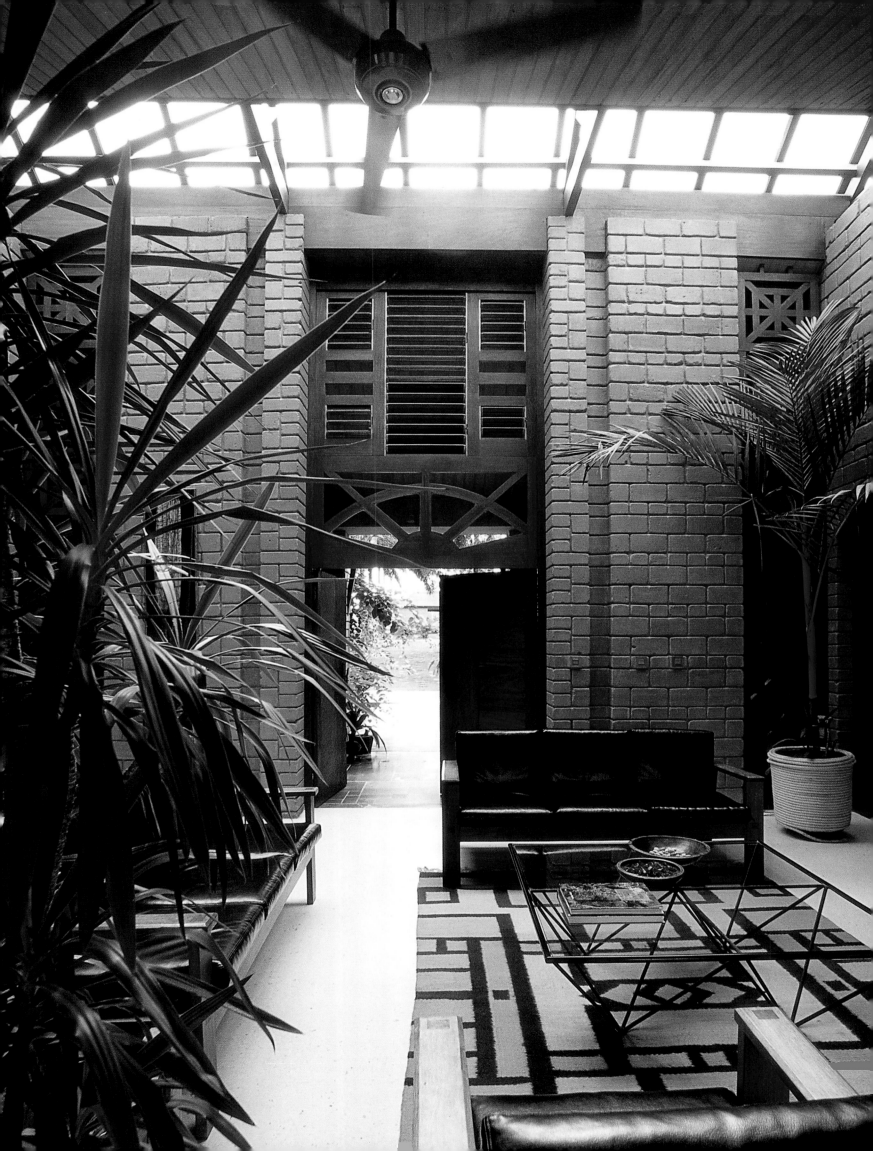

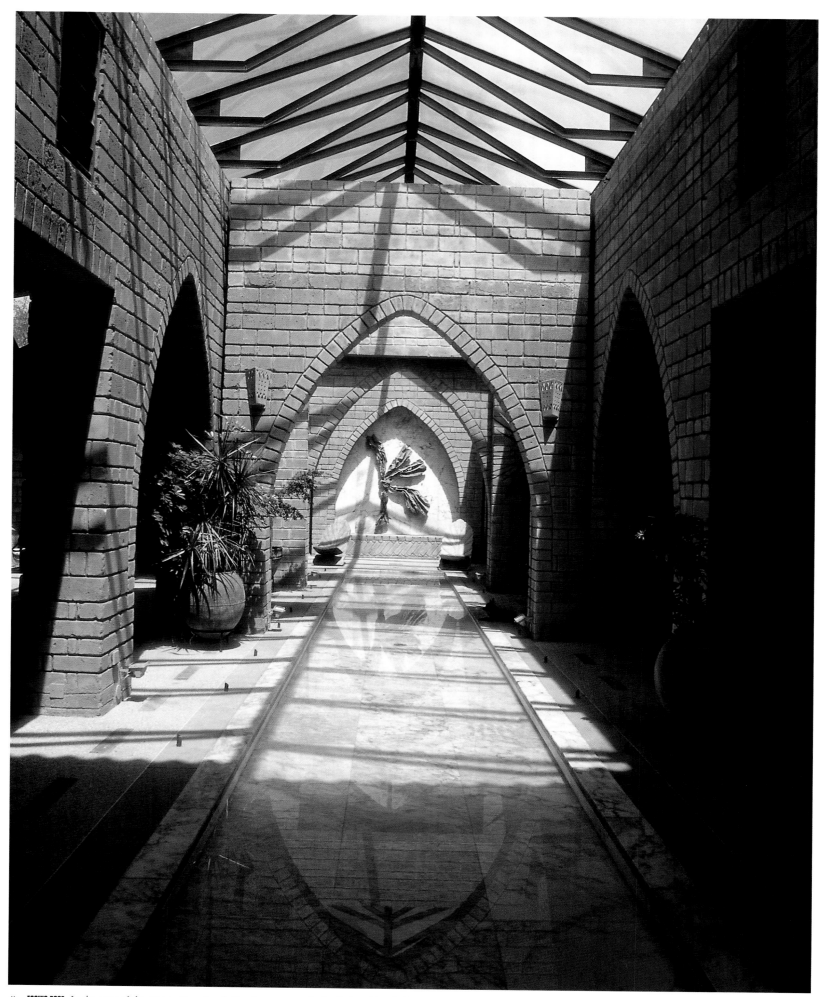

❋ **FACING PAGE** In the eyes of the owner, Yves Lambelin, these geometrically designed brick floors and walls are decorative elements in themselves. **ABOVE** An ingenious natural ventilation system avoids the drawbacks of air-conditioning. ❋ **LINKE SEITE** Nach Auffassung des Hausherrn Yves Lambelin sind die geometrisch gestalteten Ziegelböden und -mauern an sich schon Dekoration. **OBEN** Das einfallsreiche Ventilationssystem, das sich auf eine natürliche Belüftung stützt, hat nicht die unangenehmen Begleiterscheinungen einer Klimaanlage. ❋ **PAGE DE GAUCHE** Dans l'esprit du propriétaire Yves Lambelin, les sols et les murs en briques aux formes géométriques sont déjà éléments de décoration. **CI-DESSUS** L'ingénieux système de ventilation naturelle évite les désagréments de la climatisation.

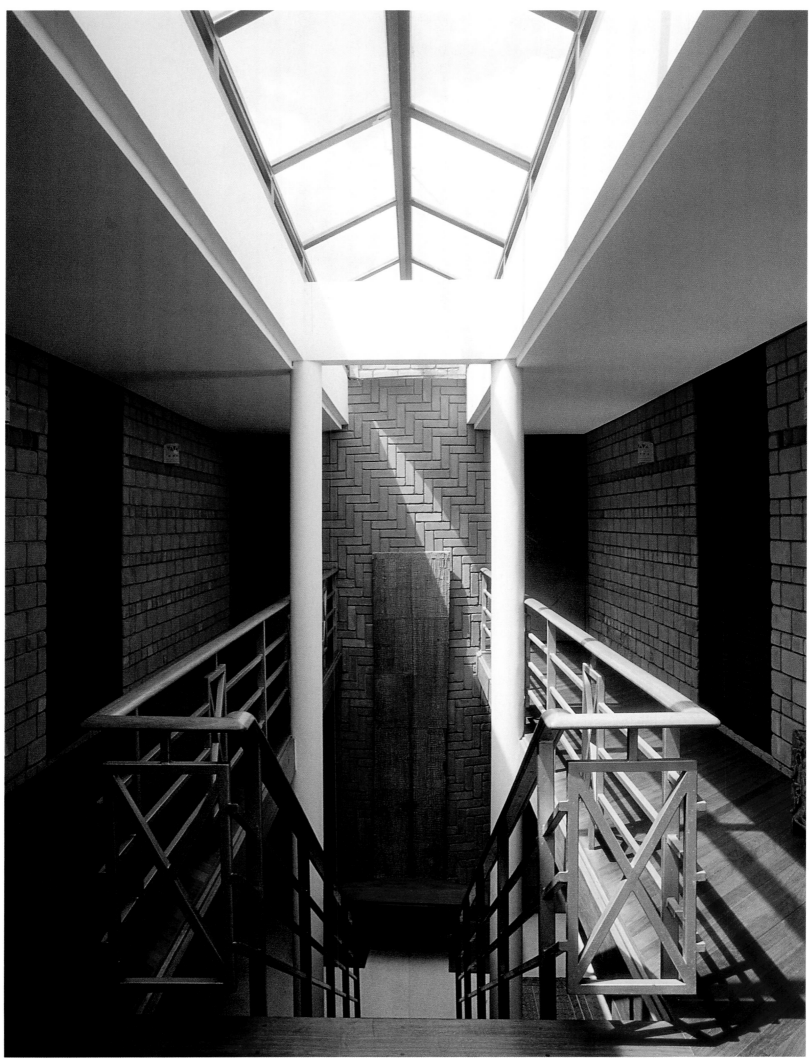

※ **FACING PAGE** Apart from its materials, the harmony of this building derives from its openings to the outside. The light varies according to the time of day, thanks to the well of sunshine that illuminates the house. **RIGHT** Under this piece of pottery from Mali, the motifs of the floor are inspired by the dance tradition of the former Zaïre. **BELOW** The armchairs and sofas in the salon were designed by Jean-Pierre Thomas, the architect's brother, who lives in Abidjan. ※ **LINKE SEITE** Neben dem Baumaterial sorgen die Fenster in diesem Haus für eine harmonische Atmosphäre. Je nach Tageszeit herrscht eine andere Stimmung, geprägt durch den Lichteinfall ins Haus. **RECHTS** Tontöpfe aus Mali auf einem Boden, dessen Muster von Tanzschritten aus dem früheren Zaire inspiriert ist. **UNTEN** Die Sessel und Kanapees im Salon wurden nach Entwürfen von Jean-Pierre Thomas angefertigt. Der Designer, ein Bruder des Architekten, lebt in Abidjan. ※ **PAGE DE GAUCHE** Outre les matériaux, l'harmonie de cette maison est donnée par les ouvertures. La lumière varie à toute heure de la journée grâce au puit de soleil qui illumine la maison. **À DROITE** Sous la poterie du Mali, les motifs du sol sont inspirés de pas de danse typiques de l'ex-Zaïre. **CI-DESSOUS** Dans le salon, les fauteuils et les canapés ont été dessinés par Jean-Pierre Thomas, designer établi à Abidjan et frère de l'architecte.

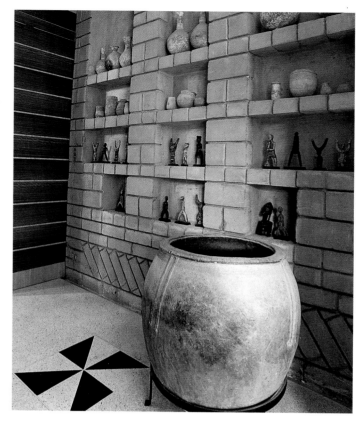

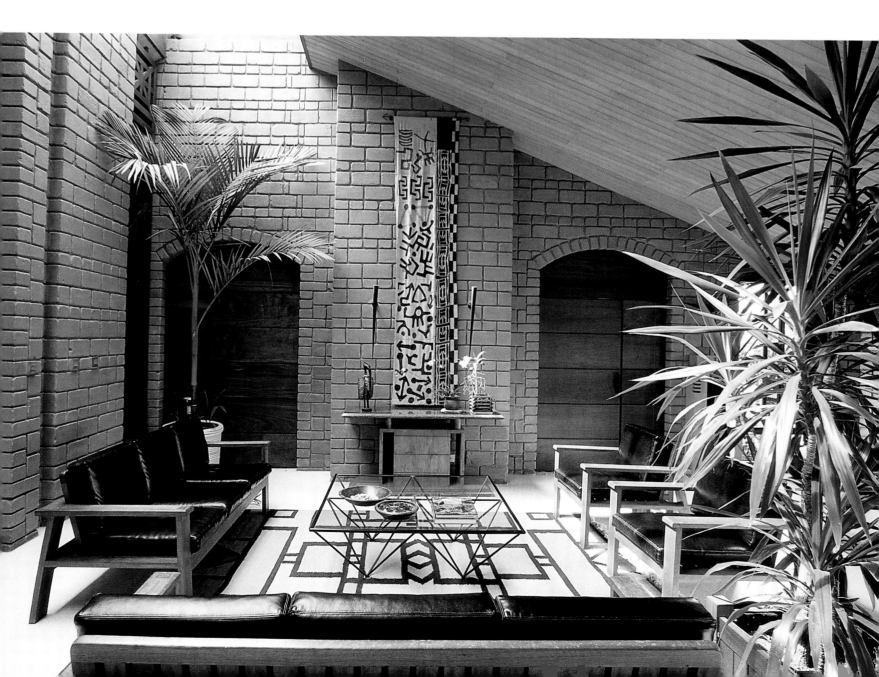

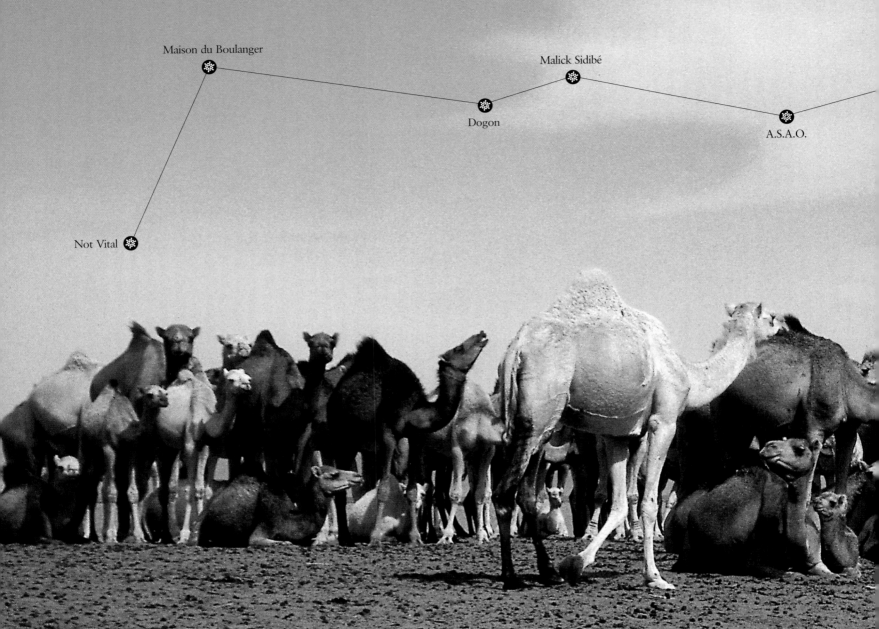

Maison du Boulanger

Malick Sidibé

Dogon

A.S.A.O.

Not Vital

# NIGER, MALI, SENEGAL, MAURITANIA

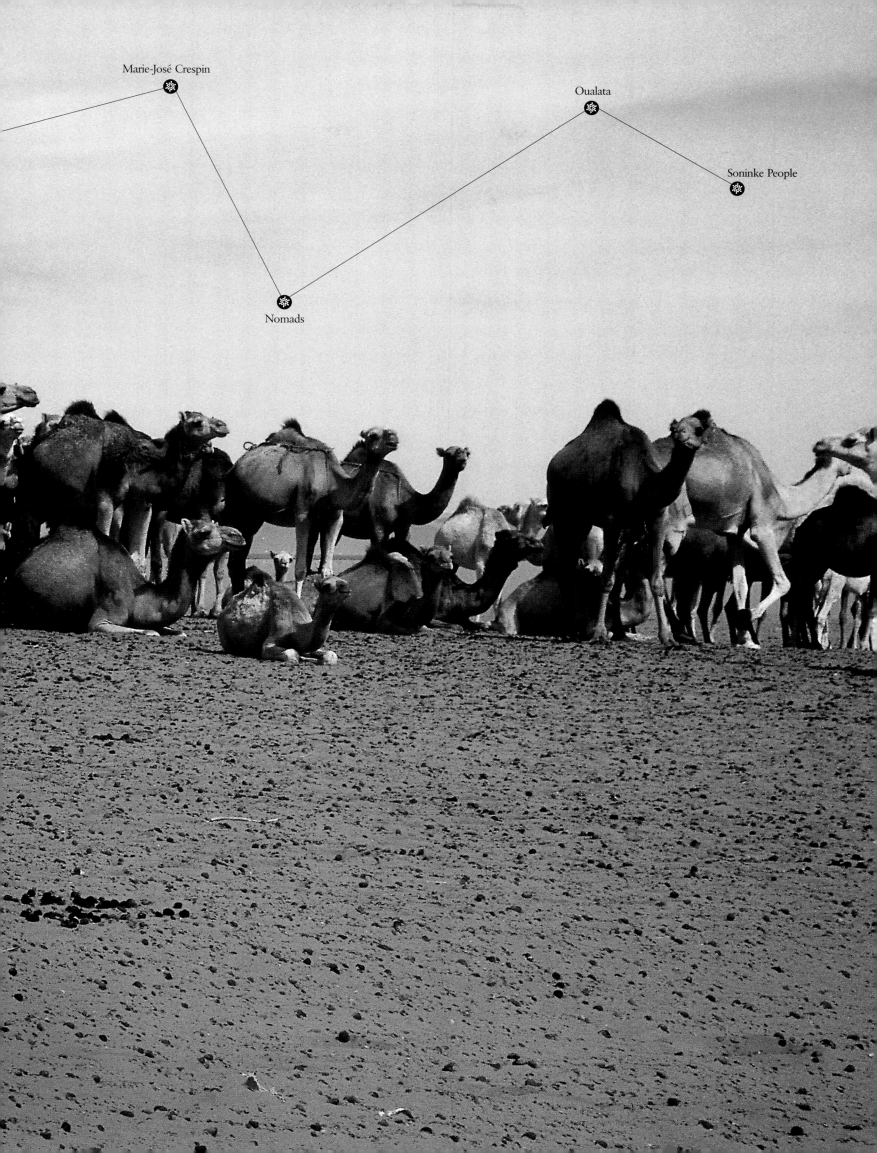

Marie-José Crespin

Oualata

Soninke People

Nomads

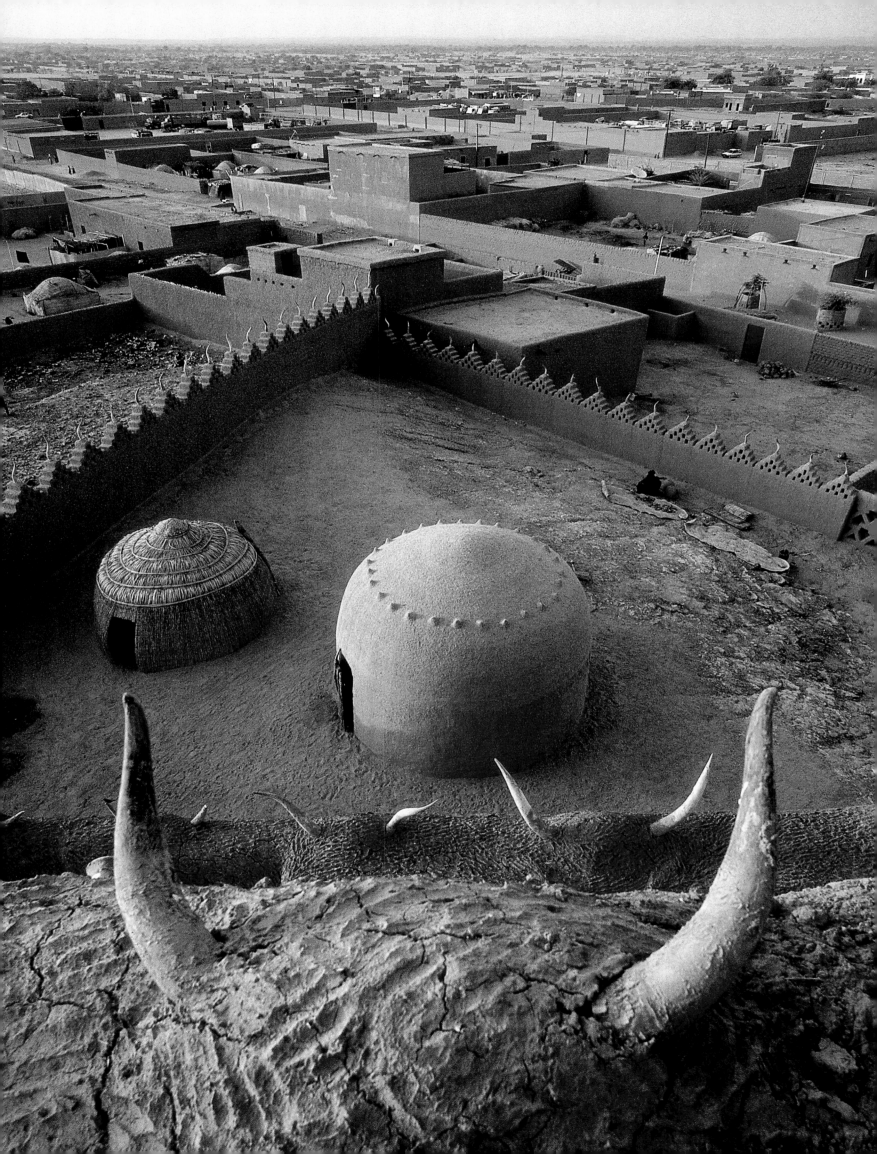

# NOt Vital
## Agadez

A sculptor living among the Tuaregs,
in whose work the animal and mineral elements are made one.

*Not Vital – half man, half animal* is the title of a documentary film about the Swiss sculptor – and indeed, nature and culture are combined in the work of this artist.

Not Vital draws his inspiration from the air of his mountain birthplace, though he lives between America, Switzerland and Italy. A lover of wide open spaces, he has also built himself a house in Niger, fulfilling his dream of an architecture truly capable of melting into the landscape. The result is perfectly adapted to Agadez, where the dunes of the Ténéré meet the mountains of Air, and represents a new departure in the artist's work. From the walls of his house you can see a city of perfectly-preserved Sudanese buildings, with walls of ochre banco (mud) and a mosque built in 1515 studded with wooden piles. The signs of wealth are clearly visible in the facades of the old parts of town, especially on the house of the chief of the bakers, with its meticulously carved and coloured walls. It is a city that appears suspended in time, peopled by blue-robed Tuaregs.

*Not Vital – Half Man, Half Animal* lautet der Titel eines Dokumentarfilms über den Schweizer Künstler. Not Vital, geprägt durch die Bergwelt seiner Heimat, lässt in seinen Werken Natur und Kultur aufeinandertreffen.

Der Künstler, der in den Vereinigten Staaten, der Schweiz und Italien lebt, liebt weite Landschaften und hat sich mit seinem Haus in Niger einen Traum verwirklicht: eine Architektur, die mit der Landschaft verschmilzt. Der Bau passt wunderbar nach Agadez, das die Dünen der Ténéré mit den Air-Bergen verbindet. Dieses Haus eröffnet Not Vital einen neuen Weg in seiner Arbeit. Es bietet ihm die Möglichkeit, die Verwandlungen des Lebens in einem einzigen Augenblick einzufangen. Von den Mauern seines Hauses blickt man auf eine perfekt erhaltene sudanesische Architektur mit ockerfarbenen Lehmbauten und eine auf Holzpfählen errichtete Moschee aus dem Jahr 1515. In den alten Stadtvierteln zeugen die fein ziselierten und kolorierten Wände vom Reichtum der Stadt. Agadez lebt, losgelöst von der Zeit, im Rhythmus der blauen Gewänder der Tuareg, die im Wind schlagen.

*Not Vital – Mi homme, mi animal*, c'est le titre d'un film consacré au sculpteur suisse. Nature et culture se rejoignent dans l'œuvre de cet artiste inspiré par l'air de ses montagnes natales.

Not Vital habite entre l'Amérique, la Suisse et l'Italie. Amoureux des grands espaces, il réalise au Niger une maison qui incarne son rêve: une architecture capable de se fondre dans le paysage. La construction s'adapte parfaitement à Agadez qui marie les dunes du Ténéré et les montagnes de l'Aïr. Cette maison ouvre une nouvelle voie dans le travail de Not Vital, elle lui permet de capter l'instant à travers les métamorphoses de l'être. Des murs de sa maison, on contemple une architecture soudanaise parfaitement conservée avec des maisons en banco de couleur ocre et sa mosquée hérissée de pieux en bois construite en 1515. Les signes de richesse s'étalent sur les façades des vieux quartiers, particulièrement du côté de la maison du «chef des boulangers» aux murs finement ciselés et colorés. La ville vit suspendue dans le temps au rythme des robes bleues des Touaregs qui claquent dans le vent.

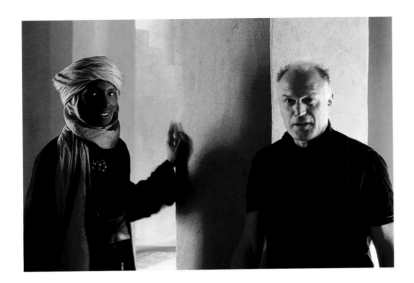

❋ **PAGE 330** The house is in the very heart of the town, with terraces decorated by Not Vital with the horns of cattle. In this society, where everything finds a use of some kind, these are among the only things that are destroyed. While watching people burning the horns that are such an integral part of his sculptures, Not Vital had the idea of integrating them into his architecture too. **ABOVE** Not Vital has created a world of his own, in which the land assumes a primary dimension. **BELOW** The sculptor's bedroom, with its warm earth tones. **FACING PAGE** A Sudanese construction, with walls of ochre mud. ❋ **SEITE 330** Das Haus im Herzen der Stadt hat mehrere Terrassen, auf denen der Künstler Tierhörner platziert hat. In dieser Gesellschaft findet alles außer Horn eine Verwendung. Beim Anblick verbrennender Hörner kam Not Vital die Idee, diese, die sonst integraler Bestandteil seiner Skulpturen sind, in die Architektur einzubeziehen. **OBEN** Hier schuf Not Vital seine ganz eigene Welt, in der dem Land eine ursprüngliche Dimension zukommt. **UNTEN** Warme Erdtöne dominieren das Schlafzimmer des Bildhauers. Eine schmale Doppeltreppe führt auf eine Terrasse. **RECHTE SEITE** Die sudanesische Bauweise mit ihren ockerfarbenen Lehmwänden. ❋ **PAGE 330** En plein cœur de la ville, la maison est dotée de terrasses où l'artiste a implanté des cornes de bétail. Dans cette société ou tout sert, les cornes sont les seules a être détruites. En voyant brûler les cornes qui font sinon partie intégrante de ses sculptures, Not Vital a eu l'idée de les intégrer à l'architecture. **CI-DESSUS** Not Vital recrée ici son univers où la terre prend sa dimension première. **CI-DESSOUS** La chambre du sculpteur est bordée des tons chauds de la terre. Un double escalier très étroit donne accès à une terrasse. **PAGE DE DROITE** Une construction soudanaise avec ses murs en banco de couleur ocre.

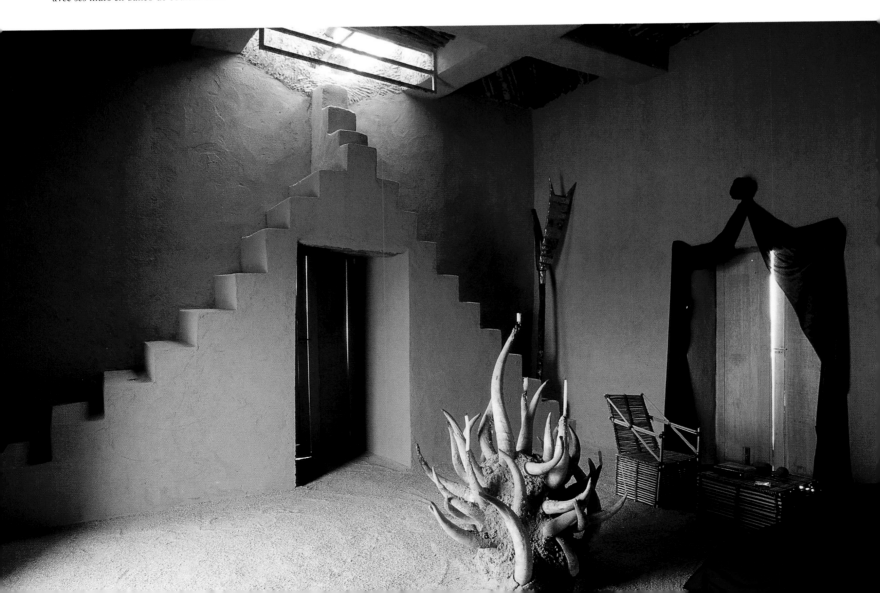

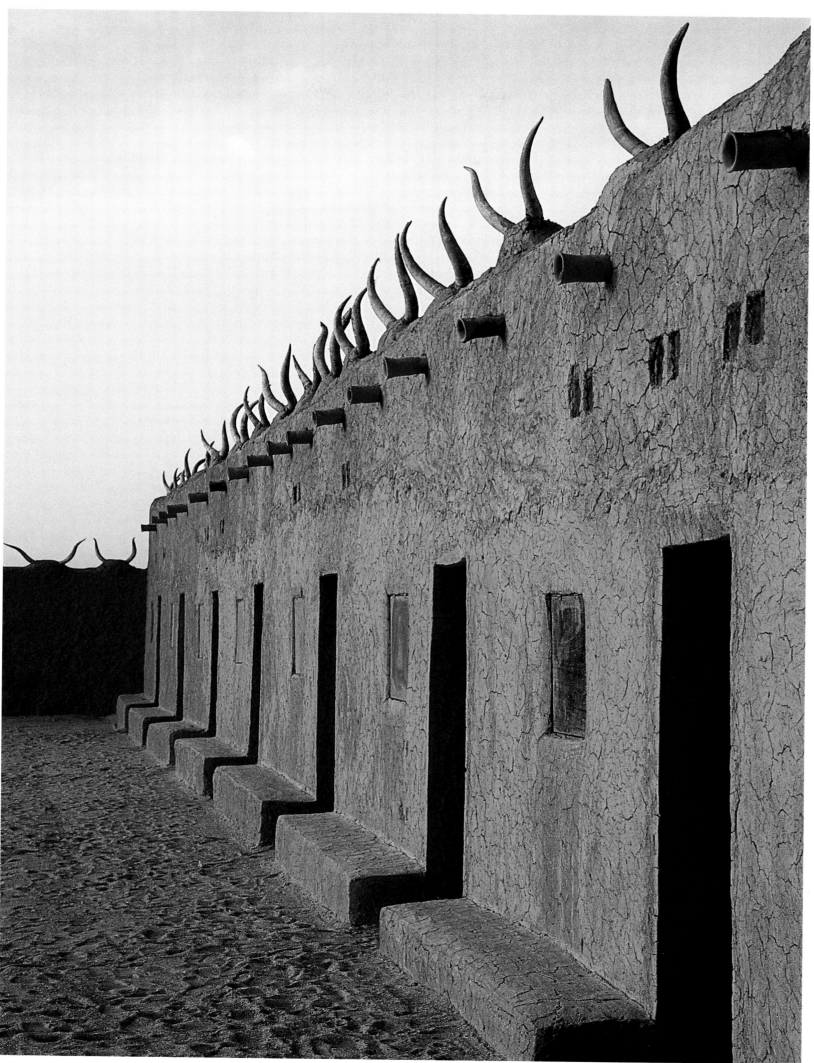

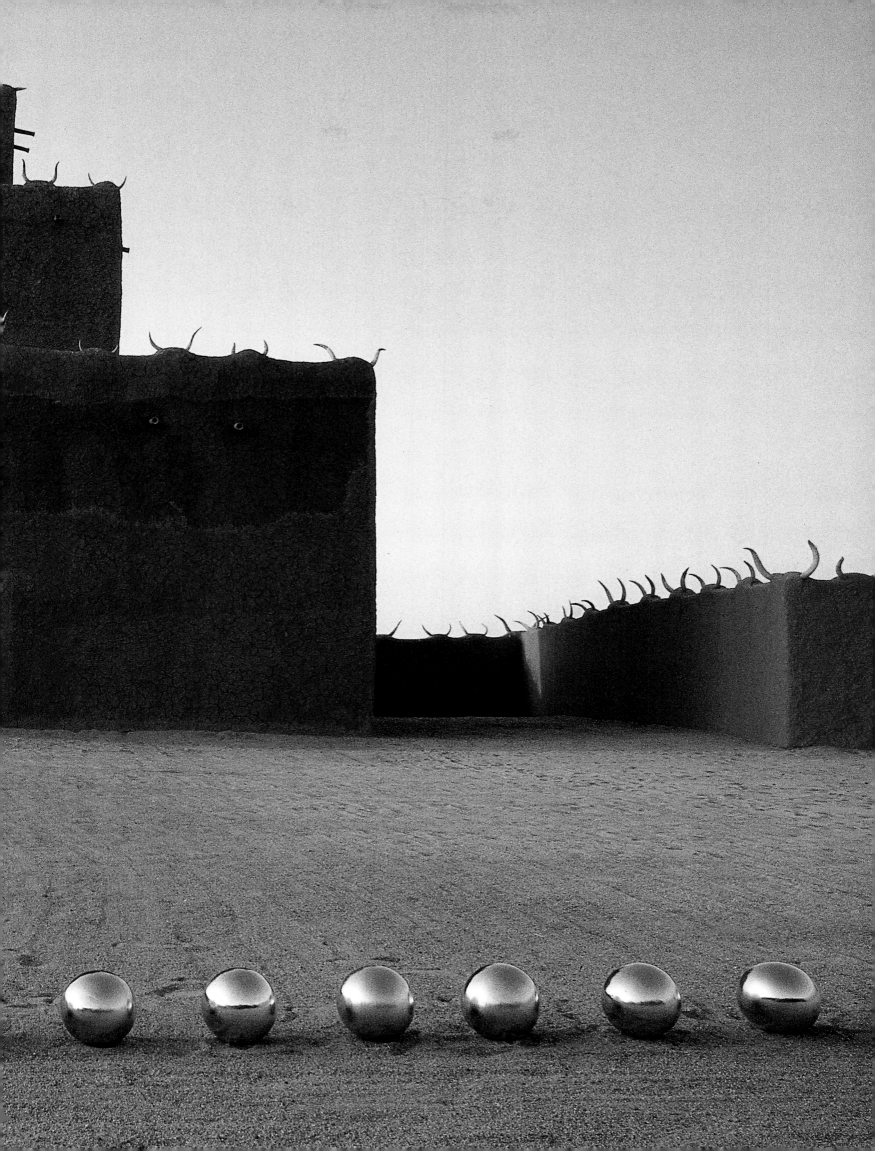

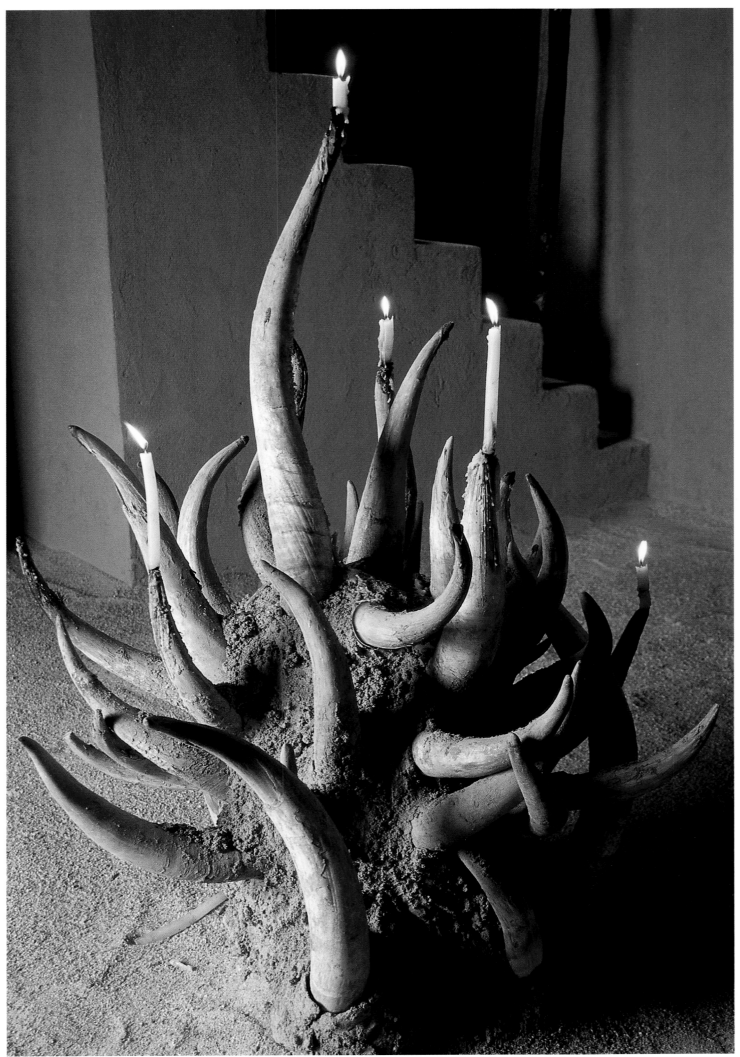

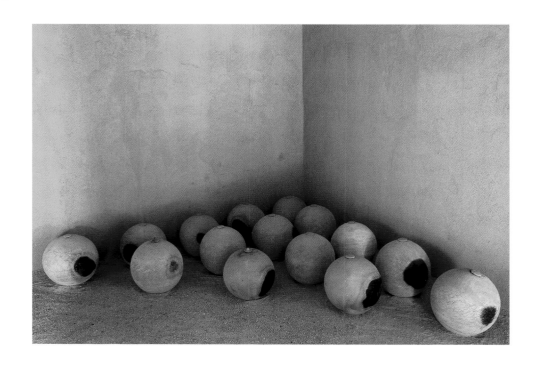

※ **PRECEEDING PAGES** Horns on the walls: a ghostly but somehow protective presence. A sculpture in the courtyard entitled *Camel*, consisting of thirteen silver balls containing the mortal remains of an entire camel. The house is on three levels, seemingly protected by the cattle horns set into the walls surrounding it. **FACING PAGE** An oversized candlestick made of a cow's horn, an ingenious lighting system. ※ **VORHERGEHENDE DOPPELSEITE** Gespenstisch wirken die Hörner, die wie Wachtposten auf den Mauern stehen. Im Hof ist die Skulptur »Camel« aufgebaut. Die 13 Silberkugeln enthalten die sterblichen Reste eines ganzen Kamels. Das Haus erstreckt sich über drei Stockwerke, bewacht von den Tierhörnern auf den Umfassungsmauern. **LINKE SEITE** Ein übergroßer Kerzenleuchter aus Tierhorn, ein findiges Beleuchtungssystem. ※ **PAGE DE GAUCHE** Un chandelier surdimensionné en corne de bétail, système ingénieux d'éclairage. **DOUBLE PAGE PRÉCÉDENTE** Présence fantomatique de la faune, ces cornes postées comme des sentinelles sur les murs. Dans la cour est exposée la sculpture «Camel». 13 boules en argent contenant les restes d'un chameau entier. La maison s'élève sur trois niveaux, gardée par des cornes de bétail que l'on retrouve sur les murs d'enceinte.

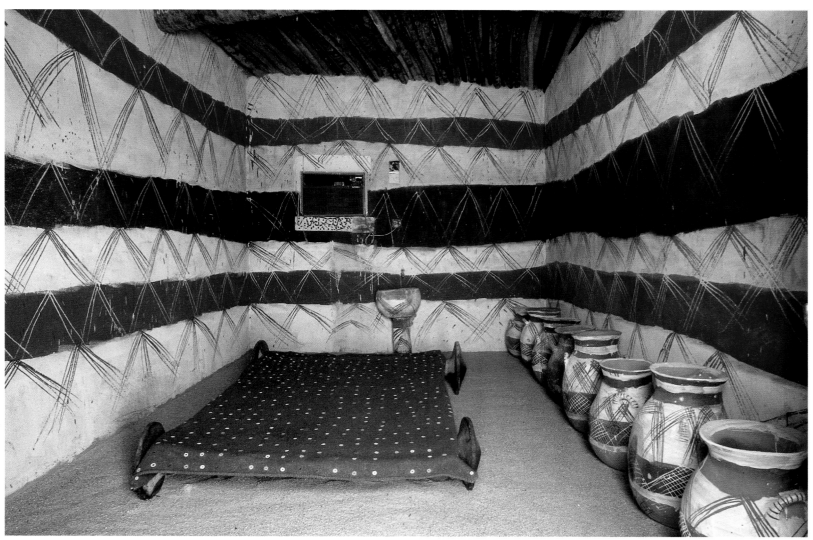

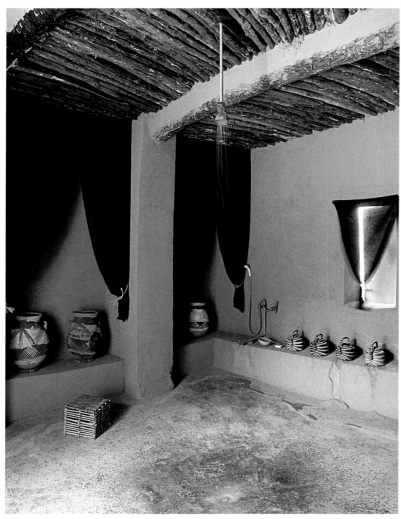
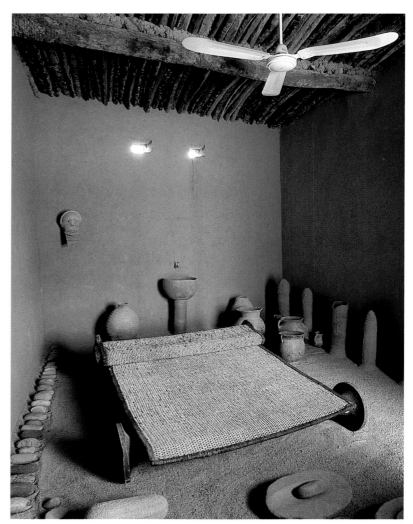
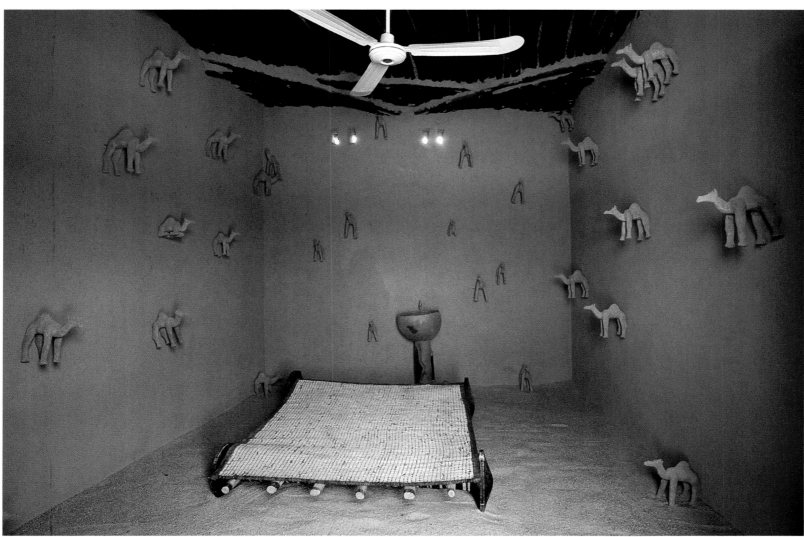

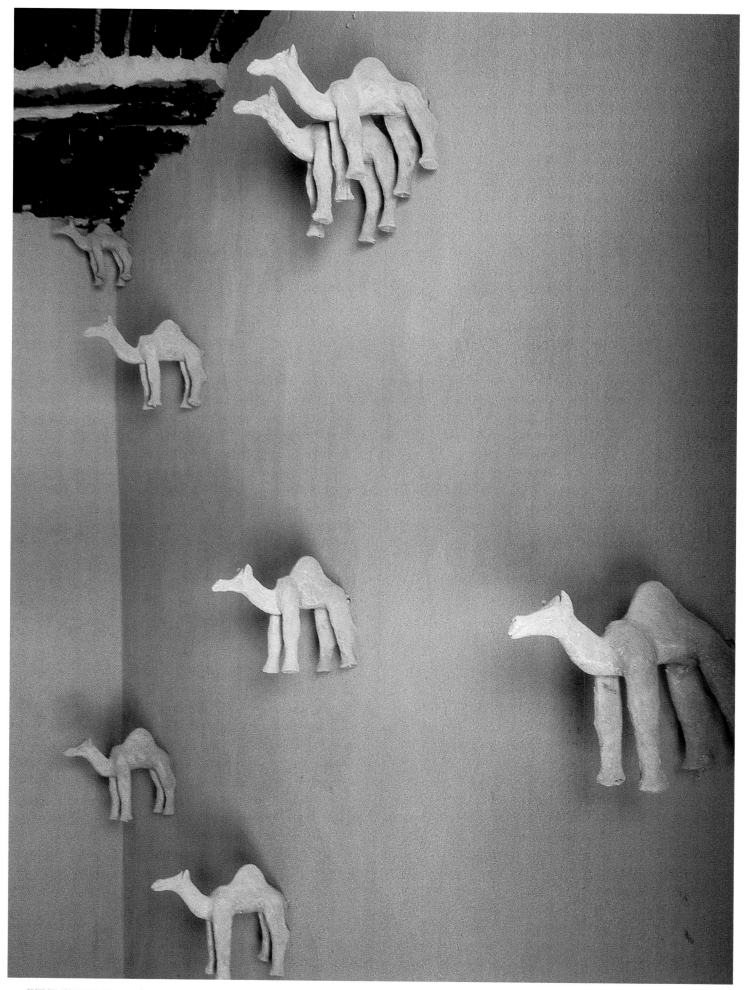

※ **ABOVE AND FACING PAGE** Not Vital's own creative work is in perfect harmony with the traditional paintings and austere Tuareg beds. ※ **OBEN UND LINKE SEITE** Not Vitals freie Kreativität harmoniert gut mit den traditionellen Gemälden und den spartanischen Betten der Tuareg. ※ **CI-DESSUS ET PAGE DE GAUCHE** La créativité débridée de l'artiste et le recours aux peintures traditionnelles s'harmonisent avec le mobilier spartiate: lits touaregs.

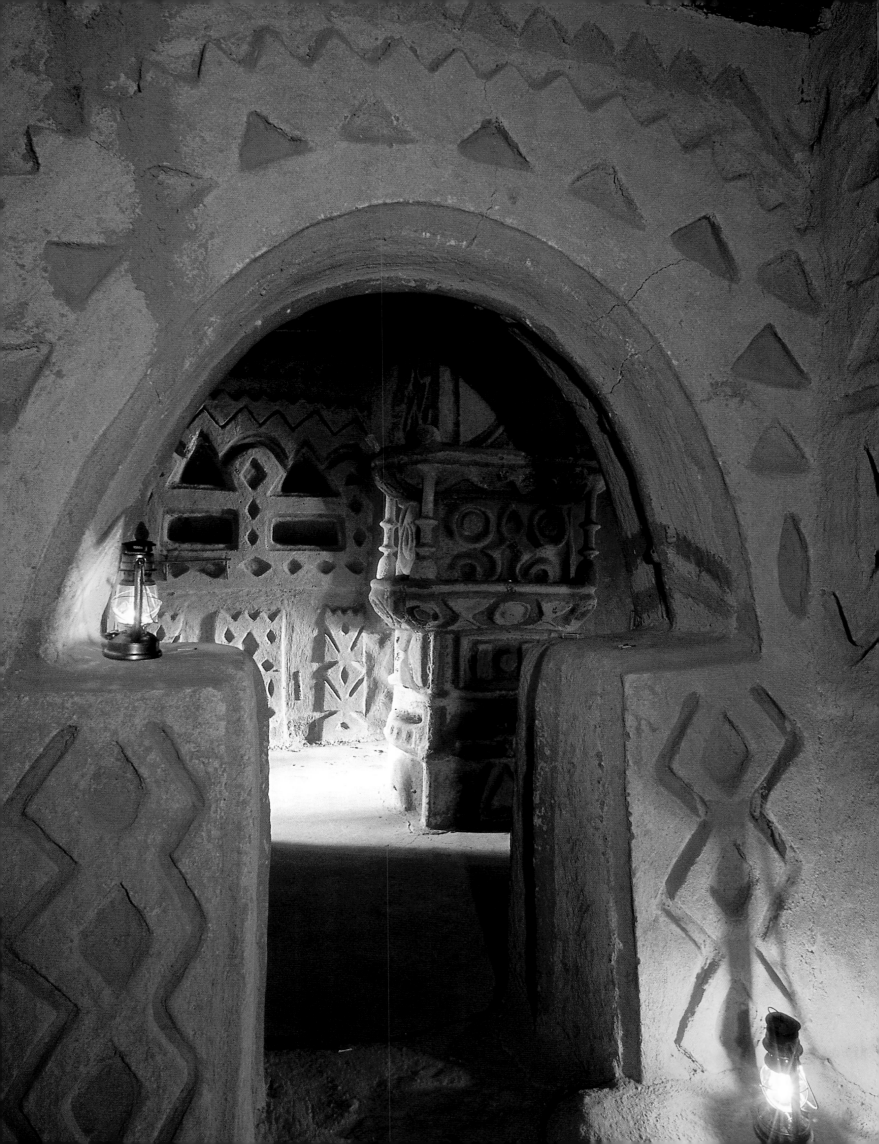

# MAISON DU BOULANGER

## AGADEZ

A traditional Tuareg house, where bread for the town has been made for many centuries.

---

In this holy city of Islam, there is no changing of water into wine. But the baker continues to make countless loaves in his traditional oven.

Here at the edge of the desert, not far from the sultan's palace from which the Imam or *cadi* oversees the spiritual life of the 159 tribes of the region, there is a palpable sense of religious sanctity. The Tuaregs who have imposed their character on Agadez have adapted the Muslim religion to their nomadic existence. Their piety and respect for the Koran run deep, but with them they have also preserved their ancestral beliefs, in which dialogue with the spirit world plays an important part. Thus, in order to heal wounds or ward off ill luck, their mud walls are decorated with talismanic motifs. On the outside of the baker's house, a dome typical of Sudanese architecture responds just as faithfully to the projecting beams and to the openings which, like fantastic corridors, lead to rooms where Tuareg and religious motifs blend comfortably with chests and niches. The contrast of bright light and deep shadow is everywhere, as is the pervasive odour of baking bread. Taste it, and you will be transfigured.

In dieser heiligen Stadt des Islam verwandelt man kein Wasser in Wein. Und doch zog einst der Bäcker aus seinem traditionellen Ofen unzählige Brötchen.

Am Rande der Wüste, nicht weit vom Palast des Sultans, wo der Imam oder *cadi* über das spirituelle Leben von 159 Stämmen der Region wacht, ist man erfüllt von religiösem Geist. Die Tuareg haben Agadez geprägt und die muslimische Religion an ihr Nomadenleben angepasst. Obwohl sie dem Koran treu und respektvoll gegenüberstehen, bewahren sie doch den eng mit der Geisterwelt verbundenen Glauben ihrer Vorfahren. So haben die Dekorationen auf den Wänden der Lehmhäuser die Funktion von Talismännern. Sie sollen Glück bringen bzw. Unglück abwenden und Krankheiten heilen. Das Maison du boulanger entspricht auch von außen der sudanesischen Architektur, mit der typischen Kuppel, den vorspringenden Balken, den Türöffnungen, die zu den Räumen führen, in deren Nischen Tuareg-Symbole und religiöse Motive der Muslime sich vermengen. Der starke Kontrast zwischen Hell und Dunkel ist allgegenwärtig so wie einst wohl der Duft frisch gebackenen Brotes. Eine Kostprobe ist eine geradezu transzendente Erfahrung.

Dans cette ville sainte, Islam oblige, on ne transforme pas l'eau en vin. Mais le boulanger, lui, tirait à l'époque de son four traditionnel une infinité de petits pains.

À la lisière du désert, non loin du palais du sultan où siège l'imam, le *cadi* qui contrôle les 159 tribus de la région, la référence sacrée s'impose dans les esprits. Les Touaregs qui façonnent Agadez ont adapté la religion musulmane à leur vie nomade. Fidèles et respectueux du Coran, ils conservent néanmoins leurs croyances ancestrales si attachées à un dialogue avec le monde des esprits. Ainsi, afin de guérir des blessures ou d'éloigner le malheur, les murs en terre de banco, semblables à des talismans, sont décorés de motifs destinés à attirer la chance. À l'extérieur de la maison du boulanger, le dôme typique de l'architecture soudanaise, répond tout aussi fidèlement aux poutres saillantes, aux ouvertures qui, tels des passages fantastiques, mènent à des pièces où s'entrecroisent motifs touaregs, signes religieux et niches voisinant avec des coffres-forts. Le contraste entre ombre et lumière est très présent ainsi que l'odeur du pain fabriqué jadis en ces lieux au rythme des tambours. En soi, une expérience transcendante.

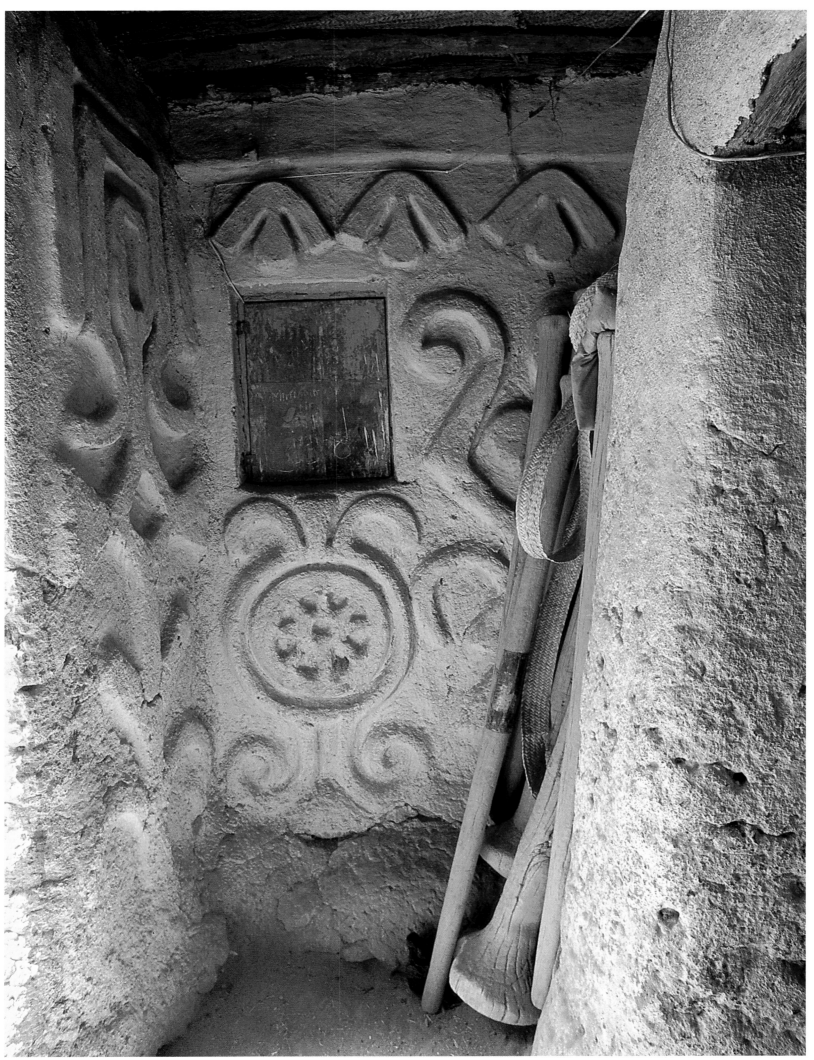

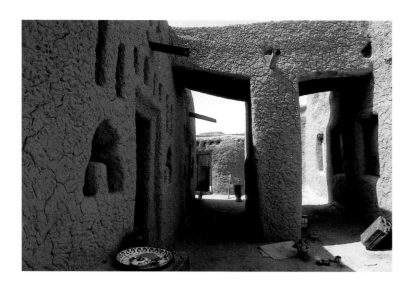

※ **FACING PAGE** The baker stacks his utensils in an earthen niche etched with Islamic motifs. **RIGHT** The passages running along the building are screened with geometrical openwork patterns. **BELOW** The ochre mud walls of the main reception room are decorated with traditional local motifs. The ceiling is a composition of tree branches.
※ **LINKE SEITE** Die Arbeitsutensilien des Bäckers in einer mit islamischen Motiven verzierten Nische. **RECHTS** Die um das Gebäude führenden Gänge sind mit geometrischen Mustern durchbrochen. **UNTEN** Der große Salon aus ockerfarbenem Lehm ist mit regionalen Motiven geschmückt. Die Decke besteht aus Holzstämmen. ※ **PAGE DE GAUCHE** Le boulanger entreposait ses outils dans une niche aux motifs islamiques ciselés dans la terre. **A DROITE** Les coursives ont été créées le long de la bâtisse avec un jeu ajouré travaillé en formes géométriques. **CI-DESSOUS** Le grand salon en terre de banco de couleur ocre est décoré de motifs d'inspiration locale. Le plafond a été façonné avec des branches d'arbres.

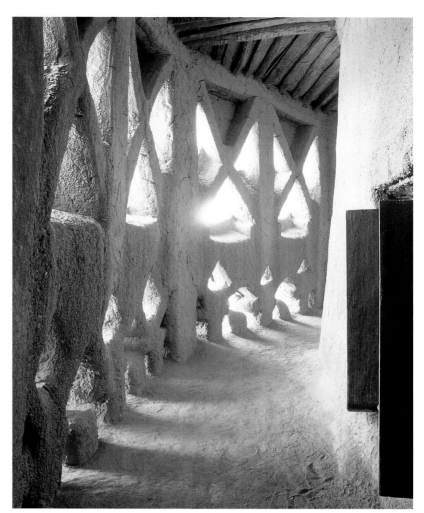

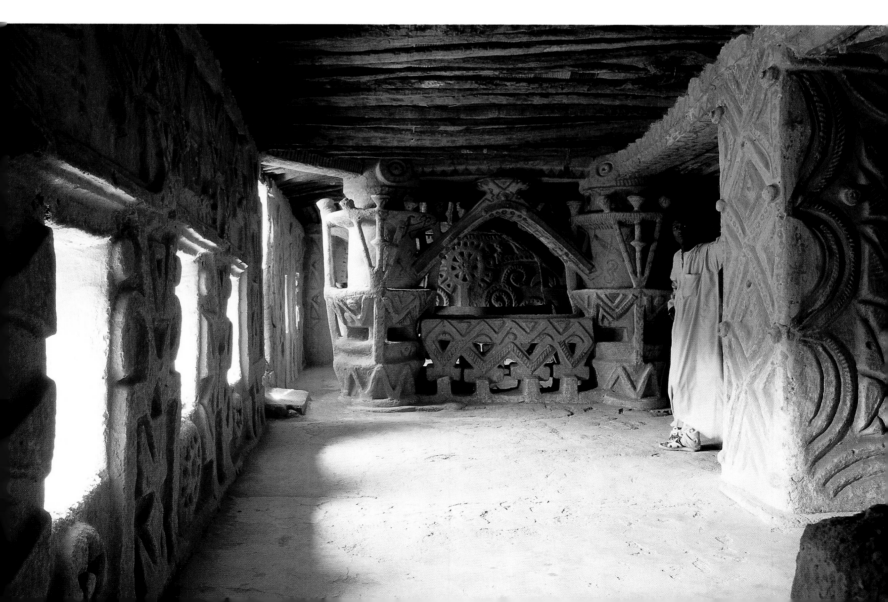

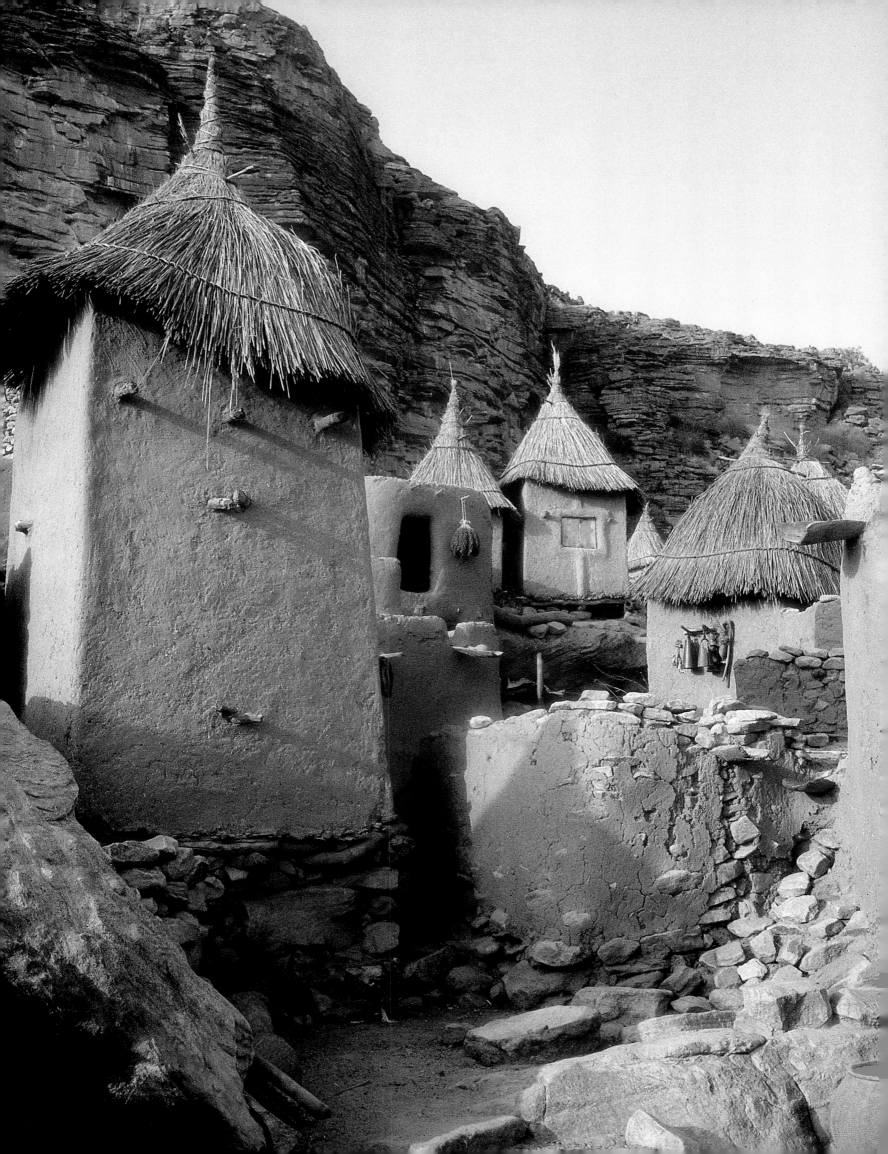

# DOGON
## BANDIAGARA FAULT

This place has fascinated travellers ever since its discovery, though its deepest meaning still baffles western logic.

Rising from the plains to a height of 800 feet, the Bandiagara fault is the most astonishing geological site in West Africa. The habitat is worthy of similar interest, to say the least.

In a zone some 200 kilometres long, the *banco* villages of ochre clay start where the cave-dwellings end. The latter were occupied by the Telem people up till the 15th century, when the Dogon arrived to build their houses and granaries at the foot and on top of the cliffs and convert the caves into tomb-sites. Today the Dogon too are still seen as somewhat mysterious. According to the ethnologists that throng the area, Dogon abodes, whether made of clay or stone, are symbolic representations of the human body. This world outside the world, which we do not understand, can impregnate a place where the dead, accused of acting against the order of the world we know, are present in every alley that twists among the huts and in every conical granary with its millet-straw thatch. At the fetish man's cave are numerous tombs; using carbon-14 techniques, researchers have established that the oldest are eight centuries old. From these eyries cut directly into the russet cliff face, the community can be seen in its authentic reality, united in the light of its cooking fires. In the far distance, the flickering lights of a Peul encampment remind us of more distant wanderings.

Der 250 Meter hohe Felsen von Bandiagara zählt zu den eindrucksvollsten geologischen Sehenswürdigkeiten in Westafrika. Die Behausungen in dieser Region sind ebenso sehenswert wie die Landschaft.

Bis 200 Kilometer weit erstrecken sich die Dörfer, gebaut aus *banco*, ockerfarbenem Lehm, am Fuß der Begräbnishöhlen in der Klippe. Bis zum 15. Jahrhundert lebte hier das Volk der Tellem, das von den Dogon vertrieben wurde, die am Fuß und oben auf der Felsenklippe Häuser und Speicher bauten, während die Höhlen den Toten vorbehalten waren. Bis heute wahren die Dogon ihre geheimnisvollen Bräuche. Den Ethnologen zufolge, die sich in dieser Region förmlich drängeln, sehen die Dogon in ihrer Behausung aus Lehm oder Stein ein Symbol des menschlichen Körpers. Diese jenseitige Welt ist für den westlichen Verstand schwer nachvollziehbar. In dieser Vorstellung sind die Toten, die beschuldigt werden, sich gegen die Weltordnung aufzulehnen, immer anwesend. Die kegelförmigen Speicher in den gewundenen Gassen sind mit Hirsestroh gedeckt. Neben der Höhle der Hohepriester liegen zahlreiche Höhlengräber (mit Hilfe der C$_{14}$-Datierung konnten Wissenschaftler das Alter der Gräber bestimmen – die ältesten sind 800 Jahre alt). Von diesen Höhlen aus, die in den rötlichen Fels geschlagen wurden, hat man einen guten Blick auf die zusammengeschweißte Gemeinschaft im Licht der Küchenherde. Aus der Ferne erinnern die Feuer eines Peul-Lagers an die ruhelosen Irrfahrten in dieser Gegend.

S'élevant sur la plaine à hauteur de 250 mètres, la faille de Bandiagara est le site géologique le plus impressionnant d'Afrique occidentale. Les habitations qui s'y trouvent sont, et c'est le moins que l'on puisse dire, à la mesure de cet intérêt.

Sur près de 200 kilomètres, les villages en *banco* (terre glaise ocre) s'enchaînent au pied de refuges troglodytes habités jusqu'au 15$^e$ siècle par le peuple Telem. Les Dogons ont débarqué dans la région à cette époque, édifiant maisons et greniers en bas et autour des falaises, tandis que les grottes, en hauteur, devenaient des lieux de sépulture. Aujourd'hui, les Dogons conservent leur part de mystère. D'après les ethnologues qui se pressent ici, leur habitat, qu'il soit en terre ou en pierre, est une représentation symbolique du corps humain. Ce monde hors du monde qui échappe à la raison occidentale, imprègne un espace où les morts, accusés d'intenter à l'ordre du monde, sont partout présents, des ruelles tortueuses aux greniers coniques coiffés de paille de mil. Du côté de la grotte des féticheurs, c'est un grand fouillis de tombeaux (à l'aide du carbone 14, les chercheurs ont daté à huit siècles les plus anciens). Depuis ces nids d'aigles creusés à même la façade rougeâtre, la communauté apparaît dans sa vérité, soudée à la lueur des foyers. Au loin, les feux d'un campement Peul rappellent une errance lointaine.

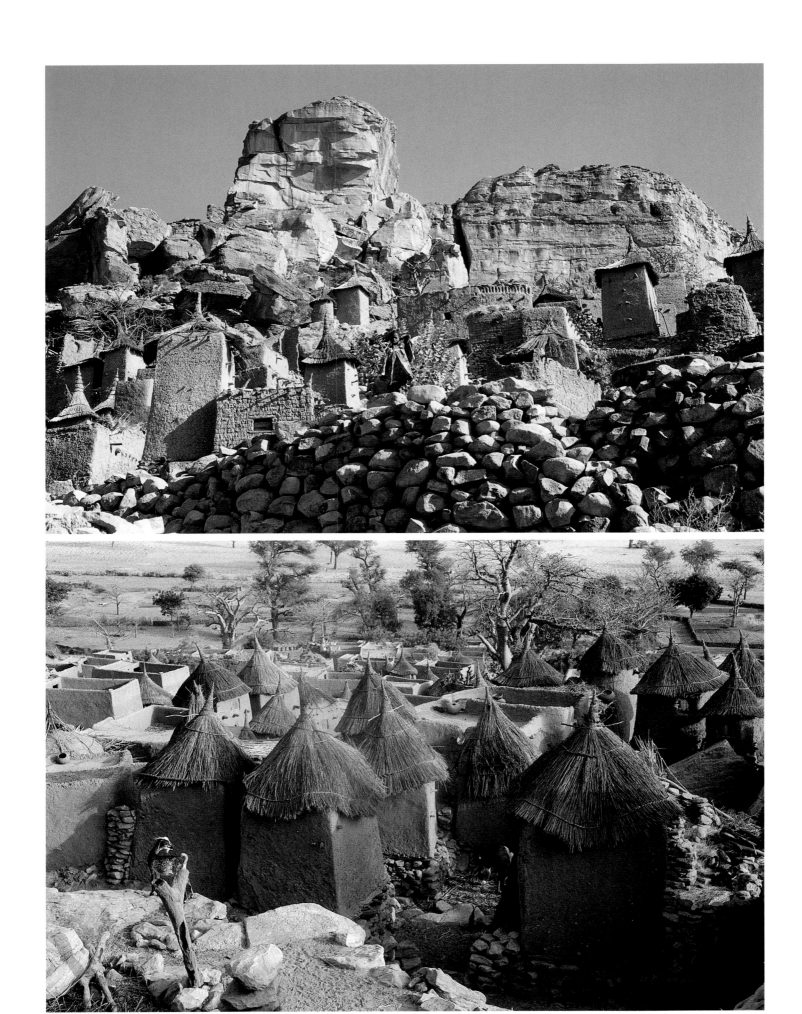

※ **ABOVE AND FACING PAGE** The *banco* (ochre clay) grain silos, thatched with millet straw, contain the food reserves of the Dogon. ※ **OBEN UND RECHTE SEITE** In den Silos aus *banco* (ockerfarbenem Lehm), die mit Hirsestroh gedeckt sind, lagern die Dogon ihre Vorräte. ※ **CI-DESSUS ET PAGE DE DROITE** Les silos en *banco* (terre glaise ocre), coiffés de paille de mil, abritent les réserves des Dogons.

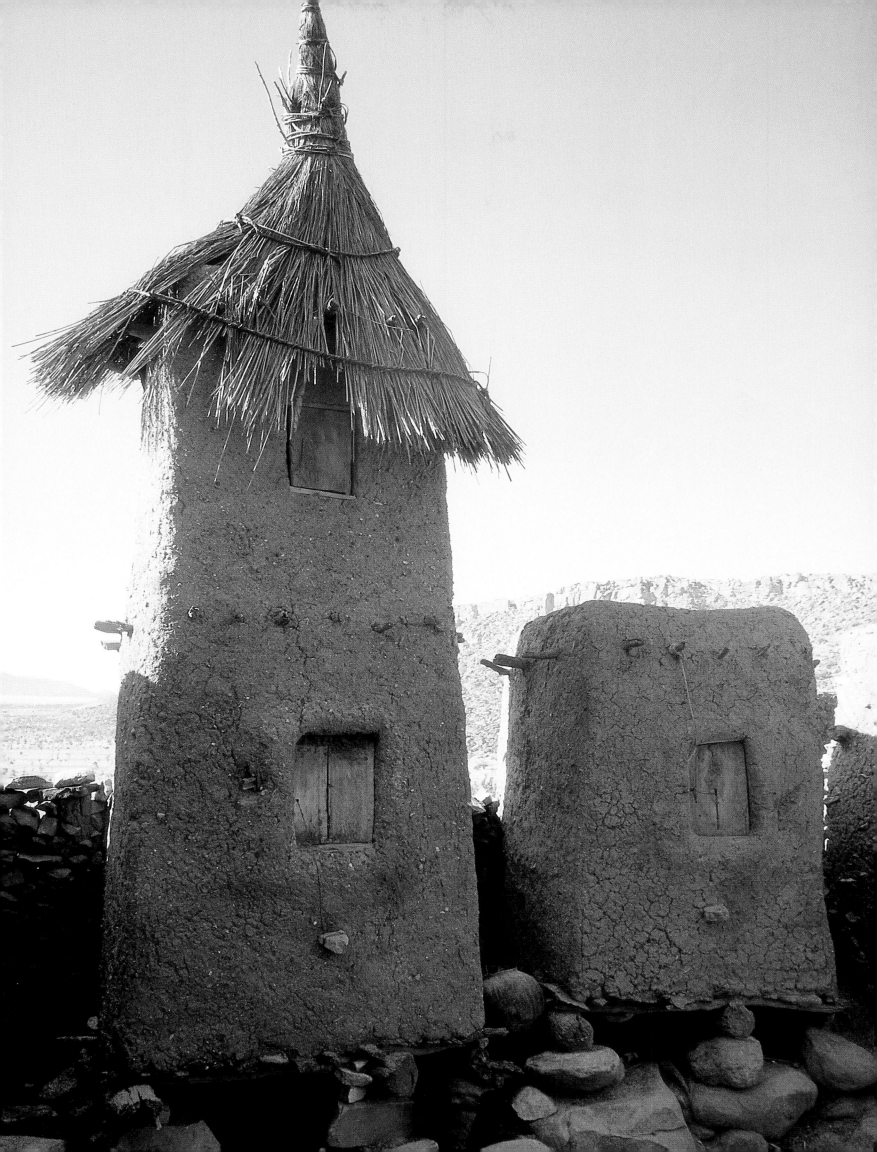

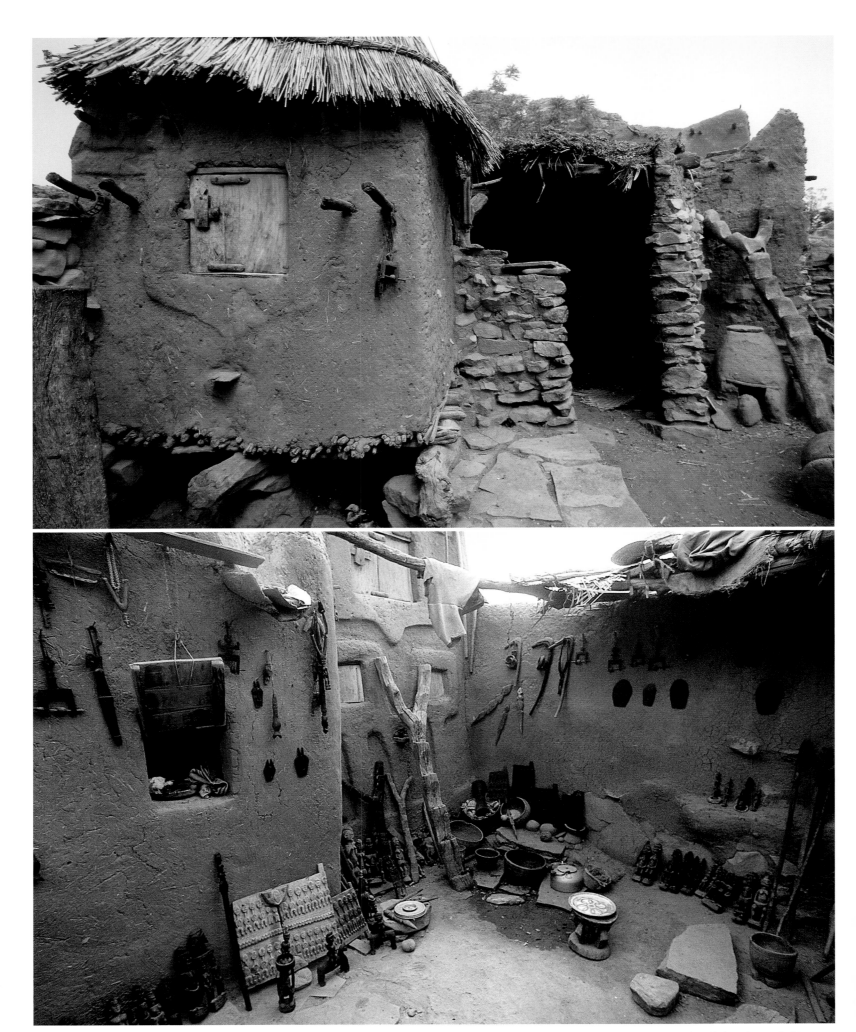

✳ **FACING PAGE** Among the Dogon, 65 different types of mask represent the denizens of the natural and supernatural worlds. Black symbolizes water, red symbolizes fire, and white symbolizes air. ✳ **RECHTE SEITE** Bei den Dogon gibt es 65 Maskenarten, die das natürliche und das übernatürliche Leben darstellen. Schwarz steht für Wasser, Rot für Feuer und Weiß für Luft. ✳ **PAGE DE DROITE** Chez les Dogons, 65 types de masques représentent les formes de la vie naturelle et surnaturelle. Le noir symbolise l'eau, le rouge le feu, et le blanc l'air.

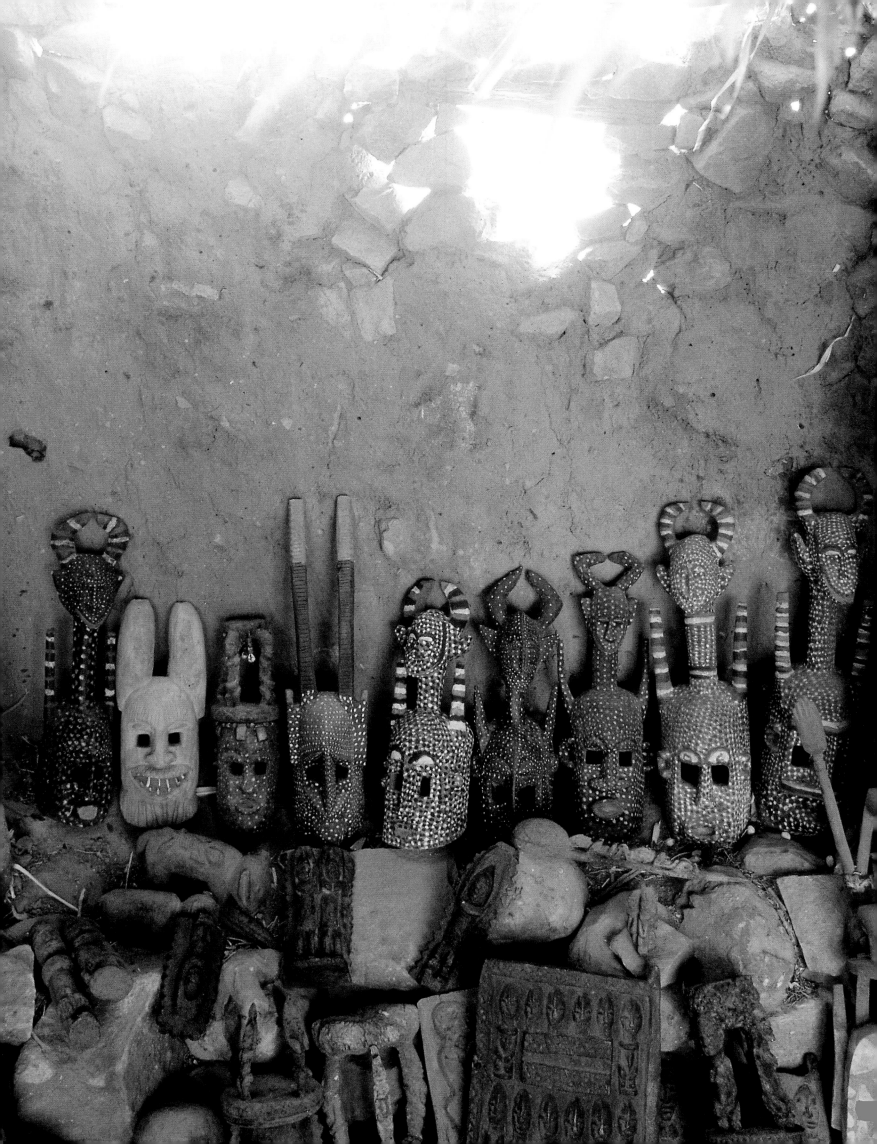

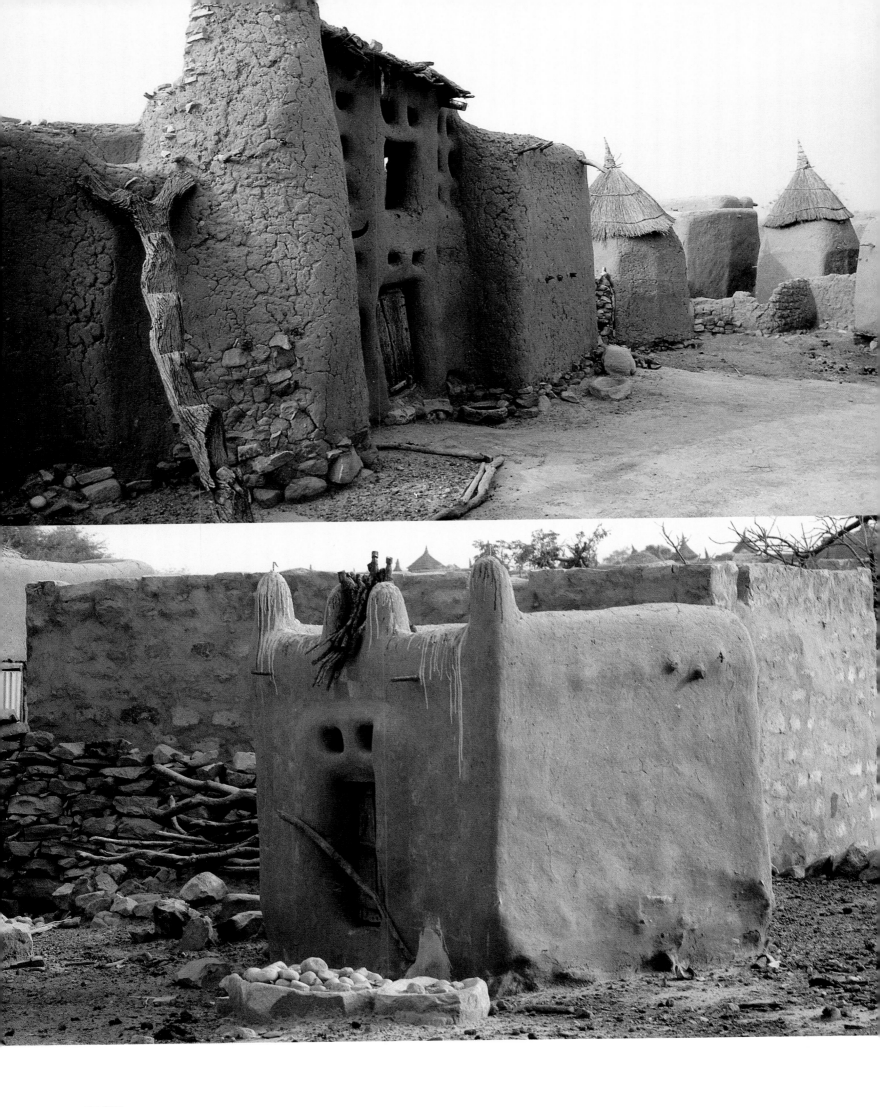

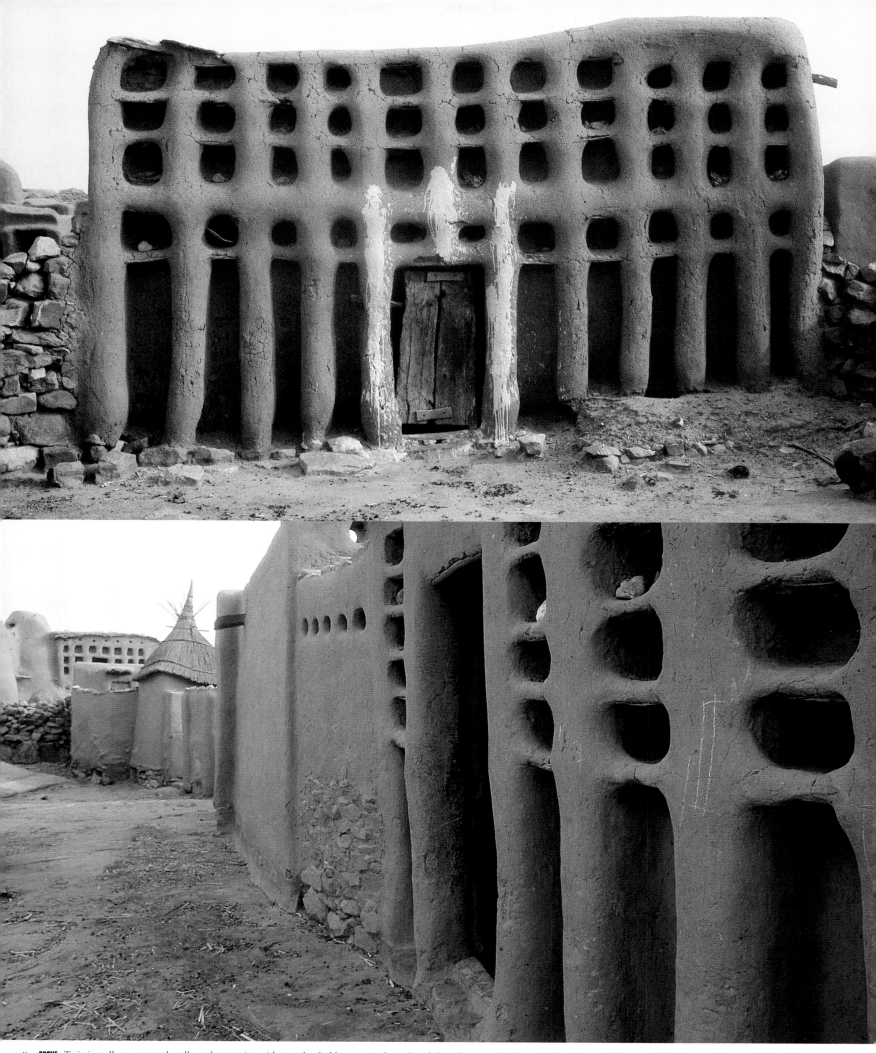

※ **ABOVE** Twisting alleys, recessed walls and granaries with wooden ladders are trademarks of the villages perched on the Bandiagara cliffs. ※ **OBEN** Krumme Gassen, Nischen in den Mauern und Speicher mit angelehnten Holzleitern sind die Markenzeichen der Dörfer an den Felsen von Bandiagara. ※ **CI-DESSUS** Ruelles tortueuses, niches aux murs et greniers dotés d'échelles en bois sont la marque des villages situés en haut de la falaise de Bandiagara.

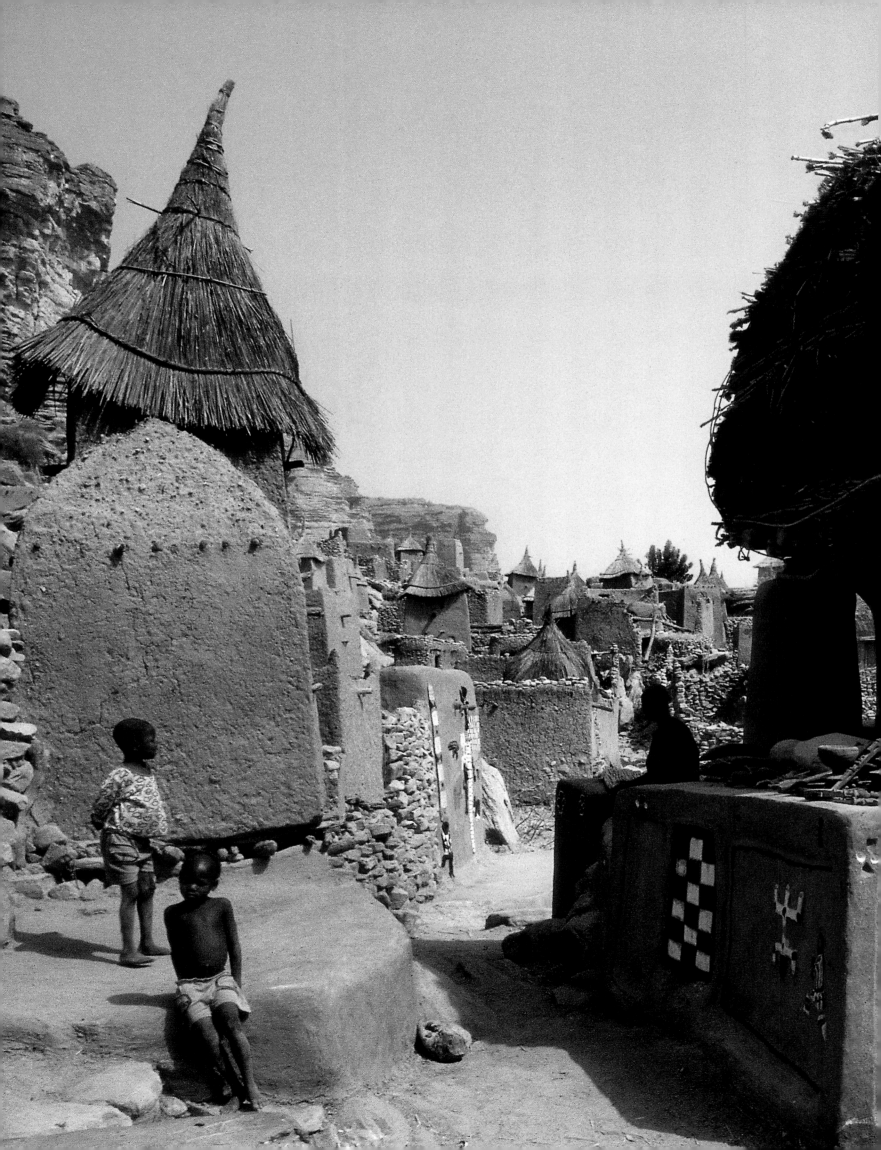

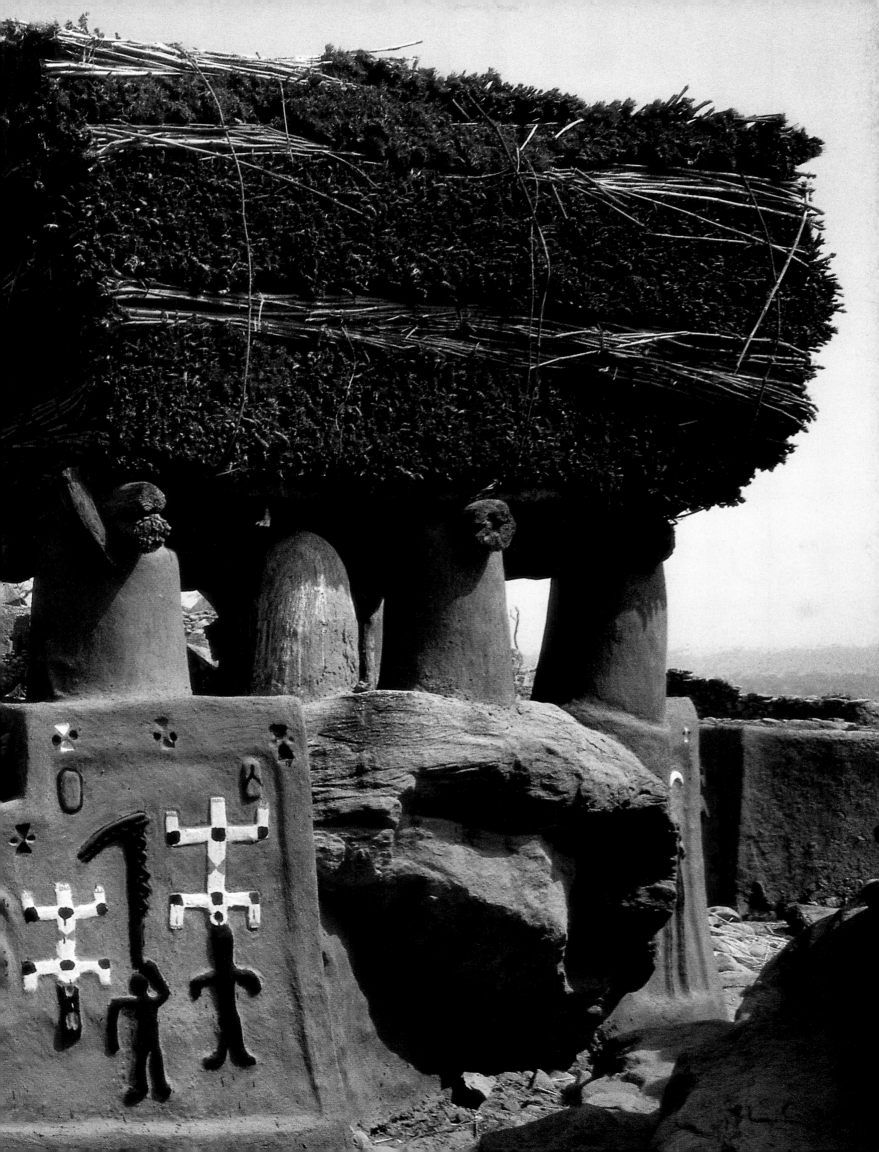

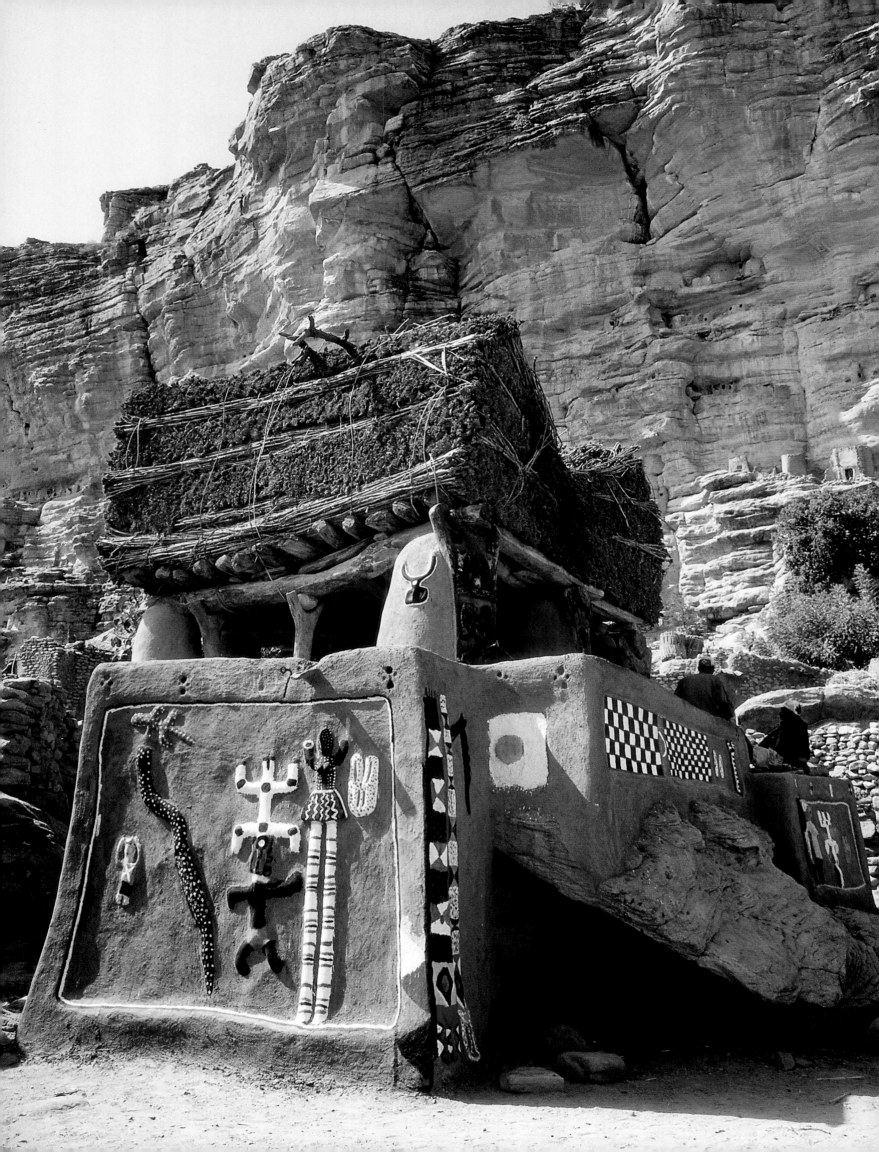

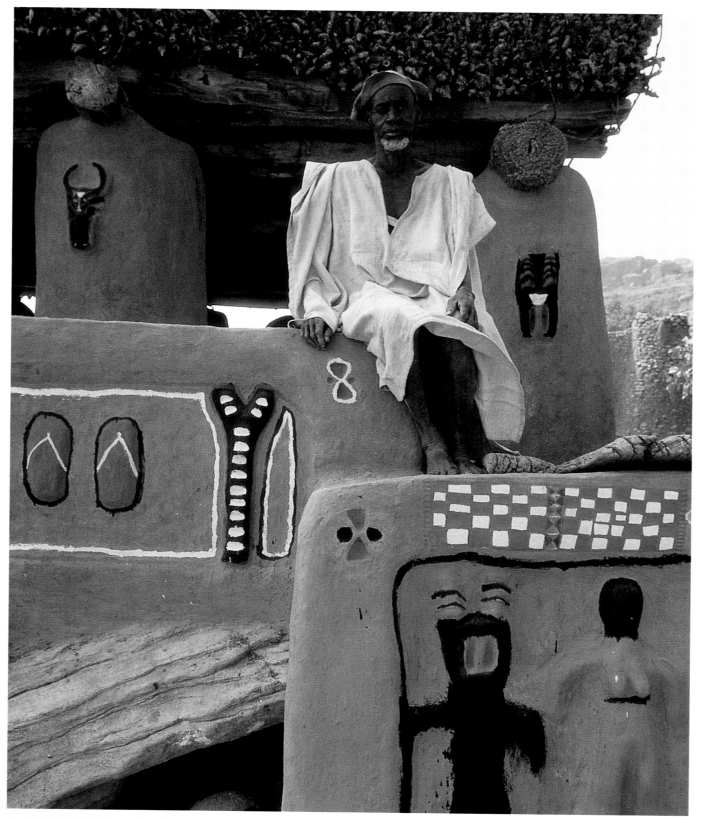

※ **FACING PAGE AND ABOVE** This palaver house in Tireli has bas-reliefs done by the old man in the picture. They represent ritual dance masks and are in the nature of a homage to the creative force of Amma, the goddess of procreation and fertility. **FOLLOWING PAGES** The Dogon believe they all have a common ancestor. The history and course of their migration is engraved on the doors of their houses. ※ **LINKE SEITE UND OBEN** Dieser alte Mann hat das Versammlungshaus in Tireli mit Reliefs geschmückt, die die Masken zeigen, die bei rituellen Tänzen getragen werden. Sie verehren die Schöpferin Amma, die Göttin der Zeugung und der Fruchtbarkeit. **FOLGENDE DOPPELSEITE** Die Dogon glauben, dass sie alle von denselben Ahnen abstammen. Die Geschichte ihrer Wanderung, die in die Türen ihrer Häuser geschnitzt ist, hält die Erinnerung an die damalige Wegstrecke in lebendiger Erinnerung. ※ **PAGE DE GAUCHE ET CI-DESSUS** Cette maison des palabres à Tireli est ornée de bas-reliefs réalisés par ce vieil homme représentant les masques de danses rituelles et rendant hommage à la force créatrice Amma, déesse de la procréation et de la fertilité. **DOUBLE PAGE SUIVANTE** Les Dogons estiment descendre tous de la même lignée. Sculptée sur les portes des maisons, une histoire de leur migration restitue leur itinéraire.

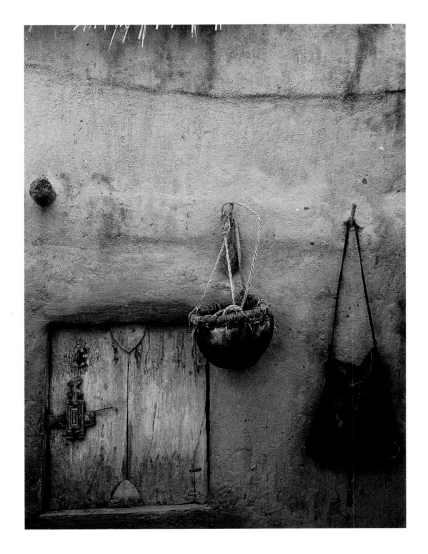

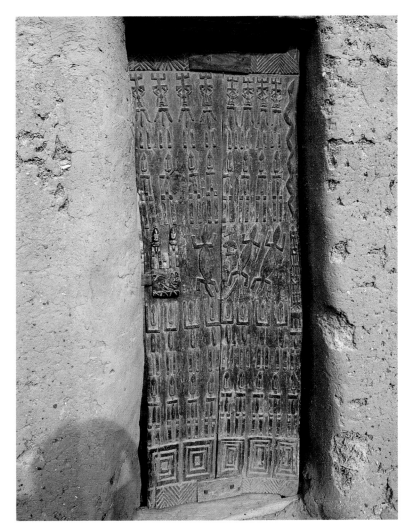

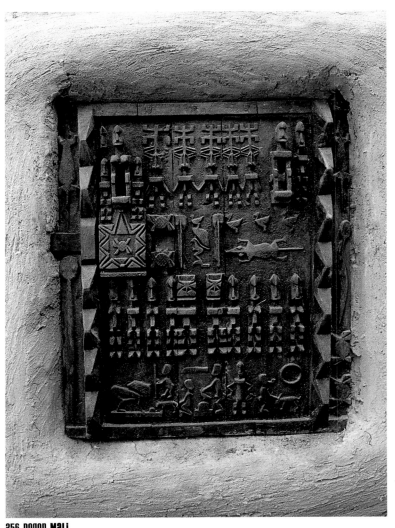

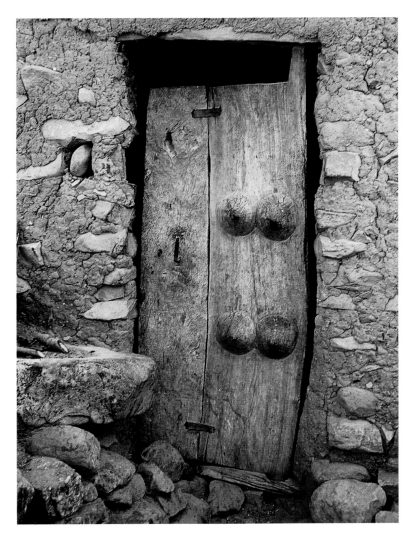

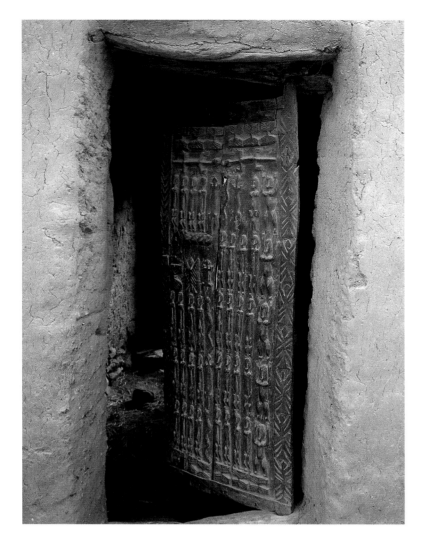
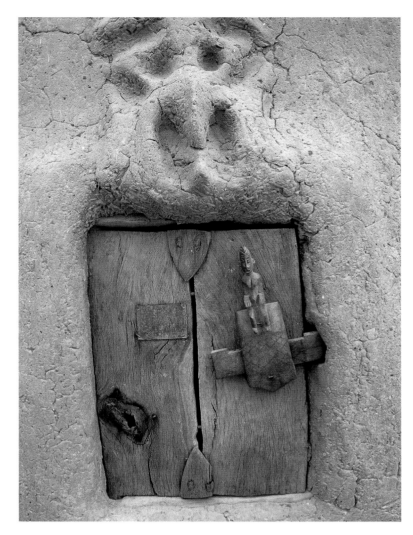
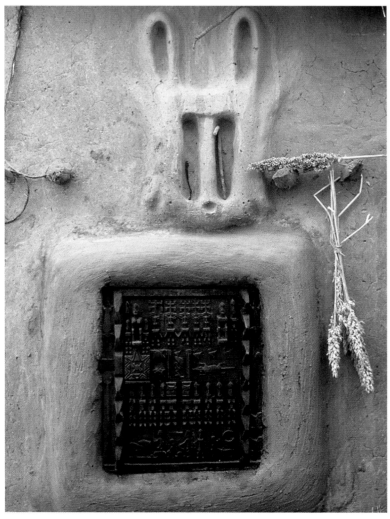
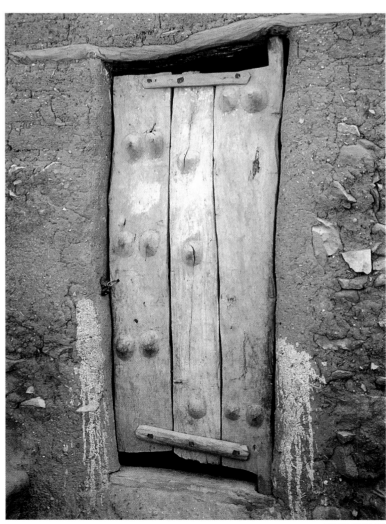

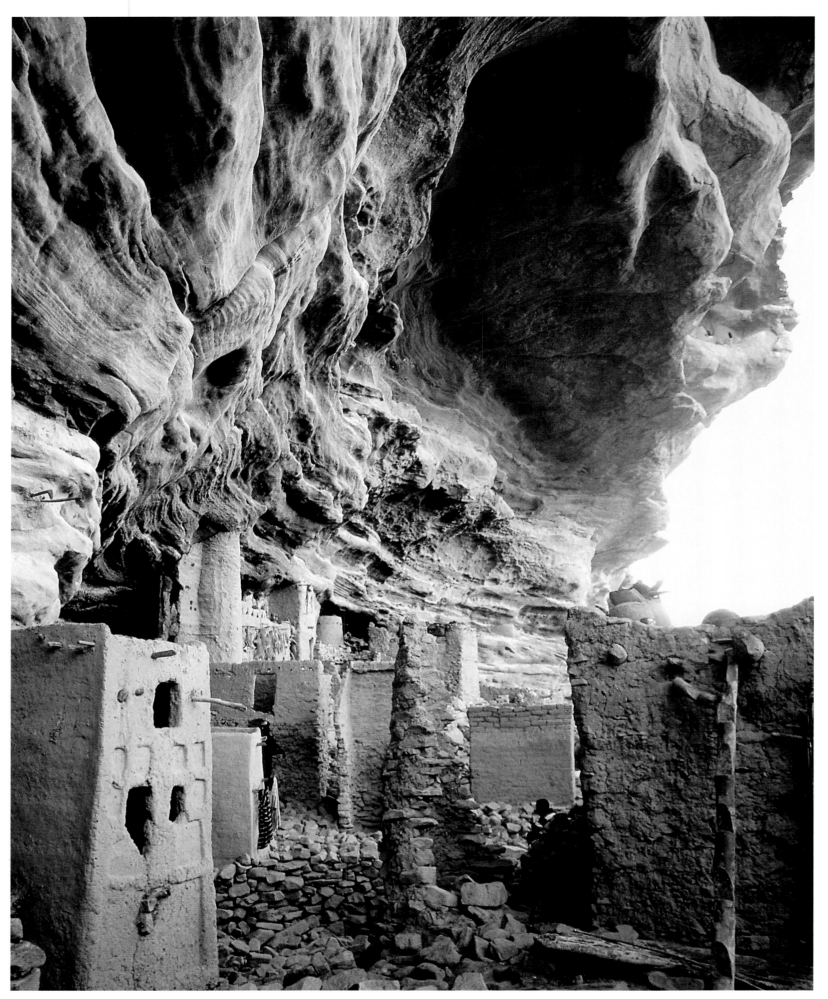

❋ **ABOVE AND FACING PAGE** High up on the cliff face, the house of the priest protects from evil spirits. Built in a spacious cave surrounded with grain stores, its façade is covered with the skins and skulls of sacrificed animals. ❋ **OBEN UND RECHTE SEITE** Das Haus des Hohenpriesters liegt in einer großen Höhle oben an der Klippe und schützt vor Geistern. Es ist von Speichern umgeben und mit Fellen und Schädeln der Opfertiere verziert. ❋ **CI-DESSUS ET PAGE DE DROITE** Située en hauteur dans la falaise, la maison du féticheur protège des esprits. Édifiée dans une vaste grotte et entourée de greniers, sa façade est recouverte de la peau et des crânes des animaux sacrifiés.

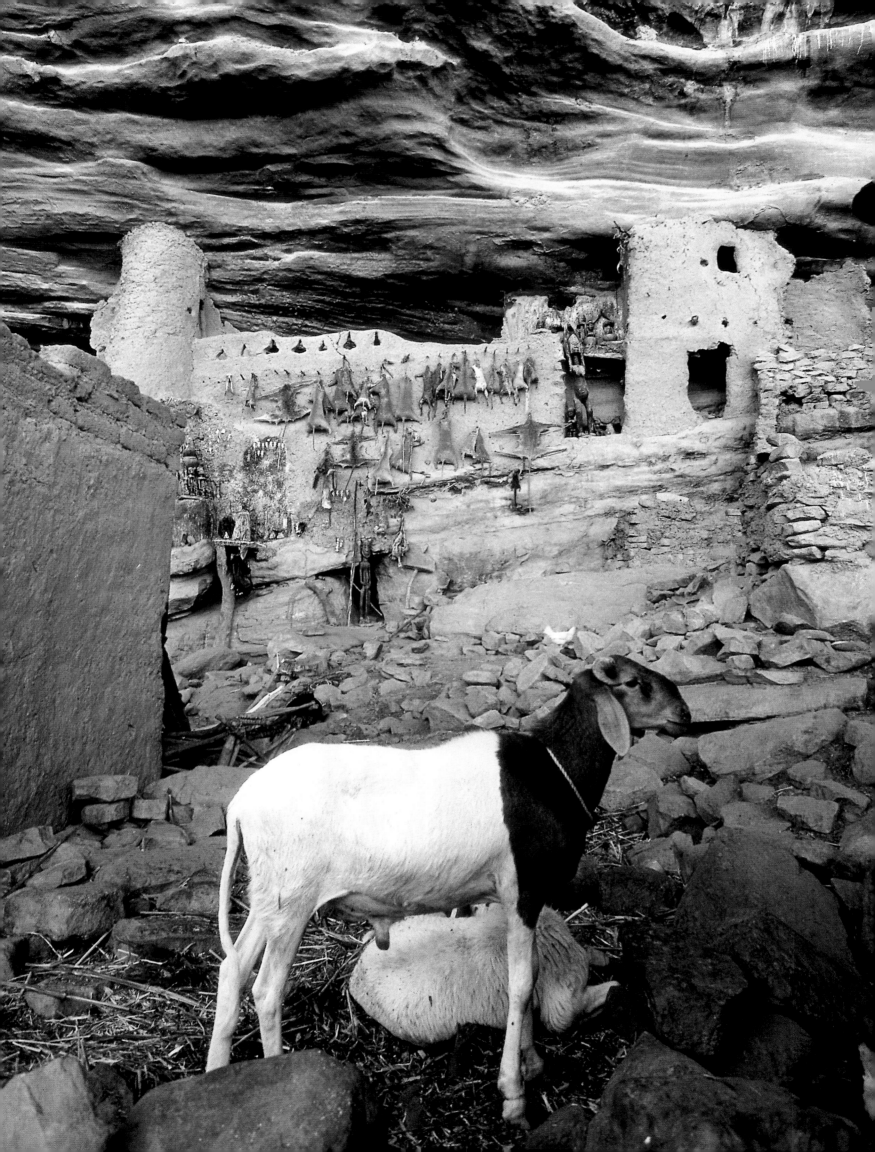

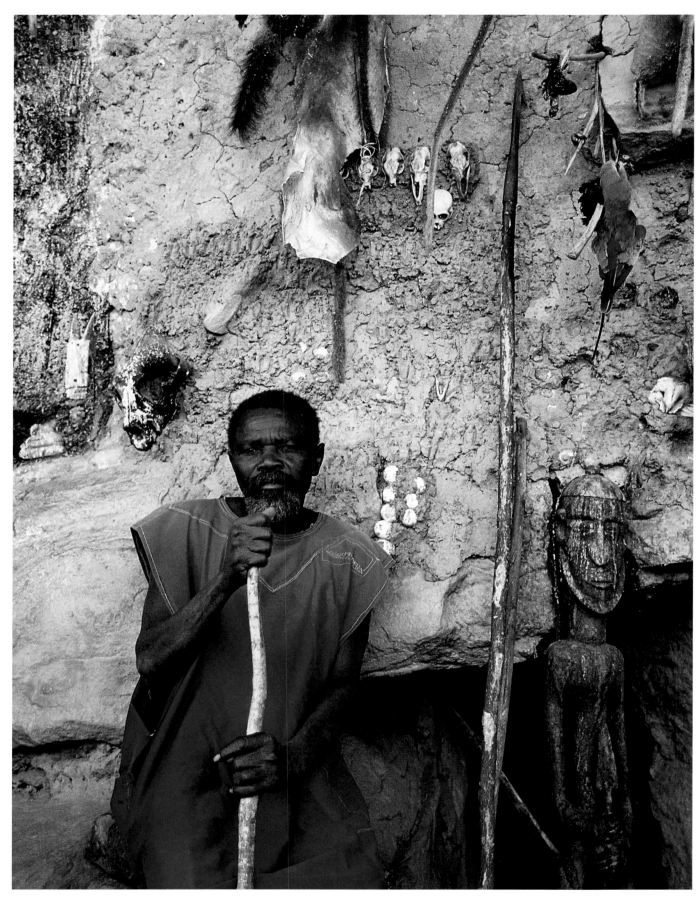

✳ **ABOVE** The priest is a central figure in Dogon society, which believes that a dead man's soul can leave his body and become a threat to cosmic order. The shaman's role is to drive away spirits such as these and re-establish "peace". **PAGES 362-367** Scenes from daily life at Mopti and Djenné. ✳ **OBEN** Der Hohepriester spielt im Leben der Dogon eine bedeutende Rolle. Dieses Volk glaubt, dass sich der Geist nach dem Tod vom Körper löst und die kosmische Ordnung bedroht. Der Priester muss den Geist vertreiben und den »Frieden« wiederherstellen. **SEITEN 362-367** Alltagsszenen in Mopti und Djenné. ✳ **CI-DESSUS** Le féticheur est un personnage central de la société Dogon qui croit que l'esprit d'un mort quitte son corps et menace l'ordre cosmique. Son rôle est de chasser cet esprit afin de rétablir la «paix». **PAGES 362-367** Scènes de la vie quotidienne à Mopti et Djenné.

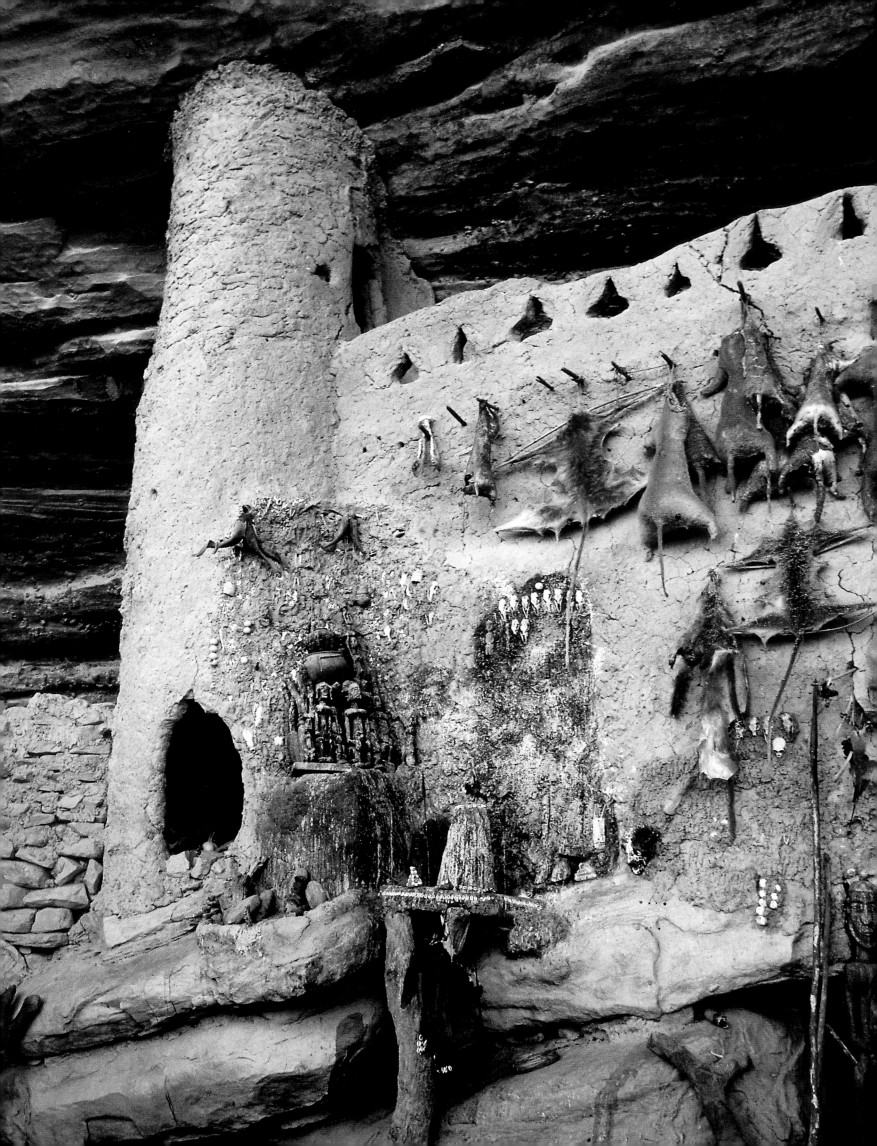

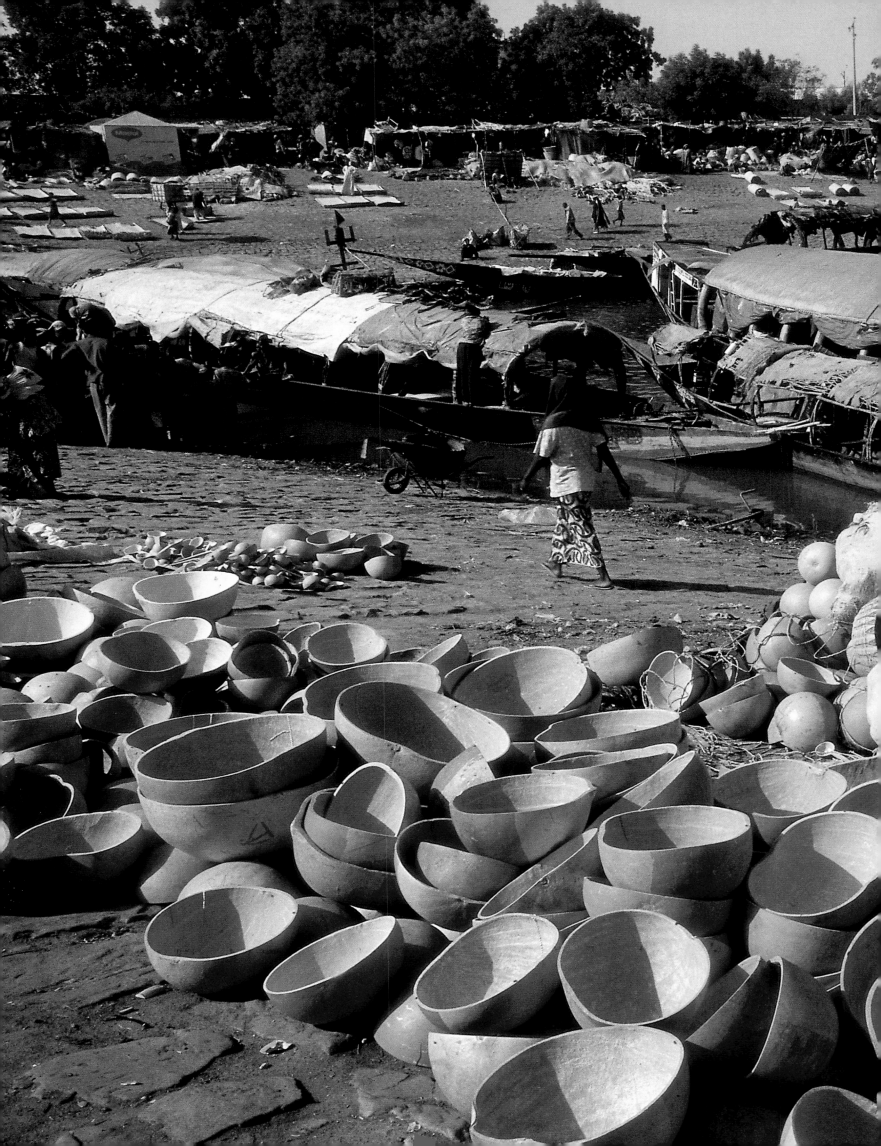

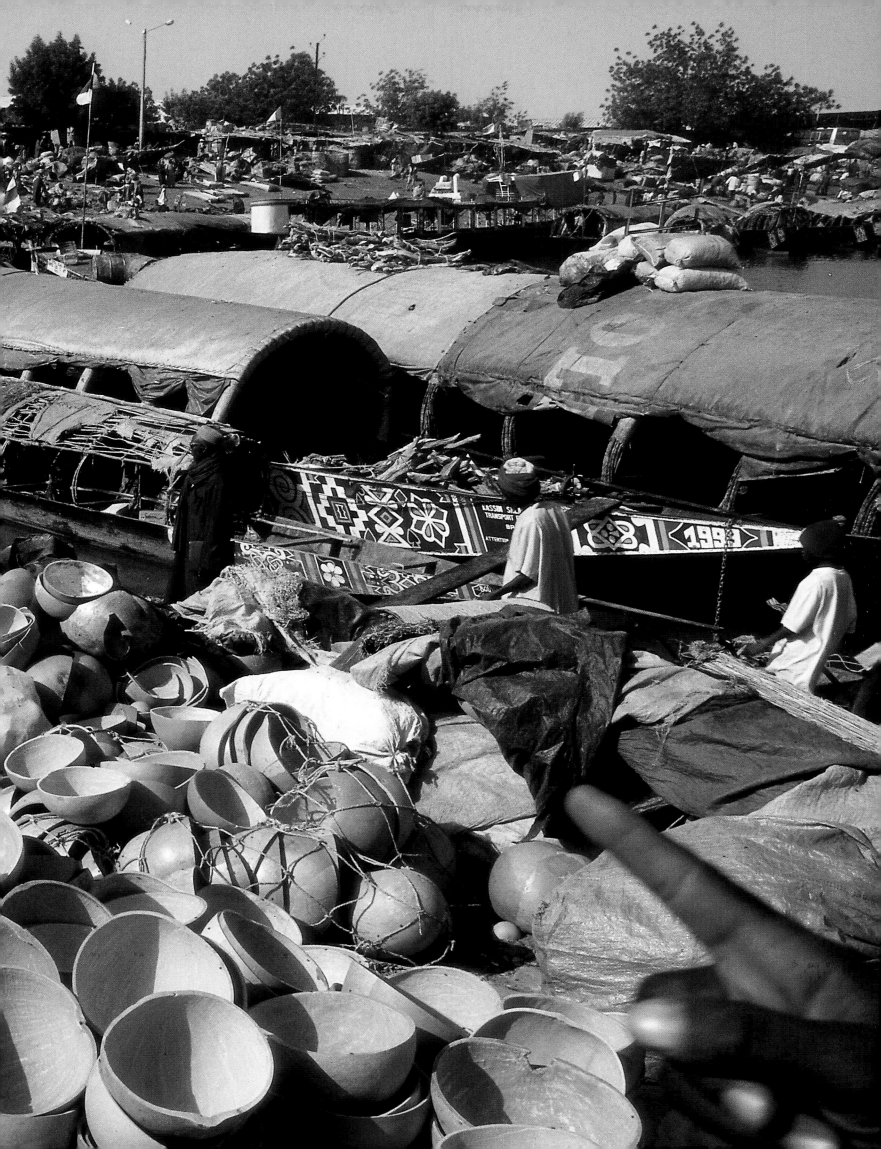

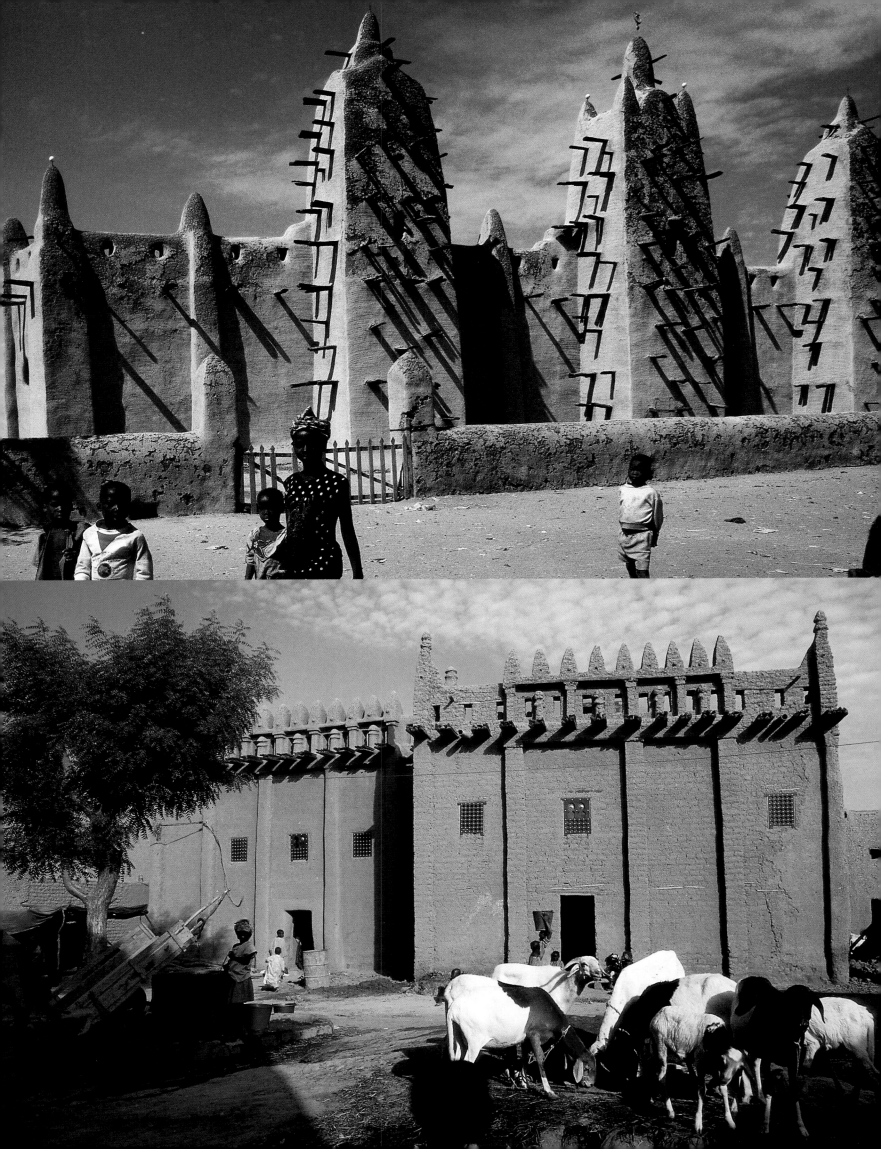

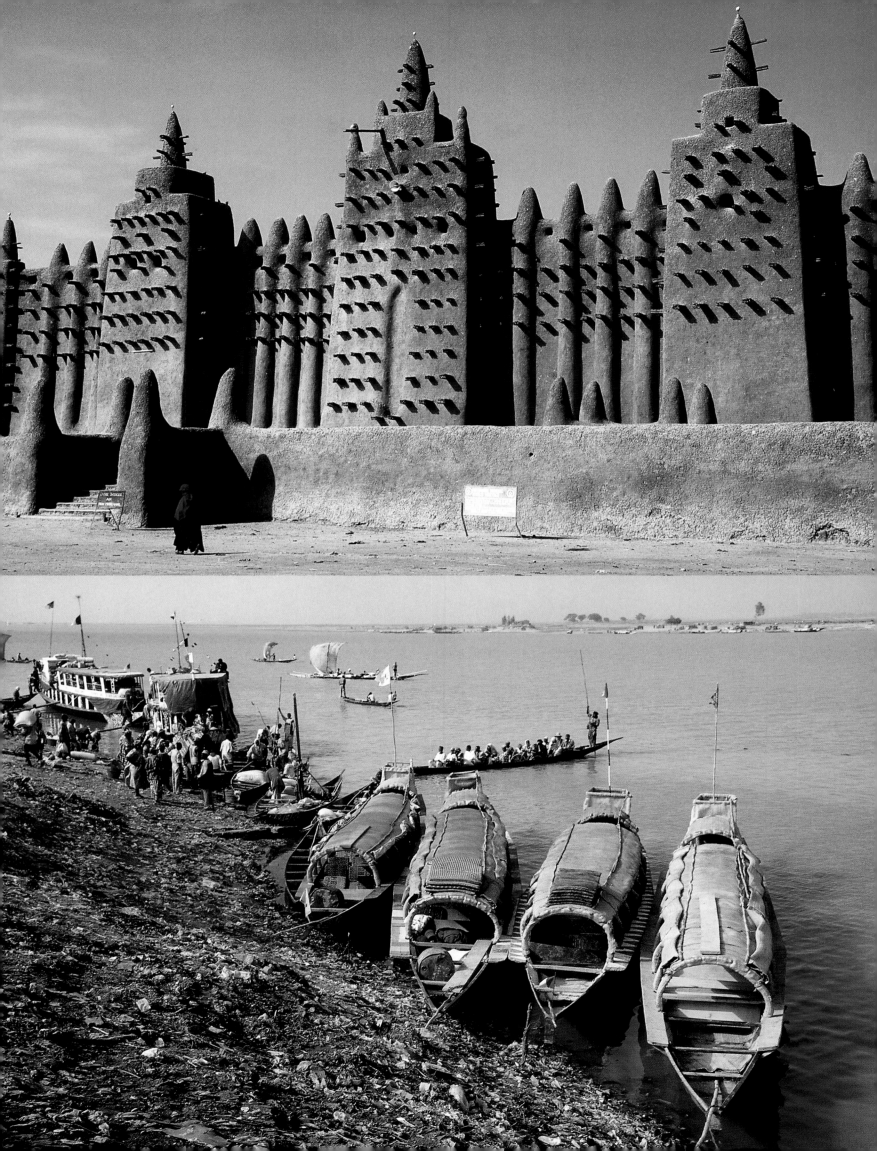

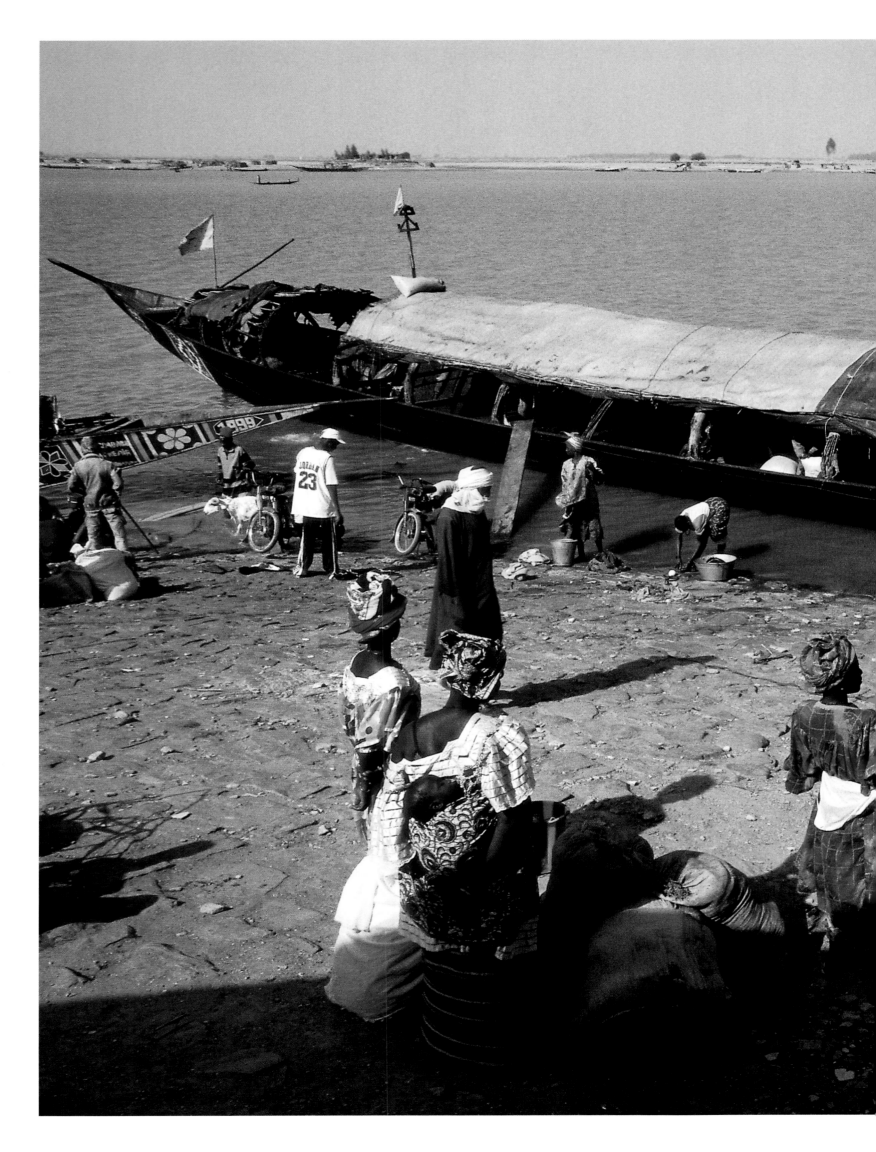

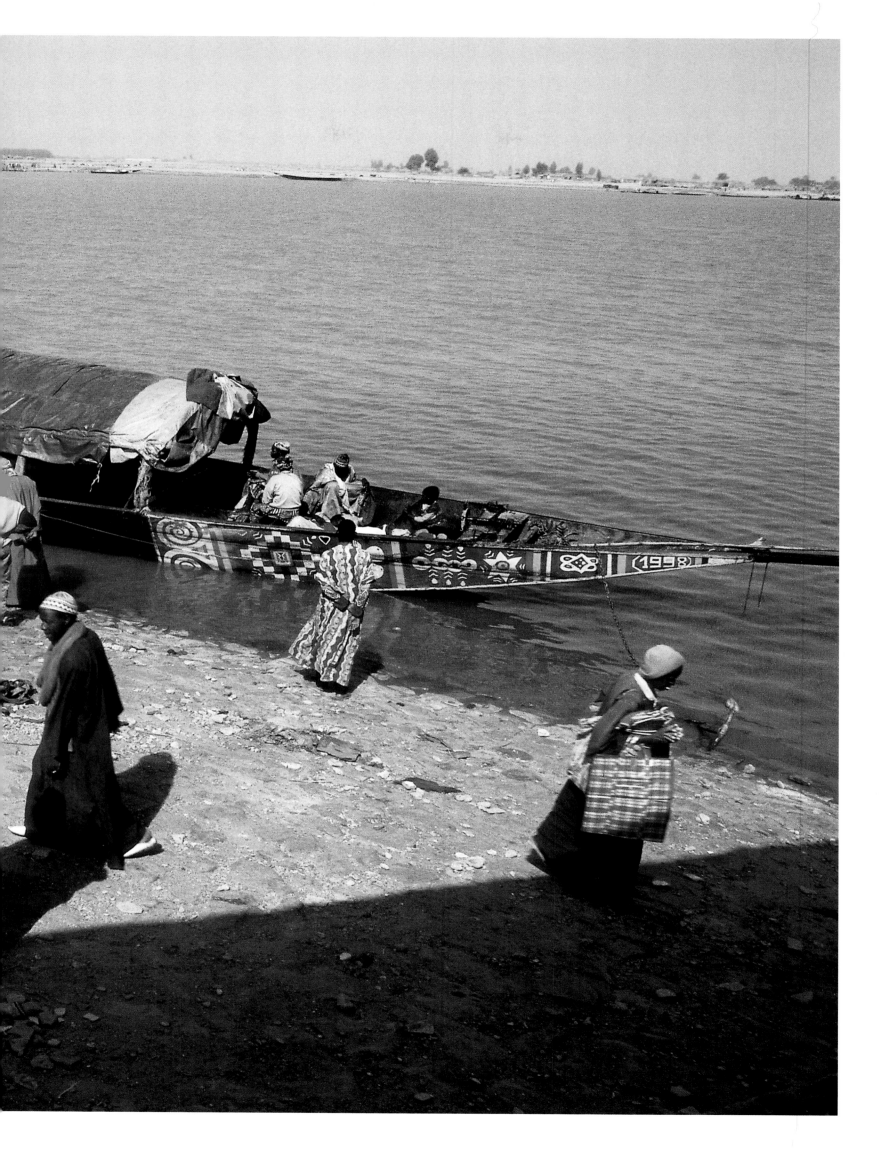

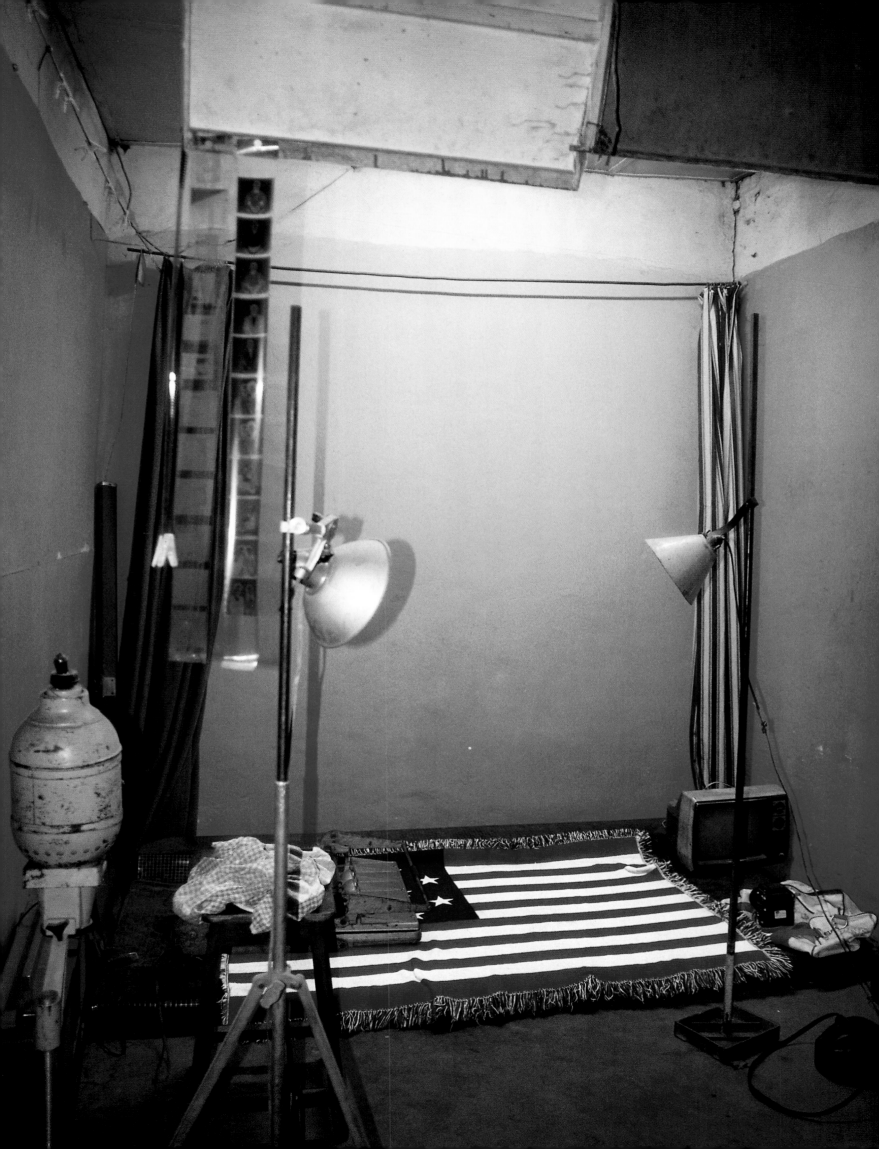

# MALICK SIDIBE
## Bamako

The world famous photographer Malick Sidibé has been working in the same Bamako studio for more than 40 years.

The Malick Studio in Bamako is a shrine for lovers of photography the world over. Now an African institution, Malick Sidibé owes his celebrity to his *Bamako by Night*, published in the 1960s.

At that time, he hung out in local nightclubs with his camera and gradually built up a portrait of a generation learning to love English pop music and sixties fashions, at the same time as it was tasting political independence for the first time. The years have passed, but Mali's national fascination with photography has endured. Now over 60, Malick Sidibé is busy training a new wave of younger photographers. The models still turn up at his studio looking their best, and in the streets outside photography is alive and well in many portrait studios and brightly-painted shops. Bamako, the capital of Mali, is Africa's darkroom; its reputation has grown apace with the development of its photography biennale. Where does all this interest originate? "In colonial times it was formally forbidden to take photographs outside," says the founder of the *Revue Noire*, Pascal Martin Saint-Leon. "So all the photographers went back to their studios and worked exclusively with portraits." Anyone coming to Bamako will be amazed at the sheer celebrity of Mali's three leading practitioners of the art – Malick Sidibé, of course, but also Seydou Keita and Madou Traoré.

Zum Studio Malick nach Bamako pilgern Fotoamateure aus der ganzen Welt. Malick Sidibé, eine Institution auf dem Kontinent, verdankt seinen Ruhm den *Bamako by Night*-Fotos aus den 1960er Jahren.

Mit umgehängtem Fotoapparat strich er damals durch die Nachtlokale und zeichnete das Porträt einer Jugend, die gerade englische Popmusik, die Mode der Sixties und ihre eigene Unabhängigkeit entdeckte. Seitdem ist die Zeit auch an der von rotem Laterit geprägten Hauptstadt Malis nicht spurlos vorübergegangen, aber das allgemeine Interesse an der Fotografie ist nach wie vor sehr lebendig. Malick Sidibé, der Generationen von Fotografen geprägt hat, ist heute über 60, aber noch immer sitzen die Modelle herausgeputzt in seinem Studio. Draußen auf der Straße blüht das Geschäft mit der Fotografie in vielen Porträtstudios und kleinen bunten Läden. Seit eine Fotobiennale ins Leben gerufen wurde, ist das Ansehen Bamakos gestiegen. Wieso ist das Interesse so groß? »In der Kolonialzeit waren Außenaufnahmen offiziell verboten«, erklärt Pascal Martin Saint Léon, der Gründer der Revue Noire. »Deshalb haben sich viele Fotografen in ihre Studios zurückgezogen und die Kunst des Porträts gepflegt.« Die Popularität der drei großen malischen Fotografen Malick Sidibé, Seydou Keita und Madou Traoré ist in der Tat erstaunlich.

Le studio Malick, à Bamako, est un lieu de pèlerinage pour les amateurs de photographie du monde entier. Devenu une institution sur le continent, Malick Sidibé doit sa célébrité à son *Bamako by Night* des années 1960.

Appareil en bandoulière, il a traîné dans les boîtes de nuit et brossé le portrait d'une jeunesse qui découvrait la musique pop anglaise et la mode des sixties en même temps que l'indépendance. Les années ont passé dans la capitale du Mali imprégnée de latérite rouge, mais l'intérêt pour la photographie ne s'est jamais démenti. Aujourd'hui sexagénaire, Malick Sidibé forme les nouvelles générations de photographes. Dans son studio, les modèles portent toujours beau pour leur séance photo. À l'extérieur, dans les rues, la photographie foisonne à travers des studios de portraits et des petites boutiques colorées. Chambre noire de l'Afrique, la réputation de Bamako s'est amplifiée avec l'organisation d'une biennale de la photo. D'où vient un pareil intérêt? «Pendant la colonisation, il était formellement interdit de prendre des images en extérieur», précise le fondateur de la Revue Noire, Pascal Martin Saint Léon. «Du coup, les photographes se sont repliés dans leur studio pour travailler essentiellement le portrait.» En voyage à Bamako, le visiteur est en effet surpris par la renommée des trois grands photographes du Mali: Malick Sidibé, donc, mais aussi Seydou Keita et Madou Traoré.

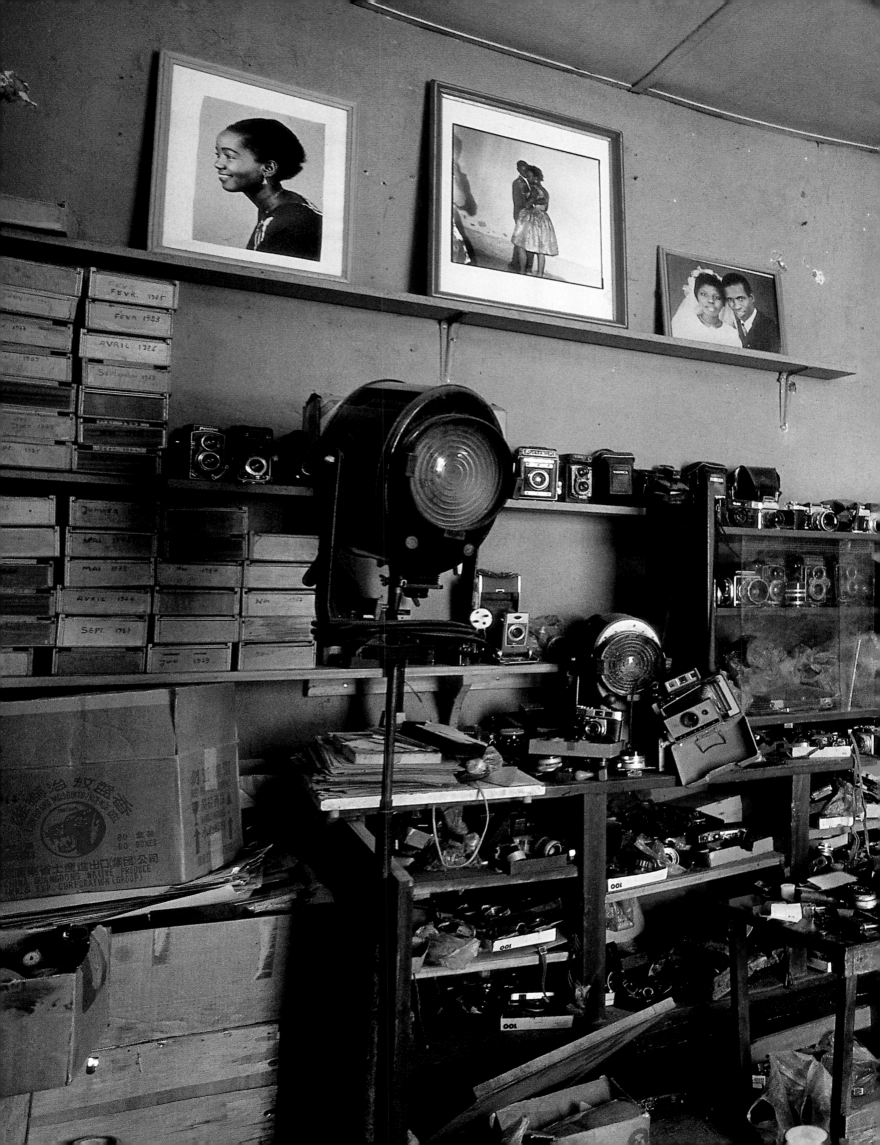

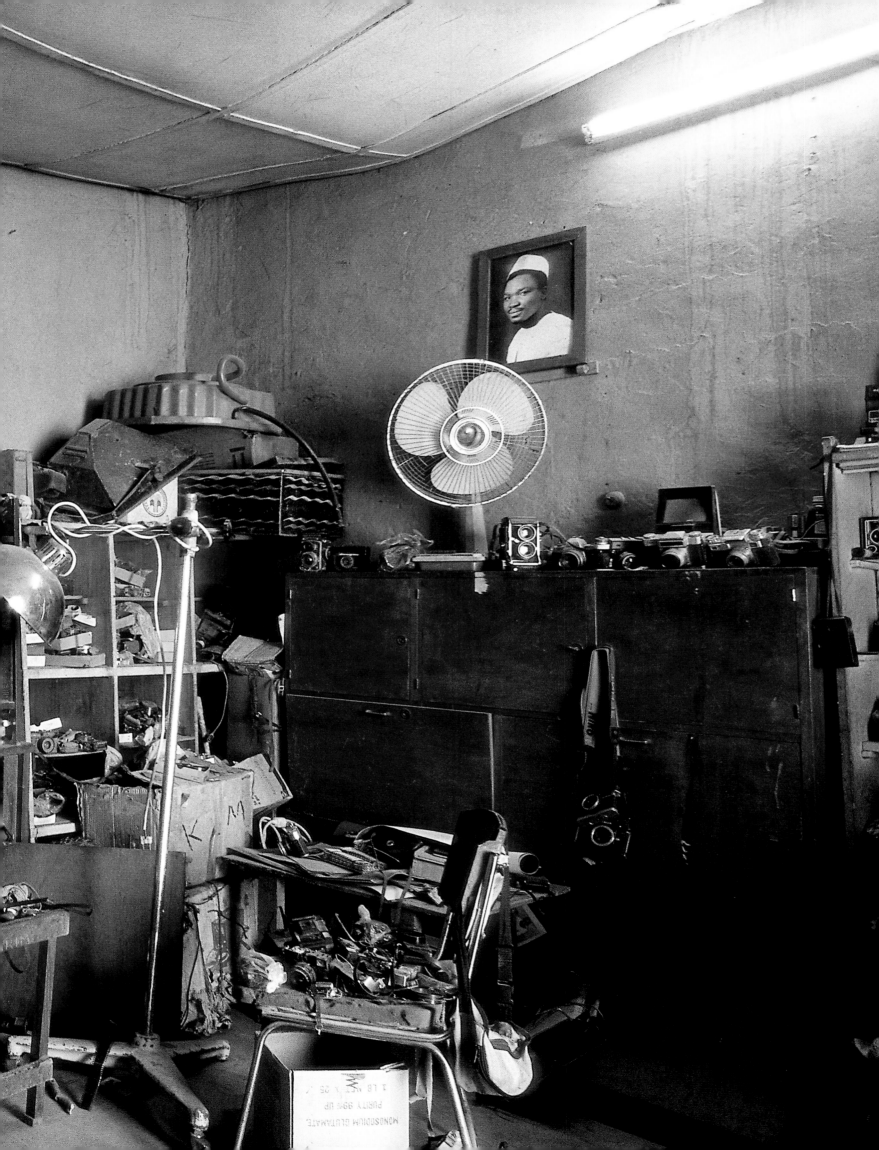

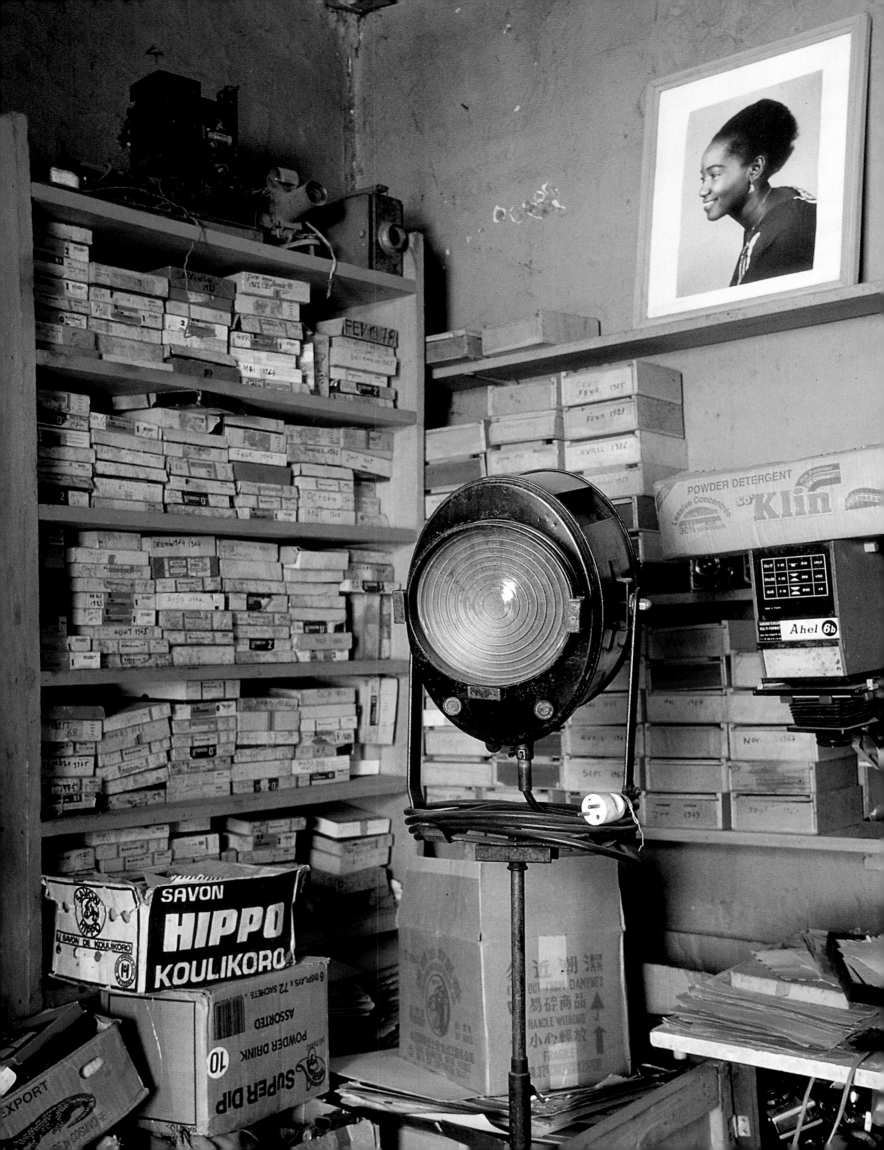

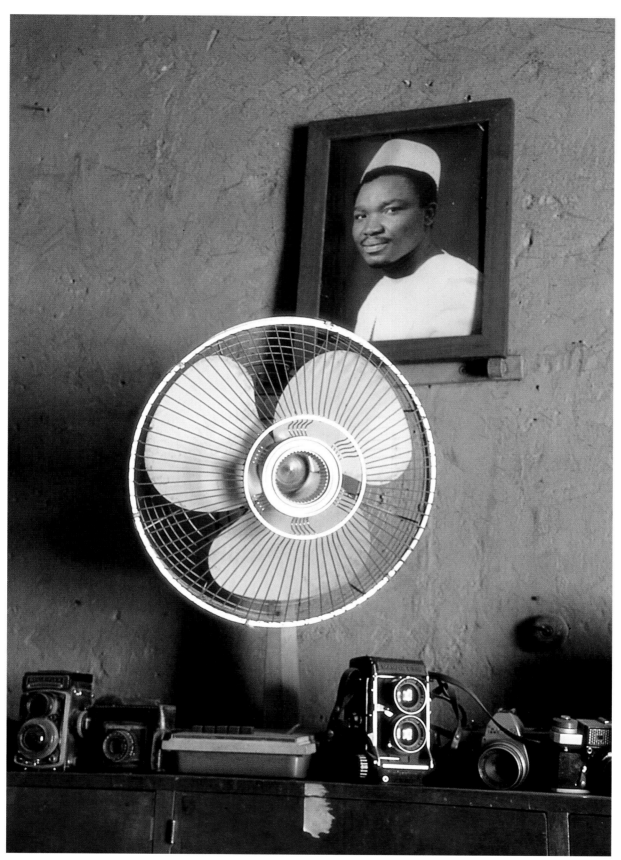

✳ **PREVIOUS PAGES, FACING PAGE AND ABOVE** Malick Sidibé records the affluent side of urban life (scooters, transistor radios, cigarettes, young people at parties in Bamako) as well as the ritual ceremonies of hunters from his own village in the bush. Apart from holding the presidency of the Mali Photographers' Group (GNPPM), he is known for his skill at repairing cameras. ✳ **VORHERGEHENDE DOPPELSEITE, LINKE SEITE UND OBEN** Malick Sidibé setzt die »Reichtümer« des Stadtlebens in Szene: Mopeds, Radios, Zigaretten und die Feste der Jugendlichen in Bamako. Gleichzeitig bildet er aber auch die rituellen Jagdzeremonien in seinem Dorf im Busch ab. Als Präsident der Vereinigung malischer Fotografen, der GNPPM, ist er zudem für die sachgerechte Reparatur von Fotoapparaten bekannt. ✳ **DOUBLE PAGE PRECEDENTE, PAGE DE GAUCHE ET CI-DESSUS** Malick Sidibé met en scène des «richesses» de la vie urbaine (mobylettes, transistors, cigarettes, fêtes des jeunes de Bamako), mais aussi les cérémonies rituelles des chasseurs dans son village de la brousse. Président du Groupement des Photographes maliens, le GNPPM, il est aussi connu pour ses qualités de réparateur d'appareils photographiques.

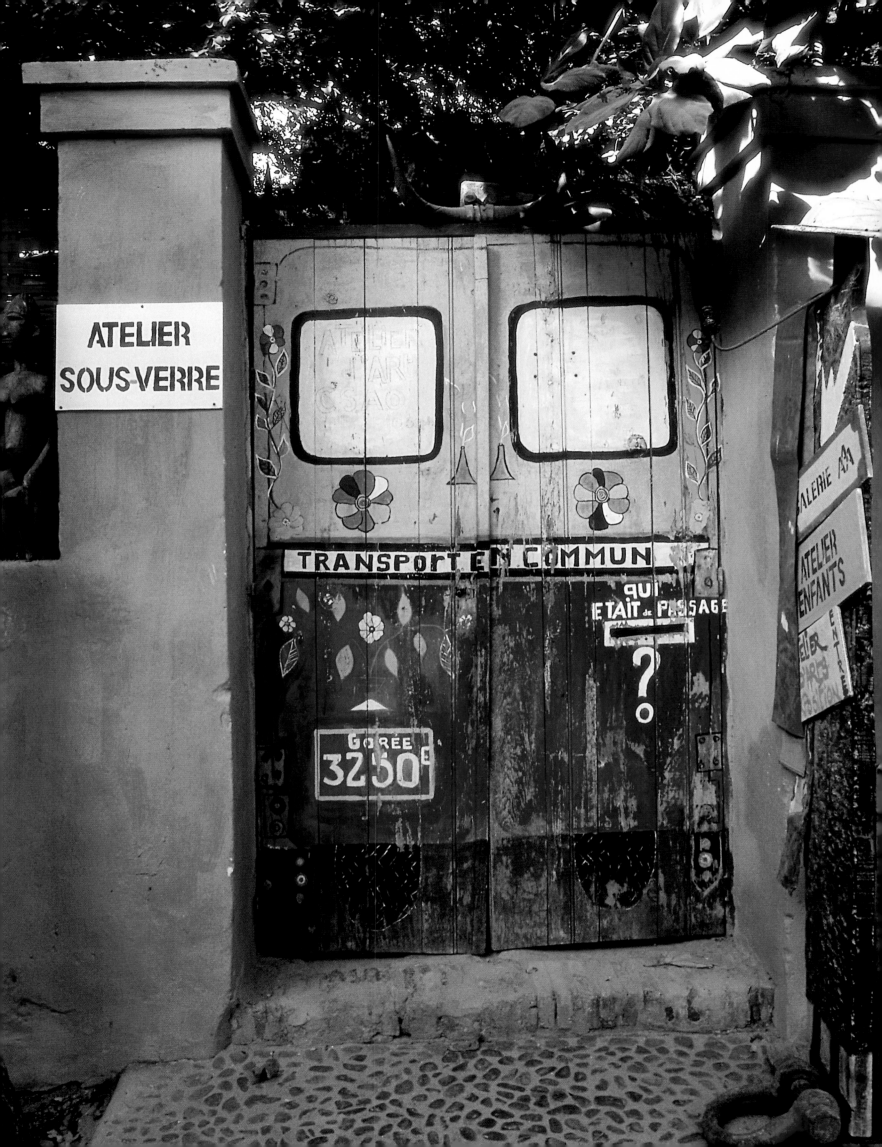

# A.S.A.O.
# Goree Island

A mid-19th century house where the melancholy past has been set aside
to celebrate the art of the present.

This studio-house on an island off Dakar has the dual function of a guesthouse and a gallery for exhibitions. Its soft ochre walls try to make you forget the cruelty of an earlier time.

The place is like its owner, a businesswoman who has done many different things in her life; having begun as a costume designer for a great film maker, she went on to become a producer for another and today divides her time between Gorée and Paris, running a company which trades with Africa. On the island, it's Amy, a young Senegalese, who takes care of the three guest rooms. "This house is full of life – you really feel good here," says Valérie. The presence of Moussa Sakho's studio adds poetry and atmosphere, with young people assembling every Wednesday for art classes. As a small foundation, the guesthouse passes on its revenues to an association that helps the Gorée dispensary; it is also dedicated to helping French children in difficulty. Valérie was originally attracted to Senegal by its clothing and printed fabrics. Today her shop in the Marais quarter of Paris is filled with everyday art, in the form of tablecloths, cushions, plastic fans, basketwork trays and mahogany dishes.

Das Haus mit Atelier auf hoher See vor Dakar dient gleichzeitig als Ausstellungsort und als kleines Gästehaus. Beim Anblick der zart ockerfarbenen Wände könnte die grausame Vergangenheit der Insel, die ihre Wirkung bis in die heutige Zeit entfaltet, leicht in Vergessenheit geraten.

Das Haus entspricht seiner Besitzerin, einer Geschäftsfrau, die bereits die unterschiedlichsten Berufe ausgeübt hat. Sie arbeitete als Kostümbildnerin für einen berühmten Kinoregisseur, produzierte Filme und leitet zur Zeit, zwischen Paris und Gorée pendelnd, ein Unternehmen, das fairen Handel mit Afrika treibt. Auf der Insel selbst kümmert sich Amy, eine junge Senegalesin, um die drei Gästezimmer. »In der lebhaften Atmosphäre dieses Hauses fühlt man sich schnell wohl«, sinniert Valérie. Die Nähe zum Atelier des Künstlers Moussa Sakho bringt Poesie ins Haus, zumal er jeden Mittwoch die junge Generation der Insel das Malen lehrt. In Form einer kleineren Stiftung werden die Gewinne des Gästehauses an eine Gesellschaft weitergegeben, die einerseits das Gesundheitsamt unterstützt und andererseits französischen Kindern in Not unter die Arme greift. Ursprünglich waren es die Kleidung und bedruckte Stoffe, die Valérie in den Senegal brachten. Seitdem präsentiert sie in ihrem Pariser Geschäft im Marais auch kunsthandwerkliche Alltagsgegenstände wie Plastikfächer, geflochtene Tabletts, Mahagoni-Teller, Matten und Kissen.

Cette maison-atelier au large de Dakar sert à la fois de chambre d'hôtes et de lieu d'exposition. Ses murs ocre et tendres tentent de faire oublier la cruauté d'un passé bien présent encore.

L'habitation est à l'image de sa propriétaire, une femme d'affaires qui croise les genres, un temps costumière pour un grand cinéaste, productrice à un autre et aujourd'hui, entre Gorée et Paris, à la tête d'une société qui fait du commerce avec l'Afrique sans omettre de lui tendre la main. Sur l'île, c'est Amy, une jeune Sénégalaise, qui veille sur les trois chambres d'hôtes. «On se sent bien dans cette maison très vivante», médite Valérie. La présence de l'atelier de Moussa Sakho ajoute de la poésie et de l'ambiance: les jeunes aiment s'y retrouver chaque mercredi pour des cours de peinture. Petite fondation, la chambre d'hôtes redistribue ses revenus à une association qui vient en aide au dispensaire de Gorée mais est aussi consacrée à l'accueil d'enfants français en difficulté. À l'origine, Valérie fut attirée au Sénégal par les vêtements et les pagnes imprimés. Sa boutique parisienne du Marais s'ouvre désormais à l'art du quotidien sous la forme d'éventails en plastique, de plateaux de vannerie, d'assiettes en acajou, de nappes et de coussins.

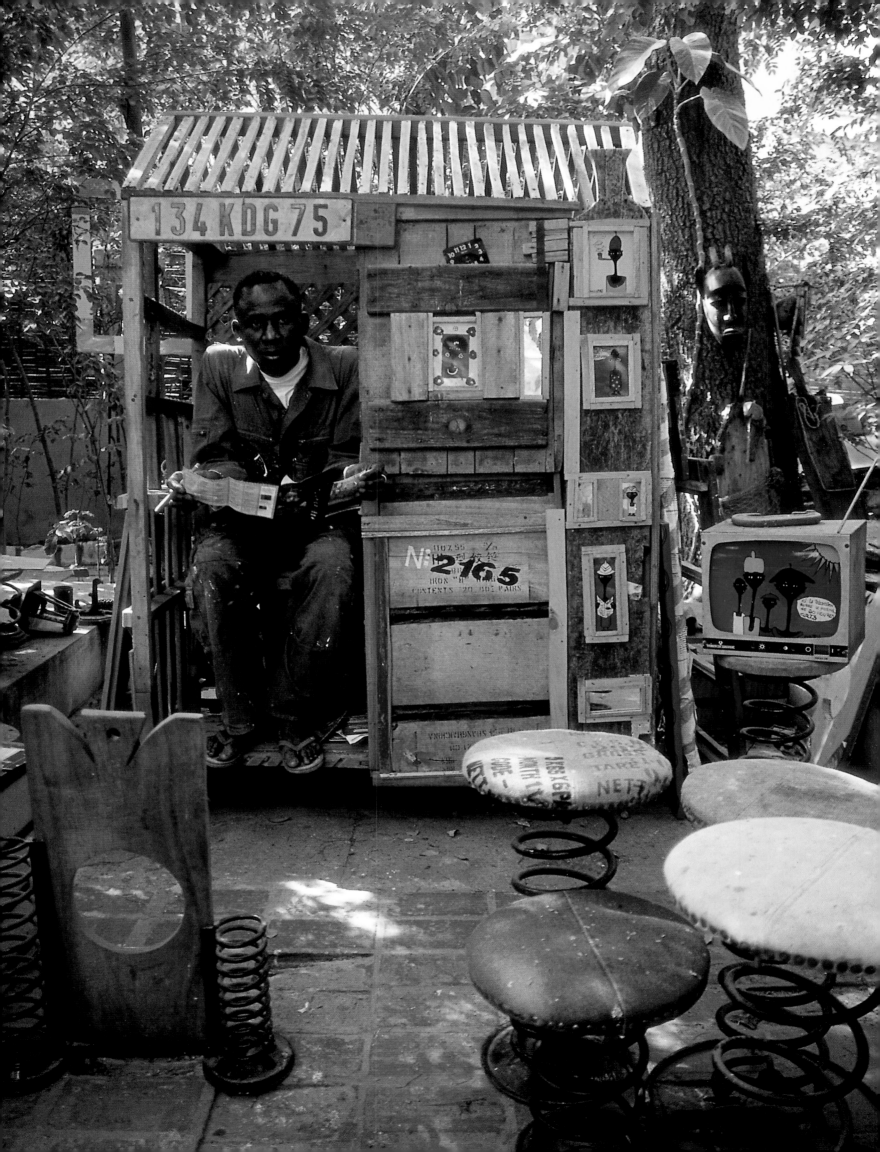

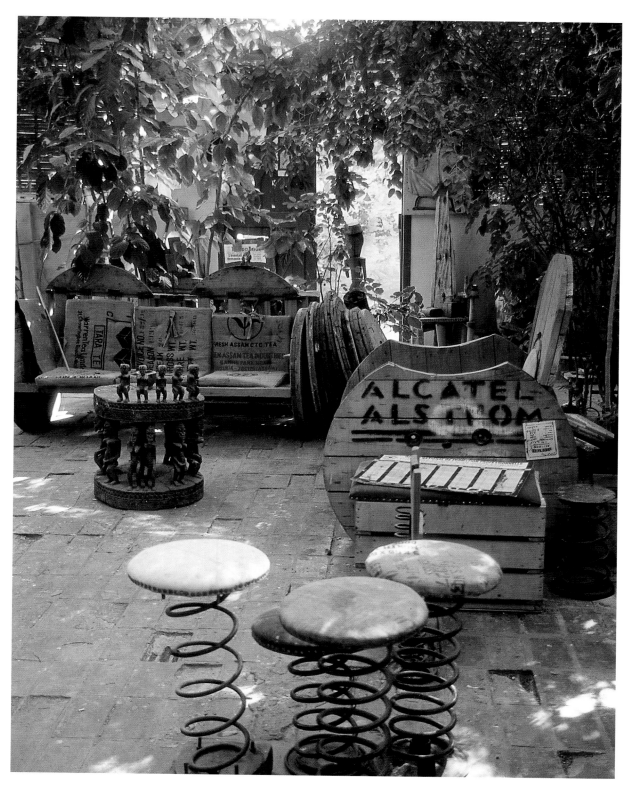

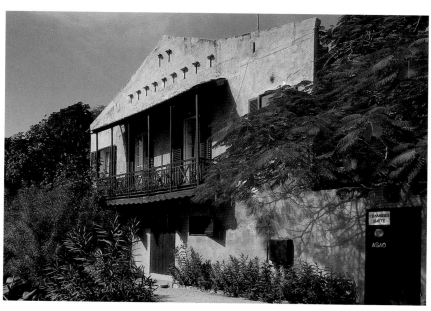

※ **FACING PAGE** Portait of Moussa Sakho, whose garden studio enlivens Valérie's establishment. **LEFT AND ABOVE** Fifteen minutes by by boat from Dakar, the house welcomes both guests and exhibitions. ※ **LINKE SEITE** Porträt Moussa Sakhos, dessen Atelier im Garten des Hauses liegt. **LINKS UND OBEN** Eine Fähre bringt die Hotelgäste innerhalb einer Viertelstunde von Dakar zu Valéries Haus, in dem auch Ausstellungen gezeigt werden. ※ **PAGE DE GAUCHE** Portrait de Moussa Sakho dont l'atelier, situé dans le jardin de la maison anime celle-ci. **A GAUCHE ET CI-DESSUS** À un quart d'heure en chaloupe de Dakar, cette maison accueille à la fois des hôtes et des expositions.

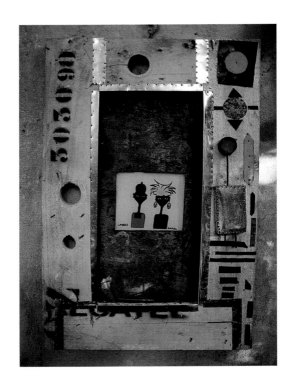
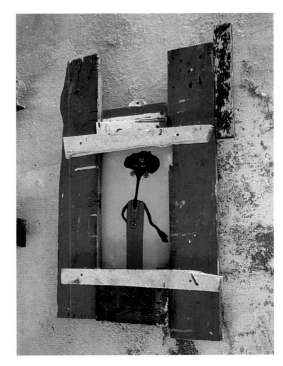
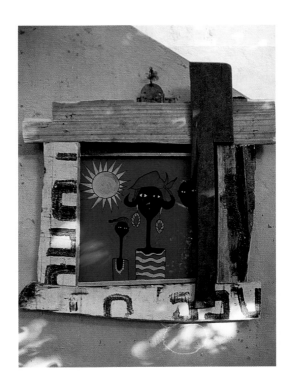

❋ **ABOVE, BELOW AND FACING PAGE** The works of Moussa Sakho (painted glass, a Senegalese speciality) are an integral part of the décor. ❋ **OBEN, UNTEN UND RECHTE SEITE** Überall hängen Werke von Moussa Sakho: Die Hinterglasmalerei ist eine senegalesische Spezialität. ❋ **CI-DESSUS, CI-DESSOUS ET PAGE DE DROITE** Les œuvres de Moussa Sakho en peinture sous verre, spécialité sénégalaise, reviennent partout dans la décoration.

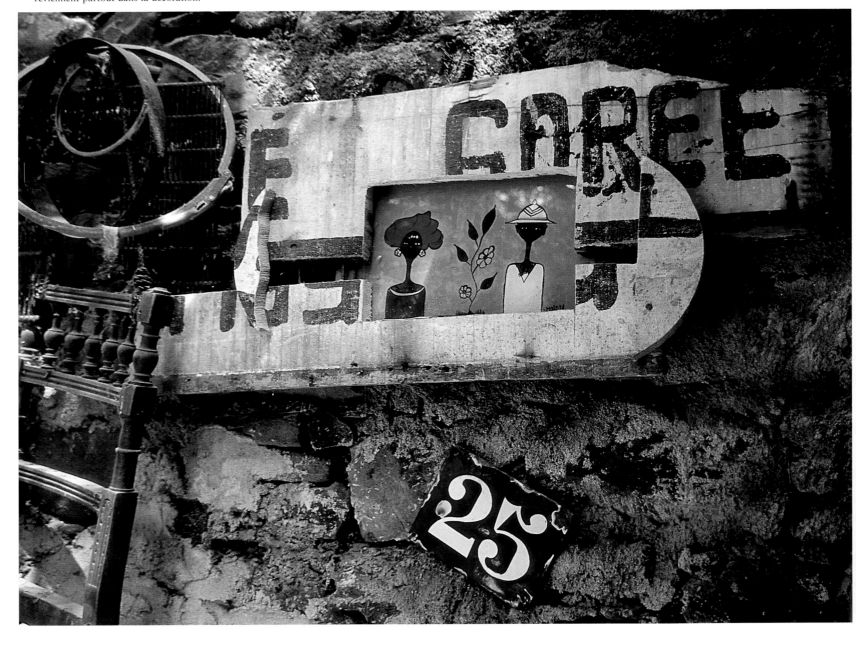

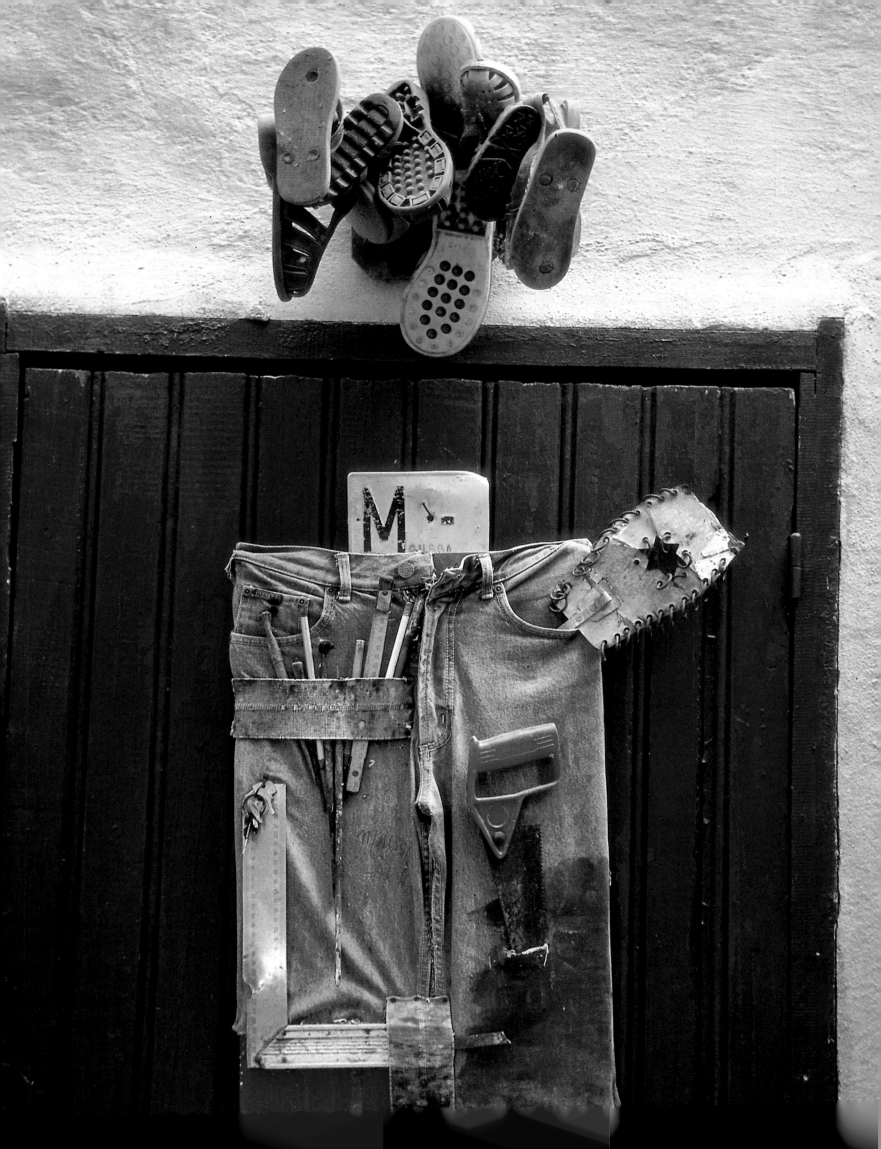

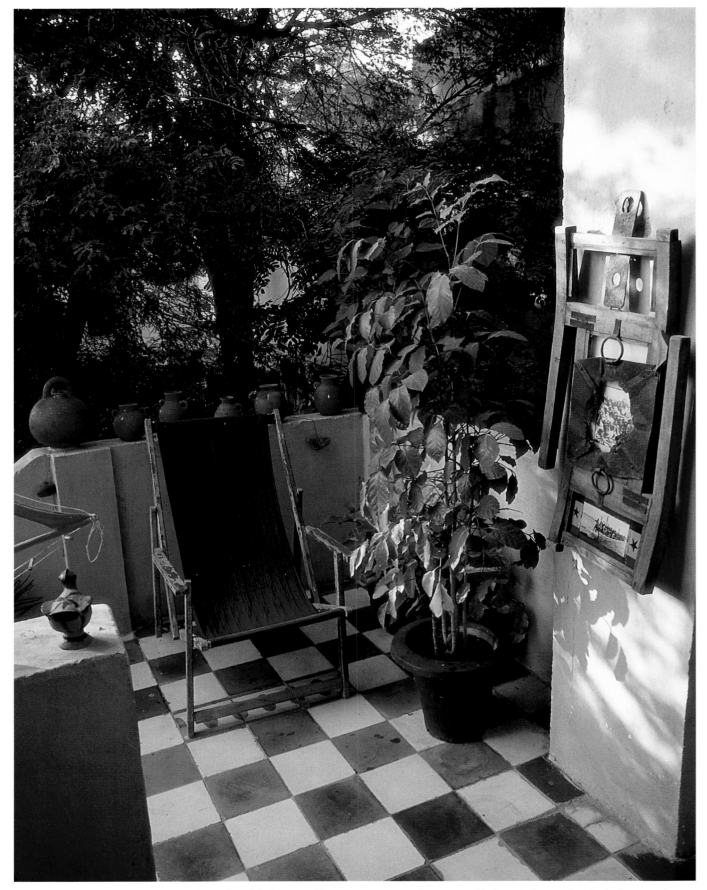

❋ **ABOVE AND FACING PAGE** The terraces and verandas of the house are like open-air rooms, with canopies of lush tropical vegetation. In the foreground, a stool from Ghana and a collection of earthenware. ❋ **OBEN UND RECHTE SEITE** Die Terrassen und Veranden des Hauses liegen umgeben von einer üppigen tropischen Pflanzenwelt unter freiem Himmel. Im Vordergrund ein Hocker aus Ghana vor einer Sammlung von Tontöpfen. ❋ **CI-DESSUS ET PAGE DE DROITE** Les terrasses et vérandas de la maison sont des pièces en plein air bordées d'une magnifique végétation tropicale. Au premier plan, un tabouret du Ghana devant une collection de poteries.

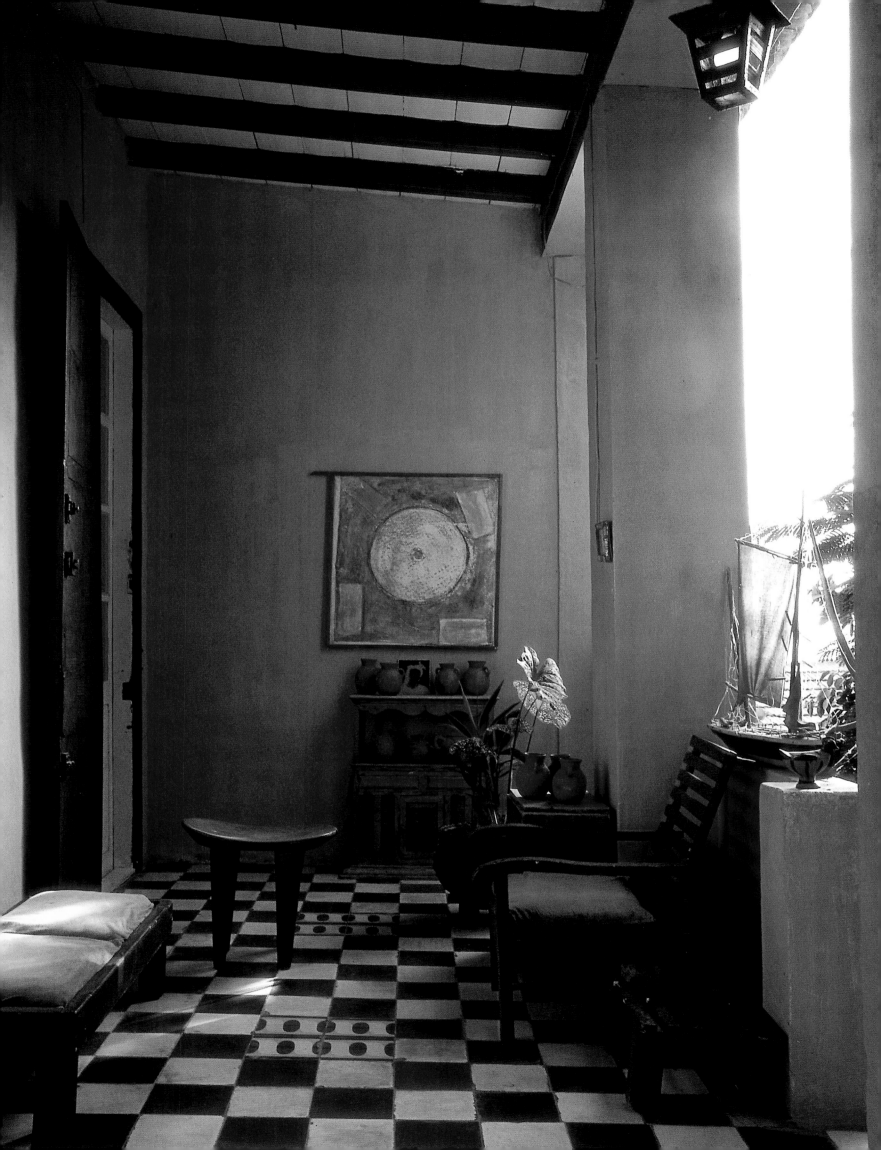

✳ **BELOW** Hidden by its screen of greenery, the house lives cheek by jowl with nature, inside and out. **FACING PAGE** Portraits on glass are a prominent feature of the simply renovated kitchen, offsetting the green and grey colour scheme and the plump-pea patterns on the walls. ✳ **UNTEN** Das innen und außen üppig geschmückte Haus liegt beinahe verborgen in der tropischen Pflanzenwelt. **RECHTE SEITE** Porträts in der Technik der Hinterglasmalerei prägen die unaufwändig renovierte Küche und betonen die grün-weiß getüpfelten Wände mit dem Erbsenmuster, das die üppige Vegetation vor der Tür aufgreift. ✳ **CI-DESSOUS** Dissimulée par un écrin de verdure, la maison se vit en intérieur comme en extérieur. **PAGE DE DROITE** Les portraits sous-verre dominent une cuisine simplement rénovée et mettent en valeur ce parti pris de vert et blanc accentué par les motifs de gros pois qui couvrent les murs, rappelant ainsi la végétation environnante.

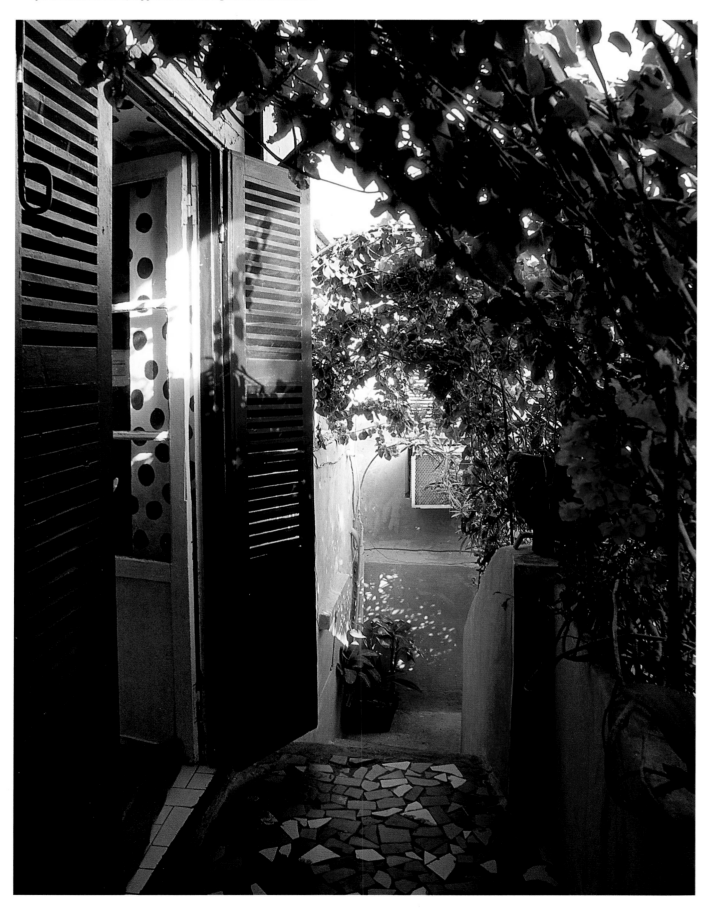

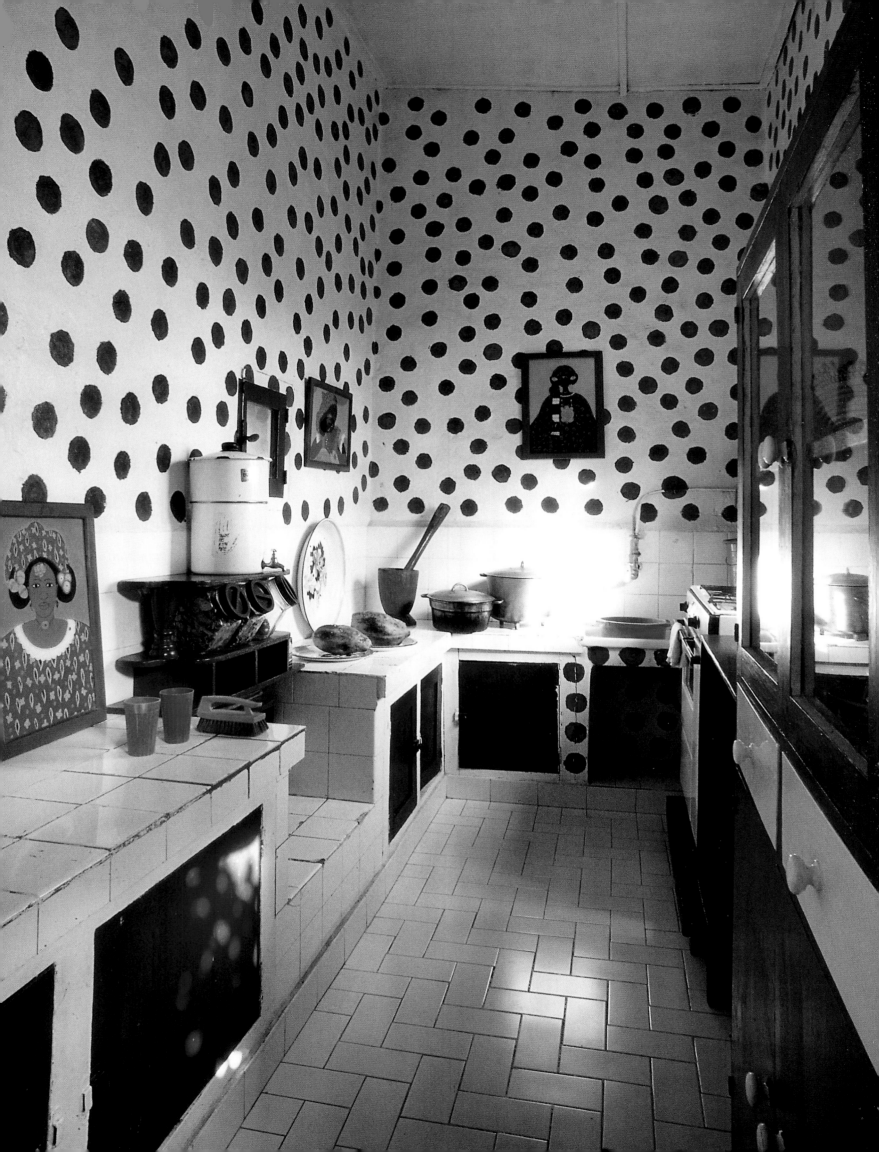

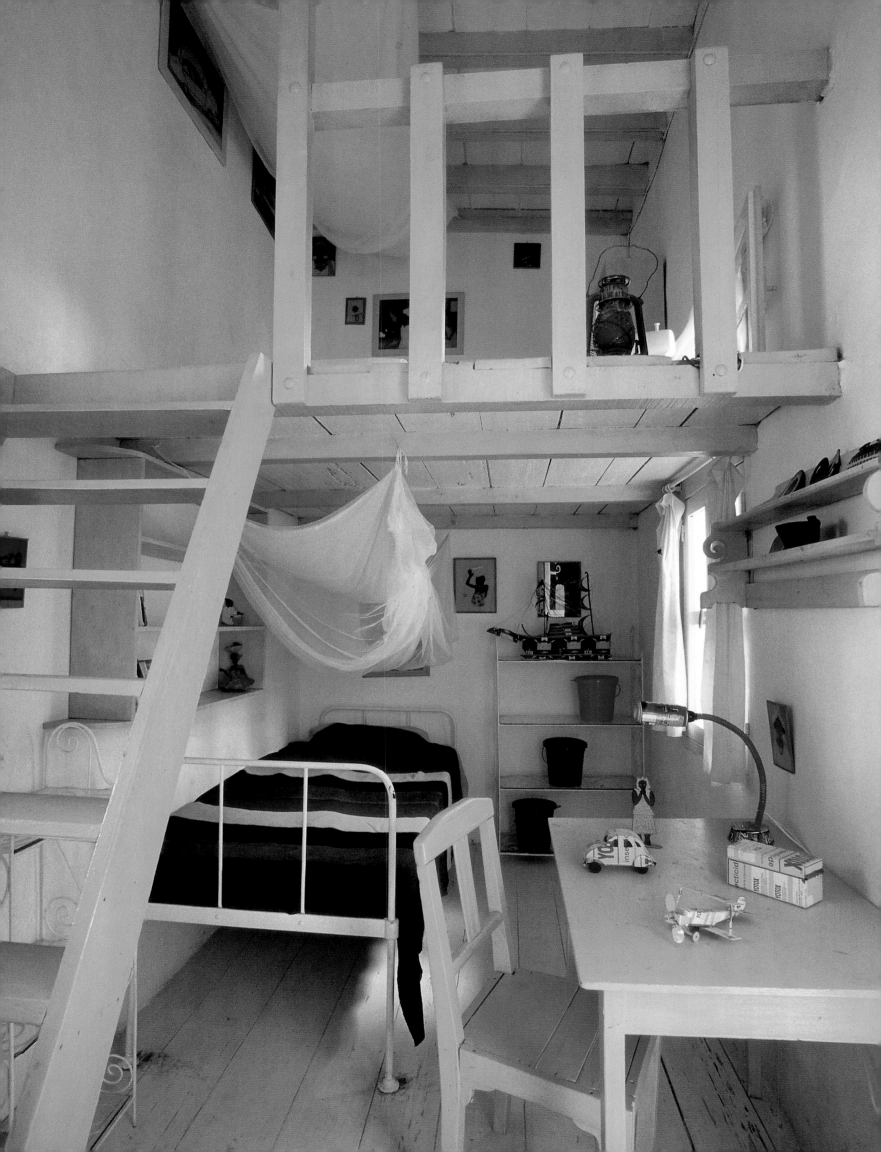

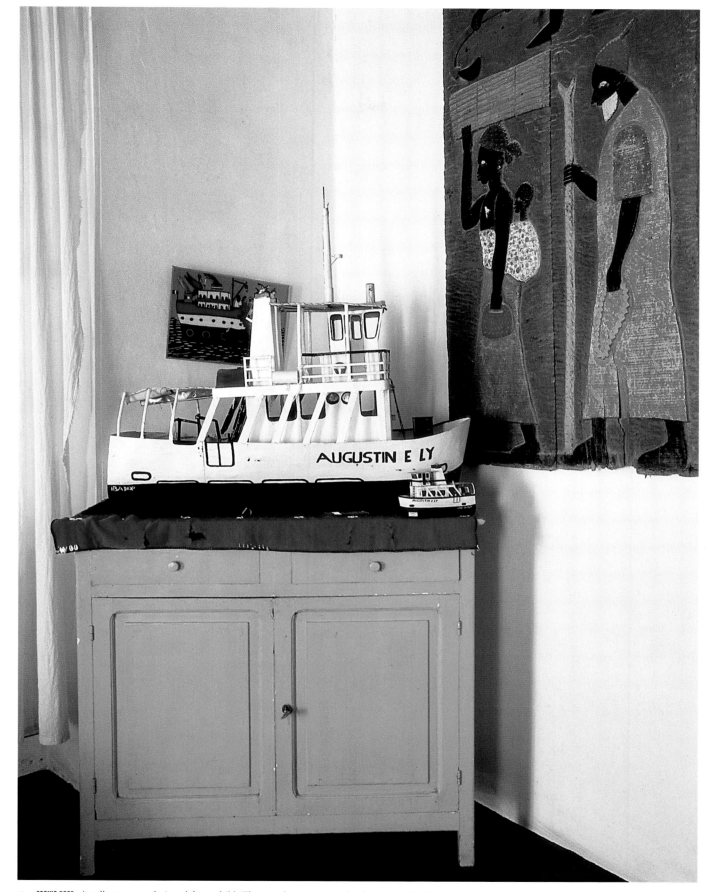

✳ **FACING PAGE** A yellow room, designed for a child. The wooden mezzanine lends a Swiss Family Robinson air, with its salvaged furniture painted yellow like the sunshine. **ABOVE** Here and there, objects made by the island's craftsmen. A few painted wooden boats have pride of place on the old kitchen sideboard, which has been refreshed with a coat of yellow-gold paint. ✳ **LINKE SEITE** Gelb ist die dominierende Farbe im Kinderzimmer. Das Mezzanin aus Holz erinnert stark an eine Hütte à la Robinson. Die sonnengelb gestrichenen schlichten Möbel wurden wieder aufgearbeitet. **OBEN** Hier und da scheint das Kunsthandwerk der Insulaner auf. Auf einer mit Gelb aufgefrischten Kommode in der Küche steht eine Sammlung bemalter Holzboote. ✳ **PAGE DE GAUCHE** Dans la chambre d'enfant, le jaune domine. La mezzanine en bois donne un aspect très cabane de Robinson avec ces meubles de récupération simplement peints couleur de soleil. **CI-DESSUS** Ici et là, les objets rappellent le travail des artisans de l'île. Quelques bateaux de bois peint se profilent sur une vieille commode de cuisine rafraîchie de jaune d'or.

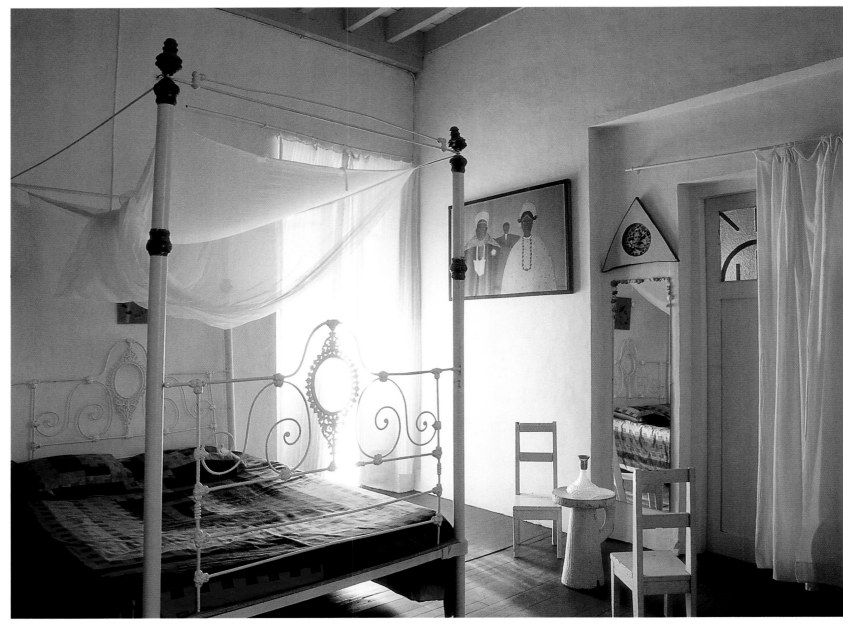

❋ **ABOVE** "We have visitors from all over the world," says Valérie, obviously delighted. She furnished the first floor bedrooms with lacquered metal four-poster beds. **FACING PAGE** Glass paintings by the artists Fallou Dolly and Djibril Sagna decorate this cupboard. ❋ **OBEN** »Unsere Gäste kommen aus aller Welt«, stellt Valérie erfreut fest. Die Zimmer im ersten Stock hat sie mit Himmelbetten aus lackiertem Metall ausgestattet. **RECHTE SEITE** Der Schrank ist mit Hinterglasmalerei der Künstler Fallou Dolly und Djibril Sagna verziert. ❋ **CI-DESSUS** «Nous recevons des visiteurs venus des quatre coins du monde», se réjouit Valérie. Elle a décoré les chambres à coucher du premier étage de lits à baldaquin en métal laqué. **PAGE DE DROITE** Les peintures sous verre des artistes Fallou Dolly et Djibril Sagna décorent cette armoire.

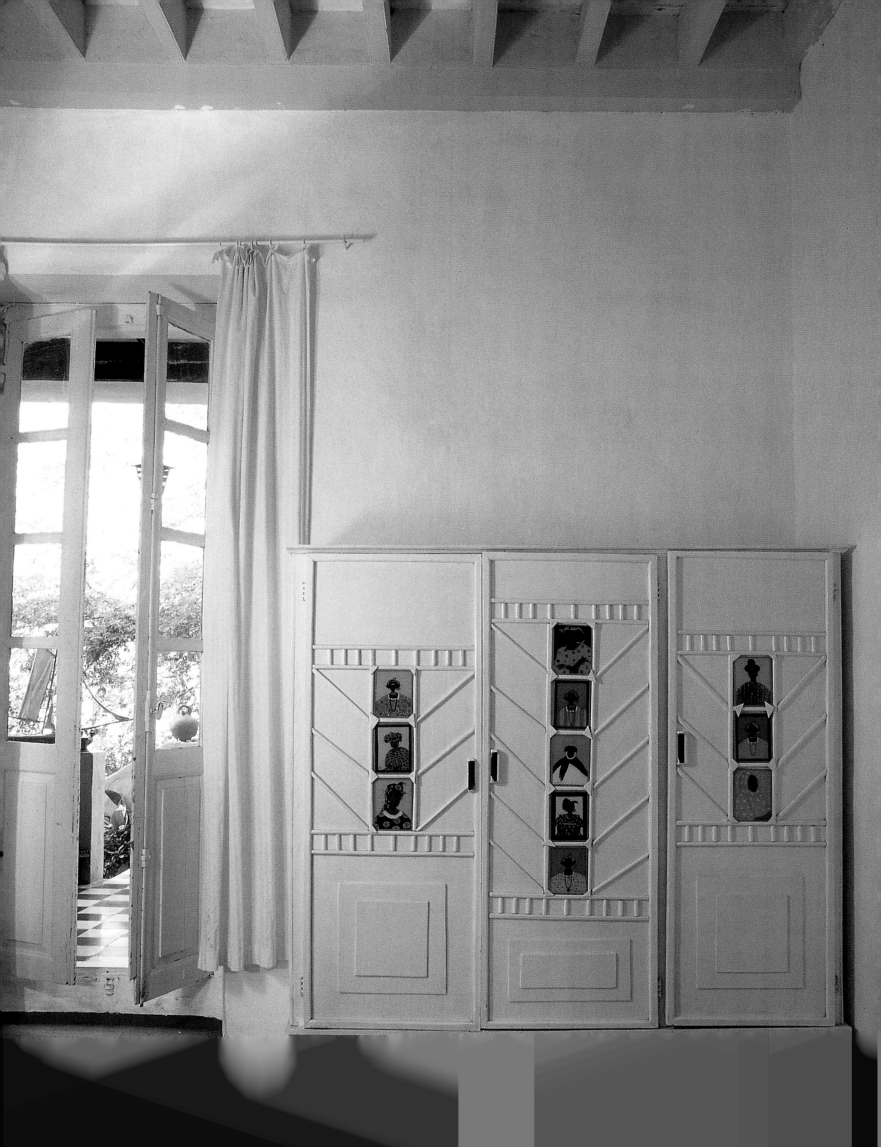

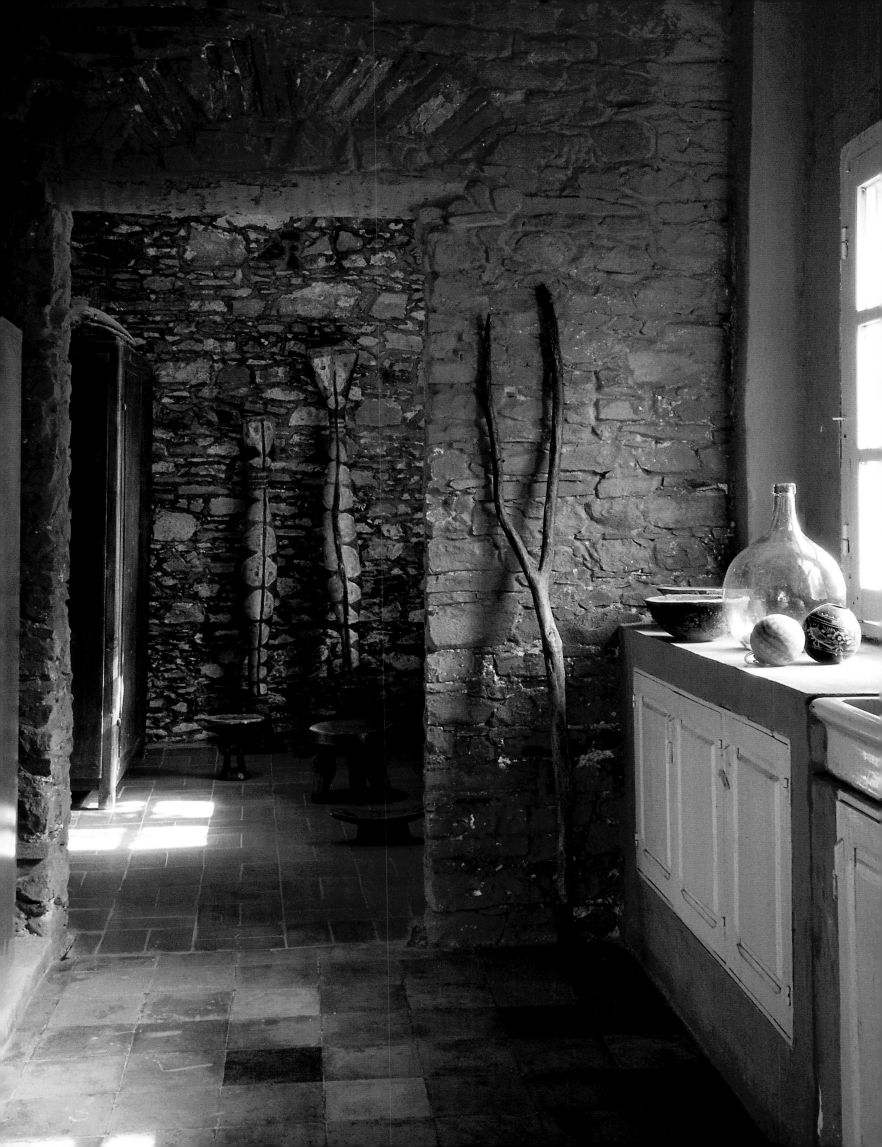

# Marie-Jose Crespin

## Goree Island

A houseful of treasures: a jewellery designer's extraordinary collection of antiques on Gorée.

This 18th century colonial house on the ramparts of Gorée was formerly the residence of a slave trader. Fronting the sea, hidden by a tangle of bonzai baobabs, bougainvilleas and mangoes, it seems to have forgotten everything: in the spacious rooms protected from the heat of the sun by pierced shutters, no trace remains of the tragic past.

On the contrary, the décor here is a joyful celebration of cross-cultural art, a riot of sculptures and African masks. The cement tile floors, the furniture fashioned from various tropical woods and the bright fabrics everywhere testify to an *art de vivre* bursting at the seams with gaiety and colour. The terrace serves as a living room, overlooking an enchanted garden dotted with 1930s *iroko* French chairs. Inside the house, the collection of ethnic objects brings together pieces from Black Africa, North Africa, Asia Minor and south America, with a few touches of modernity supplied here and there by contemporary objects. With its furniture, its lacquered doors and its patchwork of earthenware tiles, the kitchen seems locked in the 1950s. Actually it was at that time that the father of Marie-José Crespin bought the house; Marie-José played here as a child. And the house has been steadily enriched ever since, with the priceless gifts of mixture and variety.

In früheren Zeiten diente das im 18. Jahrhundert erbaute Kolonialhaus an der Stadtmauer Sklavenhändlern als Wohnhaus. Die Erinnerung ist in den Mauern des Hauses gespeichert, das mit Blick aufs Meer in einem Dschungel von Bonsai-Affenbrotbäumen, Bougainvillea und Mangobäumen steht.

In den großen Zimmern mit durchbrochenen Klappläden zum Schutz gegen die Sonne erinnert dagegen nichts mehr an die tragische Vergangenheit. Die Inneneinrichtung preist im Gegenteil, wie zur Ehrenrettung der Geschichte, die Kultur der Rassenmischung durch die ausgestellten afrikanischen Skulpturen und Masken. Eine Lebenskunst voller Fröhlichkeit und Farbe drückt sich in den gekachelten Böden, Möbeln aus exotischen Hölzern und leuchtend bunten Stoffen aus. Wie ein zusätzliches Zimmer ragt die Terrasse in den Garten hinaus – die französischen 1930er-Jahre-Stühle aus Irokoholz sind schlicht bezaubernd. Im Haus selbst wurden in einer Sammlung ethnischer Kostbarkeiten Objekte aus Schwarzafrika, Nordafrika, Kleinasien und Südamerika kombiniert. Auch die zeitgenössische Kunst ist mit mehreren Werken vertreten. Die Küche, eingerichtet mit lackierten Türen, Emailfliesen und altmodischen Möbeln, scheint in den 1950er Jahren stehen geblieben zu sein. In jener Zeit hat Marie-José Crespins Vater das Haus auch gekauft. Die Dame des Hauses hat schon als Kind hier gespielt – seitdem ist das Haus um vieles reicher geworden, vor allem aber wird hier der kulturellen und ethnischen Vielfalt Raum gegeben.

Sur les remparts de Gorée, cette maison coloniale du 18e siècle servait autrefois d'habitation aux commerçants de la pire espèce: les négriers. Face à la mer, dissimulée par une jungle de baobabs-bonzaïs, de bougainvilliers et de manguiers, les murs ont désormais la mémoire qui flanche.

Dans les grandes pièces abritées du soleil par des persiennes ajourées, aucune trace ne subsiste de ce passé tragique. Au contraire, bras d'honneur à l'histoire, la décoration célèbre une culture métissée à travers ses sculptures et ses masques africains. Sols en carreaux de ciment, meubles en bois exotiques et tissus lumineux témoignent d'un art de vivre plein de gaieté et de couleurs. Véritable pièce à vivre, la terrasse qui surplombe le jardin enchante d'emblée avec ses chaises françaises des années 1930 en bois d'iroko. À l'intérieur de la maison, la collection d'objets ethniques marie des pièces d'Afrique noire, d'Afrique du Nord, d'Asie mineure et d'Amérique du Sud. Quelques créations contemporaines posées ici et là modernisent l'ensemble. Avec son mobilier, ses portes laquées et ses carreaux de faïence en patchworks, la cuisine semble figée dans les années 1950. C'est en effet à cette époque que le père de Marie-José Crespin s'est porté acquéreur des lieux. Enfant, la maîtresse de maison y gambadait. Depuis, la maison s'est enrichie d'un des biens les plus précieux: le métissage.

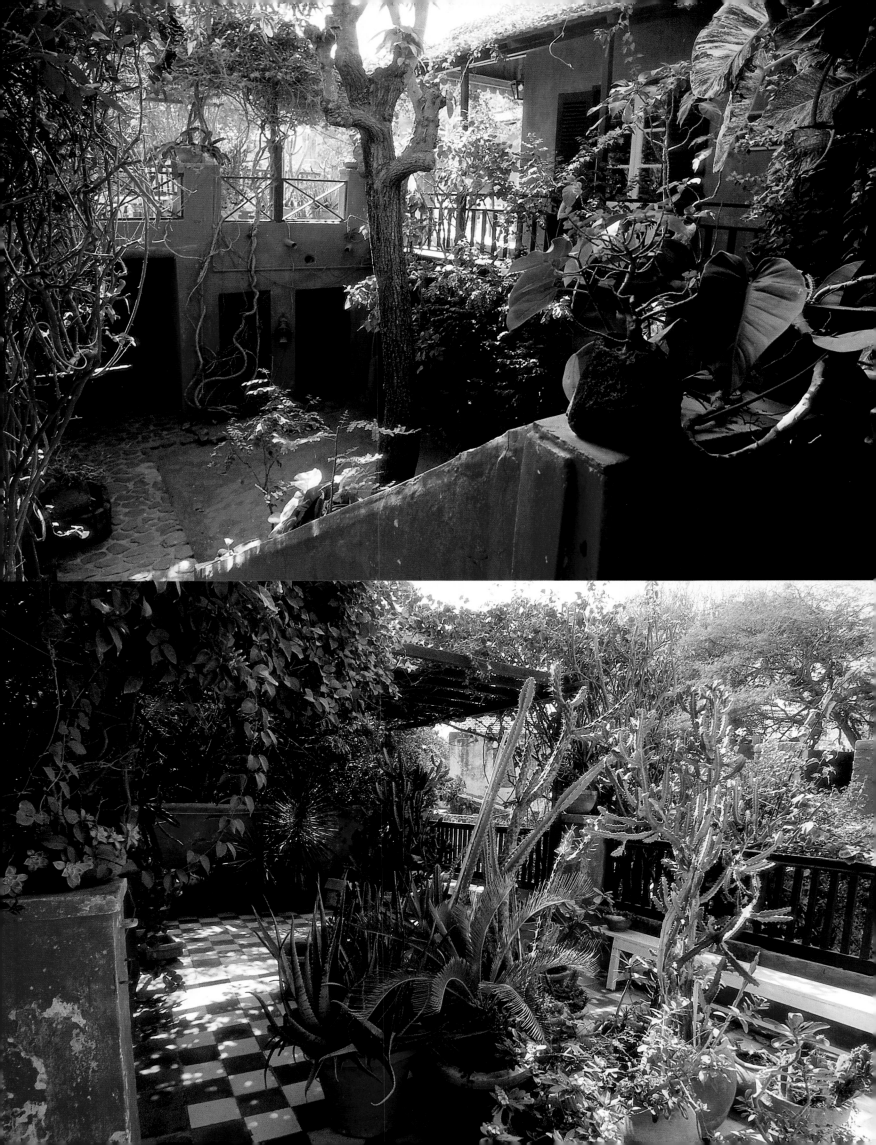

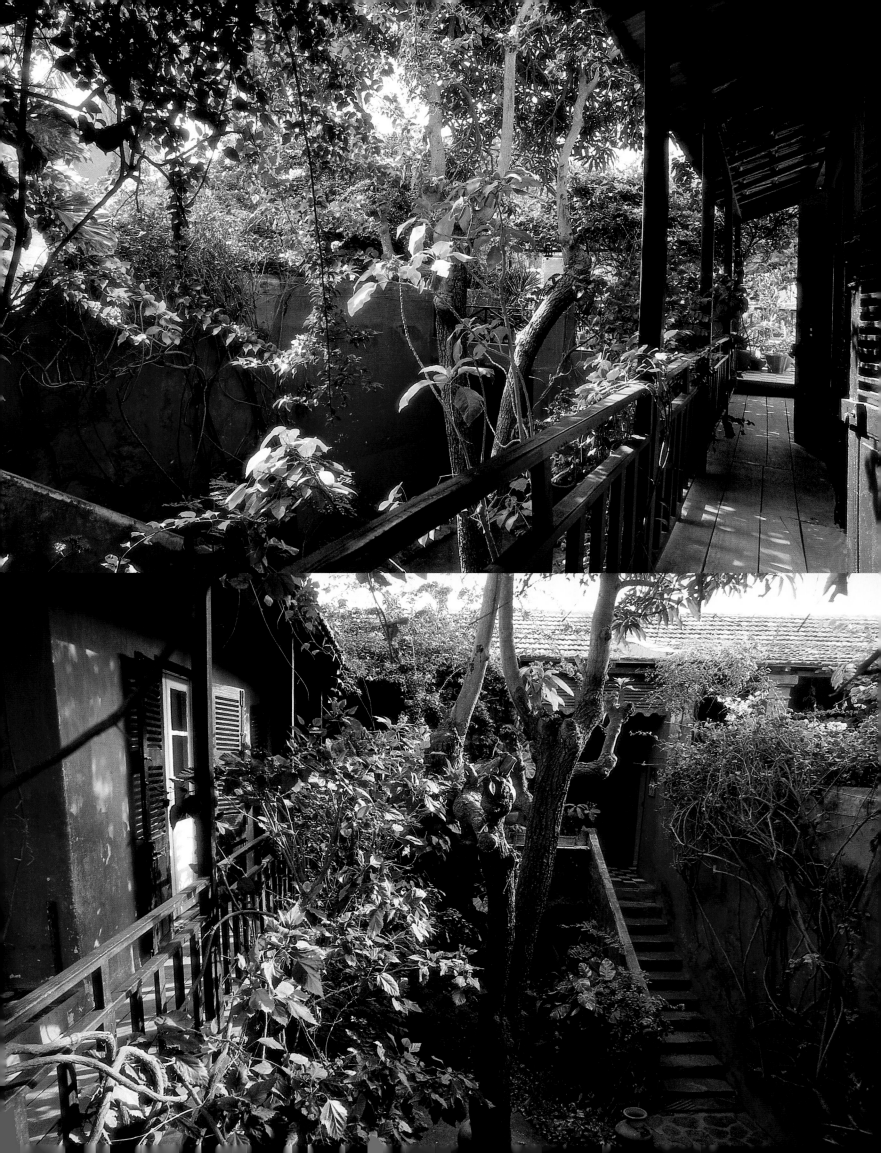

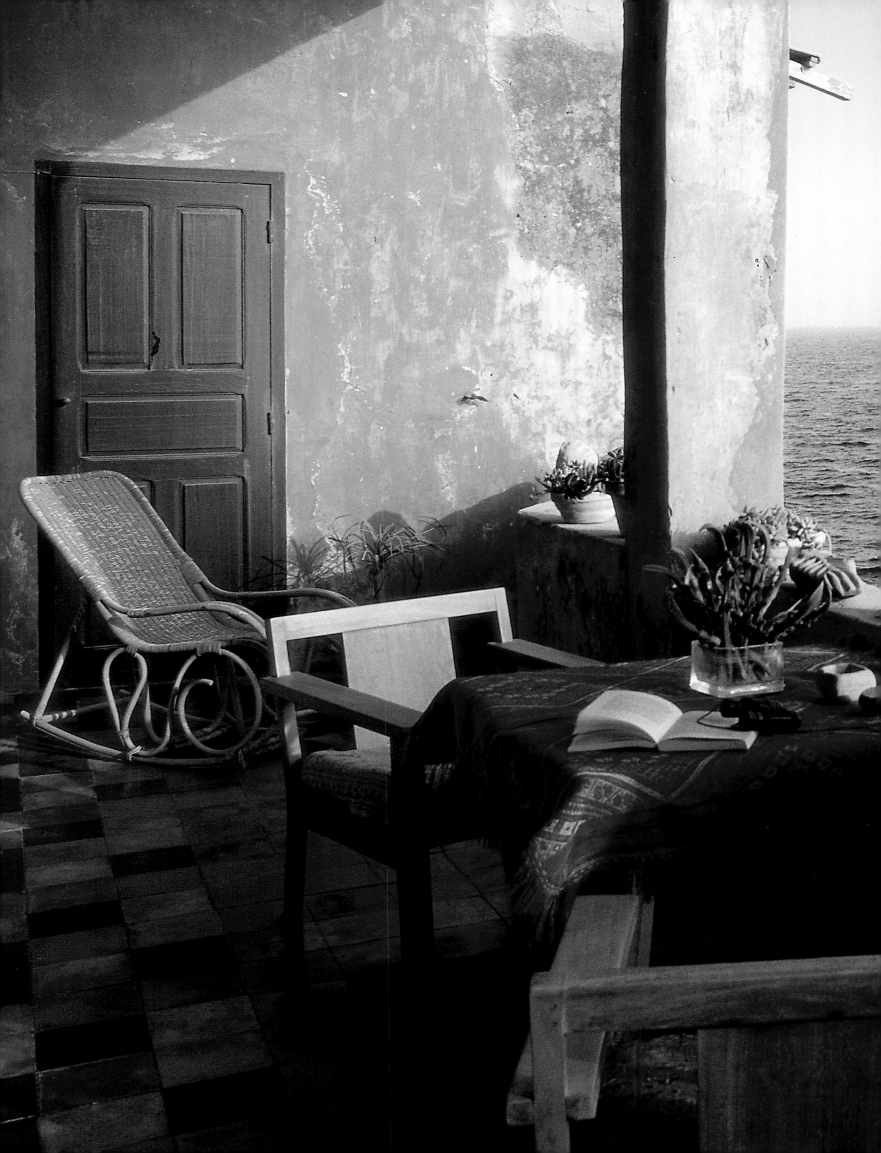

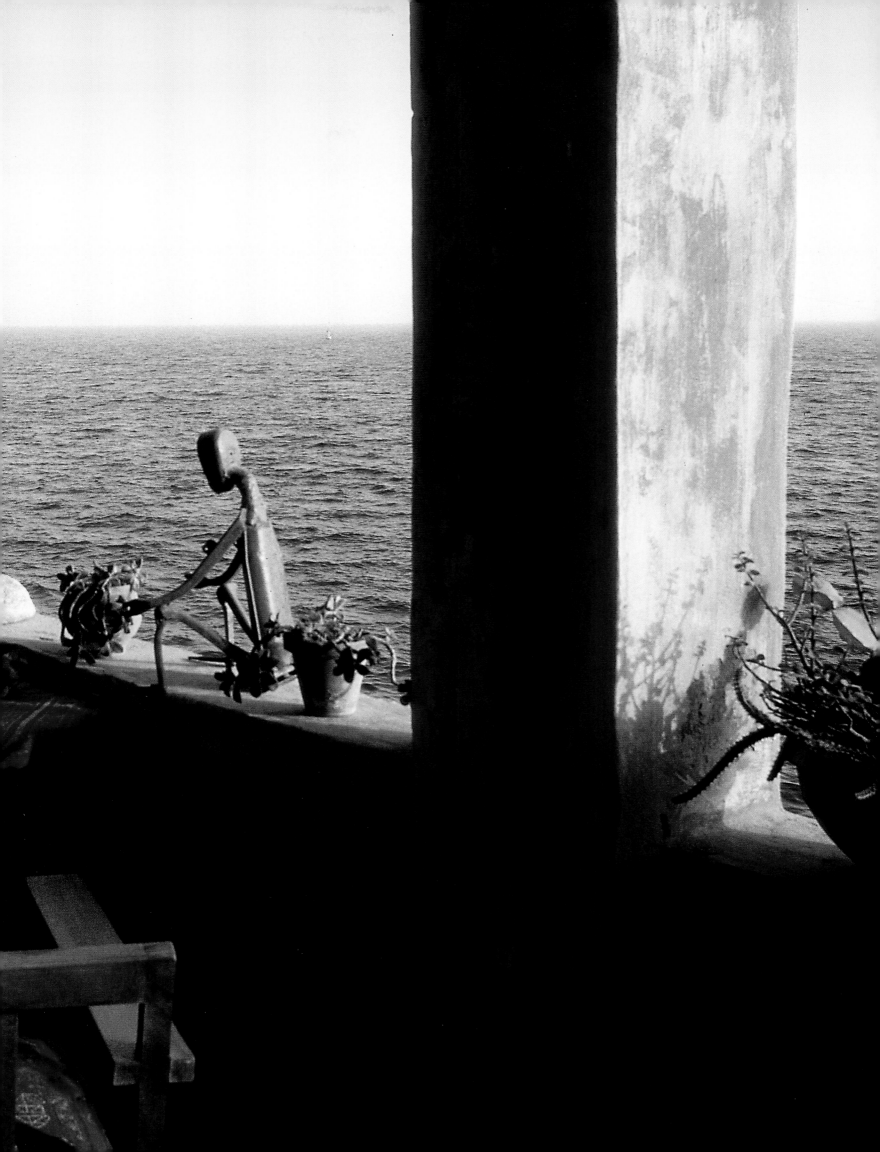

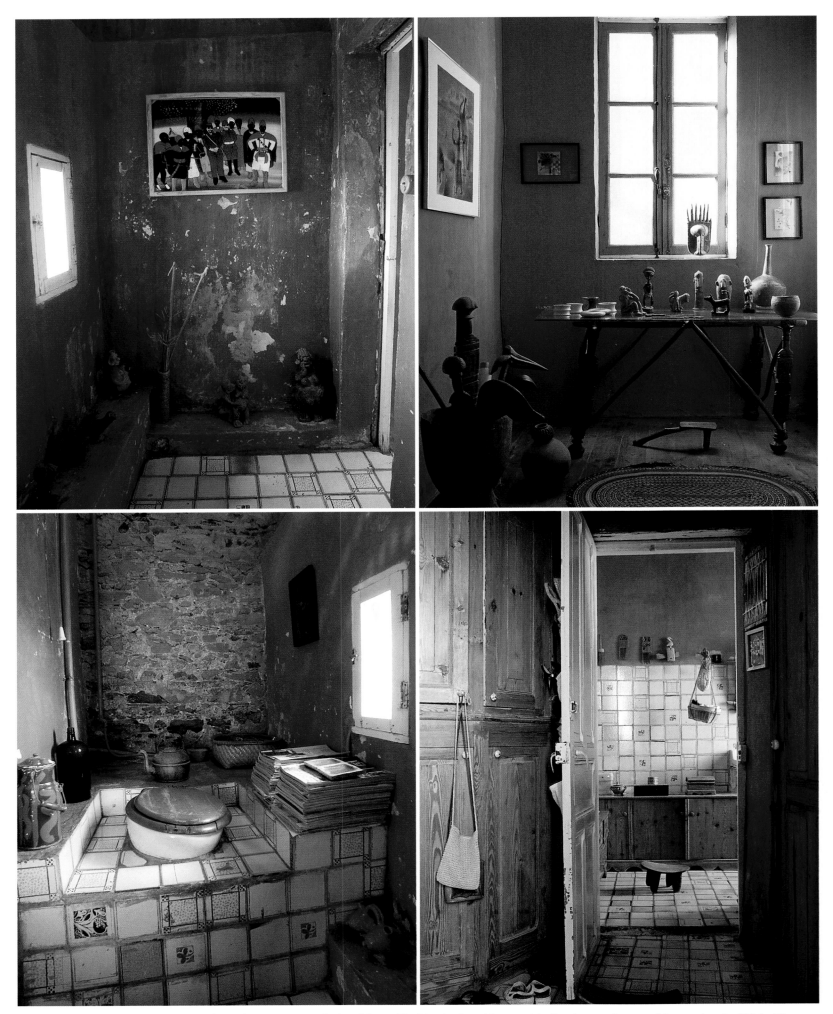

❋ **ABOVE** In the owner's study, objects found in Dakar, Mopti, Marrakesh and Lagos. The Mauritanian table was originally a baggage frame used for camels. ❋ **OBEN** Im Büro bewahrt die Dame des Hauses Objekte aus Dakar, Mopti, Marrakesch und Lagos auf. Der mauretanische Tisch war früher ein »Gepäckbock« für Dromedare. ❋ **OI-DESSUS** Dans le bureau de la propriétaire, des objets trouvés à Dakar, Mopti, Marrakech ou Lagos. La table mauritanienne est à l'origine un «porte-bagages» que l'on pose sur le dos des dromadaires.

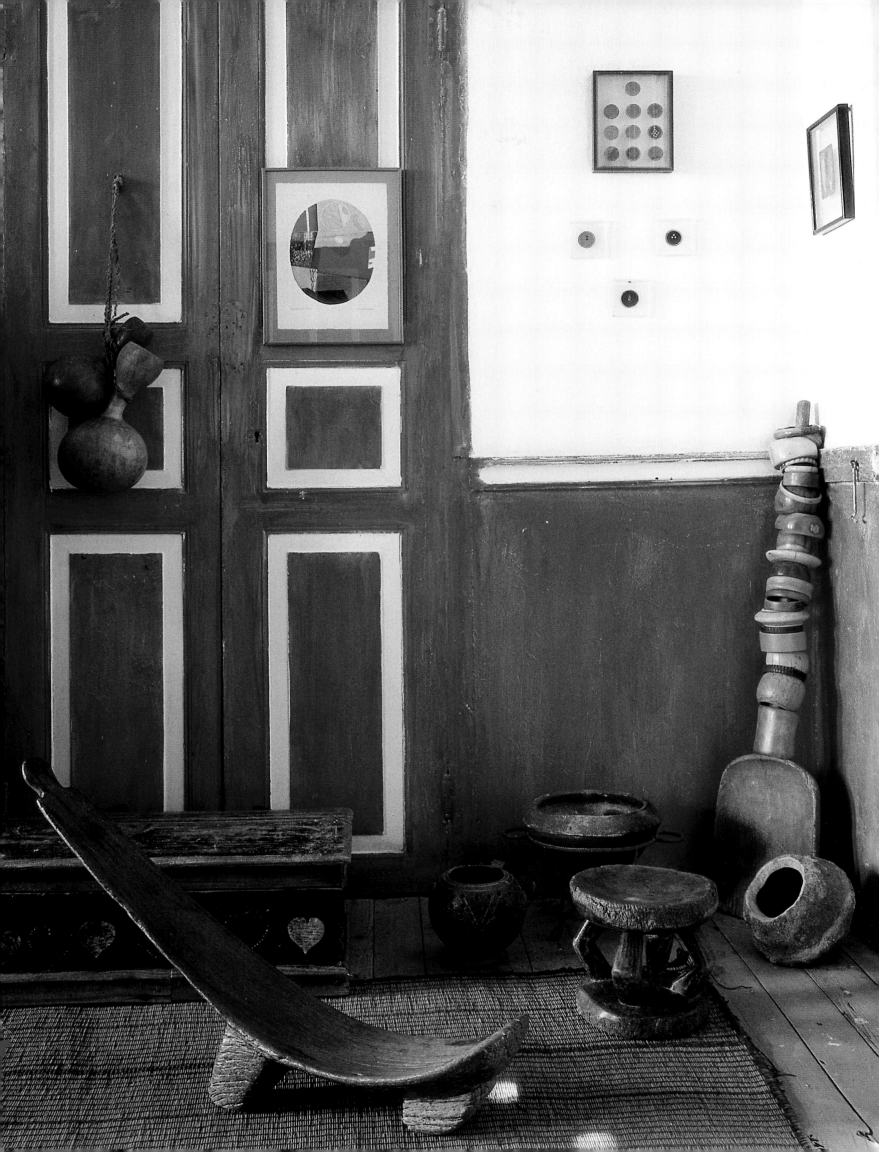

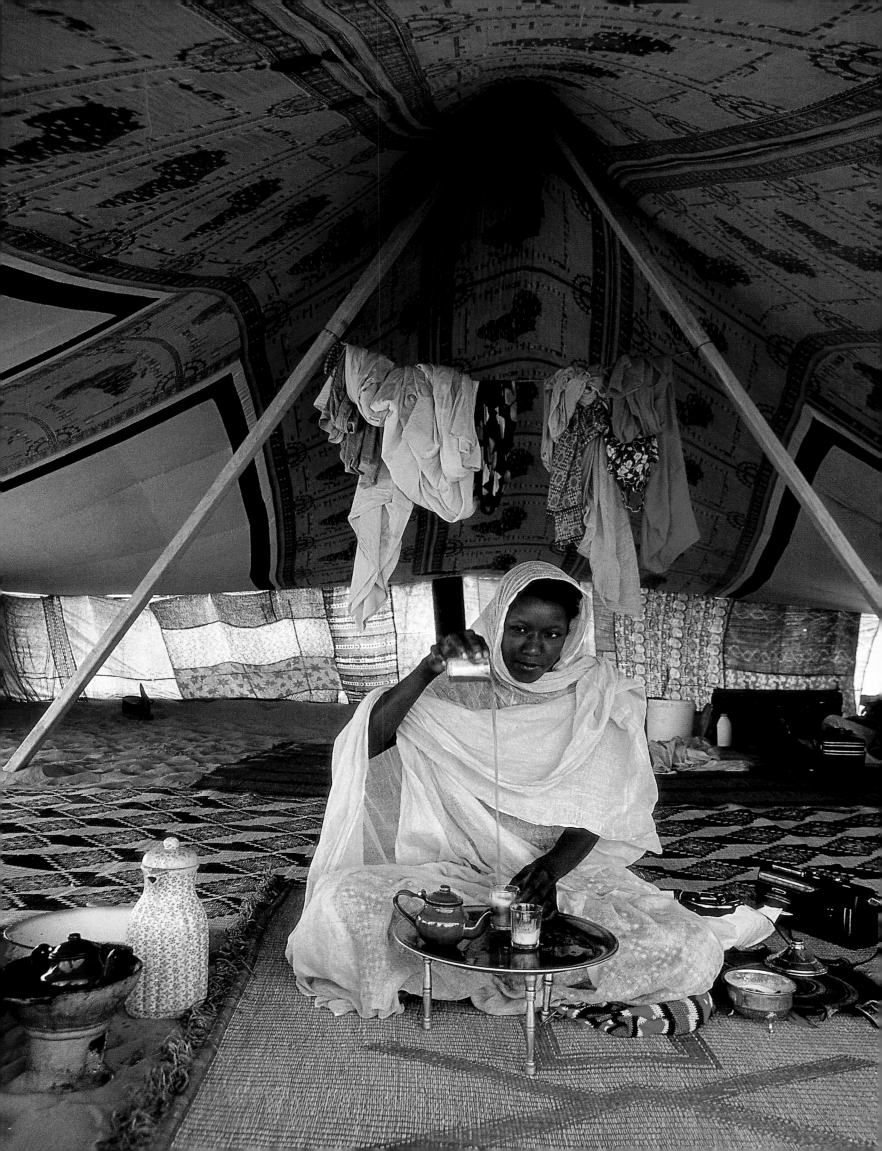

# NOMADS
## Mauritania

For the desert conditions in which they live,
the nomads have never found anything to compare with their *khaimas* (Moorish tents).

The Sahara – a place of gravelly plains, super-heated rocks and sand dunes. The men who live here have to face the most extreme conditions. Their camp is invariably the focus of a loose brotherhood. Each member of the group has his *khaima*, a tent of rectangular canvas.

Its structure consists of two V-shaped masts, joined at the top by a wooden crosspiece. The whole assembly is held down by ropes and small pegs driven in at each corner of the fabric. On the sides, geometrical motifs proclaim the identity of the occupants, while inside, piles of carpets insulate against the sand. In one corner, a kind of baggage frame contains books, clothes, and food. By definition, the *khaima* is expected to follow the rhythm of the seasons, or more precisely those of the rains, along a north-south nomadic axis which determines the migration of camels and livestock. The nomads travel with their families, of course, but the notion of hospitality is anchored deep in their tradition. Any traveller who happens on an encampment is systematically invited to take tea – three cups, no less – according to the ancient ritual. Frequently he receives gifts made by the nomads themselves; and if night falls, he will certainly be invited to sleep on a mat under the canvas.

Sahara. Steinige Ebenen, glühend heiße Felsen und Sanddünen. Die Menschen leben unter extremen Bedingungen. In den Lagern leben häufig erweiterte Großfamilien, von denen jede ihr eigenes *khaima*, ein rechteckiges Zelt aus Tuch hat.

Zwei sich verjüngende Zeltmasten bilden ein umgekehrtes V und werden in der Spitze mit einem Stück Holz zusammengehalten. Vier kleine Zeltpflöcke in den Ecken sowie Seile sichern die Konstruktion. Geometrische Muster auf den Zeltwänden verweisen auf die Stammeszugehörigkeit. Auf der Erde werden Teppiche zum Schutz gegen den Sand ausgebreitet. In einer Ecke steht etwas erhöht auf einem »Gepäckbock« eine Truhe mit Büchern, Kleidung und Lebensmitteln. Das *khaima* passt sich dem Rhythmus der Jahreszeiten an, besser gesagt den Regenzeiten. So zieht sich, bedingt durch die Wanderungen der Dromedar- und Viehherden, eine Nord-Süd-Achse des Nomadentums durch das Land. Die Gastfreundschaft ist in der Tradition der Nomaden fest verankert. Reisende, die zufällig ein Lager entdecken, werden stets zum Tee eingeladen, der dem Brauch gemäß dreimal aufgegossen wird. Häufig werden ihnen auch kunsthandwerkliche Objekte angeboten. Wenn es in der Wüste dämmert, werden sie eingeladen, auf einer Matte zu schlafen. Für die Dauer einer Nacht kann man sich dann von der modernen Welt verabschieden.

Sahara. Plaines caillouteuses, rochers surchauffés et dunes de sable. L'homme vit ici dans des conditions extrêmes. Son campement abrite le plus souvent une fratrie élargie. À chacun sa *khaïma*, cette tente de toile en rectangle.

Deux mâts en V renversés, effilés et réunis au sommet par une pièce en bois. Des petits piquets plantés aux quatre coins et des cordages maintiennent l'ensemble. Sur les parois, des motifs géométriques indiquent l'identité tribale. Voilà pour la «charpente». Sur le sol, les tapis étalés isolent du sable. Dans un coin, une sorte de porte-bagages surélève le coffre qui contient les livres, les vêtements et la nourriture. Par définition, la *khaïma* est appelée à suivre le rythme des saisons, ou plus exactement celle des pluies, en un axe de nomadisation nord-sud qui détermine les migrations des troupeaux de dromadaires et de bétail. On vit en famille, certes, mais la notion d'hospitalité est ancrée au plus profond de la tradition nomade. Le voyageur qui découvre par hasard un campement est systématiquement invité à savourer un thé, en trois fois selon le rituel. Souvent, on lui propose des objets artisanaux. Si la nuit tombe sur le désert, il est invité à dormir sur une natte. Alors, l'espace d'une nuit, il dit adieu au monde moderne.

✳ **BELOW** In the orange-tinted desert, the white canvas *khaimas* follow the rhythm of the rains, migrating alongside their owners' livestock. **FACING PAGE** The baggage frame with its coloured legs protects cushions, clothes and food from the driving sand. **FOLLOWING PAGES** The canvas sides of the tent are decorated with multicolored geometrical patterns that repeat the tribal motif sewn into the top of the tent. ✳ **UNTEN** In der orangefarbenen Wüste folgen die Nomaden mit ihrer *khaïma* aus weißem Tuch dem Rhythmus der Regenzeiten, damit das Vieh genügend zu Fressen bekommt. **RECHTE SEITE** Der »Gepäckbock« mit den bunten Beinen schützt Kissen, Kleidung und Lebensmittel vor Sand. **FOLGENDE DOPPELSEITE** Bunte geometrische Zeichen zieren die Zeltwand. Sie nehmen das auf die Zeltspitze genähte Stammesmuster wieder auf. ✳ **CI-DESSOUS** Dans le désert orange, les *khaïma* en toile blanche suivent le rythme de la pluie pour les migrations du bétail. **PAGE DE DROITE** Le porte-bagages aux pieds colorés protège du sable les coussins, les vêtements, mais aussi la nourriture. **DOUBLE PAGE SUIVANTE** La paroi de toile est décorée de signes géométriques multicolores qui rappellent le motif tribal cousu au sommet de la tente.

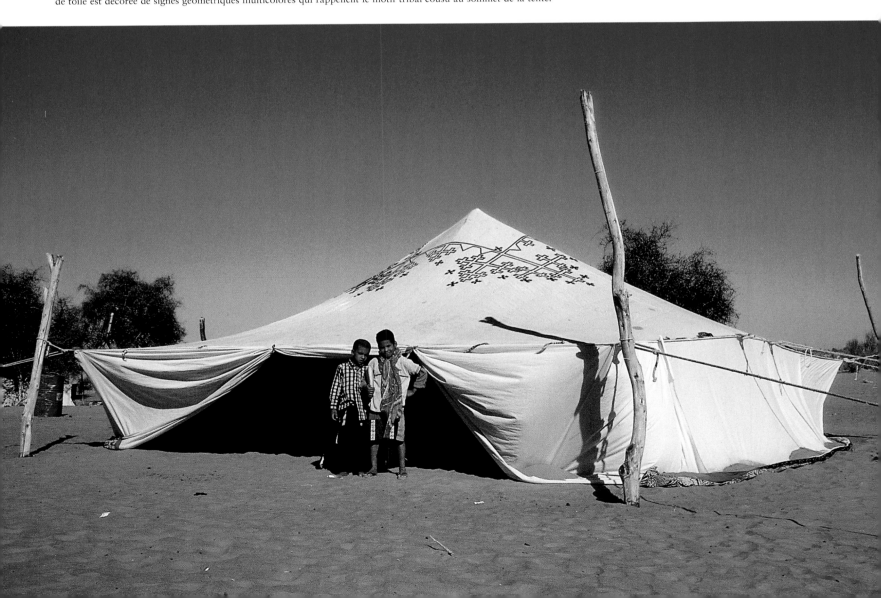

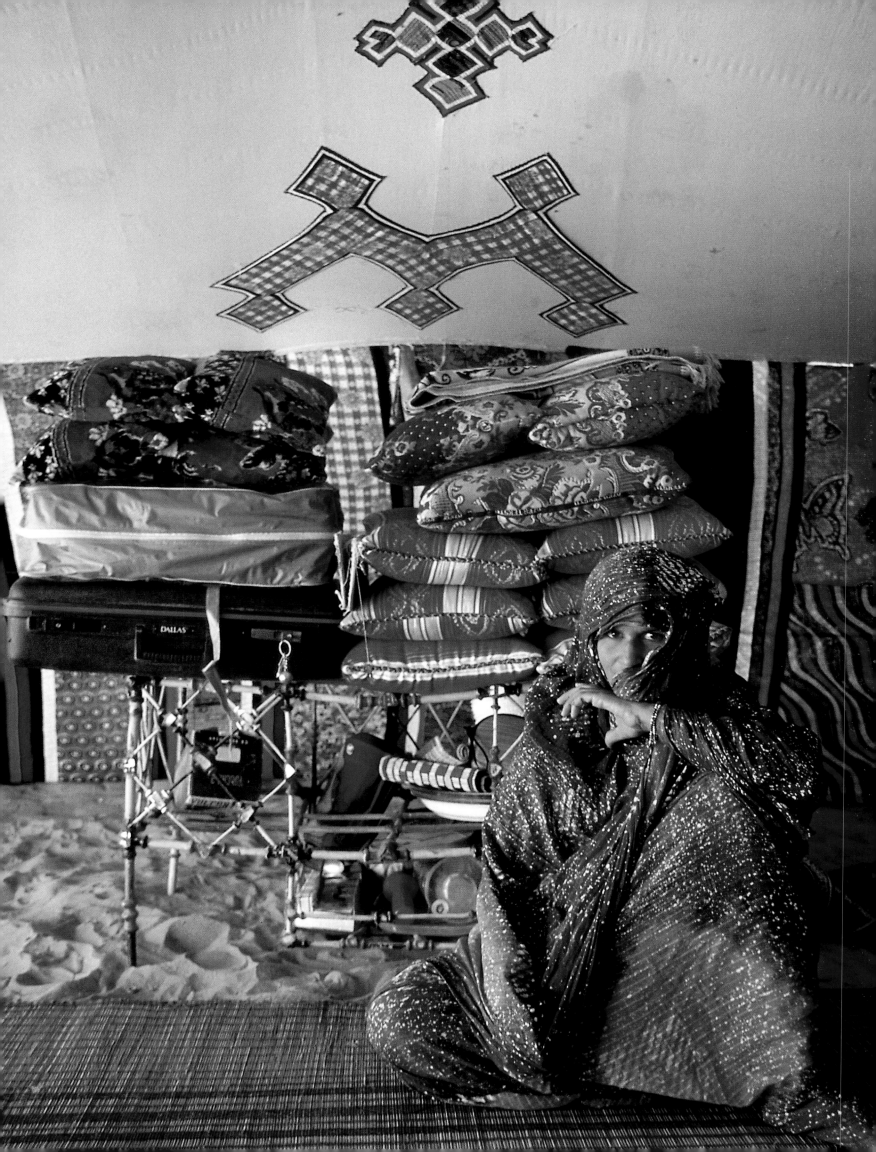

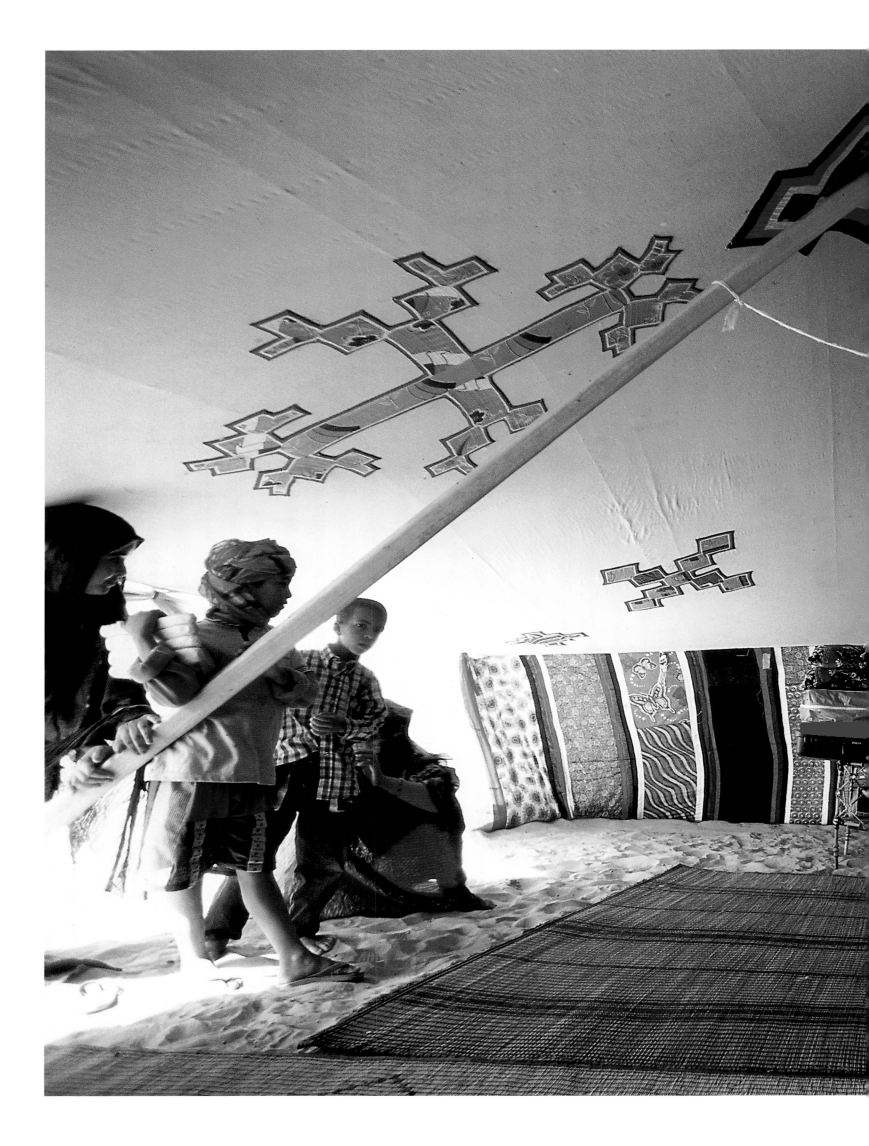

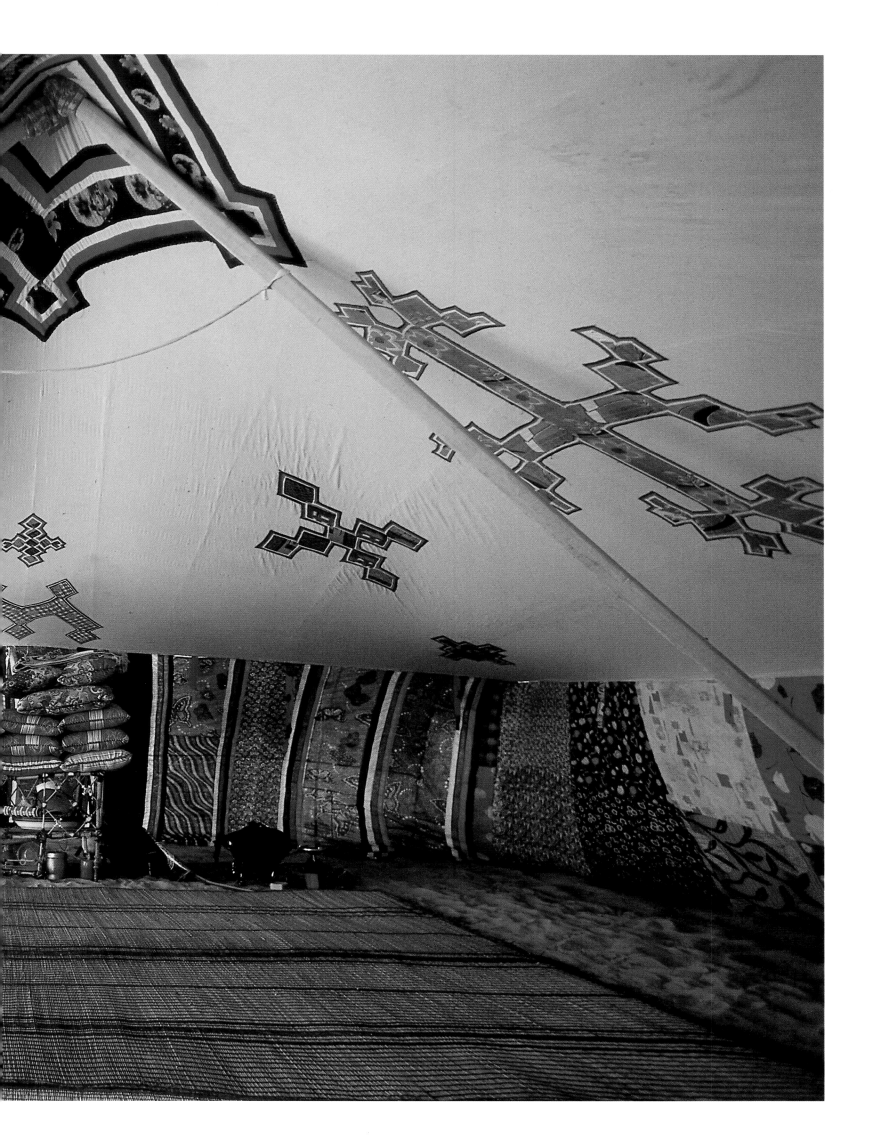

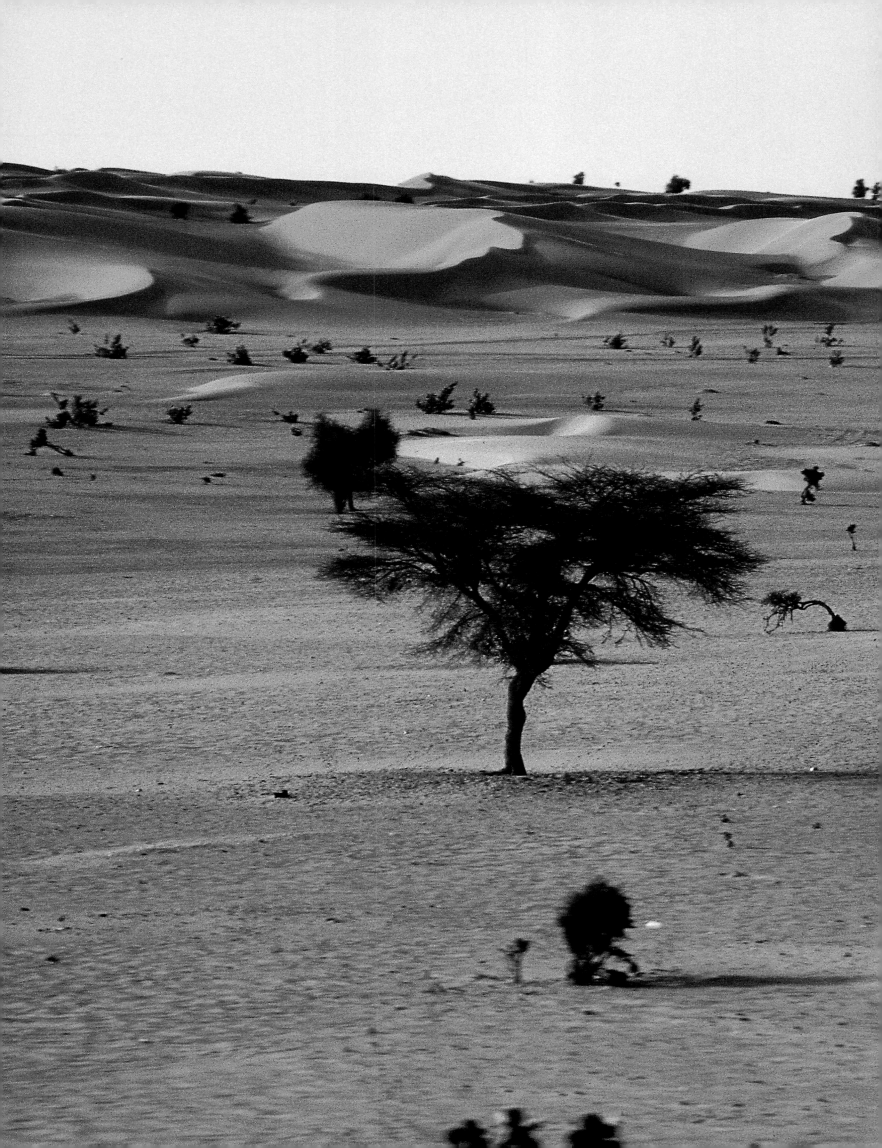

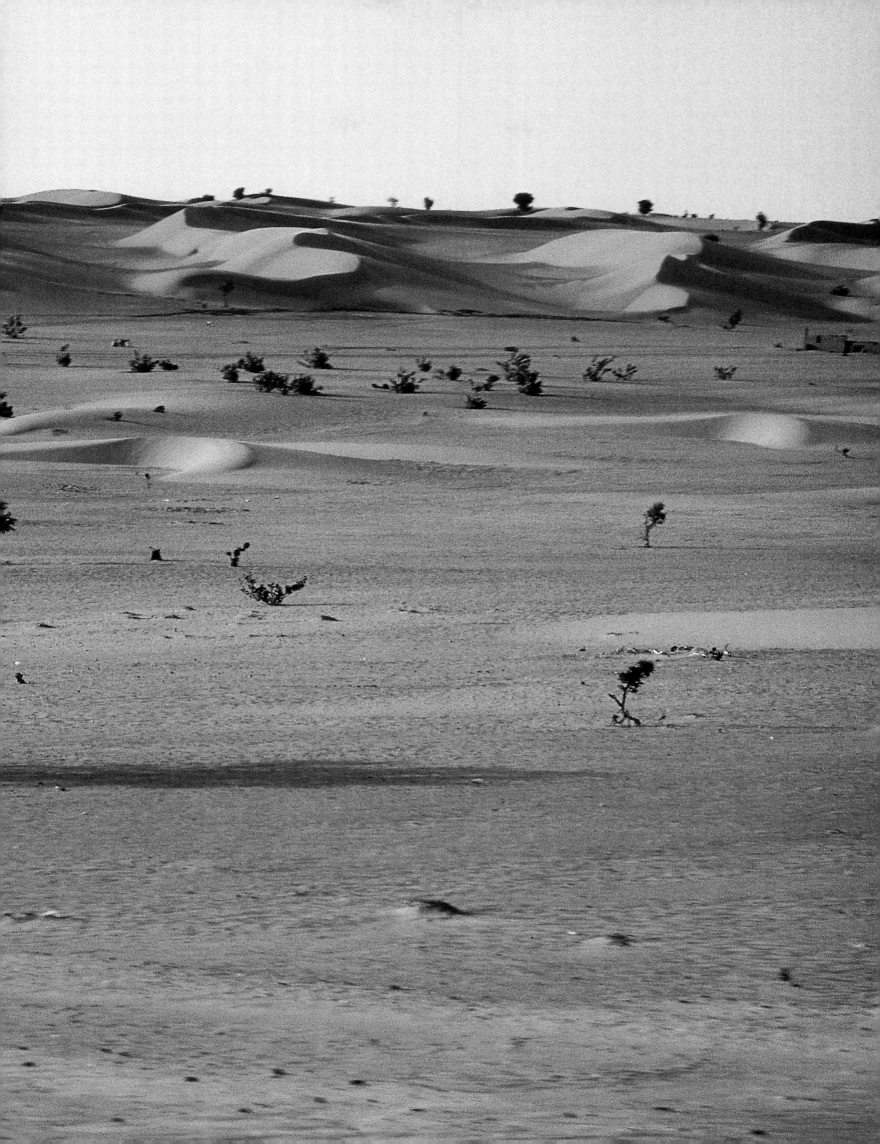

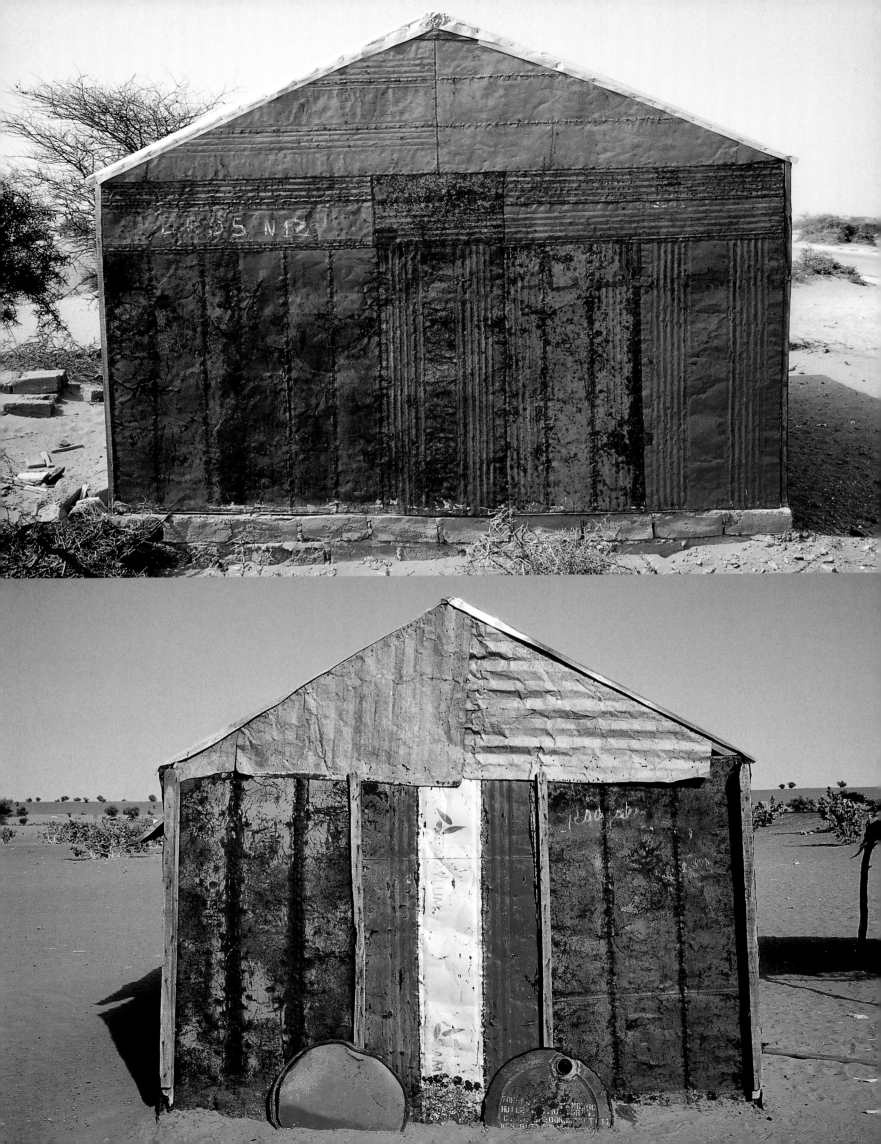

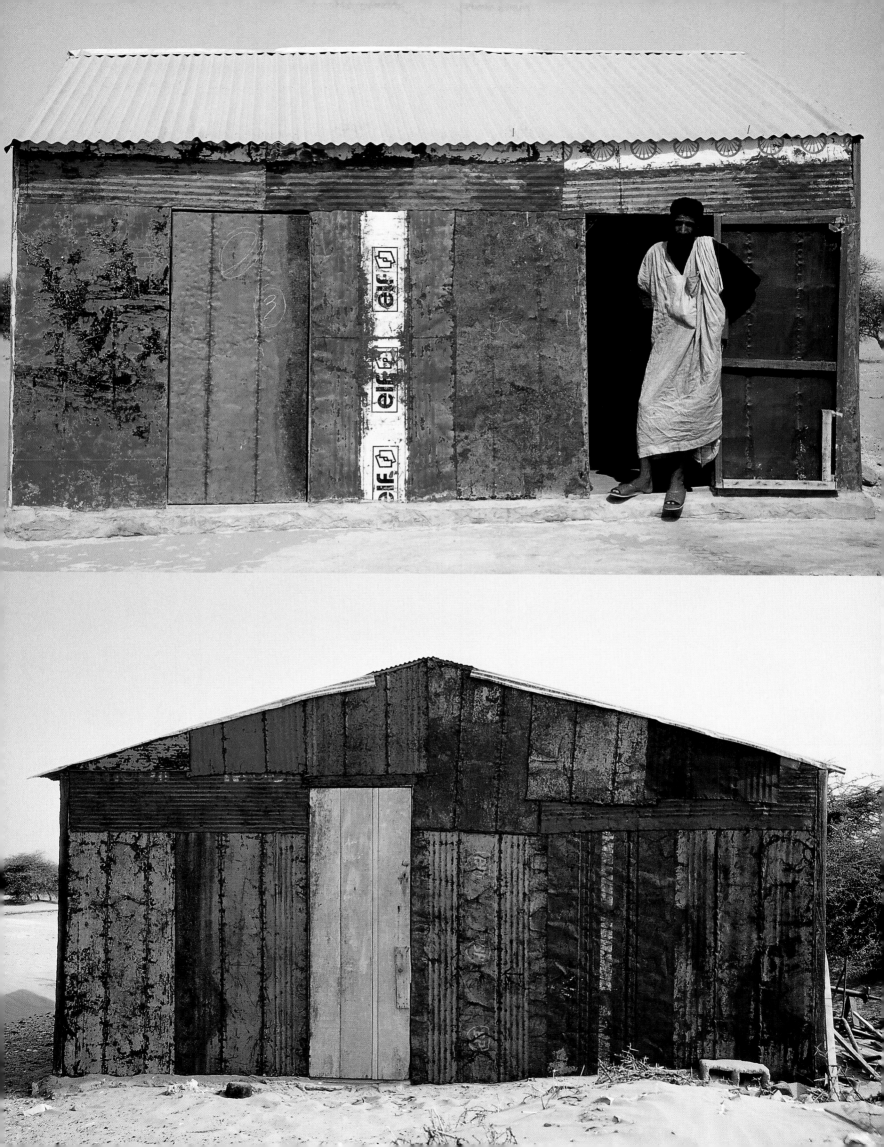

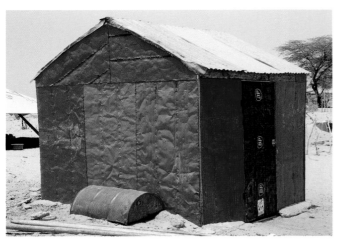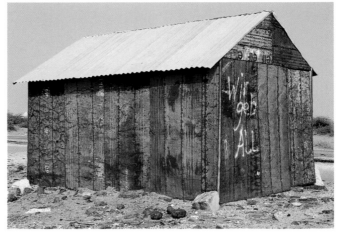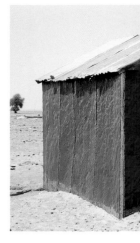
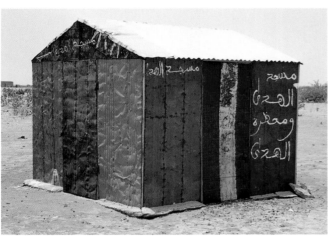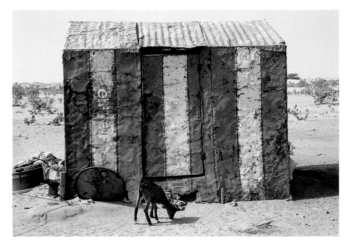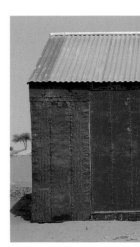
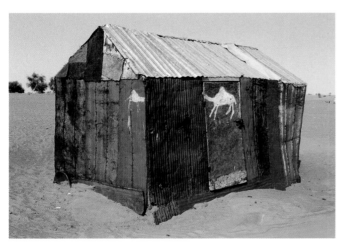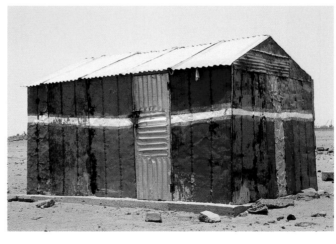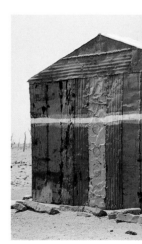
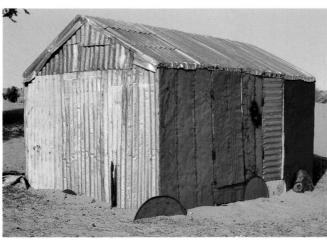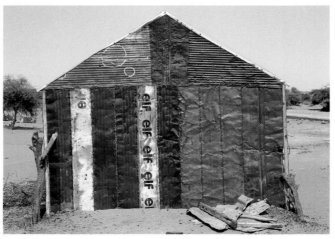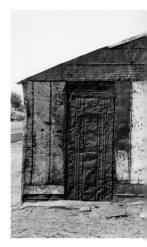

✻ **ABOVE** Drought, industrialization and various forms of modernization in their country have brought the nomads closer to the main roads. Dwellings that serve as shops and storehouses have been set up close to the tents. ✻ **OBEN** Wegen der Trockenheit sowie der Industrialisierung und anderen Ausprägungen der Modernisierung des Landes zieht es viele Nomaden in die Nähe der Straßen. Die Bretterbuden, die als Läden und Lagerstätten dienen, werden neben den Zelten errichtet. ✻ **CI-DESSUS** La sécheresse, l'industrialisation et les diverses formes de modernisation du pays ont fait affluer de nombreux nomades près des routes. Les cabanes, qui servent à la fois de boutiques et de lieux de stockage, ont été installées à proximité des tentes.

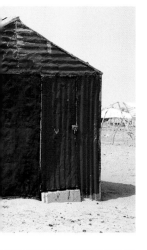
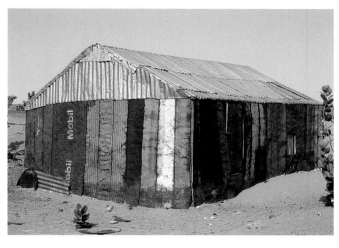
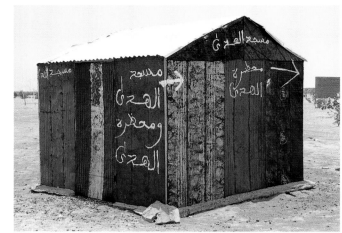
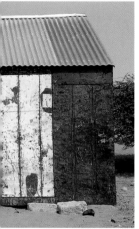
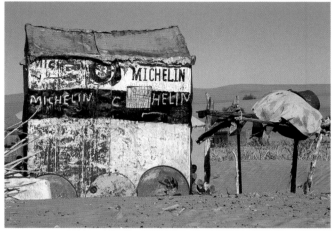
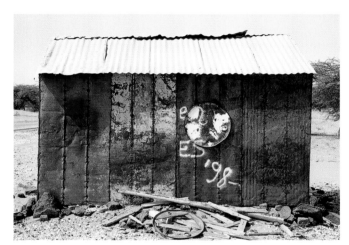
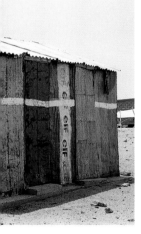
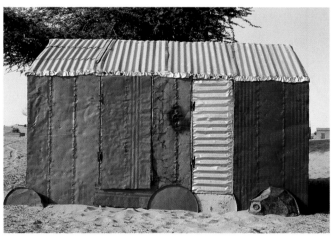
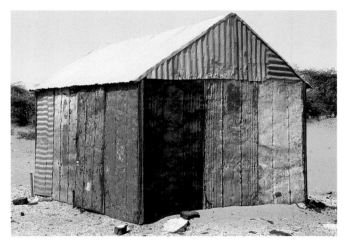
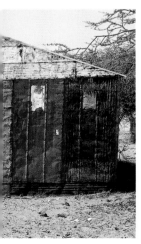
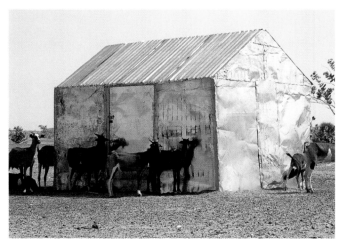
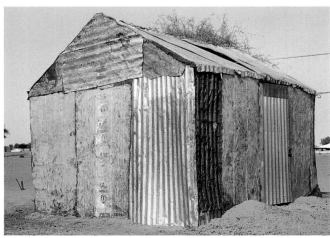

※ **BELOW AND FACING PAGE** Tradition and modernity: these coloured huts are also used as workshops and stalls by the traders along Mauritania's highways, as evidenced here on the road to Senegal. ※ **UNTEN UND RECHTE SEITE** Tradition und Moderne: Die Kaufleute, die über die mauretanischen Straßen ziehen, nutzen die bunten Hütten oft auch als Handelsplatz, wie hier auf der Route Richtung Senegal, wo diverse Gebrauchsgegenstände und Kleidung verkauft werden. ※ **CI-DESSOUS ET PAGE DE DROITE** Tradition et modernité: les huttes colorées sont aussi utilisées comme comptoirs par les marchands qui occupent les routes mauritaniennes, comme ici en direction du Sénégal, en proposant des objets d'utilité courante ou des ateliers de confection.

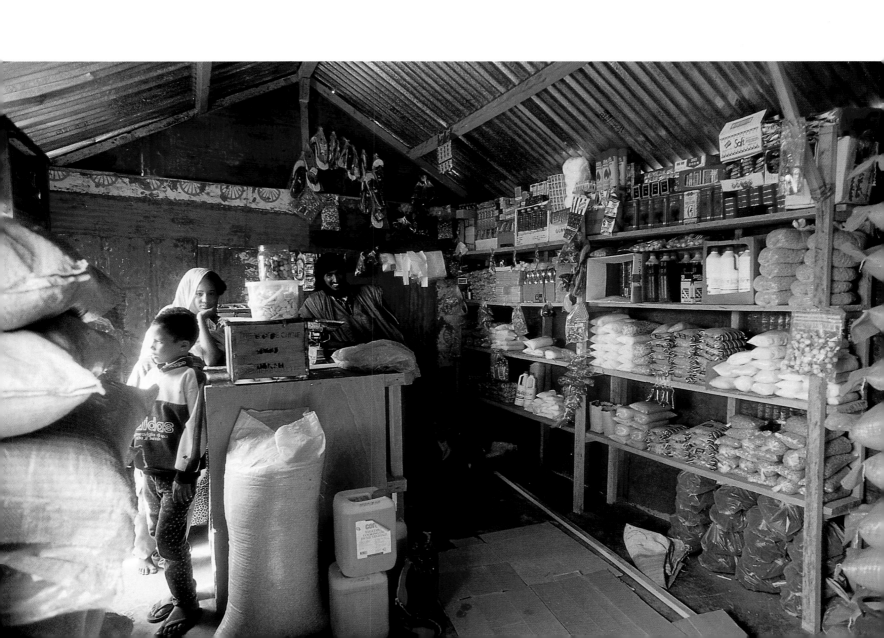

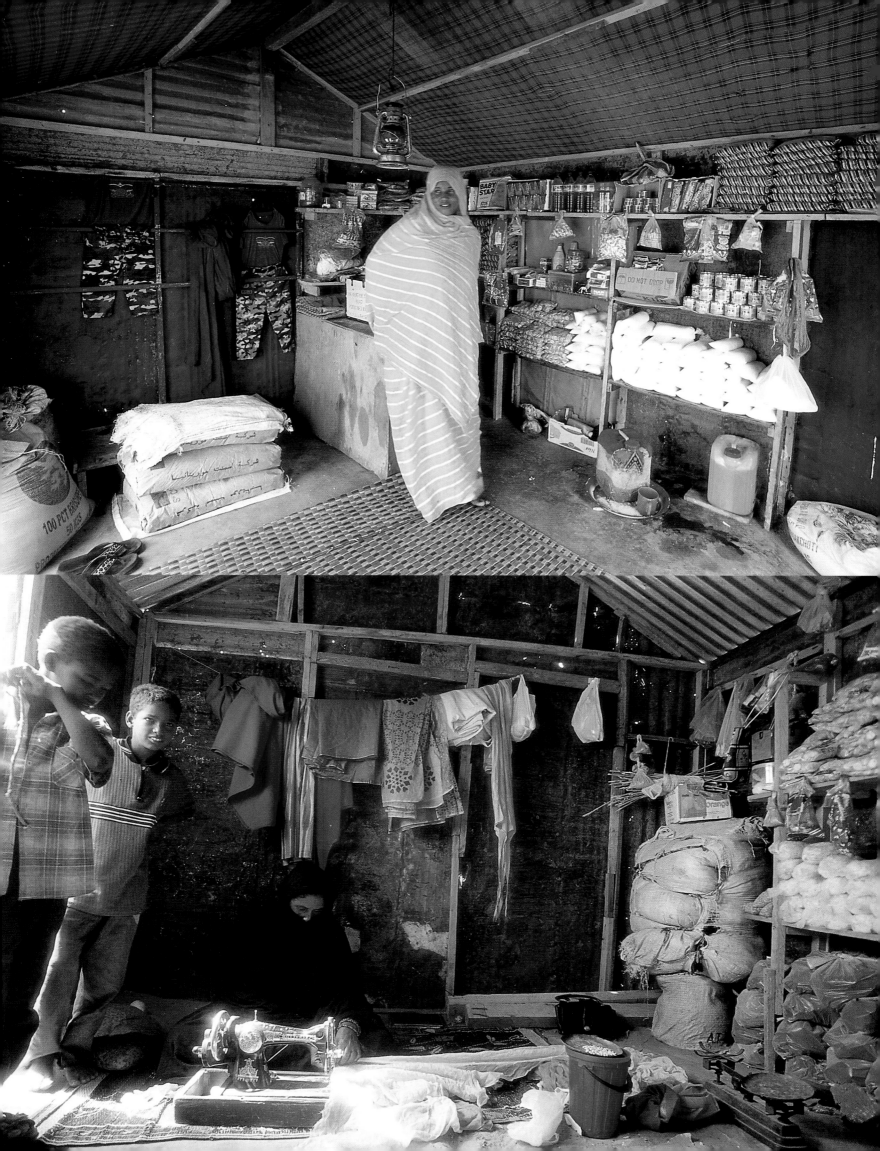

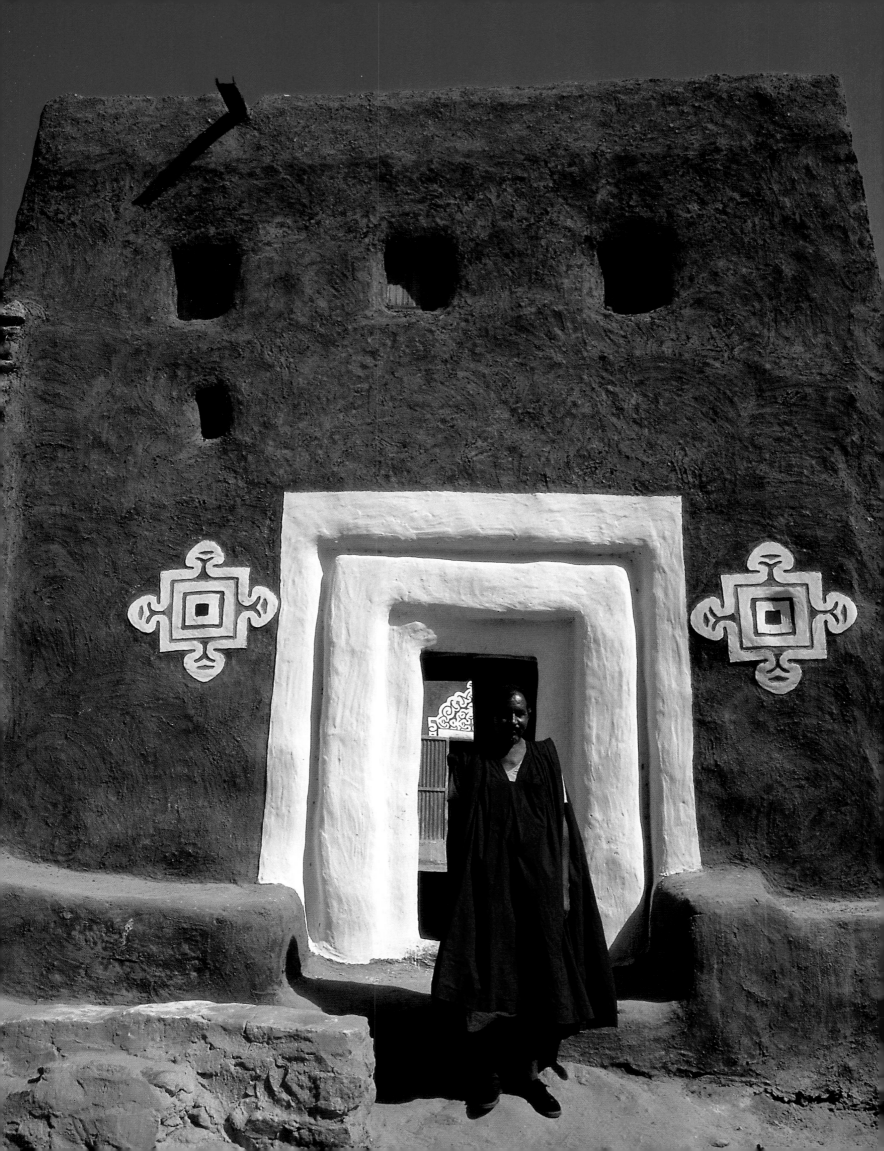

# OUALATA

# Mauritania

This city, which formerly lay at a junction of the old caravan routes, still has a secret language of its own.

From the Middle Ages to the end of the 18th century, Oualata lived contentedly from the caravans of Black Africa bringing gold from Bambuk and salt from Idjil, as well as those of Morocco laden with pottery, scents and jewellery.

Oualata, at "the edge of eternity", was only rivalled by Timbuktu. Today, in its sand-choked alleys, there are few traces of the heroic past, when sages came to study and were given free bed and board by the townspeople. There's little left, indeed, except the arabesques, restored to contemporary taste in the 1980s by one of the town's notables. Finger-painted on walls rendered with red clay (a mixture of sand and lime), these frescoes cover façades, door frames and window frames. Since the Koran forbade the representation of human beings, their decorative conventions describe the various parts of the body by way of symbols. Very present in courtyards, they are also to be found in the interiors of two-storey Sudanese style houses. Typically, the buildings consist of long, parallel rooms or else single, much larger spaces with a central pillar supporting the beams. There are recesses, too, close to the sleeping mats, where owners display their books and oil lamps. These symbolize the greatest treasures of Oualata today, namely light and knowledge.

Vom Mittelalter bis ins 18. Jahrhundert führte Oualata ein begünstigtes Dasein, denn hier machten die Karawanen aus Schwarzafrika Station, die Gold aus den Bambouk-Bergen und Salz vom Kedia d'Idjil mitführten. Die Karawanen aus Marokko dagegen waren mit Tonwaren, Parfüm und Schmuck beladen.

Oualata, »das Gestade der Ewigkeit«, hatte nur einen einzigen Rivalen: Timbuktu. Von diesen Zeiten der Blüte, als Gelehrte noch freie Kost und Logis hatten, um in Ruhe studieren zu können, ist in den Gassen, die von der gefräßigen Wüste mit Sand zugeschüttet werden, nicht mehr viel zu sehen. Übrig geblieben sind höchstens die Arabesken, die ein Notabler der Stadt im Zeitgeschmack der 1980er Jahre hat instand setzen lassen. Die Fingermalerei (in einer Mischung aus Sand und Kalk) auf den mit rotem Lehm verputzten Wänden ziert die Fassaden sowie die Tür- und Fensterumrahmungen. Da der Koran die Darstellung von Menschen verbot, illustrierte diese ornamentale Kunst die verschiedenen Körperteile symbolisch. Die verschwenderischen Muster in den Innenhöfen finden sich auch im Innern der ein- bis zweistöckigen Häuser im sudanesischen Stil. Am Eingang liegen oft längliche, parallel angeordnete Zimmer, an die sich ein großer Raum mit einem stützenden Mittelpfeiler anschließt. In den Nischen über den Schlafmatten stellen die Bewohner Bücher oder Öllampen zur Schau. Das Licht und das überlieferte Wissen sind die einzigen Schätze, die Oualata geblieben sind.

Du Moyen-Âge à la fin du 18e siècle, Oualata vivait heureuse en accueillant les caravanes d'Afrique noire chargées d'or du Bambouk, de sel d'Idjil, ou celles du Maroc bourrées de poteries, de parfums et de bijoux.

Oualata, «le rivage de l'éternité», n'avait que Tombouctou pour rivale. Aujourd'hui, dans les ruelles ensablées par un désert vorace, peu de traces sont encore visibles de ces temps héroïques où les érudits, hébergés et nourris gratuitement, pouvaient y étudier librement. Ne subsistent guère que ces arabesques remises au goût du jour par un notable de la ville au début des années 1980. Peintes au doigt sur des murs enduits d'argile rouge (un mélange de sable et de chaux), ces fresques posées à plat ornent les façades, les tours de portes et de fenêtres. Le Coran interdisant la représentation des êtres humains, cet art décoratif décrit de manière symbolique des parties du corps. Très présents dans les cours, les motifs se déploient également dans les intérieurs des maisons à étage de style soudanien. Au seuil des demeures, on découvre tantôt des pièces longues et parallèles, tantôt une salle plus vaste dont le pilier central supporte la charpente. Dans les niches, à proximité des nattes pour dormir, les propriétaires mettent en valeur des livres ou des lampes à huile. Les seuls trésors de Oualata: la lumière et la connaissance.

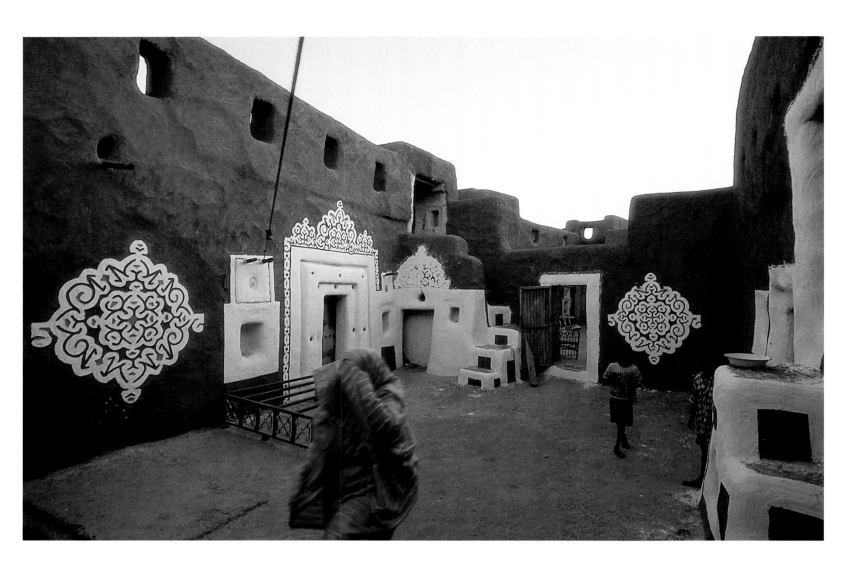

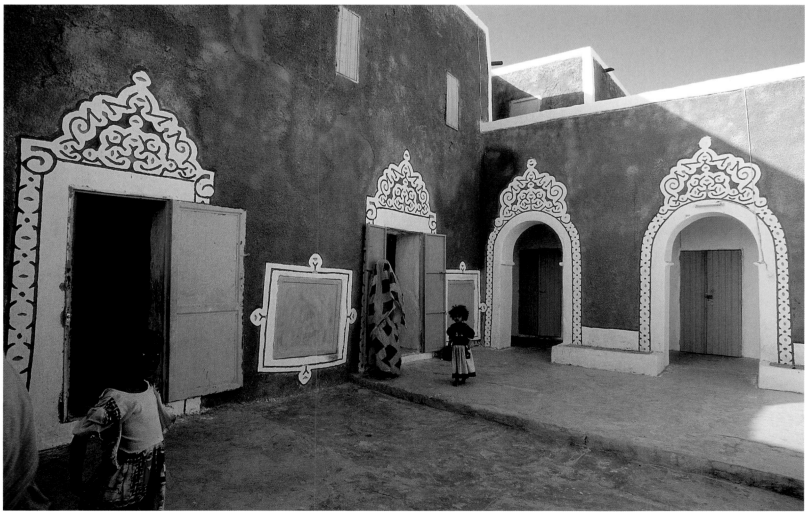

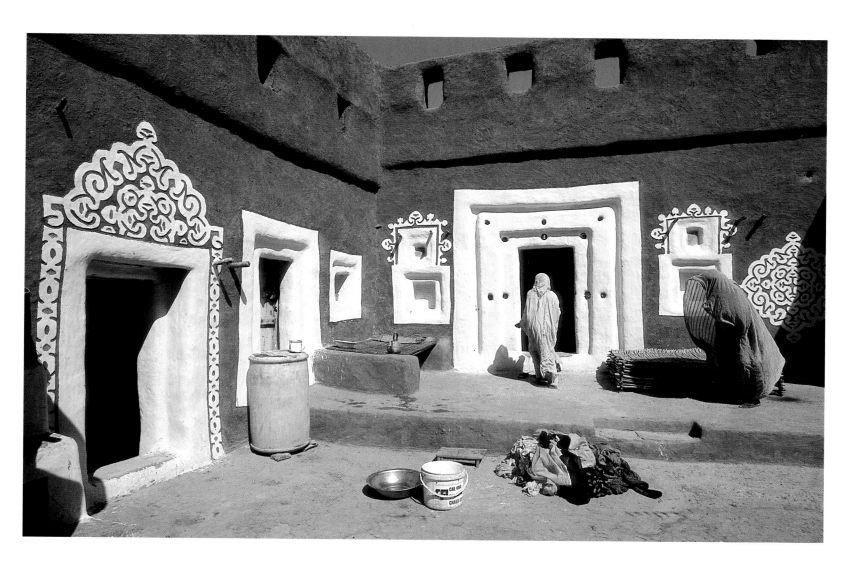
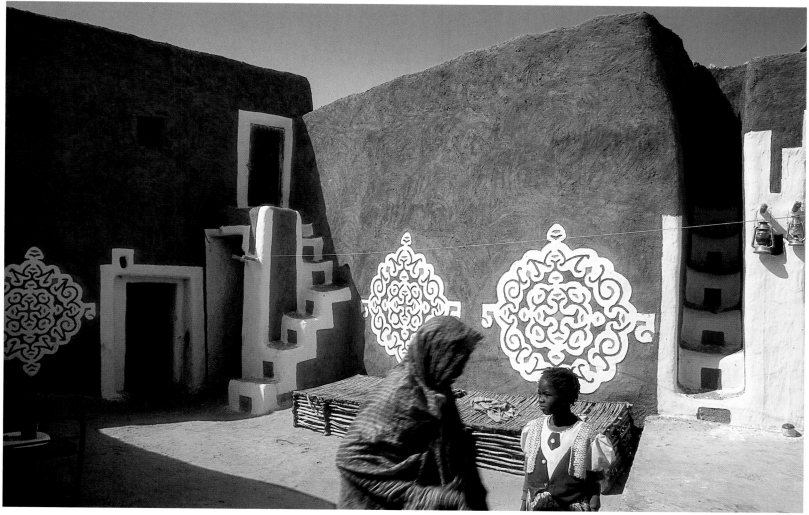

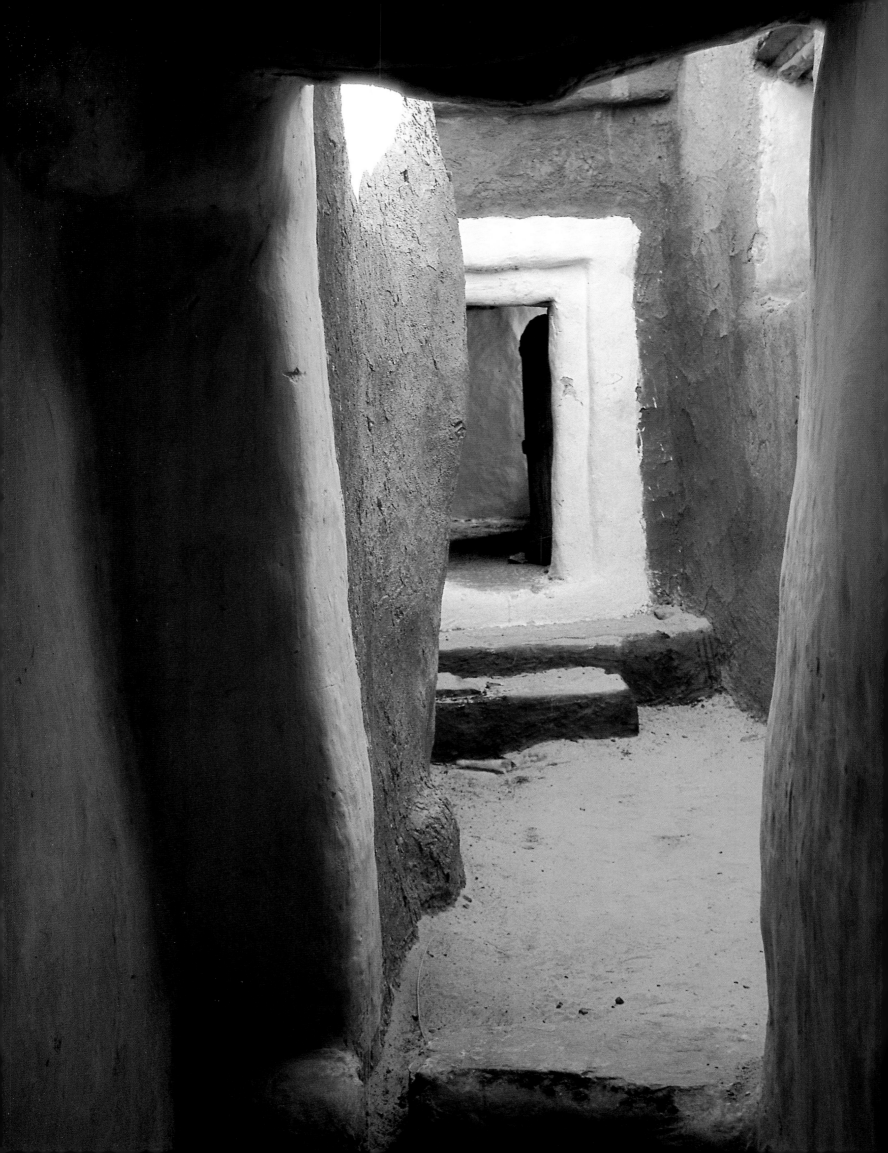

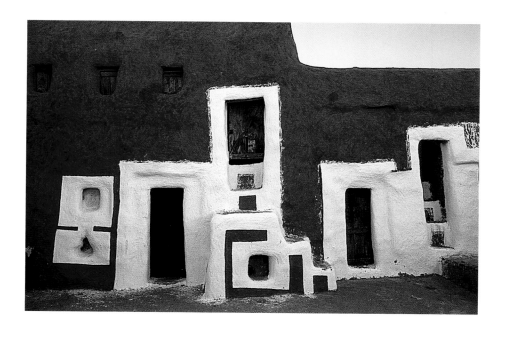

※ **FACING PAGE AND BELOW** A maze of alleyways invaded by the desert sand. Oualata is built close to a mountain slope. Between the two-storey houses, people move along paths edged by massive benches. The outer walls of the houses are all windowless, their only openings being their doors. ※ **LINKE SEITE UND UNTEN** Oualata mit seinen verwinkelten und versandeten Gassen schmiegt sich an einen kleinen Berghang. Zwischen den zweigeschossigen Häusern stehen massive Bänke. Die Außenmauern der Häuser sind glatt und fensterlos, die Türen sind die einzigen Öffnungen. ※ **PAGE DE GAUCHE ET CI-DESSOUS** Lacis de ruelles envahies par le sable, Oualata est blottie à flanc de colline. On circule entre les maisons à deux étages dans des voies bordées par des banquettes massives. Les murs extérieurs des maisons sont aveugles, les seules ouvertures sont les portes d'entrée.

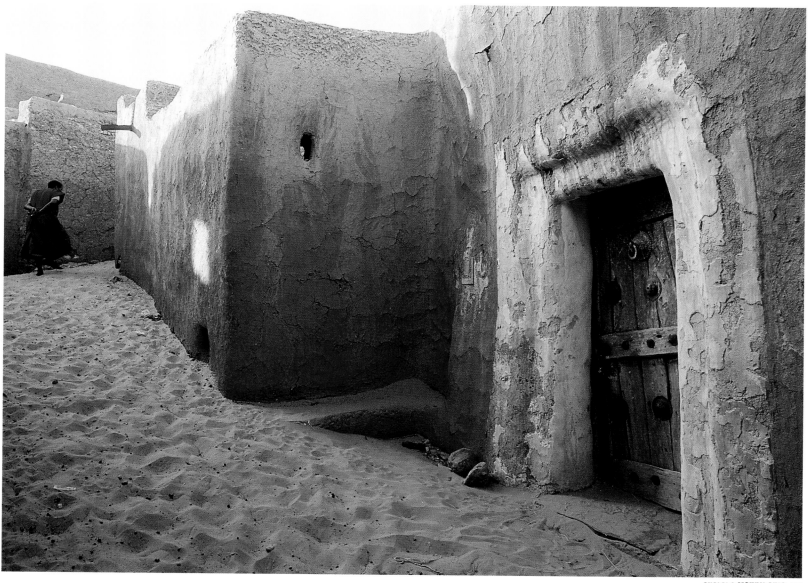

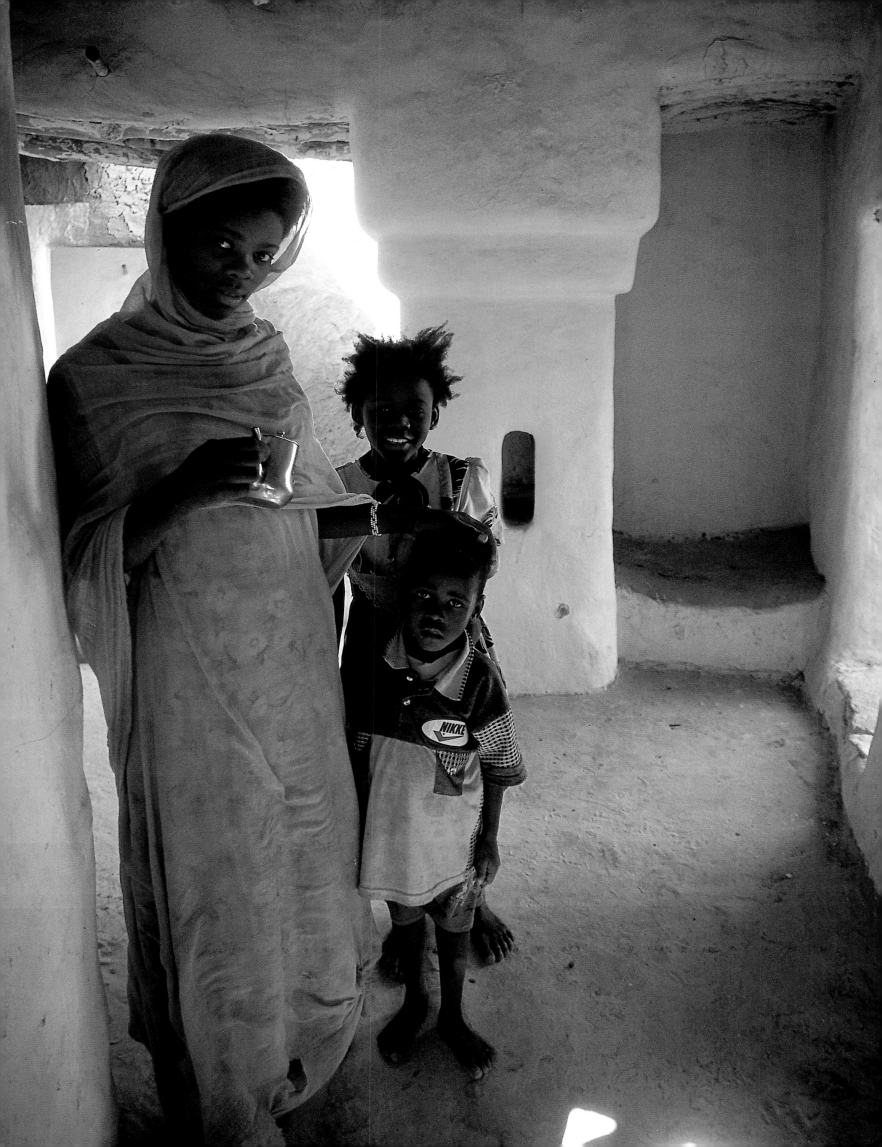

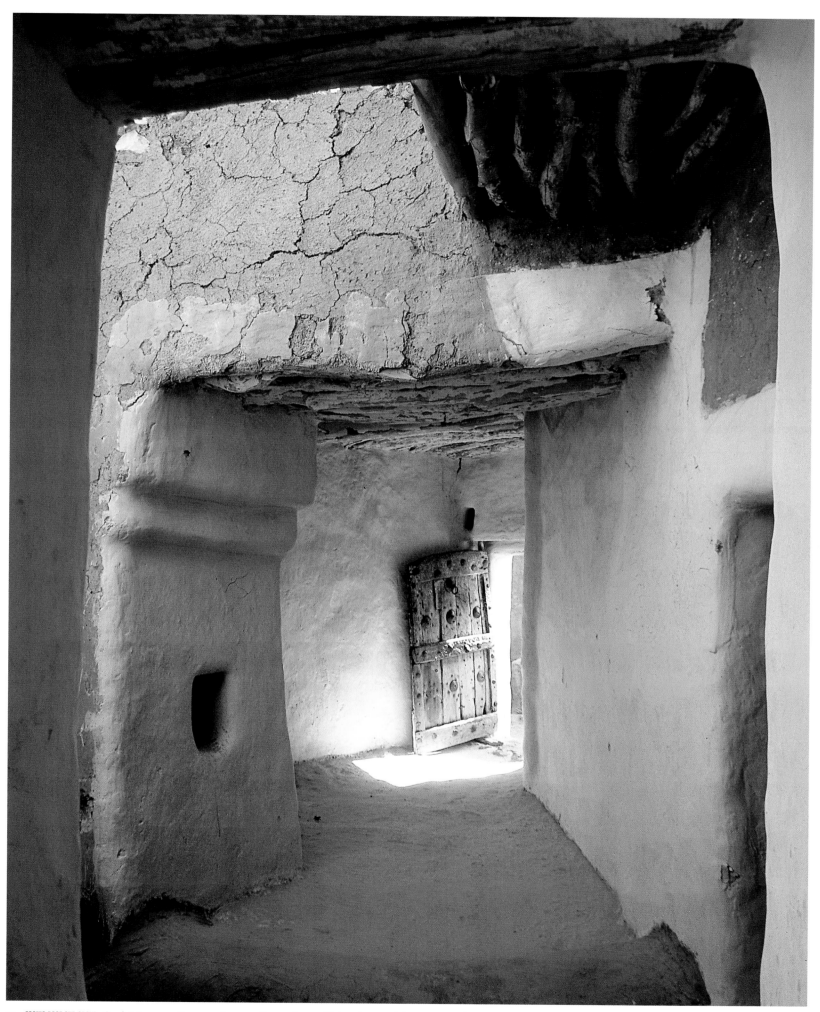

✳ **FACING PAGE AND ABOVE** Oualata's rose patterns are known all over the world, but the town's interiors are almost entirely devoid of furniture. The study of the Koranic texts appears to be its people's only source of wealth. ✳ **LINKE SEITE UND OBEN** Die Bilder der Rosettenornamentik von Oualata gingen um die Welt, doch in den Häusern stehen nur wenige Möbel. Das Studium der Koransuren ist scheinbar der einzige Reichtum der Einwohner. ✳ **PAGE DE GAUCHE ET CI-DESSUS** Si les images des rosaces d'Oualata ont fait le tour du monde, les intérieurs sont presque dénués de mobilier. L'étude des textes coraniques semble être la seule richesse des habitants.

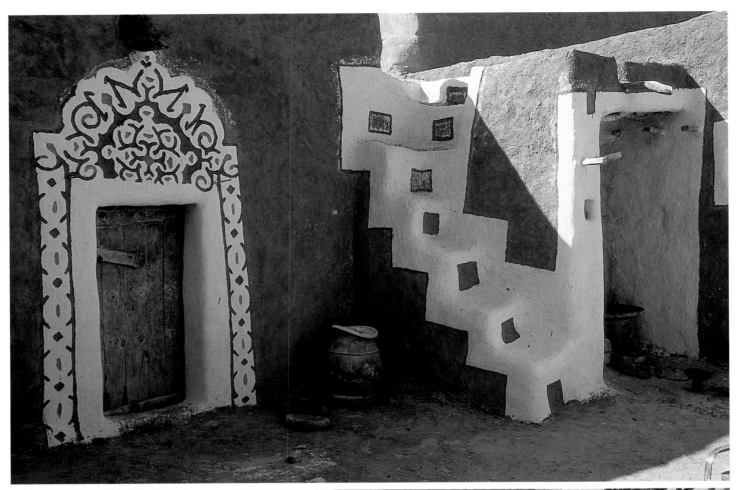

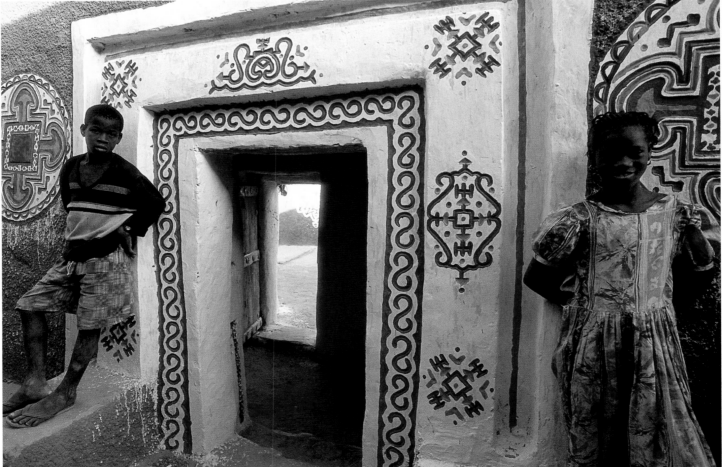

✸ **ABOVE** Oualata has been classified as a world cultural heritage site by Unesco. Its inner courtyards are decorated with motifs symbolizing human beings. ✸
**OBEN** Oualata wurde von der UNESCO zum Weltkulturerbe erklärt. Eine besondere Zierde der Stadt sind die Innenhöfe, deren Ornamentik das menschliche Wesen symbolisiert. ✸ **CI-DESSUS** Classée au patrimoine mondial de l'Unesco, Oualata affiche dans ses cours intérieures des ornementations symbolisant l'être humain.

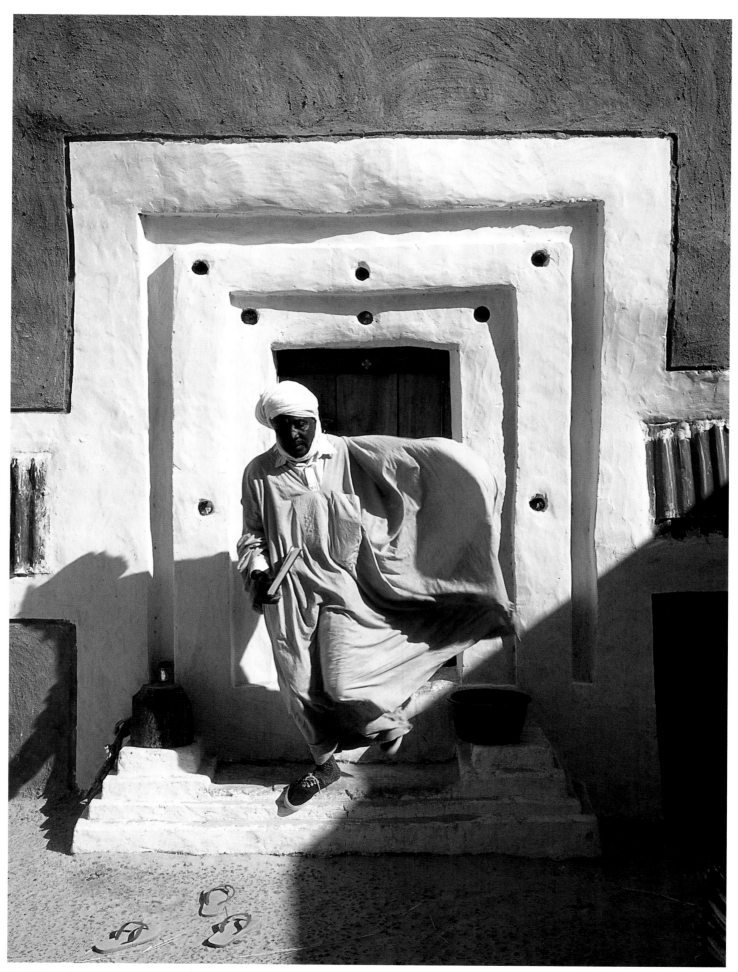

❋ **ABOVE** Oualata was formerly a refuge for Koranic scholars and one of the world's most important religious venues. ❋ **OBEN** In früheren Zeiten bot Oualata den Korangelehrten Zuflucht. Damals zählte es zu den bedeutendsten religiösen Stätten der islamischen Welt. ❋ **CI-DESSUS** Oualata servait autrefois de refuge aux maîtres coraniques, la plaçant ainsi au rang des plus importantes métropoles religieuses.

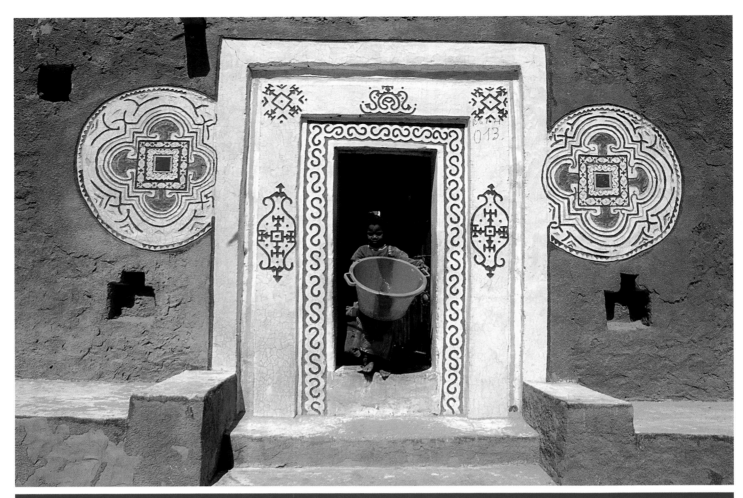

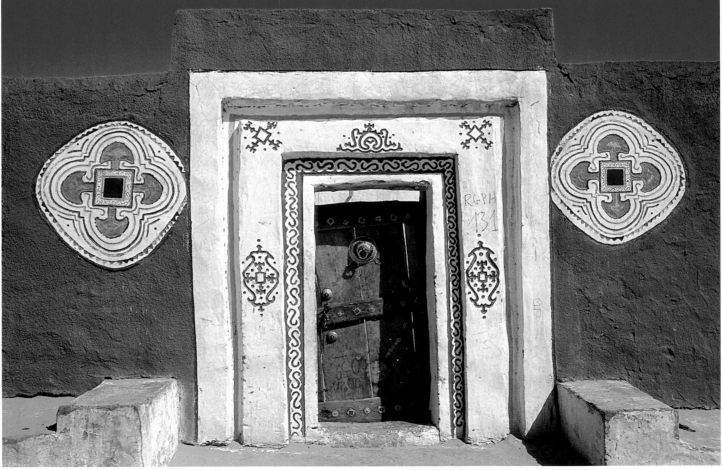

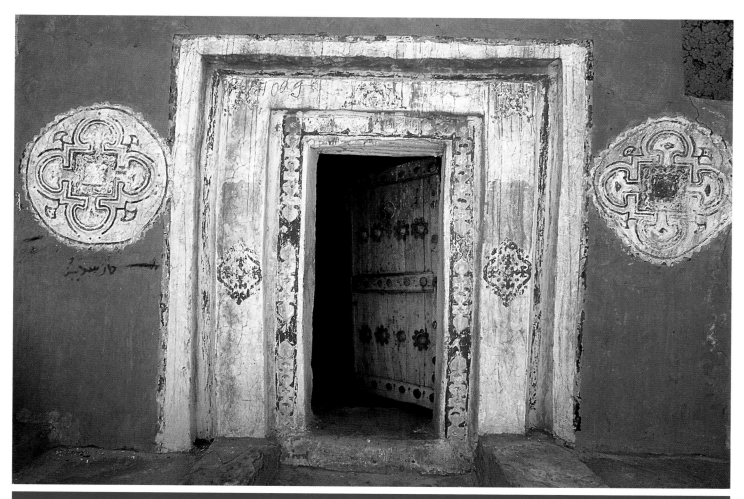

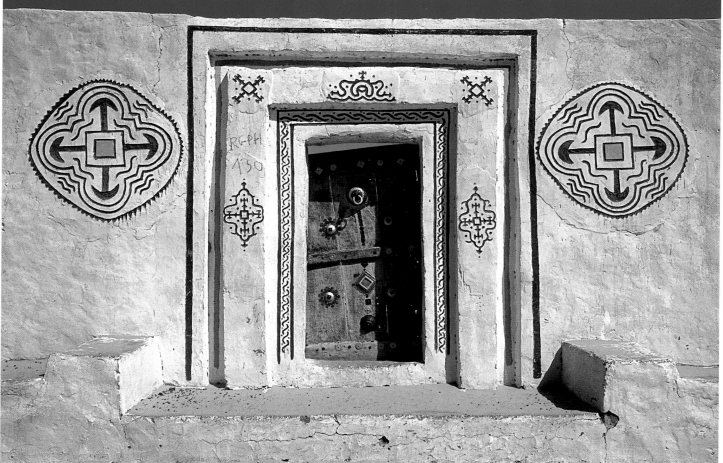

❀ **ABOVE** The doors are adorned with knockers, and latched with a simple chain. ❀ **OBEN** Die einflügeligen Türen sind mit einem Türklopfer versehen und werden mit einer schlichten Türkette verschlossen. ❀ **CI-DESSUS** Les portes à un seul vantail sont enrichies d'un heurtoir et fermées par une simple chaîne.

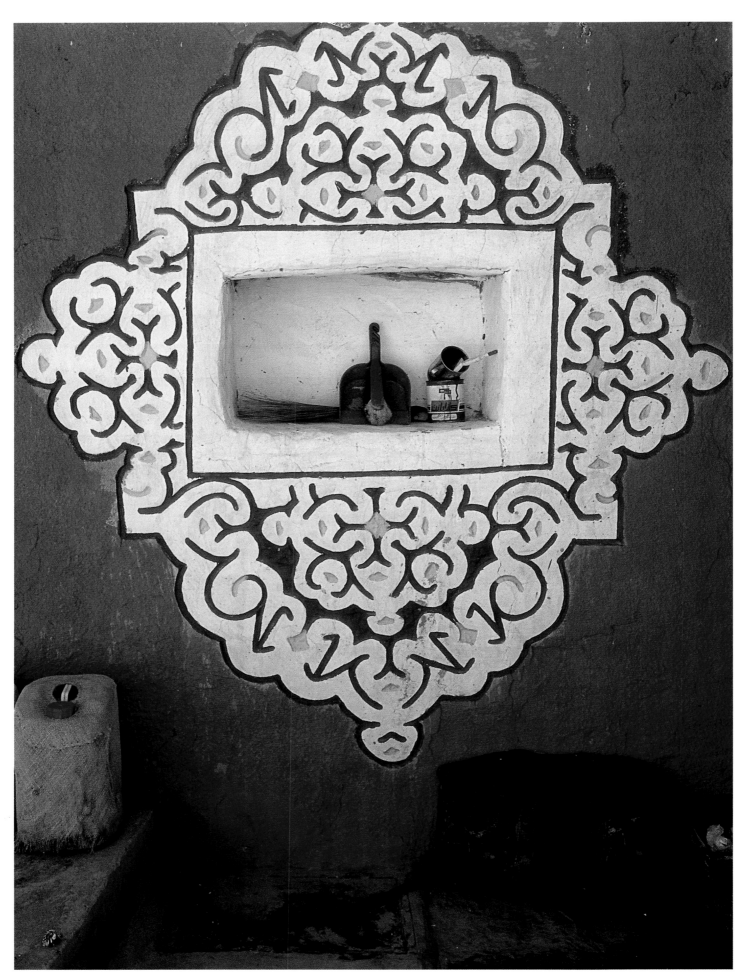

❋ **ABOVE** The motif of the "mother's thigh" is to be found in every house. This symbol of fertility, representing a part of the human thigh, is repeated in an infinite variety of ways. ❋ **OBEN** In allen Häusern findet sich das Motiv »Mutter mit Schenkeln«, ein Fruchtbarkeitssymbol, das einen Teil des Schenkels in vielen künstlerischen Variationen darbietet. ❋ **CI-DESSUS** Dans chaque maison, on retrouve le motif de la «mère aux cuisses», symbole de fécondité représentant une partie de la cuisse répétée en combinaisons infinies.

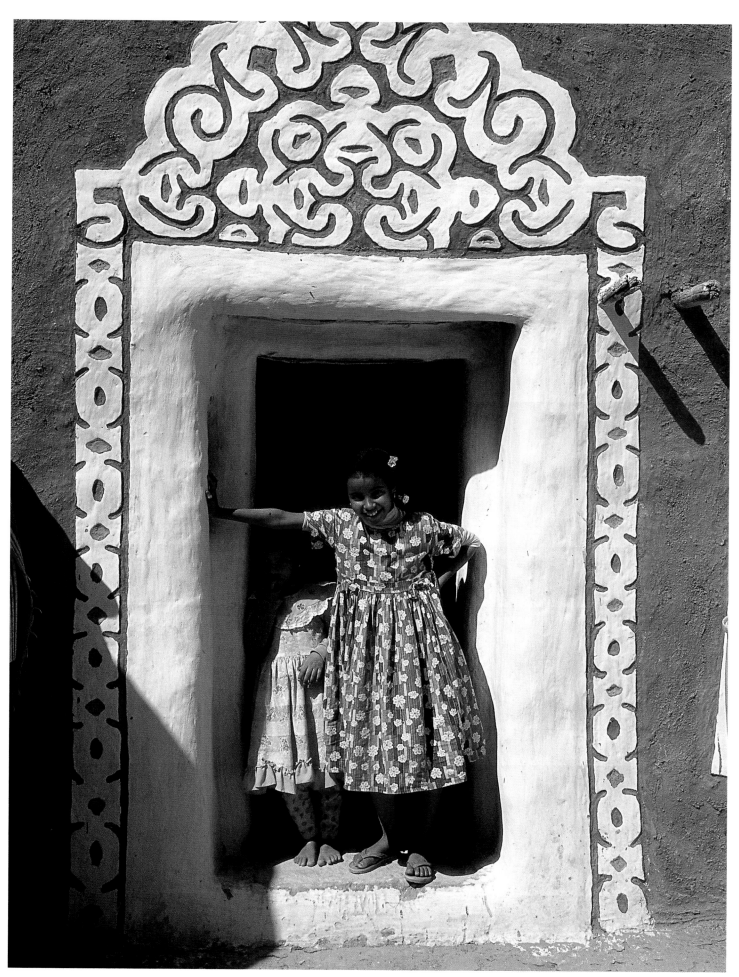

※ **ABOVE** Frescoes like these can be seen on door frames, façades and window frames all over Oualata. Here they have been finger-painted on the red clay walls of this little girl's house. ※ **OBEN** Das kleine Mädchen hat mit Fingermalerei die roten Lehmwände des Hauses verziert. Überall in Oualata sind die Fassaden und die Tür- und Fensterumrahmungen opulent geschmückt. ※ **CI-DESSUS** Peintes au doigt sur les murs d'argile rouge de la maison de cette petite fille, les fresques ornent ici comme partout dans Oualata les façades, les tours de portes et de fenêtres.

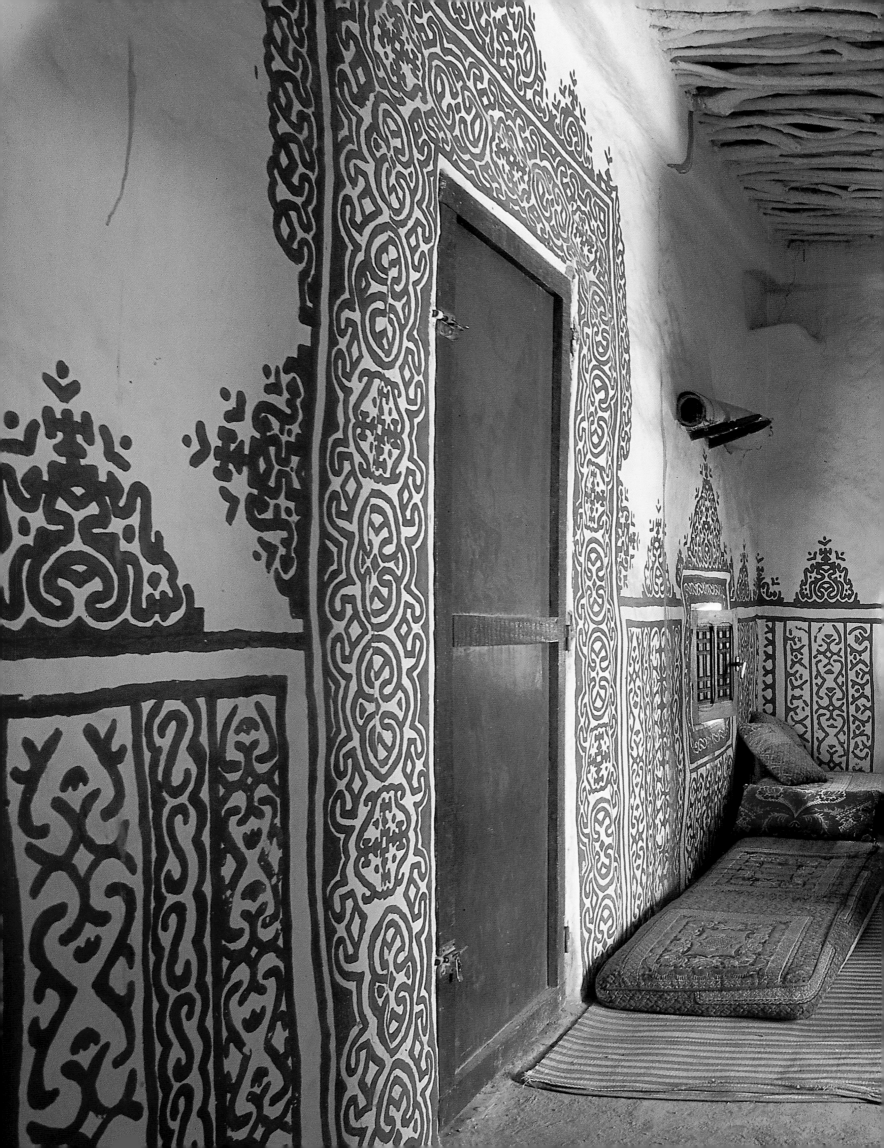

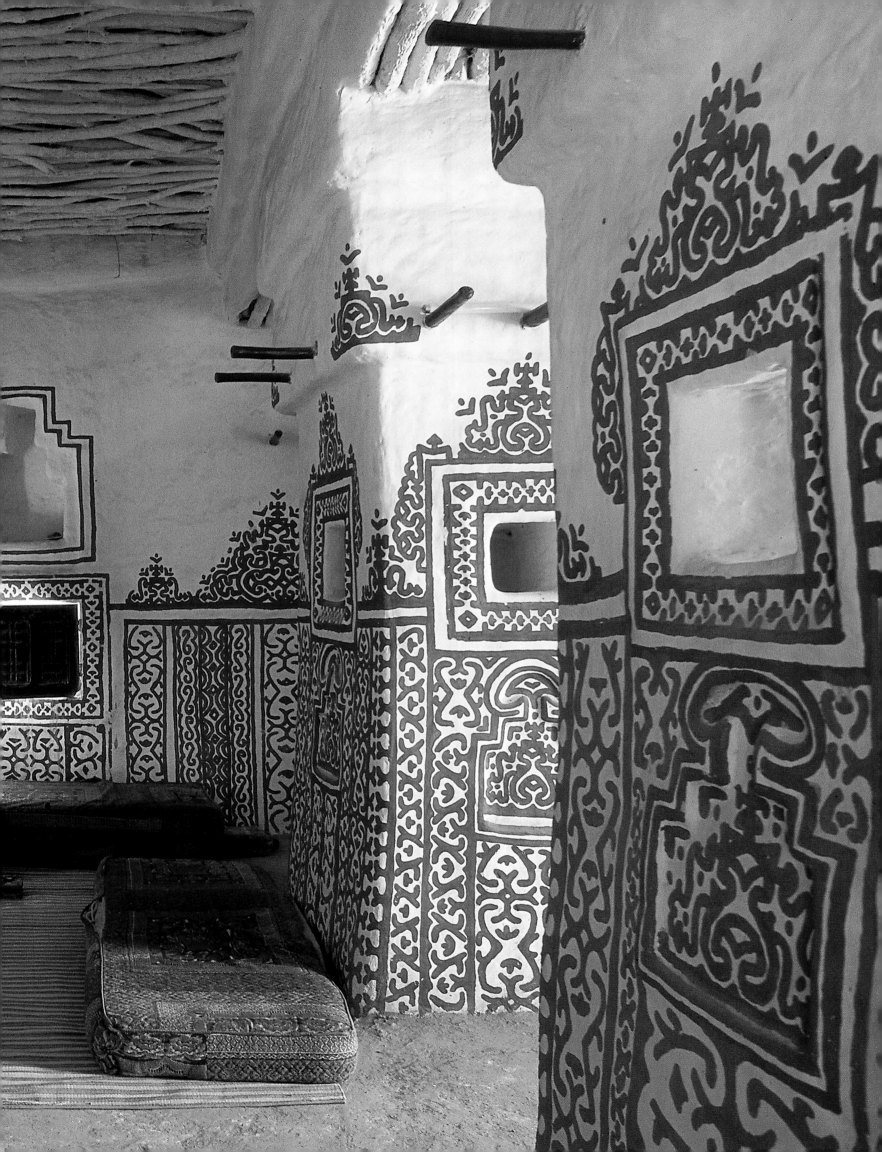

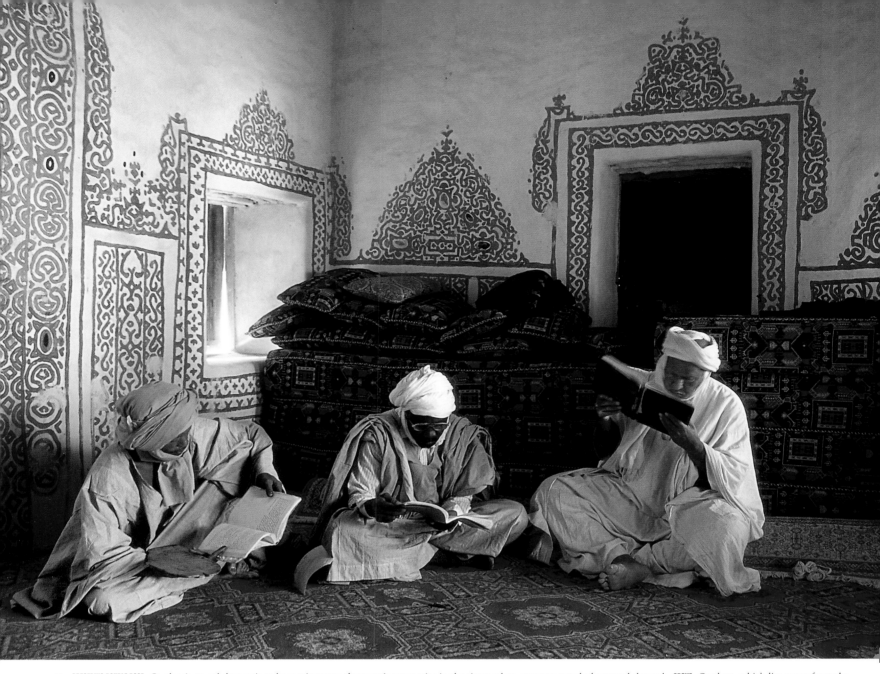

❋ **PRECEDING DOUBLE PAGE** Oualata's mural decorations bear witness to the town's prosperity in the times when caravans regularly passed through. **ABOVE** Oualata, which lies away from the roads, has remained a town of cults and cultures in which scholars still dedicate their lives to reading the Koran. ❋ **VORHERGEHENDE DOPPELSEITE** Die Wandmalereien bezeugen den Wohlstand der Stadt Oualata zur Zeit der Karawanen. **OBEN** Oualata, das abseits der Straßen liegt, ist eine Stadt des Kultes und der Kultur geblieben, in der bis heute gelehrte Männer ihr Leben dem Koranstudium weihen. ❋ **DOUBLE PAGE PRECEDENTE** Les décors muraux sont les témoins de la prospérité d'Oualata à l'époque des caravanes. **CI-DESSUS** À l'écart des routes, Oualata reste une ville de culte et de culture où des hommes consacrent leur existence à l'étude des textes coraniques.

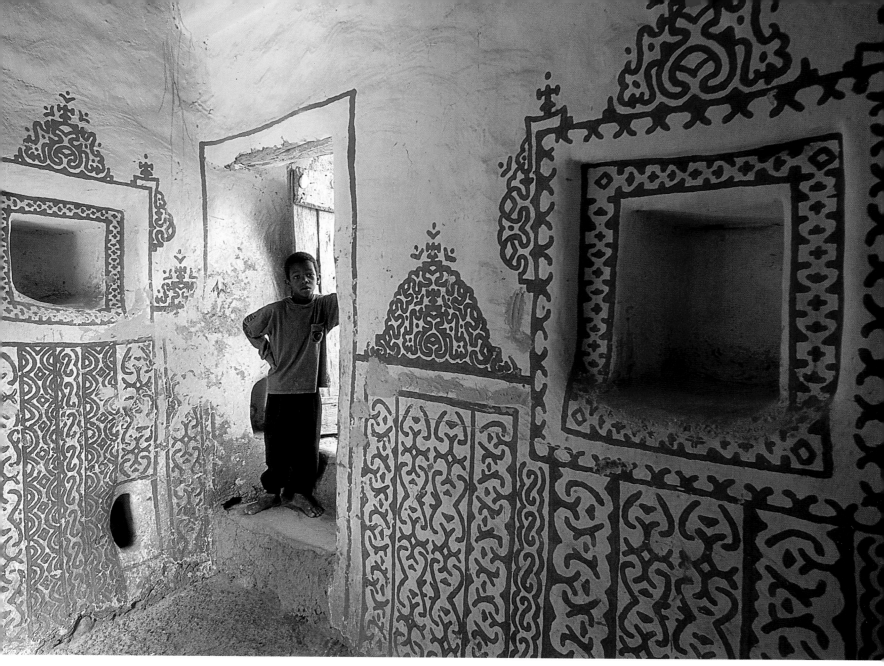

✻ **ABOVE** This child's home is typical of Oualata, with long, parallel rooms and a larger main room with a central pillar to hold up the beams. In the evening, lanterns are placed in the niches. ✻ **OBEN** Das Kind auf der Schwelle betrachtet die charakteristische Inneneinrichtung eines Hauses in Oualata, das aus kleinen länglichen, parallel angeordneten Zimmern und einem größeren Raum mit einem zentralen Stützpfeiler besteht. Abends leuchten die Laternen in den Nischen. ✻ **CI-DESSUS** Au seuil de sa demeure, cet enfant contemple un intérieur typique de Oualata fait de petites pièces longues et parallèles et d'une salle plus vaste dont le pilier central supporte la charpente. Le soir les niches s'emplissent de lanternes.

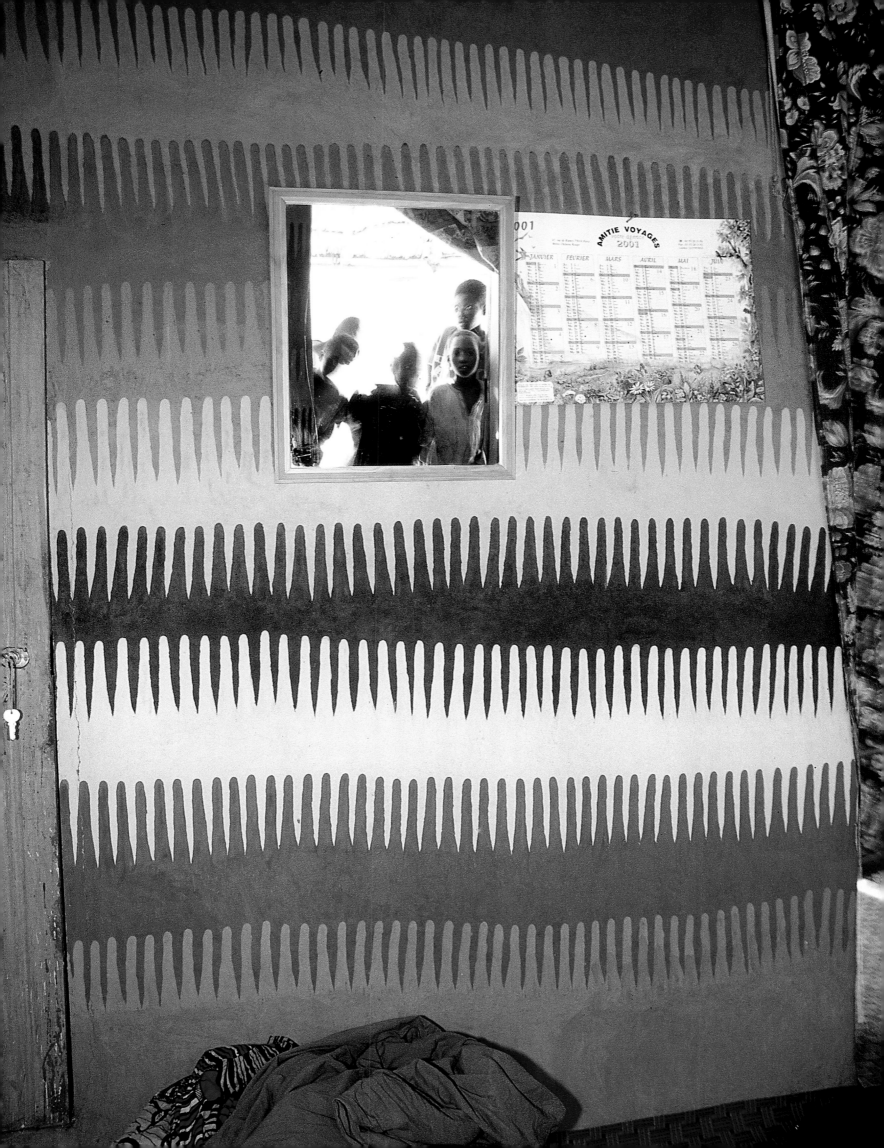

# SONINKE PEOPLE
## SELIBABI REGION

The interior of these houses is characterized
by a play of geometrical lines and beautiful figurative effects.

The entrance is decorated with flat stones in zigzag patterns. Niches set into the walls serve as shelves, but one scarcely notices them, so stunning are the colours all around. Beyond the wooden doors with their padlocks, decorative motifs literally invade the interior.

Red, brown, blue, grey or yellow, the painters of these rooms have created their composite décor with skills passed down through many generations. The original motifs of this region to the north of the town of Sélibabi were painted in mud with natural oxides. Today the women use more robust commercial paints. Naturally enough, their work has spiritual significance, emphasising the original relationship between man and his environment. Astonishingly, only one room in the house is brightened in this way with geometrical designs, and that space is the women's province as well as the focus of daily life, since all the cooking and other domestic tasks are carried out there. Photos, advertisements for cigarettes (Mauritanians smoke like chimneys) and plastic "made in China" cooking utensils serve as decorative elements. Also from the Middle Kingdom are the dishes reserved for ceremonial occasions, which hang on the walls above the woven mats.

Am Eingang bilden flache im Zickzack angeordnete Steine ein Wabenmuster. Die Mauernischen dienen als Regale, beeindrucken aber vor allem durch ihr Farbenspiel. Hinter den Holztüren mit Vorhängeschloss überziehen unzählige farbige Muster das Hausinnere.

Die überlieferte Malerei in den Farben Rot, Braun, Blau, Grau und Gelb schafft ein Interieur nach altem Vorbild. Früher wurden im Norden der Stadt Sélibabi Erdfarben mit natürlichen Oxiden verwandt. Heute bevorzugen die Frauen haltbare Industriefarben. Die spirituelle Bedeutung der Ornamentik weist auf eine ursprüngliche Verbindung zwischen den Menschen und ihrer Umwelt hin. Erstaunlicherweise gibt es aber nur einen Raum, in dem dieses Spiel mit geometrischen Formen zum Tragen kommt, nämlich dort, wo die Frauen ihren alltäglichen Aufgaben nachkommen. Sie sind für Küche und Haushalt zuständig. Die Plakate mit Zigarettenwerbung (der Anteil der Raucher in diesem Land ist unglaublich hoch) unter den Fotos sowie Küchenutensilien aus buntem Plastik »Made in China« dienen ebenfalls der Dekoration. Weiter oben zieren die für Zeremonien reservierten Teller, die ebenfalls aus dem Reich der Mitte stammen, die Wände über den Webmatten. Das hat etwas vom »Global Village«, oder?

L'entrée est ornée de décors de pierres plates en zigzag formant des alvéoles. Des niches, créées à même le mur, servent d'étagères, mais c'est à peine si on les remarque, tant le regard est attiré par le jeu des couleurs. Derrière les portes en bois fermées par un cadenas, des motifs envahissent l'intérieur.

Rouges, brunes, bleues, grises ou jaunes, les peintures créent le décor en un savoir-faire ancestral. À l'origine, dans cette région située au nord de la ville de Sélibabi, les motifs étaient peints à la boue avec des oxydes naturels. Aujourd'hui, les femmes emploient des peintures du commerce qui résistent mieux à l'usure du temps. Naturellement, ces ornements ont une signification spirituelle, soulignant l'obéissance à une relation originelle entre l'homme et son environnement. Étonnamment, seule une pièce de la maison est ainsi animée par ce jeu de lignes géométriques: l'espace dévolu aux femmes, celui de la vie quotidienne aussi puisque la cuisine et les taches ménagères leur sont réservées. Sous des photos, des publicités pour des marques de cigarettes (le pourcentage de fumeurs est hallucinant dans ce pays) et des ustensiles de cuisine en plastique coloré «made in China» servent également d'éléments de décoration. En hauteur, toujours en provenance de l'Empire du Milieu, les plats réservés aux cérémonies couvrent les murs au-dessus de nattes tissées. Vous avez dit Global Village?

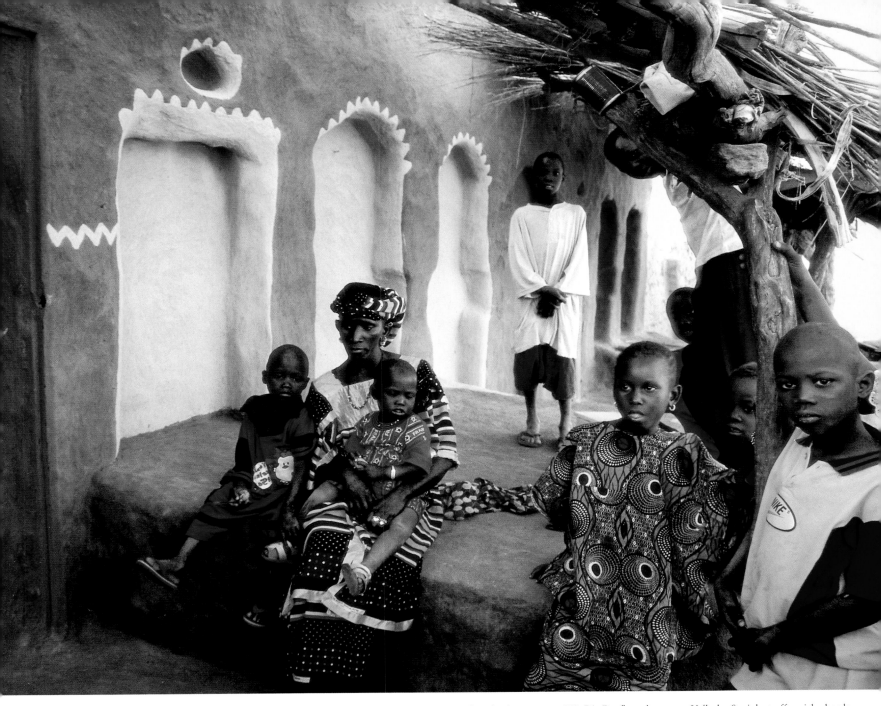

✳ **ABOVE** Soninke villagers gather to talk at the end of the day. **FACING PAGE** The entrance to an ochre-clay house. ✳ **OBEN** Die Dorfbewohner vom Volk der Soninke treffen sich abends zum Plausch. **RECHTE SEITE** Der Eingang eines ockerfarbenen Lehmhauses. ✳ **CI-DESSUS** Les villageois Soninké se retrouvent en fin de journée pour discuter. **PAGE DE DROITE** Entrée d'une maison en terre ocre.

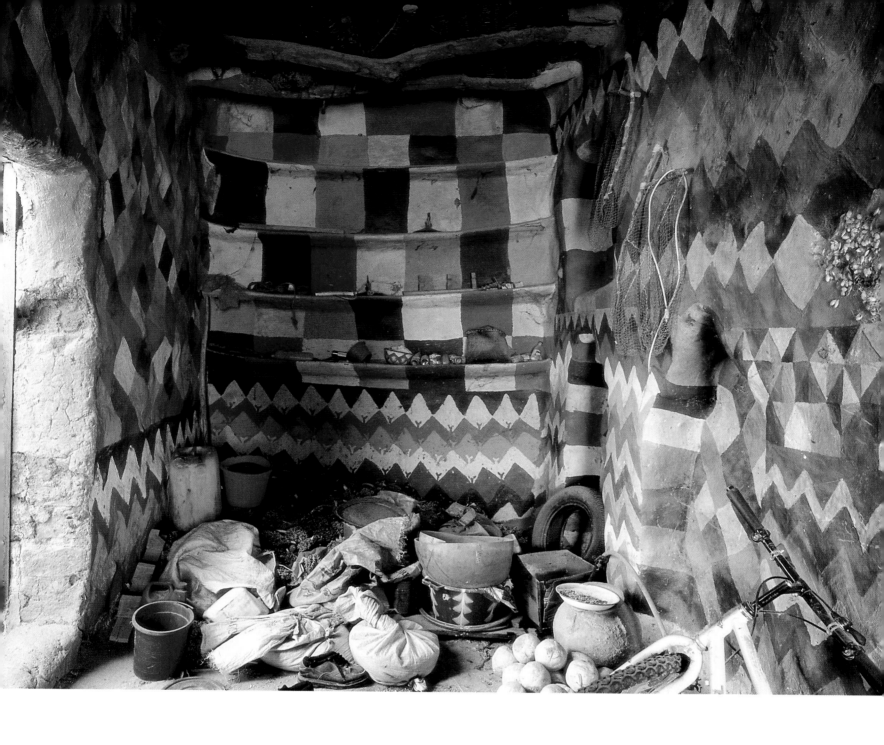

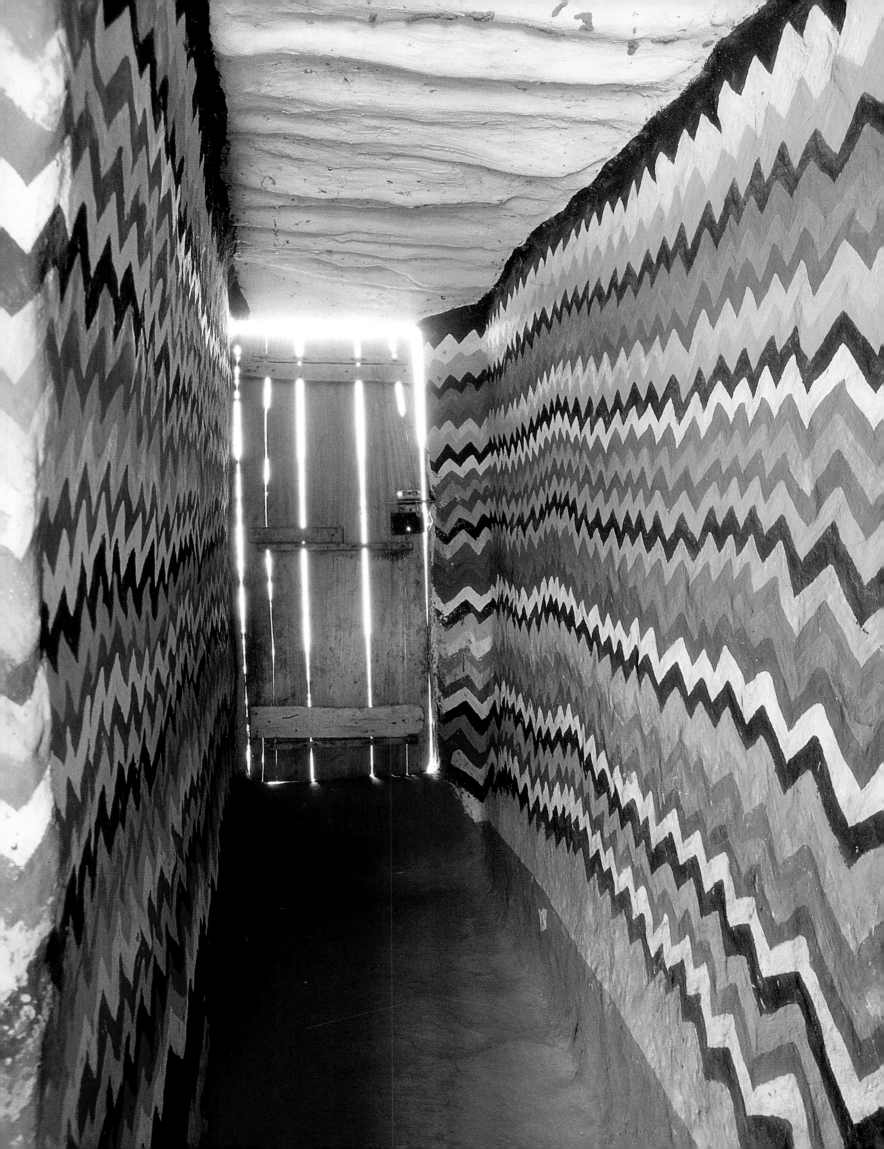

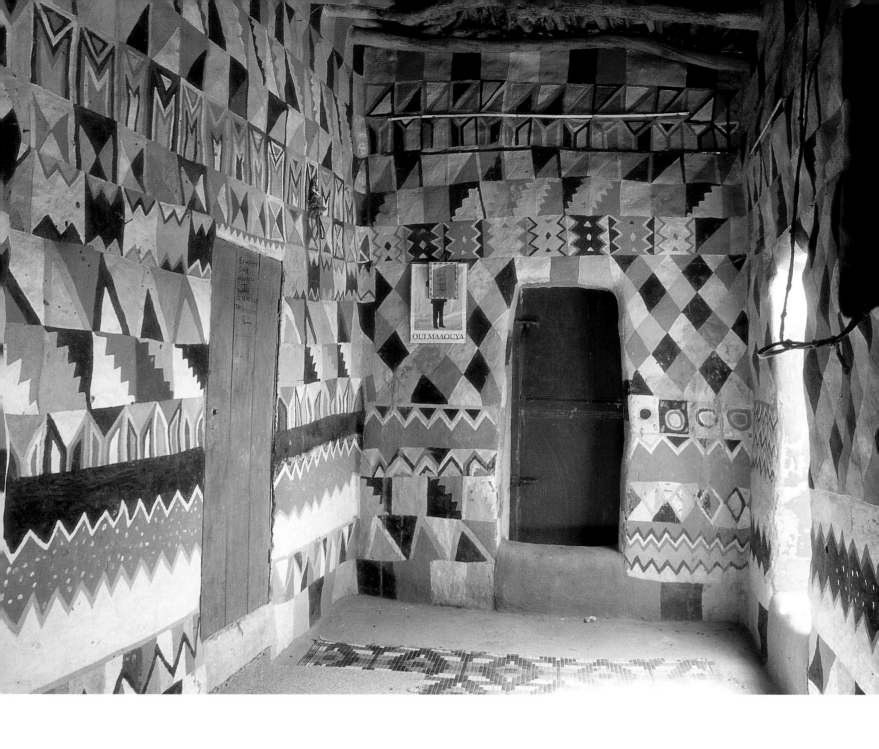

❀ **FACING PAGE** Behind the wooden doors with their padlocks, the colour seems to flow away in wavelets. **ABOVE** A cameo of ochres and browns covers this shared room with its harmoniously blended squares, triangles and diamond shapes. The absence of any kind of furniture emphasizes the sheer vigour of the wall paintings. ❀ **LINKE SEITE** Hinter den mit Vorhängeschlössern versehenen Holztüren überlagern sich die Farben im Wellenmuster. **OBEN** Die ockerfarbene und braune Malerei im Gemeinschaftsraum harmoniert mit den quadratischen, dreieckigen und rautenförmigen Mustern an den Wänden. Die Wirkung der Wandmalerei wird noch dadurch verstärkt, dass die Räume nicht möbliert sind. ❀ **PAGE DE GAUCHE** Derrière les portes en bois fermées par un cadenas, les couleurs se chevauchent en vaguelettes. **CI-DESSUS** Camaïeu d'ocre et de bruns dans cette pièce commune où, à même les murs, les formes carrées, triangulaires ou en losanges s'épousent harmonieusement. L'absence de mobilier renforce encore la vigueur de ces peintures murales.

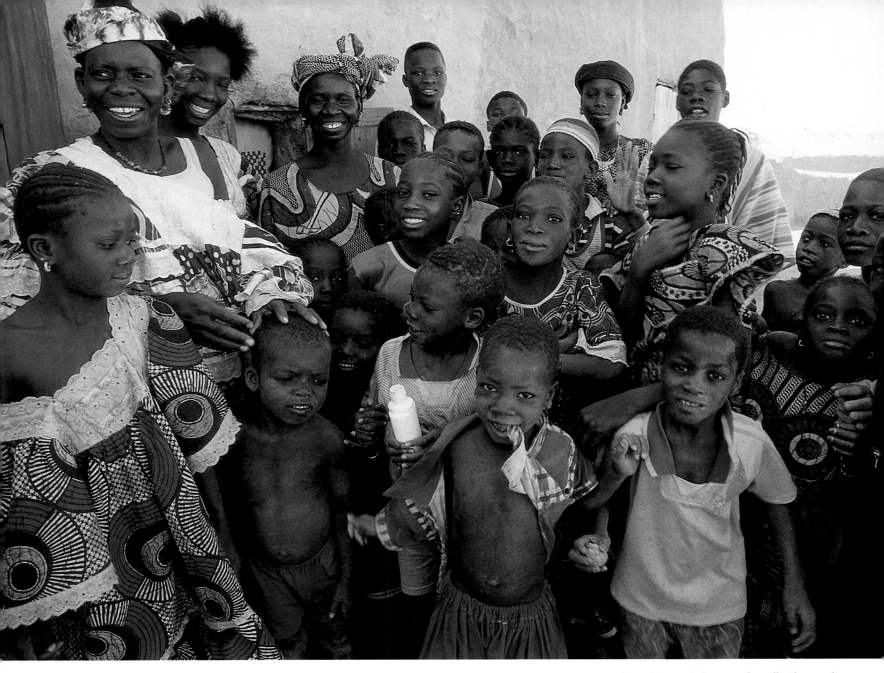

✳ **ABOVE** Just as it does everywhere else in Africa, community life takes place in front of the houses. **FOLLOWING PAGES** Square, triangular and diamond shapes on the walls. Photos, advertisements and plastic cooking utensils also serve as decorative elements. ✳ **OBEN** Das Gemeinleben spielt sich wie überall in Afrika vor dem Haus ab. **FOLGENDE DOPPELSEITEN** Quadratische, dreieckige und rautenförmige Muster werden an den Wänden stimmig miteinander kombiniert. Fotos, Werbung und Küchenutensilien aus buntem Plastik dienen ebenfalls der Dekoration. ✳ **CI-DESSUS** Comme partout en Afrique la vie communautaire est imporante devant les maisons. **DOUBLES PAGES SUIVANTES** À même les murs, les formes carrées, triangulaires ou en losanges s'épousent harmonieusement entre elles. Des photos, des publicités et des ustensiles de cuisine en plastique coloré servent également d'éléments de décoration.

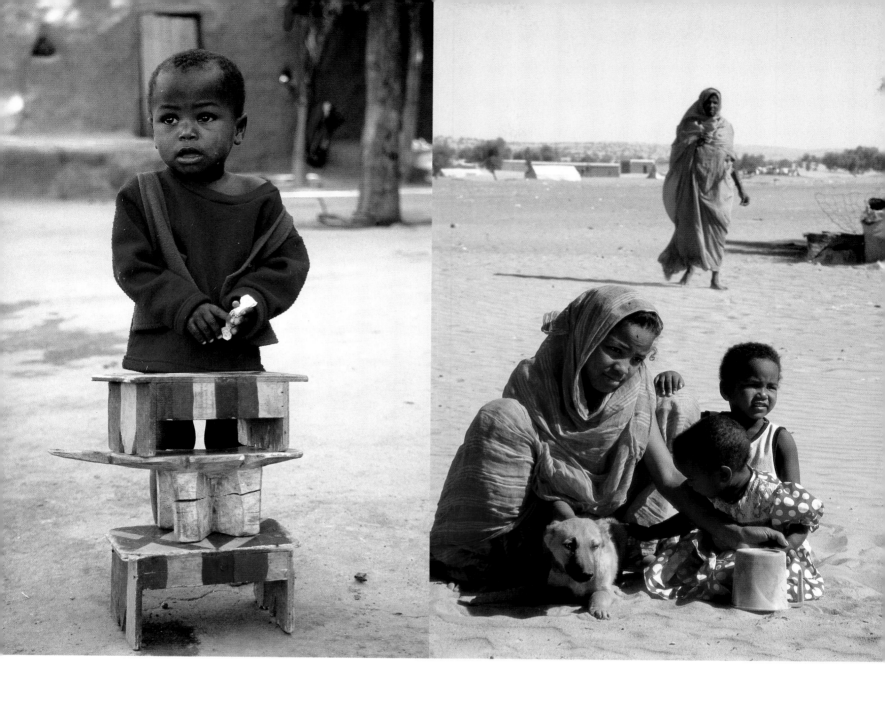

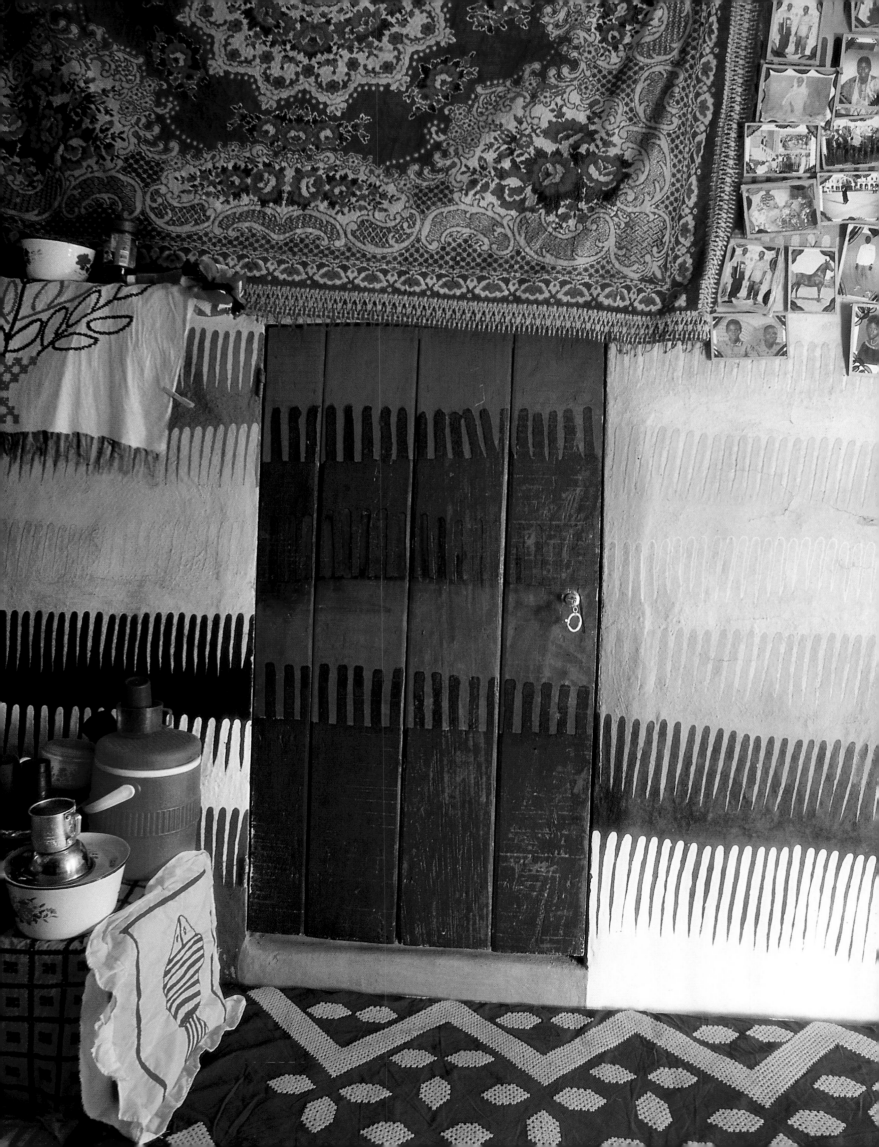

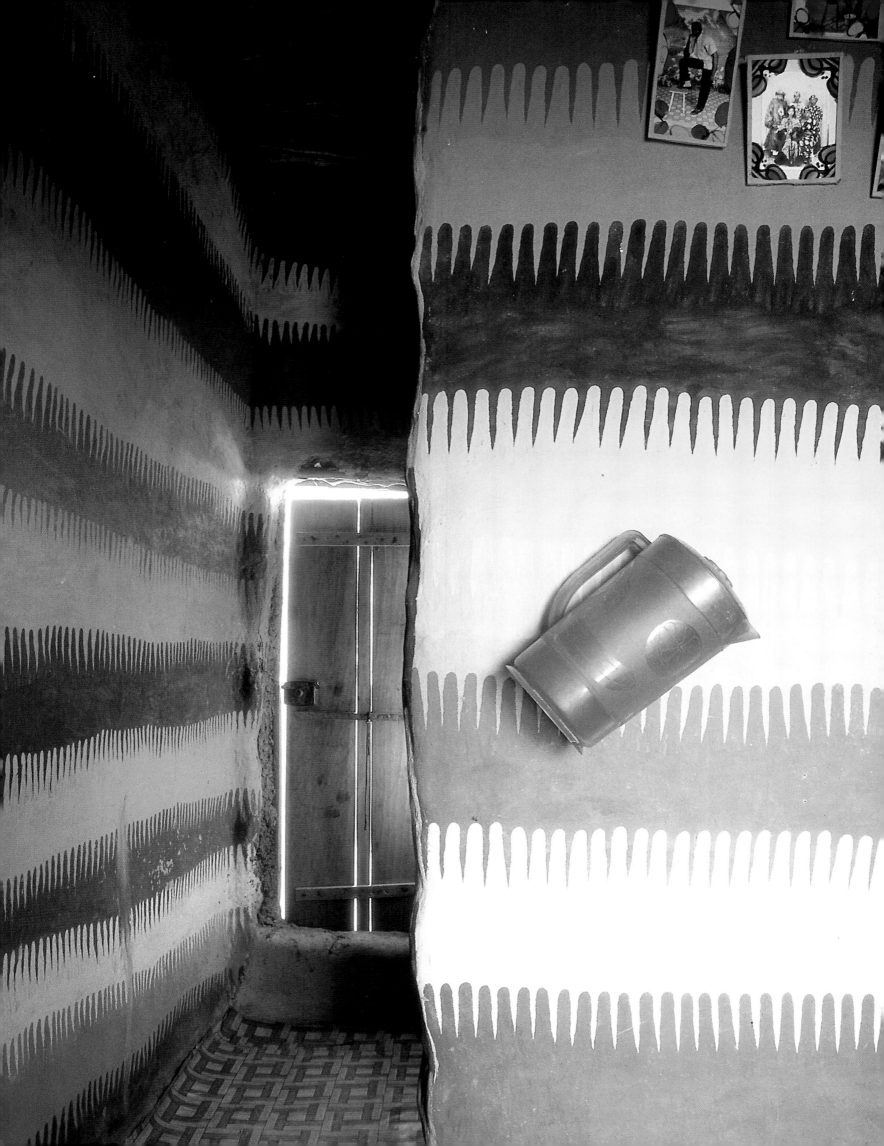

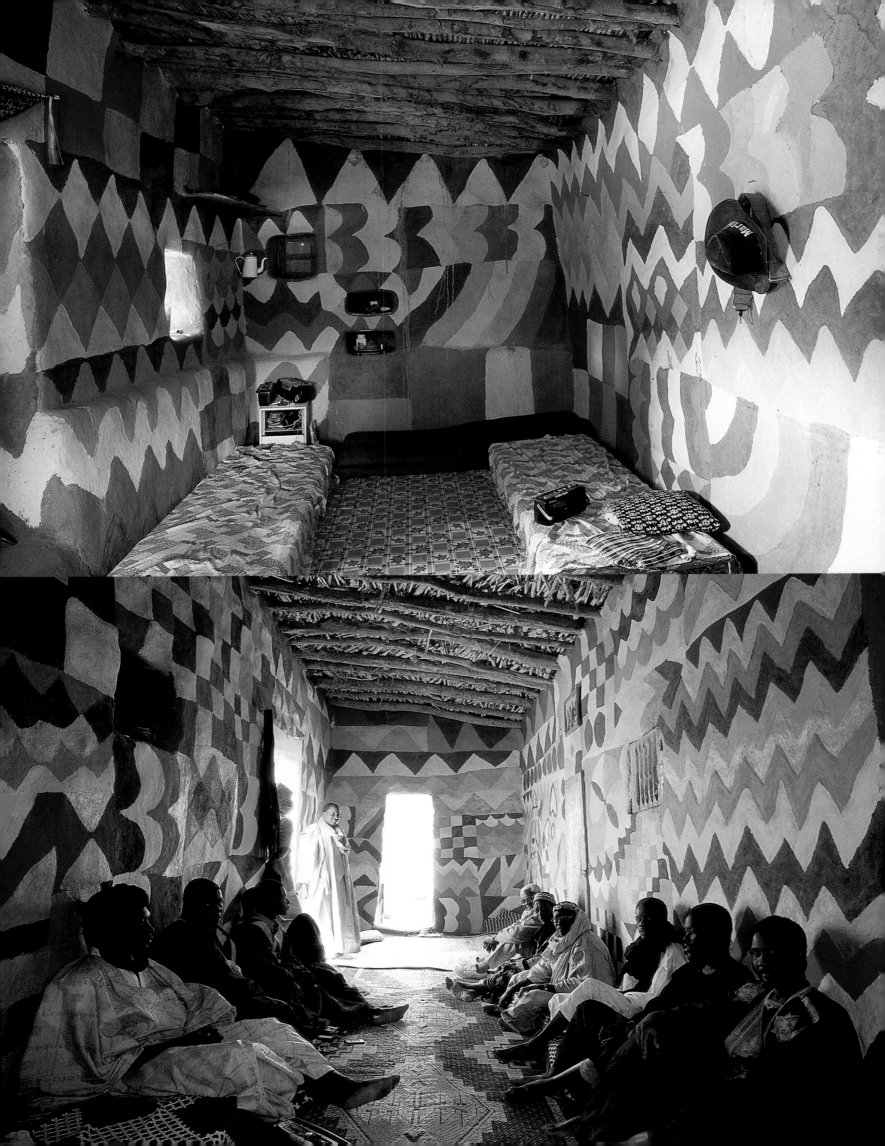

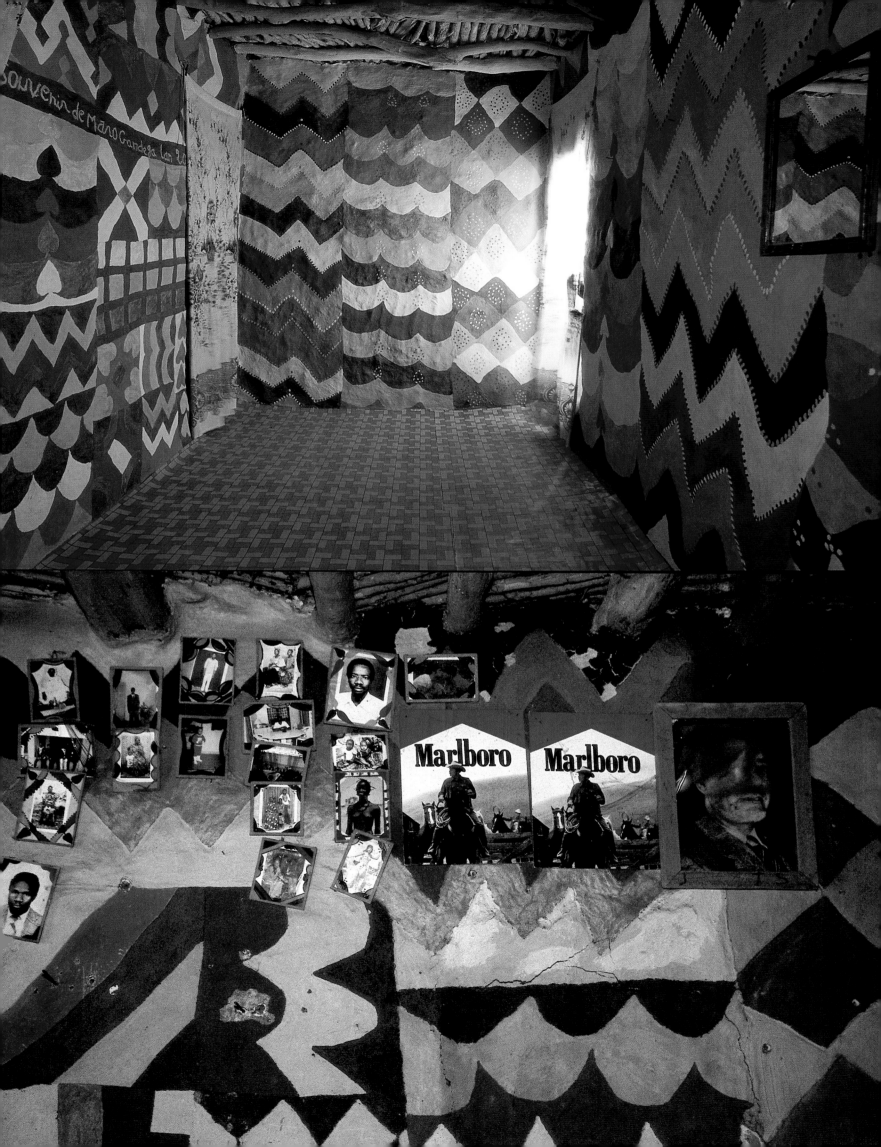

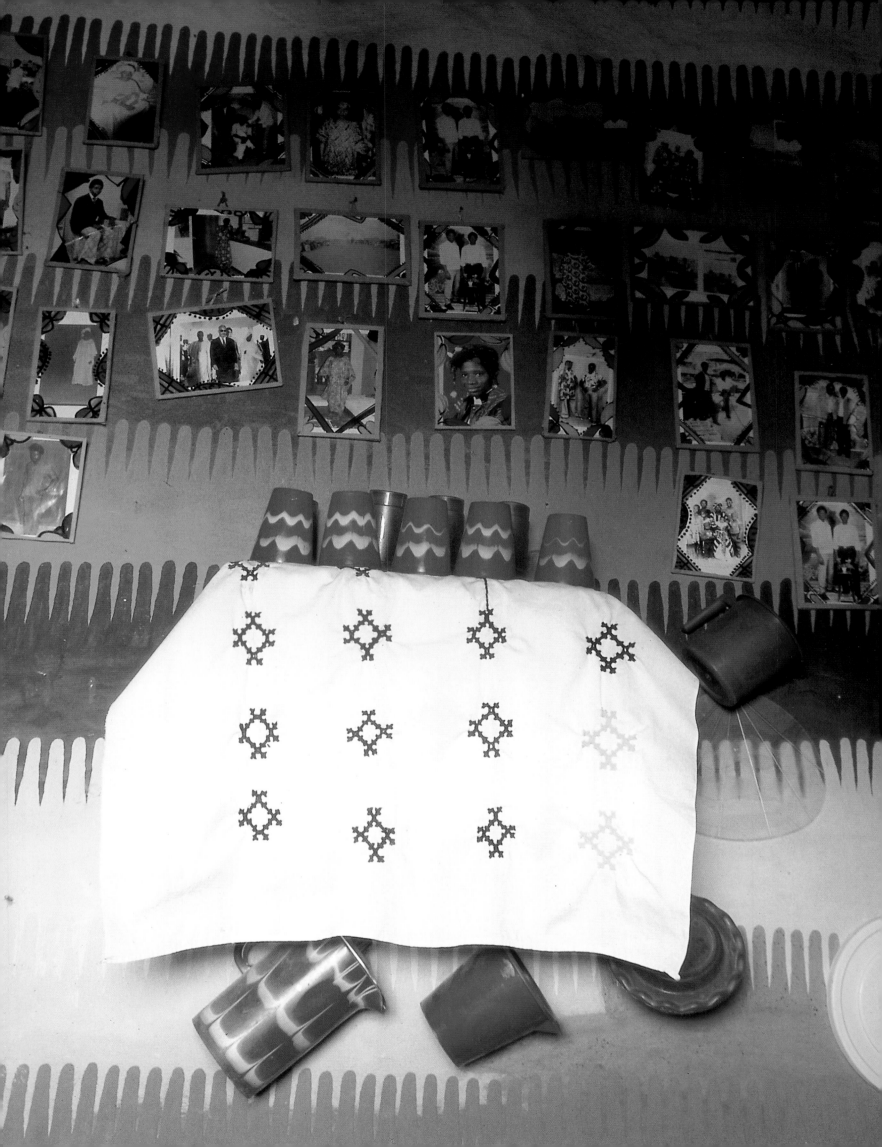

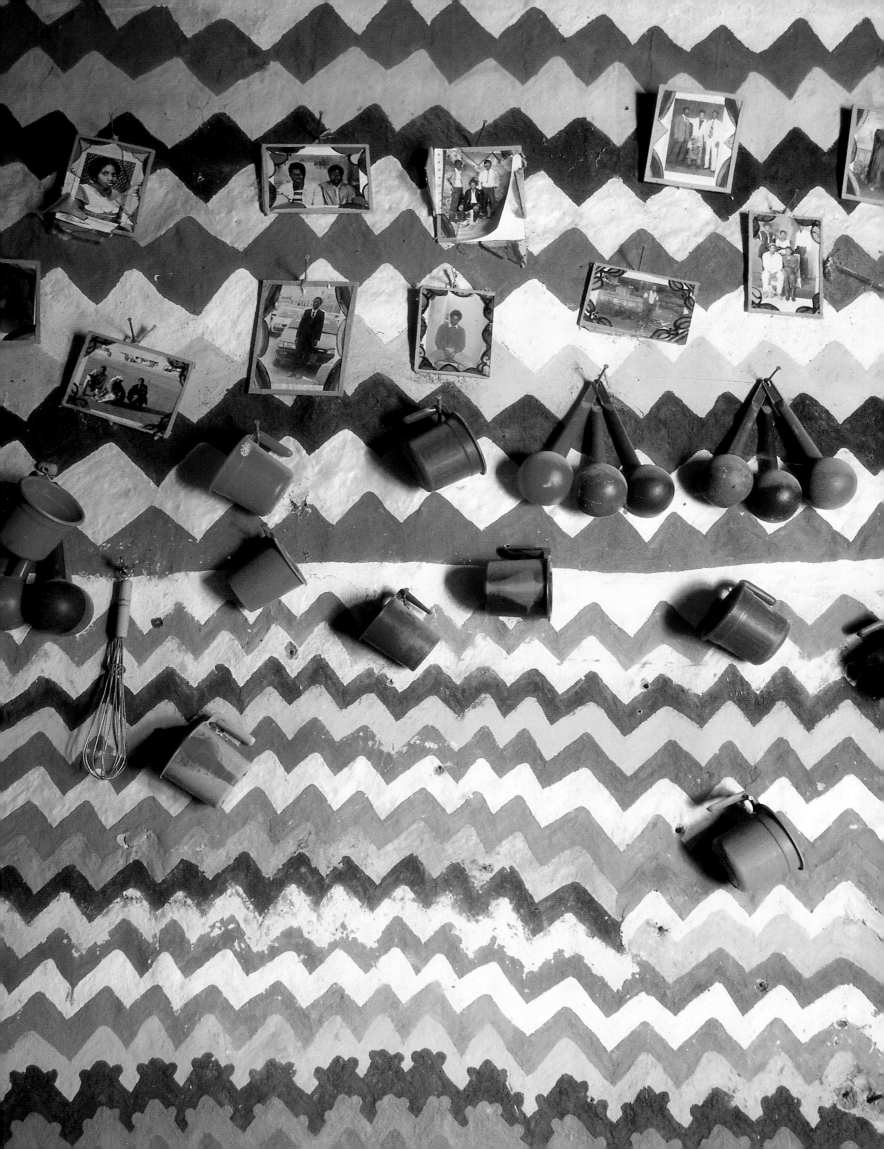

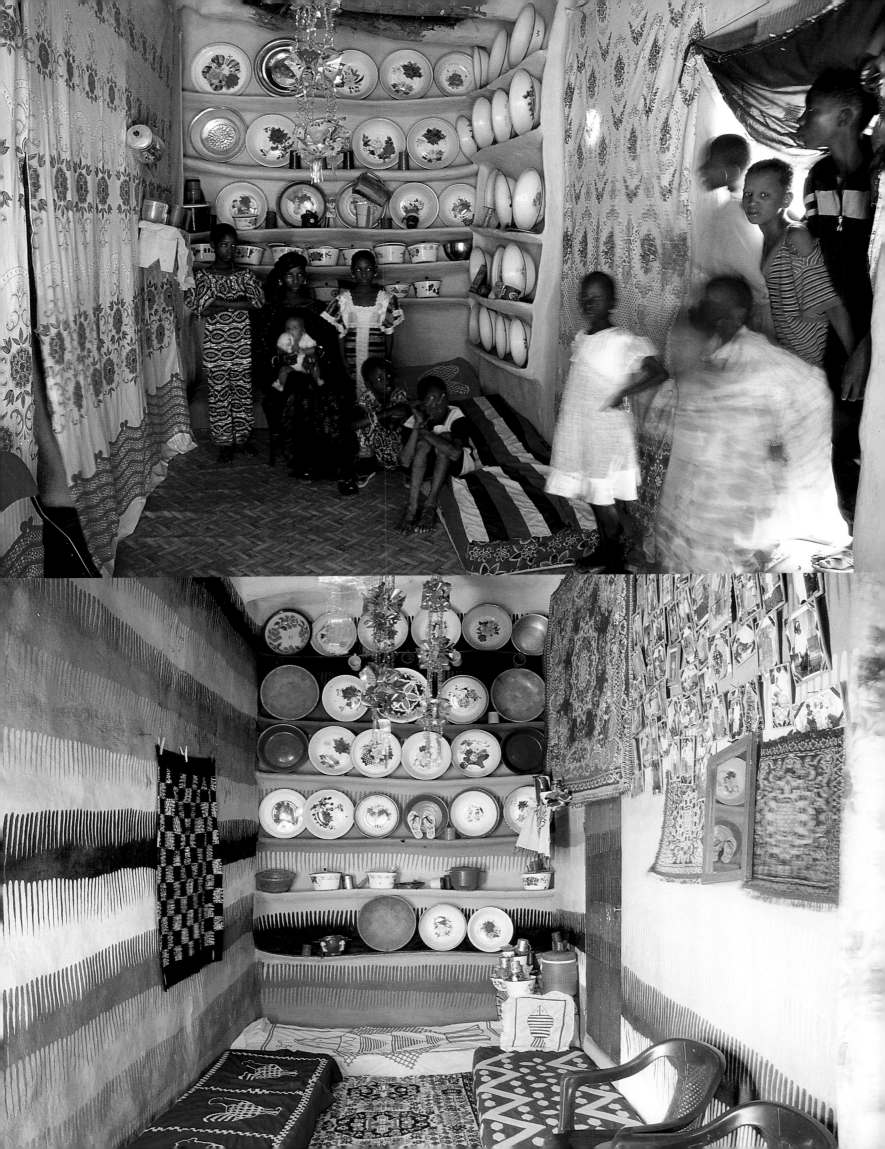

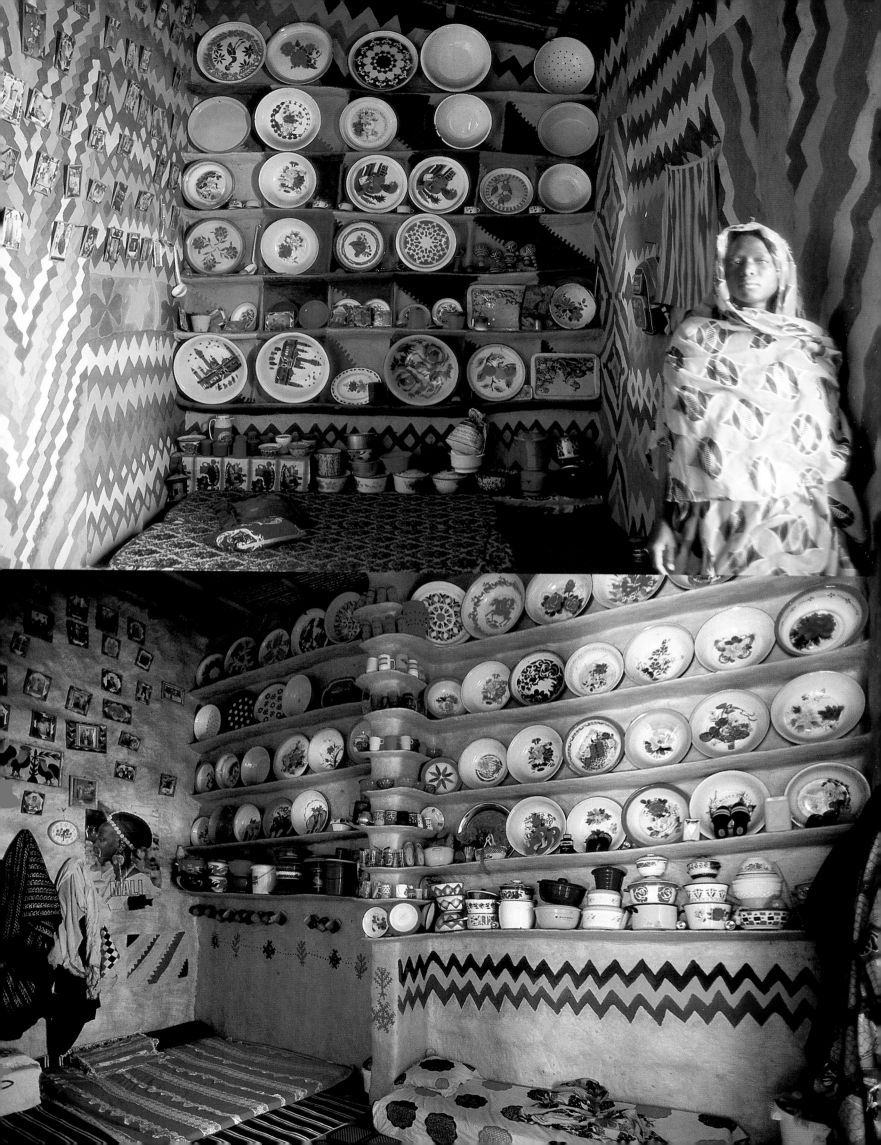

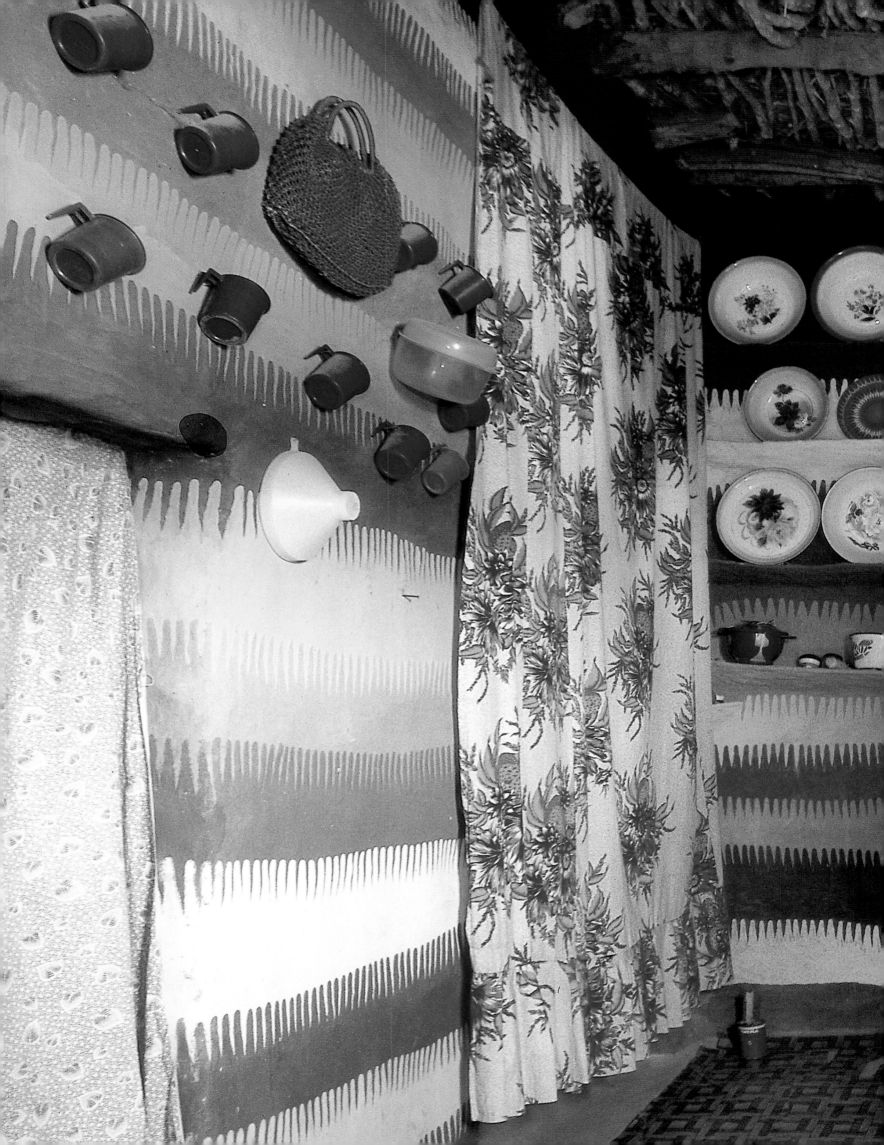

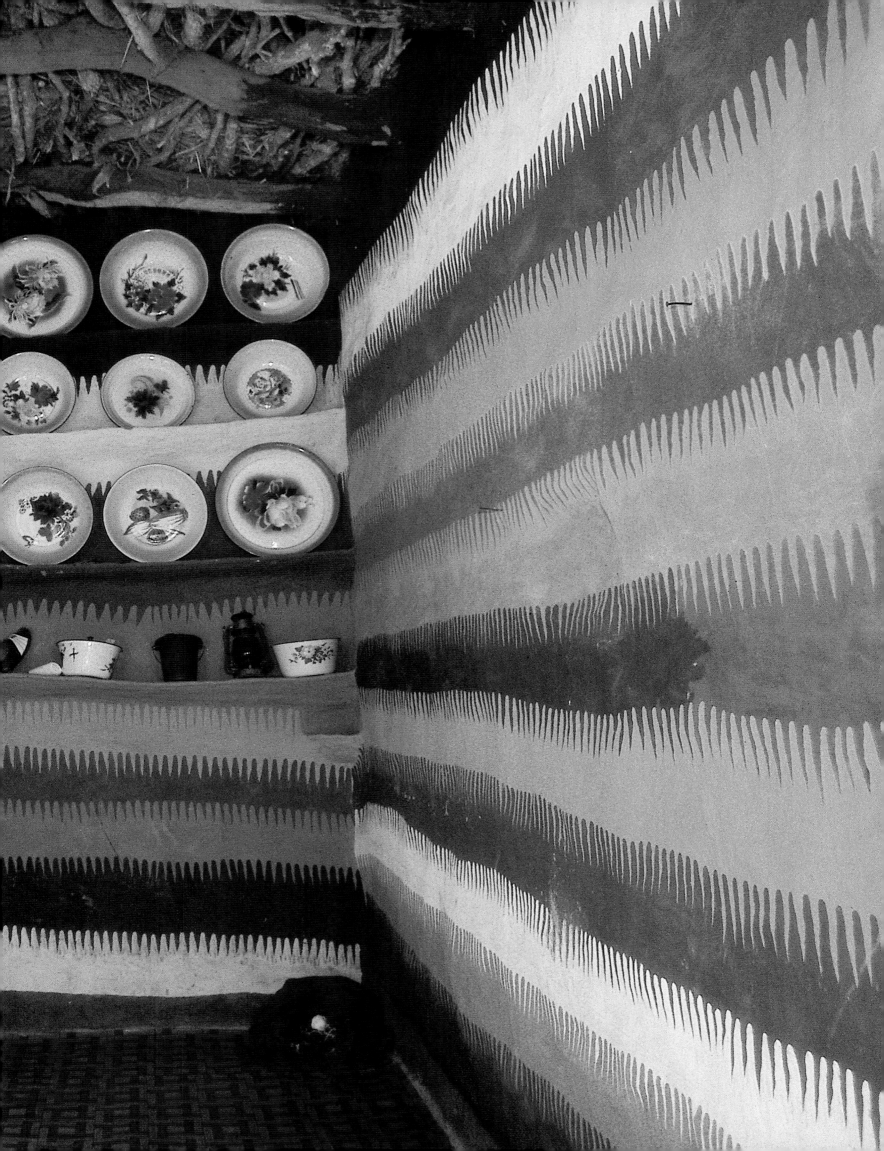

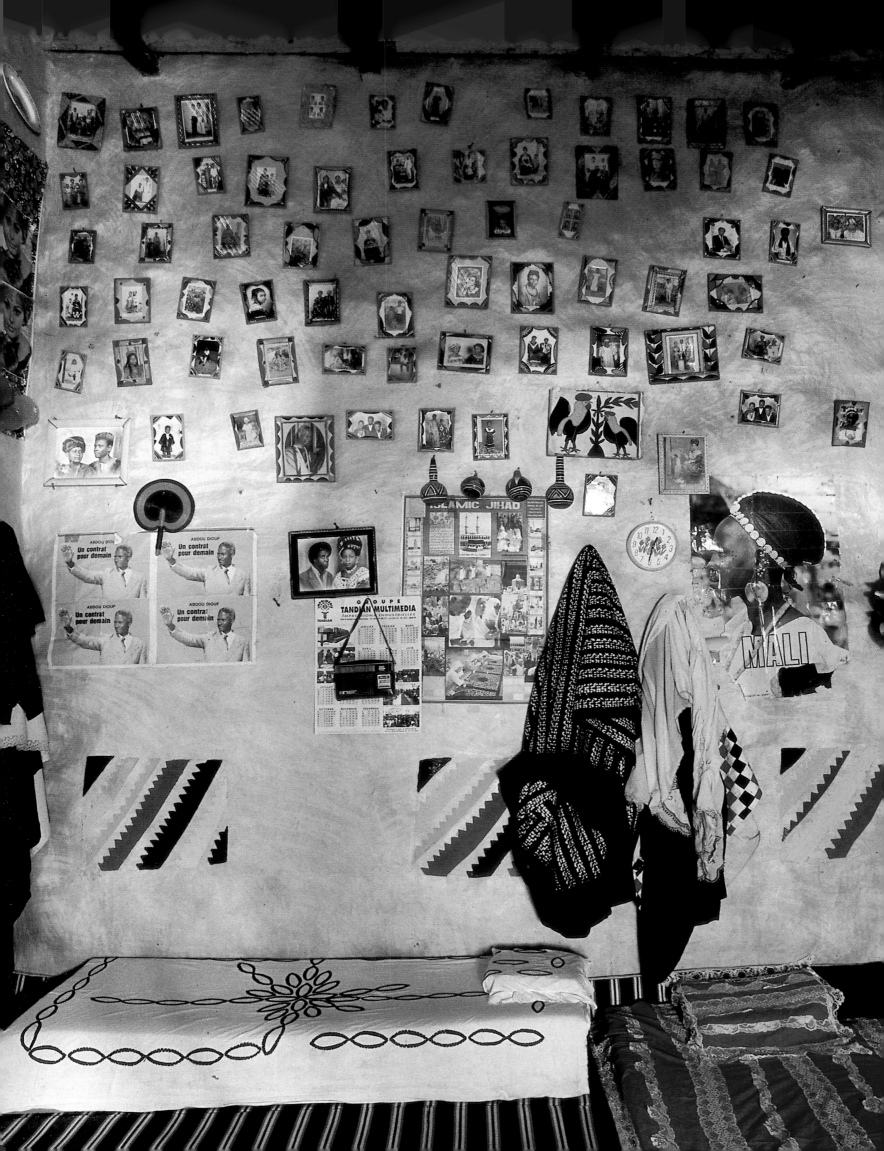

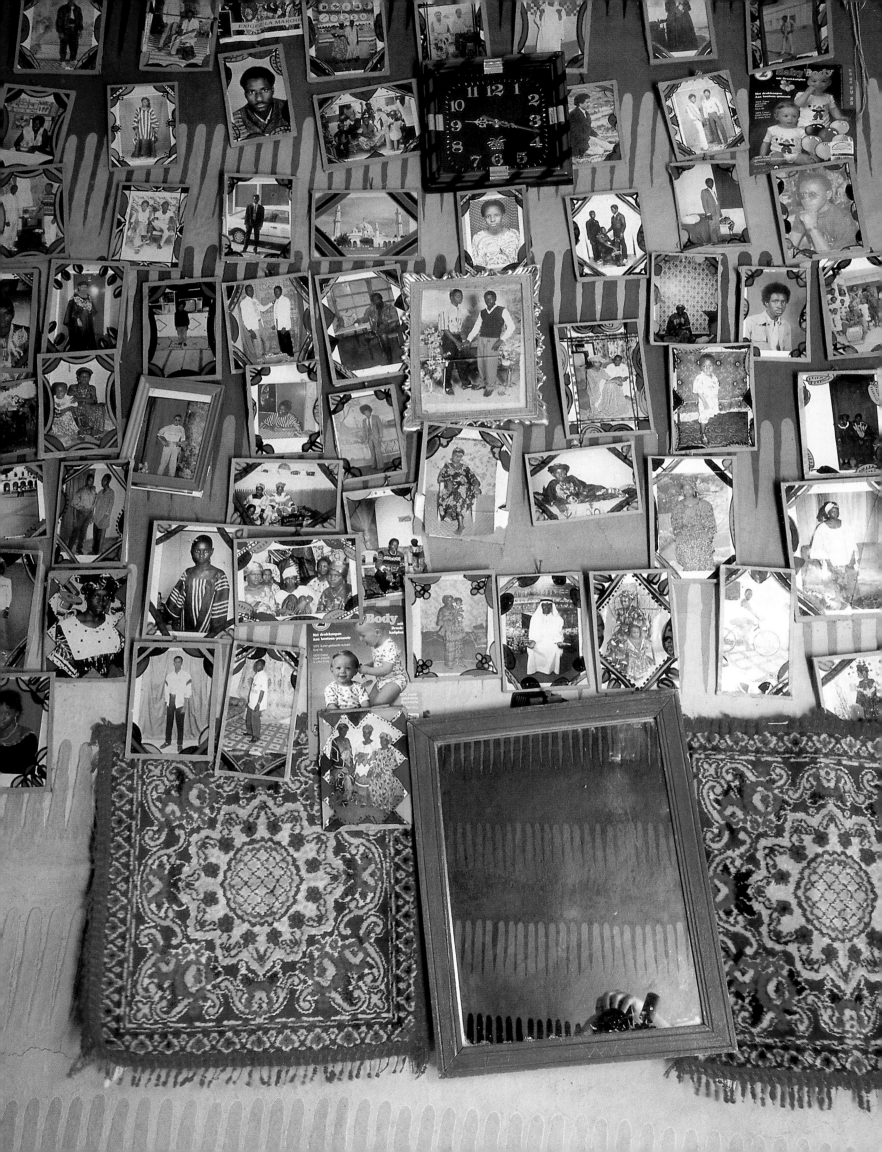

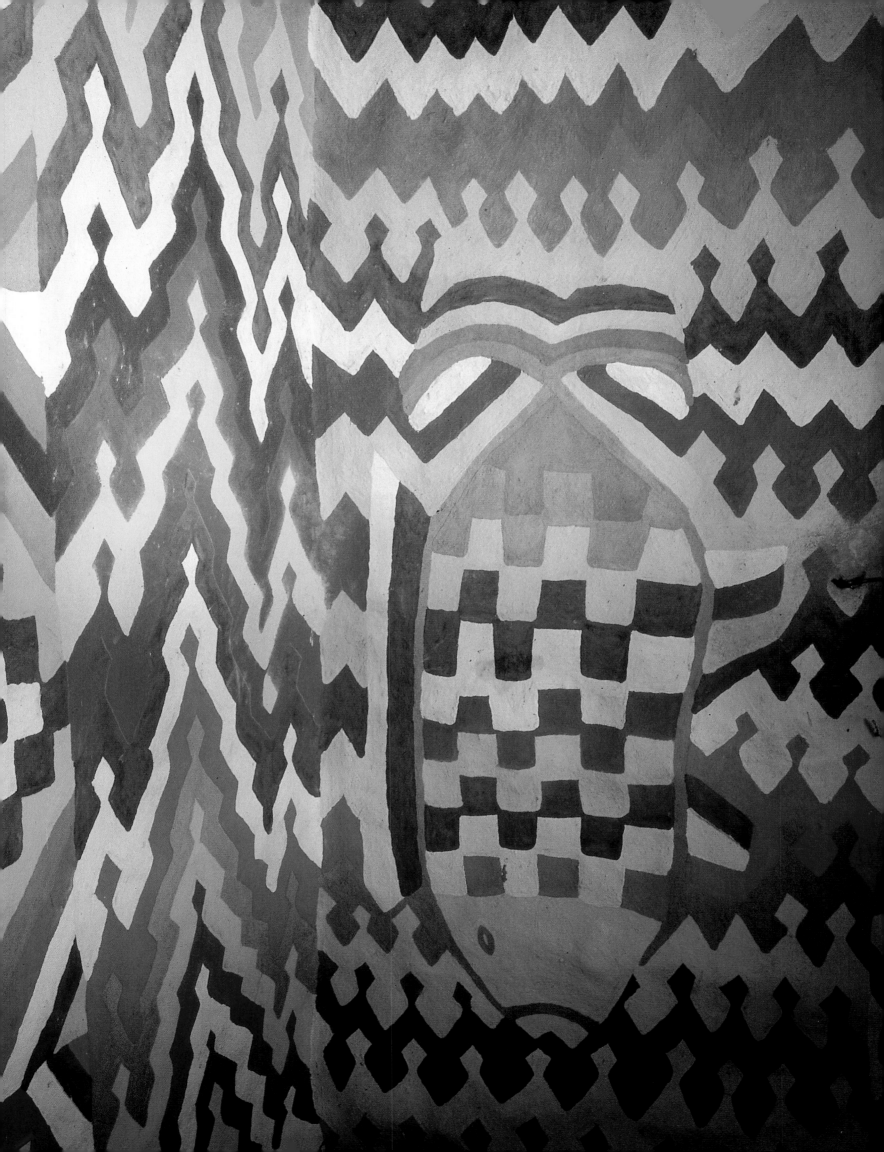

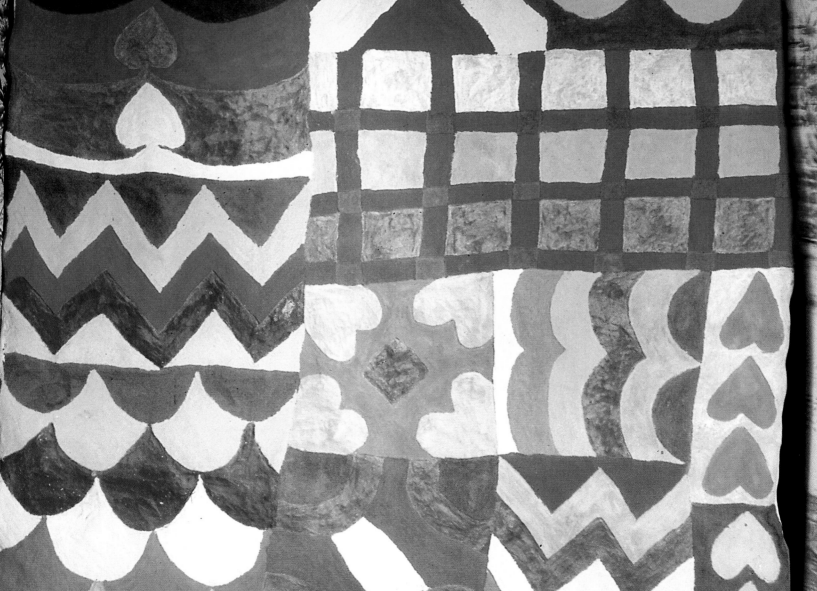

# ACKNOWLEDGEMENTS

The photographer would like to thank everyone who let her into their homes and their lives, and all those along the way who have given their time, advice and encouragement. Many thanks to all the friends who offered hospitality to her during her many travels through Africa. Without this support the book would have been impossible.

## MANY THANKS TO:

Aboudramane, Asdine Alaia, Romi Amancha, Alexandra d'Arnoux, Marie Aimée, George Arquier, Ghislaine Bavoillot, Marie-Claude Beaux, Catherine Beracassat, John Erik Berganus, Claire Bergeaud, Roussel Bernard, Jean Pascal Billaud, Françoise Blanc, Marie-Claire Blanckaerdt, Anna Bonde, Ann Bony, Christian Bouillet, Gösta Classon, Marita Coustet, Antoine and Marie Odile Debary, Jean Detière, Françoise Dorget, Rosemarie and Alan Dufour, Jérôme Dumoulin, Men Durieux, Renate Gallois Montbrun, Jean Louis Geizer, Jean Pierre Godeaut, Christine Grange-Bary, Jean Jartier, Hélène Joubert, Yves Jacques Kabasso, Matheo Kries, Patricia Laigneau, Jancy Lamom, Juan Lazzaro, Bruno de Laubadère, Étienne le Roy, Romi Loch-Davis, Aline Luque, André Magnin, Christiane Marquesi, Jean Hubert Martin, Steven R. Mendelson, Marion Meyer, Donald Namekomg, Mai Olivier, Karen Petrossian, Pierre Peyrol, Hélène Pour, Andrée Putman, Michel Reilhac, Mirella Ricciardi, Nicole Richy, Ute Rohrbeck, Sunil Sehti, Marie Paul Serre, Philippe Seulliet, Luc Svetchine, Hervé Tchakaloff, Frédérique Thomas, Rixa von Treuenfels, Alexander von Vegesack, Martin Veith, Christoph von Weyhe, Bernard Wuermser.

## IN MOROCCO THANKS TO:

Belkahia, Abdellatif Ait Benabdallah, Charles Chauliaguet, Feisal Cherradi, Françoise Dorget, Fabrice and Marcia Dubois La Chartre, Xavier Guerrand-Hermès, Amine Kabbaj, Joël Martial, Eli Moujhal, Carla and Franca Sozzani, Quentin Wilbaux.

## IN TUNISIA THANKS TO:

Jellal Ben Abdallah, Tarak and M'na Benmilled, Ahmed Djellouli, Nicolas Feuillate, Ali Ben Khalifaa, Ali Ben Khazifa, Christophe Kicherer, Mme Jacques Lanxade, Yves Marbrier, Jean-Pierre and Zeineb Marcie-Rivière, Leila Mencharie, Pierre Pes, Sadar and Zaina Sfar, Toni Facelli Sensi, Fatma and Kilani Ben Slimane.

## IN EGYPT THANKS TO:

Nagib Abdallah, Zeina Aboukheir, Loulia Damerji, Nagiba Demergé, Alain Fouquet, Titi Grace, Mustafa al Gundi, Maryse Helal, Amr Khalil, Christian Louboutin, Amina and Raouf Mishriki, Mounir and Leila Neamautalla, Jaqueline and Farouk Yunes, Vincent Grimaud and Danilles Wosny.

## IN KENYA AND TANZANIA THANKS TO:

Dr. Abungu, Rick and Bryony Anderson, Colette Belle, Bruno Brighetti, Yago Casado, Nani Croze, Dorothee and Michael Cunningham-Reid, Alan Donovan, Oria and Iain Douglas-Hamilton, Frédérique Scholl and Viviana Gonzales, Ariel Gramatidis, Mahmud Janmohamed, Ramesh N. Jobaputra, Anthony Kigondu, Sharma Lanina, Shufaa Lukoo, Mr Makweki, John Mohamed, Katharina Schmezer and Hermann Stucki, Emerson Skeens, Anita and Bernard Spoerri, Armando Tanzini, Anna and Tonio Trezebinski, Bongi Zulu, J.P. Zwager.

## IN THE SEYCHELLES, LA REUNION, MAURITIUS THANKS TO:

Corinne Asselin, Jean Barbier, Donna Bernard, Joseph Chassagne, Thierry Chokaloff, Yann Conacaud, Jacques Cuiten, Salim Currimjee, Patrice Binet Descamps, Jacques Duret, Rashio Ghanty, Catherine Gris, Edwige and François de Grivel, François Henquet, Marie-Ann Hodoul, Arnaud Lagesse, Henriette Lagesse, Martine Lagesse, Jean François Koenig, Gerard Maillot, Jacqui de Maroussem, Peter and Ros Metcalf, Jaqueline Oireaux, Marie Pierre Potier, Silvie Reol, Deborah Roubane, Pierre and Dorothea Roubanne, Pascale Vallet, Alain Marcel Vauthier, Bernard le Venneur.

## IN SOUTH AFRICA THANKS TO:

Kim Appelby, G.N. Bacon, Barbara Bailey, Beezy Bailey, Tracy Bamber, Willie Bester, Kathrine Blondeau, John and Cheryl Burgess, Sumien Brink, Norman and Janette Catherine, Christa and Michael Clark, John Clark, Adrienne Cohen, Brigitte Cross, Mike Donkin and Coenie Visser, Ian Douglas, Paul Duncan, Marmel Dutoit, Darryl and Coral Evans, Ekim Falconer, Marianne Fassler, Geordi and Boyd Fergusson, Lynne Fraser, Christophe Gallut, Gianna Ghersi, Monica Graaff, Monika Graeff, Jonathan Green and Marina Pretorius, Louise Hennigs, Nathalie Jacobson, Sue Jackson, Ian Johnson, Craig Kaplan, Joseph Kerhman, Terence Joseph Kerham, Anthony Kigondu, Barbara King, Malcolm Kluk, Julia Krone, Jean-Marc Lederman, Jenny and Desmond Loch-Davies, Pierre Lombart, Tracy Rushmere and Peter Maltbie, Trish Marshall, Annemarie Meintjies, A.C. van der Menne, Anja van der Merewe, Esther Mahlangu, Liz Morris, Hannes Myburgh, V.E. Mwabeni, Mankayi Ncediswa, Daku Sampi Nggobe, Yvonne Ntabeni, Vicky Ntozini, Cathy O'Clery, Anton Oosthuizen, Kate Otten, Sandy Ovenstone, Craig Port, Carla Pretorius, Silvio Rech and Lesley Carstens, Reyno, Peter Rich, Lew Rood, Shahn and Alice Rowe, Mandy St. Clair, Richard Santer, Bernardo James Smith, Charles Smith, Olivier Souchon, Gillian Stoeltzman, J.G.J. du Toit, Nonkosi Tshingana, Jeanie Warren, Ralph Weiden, Grant White, Ted Williams, Greg Wright.

## In Benin, Togo, Ghana, Burkina Faso thanks to:

Georges Adeagbo, Sana Allou, Ghislain F. do Behanzin, Jean-Pierre Clain, Anicet Dakpogan, Iamett-Damien, Youle Dapour, Gabin Djimasse, Micheline Egoumlety, Dominique Hazoume, Romuald Hazoume, Sabine Hentzsch, Andre Joly, Baba Keita, Konnonj, Joseph Kpobly, Bayeti Ndah, Palenkite Noufe, Nat Nunoo-Amarteifio, Abougé Inoussé Ouele, Hermann Ouele, Kabauga Ouele, Kink Ouele, Kawe Pala, Madeleine Père, Allou Sana, Nabo Sana, Thérèse Striggner Scott, David Tetteh, Cyprien Tokoudagba, Tiemoko Youl.

## In Cameroon and Nigeria thanks to:

Philippe Adrian, Hadjia Abba Ado, Musa Adolor, H.H. Aminu Ado Bayero, Henri Bulisi, Kamga David, Nike Davies-Okundaye, Michael P. Evans, Musa Hambolou, Chief Muraina Oyelami, Jean-Michel Rousset, Raymond Siaka, Remy Siaka, Takam Toukam, Philippe Gilles Petit de la Villeon, Germain Vigliano, Susanne Wenger, Abu Zaria.

## In Ivory Coast thanks to:

Elisée Brou, Pauline, Jean Luc, Sarah, and Vincent Duponchelle, Macline Hien, Monique le Houelleur, Hughe and Muriel le Houelleur, Yousouf and Monique Kone, Yves Lambellin, George Retord.

## In Niger and Mali thanks to:

Salia Male Dolo Amahiguere, Barcelo, Papa Moussa Ousman Cisse, Yves de la Croix, Asama Dara, Daodo Diabite, Boubakar Diaby, Alpha Yaya Diana, Omar Diko, Adam Douyou, the family Haidara, Jean François Lanteri, Malick Sidibé, Samuel Sidibé, Aminata Traore, Not Vital.

## In Senegal and Mauritania thanks to:

Baubau Samare Agoinit, Philippe Alquier, Diallo Bine Amadou, Mme Coulibaby, Marie-José Crespin, Tidiane Diagana, Bruno Dufour, Babcar Fall, Mr Horma, Jacques Piccard, Moussa Sakho, Amy Saw, Valerie Schlumberger, Dirk Thies, Jean Claude Thoret, Jean Paul Thorré, Mucky and Dieter Wachter.

## Special thanks to:

Michèle Champenois who helped me to recall all those many adventures for the introduction.

The publisher and the editor would like to thank Doran Ross, Los Angeles, for his skilled support, and Jean Marc Patras, Paris, for providing the transparencies of the works by Chéri Samba. They would also like to thank the Musée de l'Impression sur Étoffes, Mulhouse, France, and the Collection of The Newark Museum, Newark, New Jersey.

# ADDresses

## Accomodation (Houses, Guest Rooms, Hotels)

### Morocco

**DAR KARMA** (*Vol. I, page 58*)
Information and reservations:
Marrakech Médina
Dar el Qadi
87, Derb Moulay Abdelkader
Dabachi, Marrakech
Morocco
fon: +212 (44) 37 86 55
fax: +212 (44) 37 84 78
e-mail: marrakech.medina@iam.net.ma
www.marrakech-medina.com/riyads/index_en.htm

**DAR EL HANNA** (*Vol. I, page 71*)
Information and reservations:
Essaouira Home Collection
fon: +212 (67) 59 60 27 / fon: +33 (6) 646 430 82
e-mail: j.martial@wanadoo.fr
www.essaouirahomecollection.com

### Egypt

**ADRERE AMELLAL** (*Vol. I, page 148*)
Siwa Oasis
Egypt
fon: +20 (2) 736 78 79 / 738 13 27
fax: +20 (2) 735 54 89
e-mail: info@eqi.com.eg

**AL MOUDIRA** (*Vol. I, page 212*)
Luxor
Egypt
fon: +20 (12) 392 83 32 / 325 13 07
fax: +20 (12) 322 05 28
e-mail: moudirahotel@yahoo.com
www.moudira.com

### Kenya

**ALAN DONOVAN** (*Vol. I, page 250*)
Guest House
Information and reservations:
fon: +254 45 202 32 / +254 721 518 389
e-mail: ahalan@africaonline.co.ke
www.africanheritage.net
www.seekenya.com

In France:
Jean-Paul Merlin
As'Art
3, passage du grand cerf
75002 Paris
fon: +33 (1) 448 890 40
fax: +33 (1) 448 890 41
e-mail: asart@wanadoo.fr

**THE GIRAFFE MANOR** (*Vol. I, page 266*)
P.O. Box 15004
Langata, Nairobi
Kenya
fon: +254 (20) 89 10 78
fax: +254 (20) 89 09 49
e-mail: giraffem@kenyaweb.com
www.giraffemanor.com

**SIROCCO HOUSE** (*Vol. I, page 274*)
Guest House
P.O. Box 54667
Nairobi
Information and reservations:
Oria Douglas-Hamilton
fon: +254 (2) 33 48 68
e-mail: oria@iconnet.co.ks

**DODO'S TOWER** (*Vol. I, page 280*)
P.O. Box 24397
Nairobi
Kenya
fon: +254 (20) 57 46 89
fax: +254 (20) 57 73 81
e-mail: mellifera@swiftkenya.com

**HIPPO POINT** (*Vol. I, page 292*)
P.O. Box 1852
Naivasha
Kenya
fon: +254 (311) 301 24 / 200 98
fax: +254 (311) 212 95
e-mail: hippo-pt@africaonline.co.ke
www.hippopointkenya.com

**KATHARINA SCHMEZER &
HERMANN STUCKI** (*Vol. I, page 310*)
Information and reservations:
fon: +41 (78) 717 04 75
e-mail: lamu-house@uelischmezer.ch

### Tanzania

**NGORONGORO CRATER LODGE**
(*Vol. I, page 344*)
Information and reservations:
Conservation Corporation Africa
www.ccafrica.com

**MNEMBA ISLAND LODGE** (*Vol. I, page 372*)
Information and reservations:
Conservation Corporation Africa
www.ccafrica.com

**SALOMÉ'S GARDEN** (*Vol. I, page 358*)
Bubu
Stone Tower
Zanzibar
Tanzania
fon: +39 (051) 23 49 74
fax: +39 (051) 23 90 86
e-mail: info@houseofwonders.com
www.salomes-garden.com

**EMERSON & GREEN** (*Vol. I, page 364*)
236 Hurumzi Street
P.O. Box 3417
Stone Town
Zanzibar
Tanzania
fon: +255 (24) 223 01 71
fax: +255 (24) 223 10 38
e-mail: emegre@zanzibar.org
www.zanzibar.org/emegre

### Botswana

**MOMBO CAMP** (*Vol. I, page 414*)
**JAO CAMP** (*Vol. I, page 430*)
Information and reservations:
Wilderness Safaris
fon: +27 (11) 807 18 00
fax: +27 (11) 807 21 00
e-mail: enquiry@wilderness.co.za
www.wilderness-safaris.com

## SOUTH AFRICA

**CAMP 5** (*Vol. II, page 18*)
Information and reservations:
Makalali Private Game Reserve
fon: +27 (15) 793 17 20
fax: +27 (15) 793 17 23
Head Office
fon: +27 (11) 883 5786
fax: +27 (11) 883 4956
e-mail: reservations@makalali.co.za /
info@makalali.co.za
www.makalali.com

**SINGITA BOULDERS LODGE** (*Vol. II, page 28*)
Head Office
P.O. Box 23367
Claremont 7735
Cape Town
South Africa
fon: +27 (21) 683 34 24
fax: +27 (21) 683 35 02
e-mail: reservations@singita.co.za
www.singita.co.za

**SINGITA PRIVATE GAME RESERVE**
P.O. Box 650881
Benmore 2010
South Africa
fon: +27 (11) 234 09 90
fax: +27 (11) 234 05 35
www.singita.co.za

## Senegal

**A.S.A.O.** (*Vol. II, page 374*)
3 Guest Rooms
7, rue Saint Joseph
Gorée
Senegal
fon: +221 821 81 95

**A.S.A.O.**
2 Guest Rooms
17, avenue Malik SY
Dakar
Senegal

## More Addresses

**KITENGELA GLASS STUDIOS**
P.O. Box 15563
Mbagathi
Kenya
fon: +254 (303) 241 17 / (303) 233 51
e-mail: nani@kitengela.com / anselm@kitengela.com
www.kitengela.com

**BEEZY BAILEY ART FACTORY AND SHOP**
123 Kloofnek Road
Higgovale
Cape Town, 8001
South Africa
fon: +27 (21) 424 56 28
fax: +27 (21) 426 16 27
e-mail: beezy@beezybailey.co.za
www.beezybailey.co.za

**LOUISE HENNIGS**
13 Jarvis Street
De Waterkant
Cape Town, 8001
South Africa
fon: +27 (21) 418 11 29
fax: +27 (21) 418 45 46
e-mail: lhennigs@mweb.co.za

**AFRICAN IMAGE**
Tracy Rushmere
52 Burg Street
Cape Town, 8001
South Africa
fon: +27 (21) 423 16 19
fax: +27 (21) 423 562
www.african-image.co.za

**AFRICAN HERITAGE**
Lower Lever
Victoria Wharf
Victoria & Albert Waterfront
South Africa
fon: +27 (21) 421 66 10
fax: +27 (21) 424 73 57
e-mail: afrocarv@yebo.co.za
www.karellacarving.com

**ARTS AND CRAFTS FROM THE TOWNSHIPS**
Available from:
Khayelitsha Craft Market
34 / 562 Ncumo Road
Harare
Khayelitsha
Cape Town, 7784
South Africa
fon: +27 (21) 361 52 46
e-mail: gugs@stmichaels.org.za (Father Ningi)

**A.S.A.O. GALLERY**
15, rue Elzévir
75003 Paris
France
fon: +33 (1) 445 490 50

**C.S.A.O. BOUTIQUE**
3, rue Elzévir
75003 Paris
France
fon: +33 (1) 445 455 88
fax: +33 (1) 445 455 89

**MUSÉE DE L'IMPRESSION SUR ÉTOFFES**
14, rue Jean-Jacques Henner
BP 1468
68072 Mulhouse cedex
France
fon: +33 389 468 300
Chief curator: Jacqueline Jacqué
Curator: Annerose Bingel

# BiBLiOGRaPHY

## TraVeL aND HOTeL GuiDes

Afrique du Sud, Paris 2000 (*Guides Voir, Hachette*)

Ägypten, Ostfildern 2001 (*Baedeker*)

ALTMANN, ANDREAS: Im Herz ein Feuer. Unterwegs von Kairo in den Süden Afrikas, Wien 2001

ANDRIAMIRADO, SENNEN: Mali aujourd'hui, Paris 2001

APA GUIDE Tunesien, München/Berlin 2001 (*Polyglott*)

APA GUIDE Mauritius, Réunion, Seychellen, München 2003 (*Polyglott*)

BAUR, THOMAS: Senegal, Gambia, Bielefeld 2002 (*Reise Know-How*)

BECH, ANJA: Mauritius, München 2002 (*Polyglott Reisebuch*)

BECHT, SABINE: Tunesien, Erlangen 2002 (*Michael Müller Verlag*)

BETTEN, ARNOLD: Marokko, Köln 2000 (*DuMont Kunstreiseführer*)

BERGER, KARL-WILHELM: Kenia. Nordtansania, Dormagen 2001 (*Iwanowski's Reisebuchverlag*)

BINDLOSS, JOSEPH, SINGH, SARINA, SWANEY, DEANNA, STRAUSS, ROBERT: Mauritius, Réunion & Seychelles, Melbourne 2001 (*Lonely Planet*)

BIRNBAUM, MICHAEL: Die schwarze Sonne Afrikas, München/Zürich 2000

BOROWSKI, BIRGIT, BOURMER, ACHIM UND BRÖDEL, INA: Kenia. Kilimanjaro. Serengeti, Ostfildern 2003 (*Baedeker*)

Botswana, Melbourne 2001 (*Lonely Planet*)

BRETT, MICHAEL, JOHNSON-BARKER, BRIAN UND MARIËLLE RENSSEN: Südafrika, München/Starnberg 2000 (*Vis-à-Vis, Dorling Kindersley*)

BRIGGS, PHILIP: Ghana, Chalfont St Peter, 2001 (*The Bradt Travel Guide*)

BROCKMANN, HEIDRUN UND KRUSE-ETZBACH, DIRK: Kapstadt und Garden-Route, Dormagen 2003 (*Iwanowski's Reisebuchverlag*)

BRUNSWIG, MURIEL: KulturSchock Marokko, Bielefeld 2000 (*Reise Know-How*)

BUCHHOLZ, HARTMUT: Senegal. Gambia, Köln 2001 (*DuMont Reise-Taschenbuch*)

BURKE, ANDREW AND ELSE, DAVID: Senegal, Melbourne 2002 (*Lonely Planet*)

CARPIN, SARAH: Seychelles, Genf 2002 (*G.O. Découverte*)

CASSIDY, SHELLEY-MAREE: The Hotel Book. Great Escapes Africa, Köln 2003

CHINULA, TIONE, TALBOT, VINCENT: Zimbabwe, Melbourne 2002 (*Lonely Planet*)

COBBINAH, JOJO: Ghana, Frankfurt am Main 2002 (*Peter Meyer Verlag*)

DÄRR, WOLFGANG: Mauritius, Köln 2001 (*DuMont Richtig Reisen*)

DÄRR, WOLFGANG: Seychellen, Köln 2003 (*DuMont Richtig Reisen*)

DÖRR, ERIKA: Marokko. Vom Rif zum Anti-Atlas, Bielefeld 2001 (*Reise Know-How*)

Égypte, Paris 2001 (*Le Guide Vert, Michelin*)

Égypte, Paris 2001 (*Guides Bleus, Hachette*)

EISELE, ANJA UND SOBIK, HELGE: Tunesien, Ostfildern 2002 (*Abenteuer und Reisen, Mairs Geographischer Verlag*)

ELSE, DAVID: Zambia, Melbourne 2002 (*Lonely Planet*)

FIEBIG, HARTMUT: Kenia, Bielefeld 2001 (*Reise Know-How*)

FITZPATRICK, MARY, GREENWAY, PAUL: Madagascar, Melbourne 2001 (*Lonely Planet*)

FITZPATRICK, MARY: Tanzania, Melbourne 2002 (*Lonely Planet*)

FITZPATRICK, MARY: West Africa, Melbourne 2002 (*Lonely Planet*)

FUCHS, REGINA: Kamerun, Bielefeld 2001 (*Reise Know-How*)

GABRIEL, JÖRG: Sansibar, Pemba & Mafia, Bielefeld 2001 (*Reise Know-How*)

GÖDICKE, DÖRTE UND WERNER, KARIN: KulturSchock Ägypten, Bielefeld 2000 (*Reise Know-How*)

GÖTTLER, GERHARD, BAUR, THOMAS UND DÄRR, ERIKA: Westafrika. Band 1: Sahelländer, Bielefeld 2003 (*Reise Know-How*)

HAM, ANTHONY: Libya, Melbourne 2002 (*Lonely Planet*)

HODD, MICHAEL: East Africa Handbook, Bath 2002 (*Footprint Handbooks*)

HODD, MICHAEL, ROCHE, ANGELA: Uganda Handbook, Bath 2002 (*Footprint Handbooks*)

HOFRICHTER, ROBERT: Naturführer Seychellen. Juwelen im Indischen Ozean, Steinfurt 2000

HUDGENS, JIM AND TRILLO, RICHARD: West Africa, London 2000 (*The Rough Guide*)

HUMPHREYS, ANDREW AND JENKINS, SIONA: Egypt, Melbourne 2002 (*Lonely Planet*)

IWANOWSKI, MICHAEL: Botswana, Dormagen 2002 (*Iwanowski's Reisebuchverlag*)

JANIN, SYLVIANE: Burkina Faso. Pays des hommes intègres, Genève 2000 (*G.O. Découverte*)

KARDY, STEFFI: Kenya, Tanzania mit Zanzibar, Köln 2001 (*DuMont Richtig Reisen*)

KELLETT, FRANCISCA, WILLIAMS, LIZZIE: South Africa Handbook, Bath 2002 (*Footprint Handbooks*)

Kenia. Kilimanjaro. Serengeti, Ostfildern 1998 (*Baedeker*)

KERTSCHER, KEVIN: Afrika solo. Eine Reise, Berlin 2001

KLOTCHKOFF, JEAN-CLAUDE: Le Burkina Faso aujourd'hui, Paris 2001

KNIGHT, RICHARD: Trekking in the Moroccan Atlas, Hindhead, Surrey 2001

Le grand guide de l'Afrique du Sud, Paris 1999

Le grand guide du Kenya, Paris 2002

Le grand guide du Maroc, Paris 2002

Le grand guide de la Tunisie, Paris 1993

Le grand guide de Maurice, la Réunion, les Seychelles, Paris 2003

LEHMANN, INGEBORG: Marokko, Ostfildern 2001 (*Baedeker*)

LÜBBERT, CHRISTOPH: Botswana, Bielefeld 2002 (*Reise Know-How*)

Mali, Paris 2001 (*Objectif Aventure, Guides Arthaud*)

Maroc, Paris 2003 (*Guides Bleus, Hachette*)

MCCREA, BARBARA, MTHEMBU-SALTER, GREG, PINEHUCK, TONY UND RIED, DONALD: Südafrika mit Lesotho und Swasiland, Berlin 2002 (*Stefan Loose Travel*)

MCGUINNESS, JUSTIN: Tunisia Handbook, Bath 2002
  (*Footprint Handbooks*)
MCINTYRE, CHRIS: Botswana, Chalfont St Peter, 2003
  (*The Bradt Travel Guide*)
MILLER, ALO UND NIKOLAUS: Réunion, Köln 2002,
  (*DuMont Reise-Taschenbuch*)

NANTET, BERNARD: Mauritanie, Paris 2001
  (*Objectif Aventure, Guide Arthaud*)

OBERG, HEIDRUN: Seychellen. Mauritius. Komoren. Réunion.
  Malediven, München/Wien/Zürich 1995 (*Reiseführer Natur, BLV*)

PASSOT, BERNARD: Le Bénin, Paris 1996
Photo-guide des animaux d'Afrique, Lausanne 2001
Pistes du sud tunisien, Calvisson 2000 (*Guide Jacques Gandini*)
Pistes du Maroc, Tome 1: Haut et Moyen Atlas,
  Calvisson 2000 (*Guide Jacques Gandini*)
Pistes du Maroc, Tome 2: Le Sud, du Tafilalet à l'Atlantique,
  Calvisson 2001 (*Guide Jacques Gandini*)
Pistes du Maroc, Tome 3: De l'Oued Draa à la Seguiet el Hamra,
  Calvisson 2002 (*Guide Jacques Gandini*)
Pistes du Maroc, Tome 4: Le Maroc oriental, Calvisson 2003
  (*Guide Jacques Gandini*)

QUACK, ULRICH: Mauritius. Réunion, Dormagen 2002
  (*Iwanowski's Reisebuchverlag*)

REMY, MYLÈNE: La Côte-d'Ivoire aujourd'hui, Paris 2002
REMY, MYLÈNE: Le Sénégal aujourd'hui, Paris 2000
RICHMOND, SIMON, MURRAY, JON: Cape Town,
  Melbourne 2002 (*Lonely Planet*)
RICHMOND, SIMON: South Africa, Lesotho & Swaziland,
  Melbourne 2002 (*Lonely Planet*)
ROTTER, PETER: Bergsteigen – Safari – Trekking. Kilimanjaro.
  Tanzania, München 2001

SCHETAR-KÖTHE, DANIELA: Tunesien. Land und Leute,
  München 1996 (*Polyglott*)
SEMSEK, HANS GÜNTER: Ägypten und Sinai. Pharaonische
  Tempel und islamische Tradition, Köln 2001 (*DuMont Kunstreiseführer*)
SOREAU, FRÉDÉRIC: Maroc. Le Grand Sud, Paris 2003 (*Aujourd'hui*)
SWANEY, DEANNA: Namibia, Melbourne 2002 (*Lonely Planet*)

TONDOK, SIGRID UND WIL U. A.: Ägypten individuell,
  Bielefeld 2001 (*Reise Know-How*)
Tunisie, Paris 2003 (*Guides Bleus, Hachette*)
Tunisie, Paris 2003 (*Objectif Aventure, Guide Arthaud*)

WATERKAMP, RAINER UND WISNIEWSKI, WINFRIED:
  Ostafrika. Kenia, Tanzania, Uganda. Tiere und Pflanzen
  entdecken, Stuttgart 1999 (*Kosmos Naturreiseführer*)
WILLETT, DAVID: Tunisia, Melbourne 2001 (*Lonely Planet*)

# ILLUSTRATED BOOKS

BALDIZZONE, TIZIANA ET GIANNI: Magiciens de la pluie, Paris 2002
BALFOUR, DARYL AND SHARNA: Simply Safari, New York 2001
BEARD, PETER H.: The End of the Game, London 2000
BECKWITH, CAROL, FISHER, ANGELA: African Ceremonies, New York
  1999
BECKWITH, CAROL, FISHER, ANGELA: Unbekanntes Afrika:
  Völker und Kulturen zwischen Hochland, Wüste und Ozean, Köln 2000
BERNUS, EDMOND, DUROU, JEAN-MARC: Touaregs. Un Peuple du
  désert, Paris 1996
BERTINETTI, MARCELLO: In the Eye of Horus. A Photographer's
  Flight Over Egypt, Vercelli 2001
BETTAÏEB, MOHAMMED-SALAH, JABEUR, SALAH, HAMZA, ALYA:
  La Tunisie vue du ciel, Aix-en-Provence 1996
BURNS, NATASHA (*Text*), BEDDOW, TIM (*Fotos*): Safari Style.
  Wohnideen aus Afrika, Köln 1998

CASTÉRA, JEAN-MARC, PEURIOT, FRANÇOISE, PLOQUIN,
  PHILIPPE: Arabesque. Arts décoratifs au Maroc, Courbevoie 1998
COLBORNE, DESMOND (*Text*), DOS SANTOS, SØLVI (*Photos*):
  South Africa. Private Worlds, London 1999
COURTNEY-CLARKE, MARGARET: Ndebele. The Art of an African Tribe,
  New York 1986
COURTNEY-CLARKE, MARGARET: African Canvas, New York 1990
CRESSOLE, MICHEL: Sur les traces de l'Afrique fantôme, Paris 1990

DANTO BARRY, RAHIM: Portes d'Afrique, Paris 1999
DESJEUX, CATHERINE ET BERNARD: Afriques. Tout partout partager,
  Brinon-sur-Sauldre 2001
EINSTEIN, CARL: Negerplastik, Berlin 1992

FISHER, ANGELA: Africa Adorned, London 1987
FONTAINE, JACQUES, GRESSER, PIERRE, FAUQUÉ, NICOLAS
  (*photos*): Tunisie. Carrefour des civilisations, Courbevoie/Paris 2000
FRANCK, MARTINE, SOULÉ, BÉATRICE, VOYEUX, MARTINE:
  Ousmane Sow, Le soleil en face, Neuilly-sur-Seine 1999
FRASER, CRAIG (*Photos*): Shack Chic. Innovation in the Shack Lands
  of South Africa, London 2002

GAEDE, PETER-MATHIAS: Ein Tag im Leben von Afrika, Köln 2002
GEORGE, UWE: Sahara. Expeditionen durch Raum und Zeit, Hamburg
  2001

HUET, MICHEL (*Photos*), SAVARY, CLAUDE (*textes*):
  Danses d'Afrique, Paris 1994

KRAUSE, AXEL (*Fotos*), SEMSEK, HANS-GÜNTER (*Text*): Ägypten,
  Würzburg 2002

LA GUÉRIVIÈRE, JEAN DE: Exploration de l'Afrique noire, Paris 2002
LAINÉ, DANIEL: Rois d'Afrique, Paris 2001
LAUBER, WOLFGANG: Architektur der Dogon. Traditioneller Lehmbau
  und Kunst in Mali, München 1998

# BiBLiOgraphy

LAVAUX, CATHERINE: Réunion du battant des lames au sommet, Paris 1998

LE GABON DE FERNAND GRÉBERT, 1913–1932, Musée d'etnographie de Genève, Paris 2003

LERAT, JEAN-MARIE: Chez bonne idée. Images du petit commerce en Afrique de l'Ouest, Paris 1990

LOSSKARN, ELKE (Fotos), LOSSKARN, DIETER (Text): Südafrika, Luzern 2000

LOVATT-SMITH, LISA: Moroccan Interiors, Köln 2003

MARI, CARLO: Auf der Spur des Wassers, München 2000

MARI, CARLO: Safari, München 2003

MARTIN, MICHAEL, ALTMANN, ANDREAS: Unterwegs in Afrika, München 2002

MARTIN, MICHAEL, JAUSLY, DORIS, MAERITZ, KAY, MICUS, STEPHAN: Die Wüsten Afrikas, London 1998

MONLAÜ, LAURENT: Le voyage en Afrique, Paris 2003

MOURAD, KHIREDDINE (textes), KERBRAT, MARIE-PIERRE: Arts et traditions du Maroc, Paris 1998

NICKERSON, JACKIE: Afrika. Leben mit der Erde, München 2002

POLIDORI, ROBERT, BACCHIELLI, LIDIANO, DI VITA, ANTONINO, DI VITA-EVRARD, GINETTE: La Libye antique. Cités perdues de l'Empire romain, Paris 1998

RAUZIER, MARIE-PASCALE, TRÉAL, CÉCILE ET RUIZ, JEAN-MICEL (photos): Couleur du Maroc, Paris 1999

READER, JOHN, LEWIS, MICHAEL: Africa, Washington, D.C. 2001

RENAUDEAU, MICHEL: Dogon, Paris 2001

RENAUDEAU, MICHEL: Tableaux Dogon, Paris 2002

RICCIARDI, MIRELLA: African Visions. The Diary of an African Photographer, New York 2002

RICCIARDI, MIRELLA: Vanishing Africa, London 1977

RIEFENSTAHL, LENI: Africa, Köln 2002

Sahara. L'Adrar de Mauritanie, Paris 2002

SAINT LÉON, PASCAL MARTIN (ed.): Anthologie de la photographie africaine et de l'océan Indien, Paris 1998

SÈBE, ALAIN, SÈBE, BERNY: Sahara: Unbekannte Wüste vom Atlantik bis zum Nil, Stuttgart 2002

SLIM, HEDI (textes), FAUQUÉ, NICOLAS (photos): La Tunisie antique. De Hannibal à Saint Augustin, Paris 2001

STOELTIE, BARBARA AND RENÉ: Living in Morocco, Köln 2003

TOURNADRE, MICHEL: La Mauritanie, Paris 1996

TRIKI, HAMED, DOVOFAT, ALAIN: Medersa de Marrakech, Aix-en-Provence 1999

TROTHA, DÉSIRÉE V.: Wo sich Himmel und Erde berühren. Tuareg in der Weite der Wüste, München 2003

WENDL, TOBIAS (Hg.): Afrikanische Reklamekunst, Wuppertal 2002

WEYER, HELFRIED: Ägypten. Wüste, Nil und Sinai, Steinfurt 2002

WUERFEL, JOE (Photos), BEARD, PETER (Interview): Sensual Africa, Zurich/New York 2000

## Literary Books

ACHEBE, CHINUA:
Things Fall Apart, London 2002
Okonkwo oder Das Alte stürzt, Frankfurt 2002
Le monde s'effondre, Paris 1973

ACHEBE, CHINUA:
Arrow of God, New York 2000
Der Pfeil Gottes, Wuppertal 2003
La flèche de Dieu, Paris 1978

ADAMSON, JOY:
Born Free. A Lioness of Two Worlds, New York 2000
Frei Geboren. Die Geschichte der Löwin Elsa, München 2002

AIDOO, AMA ATA:
Our Sister Killjoy, or, Reflections from a Black Eyed Squint, London 1999
The Dilemma of a Ghost, London 1997

ALLIN, MICHAEL:
Zarafa, London 1999
Zarafa, München 2002
La girafe de Charles X, Paris 2000

ANGELOU, MAYA:
All God's Children Need Travelling Shoes, London 2002

ARMAH, AYI KWEI:
The Beautiful Ones Are Not Yet Born, London 1988
Die Schönen sind noch nicht geboren, Düsseldorf 1984

ARMAH, AYI KWEI:
The Healers: a Historical Novel, Oxford 1993

BÂ, AMADOU HAMPÂTÉ:
The Fortunes of Wangrin, Bloomington 1999
L'étrange destin de Wangrin, Paris 1982

BÂ, MARIAMA:
So Long a Letter, Oxford 2000
Ein so langer Brief: ein afrikanisches Frauenschicksal, München 2002
Une si longue lettre, Paris 2001

BÂ, MARIAMA:
The Scarlet Song, London 1995
Un chant écarlate, Dakar 1998
Der scharlachrote Gesang, Frankfurt 1996

BADIAN, SEYDOU:
Caught in the Storm, Boulder 1998
Sous l'orage, Paris 2000

BADIAN, SEYDOU:
Le sang des masques, Paris 1976

BARLEY, NIGEL:
A Plague of Caterpillars: a Return to the African Bush, London 1989
Die Raupenplage, Stuttgart 1998
Le retour de l'anthropologue, Paris 2002

BARLEY, NIGEL:
The Coast, London 1991

BECKER, FRIEDRICH (Hg.):
Afrikanische Märchen, Frankfurt 1988

BELLOW, SAUL:
Henderson the Rain King, London 1996
Der Regenkönig, Bergisch Gladbach 2000
Le Faiseur de pluie, Paris 1961
BEN HAMED CHARHADI, DRISS:
A Life Full of Holes, Edinburgh 1999
Ein Leben voller Fallgruben, Zürich 1992
BEN JELLOUN, TAHAR:
This Blinding Absence of Light, New York 2002
Das Schweigen des Lichts, Berlin 2001
Cette aveuglante absence de lumière, Paris 2002
BEN JELLOUN, TAHAR:
The Sacred Night, Baltimore 2000
Die Nacht der Unschuld, Reinbek bei Hamburg 1991
La nuit sacrée, Paris 1987
BEN JELLOUN, TAHAR:
The Sand Child, Baltimore 2000
Sohn ihres Vaters, Berlin 1986
L'enfant de sable, Paris 1995
BLIXEN, TANIA:
Out of Africa, Frankfurt 2001 (*Penguin Books*)
Jenseits von Afrika, Reinbek bei Hamburg 1999
La ferme africaine, Paris 1978
BOWLES, PAUL:
Let It Come Down, Frankfurt 2000 (*Penguin Books*)
So mag er fallen, München 1990
Après toi le déluge, Paris 1994
BOWLES, PAUL:
The Sheltering Sky, Frankfurt 2000 (*Penguin Books*)
Himmel über der Wüste, Wien 1998
Un thé au Sahara, Paris 1980
BOYLE, T. C.:
Water Music, London 1998
Wassermusik, Reinbek bei Hamburg 1990
Water Music, Paris 1998
BREYTENBACH, BREYTEN:
The True Confessions of an Albino Terrorist, London 1984
Wahre Bekenntnisse eines Albino-Terroristen, Köln 1984
BRINK, ANDRÉ:
The Other Side of Silence, London 2002

CAILLIÉ, RENÉ:
Voyage à Tombouctou, Paris 1996
CARBERRY, JUANITA:
Child of Happy Valley, London 1999
Letzte Tage in Kenia. Meine Kindheit in Afrika, Berlin 2001
CHATWIN, BRUCE:
The Viceroy of Ouidah, London 1998
Der Vizekönig von Ouidah, München 2003
CHOUKRI, MOHAMED:
For Bread Alone, London 1993
Das nackte Brot, Frankfurt 1990
Le Pain nu, Paris 1997
CHRAÏBI, DRISS:
Mother Comes of Age, Washington, D.C. 1984

Die Zivilisation, Mutter!, Zürich 1989
La civilisation, ma Mère!, Paris 1988
CHRISTIE, AGATHA:
Destination Unknown, London 2003
Der unheimliche Weg, Bern 1994
Destination inconnue, Paris 1999
CHRISTIE, AGATHA:
Death on the Nile, New York 2000
Der Tod auf dem Nil, Bern 2001
Mort sur le Nil, Paris 2003
COETZEE, J. M.:
Disgrace, New York/London 2000
Schande, Frankfurt 2001
Disgrâce, Paris 2001
COLLEN, LINDSEY:
Die Wellen von Mauritius, Reinbek bei Hamburg 1998
CONDÉ, MARYSE:
Segu, New York 1996
Segu, München 1990
Ségou, Paris 1996
COUDERC, FRÉDÉRIC:
Prince ébène, Paris 2003

DADIÉ, BERNARD B.:
Climbié, Paris 1956
Climbié, London 1984
DANGAREMBGA, TSITSI:
Nervous Conditions, London 1988
Der Preis der Freiheit, Reinbek bei Hamburg 1993
À fleur de peau, Paris 1993
DEFOE, DANIEL:
Robinson Crusoe, London 2001
Robinson Crusoe, Düsseldorf 2003
Robinson Crusoé, Paris 1997
DIAWARA, MANTHIA:
In Search of Africa, Cambridge 1998
En quête d'Afrique, Paris 2001
DIBBA, EBOU:
Chaff on the Wind, London 1986
DIRIE, WARIS:
Desert Dawn, London 2002
Nomadentochter, München 2002
L'aube du désert, Paris 2002
DOUGLAS-HAMILTON, IAIN AND ORIA:
Among the Elephants, New York 1988
Unter Elefanten, Bergisch Gladbach 1989
DUGARD, MARTIN:
Into Africa: the Epic Adventures of Stanley and Livingstone, London 2003
DURRELL, GERALD:
The Bafut Beagles, Harmondsworth 1986
Die Spürhunde des großen Fon: auf Kleintierfang in Kamerun, Wien 1957
DURRELL, GERALD:
A Zoo in My Luggage, Bath 1994
Ein Koffer voller Tiere: Ich fange meinen eigenen Zoo, Frankfurt 1992

# BiBLiOgraPHY

**DURRELL, LAWRENCE:**
The Alexandria Quartet, London 2001
Das Alexandria-Quartett, Reinbek bei Hamburg 1977
Le quatuor d'Alexandrie, Paris 1992

**EDBERG, ROLF:**
The Dream of Kilimanjaro, London 1979
**EQUIANO, OLAUDAH:**
The Life of Olaudah Equiano or Gustavus Vassa, the African,
Mineola, New York 1999
Die Merkwürdige Lebensgeschichte des Sklaven Olaudah
Equiano, von ihm selbst veröffentlicht im Jahre 1789,
Frankfurt 1990

**FANON, FRANTZ:**
Wretched of the Earth, Frankfurt 2001 (*Penguin Books*)
Die Verdammten dieser Erde, Frankfurt 1981
Les Damnés de la Terre, Paris 2002
**FORESTER, CECIL SCOTT:**
The African Queen, Harmondsworth 1980
Die „African Queen", Berlin 1999
**FORSYTH, FREDERICK:**
The Dogs of War, London 1996
Die Hunde des Krieges, München 2001
**FOX, JAMES:**
White Mischief, New York 1998
Weißes Verhängnis. Die letzten Tage in Kenya, Zürich 1988
**FRANK, KATHERINE:**
A Voyager Out: The Life of Mary Kingsley, New York 1991
**FULLER, ALEXANDRA:**
Don't Let's Go to the Dogs Tonight, London 2003

**GALLMANN, KUKI:**
African Nights, Frankfurt 1995 (*Penguin Books*)
Afrikanische Nächte, München 1999
**GALLMANN, KUKI:**
I Dreamed of Africa, London 2000
Ich träumte von Afrika, München 2000
Je rêvais de l'Afrique, Paris 2000
**GARY, ROMAIN:**
The Roots of Heaven, London 1973
Les racines du ciel, Paris 2002
Die Wurzeln des Himmels, München 1985
**GERCKE, STEFANIE:**
Ich kehre zurück nach Afrika, München 2002
**GOLDING, WILLIAM:**
An Egyptian Journal, London 1989
Ein ägyptisches Tagebuch. Reisen, um glücklich zu sein,
München 1987
**GORDIMER, NADINE:**
July's People, Frankfurt 2001 (*Penguin Books*)
Julys Leute, Frankfurt 1991
Ceux de July, Paris 1992
**GOWDY, BARBARA:**
The White Bone, London 2000

Der weiße Knochen, München 2000
Un lieu sûr, Arles 2000

**HEMINGWAY, ERNEST:**
Green Hills of Africa, London 1996
Die grünen Hügel Afrikas, Reinbek bei Hamburg 1999
Les vertes collines d'Afrique, Paris 1949
**HOFMANN, CORINNE:**
Die weiße Massai, München 2000
La Massaï blanche, Paris 2000
**HOVE, CHENJERAI:**
Ancestors, London 1996
Ahnenträume, München 2000
Ancêtres, Arles 2002
**HUXLEY, ELSPETH:**
The Flame Trees of Thika. Memories of an African Childhood,
London 1998
Die Flammenbäume von Thika. Erinnerungen an eine Kindheit in Afrika,
Bergisch Gladbach 1988

**JACQ, CHRISTIAN:**
Im Bann des Pharaos, Bern/München/Wien 2002
L'affaire Toutankhamon, Paris 1992
**JORIS, LIEVE:**
Mali Blues, Melbourne 1998
Mali Blues. Ein afrikanisches Tagebuch, München 2000
Mali Blues. Je chanterai pour toi, Arles 2002
**JOUBERT, BEVERLY ET DERECK:**
Grands chasseurs sous la lune. Les lions du Savuti, Paris 2000

**KANE, CHEIKH HAMIDOU:**
Ambiguous Adventure, Oxford 1989
L'aventure ambiguë, Paris 1998
Der Zwiespalt des Samba Diallo: Erzählung aus Senegal, Frankfurt 1980
**KANT, IMMANUEL, HENSCHEID, ECKHARD:**
Der Neger (Negerl), Frankfurt 1985
**KAYE, MARY MARGARET:**
Trade Wind, Bath 1984
Tod in Sansibar, München 1990
Zanzibar, Paris 1982
**KESSEL, JOSEPH:**
Le lion, Paris 1966
**KORNHERR, HANNELORE:**
Sehnsucht nach Kenia. Ein afrikanisches Reisetagebuch, Berlin 2002
**KOUROUMA, AHMADOU:**
Waiting for the Vote of the Wild Animals, Charlottesville 2001
En attendant le vote des bêtes sauvages, Paris 2000

**LAING, B. KOJO:**
Search Sweet Country, London 1987
Die Sonnensucher, München 1995
**LAYE, CAMARA:**
The African Child, London 1989
L'enfant noir, Paris 1994
Einer aus Karussa, Zürich 1954

**LAYE, CAMARA:**
The Radiance of the King, New York 2001
Le regard du roi, Paris 1986
Der Blick des Königs, Berlin 1983
**LESSING, DORIS:**
The Grass is Singing, London 1994
Afrikanische Tragödie, Frankfurt 1995
**LOTI, PIERRE:**
Morocco, New York 2002
Im Zeichen der Sahara, München 2000
Au Maroc, Saint-Cyr-sur-Loire 1990

**MAALOUF, AMIN:**
Leo Africanus, New York 1988
Leo Africanus: Der Sklave des Papstes, Frankfurt 2000
Léon l'Africain, Paris 1988
**MAHFOUZ, NAGUIB:**
Arabian Nights and Days, London/New York 1995
Die Nacht der Tausend Nächte, Zürich 2000
Les mille et une nuits, Arles 2001
**MAHFOUZ, NAGUIB:**
The Cairo Trilogy. Palace Walk, Palace of Desire, Sugar Street,
New York 2001
La trilogie, Paris 1993
**MANDELA, NELSON:**
Long Walk to Freedom, London 1995
Der lange Weg zur Freiheit, Frankfurt 1997
Un long chemin vers la liberté, Paris 1997
**MANKELL, HENNING:**
Der Chronist der Winde, München 2002
The White Lioness: A Mystery, Frankfurt 2003 (*Penguin Books*)
Die weiße Löwin, München 1998
**MARKHAM, BERYL:**
West with the Night, London 2001
Westwärts mit der Nacht. Mein Leben als Fliegerin in Afrika,
München 2001
Vers l'ouest avec la nuit, Paris 1995
**MARTELLI, GEORGE:**
Livingstone's River. A History of the Zambezi Expedition, 1858–1864,
London 1970
**MATTHIESSEN, PETER:**
Silences africains, Paris 1994
**MEMMI, ALBERT:**
The Pillar of Salt, Boston 1992
Die Salzsäule. Biographischer Roman, Hamburg 1995
La statue de sel, Paris 1993
**MÉNARD, JEAN-FRANÇOIS:**
La ville du désert et de l'eau, Paris 1997
**MERNISSI, FATIMA:**
Scheherazade Goes West. Different Cultures, Different Harems, New York
2001
Harem. Westliche Phantasien, östliche Wirklichkeit, Freiburg 2000
Le harem et l'occident, Paris 2001
**MERNISSI, FATIMA:**
Dreams of Trespass: Tales of a Harem Girlhood, Massachusetts 1995

Der Harem in uns. Die Furcht vor dem anderen und die Sehnsucht
der Frauen, Freiburg 2000
Rêves de femmes: Une enfance au harem, Paris 1996
**MOIRET, JOSEPH MARIE:**
Memoirs of Napoleon's Egyptian Expedition 1798–1801, London 2001

**NAIPAUL, V. S.:**
A Bend in the River, London 2002
An der Biegung des großen Flusses, München 2002
À la courbe du fleuve, Paris 1982
**NAIPAUL, V.S.:**
Finding the Centre: Two Narratives, London 1985
**NAIPAUL, V. S.:**
North of South. An African Journey, Frankfurt 1997 (*Penguin Books*)
Au nord du Sud. Un voyage africain, Monaco 1992
**NAZER, MENDE, LEWIS, DAMIEN:**
Sklavin, München 2002

**OGOBARA DOLO, SEKOU:**
La mère des masques. Un Dogon raconte, Paris 2002
**OKRI, BEN:**
The Famished Road, London 1991
Die hungrige Straße Köln, 1994
**OUOLOGUEM, YAMBO:**
Bound to Violence, London 1986
Le devoir de violence, Paris 2003
Das Gebot der Gewalt, München 1969

**PATON, ALAN:**
Cry, the Beloved Country. A Story of Comfort in Desolation, London 1998
Denn sie sollen getröstet werden, Frankfurt 1988
Pleure, ô pays bien aimé, Paris 1992

**RICARD, ALAIN:**
Voyages de découvertes en Afrique. Anthologie 1790–1890, Paris 2000
**RICHBURG, KEITH B.:**
Out of America. A Black Man Confronts Africa, San Diego, California 1998
Jenseits von Amerika. Eine Konfrontation mit Afrika, dem Land meiner
Vorfahren, Berlin 2000
**ROSS, MARK C.:**
Dangerous Beauty. Life and Death in Africa. True Stories from a Safari
Guide, New York 2001
Afrika. Das letzte Abenteuer. Die Geschichte eines Safariführers, Berlin 2000
**RUETE, EMILY:**
Memoirs of an Arabian Princess from Zanzibar. An Autobiography,
Zanzibar 1998
Leben im Sultanspalast. Memoiren aus dem 19. Jahrhundert, Berlin 2000
Mémoires d'une princesse arabe, Paris 1991

**SAX LEDGER, FIONA:**
Mr Bigstuff and the Goddess of Charm. Parties, Cars, Love and Ambition
South of the Sahara, London 2000
**SCHOLL-LATOUR, PETER:**
Afrikanische Totenklage. Der Ausverkauf des Schwarzen Kontinents,
München 2003

# BIBLIOGRAPHY

**SHAKESPEARE, WILLIAM:**
Antony and Cleopatra, Frankfurt 1994 (*Penguin Books*)
Antonius und Cleopatra, Ditzingen 1992
Antoine et Cléopâtre, Paris 1999
**SEMBENE, OUSMANE:**
God's Bits of Wood, London 1995
Gottes Holzstücke, Frankfurt 1988
Les bouts de bois de dieu, Paris 1994
**SEMBÈNE, OUSMANE:**
Xala, London 1987
Xala: die Rache des Bettlers, Wuppertal 1997
Xala, Paris 1995
**SIENKIEWICZ, HENRYK:**
Desert and Wilderness, Warsaw 1991
**SISÒKÒ, FA-DIGI:**
The Epic of Son-Jara: a West African Tradition, Bloomington,
Indiana 1992
**SOUZA, CARL DE:**
Les jours Kaya, Paris 2000
**STANLEY, HENRY MORTON:**
How I Found Livingstone, Mineola 2002
Wie ich Livingstone fand, Stuttgart 1995
Comment j'ai retrouvé Livingstone, Arles 1994
**STRATHERN, OONA:**
Traveller's Literary Companion to Africa, Brighton 1994

**TIMM, UWE:**
Morenga, New York 2003
Morenga, München 2000
**TUTUOLA, AMOS:**
My Life in the Bush of Ghosts, New York 1994
Mein Leben im Busch der Geister, Berlin 1991
Ma vie dans la brousse des fantômes, Paris 1993
**TUTUOLA, AMOS:** Palm Wine Drinkard, London 1994
Der Palmweintrinker, Zürich 1994
L'ivrogne dans la brousse, Paris 1990

**VERA, YVONNE:**
Butterfly Burning, New York 2000
Schmetterling in Flammen, München 2001
**VOLK, MORITZ** (*Hg.*)**:**
Afrika, meine Liebe. Ein Lesebuch, München 2002

**WOOD, BARBARA:**
Green City in the Sun, London 2001
Rote Sonne, schwarzes Land, Frankfurt 2000
**WRIGHT, RICHARD:**
Black Power: a Record of Reactions in a Land of Pathos, New York 1995
Schwarze Macht: zur afrikanischen Revolution, Hamburg 1956
Puissance noire, Paris 1955

**ZWEIG, STEFANIE:**
Nirgendwo in Afrika, München 2002
Une enfance africaine. Roman autobiographique, Monaco 2002

# INDEX

# imprint

© 2003 TASCHEN GmbH
Hohenzollernring 53, D-50672 Köln
www.taschen.com

© 2003 for the works by Chéri Samba:
Chéri Samba, Courtesy J.M. Patras, Paris (endpaper)

Cover volume I:
Design of Dutch Wax Fabric for Vlisco Helmond B.V., Holland, 1992

Cover volume II:
Design of the Ivoirian Wax Fabrics for Uniwax, Ivory Coast, 1989

Packaging:
"Faso Tours" design, printed by Faso Fani, Burkina Faso,
1990s, The Newark Museum, New Jersey

**EDITED BY**
Angelika Taschen, Cologne

**DESIGN**
Sense/Net, Andy Disl and Birgit Reber, Cologne

**LITHOGRAPHY MANAGEMENT**
Thomas Grell, Cologne

**LITHOGRAPHY**
lithotronic media gmbh, Frankfurt am Main

**PROJECT COORDINATION**
Stephanie Bischoff, Christiane Blass,
Susanne Klinkhamels, Cologne

**TEXT EDITED BY**
Christiane Blass, Susanne Klinkhamels, Cologne

**ENGLISH TRANSLATION**
Anthony Roberts, Lupiac

**GERMAN TRANSLATION**
Anne Brauner, Cologne

Printed in Spain
ISBN 3-8228-5771-8

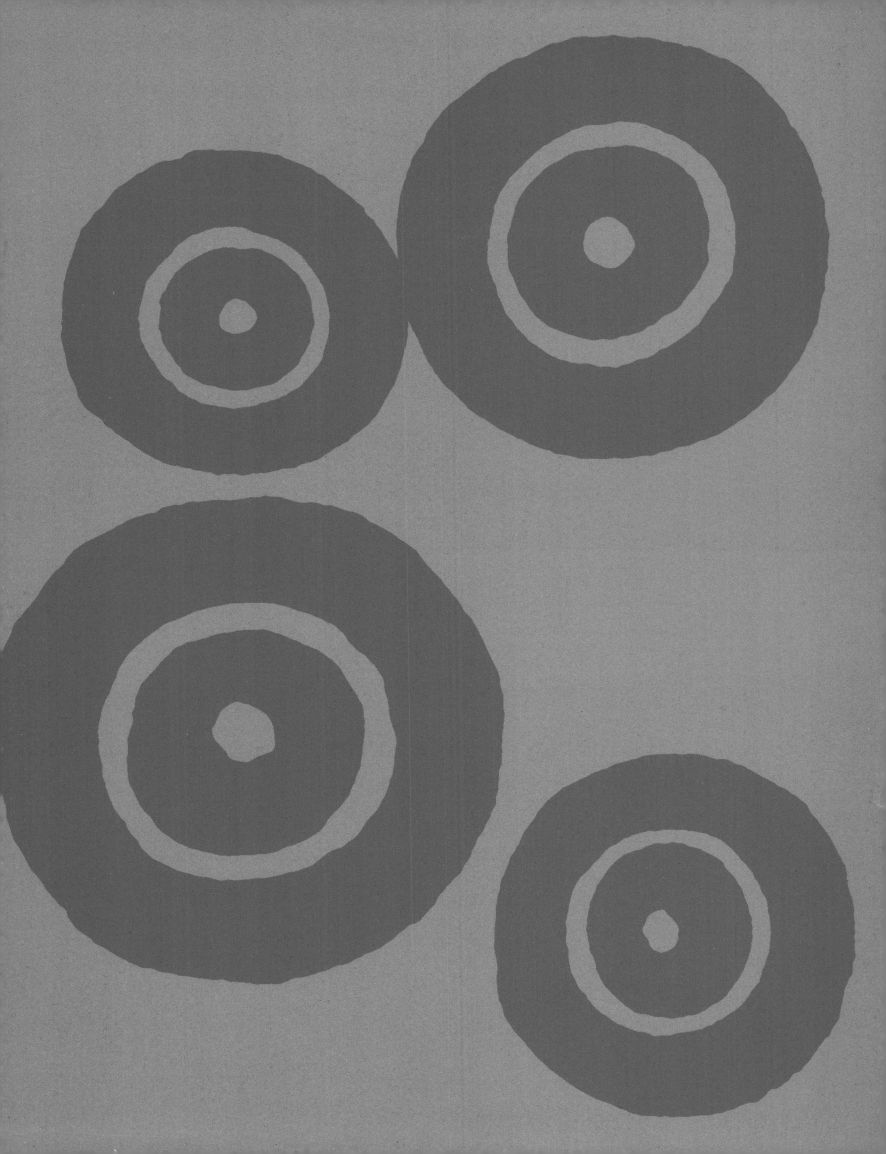

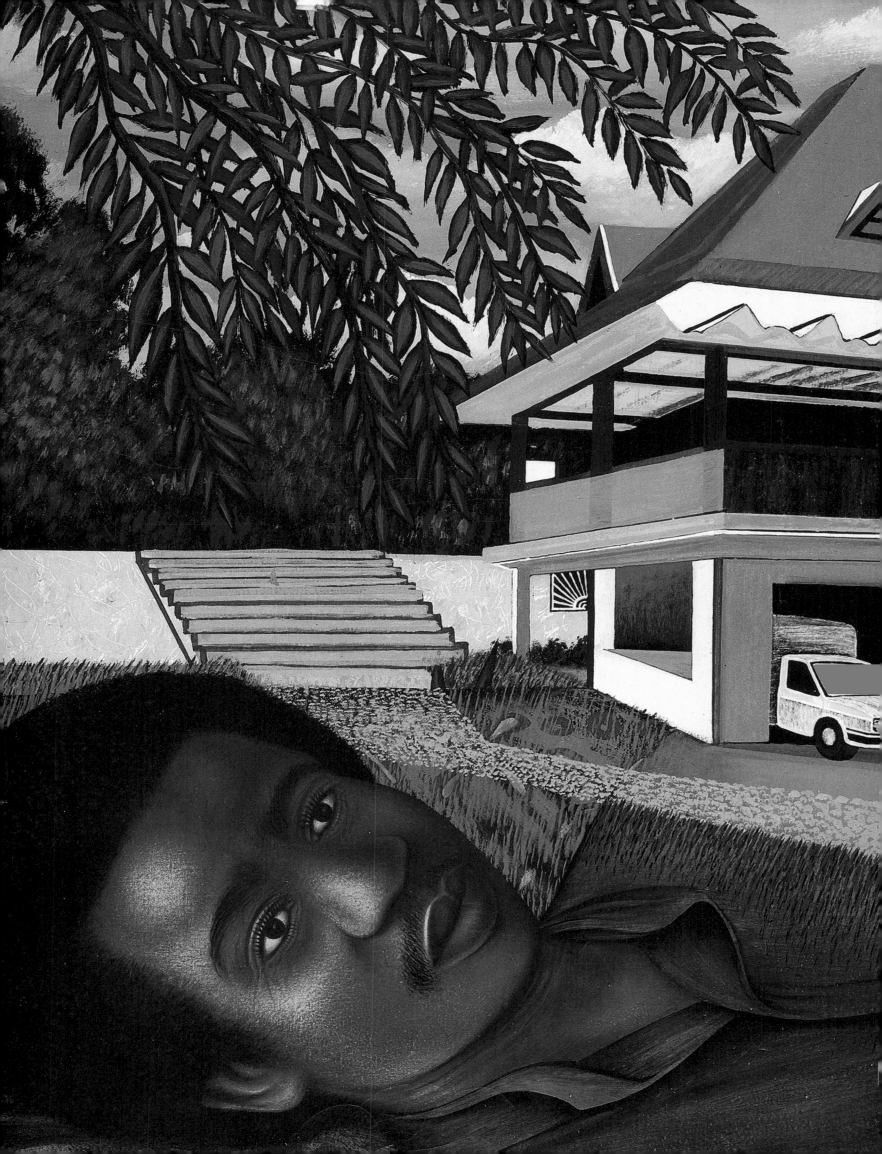